Visual dBASE Programming

MICHAEL R. IRWIN

PRENTICE HALL PTR
Upper Saddle River, New Jersey 07458

Library of Congress Cataloging-in-Publication Data

Irwin, Michael R.
Visual dBASE Programming / Michael R. Irwin
p. cm.
Includes index.
ISBN 0–13–239922–9
1. Visual dBASE. 2. Database management—Computer programs.
I. Title.
QA76.9.D3I83 1996
005.75'65—dc20 95–14060
CIP

Editorial production: *bookworks*
Acquisitions editor: *Mark L. Taub*
Cover director: *Jerry Votta*
Cover designer: *Design Source*
Composition: *Thurn & Taxis*
Manufacturing manager: *Alexis R. Heydt*

Prentice-Hall, Inc.
A Simon & Schuster Company
Upper Saddle River, NJ 07458

The publisher offers discounts on this book when ordered in bulk quantities.
For more information, contact:

Corporate Sales Department
Prentice Hall P T R
One Lake Street
Upper Saddle River, NJ 07458
Phone: 800-382-3419
Fax: 201-236-7141, e-mail: corpsales@prenhall.com

Printed in the United States of America
10 9 8 7 6 5 4 3 2 1

ISBN 0–13–239922–9

Prentice-Hall International (UK) Limited, *London*
Prentice-Hall of Australia Pty. Limited, *Sydney*
Prentice-Hall Canada Inc., *Toronto*
Prentice-Hall Hispanoamericana, S.A., *Mexico*
Prentice-Hall of India Private Limited, *New Delhi*
Prentice-Hall of Japan, Inc., *Tokyo*
Simon & Schuster Asia Pte. Ltd., *Singapore*
Editora Prentice-Hall do Brasil, Ltda., *Rio de Janeiro*

To Ron Dennis, Bill French, and Tom Rettig
for all their years of friendship and support
in the ever-changing world of databases.

Contents

Part II Basic Object-Oriented Concepts and Visual dBASE

Introduction

Welcome to the world of *Visual dBASE Programming*—your personal guide to the power of dBASE in Windows.

This book examines Visual dBASE, the language, and tools that let you build a complex object-oriented (O-O) database system. I think that Visual dBASE is an excellent database manager and one of the best Windows databases on the market today. My goal with this book is to share what I have learned about Visual dBASE, and in the process to help make your work and life easier.

This book contains everything you need to learn the programming power of Borland's Visual dBASE to a fairly advanced level. Although not a tutorial on how to create databases, you'll find that the book starts off with the basics of database programming and builds chapter by chapter on topics previously covered. In places where it is essential that you understand previously covered topics, the concepts are presented again and shown via specific tasks before continuing. Although each chapter is an integral part of the book as a whole, each chapter can also stand on its own. You can read the book in any order you want, skipping from chapter to chapter and from topic to topic. (Note that this book's index is particularly thorough, so you can refer to the index to find the location of a particular topic in which you're interested.)

The examples in this book have been well thought out to simulate the types of tables, queries, forms, and reports most people need to create when performing common business activities. There are many notes, tips, and techniques to help you better understand the product.

Although designed to supplement the Visual dBASE documentation, this book can easily substitute for the programming and reference manuals included with Visual dBASE. There are even appendixes that can be used as reference manuals for the object types of dBASE. This book follows a much more structured approach than the Visual dBASE manuals—going into more depth on almost every topic and showing many different types of examples.

Is This Book for You?

I wrote this book for people who want to understand and create Visual dBASE applications using the tools and programming language of dBASE. This book is designed for people who already have an understanding of and work with basic database concepts—creating tables, queries, and forms, and using them. In addition, you should already have some basic knowledge of programming concepts—what memory variables are and so forth.

Using basic database and programming knowledge, this book is intended for beginning, intermediate, and advanced users of Visual dBASE. With any new product, most users start at the beginning. If, however, you've already read through the Visual dBASE manuals and worked with the sample files, you may want to start with the later parts of this book. Note, though, that starting at the beginning of a book is usually a good idea so that you don't miss out on the tips in the early chapters.

I think that this book covers Visual dBASE, its tools, and its language in detail better than any other book currently on the market. I hope that you will find this book helpful while working with dBASE and enjoy the innovative style of this book.

No—If You Have No Database Experience

If you're new to the world of database management, this book does not offer you the basics necessary to work with tables, queries, and forms. Although you will find it useful later, it is recommended that you start with another book.

No—If You Do Not Want to Work in the Windows Environment

If you work in a non-Windows environment, this book and Visual dBASE will not offer any solutions for your database needs. Visual dBASE is a Windows-based database that offers powerful database management tools to assist you in building DBMS projects quickly using a graphical environment. It also offers a powerful database-oriented language that can assist you in building and maintaining database systems.

Yes—If You've Used DOS-Based Database Managers Like dBASE or Paradox

If you're abandoning a character-based database (DOS), such as dBASE III PLUS, dBASE IV, Paradox, or R:Base, in favor of a more modern graphical product, this book is for you. You'll have a head start because you're already familiar with database managers and how to use them. With Visual dBASE, you'll be able to do all the tasks you've always performed with character-based databases. This can be accomplished *without* programming, using the visual tools of dBASE or by writing code. This book will take you through each subject step by step. It will guide you through the world of O-O databases.

Yes—If You've Used Windows-Based Database Managers Like Access

If you work with existing Windows-based databases, like Access and Paradox and want the power of an O-O language, this book will apply your existing knowledge from these other products to the power of the Visual dBASE language.

Yes—If You Want to Learn Visual dBASE Programming

The Visual dBASE language is based on the dBASE language with extensions for the O-O world and Client/Server services. This book explores and explains the powerful abilities of the Visual dBASE language.

Yes—If You Work in Windows and Need a Client/Server-Based Database Product

If you are working in Windows and build Client/Server databases, Visual dBASE offers many Client/Server extensions that can ease your transition into this world. It offers you the ability to create Client/Server projects locally, and then quickly and easily upsize them to another environment.

How This Book Is Organized

This book contains fifteen chapters, which are divided into five main parts. In addition, the book contains several appendixes.

Part One—Visual dBASE Introductions, consists of the first three chapters of the book. In Chapter 1, you receive background information on Visual dBASE and an overview of some features. Chapter 2 covers an overview of the tools included with Visual dBASE. In Chapter 3, you learn about Visual dBASE objects and how to work with them.

Part Two—Basic Object-Oriented Concepts and Visual dBASE, comprises the next four chapters. You learn the issues and solutions of moving a database system from DOS to Windows in Chapter 4. In Chapter 5, you learn how to work with events and build code to respond to events in Windows. Chapter 6 teaches the basics of creating forms, and using the tools and language of Visual dBASE. Finally, Chapter 7 introduces and works with the concept of Classes and their importance.

Part Three—Advanced Programming Techniques, contains three chapters that present advanced topics on the basic tasks of programming. Chapter 8 examines how to work with memory variables, preprocessors, and compiling your code. Chapter 9 discusses advanced issues and methods of testing your application programs. Chapter 10 works with Objects and Classes in advanced ways. This chapter works with and explains containership, encapsulation, inheritance, and polymorphism—the building blocks of O-O languages.

Part Four—Working with the Outside World, comprises the next four chapters, which work with the world beyond Visual dBASE. Chapter 11 works with Multimedia. It also shows how to use dBASE as a Windows Dynamic Data Exchange (DDE) Client,

Windows DDE Server, and Object Linking and Embedding (OLE) in Windows. Chapter 12 works with the Windows Application Programming Interface (API) and external functions in Dynamic Link Libraries (DDLs). It shows how to use the external functions of Windows and other Windows applications inside dBASE. Chapter 13 builds custom controls that you can use when building your form objects. Finally, Chapter 14 discusses how Visual dBASE builds and works in a Client/Server environment.

Part Five—Building a Working Model, builds a complete working application, dLibrary, using all of the concepts and methods described in the book. Chapter 15 builds the application piece by piece.

Five appendices are included in this book. Appendix A presents a series of tables and example code for each Class built into dBASE. Appendix B is a reference of all extensions that Visual dBASE uses and creates. Appendix C is a table of new and enhanced commands of Visual dBASE versus DOS. Appendix D discusses all of the enhancements in Visual dBASE that let you work easier and more efficiently in Windows 95. Appendix E presents the functions and commands that have been added to the product dealing with Security.

Installation Instructions for the Visual dBASE Programming Companion Disk

Attention: Before installing any of the files from the companion disk, read the Disclaimer and Copyright Notice at the end of this book.

The companion disk contains the example files that are used and created in this book. The files appear in their completed form so you can avoid a lot of typing if you only want to see how certain forms work. Also included are program files that were created in each chapter, offering you a starting point for some of the more complicated examples in the chapters.

The disk is in high-density 3-1/2 inch format with approximately 1.1MB used. To install the companion disk follow these instructions. We have assumed that you installed Visual dBASE and that you want to install these example files on drive C: and that your default 3-1/2 inch floppy drive is drive A:. If this isn't your setup, substitute your floppy or hard disk drive letters or directories in place of the default. You will need 2.9MB free to extract the files on your hard disk.

The install program on the companion disk runs from . However, you can start Windows and run the SETUP program in one step from DOS.

Steps: Installing from DOS

Step 1 Insert the Companion disk in your default floppy drive

Step 2 Go to drive C:

Step 3 Type **WIN A:\SETUP**. And press the Enter key

Step 4 Follow steps 4 through 7 for the **Installing from Windows**

Steps: Installing from Windows

Step 1 Insert the companion disk into your default floppy drive.

Step 2 Activate the Windows Program Manager

Step 3 From the Windows File menu, select Run; then type **SETUP** and press Enter to run the Install program.

Step 4 Read the instructions displayed by the Install program

Step 5 Follow the Install program instructions, selecting a default directory to install to.

Step 6 Once installed, read the README.TXT file that is displayed at the end of Install program. This README.TXT file has been placed in your Default directory for future reference.

Acknowledgments

I first saw dBASE running in Windows, as an early Alpha product, back in the Ashton-Tate days of 1990. It was object oriented and Windows based. It was the most exciting thing I had seen in more than fifteen years of working with databases. I was immediately sold on this next generation of database management and access tools. I wanted this product *now*; I was sold on this new O-O technology. But, alas, I would have a long wait before it would come to fruition.

Since then, Ashton-Tate was acquired by Borland International. The product I initially saw had evolved into the product you see today. The base code was changed, scraped, rewritten from scratch, and merged with additional technology that Borland had acquired during this development period, combining technologies, and finally, shipping dBASE for Windows 5.0 (in 1994).

Although it took dBASE more than four years to enter the world of Windows, once there it has moved quickly. Since dBASE for Windows initially shipped, I've used it for numerous systems. These systems are installed worldwide. I have also had the pleasure of teaching thousands of fellow dBASE developers on how to use this product.

How do I thank and acknowledge everyone who has helped me over the years in my work with dBASE? Having worked with dBASE since dBASE 2 in the CPM days, I have had the pleasure of working with many of the truly great people of the dBASE world. These people have, over the years, directed, guided, and supported me in the field of dBASE. They have touched my life in ways that I can never repay. Because of this, acknowledging all those that have made this book a reality is an impossible task; however, the following will attempt to accomplish the task.

My first acknowledgment is to all the users of Visual dBASE and all those who have worked with dBASE over the years. Many of these dBASE people, like myself, have benefited beyond everyone's wildest dreams.

From the Ashton-Tate days, I want to acknowledge several former employees of Ashton-Tate—Marcy Glickman, Ron Dennis, Bonnie Wacker, Kathleen Noe, and Elaine Sawitzks (Tischner). Without their support, I wouldn't have had much of the exposure that has formed my expertise in dBASE.

I also want to acknowledge my colleagues, fellow charter members of dLAB—Rick Botto, Homer Branch, Russell Freeland, Charles Hager, Alan Kucheck, Tony Lima, John Pochodowicz, Cary Prague, Candy Prince, Tom Rettig, Allan Sieker, and Phil Steele. Through their support and knowledge, I was able to learn far more about dBASE than I could ever imagine. They were always there to help me. A special thanks is in memory of Tom Rettig, who has recently departed from this life. He was always there with a helpful suggestion when I was stumped with a problem. Then there were two members who joined dLAB after the first year—Mariam Lisken and Bill French. There is no way to express my feeling of gratitude to and friendship with these two special people. They immediately opened up their hearts and offered their support, suggestions, and guidance; without these two people, I would have given up on dBASE years ago.

As an instructor at all the seminars on dBASE, I can truly say that I gained more insight and knowledge of dBASE via all the people who attended. Their levels of knowledge continued to challenge me and make me a more functional analyst, programmer, and lecturer. I want to thank and acknowledge the thousands of people, worldwide, who attended and participated in these seminars.

A special thank you goes to all the development team and support staff of Borland for answering my questions and helping me solve many problems as I stumbled through the early times of the O-O syntax in dBASE for Windows and now Visual dBASE.

Another thank you goes to my agents Bill Gladstone and Matt Wagner.

I would also like to acknowledge all the folks at Prentice Hall who helped make this book a reality. This includes Mark Taub, Lisa Garboski, and Beth Sturla.

In closing, I am especially grateful to my family. Although I was preoccupied with this book over the past year, my family's love and support is what made it possible for me to complete this book. Even though I was remiss at times on my side of the relationship, my family was there to offer support and advice when I needed it most—and allow me to solve problems while offering unconditional love.

About the Author

Michael Irwin is considered one of the leading authorities on automated database management systems today. He is a noted worldwide lecturer, and an international award-winning, best-selling author and developer of Client/Server and PC-based database management systems.

Michael Irwin worked with the Metropolitan Police Department in Washington, DC, for 20 years as a developer and analyst of database systems for the Information Systems Division, retiring in June 1992. In all, he created and maintained more than 150 unique database systems during his government service. These systems include many that have gained worldwide recognition.

Since retiring from government service, he runs his own consulting firm, specializing in Database Integration, with emphasis on Client/Server solutions. The range of expertise his company offers includes database processing in and between mainframe, miniframe, and personal computer (PC)–based database systems. His company also offers expertise in working with and integrating databases across assorted hardware, operating systems, connectivity methods, and databases. Over the past three years, he has worked extensively in the Far East.

In addition to developing database systems, Michael Irwin has also authored several books and lectures worldwide concerning database issues and directions.

Part One Visual dBASE Introduction

Chapter 1
Introduction to Visual dBASE

dBASE has evolved from a simple database programming language, supporting two work areas (just fourteen years ago), to a robust worldwide industry standard for personal computer (PC) database applications. It is considered the most widely used database application product today, both licensed and unlicensed.

Since dBASE II days, it has gone from a simple programming language to a complete database application development environment. It is enthusiastically used by a wide range of people—embraced by computer professionals, as well as users who simply have to get information from their databases. It is a language, a development environment, developer tools, and end-user tools all in one package. When dBASE IV first came out, the press suggested it even had the kitchen sink thrown into the package somewhere.

Visual dBASE, the second generation of a Window's application, is a world-class object-oriented development environment.

Windows, and other graphical-user interface (GUI) environments [OS/2, Mac, Motif, and Open Look], have become the accepted standard for computer users. They are highly productive, usable environments to work in, offering a plethora of advantages, including simply making applications look great. People tend to like the "look and feel" of these environments.

Visual dBASE has been called by many people the "next generation of dBASE," the "future of database development," and other complimentary phrases. In fact, dBASE is an excellent Windows product that lets people work with databases in a graphical, event-driven environment. They can quickly and easily work with information stored in their databases using its tools and the familiar dBASE language. It has been completely redesigned to work with the event-driven model of Windows, while continuing to use a language that simply "feels" right. It, like its predecessors (dBASE, DOS, and UNIX), continues to use an English-sounding language that has been learned by millions of users over the last decade and a half.

When dBASE for Windows 5.0 was initially created, it was completely rewritten in Borland's C++ offering a true Windows application—using the services of Windows and based on the Windows messaging system. Borland touts that it will run existing dBASE DOS applications and will also create and run new, Windows-based applications. They have touted this product as "100% dBASE, 100% Windows and Client/Server ready." In fact, when the product was shipped, Borland, the proud parent, faxed a "birth" announcement to many of the Borland offices throughout the world. It looked something like this:

Birth Announcement

We are pleased to announce the newest addition to our family

Born:	*21 August 1994, at 08:00 PST*
Name:	*dBASE for Windows 5.0*
Where:	*Borland International*
	100 Borland Way
	Scotts Valley, CA
Particulars	
Weight:	*11.5 pounds*
Labor:	*234,568 hours*

The announcement of the "birth" (shipping) of dBASE for Windows 5.0

This chapter explores the problem with Windows-based databases and how dBASE fits in the Windows environment.

A New Approach

There is an old saying:

Programming is programming is programming.

This premise has held relatively true over the years—no matter what programming language you used: Assembler, C, Pascal, dBASE, or even COBOL/CICS.

With the acceptance and use of Windows-based applications, the saying should read:

Programming is programming is *not* programming.

Previously, you created applications (DOS, UNIX, VMS, etc.) deciding what would be done and when it would be done in each application. The decision was yours, the programmer. You wrote procedural code, and the code was in control. If you forgot to code something, it simply wasn't done, or, worse, the program crashed. This premise has held true since the beginning of programming back in the 1940s.

In Windows applications you, the programmer, have *no* control. In contrast, Windows and end-users rule. They decide what will be done and when it will be done. For instance, they can be running your application in Visual dBASE and decide to also run their word-processing program to type a letter while your program is doing something. Windows lets the user run more than one application at a time. This means that if you continue to program database applications based on the old model, they will fail—the program and, indirectly, yourself have lost control.

Added, database applications are becoming more complex—they use graphical controls on the data entry forms (pushbuttons, check boxes, spin buttons, etc.), support new types of data (pictures, sound, etc.), and can even use data stored in other environments.

This translates to more person-hours (in reality person-years) to develop an application. Because the capabilities of database applications continues to grow, the users are demanding more from the applications. To address the added demands of users, the time necessary to deliver a system, conception to completion, is becoming too long.

To create timely database applications based on all of this complexity and the increased need for data access, the following two technologies have emerged:

- Object-oriented development
- Client/server methodologies

The combination of these two technologies can help in eliminating the complexity of new database application projects. Visual dBASE uses them to help you quickly and accurately develop database applications for your customers.

Interface work versus database work

When you create a database application, you are really creating the following two classes of programs:

1. Interface programs
2. Information-processing programs

Figure 1–1 shows a typical Windows-based menu system. It was created in Visual dBASE, which is the main driver for a library system.

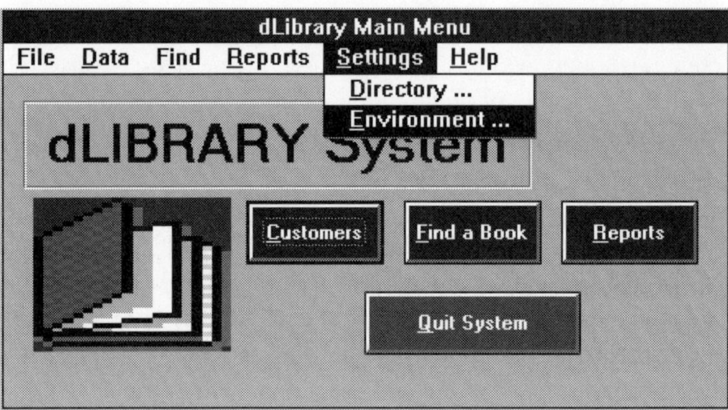

Figure 1–1. This is a main menu for a Visual dBASE application.

Notice that the menu in Figure 1–1 has both buttons and a menu bar that can be used to drive the system. This type of main menu is common in Windows applications today. It is what makes an application appear to be user friendly.

Figure 1–2 shows a Customer information form and an associated Find Customer dialog box. The Customer information form (upper left corner) can be used to view and add records. By pressing the button labeled Find Customer, the Find Customer dialog box appears, and the user can quickly select a new customer. These types of forms and their interaction is what make Windows applications appear user friendly.

These type of forms, combined together, are what the user believes is the application. In dBASE DOS applications, you can create similar functionality and interface screens; however, they will be text based and have less functionality. In addition, when you create them, two points will become painfully obvious.

1. They take a long time to create.
2. They require a lot of procedural code.

To create the forms and add all the interoperability and functionality of the forms, shown in Figures 1–1 and 1–2, would probably take the average dBASE DOS/UNIX programmer between 6,000 and 7,500 lines of code. Worse, even after they create all the driving code to run the application, it won't look as nice or operate as smoothly as the one created in the Windows environment.

In Visual dBASE, the number of lines of code to create the menu system, the three forms and all the driving procedural code behind them is less than 250 lines. Best of all, most of the code can be created using the form and menu tools built into the application. You have to write less than 30 lines of code to make it all work together.

Visual dBASE is built on the premise that the interface is the main focus of the application. Therefore, the interface is where the main focus of the programming effort should be.

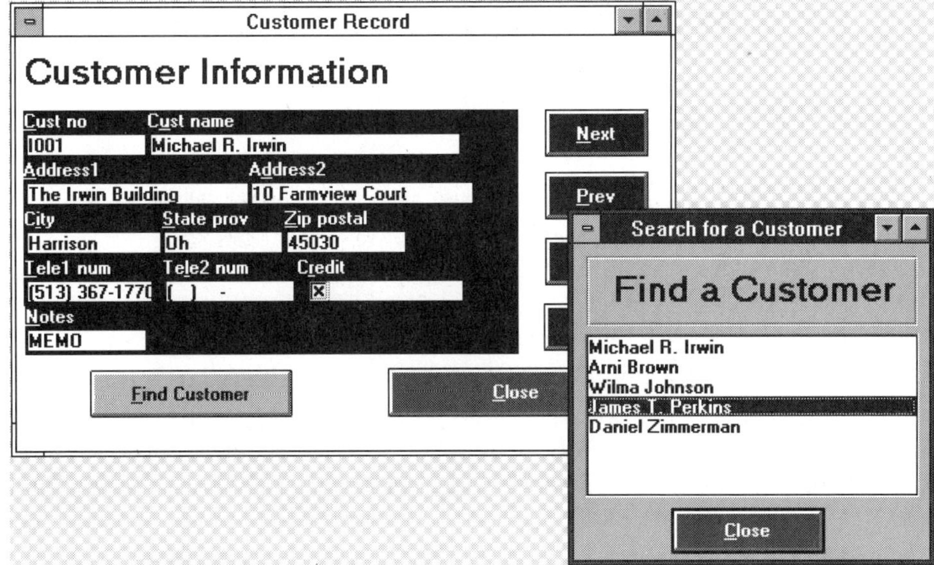

Figure 1–2. A typical form and a dialog box created in dBASE.

This simple premise will become one of the most important facets of working in Visual dBASE. You will still have to create the User Interfaces (UI) and write code that performs all the database manipulation logic. However, you will focus your main efforts on the UI, attaching the appropriate database logic to the UI.

This is a direct contradiction of traditional procedural programming. In traditional procedural programming, the programmer writes programs that totally dictate all of the database logic and attach the UI to the database manipulation code.

Working with users

Most, if not all, database applications are dependent on the people who use them. These users work with the application through the application interface that you create—the menus, forms, reports, and so forth. This is what the user honestly believes is the database application.

The user is normally sheltered from the database complexity of an application. This database complexity includes how the data is stored, how the information is placed in order, and how the tables are interrelated.

Users should be able to work with your database system with minimum database knowledge. They work with the tables/databases via the UI. Because of this, the user interface must be *usable to the user*. If users do not like how the application looks and "feels," they will use the system less efficiently or, even worse, not work with the system at all.

Database applications must address the needs of the user. From the user perspective, the stress should be on how the interface looks and interacts with its different parts. For instance, if the system uses a mouse, it should also use keystrokes that do the same thing. Users like all the graphical things in Windows. They are working with Windows applications that have toolbars, pull-down menus, check boxes, and radio buttons. They are finding that they can enter and review information quicker and more accurately using these new "controls" on their forms. They even find it easier to select choices in dialog boxes using these graphical controls.

Users are demanding more graphical looks. They are also demanding consistency between applications. They don't want to learn a different interface for each application. For instance, they don't want to have to remember the following:

> Let's see, function key F1 is help for all my DOS applications—except WordPerfect, which is function key F3. To activate the menu, I can press Alt and the first letter of my choice—or is it Ctrl and the first letter?

Users don't want, nor do they need this type of confusion. They want all the applications to appear to work the same and have them use consistent interface methods—mouse and keystrokes.

Windows and other graphical environments offer the user a graphical look and maintain consistency between applications. So, from the end-user perspective, the interface is the application and that is all that concerns them.

From a programmer viewpoint, this means that a lot of time and effort have to be dedicated to creating and maintaining the interface parts of an application.

Working with the tables/databases

Although the user interface is a critical and important part of any database application, it is only half the story. Ultimately, the application must satisfy an even more important need of the user—accuracy and usability of the information stored in the system.

To satisfy this need, the application must have programs that control and manipulate the actual information that is stored in the system. For instance, it must have a way to get information from the user and relate that information to another part of the program. Figure 1–2 shows a dialog box that gets a customer's name. Once the user selects a name from the dialog box, there must be a way to relay that information back to the customer form and update it. This type of code is part of the complexity from which the user needs to be shielded. Yet it is a critical part of the application.

The application also needs programs or code that enforce the business rules (integrity) of the system and make sure that the information being stored is accurate. These rules should include things like Cascading Deletes and Updates, data formatting, and ranges.

All of this requires the second type of program: information processing. These programs require a high degree of database expertise and require knowledge in programming them.

So database applications really require two distinct types of coding— the UI and database processing. Creating these parts of a database application tend to take a long time when writing traditional procedural code. Add the complexity of the Windows graphical environment, and the time simply gets unreasonable.

The old method = coding for all possibilities

The way most programs have been written, up until now, has been through procedural coding methods. The programmer codes everything—all the choices the user is allowed and all the things the user cannot do. The code decides what a user will do and when he or she will do it.

One step at a time

You are required to write code that considers all possibilities. For instance, the following demonstrates some typical procedural-based code:

```
*** MAINDRVR.prg
*
*
SET TALK OFF
SET ESCAPE OFF
CLEAR
USE MYTABLE
DEFINE WINDOW MyWin from 5,5 to 18,25      && create and open form
ACTIVATE WINDOW MyWin
DO WHILE .T.                               && driver to get choice
   mChoice = " "                           && starts here
  @ 0,2 TO 2,14
  @ 1,4 SAY "Main Menu"
  @ 4,2 SAY "1. Add Records"
  @ 5,2 SAY "2. Edit Records"
  @ 6,2 SAY "3. Quit"
  @ 8,2 GET mChoice
  READ
 @9,2 CLEAR TO 10,14
  DO CASE                                  && process the choice
    CASE mChoice = '3'
       EXIT
    CASE mChoice = '1'
       DEACTIVATE WINDOW MyWin
       APPEND
    CASE mChoice = '2'
       DEACTIVATE WINDOW MyWin
       EDIT
```

NOTE: An *event-driven environment*, like Windows, is one that responds to events. An event is simply some action that occurs. In Windows, if the user presses the key combination **Ctrl-Esc**, a Windows dialog box, named the Task List, appears and lets the user move to another active Windows program. The event is the actual key press. The program can look for the event and respond to the event by running another application.

With all these problems, some different method is needed for programming. That is where Object-Oriented (O-O) programming comes in. Visual dBASE is an O-O program that has object-oriented extensions added to the language.

Solving complexity

Object-oriented development is a programming methodology that solves complexity quickly and effectively.

Wouldn't it be nice if you didn't have to write programs that must control and anticipate everything? For example, wouldn't it be nice simply to create an application that has to deal with the choices of the user? These types of programs aren't concerned with the negatives (the user can't enter an invalid choice).

A better example of solving complexity and object-oriented development can be demonstrated by the two forms in Figure 1–4. Notice that the two forms, Credit Information (top left) and Personal Information (bottom right), are similar. The main difference between the two forms is that the second lacks all credit-related information (the Change Credit pushbutton, and Credit and Amount fields), and it has different text. The second form, titled Personal Information (Customer Info), was actually created from the same template (CLASS) as the Credit Information (Supervisor Screen) form. The Credit Information form (Supervisor Screen) was created first. Then another form was made, and the credit objects (fields and pushbutton) were simply made invisible.

NOTE: Creating forms from a CLASS (template).

The two forms in Figure 1–4 were created from the same thing. When you create a form and its contents (fields, pushbuttons, etc.), you actually create an object called a Form object. This object is defined and created by something called a CLASS. The CLASS is simply the template that holds the information needed to build the form, which is covered in depth later in this book.

The form, titled Credit Information, in Figure 1–4 will let the user update the credit field and the total credit line by pressing the Change Credit button.

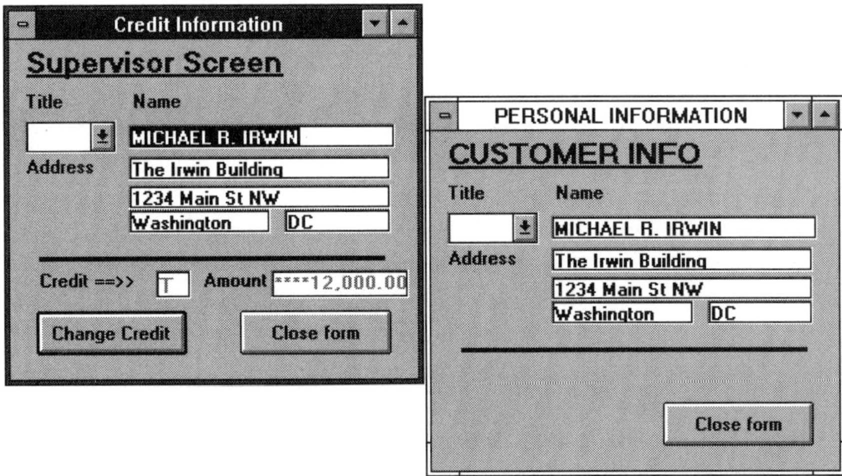

Figure 1–4. Two form objects created from the same template (CLASS).

Building programs with a single line of code

To create both forms from the same class and use them took less than fifteen lines of code. The following is the actual Object-Oriented program:

```
*** MAKETWO.prg
*
SET PROCEDURE TO TwoForm.wfm
CREATE SESSION
fSupFrm = NEW MRIFORM()
CREATE SESSION
fCusFrm=NEW MRIFORM()
fCusFrm.TxtTitle.TEXT="CUSTOMER INFO"
fCusFrm.pb1.VISIBLE=.F.
fCusFrm.ef6.VISIBLE=.F.
fCusFrm.ef7.VISIBLE=.F.
fCusFrm.t4.VISIBLE = .F.
fCusFrm.t5.VISIBLE = .F.
fCusFrm.TEXT = "PERSONAL INFORMATION"
fSupFrm.OPEN()
fCusFrm.OPEN()
RETURN
*** End of Program
```

Although it seems foreign and confusing to you now, it is really simple. The first line tells you that there is a procedure file in memory. Notice that it doesn't appear as if it was ever used. Nowhere in the code is there a **DO <program>.** Actually, the procedure file has a CLASS definition stored in it named MRIFORM. It is the template that is used to create the two forms.

The point of this code is not to understand it but rather to demonstrate that you can create two different forms (working programs) quickly with little coding.

What this program is actually doing is programming by exception. These forms (programs to view and change customer information) were created using a new command: NEW. Then the second form had several of the values in the memory variables changed. These memory variables are actually called properties, which are covered later.

So you can create a program quickly and then change a few values (memory variables or properties), and completely change the look and purpose of the program. This ability to simply change a few properties (memory variables) and create a new program is programming by exception. You do not need to program all possible user actions. In fact, you don't even specify a READ or SAYs and GETs in the object-oriented world.

This means that you don't have to redo things repeatedly. You can build on what already exists. Thus, less programming is involved, which means less complexity.

Programs for Windows

Figure 1–5 shows a Visual dBASE application has the same functionality (actually more) as the DOS application that was shown in Figure 1–3. The DOS application took more than thirty lines of code and was still text based. Using the object-oriented approach built into dBASE, you can create a true Windows application that is more powerful than its DOS counterpart.

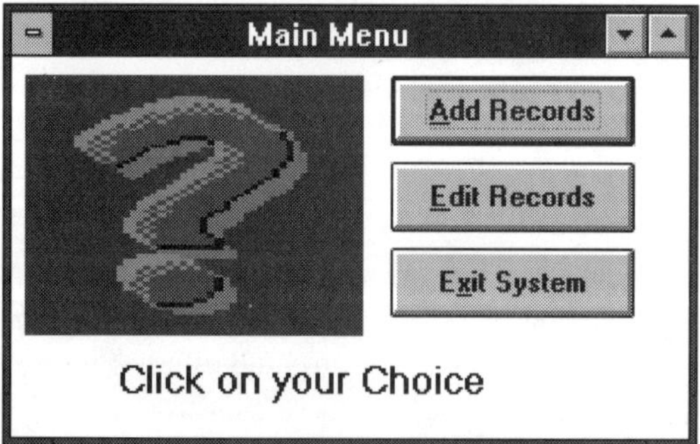

Figure 1–5. A Windows-based application to add and edit records.

The code to create this application uses familiar-sounding dBASE syntax. The following is the code to create the application:

```
*** MAINFORM.prg
*
PUBLIC zForm,t1
DEFINE FORM zFORM PROPERTY Height 10.25, Left 2, Top 1, Width
50,;
    Text "Main Menu", OnGotFocus {;frFocus()}
DEFINE IMAGE iPict OF zFORM PROPERTY  Height  7,  Left  1,;
    Top 0.5,; Width  25, DataSource "RESOURCE #124"
DEFINE PUSHBUTTON pb1 OF zForm PROPERTY Height 1.88, Left 28,;
    Top 0.50,Width 18,Text "&Add Records", OnClick {;pbClk1()}
DEFINE PUSHBUTTON pb2 OF zForm PROPERTY Height 1.88, Left 28,;
    Top 2.80, Width 18, Text "&Edit Records", OnClick {;pbClk2()}
DEFINE PUSHBUTTON pb3 OF zForm PROPERTY Height 1.88, Left 28,;
    Top 5.10, Width 18, Text "E&xit System", OnClick
{;form.close()}
DEFINE TEXT t1 OF zForm AT 8,8 PROPERTY FontSize 12, Alignment
3,;
    Height 1.40, Width 28, Text "Click on Your Choice"
OPEN FORM zFORM
*
PROCEDURE pbClk1
   zForm.t1.text = "Adding Records"
  APPEND
PROCEDURE pbClk2
   zForm.t1.text ="Editing Records"
   EDIT
PROCEDURE frFocus
   zForm.t1.text = "Click on your Choice"
*** End of Program
```

Did you notice that the code sounds and looks like dBASE? It uses new commands—dBASE-sounding commands. This small program is actually an Object-Oriented (O-O) program. It uses object-oriented techniques built into dBASE. The program used dBASE-like commands, although you could have written it using totally new O-O syntax. The remainder of this book explores how you can create Windows applications in dBASE using both dBASE commands and O-O commands.

A New Environment

Visual dBASE is a true Windows application. It takes advantage of the graphics built into Windows. As a true Windows application, you can take advantage of all your Windows knowledge when working with dBASE.

Why Windows? Applications created in these environments are considered easy to use. They offer a graphical look and feel for the end user.

The Windows model

The Windows model offers three advantages.

- Graphical environment
- Consistency in program usage
- Interoperability between applications

It was built with the following simple premise:

Create an environment that can be used to reflect the way people work.

Windows puts users in control—not programs. It lets users do multiple tasks at the same time. Users need to focus on getting a task done—not operating an application.

Because of this simple idea, programs created for Windows focus on the user. Remember: Windows-based applications are never in complete control. Understanding this, you will find that you will be creating programs that concentrate on tasks rather than applications. These tasks are the things that the user will need to do.

New ways to work with information

Windows itself provides many shared resources (fonts and printers) and features Dynamic Data Exchange (DDE) and Object Linking and Embedding (OLE) that can be use to enhance your dBASE applications in Windows.

Windows colors and fonts

Visual dBASE uses Windows fonts for sending text to the screen or the printer. This means that you can change the look of your application by using any color that is supported by your monitor. If your monitor supports 1,024 × 768 and 256 color, dBASE supports 1,024 × 768 and 256 colors. Colors can be set based on the red, green, and blue (RGB) values. For instance, you can use the new command, DEFINE COLOR, with the SET COLOR TO command to set colors like the following:

```
DEFINE COLOR mCol1 91, 112, 82
DEFINE COLOR mCol2 207, 58, 41
SET COLOR TO mCol1/mCol2
? "HELLO"
```

NOTE: The **DEFINE COLOR** <var_name> RED_Value, GREEN_Value, BLUE_Value command lets you specify the RGB values in the range of 0 to 255 for each.

You don't have to remember all the different color combinations, rather, you can use a new dialog box to help you set the RGB values. The function GETCOLOR() activates the color picker. This command works in conjunction with the DEFINE COLOR command. For instance, the following code lets the user select the colors to set:

```
xCol = GETCOLOR("Pick the foreground color")
DEFINE COLOR fgCol &xCol
```

These color commands work with the colors associated with the DOS world. In addition to these commands, dBASE has a property called ColorNormal that can be used to change the color of any "object"—forms, texts (equivalent to the @... SAY), and entryfields (equivalent to the @... GET). When you begin to work with these objects, you can also specify the hue, saturation, and luminescence giving you more than one million color combinations. For instance, type the following commands in the Command window to create an empty form and then set its color:

```
my1stForm = NEW FORM()
my1stForm.OPEN()
my1stForm.ColorNormal = "W/B+"
```

The preceding code will create a form, open it, and set the background color to bright blue. You may want to set the color to a light blue-green-gray. To do this, you can use the color picker in the form designer or simply enter the correct value (hex notation). For instance, enter the following to change the color of the form, my1stForm, to light blue-green-gray:

```
my1stForm.ColorNormal = "W/0xffff80"
```

Notice that the color is foreign to you—white over something known as "0xffff80". Before, you had to remember only five color codes (N, W, R, B, and G) and make sixteen colors using the plus sign (+); now you can try to remember more than a million. You can really fine-tune your color settings when working with objects (forms, pushbuttons, check boxes, etc.).

You have this same flexibility when working with Windows fonts. You can select any font, size, or mask (underline, bold, etc.) that Windows supports.

The best part of all of this is that you can distribute an application with the fonts that you selected. If the client's machine doesn't support them, Windows will select one of the fonts or colors that is closest to it—that is supported by the machine.

Setting colors using a Windows color scheme

➡ In addition to the standard method of indicating color values in Visual dBASE, you can also specify colors-based color values of the current Windows system color palette. Using special system strings, you can specify any colors from the currently defined Windows color scheme based on the Windows screen elements colors. The following table shows the dBASE system color strings and their associated Windows screen elements:

Table 1–1. Associated Color Strings and Windows Screen Elements

Window Screen Element	dBASE Color String Name
Desktop	BACKGROUND
Application Workspace	APPWORKSPACE
Window Background	WINDOW
Window Text	WINDOWTEXT
Menu Bar	MENU
Menu Text	MENUTEXT
Active Title Bar	ACTIVECAPTION
Inactive Title Bar	INACTIVECAPTION
Active Title Bar Text	CAPTIONTEXT
Inactive Title Bar Text	INACTIVECAPTIONTEXT
Active Border	ACTIVEBORDER
Inactive Border	INACTIVEBORDER
Window Frame	WINDOWFRAME
Scroll Bars	SCROLLBAR
Button Face	BTNFACE
Button Shadow	BTNSHADOW
Button Text	BTNTEXT
Button Highlight	BTNHIGHLIGHT
Disabled Text	GRAYTEXT
Highlight	HIGHLIGHT
Highlighted Text	HIGHLIGHTTEXT

As Table 1–1 demonstrates, you can set colors based on the color scheme of Windows currently in use by the user.

User controllable Form colors. By using the dBASE color strings in lieu of hard-coded colors, each user can match your application's form colors with their currently defined Windows system colors. If users want to change the system colors, they can change them using the Windows *Control Panel* program. This eliminates the need to create hard-coded colors users must live with or a program within an application, allowing users to define the colors they want.

By default, Form objects are assigned the color of the Button Text/Button Face. This includes the Form, Browse objects, Check boxes, Pushbuttons, Rectangles, and Radio Buttons.

✔ **Changing the Windows system color palette**
If the System color palette is changed while your form is running, the form or any controls in the form that use these values will change automatically. This ability is only available in Visual dBASE. It is not available in dBASE for Windows 5.0.

! **ColorNormal values and the Form designer**
Since the Form designer now generates these dBASE color strings for colors, you will not be able to run your Visual dBASE forms in dBASE for Windows 5.0 without first changing all these values back to physical colors.

Windows printer support

Unlike DOS applications, the Windows environment provides printer support at the environment level. Windows operates and controls the printer drivers—not the application. This means that you can use any printer driver built into Windows without worrying about: "Will I have to change the code that controls the fonts and print attributes (bold, etc.) if the user changes printers?" As long as Windows supports the printer, dBASE will work with it, and you won't have to change anything in your program—Windows takes care of it.

Visual dBASE takes advantage of all the Windows printing facilities, including the Print Manager. While in dBASE you can use another new function, CHOOSEPRINTER(), to display a printer setup dialog box like the one in Figure 1–6.

This dialog box lets you change printers, select paper size, and change orientation (landscape or portrait). Once it does, the new selection automatically updates the printer system variables: _pdriver, _porientation, and _plength.

Linking to other Windows applications

Besides working with the clipboard and directly using Windows resources, you can work with two Windows features: Dynamic Data Exchange (DDE) and Object Linking and Embedding (OLE).

DDE goes beyond the capabilities of the clipboard by allowing two different Windows applications to share and exchange data (information) and instructions. DDE needs one program to be the client (user or requester) and the other to be the server (program that can work with the information—picture, sound, etc.). dBASE can work with DDE as both a client and a server.

OLE is an extension of DDE. It lets you use an external Windows application directly from a dBASE field (in a table or form). This means that you can store an Audio Visual file (AVI) in a dBASE table (an OLE field) and then show the movie from inside dBASE.

Chapter 2
Visual dBASE Tools Overview

To start Visual dBASE (or dBASE for Windows 5.0), go to the Windows Program Manager and double-click on the Visual dBASE program icon in the group. The icon should look similar to the one in Figure 2–1.

Figure 2–1. The Visual dBASE icon.

NOTE: Visual dBASE has several icons that can be associated with dBASE. Figure 2–2 shows some of them. You can change the icon by selecting File >> Properties ... >> Change Icon while in the Program Manager.

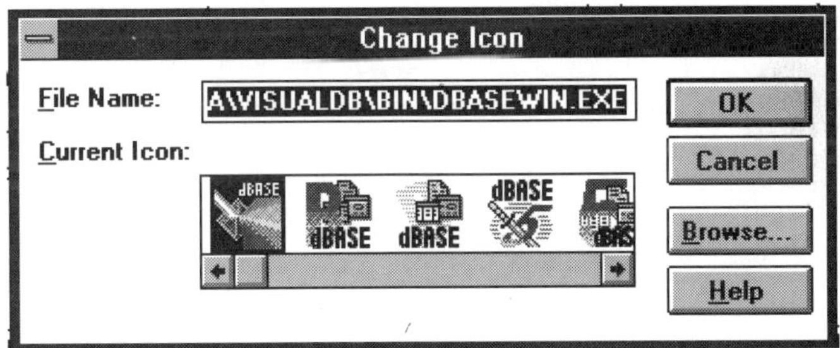

Figure 2–2. A few of the different Visual dBASE icons.

When you double-click on the dBASE icon, the Borland splash screen will appear with the registered user's name and the copyright notice. This will be followed by the Visual dBASE desktop as shown in Figure 2–3.

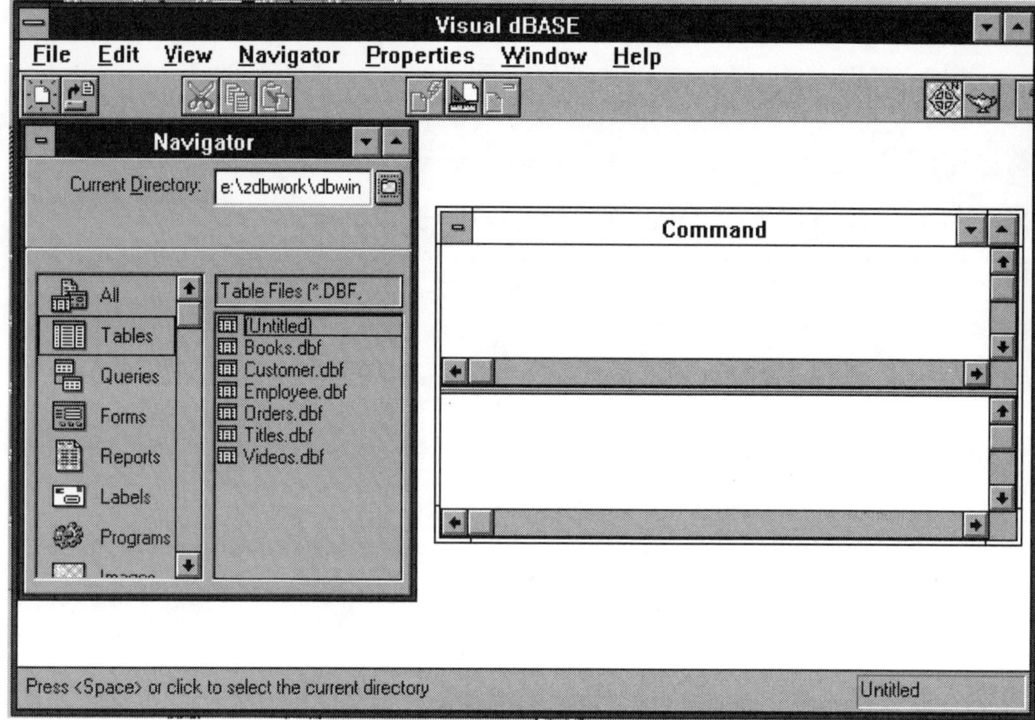

Figure 2–3. The Visual dBASE desktop.

THE VISUAL dBASE DESKTOP

dBASE is a true Windows applications; as such, the desktop exists in its own window. This window has six visible parts.

- Frame and title bar
- Menu bar
- SpeedBar
- Navigator window
- Command window
- Status bar

Remember: dBASE is now an object-oriented application. As an object-oriented application, everything in dBASE is an object, which includes the application, or desktop, itself. The desktop is an object and even has a name: **_APP** (short for system application). Each of the parts of the desktop are individual objects. These objects exist and work independently. The object nature of dBASE is integral to understanding how dBASE and the desktop works; although the object side is covered later in this book, it is important to remember that everything in Visual dBASE is an object.

The title bar

The *title bar*, along the top of the desktop's window, is part of the windows frame. It is an object, and it has four parts—a system menu (on the left side), two size buttons (on the right side), and the title bar (in the center). Figure 2–4 shows the title bar, which is part of the frame window.

Figure 2–4. The dBASE desktop title bar.

These parts are known as *controls*, in dBASE. A control is anything (an object) that is part of the user interface (the visible parts). These desktop controls are how you work with the desktop, actually its window. You can minimize the window by clicking the minimize button or maximize it to the entire screen by clicking on the maximize button.

Because it is object oriented, the title bar also has a name: **framewin**. You can work with the title bar object. For instance, you can change the **text** that is on the title bar. Maybe you would like to have your name come up on the title bar. To change the text on the title bar, go to the command window and type in the following command:

```
_APP.framewin.text = "Michael Irwin's Visual dBASE"
```

Notice that the text changed on the title bar. You have just worked with object orientation. You told dBASE that you wanted the text on the title bar to change. You did this by telling it to look at itself (_app), find another object that is inside it (framewin) and change the value of the text (text is actually something known as a property of the object named framewin).

So the title bar has the name of the dBASE application or any name you want to give it. It has a system menu, like most Window's applications, and a minimize and maximize button.

The menu bar

Directly below the title bar is the main menu. It should look similar to the one in Figure 2–5. You can click on any word on the menu bar to open the associated pull-down menus and perform the associated tasks. Alternatively, you can do the same thing by pressing the **Alt** key, and the underlined letter of any menu item.

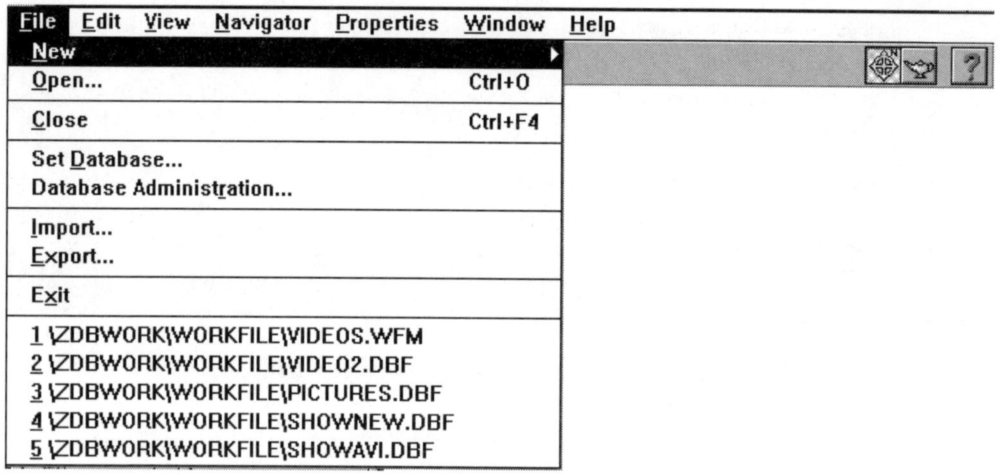

Figure 2–5. The dBASE desktop menu bar with a pull-down menu active.

➡ **Menu changes between versions**
There are several new menu items in Version 5.5. For instance, the File menu in version 5.5 has two database options as shown in Figure 2–5; version 5.0 doesn't have them.

The menu bar in Figure 2–5 shows the pull-down menu of the File choice active. A couple of the choices show keystroke combinations associated with them. For instance, **Ctrl+O**, is associated with the **Open** menu choice. These keystroke combinations are known as hot keys or shortcut keys. By pressing them, you can eliminate having to go through the menu to perform some action.

The menu choices and their associated pull-down menus change with the task being performed. For instance, when you create a new table (database), the menu bar removes the Navigator prompt and adds a new one titled Structure.

The SpeedBar

The *SpeedBar* is the row of icon buttons immediately below the menu bar. Figure 2–6 shows the SpeedBar. The SpeedBar, in Borland products or toolbar in Microsoft products, is a series of buttons that are used to perform common tasks quickly. You simply click on the button that you want to use.

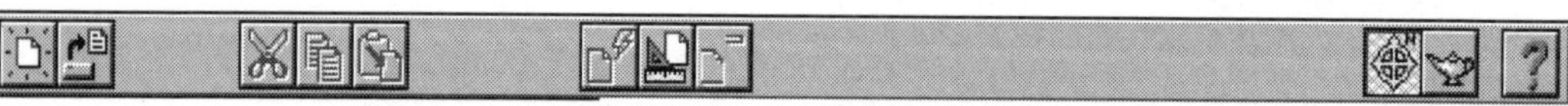

Figure 2–6. The dBASE desktop SpeedBar for the Navigator.

The SpeedBar, like the menu, changes based on the task that you are performing. The SpeedBar in Figure 2–6 is the one associated with the Navigator. Figure 2–7 shows three additional SpeedBars: the Command Window SpeedBar, Query SpeedBar, and a Form SpeedBar.

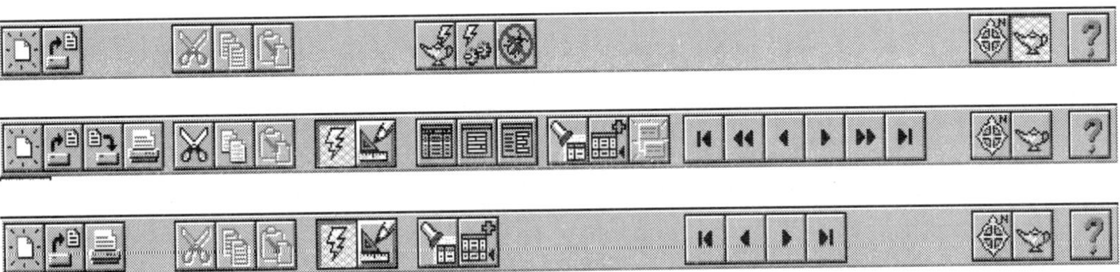

Figure 2–7. Three different dBASE desktop SpeedBars: the Command Window, a running Query, and a running Form.

By looking at the four SpeedBars in Figures 2–6 and 2–7 you can start to see six groupings of icons/buttons. The SpeedBars can be grouped into the following six areas:

1. File/Print
2. Cut/Copy/Paste
3. Run/Design
4. Task Specific
5. Navigational/VCR
6. Desktop

The File/Print SpeedBar group

This group comprises two to four buttons. It is along the left side of the toolbar. These icons enable you to create a new object, save an object, open an object, and print the object.

The Cut/Copy/Paste SpeedBar group

The next group, from the left, consist of three buttons that can be used to cut, copy, and paste to/from the Windows clipboard. You use these buttons to copy and move text or other objects when working with the design surfaces or memo fields in dBASE.

The Run/Design SpeedBar group

This is the third group of buttons on the tool bar. It has from two to three buttons. These buttons are normally used to run (execute) an object or go to the design surface to create or modify an object. If you are in the Navigator, the highlighted item will be run or designed. If the object is active, you can use these buttons to toggle between run/design modes.

The run button has a picture of a lightning bolt, and the design button consists of a pencil tip, angle template, and ruler.

When the Command Window is active, you are given three options: to run the existing line in the command window, run a program, or debug a program.

The task-specific group

These buttons sit in the middle of the SpeedBar. They are there to assist you with the task being performed. For instance, in Figure 2–7, the bottom two SpeedBars show several task-specific buttons. The bottom one has only two buttons: Search for a record (flashlight on a table) and Add a new record (table with a green plus sign at the top right). These buttons are task specific—changing with the task being performed.

The Navigational/video cassette recorder (VCR) group

This group is used to navigate through an active form, report, table, or query. They are only displayed when you are running one of the objects. They are located at the center right of the SpeedBar, as shown in two of the bars in Figure 2–7. Notice that they look similar to the buttons on a VCR—thus, their name.

NOTE: Navigational buttons in Design surfaces

There are no navigational buttons in the Design surfaces of dBASE. Instead, the space used by navigational buttons is dedicated to additional task-specific buttons.

The Desktop

The last few buttons on the SpeedBar are located at the extreme right of the bar. The two on the left let you open, or activate, the two main windows of the desktop: Navigator (Navigational Compass, like on a ship) and Command (Genie's lamp: "your wish is my command"). The button on the extreme right is the Help button.

➡ **Desktop/Tutor group and the Desktop section**

Version 5.0 of dBASE for Windows offers two additional buttons in most menus with the Desktop section—the tutorial buttons. They are the Expert button (a light bulb: "I see the light") and the Tutor button (a graduate with a mortarboard on, or a graduation cap). These buttons are missing in Visual dBASE, being incorporated in help. The Expert button is used to activate an expert builder. In version 5.0 of dBASE for Windows, there is only one expert—the form builder. The Tutor button activates the dBASE tutorial. You can use the tutorial with your files to learn how to do something.

The Navigator Window

On the left-hand side, in the open area of the desktop, is the dBASE Navigator. The *Navigator* replaces the dBASE DOS Control Center. Figure 2–8 shows the Navigator. Your navigator may be slightly different, depending on the options (properties) you have set. The Navigator is an independent object. It has its own window frame, title bar, and so forth. It can be minimized, maximized, and resized like many other Windows frames.

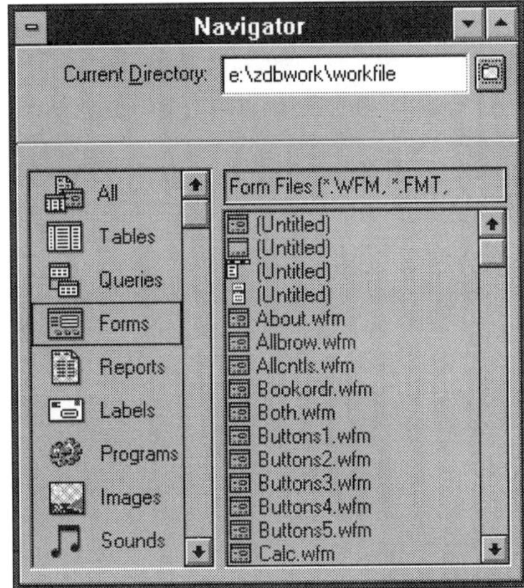

Figure 2–8. The dBASE Navigator.

The Navigator is used to organize and display the different file types (tables, queries, forms, reports, etc.). It is similar to the catalog file in dBASE DOS, except that it is directory oriented.

Like the Control Center in dBASE DOS, the Navigator is used to manipulate graphically the different file types, objects, of dBASE. It is used to display the primary file types and details about them. You use the Navigator to

- Display information in dBASE, Paradox, and SQL tables
- Run files—open queries, forms, reports, and run programs
- Modify files—open designers and other tools
- Change directories and search paths

The Navigator can be broken into four distinct sections:

- Top—Directory/Path Information section
- Left—File Type Selection area
- Right Top—File Skeleton Information section
- Right—File Details Container section

Directory/Path information section

The top portion of the Navigator is the Directory/Path section. It shows you the current directory dBASE is looking at for its files. It may also display two other areas: the **Search Path** being used to display files (not shown in Figure 2–7) and a **Tables from . . .** area.

Directories

The Current Directory is the main directory that dBASE will use to search in. The Search Path is one or more *additional* directories that is used by dBASE to search in for the files being used by the Navigator. You can display the search path by selecting Properties >> Navigator Properties . . . Use Supplemental Search Path from the main menu. This will activate another combination box in the top portion of the Navigator. Figure 2–9 shows the top portion of the Navigator with the Search Path active.

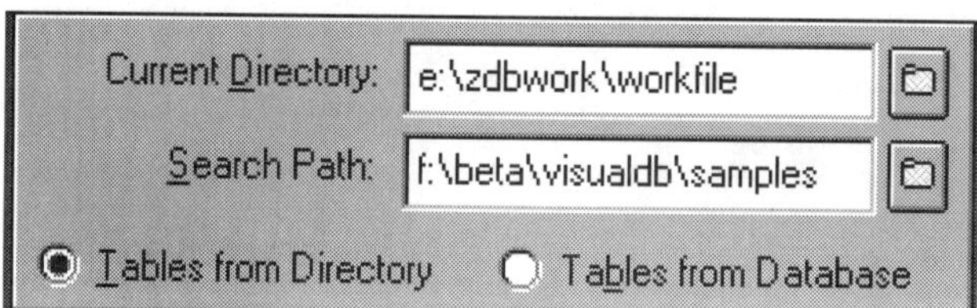

Figure 2–9. The search path active in the Navigator.

The directory area of the Navigator has two buttons alongside of the combo boxes. These two buttons (icon of a file folder) will activate the Choose Directory dialog box. This dialog box can be used to set directories.

Tables from . . .

When you use SQL databases on your system, dBASE shows you the two radio buttons that are located at the bottom of Figure 2–9. These buttons let you select tables from a directory or from an SQL database (local or remote).

To make these two options visible, you have to run the BDE Configuration Utility, named BDECFG.EXE, from the program manager, and specify databases and alias names. For demonstration purposes, you can follow these steps:

1. Quit Visual dBASE.
2. Open Program Manager and Run the BDE Configuration Utility program.
3. Select the "ALIAS" tab, along the bottom of the window.
4. Click on NEW alias button to activate the Add New Alias dialog box.
5. Type in the name **MyCustomerTable** in the New Alias Name field.
6. Click on the **OK** button to close the dialog box and return to the BDE window.
7. Select File >> Save from the menu.
8. Quit the BDE Configuration Utility program.
9. Restart Visual dBASE.

Now your Navigator should appear similar to the one in Figure 2–9.

When you select the **Tables from Directory** button, you will see the names of all dBASE and Paradox tables in the current directory, or path (if the path is set). By selecting the **Tables from Database**, you are shown the names of all the tables in the active SQL database.

If you do not want to use SQL tables, return to the BDE utility and remove the Alias name you created. The next time you run Visual dBASE, the selection will be gone.

NOTE: BDE Configuration Utility

The Borland Database Engine (BDE) configuration utility was called IDAPI in previous versions of Borland products. BDE and IDAPI are referring to the same database engine and reference use of tables in the Client/Server model.

File type selection section

This section is located along the left side of the Navigator. It is used to select the primary type of files that you want to see. You can select **All, Tables, Queries, Forms, Reports, Labels, Programs, Images, Sounds, Catalogs,** and **Custom**. Figure 2–10 shows the file type selection section of the Navigator.

Figure 2–10. The file selection section of the Navigator.

To select and view only Form files, click on the name Forms or the form icon in the left side of the window. When you select one of the file types, dBASE will display the names of the files in the right window.

If you click the All category, dBASE will display all the files that it uses—tables, queries, and so forth. dBASE uses a different icon next to name for each of the file categories.

In Visual dBASE, if you make the Navigator window too small to display all of the categories of files, a vertical scrollbar will be attached to the right side of the section. Figure 2–10a shows the same File selection section with the scrollbar activated. To display more selections, simply use the elevator scrollbar.

Figure 2–10a. This is the File selection section with a vertical scrollbar activated.

The very last category—Custom—is user controllable. You can specify any nonprimary file types that you want to display in the Navigator. In Visual dBASE, the default skeleton is: *.cc, *.vbx, *.h, *.def. However, you can change this to anything you want.

File Skeleton Information section

After you select the file category of the type of files that you want to work with, dBASE displays information in a small area below the Directory section and above the file named Container. It looks similar to the one in Figure 2–11.

Form Files (*.WFM, *.FMT, *.CFM, *.MNU, *.POP)

Figure 2–11. The File Skeleton Information section of the Navigator.

Figure 2–11 shows the file skeleton for the forms with which dBASE can work. If you click on a different category, like tables or queries, the new section will reflect the file types for it; for instance, tables will be "*.dbf, *.db", and queries will be "*.qbe, *.vue, *.qry".

This section is used to display the skeleton for the type of files that dBASE will display in the file named Container, below it. Normally, this section is not modifiable by the user; however, if you select the Custom file type, the user can specify what types of files they wish to display. Figure 2–12 shows the File Skeleton Information section for Custom with the user specified: "*.avi, *.vbx". This user selection will show Video for Windows, audio visual files, and visual basic files.

Figure 2–12. The File Skeleton with user-supplied Skeleton Information.

File Details Container section

Below the File Skeleton Information section and to the left of the File Type Selection section is the File Details Container. This section shows, at a minimum, an icon and the name of each file for the specified type (Tables, Forms, etc.) In addition, it can also display file specific information (date, time, and size). It shows only the files matching the category of files selected in the section on the left side of the Navigator. Figure 2–13 shows the container with the form files (*.wfm, *.mnu, . . .) in the current directory.

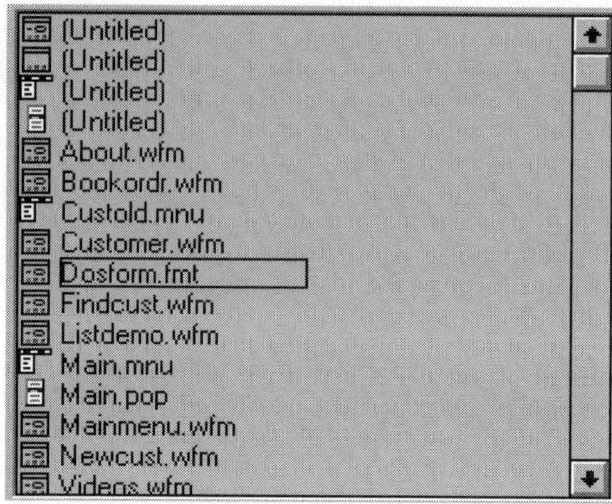

Figure 2–13. The file name container of the Navigator.

Notice that the file container has a vertical scrollbar along the right side of the container. If there are too many file names to display in the current container, the scrollbar is activated so that you can display additional items.

Each file in this container has a name and an associated icon. The icon, aligned to the left of the file name, or atop of it—if View >> Large Icons is active—visually tells you what type of file it is. For instance, Figure 2–13a shows three large icons for the most common types of form files in Visual dBASE: Main.mnu is a Menu file, Main.pop is a PopUp file (SpeedMenu), and Mainmenu.wfm is a form file.

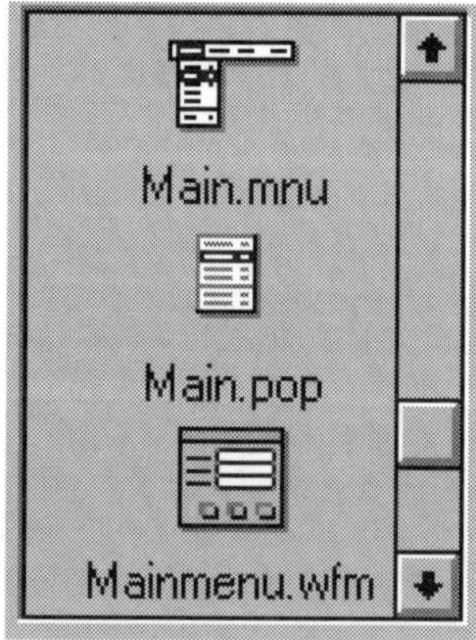

Figure 2–13a. This is the files container with three files and associated icons.

This section, the file detail container, is the main driver of the Navigator. Using this section, the user can do four basic things with the files in this section:

Select. Clicking with the left mouse button, on the file (object) name, will select the object (file). The file name will be highlighted.

Work. Double-clicking with the left mouse button, on the object name, will run (or work) with the object. For example, if you double-click on a table or query, dBASE opens the table and displays the information in a default mode (usually browse).

Question. Single–*right* clicking, the object name, opens a ***SpeedMenu***, showing any actions that can be done with the object. Once the SpeedMenu is open, you can select any of the choices available.

Modify. Double–*right* clicking on the object name will open the object in design mode, letting you modify the design or structure of the object. For instance, double–right mouse clicking on a form name will take you into the form designer.

You can perform these same actions through menu choices or keystrokes while you are in the Navigator.

The Command Window

Like the Navigator, the *Command Window* is a separate object. It has its own frame (window) and can be manipulated like most other windows. It normally appears in the right side of the open area of the desktop. Yours will probably resemble the one in Figure 2–14.

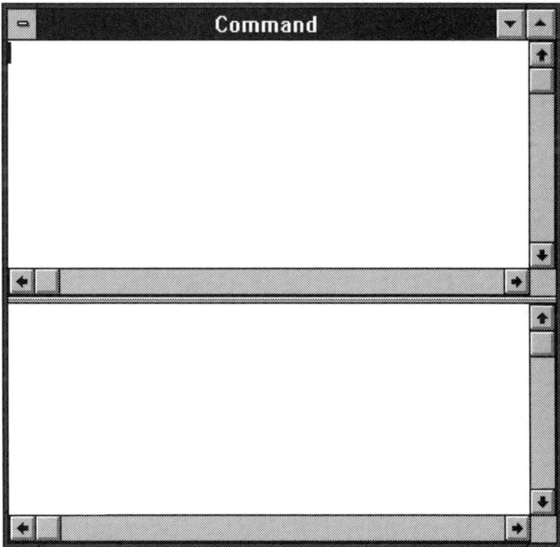

Figure 2–14. The Command window.

The command window serves two purpose. First, it takes the place of the familiar dot prompt in dBASE DOS. You type commands in the command window, just like you did at the dot prompt. Second, the command window is used to run DOS based dBASE applications and display the results of interactive commands.

To accomplish these two tasks, the command window comprises two panes: an ***Input*** and a ***Results*** pane. The Input pane is the portion where you type in dBASE commands, and the Results pane is where the results are displayed. The default positions are the Input pane on top and the Results pane below. However, you can change the positions from one over the other to side by side.

Input pane

Figure 2–15 shows the input pane of the command window. The input pane is where you type dBASE commands like the ones in Figure 2–15: **USE CUSTOMER, BROWSE, ? DATE(),** etc.

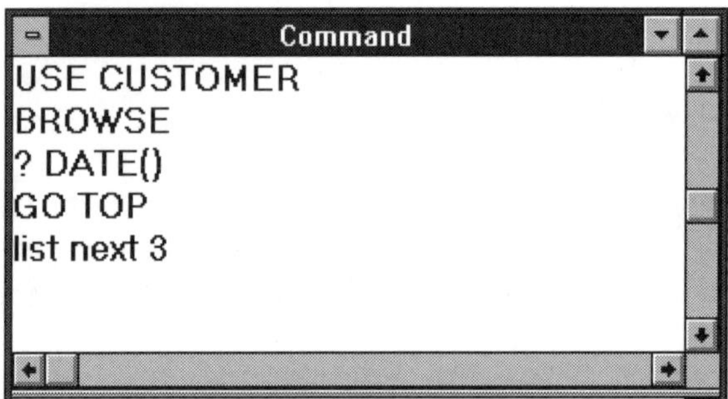

Figure 2–15. The Input pane of the Command window.

The input pane will maintain the last 1,000 lines of commands that you type in it. To redo a previous command, you use the up arrow key or mouse to go to the line and press **Enter** while sitting on the line. Each line can be up to 4,096 characters long.

You can enter more than one command on a command line. Simply separate each command with a semicolon. For instance, you type the following commands on one line:

```
CLEAR; FOR x = 1 to 10; ? "Your number is"+STR(x); NEXT
```

Results pane

The results pane is where the results are placed. Figure 2–16 shows the results of the Date() function executed in the input pane. When you run a dBASE DOS application, it is actually executed in the results pane of the command window.

Figure 2–16. The Results pane of the Command window.

Resizing the panes of the Command window

The command window can be resized like any other window's frame. In addition to the window, the panes can also be resized. To reissue a pane, select the ***center divider*** between the two panes and drag the divider up or down (or left/right) to increase or decrease a window pane. The center divider is the line between the two panes. It should look similar to the one in Figure 2–17.

Figure 2–17. The Center Divider Line of the Command window.

The status bar

The *status bar* is the last area of the desktop and sits at the bottom of the main window (frame). It is used to display messages and information about the current menu bar choice or SpeedBar item. Figure 2–18 shows the status bar with a message on the left side of it. This is the status bar that is active when the Navigator is active.

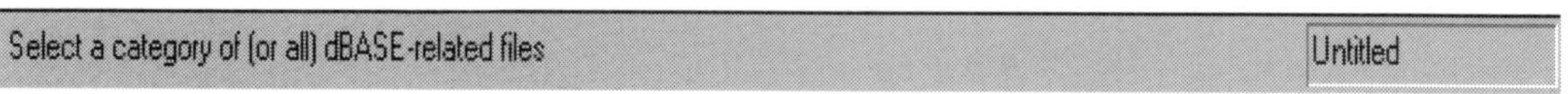

Figure 2–18. The status bar of the desktop.

The status bar in Figure 2–18 actually has two areas. The left side shows a message based on the highlighted item. The right side gives additional information. In this case, there is no additional information. Figure 2–19 shows the right side of two additional status bars. Notice that it displays more information.

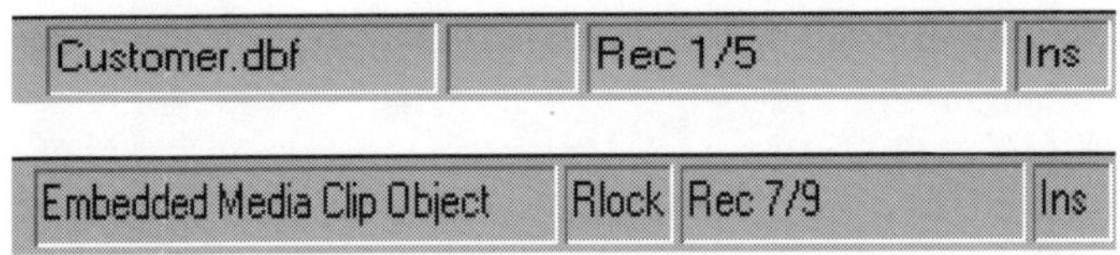

Figure 2–19. The right side of two status bars.

As Figure 2–19 shows, the right side of the status bars in Figure 2–19 shows different information, based on the activity that you are performing. The top one, the command window status bar, shows the name of the open table—Customer.dbf and the record number. The bottom one shows the information for an OLE field that is open in a browse window.

SOME IMPORTANT TOOLS IN VISUAL dBASE

In addition to the dBASE's desktop, there are several tools that can help you when working with dBASE and creating applications. These include

- SpeedMenus
- Help systems
- Dialog boxes for properties
- Expression builder

SpeedMenus

Figure 2–20 shows a SpeedMenu for the form named Mainmenu.wfm.

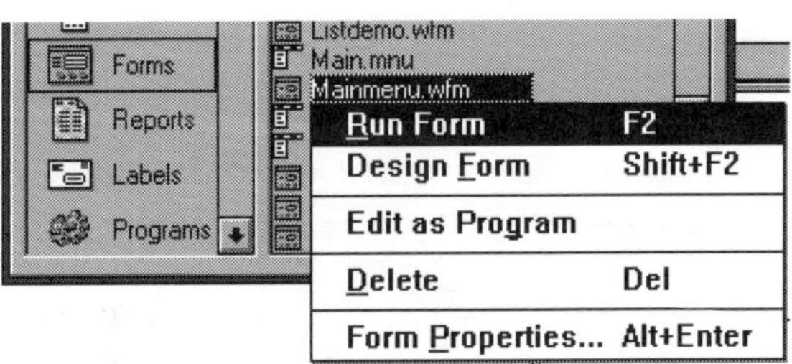

Figure 2–20. A SpeedMenu in Visual dBASE.

A *SpeedMenu* can be thought of as a Menu-on-Demand. When you *right* mouse click on an object, dBASE activates a minimenu, called the SpeedMenu. This menu makes an object's frequently used commands quickly available to perform operations on the object.

The SpeedMenu in Figure 2–20 lets you activate the Form Properties dialog box, delete the form, run it, or edit it as a program or in the form designer. All the available choices in any SpeedMenu will work with the object that the SpeedMenu is active for.

dBASE Help system

Visual dBASE has several options for helping you work with dBASE. It has traditional help where you type HELP with the keyword as well as experts and an interactive tutorial built into the product.

The Help Engine

dBASE uses the Help Engine that is built into Windows. You can activate the Help Engine by typing (in the Command window) HELP followed by the command you want help on or selecting Help from the menu bar. Once active, the Windows help system activates with the dBASE help file. Figure 2–21 shows the Help window active with help for keystrokes in dBASE.

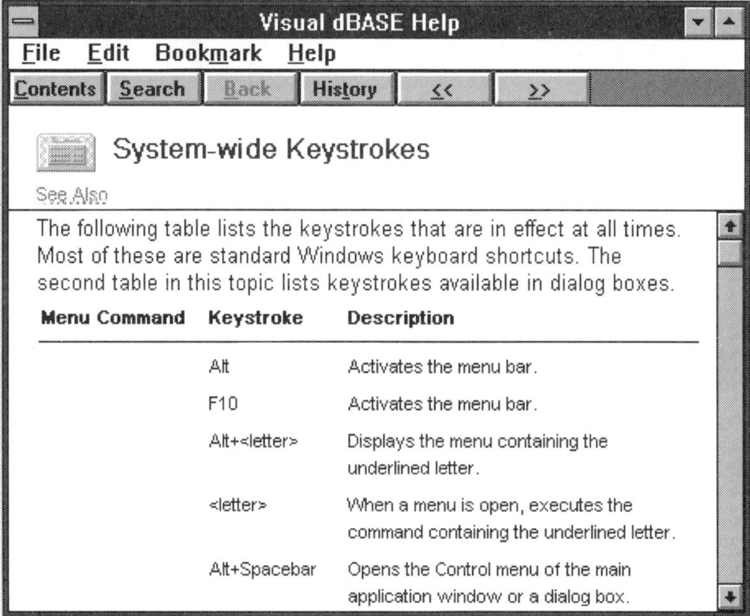

Figure 2–21. The Help Engine in Visual dBASE.

This Help Engine is the same one used by all Windows applications. You can build your own Help files and use the same engine in your Visual dBASE applications.

The Experts

dBASE offers *Experts* to help you create objects. In this first release of dBASE for Windows, there was only one Expert—the form expert. However, with the release of Visual dBASE, there are several experts, including a table design expert, form, report, and label experts. Figure 2–22 shows the first screen of the form expert. Experts are a series of dialog boxes that prompt the user through building an object.

Figure 2–22. The Form Expert.

The form builder expert uses five dialog boxes. It goes from one dialog box to the next, with the user answering a few simple questions on each. Once completed, the expert will build a form. This form can be a single- or multiple-table form (using a query).

The Interactive Tutors

dBASE offers tutors to guide you through performing tasks in dBASE. It lets you work with your data or the sample data provided by the tutor. To run the tutors, select Interactive Tutors from the Help menu on the menu bar. The Tutors will walk you through tasks step by step. Figure 2–23 shows the main screen of the Interactive Tutors.

It offers you advice and step-by-step instructions when working with Visual dBASE. To use it, simply select the category (on the right side) and the topic (on the left side). dBASE will run the tutorial. Figure 2–24 shows the interactive tutor working with some sample data teaching a user how to append records to a table.

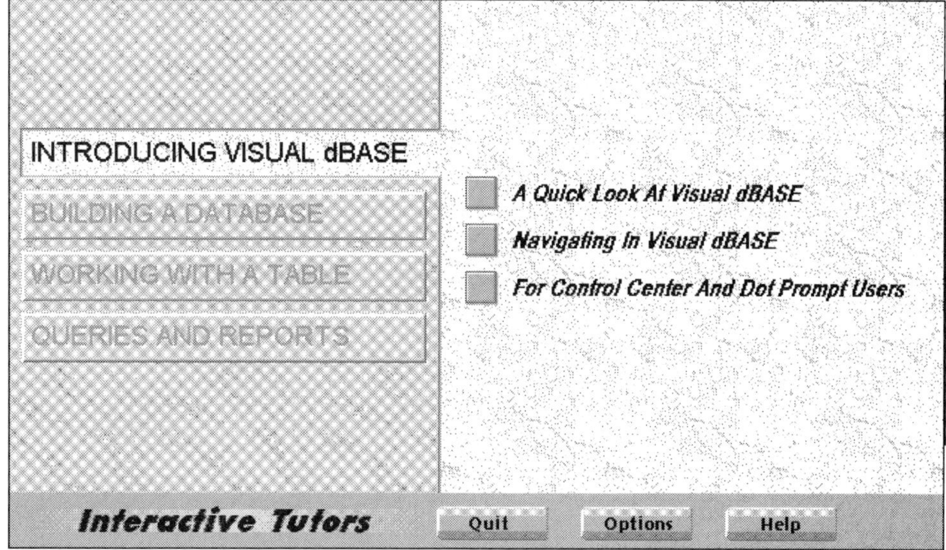

Figure 2–23. The main screen for the Interactive Tutors.

The tutors dialog box in the bottom right corner of Figure 2–24 explains the steps necessary to complete the task. The tutorial placed a large arrow pointing to the Table menu choice of the main menu. The arrow is part of the tutorial. The data in the Browse window is active. The tutor visually aids the user in taking the appropriate steps to complete the task.

The Properties dialog boxes

In the world of objects, all objects are made up of properties. When you work with objects, you manipulate them (objects) by changing the values of their properties. Properties are the characteristic values, the memory variables that are used to create an object. Everything has properties—the desktop, the Navigator window, the Command window, or a form. Figure 2–25 shows the Properties dialog box for the desktop. It can be activated by selecting the Properties >> Desktop Properties . . . choice from the menu bar. Additionally, you can activate it by simply typing the command SET in the command window.

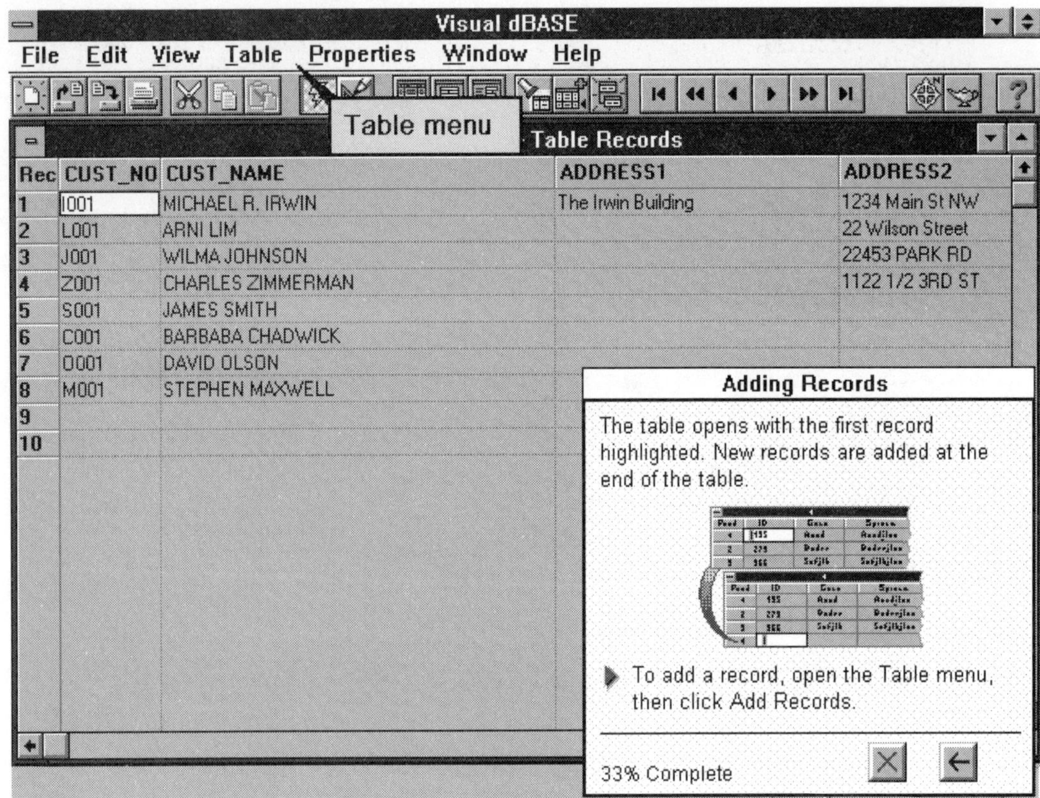

Figure 2–24. The Interactive Tutor for adding records to a table.

These dialog boxes let you interactively change any properties of the object. The desktop dialog box has six tabs (bottom of dialog box) that display different pages of properties that can be set by the user. The **application** tab is currently active. Notice that you can change the position of the SpeedBar, turn the status bar on/off, and so on. You can select the other tabs to see what other properties can be set for the desktop.

The desktop properties are similar to the SET commands of dBASE DOS. Think of them as memory variables that are used by the object. For instance, activate the Command window Properties dialog box by selecting the Command window and then choosing the Properties >> Command Window . . . choice from the menu. Another way would be to select Command window Properties . . . from the SpeedMenu (right mouse click). The Command Window property dialog box (Figure 2–26), lets you change fonts in either pane and determine the position of the Input pane (top, left, right, bottom).

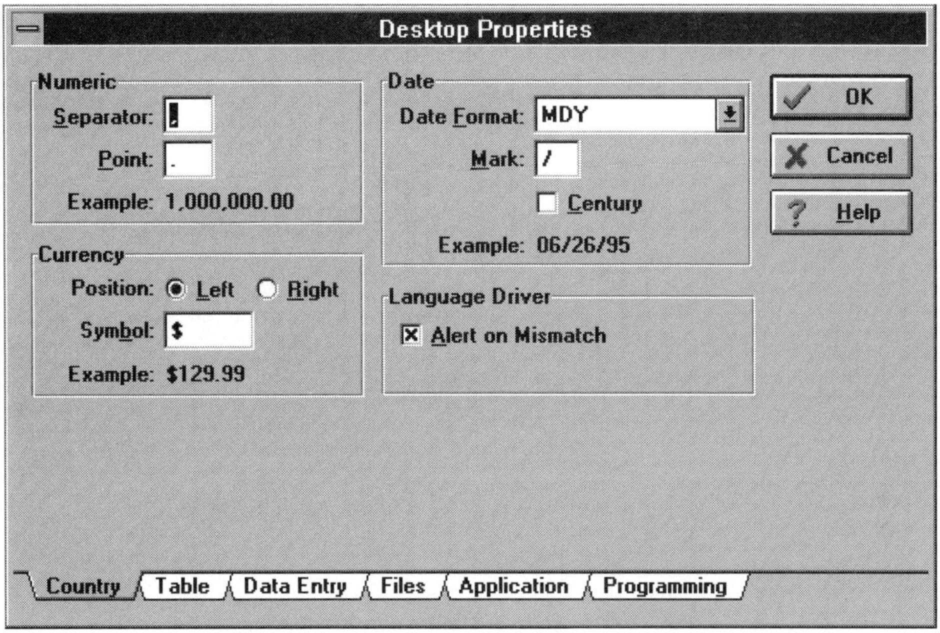

Figure 2–25. The Desktop Properties dialog box.

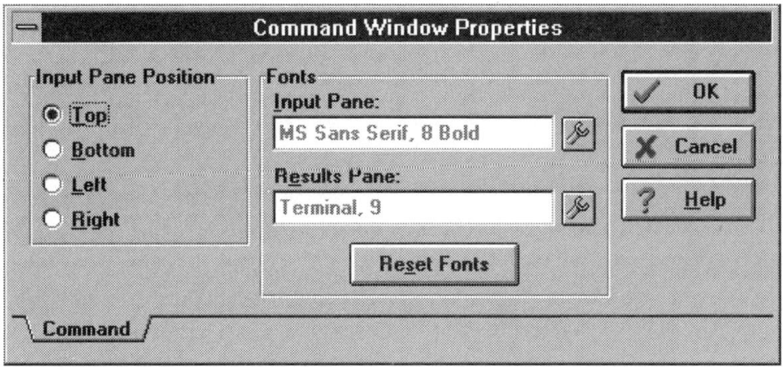

Figure 2–26. The Command Window Properties dialog box.

Property dialog boxes let you manipulate the properties of any object interactively. By using them, you won't have to remember every property for every object.

Later you will learn to use the Inspect() function to inspect properties interactively for the objects you create.

The Expression Builder

Another tool that is available to you is the Expression Builder. You can use this tool to help you construct *expressions* that you may need to include in some operation. The Expression Builder dialog box looks like the one in Figure 2–27.

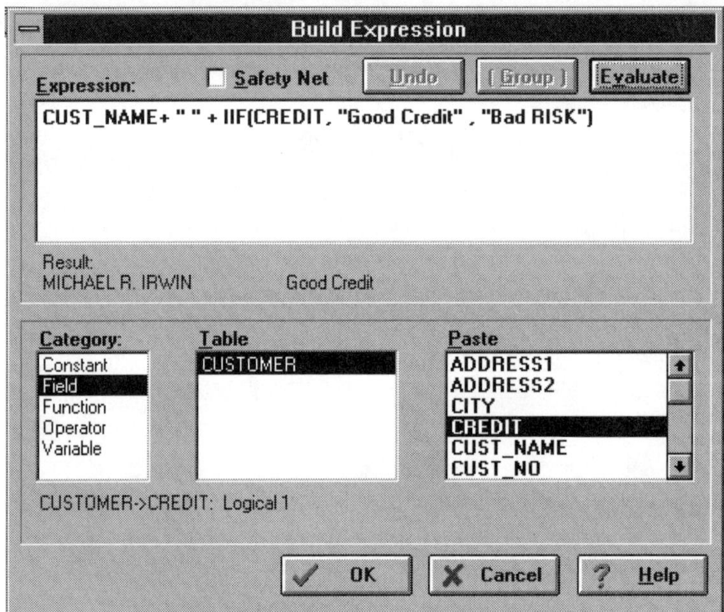

Figure 2–27. The Expression Builder dialog box.

To activate the Expression Builder you can select Edit >> Build Expression . . . from the menu or press Ctrl+E from several surfaces. For instance, while in the Command window, select the choice from the Edit menu. Once the Expression Builder is active, it can be used to build expressions using simple prompts and selections. The Expression Builder can be used in the Command window, Program Editor, and the Query builder (with calculated fields).

There is a check box located at the top left corner of the Expression Builder dialog box labeled Safety Net, like in Figure 2–27. By enabling this, your expression will be entered via selections, thus verifying its accuracy as it is entered. The user will not be able to type the expression directly into the box.

Once the Expression has been built, it can be tested by pressing the "Evaluate" button. Figure 2–27 shows the expression tested and displayed in the Result: area below the Expression Builder box (above the Category list box). In this case, it says "Michael R. Irwin Good Credit."

You can also activate the Expression Builder in your code by using the new GETEXPR() function.

Chapter 3
Introduction to Objects and Visual dBASE

It has been said that "Objects are the important elements of programming for the future." In part, this is said because objects can be reused and customized with minimal effort. To change an object's behavior or abilities does not require that your re-create the object to change something. It is like people: You don't have to re-create them to change their actions. Rather, you simply educate them. Objects are similar; once they are created, you can add, change. or delete parts of them.

One of the most important tenets of objects is that when you use an object, it doesn't have to be redeveloped (or re-created) each time. Once created, it always exists.

WHY OBJECT ORIENTED?

The primary purpose of the object-oriented approach is to solve *complexity* quickly. The more complex a programming project is, the more you should consider designing and programming it in an object-oriented manner.

Today, most object-oriented programming is being performed in third-generation languages like C++ and Smalltalk. These development languages have already proved the benefit gained by use of object-oriented methodologies.

The object-oriented approach is not new; it is more than 20 years old. Over the last three to five years, it has quickly grown and matured. However, it is still in flux and doesn't even have a common standard among object-oriented languages; even the terminology isn't standardized. For example, something called data in C++ is known as properties in some other object-oriented languages. This lack of commonality among object-oriented languages can be confusing. To dBASE people, it is even worse—data are stored information in a table or database, not properties or memory variables with values. This book explains the terminology in the object world from the Visual dBASE perspective, and, where appropriate, it is compared with terminology from other object languages.

Common concepts of the world of objects

Even though there is no standard among object languages, there are four principles that remain true in the object world.

1. Everything is an object.
2. Objects consist of two categories of parts.
3. All objects live independently.
4. All objects are constructed the same.

Everything is an object

Everything you create and use in dBASE is an object. The objects are the forms, browse windows (in its own form), pushbuttons, texts objects (equivalent to @ . . . SAY in dBASE DOS), entryfield objects (equivalent to @ . . . GET in dBASE DOS), menus, check boxes, and so forth.

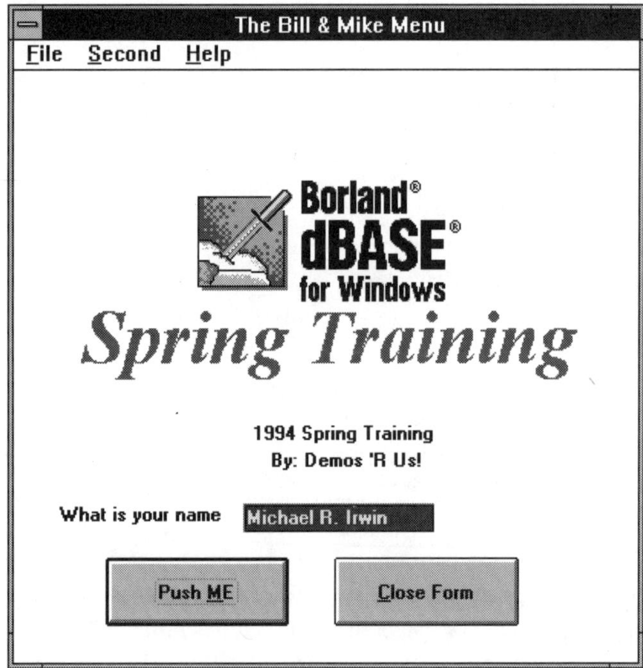

Figure 3–1. A typical form with many other objects in it.

The form in Figure 3–1 is actually an object—a form object. A form object can be a complete application or just a form that is called from another form. The form object usually has other objects inside it: a menu object, an image object, some text objects (similar to the @ . . . SAYs of DOS), an entryfield object (similar to the @ . . . GET of DOS), and a couple of pushbutton objects. Everything is an object in dBASE.

Each object is physical and can be described by its own distinguishing features or characteristics. For instance, each form has its own size (height and width), positioning (top/left corner of the screen), color, text on the title bar, ability to be maximized, minimized, moved, and so on. You can describe each form by identifying its specific features (characteristics). Each form you create will have the same characteristics, called properties. The values of those properties, though, can be different from form to form.

An analogy would be people. Each person is an individual. Each person has properties (characteristics). They have a size (height and weight), eye color, skin color, extremities (arms and legs), and usually two arms and two legs. When you try to describe a person to someone you usually describe the physical characteristics first. Then you describe some of their other qualities, such as disposition and expressiveness.

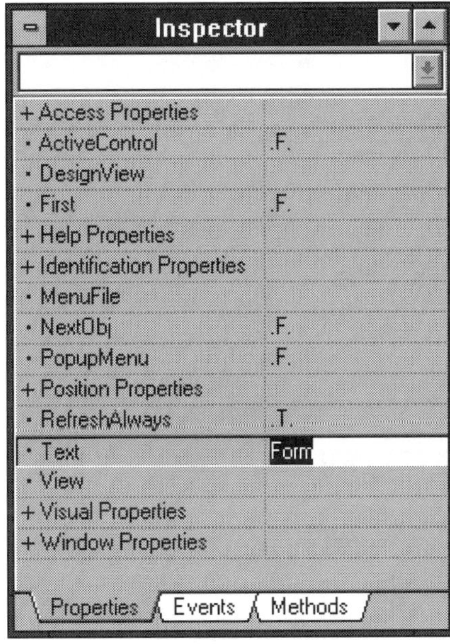

Figure 3–2. The property inspector showing some of the properties (characteristics) of a form.

Figure 3–2 has the Property Inspector open. It is showing the properties for a form named "f." To activate the Property Inspector you use the Inspect() function with the name of the object you want to examine. This can be done in the Command window by issuing a command like the following:

```
INSPECT(f)
```

NOTE: Starting the Property Inspector. Notice that you do not have to use the print statement (?) before the function name. Once active, the Property Inspector lets you visually examine and change the properties (characteristics) of an object.

The point of this section is that everything you work with in dBASE is an object.

Objects consist of two categories of parts

Every object that is created, or constructed, has the following two distinct sections:

- Properties
- Methods

Properties, known as data to C++ people, can be thought of as *memory variables* with values. These memory variables, properties, are broken into two subgroups: characteristic properties and event properties.

Methods are the programs (functions and procedures) that work on the object.

Characteristic (general) properties. The characteristic, or general, properties are the ones that actually create and determine the functionality of an object. They are the descriptors and physical attributes of an object. For instance, a form object has position and size, there are four properties that are used to describe them—height, width, top, and left. Figure 3–2 shows several properties for a form. A form also has the ability to be moved—it is also controlled by a property, the Moveable property. There are even visual properties for a form—ColorNormal, ScrollBar, and MousePointer. They are used to specify a color, authorize the use of a scroll bar, and set the type of mouse pointer to be used when in the form.

Event properties. The other type of properties, event properties, are the ones that wait for an event to occur. When the event occurs, the event property traps it and tells dBASE what to do. For instance, some of the event properties for a form are OnOpen, OnClose, OnHelp, and OnMove. These properties are used to run some program or perform some action when the event occurs. The OnOpen property is used to perform some action when the form is opened.

So event properties are used to run some program or take some action, automatically, when an event occurs.

Object methods. The methods of an object, known as code to C++ people, can be thought of as the functions and procedures that actually work with the object. For instance, when you want to open a form, you tell the form to open itself. It will look inside itself and find its Open() method (or function) and run it. If you want to print the form, you tell the form to use its own Print() method, and it will print itself.

Methods are the programs that are inside the object and only work with that object. They are used to change a form's property value or to perform some other function—like open and close.

All objects consist of two categories or parts: properties and methods.

Objects are created the same

All objects are constructed the same. For instance, if you create a form, you have created something that looks like a dBASE window (has a border with the middle empty). Once created, you will probably want to put other objects inside it. To create a form named MYFORM, type the following command in the Command window:

```
MyForm = NEW FORM()
```

In the DOS world, you create a window, open the window, and then add @ ... SAY and @ ... GET commands to put something in the window. In the Visual dBASE world, everything is an object—the form, the text (@ ... SAY) and the entryfields (@ ... GET). So the form is an object that is empty. If you want to put something else inside it, you need to create other objects (text, entryfields, pushbuttons, check boxes, etc.) and place them inside the form.

When you create any object, you create it by using a template of code that is used to make it real—it is known as a Class. In dBASE, all objects come from a Class. Each object is created in the same manner, from a Class. The Class holds the construction information that will be used to create the properties and methods for each object it creates.

If you create two different forms from the same Class, both forms will have the same properties and methods when they are initially created. Once these objects are created, you can change the values of their independent properties (change the memory variable values). Remember, when you initially created them, they will start life identically—something like identical twins.

In addition to consistency of creation between two like objects, all objects are created using similar syntax. Because all objects come from Classes, the syntax used to create all objects is the same. The difference is some of the specifics. For instance, the following code will create a new form named MikeForm and place a pushbutton inside the form named, MyButton:

```
MikeForm = NEW form()
MyButton = NEW pushbutton(MikeForm)
```

Notice that the method used to create both objects was the same. The difference is that you had to tell the pushbutton where it should go (into the form named MikeForm). Once you create the form object and its pushbutton, you can open the form by calling one of the forms methods (programs). Issue the following command:

```
MikeForm.Open()
```

Notice that there is a dot (period) between the name of the Object and the Open() method, or function.

Objects live independently

The final concept to understand when working with objects is that all objects exist independently. This concept is consistent between all object languages. Each object consists of properties and methods. The values of those properties can be different in each object. For instance, all form objects have a property named Height (to specify the height of the form). The value of the Height property can be different for each form object. One form can be opened, and two others can be closed (two can be blue, one red, etc.). If you close one form, the other two are not affected; each object lives independently.

Properties and methods of each object only work with that object. Because the properties and methods of an object only work with that object, they are hidden or contained within the object. This lets each object work independently from another object. Because each object has to exist and work independently, it needs to be totally self-contained. When a form needs to move, it calls its own move routine (actually it simply changes some properties—Top and Left); if it needs to be closed, it looks inside itself and runs its own close routine.

Benefits of object-oriented development

It is said that object-oriented languages allow you to create and maintain applications quicker and more effectively. So when do you use object-oriented methods?

When to use object-oriented development

Object-oriented development is beneficial for the following:

- *Large, complex projects.* Using object-oriented techniques, you can quickly and easily create an application that "models" the real world. This is accomplished by creating code and associating it with a specific object's behavior (or action). The code becomes task oriented instead of procedural in nature. This simply means that you program by exception rather than program in all possibilities.
- *Application projects that are modified often.* Applications created in an O-O language are usually easy to update and maintain. Once you define the classes that create your objects (covered later), you can easily modify their functionality by creating (deriving) subclasses and modifying them. This eliminates the need to ever have to touch the original code.

- *Multiple programmer projects.* When working with objects, you "hide" the memory variables (called properties), their values, and the methods (subroutines/functions) in the object. This makes it possible to create different parts of an application with different programmers and not require strict variable naming rules. You won't have to worry about having pages (or books) of system documentation tracking all known memory variables and procedure or function names.

Notice that all three reasons to use O-O development—large projects, remodifiable projects, and multiple-programmer projects—draw attention to a specific type of development: database management projects.

Database object-oriented development

Database management systems (DBMS) are applications that tend to be large and complex, and are always modifiable. Most, if not all, DBMS applications grow. They take on a life of their own. The system that you originally installed at the client's location will change over time. Users will want more functionality, or enhancements and modifications for their system. This is normal—as a system is used, new and creative ways to use it are revealed. Thus, the system grows. In addition, many projects are being developed by small teams of programmers (two to five people).

So if the goal of O-O development is to solve complexity quickly and it is ideal for applications requiring constant maintenance, O-O languages should be developed to work in and with DBMS. Visual dBASE has an O-O language that is a natural extension of the database manipulation language. It, unlike C++ and Smalltalk, is a fourth-generation language—made specifically for database work.

It Is All about Words

It is easy to learn and understand the basic concepts of O-O.

- Everything is an object.
- Objects consist of two categories of parts.
- All objects live independently.
- All objects are constructed the same.

What isn't easy is the terminology, or the words of the Object world. O-O development concepts make sense to a programmer—until the names appear. The words are ones you really do not want to learn. You don't have to learn them; rather, you simply need to know how to use O-O to get your job done.

The "What" words

When you start learning object orientation you hear words like the following:

- Class
- Object
- Members
- Data or properties
- Code or methods
- Constructors
- Method declarations

This book has already used several of these words. As you work with objects, you will tend to learn a new vocabulary—the "what" words of the object world.

Remember, they are only words. You don't have to memorize them. You only have to understand what objects are and how to work with them.

Putting definitions to the words

Table 3–1 defines most of the "what" words.

Table 3–1. The "What" Words of O-O.

Term	Meaning
Class	It is a template or specification that creates objects. It has constructor code and method declarations inside it. These are a series of commands used to create the objects (properties and methods). Each Class can create many of the same object. All the objects created by the Class will be identical (e.g., a form Class, a pushbutton Class, a browse Class, etc.).
Constructors	This is the code that is inside a Class definition that is used to create the properties (memory variables) and assign their default values of an object. The Class used constructor code to create the object physically.
Method Declaration	These are the actual functions and procedures that are used by the object. Because a Class can create several objects, all identical, the Class physically maintains the actual code for the methods. The declaration is the actual procedure or function that is used by the object. The object maintains a pointer to its methods (which live in the Class).

Table 3–1. The "What" Words of O-O, continued.

Term	Meaning
Object	It is a thing that is created, instantiated, from a Class. It is made up of memory variables (properties) and functions/procedures (methods).
Members	They are the collection of properties and methods in an object. Each property or method is a "member" of the object.
Property	It is a memory variable and its value defines an object. It is the characteristic values (e.g., size and color) and action values (e.g., sizable and moveable) of an object. Besides characteristic properties, there are also event properties. These memory variables are used to tell the object to run a method (program) when an event occurs against the object.
Method	It is a function or procedure that belongs to an object. The object's function or procedure only works with that object (e.g., the Open() and Close() methods of a form object).
Member Access Operator	When you work with the members (properties or methods) of an object, you must specify the object name to use and then the name of the property or method. To separate the two parts (object name and member), you use a period (dot) between the names (e.g., myForm**.**Top, myForm is the name of the form object; Top is the name of the property).
Member Call Operator	When you want to run one of the object methods, you call it by the name of the object, the dot (member access operator), the name of the method (function or procedure), and end it with the left and right parenthesis—( ) (e.g., myForm.Open(), myForm is the name of the object; Open is the name of the method). The parentheses tell dBASE that it is a method of an object.

The Class

To tie them all together, a Class is a program that contains two parts: Constructor code and Method Declarations. The Class creates objects. A form Class creates forms, a pushbutton Class creates pushbuttons. A Class can create any number of objects; however, every object that it creates will be the same.

A Class is code. The class, itself, is simply some program that someone wrote. DBASE has many different classes built into the product (Form, pushbutton, browse, etc.). The following code was created in a procedure file by typing MODIFY

COMMAND MYPROCS.PRG in the command window. It is an example of a Class that was created for objects that can be used to track inventory.

```
*** MYPROCS.prg
*
* Procedure file with Class definitions
*
CLASS MyInvItem
     *
     * the following is the Constructor code
     *
     this.Type = "Item Name Here"
     this.MadeBy = "Widget Intl"
     this.Weight = 100
     this.Cost = 1.00
     this.Quantity = 100
     *
     * the following is the method declarations
     *
     PROCEDURE QuantityDown
          parameter n
          IF TYPE("n")="L"
               this.Quantity = this.Quantity - 1
          ELSE
               this.Quantity = this.Quantity - n
          ENDIF
          return
    PROCEDURE QuantityUp
          parameter n
          IF TYPE("n")="L"
               this.Quantity = this.Quantity+1
          ELSE
               this.Quantity = this.Quantity+n
          ENDIF
          return
ENDCLASS
```

The preceding code is not practical; however, it does show that a Class is simply some code that exists in memory that will be used like a User-Defined Function to create objects. This code creates a Class named MyInvItem, and it is inside a procedure file named MYPROCS.prg.

To create a Class, you begin the Class with the word CLASS and end it with the word ENDCLASS, both on their own lines. The code placed in between these two commands, called *constraints*—CLASS . . . ENDCLASS—is the Class itself. Notice that this syntax is consistent with other dBASE commands (DO WHILE . . . ENDDO, IF . . . ENDIF, . . .). Between the two Class constraints are the main parts—*Constructor code* and *Methods Declaration*. The Constructor code simply creates all the properties for the object (e.g., Type, MadeBy, Weight, etc.). The Methods Declaration is the actual procedures or functions that will be used by the object (e.g., QuantityDown or QuantityUp).

The Object

The Object, which is created by a Class comprises two parts: properties and methods. The properties are the memory variables that are used to identify or make up the object (characteristics and actions available to it). The methods are the actual functions and procedures that the object uses. An object's methods will only work with that object. All the objects created from a class will, when they are initially created, have the same property values and methods.

An object is created. To create an object, you must first have a Class for it to be created from. For example, to create two inventory items (actually two MyInvItem objects) from the Class MyInvItem (created earlier), you would use some code like the following. The code could be in a program or typed in the Command window.

```
SET PROCEDURE TO MYPROCS
Item01 = NEW MyInvItem()
Item02 = NEW MyInvItem()
```

The syntax can be generalized using the following formula:

<Object Name> = NEW <Class Name([options/parameters if needed])>

In this case, you created two MyInvItem objects and gave them different names: Item01, Item02. To create them, you used the O-O command *New*. They are created from the Class named MyInvItem.

Object type. The type of object is usually identified by the name of the class (or the parent class; more on Class hierarchy follows later in the book). In this case, you created two MyInvItem objects. They are categorized MyInvItem because they came from the original Class named MyInvItem. If you create a form object, it comes from the FORM Class. If you create the Class, you can name the type of object you want. In this case, you created two MyInvItem or Inventory Item objects.

The object's properties. Other than their names, both of these objects (MyInvItem objects) are identical. They both have the same memory variables (properties) named Type, Weight, MadeBy, Cost, and Quantity. The values in their memory variables are exactly the same (type = "Item Name Here"). They both have two methods: one to increase the value in the Quantity property and one to decrease the value in the Quantity property.

Once created, the Objects exist; they are alive. You can check the values of their properties by using commands you have used in the past. For instance, type the following:

```
? Item01.Type
```

dBASE responds with **Item Name Here** in the results pane of the Command window. Now type the following commands and note their values:

```
? Item02.Type
? Item01.Weight
? Item02.Weight
? Item02.Quantity
```

Both objects exist, and both objects are the same (except their names). They both have the same properties and methods. You can change the value in the Item01's type by entering the following command:

```
Item01.Type = "Hammer, claw"
```

This gives Item01 a new value (**Hammer, claw**) for its Type property. Only Item01's type was changed; Item02.type still equals "Item Name Here."

You can change the value of an object's properties (memory variables) by simply assigning a new one. Remember, when you first create the object, the object's property values are initially set by the Class that created it.

The object's methods. In addition to properties, objects can have methods. In the case of our two MyInvItem objects, there are two methods. One increases the value of the Quantity property, and one decreases it.

To run, or use, an object's method, simply call it by specifying the object name and then the method name. All methods are called the same way you call a function (even if they are procedures). Type the following commands in the Command window:

```
Item02.QuantityDown()
Item01.QuantityUp(32)
? Item02.Quantity
? Item01.Quantity
Item02.QuantityDown(12)
? Item02.Quantity
```

The "How" words

These are the words that really scare people away from the O-O world. Some of these words follow:

- Containership
- Encapsulation
- Overloading
- Inheritance
- Instantiation
- Polymorphism

Just hearing these words, you want to immediately think of a simpler time. A time when you could jump in bed and throw a cover over your head to make the "bad" dream go away.

Maybe the "How" of object oriented is just a bad dream!

Well, sorry to say, the "How" of O-O language is important, but the words used to describe the "How" are not. So you need to learn "how" it works, but don't let the words scare you. Remember, they are only words. To paraphrase a famous saying from a child's tale, "Sticks and stones can break my bones, but words will never harm me."

"How" words—what do they mean?

Table 3–2 shows the important "How" words and gives a brief explanation for them.

Table 3–2. The "How" Words of O-O.

Term	Meaning
Instantiation	When you create an object from a Class, it is known as instantiation. You are actually making an *instance* of the Class when you create an object. The actual creation of the object is called instantiation.
Encapsulation	The members of an object are "hidden" inside the object. Because of this, two different objects can have the same property name (memory variable name)—yet contain different values. This act of hiding the members and their values in an object is known as encapsulation.
Containership	After you create a form object, you will probably want to place other objects inside it—pushbuttons, entryfields (@ . . . GET), text, etc. Once the objects are placed inside an object, they are contained within the object. If you close the form object, the contained objects also go away. If you open the form object, everything contained inside it is still there, so it opens also. Containership is the act of containing one object in another object.

Table 3–2. The "How" Words of O-O, continued.

Term	Meaning
Inheritance	When creating a Class, you do not have to create a Class from scratch. Rather you can re-use all the existing resources (Constructor code and Method Declarations) of another Class. Then you can modify or add new resources to the new Class. The new Class would be a descendant of the Class that it copied, and it "inherited" the resources. This way you don't have to re-create new Classes from scratch.
Polymorphism	This is the ability to have two different objects call a method that has the same name, but the methods will do different things (i.e., two methods exist that have exactly the same name, yet they do different things). Which method is used is determined by which object calls it. It is like having two different functions sitting in memory that have the same name. Depending on what parameter or information you send to dBASE, it will decide which function needs to be executed.
Overloading	This deals with inheriting resources from another Class. If a Class is created that starts from the basis of another class, the Method Declarations that are copied into the new class can be redefined. Once they are redefined, any objects created from the new Class will use the new method rather than the one that was inherited. This ability to have an existing method, which is inherited, ignored and a new one put in its place is known as overloading.
Class hierarchy	When you create your own Classes based on other classes, you are building a hierarchy of Classes, or a pecking order where some classes come from other classes. This is also known as subclassing.

Table 3–2 defines all the "How" words of object-oriented. You are not expected to understand everything that is covered here. Rather, this table is placed here to be used as a reference as you learn the "how" of O-O language. It is just preparing you for the "culture shock" of the object world.

Think about this portion of the chapter as all the "legal stuff" that we have to get through (it is required by law). With all of these words presented, it is now time to learn the object world. You will accomplish this task by working with examples and learning by working with them.

Working with Simple Objects

If you have been typing in the examples up until now, you have already worked with the principal object in dBASE—the form object.

As pointed out in an earlier chapter, when you look at Visual dBASE, you are looking at *objects*. Most of the objects already exist when you start dBASE. The objects of the user interface (UI) include the dBASE window (frame), menus, SpeedBars, Command window, Navigator, ... Everything you can 'see' is an object. You can also create your own objects, like forms and their contents.

Creating a form object

For example, to create a form, which is similar to a window in dBASE DOS, you would type in the following command in the Command window:

```
MyPersForm = NEW FORM()
```

If TALK is ON, dBASE will let you know that it created the object by displaying the word **Object** in the *results pane* of the Command window (bottom half). In the preceding example, you used the object extension, **NEW**, to create the object. In addition to extending the language with an O-O language, dBASE also has dBASE-like syntax that will help you do the same thing, in a more familiar way. The following two commands do exactly the same thing; they create a form object, name it, and give it text for the title bar:

```
DEFINE FORM MyPersForm
MyPersForm = NEW FORM("MyPersForm")
```

The first command sounds like a dBASE command. The second, although it may appear awkward at first, tends to grow on you with its simplicity.

The NEW command

The NEW command is probably the most powerful command added to dBASE. It lets you create any type of object. When you use it, you use the following simple syntax:

<name of object to create> = NEW <name of class used to create it([options])>

When you create the NEW object, dBASE creates all the properties and methods for the object automatically using the Class definition.

If you need to create a form, you can use the NEW operator; you can also use the NEW operator for a check box, entryfield, text, or any object.

Once you create the object, you are ready to work with it. To work with the object, you need to manipulate and work with its properties (memory variables) and methods (functions and procedures).

Programming by exception

When you work with objects in an O-O language, you are really programming by exception, or property programming. Because an object is self-contained and self-living, you work with objects independently. Programming is accomplished by changing property values or writing methods that will be used by the object when an event occurs.

To work with the members (properties and methods) of an object, you can use the member access operator.

Working with object members and the dot operator

To work with an object's members, you must tell dBASE the name of the object and which member to use. This is done with the help of the *dot operator*. The dot operator (a period between the two names) is formally known as the *member access operator*. It is used as a joiner to link the object name with the member name. The general syntax for using the dot operator is

<object name>**.**<member name>

The following code can be typed into the Command window interactively:

```
MyPersForm = NEW FORM()
AnotherForm = NEW FORM()
MyPersForm.OPEN()
```

NOTE: If you are going to place this code in a program and run it from a program, you must add the command PUBLIC MyPersForm on the first line of the program. This is necessary to work with the form interactively at the Command window. If you are creating this form in the Command window, this step will not be necessary.

You just created two form objects and used the dot operator between the name of the object, MyPersForm, and the method, Open(), to open one of them. Now that the MyPersForm is open, you are ready to do some additional work with the object. Click back into the Command window to make it active and type in the following commands:

```
? MyPersForm.Width
? MyPersForm.Height
MyPersForm.Text = "Mike's Form Title"
MyPersForm.Width = 35
MyPersForm.Height = 12.5678
MyPersForm.Top = 6.55
MyPersForm.Left = 5
MyPersForm.ColorNormal = "/W*"
MyPersForm.Close()
```

Now you have worked with several of the form's (MyPersForm) properties (memory variables). You checked to see what the width and height of the form named myPersForm was. Then you changed its text title, color, size, and position. You have begun to program by exception.

You have also worked with the Open() and Close() methods that belong to the object named MyPersForm. To manipulate the properties and methods of the object, you use the dot operator.

As you work with this coding method, it will become second nature. Right now it seems foreign; however, as you use it, it will seem natural. Using the dot, or member access operator, is known as *dot notation.*

You only worked with one form object—MyPersForm—even though you made two form objects—MyPersForm and AnotherForm. Now open both forms using the following commands:

```
AnotherForm.Open()
MyPersForm.Open()
```

The forms should look similar to the ones in Figure 3–3.

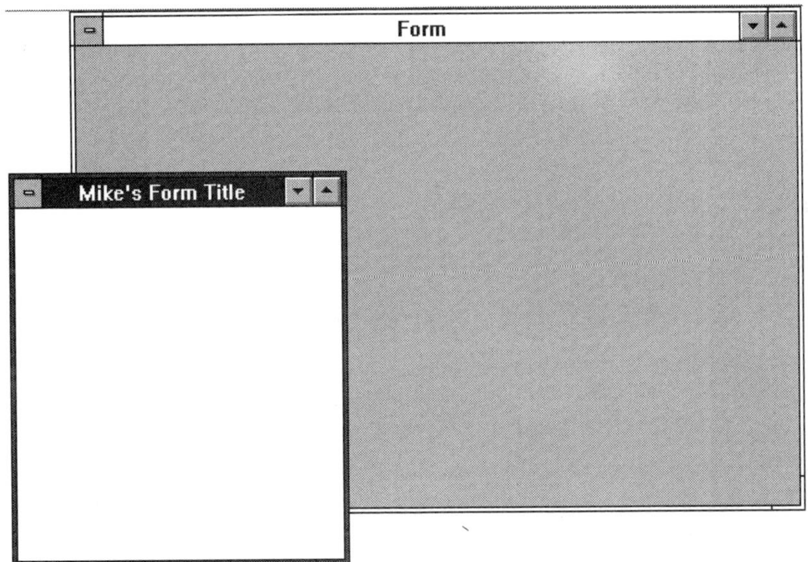

Figure 3–3. Two forms created from the same Class.

Notice that the changes you made to MyPersForm did *not* affect the other form named AnotherForm. When you initially created both forms, they were identical (except their names)—same size, text ("Form"), and color. Because they both came from the same Class, their properties and methods are the same. You used dot notation to change several of the properties of the form named MyPersForm, while leaving the other form alone.

Once you make changes to the properties they are *permanent*. When you closed the form MyPersForm and then reopened it, the changes that were made before closing were still effective.

Creating objects for the form

With the form, MyPersForm, open, it is time to create a couple of pushbuttons and text objects to put inside the form. The following code creates two pushbuttons and two text objects (inside MyPersForm):

```
MyButton1 = NEW Pushbutton(MyPersForm)
MyButton2 = NEW Pushbutton(MyPersForm)
MyText1 = NEW Text(MyPersForm)
MyText2 = NEW Text(MyPersForm)
MyButton1.Top = 1.2
MyButton1.Width = 20
MyButton1.Left = (MyPersForm.Width/2)-10
MyButton1.Text = "Close Another Form"
MyButton2.Top = (MyPersForm.Height)-2
MyButton2.Width = 20
MyButton2.Left = MyButton1.Left
MyButton2.Text = "Close this Form"
MyText1.text = "Hello this is a Text object"
MyText1.top = 4
MyText1.width = 30
MyText2.text = "Text objects are like @ SAY"
MyText2.top = 5
MyText2.left = 3.5
MyText2.width = 30
```

If you typed these commands one at a time in the Command window you noticed that each object was immediately placed in the top, left corner of the form after creation. Then each block of code manipulated the properties of individual objects (MyButton1, MyButton2, MyText1, and MyText2). Your form should now look similar to the one in Figure 3–4.

If you try the buttons, in Figure 3–4, you will see that they do nothing. You have not told the button objects what to do if the user presses them. All you have done is created the buttons, telling them where to live, in the form, and assigned text to them.

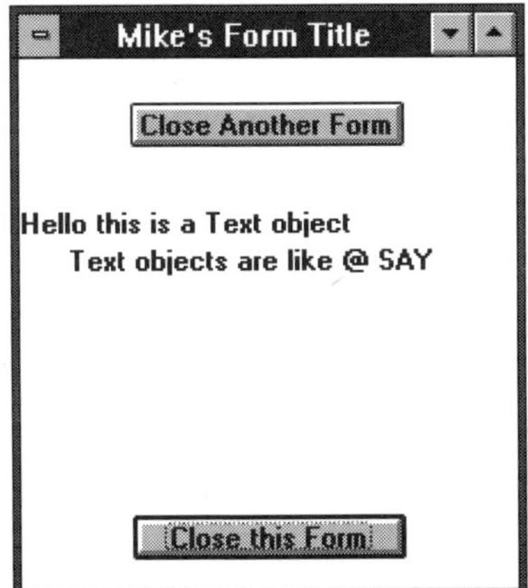

Figure 3–4. A form object with four other objects placed inside it.

Object containership

The four objects you just created are contained inside the form MyPersForm. When you move the form, the object inside it also moves. If you minimize the form, the objects inside it also minimize. This concept is known as containership—one object is contained within another.

Now close the form using the command

```
MyPersForm.Close()
```

All of the objects inside the form closed with the form. Now the question: If you open the form will the objects contained inside it still be there? Try it with the following command:

```
MyPersForm.Open()
```

The DOS way. When you create a window in dBASE DOS and place text (@ . . . SAYs) and entryfields (@ . . . GETs) inside it, they are not kept inside. Instead, you create the window, and then put all the SAYs and GETs in the windows. When you close the window, everything in it goes away. However, when you reopen the window, it is empty again. This means that you must write code that does the following:

1. Define the window
2. Open the window

3. Puts the SAYs in the window (many SAYS)
4. Puts the GETs in the window (many GETS)
5. Close the window

Repeat the process of steps 3 to 5 repeatedly.

OPEN ... SAY ... GET ... SAY ... GET ... CLOSE

OPEN ... SAY ... GET ... SAY ... GET ... CLOSE ...

You have to replace everything in the window repeatedly. Redundant, repetitive processing of the same thing is required. You have to constantly control what is going on in a procedural manner, one step at a time.

The Object way. When you opened the form MyPersForm using the command MyPersForm.Open(), all the objects already placed inside the form are still there, and they are also activated with the single command <form name>.Open(). They are associated with the form as if they had become a part of the overall form. The push-button objects and the text objects are still individual objects, yet they are associated with the form because they are *contained* in the form.

To draw an analogy to DOS, you do the following:

1. Define the form
2. Define all the objects to go inside the form
3. Open the form
4. Close the form

You no longer re-create SAYS and GETS when the form opens.

OPEN ... CLOSE ... OPEN ... CLOSE

Using dBASE-like syntax for objects

Up until now, you have created objects using the NEW object operator (command). Must you use this type of notation to create an object? No. You can also use dBASE-like commands to create the objects. This means that you can continue to use familiar dBASE-like commands to do the same thing.

The dBASE DEFINE <Object> command

dBASE lets you create objects using the DEFINE <object> Command. For instance, the following code will create a form and place a pushbutton on the form:

```
DEFINE FORM ThisForm PROPERTY text "Main Form",          ;
      ColorNormal "W/R", width 35, height 12.5
DEFINE PUSHBUTTON MyButton OF ThisForm PROPERTY          ;
      text "&Close Form", top 2, left 3.5
OPEN FORM ThisForm
```

This dBASE-sounding syntax will create a form and place a pushbutton inside the form. Notice that you can set the property (memory variable) values directly using the DEFINE command. This eliminates the need to set each property individually, as you did using the NEW command.

Which is better: NEW or DEFINE?

Either method of creating objects will work. Both have their advantages and disadvantages. As you work with dBASE and the object model, you will find that a combination of command usage is common.

Pluses/minuses of the NEW command. The NEW command tends to be the best way to create quickly any object from a Class that has most of the default property values you need for the object. Using the NEW operator also makes it easier to reference an object (the name of the object) directly—whether it is contained in another object or not.

Pluses/minuses of the DEFINE <object> command. The DEFINE command is good for those times when you need to change many of the default property values, or you want to add your own custom properties. It will require that you reference any contained object following the object path. This will be explained more in a later chapter.

The REDEFINE <object> command

In addition to the NEW operator and the DEFINE command, Visual dBASE offers another command: REDEFINE, which is useful for modifying an existing object. To demonstrate its usefulness and methodology, type in the following commands:

```
aNewForm = NEW Form()
aNewForm.Height = 10
aNewForm.Width = 35
DEFINE PUSHBUTTON MyButton OF aNewForm PROPERTY;
      text "&Close Form", top 9, left 3.5
aNewForm.Open()
```

Now that the form is open, you see that the pushbutton is too far down and not far enough to the right. So you attempt to re-create the pushbutton with the command

```
DEFINE PUSHBUTTON MyButton OF aNewForm PROPERTY ;
           text "&Close Form", top 7.5, left 18.5
```

When you retype in this command with the new top and left locations, Visual dBASE reports an error: **Cannot have more than one form object with the same name: MYBUTTON**.

So what do you do? Do you re-create the entire form and its contents (in this case, one button)? Do you erase the pushbutton and re-create it? The answer to all three of these questions is *no*.

Simply change the second DEFINE command to a **REDEFINE** command.

```
REDEFINE PUSHBUTTON MyButton OF aNewForm PROPERTY ;
           text "&Close Form", top 7.5, left 18.5
```

The REDEFINE command lets you change the values of an existing object without having to destroy (or RELEASE) the object first.

Understanding properties

All objects are made up of two parts: properties and methods. The *properties* of an object are the features or traits associated with the object. These features include things like the following:

- Location (on the screen or in the form)
- Color
- Size
- Font type (e.g., size, bold, or italics)
- Accessibility (e.g., visible or enabled)
- Text

These properties are actually part of the object. They can be thought of as memory variables with values.

Viewing a form's properties

Most of an object's properties can be set or changed. To examine an object's properties you can use the *Inspect()* function. Using the form MyPersForm, go to the Command window and type in the following command:

```
Inspect(MyPersForm)
```

NOTE: If you get an error that says the memory variable "MyPersForm" does not exist, you will need to do one of two options: (1) re-create the form MyPersForm with the command "MyPersForm = NEW FORM() or (2) you must have created the form and the objects inside it in a program. Make a PUBLIC declaration for the form MyPersForm on the first line of the program.

Visual dBASE activates the *Inspector dialog box* similar to the one in Figure 3–5. Notice that a vertical scrollbar is attached to the right side of the dialog box. If the properties in the box are longer than the viewable area of the Inspector dialog box, a scrollbar is automatically attached.

The Inspector dialog box, also referred to as the *Property Inspector*, has three tabs across the bottom, representing the three pages of items that can be examined. From left to right they are titled: **Properties, Events,** and **Methods**. Click on the Property tab to see all the "general" properties for the form MyPersForm.

Figure 3–5. The Property Inspector dialog box showing the properties for the form MyPersForm and the three tabs across the bottom.

The Property Inspector dialog box is inside a window frame. Like other Windows frames, it can be resized, minimized, and so forth. It has two columns: The left column displays the names of properties (or the category name); the right column holds the value of the property.

Cascading property menu. The individual cells of the left column may hold a property name or the category name for a group of properties. Figure 3–6 shows the left column of the property inspector with several *category* titles displayed. You can quickly identify them by the plus (+) or minus (–) sign in front of the category name.

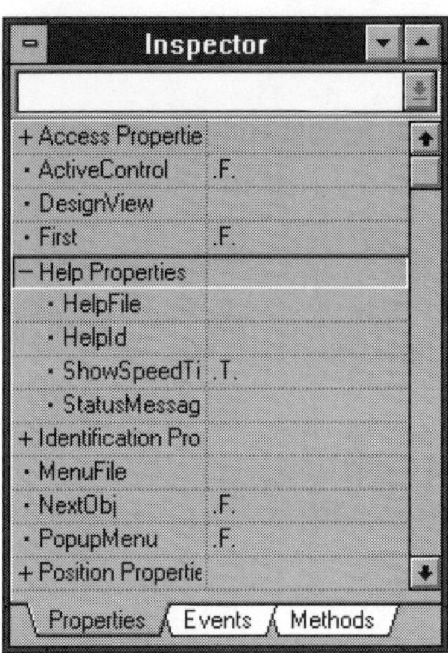

Figure 3–6. The left column of the Property Inspector showing the category listing of properties.

Looking at the property name column in Figure 3–6, you see one of three signs on the left side of each cell: a plus sign (+), minus sign (–) , or a dot (•). If the cell on the left holds a category title, it can be expanded (+) or collapsed (–). When expanded (opened to show all the properties that fall within this category), it will display a minus sign. When collapsed (no properties are seen for this category), it will display a plus sign.

To open or close a category, simply double click on the name of the category. All the cells with a dot (filled circle) to the left of the name are the actual properties of the object.

Using the Property tools. Some properties offer specialized tools to help you assign a value to their property. If the property has a tool to help you, it will display a "wrench" icon on the right side of the value cell when the property gains focus (you click in the property cell). For instance, Figure 3–7 shows the tool button (wrench) for the property ColorNormal, under the Visual Properties category.

Figure 3–7. The Property tool button (wrench) for a property.

To activate the ColorNormal cell, expand the Visual Properties section, and then click in the ColorNormal cell—the tool button will appear to the right side of the cell. Clicking on the property tool button will activate the Color Builder dialog box, as shown in Figure 3–8.

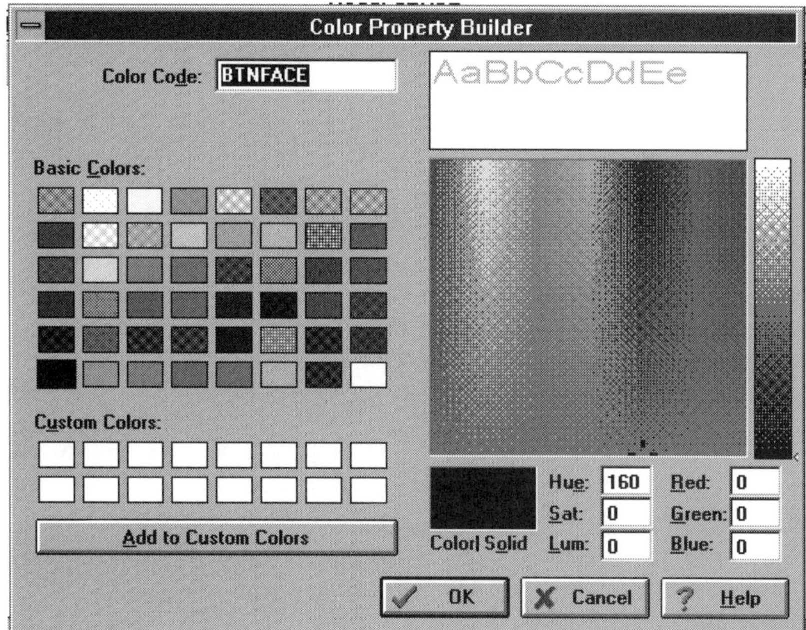

Figure 3–8. The Color Builder dialog box.

The Color Builder dialog box can assist you when setting a color value for an object. In this case, you are setting the color of the form, so it allows you to set a single color. Notice that the color code Entryfield has a value of BTNFACE, a Visual dBASE keyword for the button-face color of the currently active Windows scheme. You can enter any of the dBASE color scheme words here, or the familiar N, R, G, W, B values, or even new values like 0XC0DCC0 (pale green) or 0X4080 (reddish brown). These final values are the Hex codes for colors. Visual dBASE lets you use any valid Windows color your monitor can support.

Working with properties

As Figures 3–5 to 3–8 show, a form object has quite a few properties. Most of their names are identifiable and descriptive: Height, Width, Top, Text, ScaleFontName, and ColorNormal.

Changing property values with the Object Inspector. You can change properties directly in the Object Inspector or through code (in a program or in the Command window). For example, to use the object inspector to change the top, left position of the form, go to the Top property, and type in a new value. Then go to the left property, and change its value. Notice that the form object MyPersForm immediately moves when you change either value.

Properties values are immediate. Because a property of an object is simply a characteristic trait or peculiarity, which is used to define or describe the object, when you change it, the object reacts immediately.

The property is actually a trait about the object that is stored in a memory variable. The memory variable (property) is used to hold the value of a particular characteristic.

The event properties

Besides "general" properties, objects have a special type of property known as the *event* property. Unlike standard properties, the event properties are used to trigger the object into doing something when the event occurs.

The event. To understand event properties, you should have a good working knowledge of what an event is. It is said that Windows is an event-driven environment. This means that Windows and Windows applications respond, or react, when an event occurs.

According to the *American Heritage Dictionary* (third edition, version 3.0A, electronic edition, Copyright © 1993, WordStar International, Copyright © 1992, Houghton Mifflin Company), an event is

> **Event** *n.*, **1. a.** Something that takes place; an occurrence. **b.** A significant occurrence or happening. **2.** The final result; the outcome.

So in Visual dBASE an event is when something happens, or when

- A form opens
- A form closes
- An object gets focus
- A user presses a pushbutton
- A user presses a key

Anytime some action occurs (e.g., pressing a pushbutton), an event has occurred. Some events (actions) are user controlled (pressing a key) and are called *external* events. Some events are not controlled by the user (a form opening) and are called *internal* events.

Trapping the event. The actual event is the pressing of a pushbutton or the opening of a form. The *event property* is the item (property) that is used to trap the event.

To see the event properties of a form, click on the **Events** tab of the Inspector. Figure 3–9 shows some of the event properties that are associated with a form.

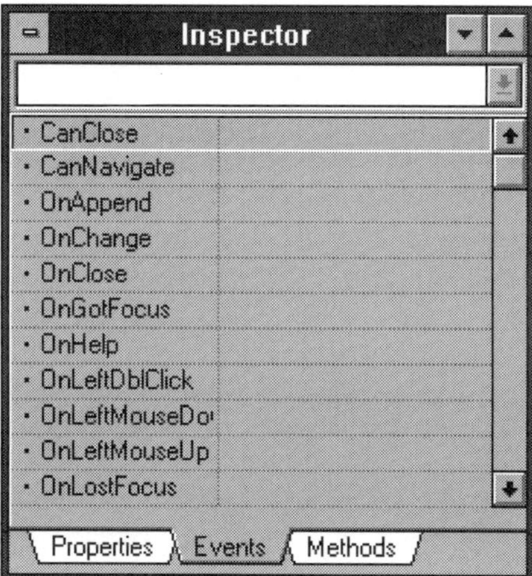

Figure 3–9. The Property Inspector showing the event properties of a form.

Notice that the event properties usually begin with the word **On**—OnAppend, OnOpen, OnClose, OnGotFocus, OnLeftDblClick, or OnMove. Event properties are action type properties, so if you see the prefix "On" before the name of the property, you will know that it is an event property.

The event property will wait until something occurs, then if the event occurs, it will run the program or execute the codeblock (like an unnamed function) that is associated with it. For instance, you should still have your form object, MyPersForm, open and it should have a pushbutton in it named MyButton2 (the one that says "Close this form"). You can associate (assign) some code to the **OnClick** property of the pushbutton object by typing the following command in the Command window:

```
MyButton2.OnClick = {;form.Close()}
```

You have just attached a codeblock—**{;form.Close()}** to the event property OnClick. Once you do this, click on the button at the bottom of the open form. The form closes. You have just attached some code to an event property.

If you attach code to an event, you have attached an *event handler* to the event.

Event handlers. The *event handler* is simply the method or codeblock that is executed in response to an event. The event handler is usually some traditional procedural (flow-of-control) code. Instead of a codeblock in the preceding example, you could have created a procedure or function that will close the form. Then assign the procedure name to the event.

Understanding methods

In addition to properties (general and event), objects also have *methods*. A method is *program code* (a subroutine like a function or procedure) that is used by the object to take some action. It is also directly associated with the object. To see what methods are associated with the form object, MyPersForm, click on the **methods** tab (the last one on the right) of the properties inspector. Figure 3–10 shows the methods that are associated with the form MyPersForm.

Figure 3–10. The Properties Inspector showing the methods associated with a form.

Notice that the form has fifteen different methods associated with it. The two that you have already used are the Open() and Close() methods. These methods are built into the Class FORM. The Class FORM is the Class that you used to create your form MyPersForm.

Methods live in Classes

Unlike properties, the methods of an object are associated with the object through a function pointer. They do not actually live in the object; rather, they exist in the Class. In other words, the method is only created once—in the Class that creates the object. It is created in the method declaration section of a Class. Any object created by the Class can use the methods that are in the class.

By only creating the method one time, there is no wasted code, or code bloat, added to the objects. Because the actual method is in the Class, a function pointer is needed to tell the object where to find the method that it must execute.

The function pointer of a method. The function pointer simply points to the point in memory where the object can find the code that it needs to perform the method. This means that the Class must be sitting in memory at all times, active, like a procedure file. All of the Classes built into dBASE are always available for the objects to use.

NOTE: Although covered later, if you create your own Classes, you will have to place them in a procedure file and load them in memory, before using them. A class must be in memory to create objects and let those objects use the methods declared inside the Class.

Working with an object's methods

To execute an object's method, simply call the method by specifying the name of the object and the method to use. The general format is

```
<Object name>.<Method Name>()
```

When you opened the form object, MyPersForm, you typed the following command:

```
MyPersForm.Open()
```

Notice that you join the name of the method with the object name by using the dot operator.

Using the member call operator. Every time you call a method, you have to place parentheses—( )—after the name of the method. These parentheses are known as the *member call operators*. All methods, functions, procedures, or codeblocks are always referenced by the member call operator after the name of the method. This syntax is exactly the same as when you call functions in dBASE.

Passing parameters to a method. If you create your own methods and need to pass parameters, you simply place the parameters to be passed in between the member call operators (parentheses). This is exactly the same as using a dBASE function. For example, you have a Class with the following structure:

```
CLASS Employee
   this.EmployeeID = "ID001"
   this.FullTime = .T.
   this.HoursWorked = 40
   this.HourlyRate = 22.55
   this.OT = 0
```

```
    Func CalcOverTime(lFullTime)
    LOCAL lFullTime
    IF lFullTime .AND. (this.HoursWorked > 40)
          this.Ot = this.HoursWorked—40
    ENDIF
ENDCLASS
```

Then you create an object from this Class by typing in the following command:

```
Emp1 = NEW EMPLOYEE()
```

After creating the object Emp1 and working with it for some time, you need to run the object's method to determine if Emp1 is due any overtime (OT). If Emp1 worked over 40 hours, then the OT property should be updated to reflect the number of overtime hours that were worked. This is done by the method named CalcOverTime().

To run the CalcOverTime() method, you simply call it as you do any other method. In this case, it needs a parameter: the status of the employee (full- or part-time). This information is stored in a property named FullTime. The syntax to call the method would be:

```
Emp1.CalcOverTime(Emp1.FullTime)
```

Then you can check the OT property, to see if any OT hours were worked. If the employee is full-time and worked more than 40 hours, then OT will reflect the number of hours of OT worked. For instance, update the HoursWorked property and then run the CalcOverTime() method and finally check the OT property.

```
? Emp1.OT
Emp1.HoursWorked = 55
Emp1.CalcOverTime(Emp1.FullTime)
? Emp1.OT
```

The OT property first showed 0; now it shows 15. You passed one parameter to the method CalcOverTime. So passing parameters to a method is the same as passing them to a function.

Part Two Basic Object-Oriented Concepts and Visual dBASE

Chapter 4
Moving from DOS to Windows

When you compare a dBASE DOS application and a dBASE Windows application, the first point that is obvious is the User Interface (UI) differences. The DOS application visually appears plain and unappealing. It just doesn't look as efficient. Comparing dBASE DOS to Windows is like comparing the meal you ate at home last night with the dinner you enjoyed at a plush restaurant. The food last night at home was good (some say "just OK"), but, reminiscing, you might ask: "Remember that fantastic meal we had at XYZ restaurant?"

The greatest chefs in the world say that the real secret to great food is in the presentation: If it is visually appealing and has a pleasant aroma, the meal will be great. This philosophy is similar to a great computer application: If the UI looks great and it responds well, the program is great.

This fact has been one of the driving forces for the acceptance of Windows as a working environment—programs simply look and feel good in Windows.

When you look at dBASE DOS versus Visual dBASE, the Windows application looks great. This is true, even when you consider the difference between the DOS tools and those in Windows. The familiar dot prompt is gone. The Control Center has disappeared. Some of the keystrokes are even different. Conversely, Visual dBASE is a *true* Windows application. The user interface has all the functionality and visual presentation features of a GUI. It works with the Windows print services, monitor and font drivers, and Help engine. It lets you create graphical menus, forms, and dialog boxes. These forms use graphical controls like check boxes, spin buttons, pushbuttons, drop-down list boxes, and others. To the user, things simply appear to work differently in Windows.

Using Your Existing DOS Code and Data

Borland said that dBASE for Windows 5.0 (and Visual dBASE) will run your DOS applications, unchanged. For many DOS applications, this will be true, but it is *not* 100 percent assured. Added, the DOS applications that it does run will offer you a few surprises.

Text based versus graphical

Because dBASE DOS applications are text based (versus graphical), they use nonproportional fonts and are limited to eighty characters across a line, by twenty-five lines of code. To attempt to run them in a Windows GUI environment as a graphical program could prove disastrous. There is no way for the program to know the graphics mode, font proportions, or the ANSI versus ASCII versus OEM character set differences. Things that were lined up in DOS may be skewed in Windows: A full screen in DOS could prove to be too small or too large in Windows; what was a line in DOS is now a "funny little *a*."

This type of problem and other problems suggest that the UI portion of dBASE DOS applications should be converted.

The DOS idiot box

You can run your dBASE DOS application in Visual dBASE. Most probably, your DOS application will run unchanged. However, it will run where you probably didn't expect it to—in the *Results pane* of the Command window. Figure 4–1 shows the dBASE Business.prg running in Visual dBASE. Notice that it is running in the Command window.

The application running in Figure 4–1 is a DOS application (it comes with every copy of dBASE DOS III+/IV). It is automatically mouse enabled in Windows. However, it is text based and looks awkward in Windows. Notice that it doesn't look or feel like a Windows application.

Unexpected surprises

Most dBASE DOS applications will run unaltered in Visual dBASE. However, you need to be prepared—there can be a few unexpected surprises when you run them in Windows.

DOS applications and Windows fonts

Figure 4–2 shows the Business DOS application running in the Command window. Notice that the graphics and text are skewed.

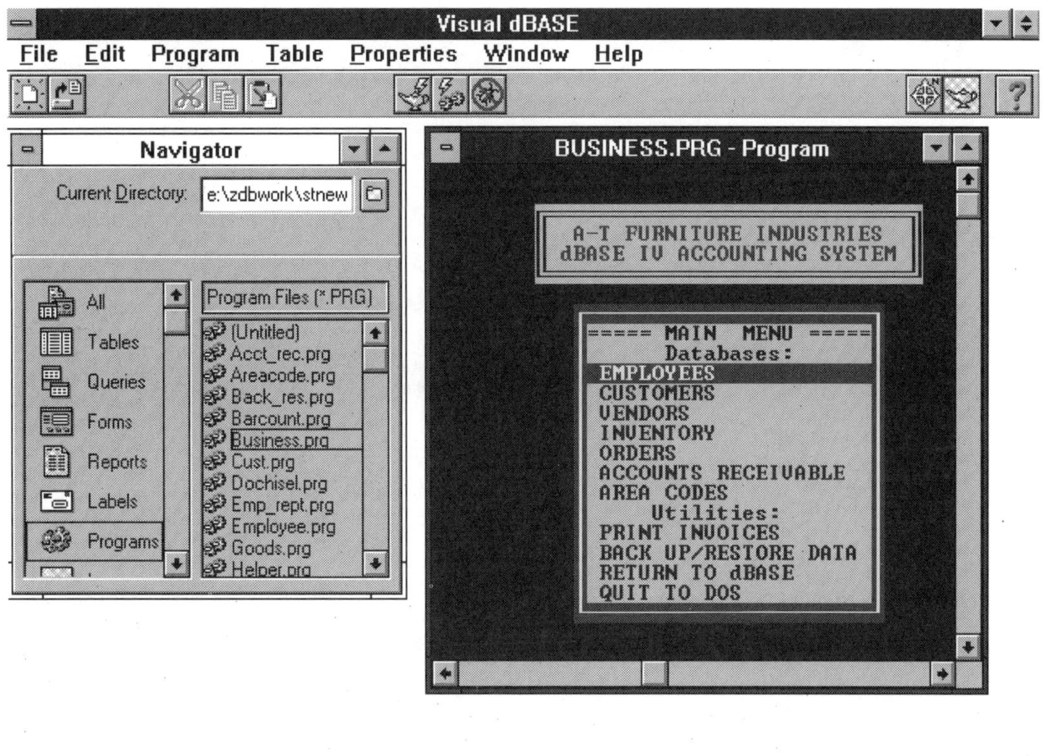

Figure 4–1. A DOS application running in Visual dBASE.

The Employee data entry/view screen, in Figure 4–2, has a serious problem. It is difficult to read the text on the screen. Yet, the pop-up atop of the screen appears to be fine. What happened?

The font set for the Results pane of the Command window is 12-point New Times Roman. Even though it is a standard Windows font, the ANSI values for the graphics (lines in the format file) are different from its DOS counterpart. This means that you need to reset the fonts for the Results pane to Terminal 9.0 (the default). Figure 4–3 shows the Command window Properties dialog box. Because the DOS applications all run in the Results pane of the Command window, only this pane must be reset to the default value.

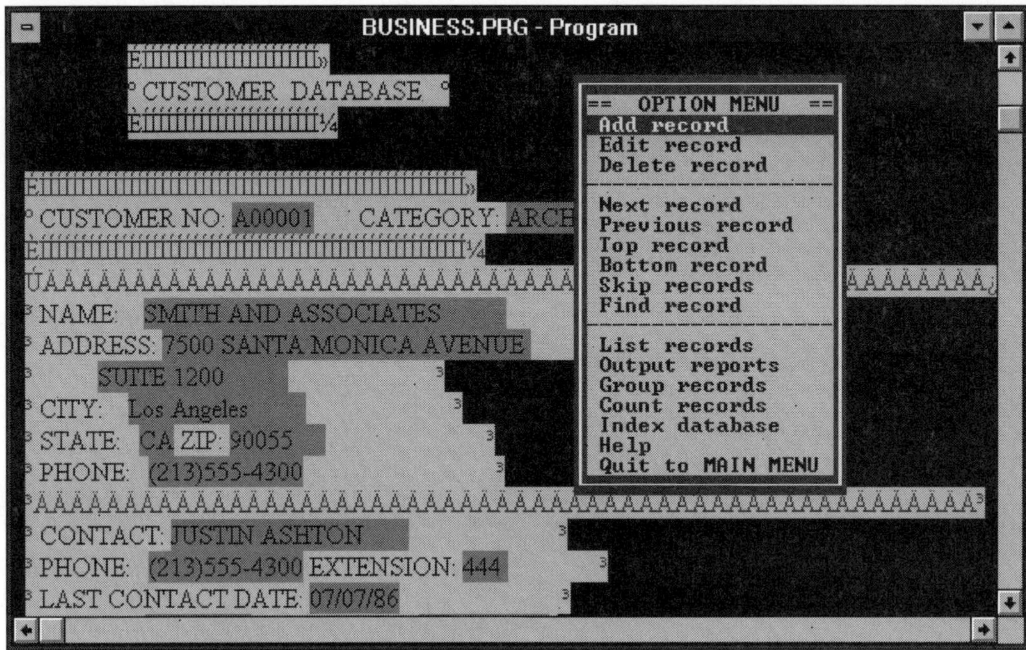

Figure 4–2. DOS application running with a bad Windows font.

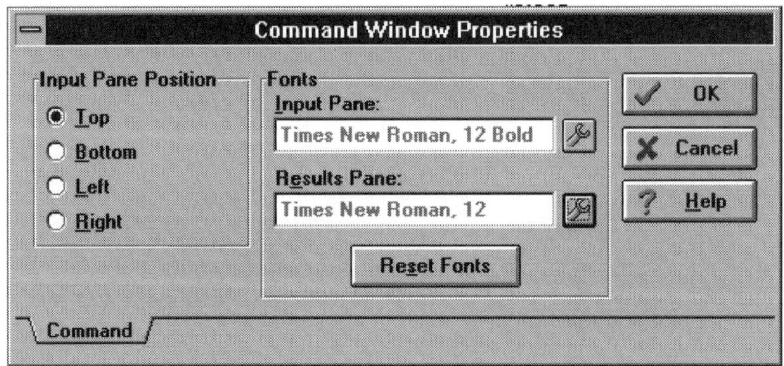

Figure 4–3. Fixing the Results pane font for running dBASE DOS applications.

To activate the Command window Properties dialog box select Properties >> Command Window Properties . . . , or select the choice from the SpeedMenu (right mouse click while in the Command window). Once the dialog box is active, you can pick the correct font for the Results pane or press the pushbutton titled "Reset Fonts" to change all of the fonts back to their default values. You will see your DOS application graphics immediately correct itself.

Running DOS pseudocompiled code (.dbo files)

Visual dBASE will *not* run your DOS-compiled files. The DOS-compiled files are the ones that have an extension that ends in *o* (e.g., .fmo or .dbo). You will need to have the original program files available. In Windows, dBASE will recompile the programs into Windows pseudocompiled code.

NOTE: *Pseudocompiled code* is code that is converted from its source form to tokenized code. By pseudocompiling the code, it will execute quicker. Normally, a noncompiled environment like dBASE III plus needs to interpret every line of code as it is run. This means that each line of code will need to be checked for accuracy and then executed every time the program is run. In dBASE IV and dBASE 5.x (DOS and Windows), dBASE goes through the code the first time it is run and verifies it, converting it to a new format. This new format is known as tokenized code. The tokenized code is not true compiled code (machine language), nor is it source code—it is in between. This tokenized code does not need to be reverified each time, but it still requires some runtime code to execute it.

BROWSE or EDIT in a DOS window

The following code will be used to demonstrate some problems you may encounter when running your DOS applications in Visual dBASE. It assumes that you have a table named Employee to open and a dBASE DOS format file named DOSFORM. You can use any table in its place and any format file; simply change the code to use your own table and format file.

```
*** DOSBROW.prg
*
set talk off
clear
*
*  Structure of Employee.DBF file is
*
*   Field  Field Name     Type       Length  Index
*       1  LASTNAME       Char        15       N
*       2  FIRSTNAME      Char        10       Y
*       3  DEPARTMENT     Char        15       N
*      -------------------------------------------
*    ** Total **                                41
*    DOSFORM.FMT file contents are
*
*       @ 02,02 say "Last"
*       @ 02,12 get Employee->Lastname
*       @ 03,02 say "First"
*       @ 03,12 get Employee->Firstname
```

```
*       @ 04,02 say " Dept"
*       @ 04,12 get Employee->Department
*
use employee in select()
select employee
define window mainmnu from 2,2 to 15,30 panel
define window lookrec from 16,15 to 24,60
define window fullscrn from 3,2 to 24,60
activate window mainmnu
@2,1 say "Main Menu"
@4,3 say "1. Edit records"
@5,3 say "2. Edit/Format (do LAST)"
@6,3 say "3. Browse records"
@7,3 say "4. Look at code"
@8,3 say "5. Exit"
do while .t.
  mCH='5'
  @10,3 get mCH valid mCH$"12345"
  @10,6 say "<<=== Enter choice"
  read
  do case
    case mCH='5'
      exit
    case mCH='1'
      acti wind lookrec
      edit
      deac wind lookrec
    case mCH='3'
      browse window lookrec noedit nofoll noappe nomenu
    case mCH='2'
      acti wind lookrec
      set format to DOSFORM
      edit
      set format to
      deac wind lookrec
    case mCH='4'
      acti wind fullscrn
      modi comm dosbrow
      deac wind fullscrn
  endcase
enddo
deactivate window mainmnu
use
return
*** End of DOSBROW.prg
```

This code is typical of how people used dBASE DOS windows in programs. They mix windows with commands like EDIT, BROWSE, SET FORMAT TO, @ . . . SAY/GET. Depending on how you mix these command in an active window, Visual dBASE may give you unexpected results.

A lot of DOS applications use a dBASE window (DEFINE WINDOW FROM . . .) to display and edit information (@ . . . SAY/GET commands). If you activate a DOS window in Visual dBASE and place a series of SAY/GET commands in it, everything will work correctly. Everything will work as expected when you use hard coded @ . . . SAY/GET commands with the READ command in a window.

If you use the EDIT command with a Format file in an active window, dBASE for Windows will create a text-based entry screen, as expected. Figure 4–4 shows an active DOS window with information inside it.

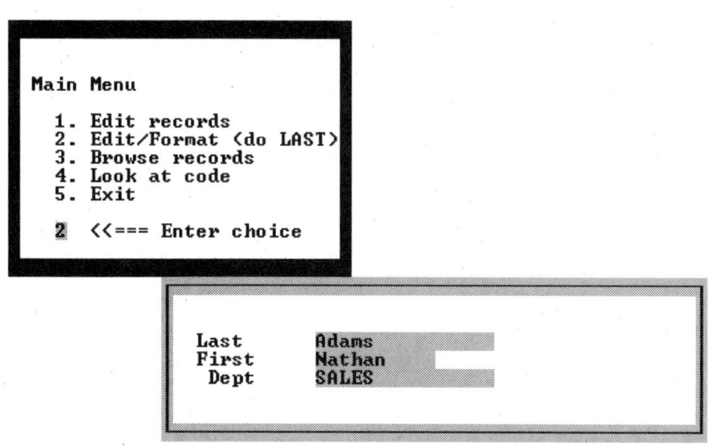

Figure 4–4. A DOS window with information inside it.

Everything appears OK. Even though the entry portion of the program (in Figure 4–4) is text based, it appears consistent with the menu portion.

Now look at Figure 4–5. The DOS-based code in Figure 4–5 simply uses the EDIT and BROWSE command (independently) in an active DOS window.

Figure 4–5 shows two different windows—one for BROWSE and one for EDIT. The DOS application only activates one window at a time. Notice that both of these windows demonstrate a problem. Both the EDIT and BROWSE commands, when used in a program with an active DOS window, will appear and act graphical. Actually, what has happened is Visual dBASE opened the DOS-based window and then placed a graphical EDIT in the window. (This was also true for the BROWSE). This can be a real visual problem for end users. They see a Windows-like BROWSE/EDIT that works like a Windows applications (BROWSE fields can be moved, resized, etc.). Everything else in the application is DOS text based—confusing and, at a minimum, not visually appealing.

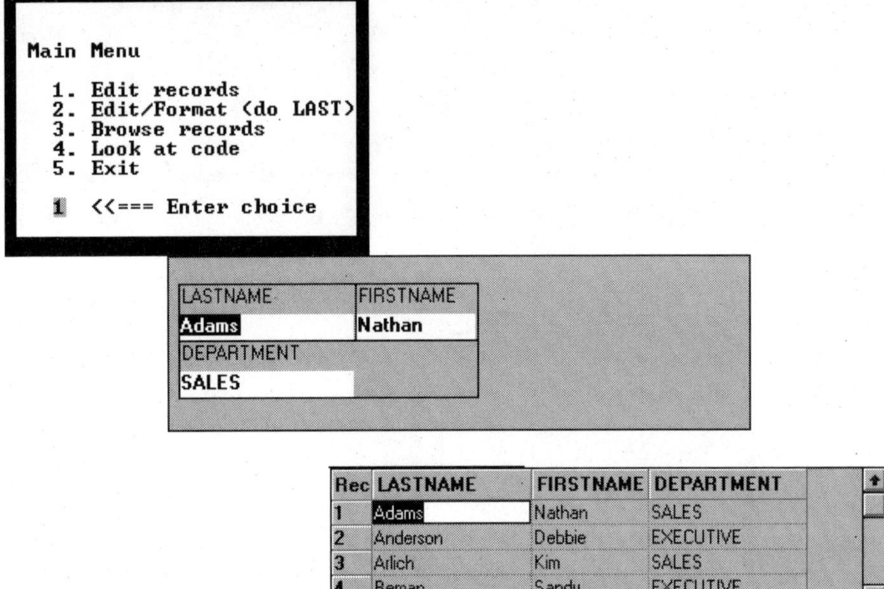

Figure 4–5. Running the EDIT command in an active DOS window.

When working with BROWSE and EDIT in DOS applications, you may need to go back and modify your applications, if they use dBASE Windows.

BROWSE and EDIT will automatically use any active dBASE window in Visual dBASE, even if you do not specify a window. To demonstrate this, change the preceding code for several case statements to the following:

```
case mCH='1'
   edit
case mCH='3'
  browse noedit nofoll noappe nomenu
```

If you run the DOS code in Windows with the preceding change, you will see that the EDIT and BROWSE commands will use the active window for the menu—the window that is used for the menu choices 1 through 5. Figure 4–6 shows the results of selecting choice 3 in the program, and demonstrates that you should be careful when running a dBASE DOS application in Visual dBASE if it uses EDIT/BROWSE and dBASE windows.

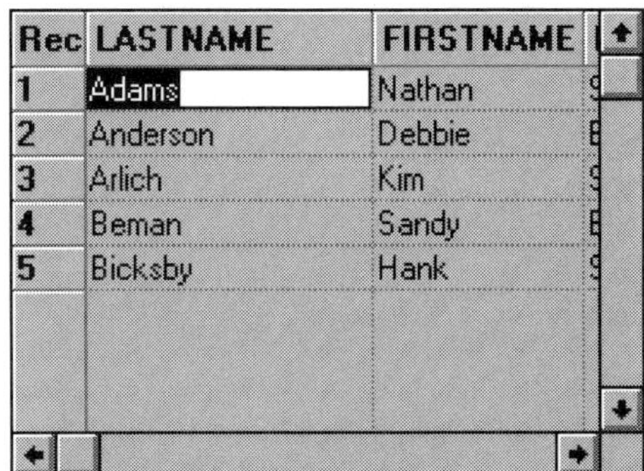

Figure 4–6. The BROWSE command with any active dBASE window.

Creating new objects

If your code has commands that create new objects (CREATE), Visual dBASE will activate an independent Windows-based frame (window) to create the object in. This again means that your code will display both text- and graphics-based parts.

DOS language compatibility issues

There are a few dBASE DOS commands that are not supported in Visual dBASE. Many of the commands are obvious, such as SET SCOREBOARD, SET CLOCK, and ASSIST. These commands just aren't appropriate for the Windows environment. There are others that are less obvious.

Commands and functions that won't work

With Visual dBASE, the second release of dBASE for Windows, several DOS features have been supported and greatly enhanced to support the client/server model of dBASE. The following is a list by category of DOS commands that are not supported in dBASE for Windows 5.0 and Visual dBASE:

System variables

_pecode

_pscode

_pwait

Macros

SAVE MACROS

RESTORE MACROS

PLAY MACRO

Binary files (.BIN)

LOAD

CALL

CALL()

RELEASE MODULE

NOTE: Although dBASE Windows cannot use .bin files, it does support .DLLs and the .bin files could be rewritten into Windows .DLLs.

---

dBASE DOS clock

SET CLOCK

SET HOURS

NOTE: dBASE Windows uses the environment clock (Windows clock) instead.

Template commands

DGEN()

DEXPORT

History buffer

SET HISTORY TO

SET HISTORY

LIST HISTORY

DISPLAY HISTORY

NOTE: Visual dBASE does not have a dot prompt. Instead of a dot prompt, it uses a Command window. You can scroll through the last thousand commands in the Command window and re-execute any of them by simply pressing the **Enter** key.

Control center

ASSIST

SET INSTRUCT

NOTE: dBASE Windows does not have a Control Center, so these commands are inappropriate for Windows. The Navigator has replaced the Control Center.

Debug commands

SET DEBUG

SET TRAP

NOTE: Visual dBASE has a fully integrated debugger that is more powerful and productive than the DOS counterpart.

Miscellaneous SET commands

SET SCOREBOARD ON/off

SET DBTRAP ON/off

SET COLOR ON/off

SET HELP TO ON/off

SET STATUS ON/off

Miscellaneous functions

ISMARKED()

dBASE command support based on which Windows version. The Windows versions of dBASE acts differently or offers support for the following four groups of commands based on the Windows version being used:

Transaction processing

Security

Multiuser

SQL

Transaction processing commands follow:

BEGIN TRANSACTION ... END TRANSACTION

ROLLBACK

RESET

COMPLETED()

ISMARKED()

ROLLBACK()—works differently from DOS

NOTE: Although Visual dBASE, and version 5.0, do not support these transaction commands, they do have transaction processing and use three new functions: BeginTrans(), Commit(), and Rollback(). These functions are new or work differently, but they are comparable with their DOS counterparts.

➡ **The BeginTrans() function**
Visual dBASE has added even more functionality to transaction processing, allowing the user to specify an isolation level of the type of read supported by a back-end database in the client/server model.

Encryption
The following commands will only work in Visual dBASE. Version 5.0 does not support any type of dBASE-related table encryption.

PROTECT

LOGOUT

SET ENCRYPTION

NOTE: dBASE for Windows 5.0 does not support dBASE table encryption. If dBASE DOS files are encrypted, they will have to be un-encrypted if you want to use them in dBASE for Windows. Conversely, it does recognize and support encryption and password protection of Paradox tables. If you need to have protected data, via encryption, you can use Paradox to create and encrypt Paradox tables that can then be used by dBASE Windows. It also supports any encryption and security that exists in SQL tables under the client/server model.

➡ **Encryption and Visual dBASE**
Visual dBASE fully supports dBASE DOS security, enabling it to read and write to DOS-encrypted tables (assuming the user can login to the table's assigned group). This support is for dBASE tables only; PROTECT will not allow you to apply security for other table types.

Multiuser commands
The following two commands are not supported by Visual dBASE or dBASE for Windows version 5.0:

LIST USERS

DISPLAY USERS

These two commands are *only* supported by Visual dBASE (version 5.0 does not offer support for them):

ACCESS()

USER()

Like dBASE DOS, Access() will return the access level of the current user, based on the value assigned with PROTECT. User() will return the current user name, also based on assignment with the PROTECT command.

NOTE: In addition to these commands both dBASE for Windows 5.0 and Visual dBASE offers support for all the other multiuser commands including automatic record locking.

SQL

The following two SQL-related dBASE DOS commands are not supported in either version of Windows dBASE:

SET SQL

SET PAUSE

NOTE: Visual dBASE and dBASE for Windows 5.0 does have a new function, SQLEXEC(), that is used to perform SQL commands directly against SQL tables on a server.

➡ **SQL support in Visual dBASE**

In addition to the SQLEXEC() function, Visual dBASE allows the user to perform SQL operations against local and remote data by embedding SQL statements (called *ESQL* in dBASE) directly into a dBASE program. By directly embedding SQL statements into a program, the user no longer needs to specify an explicit SQL mode using SET SQL On/Off. The SQL statements are simply pass-through directly to the SQL server if the client/server model is used or perform directly against Paradox and dBASE tables using local SQL. In addition, the programmer can use SQL procedures stored on a remote server using the Windows EXTERN function to call the procedure.

To access remote SQL servers will require that you install Borland's SQL links and set up remote server aliases through the Borland Database Engine.

Total number of command unsupported in Windows. Although these commands appear to be a lot, they represent less than 1 percent of all the dBASE commands and functions available to you as a dBASE programmer and user.

Performing some familiar tasks

There are other incompatibilities between dBASE DOS and Windows. You should be aware of these problems. Most of these inconsistencies are familiar to you. However, they may not be considered when working with dBASE DOS applications in Windows.

Error message numbers

More than 40 percent of the error messages in Visual dBASE return a different number from their DOS counterparts. If you have error-trapping programs that look for an error number, check the code against the *dBASE Manual* to verify the error numbers for which you are trapping.

CONFIG.DB file

Visual dBASE will not read or use any setting in the dBASE DOS Config.db file. Instead, it uses a new file with the extension .INI (for initialization file). If you have any default values set up in the Config.db file, you will have to move them to the new dBASEWIN.INI file.

The dBASEWIN.INI file

The initialization file (.INI) is the one that most Windows applications use to initialize the program. The dBASEWIN.INI file replaces the old Config.db filed from DOS. It should exist in the same directory as the dBASEWIN.EXE file.

Like the old Config.db file, Visual dBASE will attempt to load the dBASEWIN.INI file automatically from the working directory of your application. If the dBASEWIN.INI file isn't located there, Visual dBASE will then look for the directory containing the executable file dBASEWIN.EXE. If it doesn't find the dBASEWIN.ini file, dBASE will automatically create one in the same directory with the dBASEWIN.EXE file.

NOTE: Specifying a *.ini file to use
Although dBASE requires the default dbasewin.ini file reside in the same directory as the working directory or in the directory where dBASEWIN.exe is located, you can tell dBASE to use a different .ini file. If you need to start dBASE with a different dbasewin.ini file, you can do so using the **-C** option switch on the command line when you start dBASE.

Restoring the default dBASEWIN.INI settings. If you need reset the dBASEWIN.INI file to its initial set of defaults, follow these steps:

1. Quit Visual dBASE.
2. Delete the DBASEWIN.INI file.

3. Start Visual dBASE.

The next time you start Visual dBASE, the program will not find the dBASEWIN.INI file and automatically create one. The new *.ini file will not contain the User Name and Company information that was supplied when the program was first installed. If you need this information placed in the *.ini file, you will have to edit the file and add it.

dBASEWIN.INI is self-updating. The dBASEWIN.INI file is self-updating. It, like many Windows *.ini files, is constantly being updated as you work with Visual dBASE. When you leave Visual dBASE, the existing settings of several user interface settings will be saved. The next time you start dBASE, the program will maintain the changes made from the previous session.

Many dBASEWIN.INI sections aren't even written to the file until you take some action that requires an addition to the *.ini file.

dBASEWIN.ini sections

The dBASEWIN.ini file comprises several sections. Each section begins with a section name enclosed with brackets and it sits on its own line (e.g., [Navigator], [Fonts], etc.). The following are the main sections and an explanation of their purpose:

[Catalog]
Contains the settings for the Catalog window.

[CommandSettings]
Contains the Desktop settings, like any system procedure file (SYSPROC), the current directory, the home directory of dBASEWIN.exe, country information (date, currency, etc.), default database type, path, location of the dBSYSTEM.db file (security), etc.

[CommandWindow]
Contains settings for the Command window, such as maximized, minimized, position, open or closed, and the Input pane position.

[ControlsWindow]
Settings for the Form designer's Control Palette window.

[CustomControls]
Maintains the loaded Custom Control (*.CC) files that have been loaded with File >> Set Up Custom Controls. It can maintain up to ninety-nine files in the form CC0=<path\filename>, CC1 = .

[DeskTop]
Contains additional settings for the desktop, beyond the section [CommandSettings].

[Dialogs]

Contains the position settings for five dialog boxes: More, Find Text, Replace Text, Find Records, and Replace Records.

[DLLs]

Lists the DLLs and VBXs that have been loaded from the File>>Set Up Custom Controls menu in dBASE. It can maintain up to 99 files in the form DLL0=<path\filename>, DLL1 = .

[ExpressionBuilder]

This section has a single value, SafetyNet, for the status of the safety net.

[Fonts]

Used for DOS compatibility only—for the STYLE options of ? and ?? commands.

[FormDesigner]

Settings for the Form Designer like Grid information, Ruler setting, and Scheme information.

[IDAPI]

Allows you to specify a specific *.ini file for the BDE (previously known as the IDAPI engine). The CONFIGFILE01 value is assigned the name of the BDE *.ini file.

[ImageViewer]

This section contains one setting, SizeToFit, for the Image Viewer.

[Install]

Contains the values for Username and Company. If you ever delete the dBASEWIN.INI file, this section will have to be edited manually.

[MemoEditor]

Contains the editor properties for the internal text editor of a memo field.

[MRU_Files]

Maintains the most recently used (MRU) files by dBASE in the File menu when dBASE starts and the number of MRUs to show (from three to seven).

[Navigator]

Contains settings for the Navigator like position, the search path, icon information, and sort order for icons in the Navigator.

[ObjectProperties]

Settings for the Object Properties window (Inspector).

[OLEViewer]

This section contains one setting, SizeToFit, for the OLE Viewer.

[OnOffCommandSettings]
Contains many of the SET command settings like Currency (LEFT, right), Century (OFF, on), Exclusive (OFF,on), Autosave (OFF, on), Bell (ON, off), Talk (ON, off), and so forth.

[Printer]
Maintains the printer settings for printers in Visual dBASE.

[ProcedureEditor]
Maintains the information used by the Procedure Editor in the form designer.

[ProgramEditor]
Holds the information concerning the editor properties of the Editor window (invoked by MODIFY COMMAND).

[QueryDesigner]
Has only one setting, ComplexIndexes, used to determine if complex keys will be shown in the skeleton.

[TableRecords]
Contains information for the Table Records properties. It also contains information for individual table windows. When you open a table in BROWSE, single record, or miniform, the information is maintained as well as the field positions, if changed, and any flags (e.g., NoEdit, NoDelete, etc.). This section can maintain this information for any number of tables, although the default number is 10.

[TableStructure]
Maintains information about the table structure window.

[TextEditor]
Contains the editor properties from the internal text editor (MODIFY FILE).

Looking at these sections, two of them hold the same information that used to be in the Config.db file: [CommandSettings] and [On/OffCommandSettings]. These are where you will place your default value information that was previously in your Config.db file.

User-defined functions

Visual dBASE has many new functions. If you have a user-defined function (UDF) with the same name, dBASE will run its internal function rather than your UDF. The appendix has a complete list of all new and enhanced commands and functions in dBASE for Windows 5.0 and Visual dBASE.

Queries

There are several major changes between DOS queries and Windows. The following are the areas of concern.

Aggregate operators

If you use *aggregate* operators (e.g., count, sum, etc.) in your DOS queries, they will not work in Visual dBASE. Visual dBASE performs aggregate summations outside of the Query Design surface. They can be performed by menu options or by writing code to perform the aggregate operator. If you need to perform a Count or a Calculation, open the table or query in a BROWSE window, and then select the menu choice: Table >> Table Utilities. You will be limited to a single calculation at a time. If you need to perform another calculation, you will have to go through the menu choices again.

Temporary (speed-up) indexes

You can't keep temporary indexes in Windows queries; this choice is gone. You will have to go into the query and modify the relation, creating a new index.

.NDX indexes (III +)

To use III+ indexes (.ndx), you will have to change the code that uses the query and add the command SET INDEX TO before running the query. This is also true if you need to use a III+ index when creating a query.

Update queries

Update queries will not work in the Windows version of dBASE. It doesn't use them or recognize them. You will have to either write an application to perform the update or use the Table menu items while BROWSING the table.

The keystrokes

dBASE lets you trap for keystrokes using the ON KEY LABEL command. This is useful for assigning a procedure or UDF to a "hot key" combination. Visual dBASE has a series of reserved key combinations that you should not use. Table 4–1 lists the key combinations you should not use.

If you trap for these keystrokes, Windows will steal them first—your code will do nothing.

Table 4–1. Reserved Key Combinations.

Reserved Key Combination	Purpose (in Windows)
Ctrl + Esc	Activate the task manager dialog box
Ctrl + F4	Close the active group or document window
Ctrl + F6	Cycles through all open windows in an application
Alt + Esc	Switch forward between all open applications
Alt + Tab	Switch backward between all open applications
Alt + F4	Quit the active application or Windows
Alt + Print Screen	Capture the active window to the Clipboard
Alt + Spacebar	Open System (Control) menu of current application
Alt + Hyphen (minus sign)	Open System menu of active window in application
Print Screen	Copy the image on the screen to the Clipboard
Shift + Alt + Tab	Cycle through applications (hold Shift + Alt; press Tab)

Creating format screens

dBASE only uses format screens for DOS applications. Therefore, Visual dBASE does not have a format screen builder. Rather than format screens, it uses O-O forms and has a form designer to help you build them.

Creating reports and labels

dBASE uses Crystal Report Writer for Windows to create reports and labels. This program has graphical tools that lets you build reports quickly. However, it does not create source code that can be modified by hand. Visual dBASE will run reports that are built in dBASE IV DOS or by using dBASE code as well as reports created in Crystal.

File formats

Visual dBASE and version 5.0 will use existing dBASE files, .DBFs, .DBTs, and .MDXs, with no change. They can be used in a network environment with dBASE IV applications without problems. If you add one of the new field types to a database structure, the table will not work with previous versions of dBASE.

THE VISUAL dBASE FILES

dBASE can work with dBASE or Paradox, separately or together. You can join a Paradox table with a dBASE database, and so on.

dBASE databases (tables)

dBASE offers two new field types in dBASE databases: OLE and binary. If you add either of these two new field types to a .DBF or .DBT file, you will not be able to use the tables in previous versions of dBASE.

Field types supported by Windows versions of dBASE

Visual dBASE can use and create both dBASE and Paradox files. If you only use the field types in dBASE IV, Windows can concurrently use it with other versions of dBASE. It has maintained file consistency, where possible.

Table 4–2 shows all the field types supported by dBASE.

Table 4–2. dBASE field types.

Field Type	Purpose
Character	Holds text-based data—names, address, zip/postal codes, etc.
Numeric	Hold numbers used in financial and general calculations
Float	Holds numbers used in scientific calculations
Logical	Holds a logical true (.T.) or false (.F.)
Date	Holds an internal number that represents a date
Memo	Holds a block address in .DBT file to point to a memo
Binary	Holds a block address in .DBT file to point to any binary data
OLE	Holds the reference information to a linked object or stores the document from an OLE server application

Because dBASE is now a Windows program, it also offers support for multimedia—pictures and sound. To do this, it uses the two new field types at the bottom of Table 4–2: binary and OLE.

Binary field type

A *binary* field is actually a memo field that has been designated to hold images and sound. Because dBASE offers support for sound (.WAV) and graphic (.PCX, .BMP, etc.) files automatically, this field also holds a TYPE number to tell it what type of binary data is being stored. If the type is one that dBASE supports, it will work with it directly. If it is a type that dBASE does not work with, it can still be stored; however, you will have to supply a way to use it. There are two advantages to binary fields:

1. You can store any type of binary data; the data can be independent.
2. You can store text in a binary field.

OLE field type

dBASE can store any type of binary data (also known as binary large objects [BLOBs]) in a BINARY field. However, if you want to work with data types that are not directly supported by dBASE, you may want to use the OLE field type. This field can *point* to an external object (graph, picture, sound, audio visual file, etc.) and the name of the program that can work with it. dBASE fully supports DDE and OLE for working with additional data types not directly supported by it.

OLE fields can require less storage space than a binary field. You may want to consider this when deciding which new field type to use for storing binary data. The two advantages to using OLE fields are

1. Save disk space by linking to a file rather than copying or embedding the file.
2. Edit the data, once embedded or linked, by opening the server application.

Paradox tables

Visual dBASE uses and supports Paradox 5.x and 6.x tables, in addition to dBASE tables. Table 4–3 shows the field types and compares Paradox table information with dBASE table information.

As Table 4–3 shows, Paradox tables have many field types when compared with dBASE. In addition to richer field typing, Paradox tables also have the ability to attach business rules (a validation file) to the fields, and passwords enable the table. dBASE will recognize and use the validation rules and password protection of a Paradox table. dBASE will *not* create a validation file or protection against a Paradox table—Paradox will have to do it.

Table 4–3. dBASE Databases versus PARADOX 5.x Tables.

	dBASE	Paradox
Field types	Character, Numeric, Memo, Logical, Date, Float, OLE, Binary	Alphanumeric, Number, Money, Date, Short, Memo, Binary, Formatted Memo, OLE, Graphic, Time, Time Stamp, Long, Logical, Bytes, BCD, Autoincrement
Field naming	1. Maximum of ten characters 2. First character must be non-numeric 3. Alphanumeric and underscore allowed	1. Maximum of twenty-five characters 2. First character may not be a space 3. dBASE will not accept a name with a space in it (you can still reference a field with a space in it by encompassing the name inside colons—:my field:)
Indexing	Ascending/descending	Ascending or none

Types of files dBASE supports

dBASE creates and uses many file types—some old, some new. You already know several: .DBF, .DBT, .PRG, etc. Table 4–4 shows all the main file types that dBASE creates and uses:

The file types shown in Table 4–4 are the main file types that Visual dBASE and dBASE for Windows 5.0 creates or uses (like EXE, DLL, and VBX).

Table 4–4. Main File Types That dBASE Creates and Uses.

Type	Extension	Backup	Compiled	Comments
Tables/ databases	DBF	DBK	—	dBASE table
	DBT	TBK	—	dBASE memo
	DB		—	Paradox table
	MB		—	Paradox memo
	Client/server	none required	—	SQL tables
	Supported "SQL tables"			
Table-related files	VAL		—	Paradox Validation file
	LCK		—	Paradox Lock management
Indexes	NDX		—	dBASE III Plus
	MDX	MBK	—	dBASE IV and 5.0
	PX		—	Paradox primary index
	Xnn		—	Paradox secondary one field
	Ynn		—	Paradox secondary one field
	XGn		—	Paradox secondary multifield
	YGn		—	Paradox secondary multifield
Queries	QBE	QBK	QBO	dBASE Query file
	UPD		—	QBE update query file
	VUE		—	dBASE View binary file
	QRY		—	dBASE III Query file
Forms	WFM	WFK	WFO	dBASE Form
	WFM		BFM	VBX binary data in form
	FMT		FMO	dBASE DOS form

Table 4–4. Main File Types That dBASE Creates and Uses, continued.

Type	Extension	Backup	Compiled	Comments
Reports	RPT		—	dBASE reports (editable)
	RPC		—	dBASE cross-tab (editable)
	FRM		—	IV DOS (not editable)
	FRG		FRO	IV DOS (generated code)
Labels	RPL		—	dBASE labels (editable)
	LBL		LBO	IV DOS (not editable)
	LBG		—	IV DOS (generated code)
Programs/	PRG	BAK	PRO	dBASE source code
header	H		—	dBASE header (number include)
Images	BMP		—	Windows bitmap graphic
	PCX		—	Paintbrush bitmap graphic
	TIF*		—	Tag Image File (version 5.0)
	ICO*		—	Windows Graphic icons
	WMF*		—	Windows Metafiles
	EPS*		—	Encapsulated PostScript
Sounds	WAV		—	Windows sound file
Catalogs	CAT		—	dBASE catalog file
Menus	MNU	MNK	MNO	dBASE menu file
Custom Controls	VBX		—	Visual Basic control
	CC		—	dBASE custom control
Memory	MEM		—	Saved memory variables
External	EXE		—	non–dBASE programs
	DLL		—	non–dBASE DLLs

Table 4–4. Main File Types That dBASE Creates and Uses, continued.

Type	Extension	Backup	Compiled	Comments
Miscellaneous	FNF		—	Expression builder dBASE file
	CVT		—	Change detection field table
	HLP		—	Help file
	HDX		—	Help keyword index file
	COV		—	Coverage file (testing)
	PRF		—	Print form file
	PRT		—	Printer output file
	SCN		—	Image file of results pane
	WIN		—	IV window save file
	INI		—	Initialization file

* These file types are *not* supported by version 5.0 of dBASE for Windows.

Converting Your Data

If you work with dBASE IV encrypted files, dBASE for Windows 5.0 will not be able to use them. Before they can be used, you will have to de-crypt the tables (databases). However, Visual dBASE can use encrypted DOS files directly.

Un-encrypting the data

To un-ecrypt a dBASE IV table you will need to use the following commands:

```
SET ENCRYPTION OFF
USE <table name of encrypted file>
COPY TO <new table (not encrypted)> WITH PRODUCTION
CLOSE DATABASE
```

Once you have copied the un-encrypted file and its production .MDX files to a new database (and .mdx file), you can begin to use the table in dBASE.

Protecting the data

If you are using dBASE for Windows 5.0, and you must have your tables protected, dBASE can use and support the protection mechanism of Paradox tables as well as the protection built into SQL tables (Oracle, Sybase, etc.). You can move your data to one of these file types.

If you are using Visual dBASE, you can use the Security commands built into dBASE to secure your dBASE tables—PROTECT.

Using Paradox .db tables

If you need to protect a Paradox table (attach a Paradox .VAL), you will have to use Paradox to actually create the .VAL file. Once it is created, dBASE can use the table and move records to the table.

Assuming that a Paradox table with validation rules is built, you can use the following commands to move nonprotected dBASE data to a Paradox table if the field names are the same:

```
USE <Paradox table> TYPE PARADOX
APPEND FROM <dBASE table> TYPE DBASE
```

Using the new TYPE keyword, you can tell dBASE to work with a dBASE or Paradox file. Now you have your data moved into a Paradox table that has validation attached to it.

NOTE: If the field names are not the same, you will have to write some code that opens both tables and steps through the dBASE table moving the records over to the Paradox table using the REPLACE command.

Using SQL tables

If you are using a client/server environment and are connected to a server (e.g., Oracle, Sybase, SQL Server, or InterBase), you can also move your data to or from the server. You would open the server database, use the table in the database, and simply append the records into the table.

Converting Your Code

As you begin to work with objects and the Windows event model, you begin to think about moving your application into the Windows world. Sure, your existing dBASE application can run in Visual dBASE unchanged. The program remains text based and because it is in Windows, it has a serious flaw—it has *no* control.

In Chapter 1, you ran a dBASE DOS application, and, while it was in an active READ state, you quit Windows—the dBASE DOS program was *not* in control. In fact, Windows didn't even warn you that the program was running.

In the previous chapter, you worked with the new dBASE Object model and are probably beginning to see the advantages of the object model. You have created and used different visual controls (objects) that are graphical (check boxes, pushbuttons, etc.). These new applications look good and seem to work great.

So you are considering moving your existing application.

Modify or rewrite?

You have to decide if you should simply rewrite everything from scratch or modify your application a little at a time.

In the previous chapter, you worked with forms and form objects. You found out that the @ . . . SAY and @ . . . GET commands are dead in the Object world. You probably realize that all of the User Interface parts of your application will have to be converted. These include all the READ, WAIT, @ . . . TO, ? and ?? commands as well as the @ . . . SAY/GETs. You can still use all of them, but they will only work in the Results pane of the Command window and remain text based.

You also realize that the event model will have to be dealt with. Some events, like leaving a program that is running a REPLACE or some other critical commands, must be controlled.

New model—new methods

If you want to migrate to the Windows environment and create true Windows applications in dBASE, you will have to use the Event and Object models. This means you will have to change your way of thinking from procedural to task oriented.

Once you begin to think about performing tasks in your application, you are ready to decide what to do with your applications.

Converting DOS programs

Several portions of your programs can be converted from their DOS form into their new Windows form without recreating them. These resources include menu, forms, reports, and labels. dBASE has included the dBASE Component Builder in the package to convert these DOS resources for you. All of these DOS resources share definitions and parts that can be translated into objects.

Writing new code

If you convert your DOS resources into Windows objects, you may have to write some code that will help you control these new objects. You may have to attach code to events like leaving a form. Any references to UDFs in your DOS format screens (@ . . . GET <var> VALID <UDF()>) will be moved to the appropriate event property in the new form object.

WORKING IN A TASK-ORIENTED PROGRAM ENVIRONMENT

When you work with Windows applications, you need to change your method of thinking from procedural to task oriented. In a later chapter, you will build an application from scratch—using some tables you will create forms, reports, and labels.

The task way

Because a Windows application is task oriented, you need to think through all the tasks the program will perform. Task-oriented thinking is not new to database work. When you perform your system analysis, you start by planning out all the tasks that the system will perform.

Start general

Group tasks into general categories: reports and forms. The reports are easy—think about the current forms that the system uses (and the ones that you want to create). The forms can be a little more difficult—you'll need entry forms, view forms, and forms called by other forms.

Tune the task

Once the forms and reports are determined, you can start to tune the tasks—work with a main form, run a report, edit records, or activate a form from another form. As you build your task list, you will begin to see the tasks fall into place. Once this is done, you are ready to go to the next step.

Determine task interaction

With the tasks determined, you can begin to analyze how the tasks will interact with each other. Will the personnel form need to open the pay record history form? Do you need to look up a customer based on an invoice number?

As you reveal the task interaction, you will realize that you are already thinking task oriented.

Task-oriented thinking is focused on the user

Because task-oriented programming is focused on the user, you'll begin to think about building applications from the UI viewpoint. In fact, task-oriented methodologies demand that the main focus be UI driven.

Applying task-oriented thinking to programming

Now that you are thinking task oriented, you are ready to apply it to your dBASE applications in Windows. To build the parts needed by a task, you will use dBASE objects. These objects will be the main focus of your application. You simply build the forms, menus, and reports needed for your system. Once they are built, you attach code to the event properties of the objects (form, entryfield, check box, etc.) and run the application.

In other words, you create the forms, dialog boxes, and other objects. Once you create the user interface portion, you attach code to it. If you need to validate some data, you can attach the validation code to an event at the entryfield (equivalent to an @ . . . GET in DOS) level or at the form level. If you need to update records or perform some database action, you would attach the code for that action to another object (perhaps a pushbutton).

The UI will be created using object technology; the database work will be created writing traditional database manipulation code.

Using the dBASE Object Component Builder

The purpose of this utility is to bring much of the DOS-based dBASE resources to Windows without recoding them. Menus, forms, reports, and labels all share some fundamental definitions and attributes that can be easily translated into dBASE objects.

Typically, dBASE DOS applications comprise many format screens (forms), labels, and reports. They also tend to include a single menu structure. You can convert all of these into their Windows counterpart.

First you need to organize your work. *Back up* all of your existing application source files before starting the conversion. This should include all the files that the Component Builder will process.

The conversion approach

Consider taking these steps when converting your resources:

1. Create a directory where all the conversion work will be completed.
2. Copy all the files to convert to the newly created directory. (This automatically gives you a backup copy of the files—the originals.)
3. Create a dBASE catalog file containing all the **.FMT, .PRG, .FRM,** and **LBL** files that you want to convert. You should create this catalog file in Visual dBASE. You can use drag-and-drop to move all files (except .FMT files) from the Navigator window into your new catalog. You can move the .FMT files by adding them using the Catalog >> Add Item . . . (Ctrl + A) menu choice while the Catalog file is active.
4. Start the dBASE Component Builder.
5. From the Component Builder's Files menu, select the catalog option and select the catalog that you created, containing the files to be converted. The Component Builder will automatically convert each support file in the catalog sequentially.
6. Once completed, you can view the generated code using a text editor. The menus, forms, reports, and labels are ready to be used or further customized using the design surfaces in dBASE.

NOTE: The *only* .PRG files that should be converted are those that contain menu structures. If the programs contain the equivalent code of a format file (@ . . . SAY/GET commands), you should modify the program to match the format file structure. To modify the program, go into a text editor and place all the SAY and GET commands on their own lines, using their own @ coordinates. Once you modify a format type program file, rename it giving it the extension of .FMT, and reconvert the file.

Running the Component Builder

You can run the Component Builder by launching it from the Program Manager. It will start dBASE and run the program. If you are already running dBASE, you can simply run the application by DOing it in the Command window. To run the program, type the following command in the Command window:

```
DO C:\VISUALDB\UTILITY\CB.PRO
```

You have to specify the drive and directory name where the program is located. When you install dBASE, it placed the Component Builder program in a directory, named UTILITY, below the dBASE Windows directory. If you specified a different drive or a different directory, you will need to use that name. For instance, the author installed dBASE on drive E: in a directory named VDBWIN. The command would be

```
DO E:\VDBWIN\UTILITY\CB.PRO
```

Once the program starts, you should see a form similar to the one in Figure 4–7, which shows the Component Builder with the File menu open.

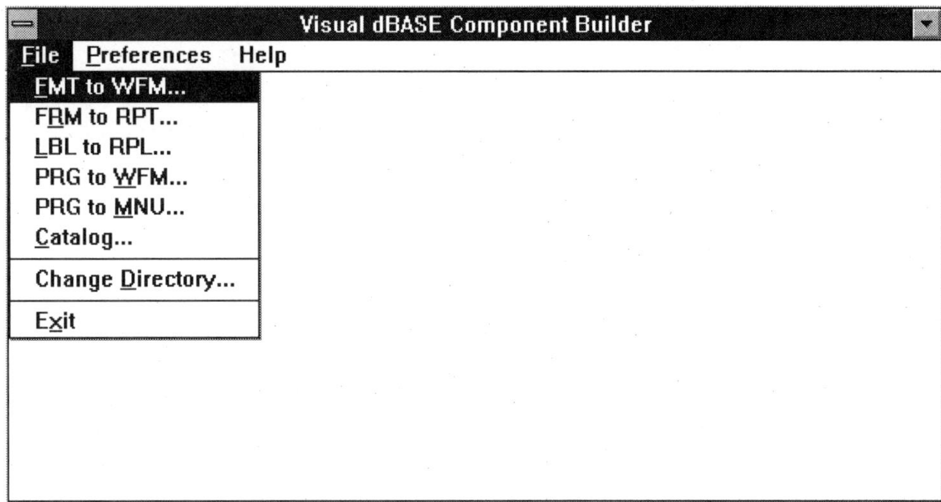

Figure 4–7. The Component Builder.

Using a Catalog file for the conversion

As the file menu shows in Figure 4–7, you can convert individual files or files located in a Catalog file. To convert more than one file automatically, place them in a catalog file and while you are running the Component Builder, select File >>Catalog . . . from the menu. Then select the name of the catalog file that holds your files to be converted.

dBASE will then open a dialog box and begin converting your code. You can watch the status of the conversion as the builder works with your files. Figure 4–8 shows the status dialog box as the converter is working.

Figure 4–8 shows two windows: the update window and the Report Intro Band dialog box. The Component Builder is updating a dBASE IV report source file. Notice that the dialog box asks if you want the Intro Band included in the report. The primary window—The Object Update—shows the status of the conversion process.

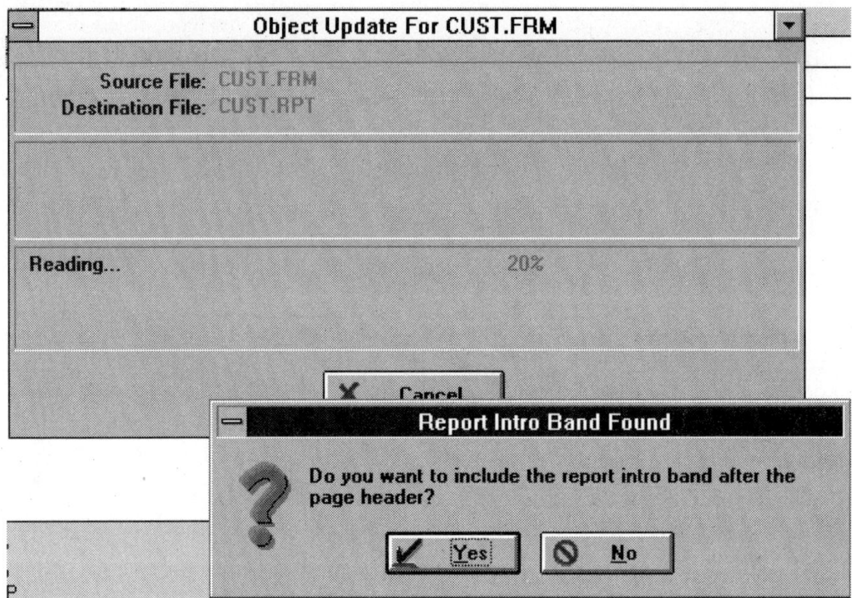

Figure 4–8. The Component Builder dialog box as it was working.

> **!** **Display of progress during conversion**
> Visual dBASE's Component Builder may appear to freeze up while converting individual objects. If, after reading a source file, the screen displays a 75 and no message and appears to be locked up, it is *not*. The program is reading and processing the existing source file. If you check your hard-drive light, you will see that the program is running okay. Just wait; it may take up to two minutes before you will see another message.

Converting individual files

You can convert a single program or a group of programs (like you did using the catalog option). To select one program at a time, select the correct file type from the File menu, and then select the name of the file you want to convert. The converted will automatically convert it.

The conversion process

The process of converting DOS to Windows is straightforward. Table 4–5 shows the type of files being converted and what they are converted to.

Table 4–5. The Conversion File Types.

IV	Windows	Notes
PRG	MNU	Only extracts the menu-related code
FMT	WFM	Converts the screen controls and their layout
FRM	RPT	Converts the report fields and their layout
LBL	RPL	Converts the field and layout information

➡ **Converting PRGs to WFMs**
In Visual dBASE, the Component Builder can also extract @ . . . SAY/GET code and create a windows format file (WFM). The dBASE for Windows 5.0 does not convert .PRG files directly to WFM.

How the converter works

The converter takes your DOS source code and converts it to Windows source code. While it is converting it changes the code from procedural- into object-based code. As it moves your code, it actually changes many of the commands in the code. Table 4–6 shows the DOS command and what it is converted to in Windows:

Table 4–6. dBASE DOS Commands to Windows.

dBASE IV Command	Visual dBASE Object
DEFINE MENU	CLASS <menuName>
DEFINE PAD	DEFINE MENU <padName.menuName>
DEFINE BAR	DEFINE MENU <barName.padName.menuName>
ON SELECTION	<barName.padName.menuName.onClick>
@ . . . SAY	DEFINE TEXT
@ . . . GET	DEFINE ENTRYFIELD
@ . . . TO	DEFINE RETANGLE
@ ... FILL TO	DEFINE RECTANGLE <with color>

As Table 4–6 shows, the converter simply changes the DOS bases' procedural code into object code.

Files that can be converted

In the DOS world, you approach the user interface differently from Windows. Because of this, it is impossible to have 100 percent compatibility between dBASE DOS and Windows. This is especially true if you need to exploit the graphical capabilities of Windows. However, you can move your menus, forms, reports, and labels over to Windows and begin to exploit the GUI environment.

Files that need to be converted (and can be converted) include **PRG, FMT, FRM,** and **LBL** programs. They only have to be converted if you intend to run them as windows like programs. Once converted, you will probably have to add code and additional controls to make them more functional (like pushbuttons to skip through a table, etc.)

PRG to MNU. Converting a dBASE IV menu structure to Windows is easy. The converter assumes you have a program file (.PRG) that contains the DEFINE MENU commands. It will go through the code and convert all the menu code into a menu CLASS.

It will not convert any other code in the .PRG file—only menu code.

FMT to WFM. The converter can convert 100 percent of the FMT code into a form object. It takes all the @ . . . SAY/GET commands and the associated options and transforms them to TEXT and ENTRYFIELD objects and sets their properties according to the information in the DOS format (.FMT) file.

FRM to RPT. Like the format file conversion, the converter will take the style and format information in the DOS report form and convert it into a file that Crystal Reports can load and modify. Crystal reports may not convert a dBASE IV report correctly if the dBASE IV report has a Report Header section. Crystal does not support this option—rather, the Converter will prompt you to include the Report Header in the Page Header Section in Visual dBASE.

LBL to RPL. DOS label files will convert the label information into files that Crystal Reports can use. This includes any label forms that were created with defining the form in DOS.

PRG to WFM. The Component Builder has added a new choice to Visual dBASE (not available in version 5.0), allowing you to update @ . . . SAY/GET code in a .PRG to a Windows file menu (WFM). Individual dBASE IV .PRG files can be selected to generate a new .WFM file. The option is an interactive process that makes it possible to select several different @ . . . SAY/GET command lines and pass these marked lines of text to the Component Builder for processing.

 **Converting dBASE for Windows 5.0 PRGs to WFM**

You can convert your @ ... SAY/GET programs to .WFMs in dBASE for Windows 5.0 by simply renaming the .PRG to .FMT and running the converted against the .FMT.

Chapter 5
Working with Events, Event Handlers, Methods, and Codeblocks

When working with Visual dBASE or dBASE for Windows 5.0, there are two key points to consider.

1. dBASE is an Event-Driven Application
2. dBASE is an Object-Oriented Application

Because it is a true Windows application, it is an event-driven application. Because it is event driven, the Object-oriented paradigm tends to be the best way to build applications for the environment. Events, trapping for an event, and performing some action based on an event is the answer to working in the Windows environment.

Although you have already discovered and worked with events and event processing in earlier chapters, this chapter covers events, event handlers, methods, and codeblocks in detail. Some of the information may seem repetitive—it is.

The Event

An event is simply an occurrence of something. It can be the pressing of a key, the electrical power going off, or moving a mouse. It is some tangible action and can be described in words. The actual action of moving a mouse is the event.

You have worked with events in dBASE programming for a long time; you probably are not aware of it. Every time you program for an ON ESCAPE command, you are working with events. You are telling dBASE to look for the user pressing the Escape key and when it occurs do some command or program.

So from a dBASE perspective, events are built-in triggers, or interrupts, which are used to run some specific code when the event occurs.

Windows is an event-driven environment

Windows is called an operating system by some. By definition, an operating system works with the computer at the system level. It performs the low-level functions needed to operate the computer (read and write to the input/output devices—screen, printer, drives, etc.). Windows is incapable of maintaining complete control of the system; thus, it relies on DOS to do low-level operating system work. In part, Windows is like a shell that sits on top of DOS, working in cooperation with DOS. However, Windows is also a working, processing environment. It has a common Print engine, Help engine, and other resources that other programs can use. This suggests that Windows is an operating environment (versus a system) because other applications operate inside it.

Windows is an event-driven environment. It is always in control of the environment, even when other programs are running in Windows.

DOS and programs

DOS is an operating system that runs applications. It only lets one application operate at a time. The application is given control when it is running. When you run dBASE in DOS, the program, dBASE, is in control of what goes on inside the program. It maintains complete control. If you need to do something else and dBASE doesn't support it, it can't normally be done. This is true for all DOS applications—they are in control. In fact, if you create a compiled DOS application, and run it in DOS, your compiled dBASE application will be in complete charge of what goes on—DOS doesn't interfere. DOS turns over control of the computer to the DOS application. It works with one application at a time.

TSRs and DOS. Even though DOS turns over complete control to a program, it offers a way for other applications to work at the same time—interrupts. Terminate but Stay Resident (TSRs) programs use these interrupts to sit in memory waiting to run while another DOS application is working.

People wanted the ability to do more than one thing at a time. They wanted the ability to do some other task while in the middle of an application. SideKick, by Borland, was an excellent example of a TSR that lets users do something else while running a DOS application. TSRs let a person activate the TSR program by pressing some keystroke or key combination. The TSR program "wakes" when the user presses the "activation key" and lets users work in it until they are done, and then return to the original program. This "waking up" is really DOS turning over complete control to the TSR program—putting the TSR program in complete control.

The way TSRs work is simple; they load in memory and poll one of the DOS interrupts that are sitting there looking for some action (like a key press)—an event to occur. DOS has several interrupts that can be used to check for events. They are used by DOS and other programs to halt execution of an existing program and do something. The DOS clock interrupt is used to refresh the internal clock.

The TSR sits there, polling an interrupt, waiting for the keystroke combination it needs to "wake it up." When it occurs, the TSR suspends the application that is currently running in memory and then it, TSR, steals the central processing unit (CPU) to do what it has to do. Once done, the program reactivates the other program, and it goes back to sleep—waiting for the event to occur again.

Memory is a problem. DOS has a limiting factor—it can quickly run out of memory. It can only work with the first 1 megabyte of memory, and everything it runs must be in the first 640 kilobytes of memory—not a lot of space to put programs in today.

Windows and its applications

In contrast, Windows is an environment that works with DOS to use all memory, including the memory above 1 megabyte. It is considered a user environment because it is geared to work the way people work—oriented to completing tasks, including getting information from (or doing) multiple applications at a time.

People tend to perform more than one thing at a time. They can be doing one thing, stop for a moment, do something else, and return to the first one. For example, while writing something, they may need some information, and look something up in a dictionary, thesaurus, or even an encyclopedia. While doing some file downloading in a communications program (that may take hours), the user may also decide to do some word-processing or database work. The person doesn't care about the single application that is running (like the communications program); he or she is concerned with completing a task—getting something done without wasting time.

Windows allows user to perform tasks. Windows is an event-driven environment geared toward completing tasks. It lets users perform more than one action at a time. In the Windows environment, you can be working with two forms or applications at the same time. They can be running independently or in cooperation with each other (sharing information). It is possible to have your Windows word processor performing spellchecking on a document; at the same time, your dBASE application can be doing a series of record replacements on a dBASE table.

Windows looks for events. The Windows program being used by a person does *not* completely control what the user can do—Windows does. The program is *never* in complete control—Windows is. It sits there waiting to see if some event occurs (like a key combination or a mouse action). If a recognized event occurs, then Windows takes control and performs some action.

As an example, a person can be running any Windows application, and press the **Ctrl-Esc** key combination. When the **Ctrl-Esc** keys are simultaneously pressed, Windows will activate the Windows task list dialog box. Once active, the user can switch to any other active Windows program—leaving the current one still running in Windows.

Windows is always sitting there looking for some action, or event, to occur. If it is an event that Windows recognizes, it will take some action. Windows is always in control.

The user is in control. Because Windows is always in control, it means that the *user* decides what to do, not the Windows application or the programmer who created it. A good Windows application recognizes that Windows is in control and works with the Windows environment by supporting the event-driven environment.

What is event-driven programming?

True Windows applications take advantage of the event model built into Windows. They are written to support the event-driven environment.

In traditional dBASE DOS programming, you build an application by writing dBASE code one line after the other. You create menus that drive the system. The menus, while they are running, are in control. They are used to launch predefined procedures—which are given complete control over the user. The user can only perform *predetermined* actions—ones that are programmed into the application.

This means that you, the programmer, are in control in environments like dBASE for DOS. Whatever you write in a program is what the user can do. As a good procedural programmer, you write programs that have good error checking. When you create a menu, you check for a valid menu choice and if a bad choice is given, you tell the user to choose again. The code is in complete control.

Working with the events

True Windows applications are developed to look for events and respond to events. They rely on the events model to accomplish tasks. Windows is a graphical environment that has many different types of graphical controls. These controls can be used to enhance the appearance and effectiveness of a Windows application. A control is an object that is part of the user interface (the visual parts of a program). Figure 5–1 shows a few Windows graphical controls in a dBASE form.

Figure 5–1 shows many different types of controls, starting with the top left (and going from left to right): images, rectangles, pushbuttons, spin buttons, combo boxes, list boxes, check boxes, and pushbuttons. These graphical control objects are useful; they offer both a visually pleasing appearance and a functional way to work with information.

Graphical controls, themselves, have events. For instance, if you press on the pushbutton, it physically changes form (looks like it was pressed in). If you click on the check box, a small **x** will be toggled on and off. These controls respond to events. In the case of the toggling of a pushbutton, a check box, or a radio button, it is automatic.

You can also control what happens when working with these control objects. For instance, you can assign a program to an event on the pushbutton. If the user presses the pushbutton, a program runs that will leave the form (or even close it). You work with events to perform tasks.

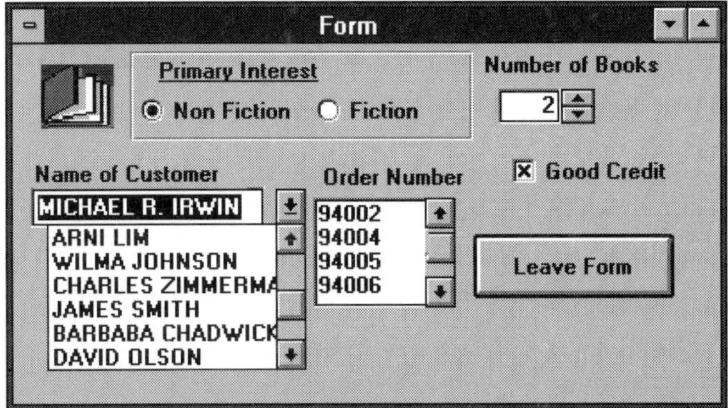

Figure 5–1. Graphical controls that can be used in Visual dBASE programs.

The event-driven process. The process of using events is known as *event driven.* Windows is an event-driven environment. Windows responds to events and uses events with internal messages to communicate with its programs. Windows programs work with Windows events and messages to communicate with other Windows applications. True Windows applications also work with their own events.

dBASE, like other true Windows applications, is event-driven. It supports the event process of windows and uses the same event-driven process to accomplish tasks.

Visual dBASE events

Working with dBASE event-driven applications does require learning some new coding techniques. First, you program tasks—you use a pushbutton to trigger a customer record update or to add new records to an order form.

Remember Windows allows the user to leave one application and go to another one (or worse, leave Windows). This means that you need a way to keep a user from leaving a critical database task (like updating records) until the task is complete.

Looking for events and doing something based on the event is the answer. In the case of a user trying to leave the form (the form loses focus) when it is doing a critical task, you can look for the event and trigger a program that returns them to the form until the event is completed. In this case, you would use the event property, OnLostFocus, to attach some code that would bring the user back to the form.

The event is the action

In the preceding example, the action of leaving the form is the event. The event is some action. It can be caused internally or externally. Events are constantly occurring in dBASE forms—users are pressing keys, the mouse is moving, and tables are being opened for queries and forms.

Internal events. *Internal events* are those actions that the user has minimal control over. For instance, if a form is linked to a query, the form automatically opens the query when it opens, and the query opens the underlying tables for the form to use. The actions of opening the query and the tables are internal events.

Internal events are performed by the application itself. Another example of an internal event is when the user clicks on a check box. The check box automatically toggles a small **x** on and off in the box to reflect a true (**x** on) or false (**x** off). This is also true for other form controls like the combo box, spin button, and radio button.

External events. In addition to internal events, there are *external events*. An external event is one that is performed by some external force. This external force is normally the end user. When end users move the mouse, clicks a mouse button, or presses a key, they are performing an external event.

Old dBASE events. Events are not new; dBASE DOS has events. Every time you use a VALID clause on an @ . . . GET statement, you are working with an event. You rely on an event to occur—change the contents of the field, and then have dBASE run some code to check the validity of the input in the field. Every time you code an ON ESCAPE DO <program> you are telling dBASE to handle the pressing of the **Esc** key by running the <program>.

The problem with the ON KEY [LABEL <key>] and ON ESCAPE commands in dBASE DOS is that they are single global sets. They are active across all programs and for all actions.

Responding to events. In Visual dBASE, each object in a form can respond differently to the same event. The Got Focus event of a form may open another form, while the Got Focus event of a pushbutton may activate an entryfield. All the objects in a form, and the form itself, have event properties. Many of the event properties are the same between objects (controls). For instance, most object controls in a form, and the form itself, have an event property that determines if the object Got Focus.

Because each object can have a property that checks for its focus, you can't globally set an OnFocus command. dBASE will not know which OnFocus you are referring to—the form's OnFocus, the pushbutton's OnFocus, and so on.

Event properties find the event

The event property is a property of an object that is used to check for the occurrence of an event against the object. The event property is used to trigger some *Event Handler*.

Figure 5–2 shows twenty of the twenty-three event properties that are associated with a form in Visual dBASE. These properties are used to trap for their corresponding events and trigger an event handler.

> ➡ **The event properties of Visual dBASE**
> The CanClose event property is new to Visual dBASE. It is not available in dBASE for Windows 5.0. It is used to determine if the user has attempted to close the form. If the user tries to close the form, it will run a program specified.

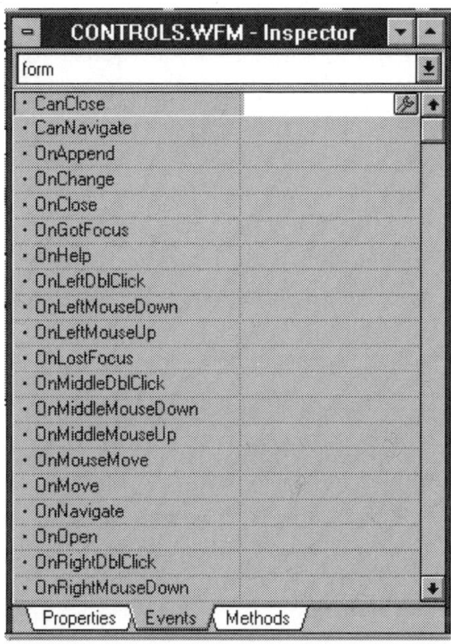

Figure 5–2. The event properties of a form.

The event properties. There are twenty-nine different event properties used by the nineteen control objects of a form in Visual dBASE.

> ➡ **New controls and properties**
> Visual dBASE has added two new control objects for a form to use: shape and paintbox. In addition, it has added five new event properties, totaling twenty-nine event properties that can be used.

These event properties are used to trap associated events. Many of these are common among the objects. Table 5–1 shows the event properties in dBASE and the objects that use them:

Table 5–1. Control Objects and Their Event Properties.

Event property	FORM	TEXT	ENTRYFIELD	COMBOBOX	SPINBOX	LISTBOX	PUSHBUTTON	CHECKBOX	RADIOBUTTON	LINE	RECTANGLE	BROWSE	EDITOR	IMAGE	VERT SCROLLBAR	HORI SCROLLBAR	OLE	TABBOX —new—	SHAPE —new—	PAINTBOX —new—
CanClose (*new*)	X																			
Key			X																	
OnAppend	X											X								
OnChange	X		X	X	X			X	X			X	X		X	X	X			
OnChar (*new*)																				X
OnClick							X													
OnClose	X																X			
OnFormSize (*new*)																				X
OnGotFocus	X		X	X	X	X	X	X	X			X	X		X	X	X	X		X
OnHelp	X		X	X	X	X	X	X	X			X	X		X	X		X		
OnKeyDown (*new*)																				X
OnKeyUp (*new*)																				X
OnLeftDblClick	X	X	X	X	X	X	X	X	X		X	X	X	X	X	X		X		X
OnLeftMouseDown	X	X	X	X	X	X	X	X	X		X	X	X	X	X	X		X		X
OnLeftMouseUp	X	X	X	X	X	X	X	X	X		X	X	X	X	X	X		X		X
OnLostFocus	X		X	X	X	X	X	X	X			X	X		X	X	X	X		X
OnMiddleDblClick	X	X	X	X	X	X	X	X	X		X	X	X	X	X	X		X		X

Table 5–1. Control Objects and Their Event Properties, continued.

Event property	FORM	TEXT	ENTRYFIELD	COMBOBOX	SPINBOX	LISTBOX	PUSHBUTTON	CHECKBOX	RADIOBUTTON	LINE	RECTANGLE	BROWSE	EDITOR	IMAGE	VERT SCROLLBAR	HORI SCROLLBAR	OLE	TABBOX _new_	SHAPE _new_	PAINTBOX _new_
OnMiddleMouseDown	X	X	X	X	X	X	X	X	X		X	X	X	X	X	X		X		X
OnMiddleMouseUp	X	X	X	X	X	X	X	X	X		X	X	X	X	X	X		X		X
OnMouseMove	X	X	X	X	X	X	X	X	X		X	X	X	X	X	X		X		X
OnMove	X																			
OnNavigate	X											X								
OnOpen	X	X	X	X	X	X	X	X	X	X	X	X	X	X	X	X	X	X	X	X
OnPaint																				X
OnRightDblClick	X	X	X	X	X	X	X	X	X		X	X	X	X	X	X		X		X
OnRightMouseDown	X	X	X	X	X	X	X	X	X		X	X	X	X	X	X		X		X
OnRightMouseUp	X	X	X	X	X	X	X	X	X		X	X	X	X	X	X		X		X
OnSelection	X																			
OnSelChange						X												X		
OnSize	X																			
Valid			X		X								X							
When			X	X	X	X	X	X	X			X	X		X	X		X		

As Table 5–1 shows, most control objects have many event properties that can be used to look for an event and trigger some event handler.

Most event properties begin with the word **On**. It is a quick way to identify the property as an event property versus a general property. These properties are there to look for some event.

The event properties are self-explanatory. OnAppend looks for the event of appending a record, OnClick looks for the event of clicking on the object (pushbutton), and OnMove looks for the event of moving the object (form).

Event (property) order

Because there are so many event properties (looking for events) that can be associated with an object, is there some order of occurrence for the event properties? In other words, if you associate some code with an event, can it trigger some other event code?

Event precedence. Some events can cause other events to occur. If you click on a pushbutton (in a form that is already active) and the pushbutton doesn't already have focus, the following events occur:

1. The *When* event handler will be executed to determine if the button is allowed to get focus.
2. If the button can have focus, its *OnGotFocus* event handler will be executed.
3. Then the button's Onclick event handler will be executed.

The sequence of events and the activity of the event properties gets even more complex if another control in the same form has focus, when the pushbutton is clicked. If the control object has a Valid or OnLostFocus event property, their event handlers will execute before the control relinquishes control to the pushbutton. This increased the sequence to five different programs being executed.

Add working in a different form, from the one that you push a button in, and you have just added at least three more event handlers to the pack—the form you are leaving has three possible event properties (OnMouseMove, OnClose, and OnLostFocus), and the form you are coming into has several that may activate (OnMouseMove, OnGotFocus, OnOpen, OnNavigate, and OnSelection).

So a single mouse click can cause many (five or more) events to occur.

Event conflicts. When working with pushbutton event properties, you need to be aware of a possible problem. The OnClick versus the OnLeftDblClick can be problematic. If you assign an event handler to both the OnClick and the OnLeftDblClick, such as in the following code, the OnLeftDblClick may *never* take effect.

```
F = NEW MyFORM()
f.open()
CLASS MyFORM OF FORM
   this.Left = 14.5
   this.Top = 0.2344
   this.Height = 8
```

```
   this.Width = 30
   DEFINE PUSHBUTTON PUSHBUTTON1 OF THIS PROPERTY;
         Top 2.5, Left 6, Height 2.4, Width 16, Text
        "Press ME" ,;
         OnLeftDblClick CLASS::DoubleIt, OnClick
         CLASS::GotOne
   DEFINE TEXT TEXT1 OF THIS PROPERTY;
         Top 1, Left 6, Width 22, Text "No 1 button click"
   DEFINE TEXT TEXT2 OF THIS PROPERTY;
         Top 6.5, Left 6, Width 22, Text "No 2 button
click"
   Procedure GotOne
   form.text1.text="ONE Click"
   form.text2.visible=.f.

   Procedure DoubleIt
   form.text2.text="DOUBLE CLICK"
   form.text2.visible=.t.

ENDCLASS
```

This code may cause a problem. The OnClick (single click event) will take effect before the OnLeftDblClick (double click event). This means that the OnClick event handler will *always* trigger. Although you can get the OnLeftDblClick to occur, it will *also* always trigger the OnClick.

In addition to the problem of the single versus double click, there is an order of precedence when working with the event properties that trap for the three mouse buttons (down, up, and double click). If you assign event handlers to all three of these events, the following is the order of capture:

1. OnLeftDown	1. OnRightDown	1. OnMiddleDown
2. OnLeftDblClick	2. OnRightDblClick	2. OnMiddleDblClick
3. OnLeftUp	3. OnRightUp	3. OnMiddleUp

If you are using a pushbutton, the OnDown event will also occur before the OnClick.

Which event property should you use?

Because there are so many event properties that can be used to trigger an event handler (some program code), which one do you use? The key to this question is easy: Do not think about *all* the events that can occur when a form is active—just the ones that can be used to complete your task.

Coding event properties. When working with event properties only concern yourself with the ones that you need to use. Table 5–2 shows several of the more common events that you may want to control.

Table 5–2 shows the most common events that are used in programming event-driven applications. As you can imagine, using these few events will probably fulfill 80 percent of your trigger needs.

Table 5–2. Common Events for Control Objects.

Control	Event	Event Property	When to Use
ALL—forms, pushbuttons, and entryfields	Press F1	OnHelp	To display some help when the user presses F1 while the pushbutton has focus
Pushbutton	Clicking	OnClick	Have something occur when the user presses the button
Form	Opening	OnOpen	Have something occur when the form opens, such as open another form etc.
	Getting focus	OnGotFocus	If more than one form is open and you want to refresh the form when it is made, the active point of control (focus)
	Losing focus	OnLostFocus	Do something when the form losses control; if the form is doing some critical activity, this Property can be used to regain focus
	Closing	OnClose	Have the form do something when it closes, such as close any associated forms
Entryfield, pushbutton, check box, and combo box	Changing contents	OnChange	To trigger some program that can check the contents when something changes in the object
	Entering object	When	Trigger an event to determine if the user can enter the object (give it focus)

Default event property actions. The default property action for an event is simply to ignore the event. If you don't assign any code to the event property, the event property can't trigger based on the event. dBASE simply ignores that event and goes on to the next one to see what event handler is associated with it, until all the events have been processed.

Associating initialization and cleanup code with an object

Many forms that you create in dBASE will require setup code to initialize the environment as the form opens. Likewise, you may have to perform some cleanup code when the form closes. Using the form's onOpen event to initialize actions and the onClose event to assign cleanup code is the answer.

In fact, most control objects on a form can also use the OnOpen event property to perform initialization. These two properties are the easiest one to use.

- OnOpen property is used to assign code that performs start (initialization) procedures, such as opening tables not used directly by the form, declaring or reinitializing memory variables, and so on.
- OnClose property is used to perform cleanup procedures, such as releasing a memory variable or closing a table.

The order of event execution when opening a form. When a form is opened, the form frame (window) gains focus. Then the control objects inside the form are evaluated to determine if they can gain focus. The first available control (that can gain focus) then gets the focus. The following is the order of event precedence for opening a form:

1. The form checks to see if any contained control objects can gain focus (the When event handlers will be executed for all contained objects).
2. The form's OnOpen event handler for the form executes. The window opens and it gets focus.
3. If there are any active controls (that can gain focus), the OnOpen event handlers of each control is executed.
4. The form's OnGotFocus event handler activates. The first contained control object in the tabbing order is given focus.
5. The OnGotFocus event handler of the first control (which now has focus) activates.

As you can see by the sequence of events, at least five event handlers can be triggered.

The order of event execution when closing a form. When a form is closed, the form frame (window) and any contained control objects lose focus. Then the form closes (disappears from the screen). The following is the order of event precedence for closing a form:

1. The current contained control's Valid event handler executes. If it returns a false (.f.), the form cannot be closed.
2. The current control's OnLostFocus event handler executes.

3. The form gains focus, and the form's OnLostFocus event handler triggers.
4. The form's OnClose event handler executes.

As you can see by the sequence of events, four different event handlers can be triggered. If the Valid property of the current control returns false, then the form will not be closed until it returns a true.

EVENT HANDLERS

Up until now, you have heard a lot about *event handlers*. The event handler is a procedure, function, or codeblock. It is the code that is run when an event occurs. It is normal procedural (flow-of-control) code.

The code inside the event handler executes one line of code at a time. It can contain branching (IF . . . ENDIF, CASE . . . ENDCASE) and looping (DO WHILE . . . ENDDO) commands. It is simply a subroutine that performs some action.

The only difference between an event handler and traditional procedural code is the way the code is used.

Assigning event handlers

In event-driven applications, the programmer creates and assigns event handlers to events. When the event occurs the procedure, function, or codeblock (event handler) executes.

Using external procedure files

You can create procedures, place them in memory (in a procedure file), and use them as event handlers. For instance, the following procedure file has a single procedure in it, named ButtonClick:

```
*** MIKEPROC.prg
*
PROCEDURE ButtonClick
  * change a window's text (title caption)
  MainWindow.Text = "You pushed the Button"

  * change the button's text and size
  MainWindow.TheButton.Text = "Help Me"
  MainWindow.TheButton.Width =
  MainWindow.TheButton.Width*1.2
RETURN
```

Once the procedure is created, you can assign it to an event property and have it execute. The procedure must already be in memory for the object to use it. The following code will load the procedure, create a form with a pushbutton in it, and assign an event handle, ButtonClick, to the pushbutton's OnClick event, finally opening the form:

```
Public MainWindow
SET PROCEDURE TO MikeProc
MainWindow = NEW FORM("Main Form")
DEFINE PUSHBUTTON TheButton OF MainWindow
MainWindow.TheButton.OnClick = ButtonClick
MainWindow.Open()
```

If you type these commands in the Command window or create a program and run them, you will see how the event handler works. The line that assigns the Event Handler (procedure) is the fourth line: "**MainWindow.TheButton.OnClick = ButtonClick**". It attaches the procedure (Event Handle), ButtonClick, to the event property, OnClick. Whenever you click on the pushbutton named TheButton, the program will execute.

NOTE: The code in the preceding example refers to the pushbutton by referencing the form first. Because the pushbutton is inside the form (contained) and was declared using the DEFINE command, you must reference it by the full path of containership.

<form name>.<object name>.<property name>

Every time you click on the pushbutton, it will get wider, and the text of the Window and the button will change. You will only see the text change one time. In this case, the event handler is outside of the object in a procedure file.

Using methods (internal procedures) as event handlers

In addition to creating event handlers in external procedure files, you can create event handlers that will be inside the object itself. These procedures are known as *methods*.

An Event handler can be a method that is stored in the Class. Remember all objects (including forms) come from a Class. The class creates the object and holds all of the objects methods inside of it. Although you haven't worked with a class yet, the following code shows the same procedure stored inside a Class definition:

```
*** MYPROCS.PRG
*
CLASS MYNEWFORM OF FORM
   this.Height = 10
   this.Left =  1
   this.Top =  1
   this.Width =  40
   this.Text = "Sample Form"
   DEFINE PUSHBUTTON TheButton OF this PROPERTY;
     Height  2, Left 1, Top 1, Width 10, Text "Button 1",;
```

```
        OnClick CLASS::PUSHBUTTON1_ONCLICK
      Procedure PUSHBUTTON1_OnClick
        * change a window's text (title caption)

        form.Text = "You pushed the Button"
        * change the button's text and size
        if this.Text = "Help Me"
          this.text = "Button 1"
        else
          this.text = "Help Me"
        endif
        this.Width = this.Width*1.2
        RETURN
ENDCLASS
```

This code creates a new type of form class named MyNewForm. It inherits all the default properties and methods of the built-in Class FORM. Then it changes the default values for five of the properties (Top, Left, Height, Width, and Text). Then it creates a pushbutton that will be placed in the form and assigns the internal event handler to the OnClick event property of the pushbutton.

Once the class has been created, it can be placed in memory like a procedure file, and the following code can be used to create a form object that will use the internal Event Handler:

```
SET PROCEDURE TO MYPROCS
xForm = NEW MyNewForm()
xForm.Open()
```

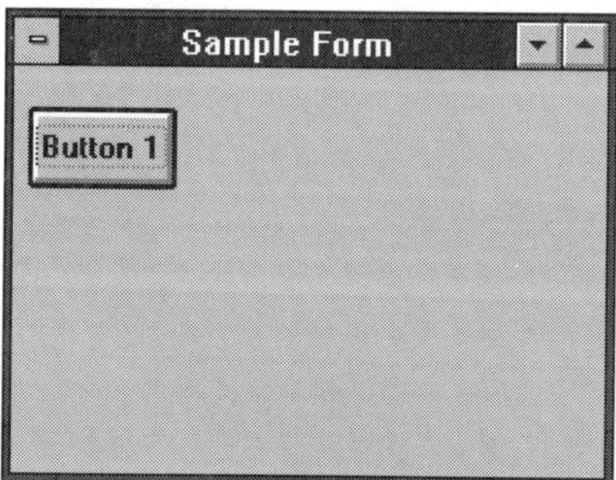

Figure 5–3. A form with a pushbutton that has an Event Handler attached to the button.

Figure 5–3 shows the form, xForm, immediately after it is opened. Notice that it has a single button and the text (title) of the form is "Sample Form"; also the text on the button is "Button 1."

Now that the form is open, clicking on the button will trigger the OnClick property, which will run the internal Event Handler, CLASS::PushButton1_OnClick. This procedure is actually made part of the Class. Figure 5–4 shows the new text on the form and button as well as a larger pushbutton. These changes were made by the Event Handler that is stored inside the Class.

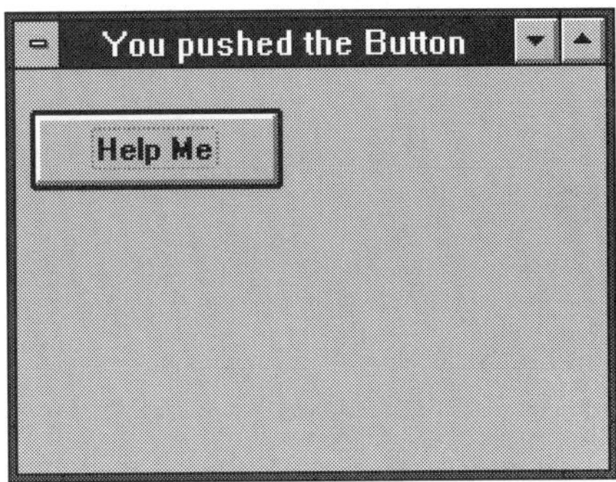

Figure 5–4. The same form as Figure 5–3 once the pushbutton has been pushed.

If you continue to press the pushbutton in the form, xForm, the button will continue to get wider and wider.

Generalizing your event handler code

Where possible, you should create event handlers that use generic references to the objects with which they will work. The preceding example Class definition uses two special reference variables. The two special reference variables are *form* and *this*.

Form reference. The *form* reference is a special keyword variable that will refer back to the actual form that is currently active. By using the form reference, you will not have to hard code the name of the form in the procedure file. The keyword *form* can be thought of as a special macro name or place holder that will be replaced with the actual name of the active form.

This reference. The *this* reference is another special keyword variable that will refer back to the active control object (the one that has focus) that called the code that has the *this* keyword in it. By using the this reference, you will not have to hard code the name of the control object (<form name>.<control object>) in the procedure file. The keyword *this* can be thought of as a special type of macro or place holder that will be replaced with the actual name of the active control object in the form.

The following two event handlers demonstrate hard-coding versus generic procedures. Either of these two procedures could be placed inside a Class definition or even a procedure file, and used as an event handler.

Table 5–3. Hard-Coding versus Generic Procedures.

Hard-Coded Event Handler	Generic Event Handler
PROCEDURE ClickIt	PROCEDURE ClickIt
* change the window text	* change the window text
MainForm.text = "You changed me!"	form.text = "You changed me!"
* change the button's text	* change the button's text
MainForm.TheButton.text = "YES!"	this.text = "YES!"
RETURN	RETURN

Notice that the Generic event handler (external procedure) uses the keywords *form* and *this* to change properties in a form.

The second method is more efficient than the first. The second one has become more generic by using two special references (form and this).

The following code can be used to demonstrate the use of both the *this* and *form*:

```
*** REFDEMO.prg
*
xf = NEW MyForm()
xf.open()
CLASS MyForm of FORM()
   DEFINE PUSHBUTTON PUSHBUTTON2 OF THIS;
       PROPERTY;
         Top 2, Left 8, Height 2, Width 16, Text
         "ProcDemo",;
         OnClick CLASS::ClickIt
   Procedure ClickIt
       form.text = "You changed me!"
       this.text = "YES!"

EndClass
```

Notice that the Procedure ClickIt uses both the *form* and *this* references. When you run this code with DO REFDEMO, the use can click on the button. Clicking on the button, the forms text on the title bar changes to "You changed me!" (f*orm*) and the text on button changes to "YES!" (*this*).

NOTE: *Form* and *this* will be covered more in depth in later chapters.

This and form—one level *only*. When working with the *form* and *this* reference variables, you must remember that they will only work one level deep. If you try to use *form* and *this* in a lower called procedure, you will get an error. In other words, you can use these special reference variables in the procedure that is directly linked to the event (<object name>.OnClick = MyProc; MyProc can reference *this* and *form*). Another procedure cannot reference these variables.

To use the information from *form* and *this* in a lower-level procedure, you must pass these special reference variables as parameter(s). The following code demonstrates this:

```
PROCEDURE ClickIt
    form.Text = "You pushed the Button"
    this.Text = "Help!"
    DO ReSizeBtn WITH this
RETURN
PROCEDURE ReSizeBtn(xRef)
    xRef.width = xRef.width*1.5
RETURN
```

The second procedure, ReSizeBtn, is called by ClickIt. ClickIt is directly linked to the OnClick property by some code like this—MyButton.OnClick = ClickIt. ClickIt can use the special reference variables *this* and *form*. ReSizeBtn cannot use these reference variables; instead, the reference variables must be passed as parameters.

What do event handlers do?

Event handlers normally execute some code performing one of the following actions:

- Affect the object itself, such as changing a property value or triggering an object method
- Affect the underlying tables, such as replacing fields with new values, or opening another form or closing a form

The most common event handler is one that performs an action in response to mouse clicks. These types of event handlers are linked to the OnClick event property of a menu item or a pushbutton.

Types of event handlers

You have already worked with two of the basic types of event handlers—external and internal procedures. There are six different types of event handlers:

- Internal procedures (methods in Classes)
- External procedures (procedure files)
- Internal UDFs (methods in Classes)
- External UDFs (procedure files)

- Internal statement codeblocks (directly linked to event property)
- Internal expression codeblocks (directly linked to event property)

As pointed out earlier, event handlers are plain, old-fashioned, procedural codes. They can be procedures, functions, or codeblocks. They contain the same type of code that you have written in the past.

Technically, codeblocks are event handlers; however, they have no name. Instead of giving the event property the name of the event handler to process, you assign the actual code that you want the event property to process.

NOTE: Codeblocks and functions
Although covered in depth later in this chapter, a codeblock is like a function or procedure that is unnamed. The code of the function or procedure is written and enclosed in braces ({ }).

Which type of event handler is best?

Normally, if the code is small and will not be re-used, a codeblock is the first choice. If the code can be used by a lot of different objects (from different Classes), then the next choice is to make the Event Handler an external procedure or function. Finally, if the codeblock is to be used by objects from the same Class or a derived Class (Subclass), then an internal procedure or function is best.

As for the procedure versus function argument—if the event handler must return a value, then it must be a function. If no value is to be returned, you should create a procedure.

Calling an event handler

When you call the event handler, you simply assign its name to the event property following one of these formats:

<object name>.<Event Property name> = <Event Handler name>

<object name>.<Event Property name> = <Event Handler codeblock>

For example, the following examples call event handlers:

```
MyButton.OnClick = {;form.Close()}           Codeblock
MyForm.OnClose = CLASS::ResEnvirn            Internal method
MyCusForm.OnOpen = PetFrmOpen                External
procedure
```

Attaching an event handler in the Forms Designer. Notice that they all have something in common—the name of the object is attached to an event property, and the event handler is assigned by using the equal sign. This is how you would do it in code. You can also attach an event handler to an event property by using the property inspector in the form designer. Figure 5–5 shows attaching an event handler to an event property in the forms designer.

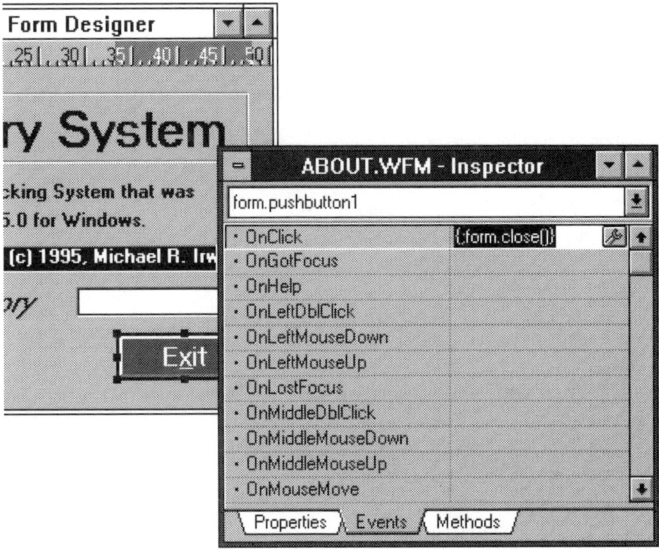

Figure 5–5. Attaching an event handler to an event property in the Property Inspector.

There is a one minor problem when setting event handlers in the form designer. You *cannot* easily assign an external event handler (one in a procedure file) to an event. Setting external event handlers can only be done through code (or in the Command window).

Event handlers and the Inspect() function. You cannot attach an event handler to an event property using the Inspect() function from the Command window. However, if you attach an event handler to an event property in code and then use the Inspect() function, you can see what handlers have been attached. Figure 5–6 shows the Property Inspector, called using the Inspect() function. Notice that the event property OnClick is assigned an event handler named ClickIt.

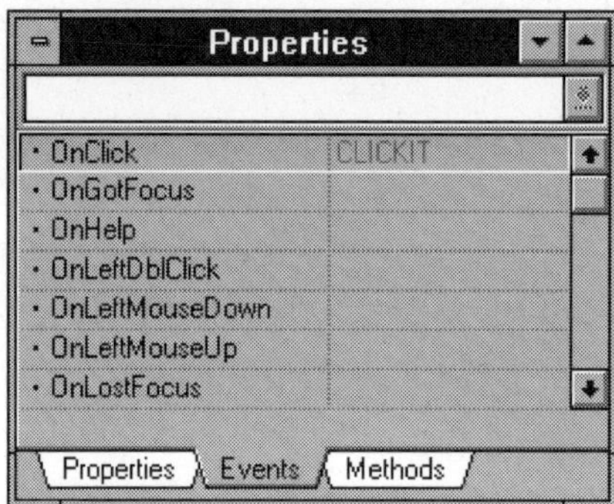

Figure 5–6. Using the Property Inspector to view event handler assignments.

Notice that the name of the Event Handler is dimmed in Figure 5–6. This lets you know that you cannot change the value—only review it.

Creating event handlers in the form designer

The examples so far have worked with external code or have shown the structure of a Class definition that used a method internally. The easiest way to assign event handlers is when you are creating a form and its contained control objects in the form designer. The following examples use the form designer to build an event handler.

Before beginning you will need to enter the form designer by following these steps:

1. Enter the form designer by typing the command CREATE FORM TestEvt in the Command window.
2. Place a pushbutton (the control object with an OK on the button of the control palette) anywhere on the form, and select the pushbutton.
3. Activate the Object Property Inspector by right mouse clicking and choosing Inspector from the SpeedMenu.

➡ **The Inspector choice of a SpeedMenu**
The original dBASE for Windows 5.0 called the Object Property Inspector choice of the SpeedMenu is Object Properties. Borland has changed the name of this menu choice to reflect more accurately the actual action—an Inspector dialog box is opened displaying the objects properties and methods.

Figure 5–7 shows the SpeedMenu active with the Inspector choice active.

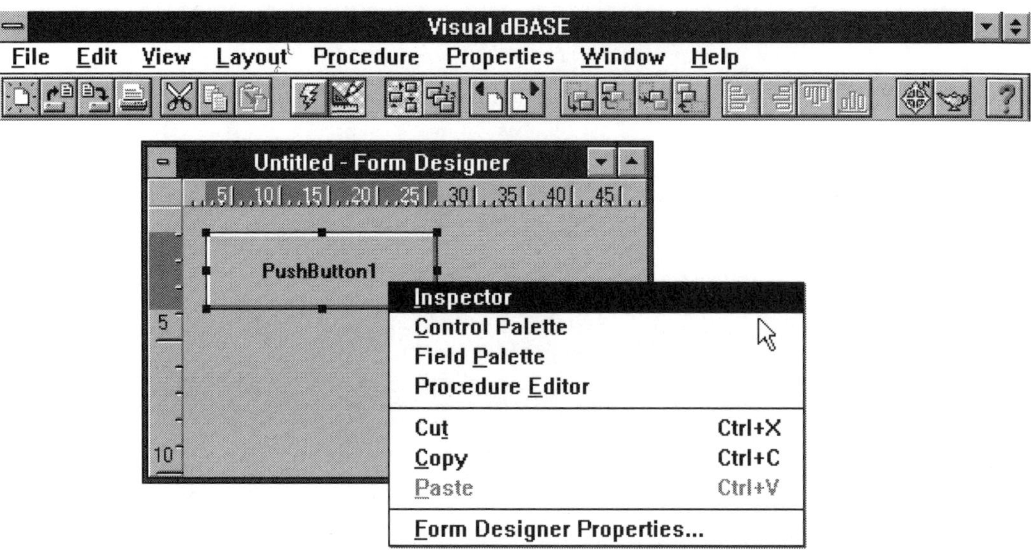

Figure 5–7. The SpeedMenu, selecting the Property Inspector dialog box.

Creating an event handler in a form

With the Object Property Inspector active, select the tab named **Events**. Once the event properties are shown, select the OnClick property of the pushbutton. Your screen should look similar to Figure 5–8.

The Procedure Editor. Notice the small icon (picture) of a wrench located at the left side of the OnClick cell. This wrench button is a *tool* button. Clicking on the button will activate the *Procedure Editor*. Click on the tool button.

The Procedure Editor is an editing window that can be used to create procedures. It is a mini–word processor. When it opens, it appears at the bottom half of the screen and will look like Figure 5–9.

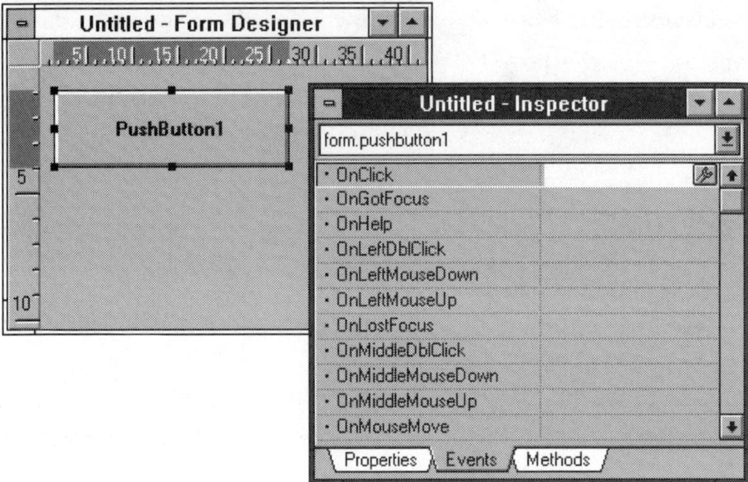

Figure 5–8. The OnClick property is selected in the Property Inspector.

Figure 5–9. The Procedure Editor.

Type in the small procedure program that is in Figure 5–9. Notice that dBASE has automatically assigned a name to the procedure (Procedure PUSHBUTTON1_OnClick).

```
Procedure PUSHBUTTON1_OnClick
   this.text = "Bye, Bye"
   sleep 3
   this.text = "Hello again"
RETURN
```

You have just created an event handler using the Procedure Editor of the form designer to create an event handler. It is not necessary to close the Procedure Editor; however, it can be closed by simply double clicking on the frames system menu (top left corner).

The event handler that you just created is actually a procedure. It will be placed inside the Class definition of your form.

Now you can save your work and run the form. When it first starts, the button's text is "Pushbutton1." If you click on the button, you will see the text change—twice. Figure 5–10 shows all three pushbutton texts that will occur as you press the button.

Figure 5–10. From left to right: the form open, the button pressed, and the button after being pressed.

The text on the button "Hello Again" will now toggle between it and "Bye, Bye" as you press the button.

WORKING WITH METHODS

In the previous example, you created your own method to be used as an event handler.

If you recall from earlier chapters, a method is simply a procedure, function, or codeblock that lives in the object; it is a part of the object. Technically, it is stored in the Class that was used to create the object, and the object has a function pointer inside it that tells it where to go find it.

Examining methods in form designer

Return to the form designer, with your form named TestEvt, and activate the Property Inspector, then click on the **Methods** tab with the pushbutton selected. You should see the methods of the pushbutton. Figure 5–11 shows four methods that are associated with the pushbutton: MarkCustom, Move, Release, and SetFocus.

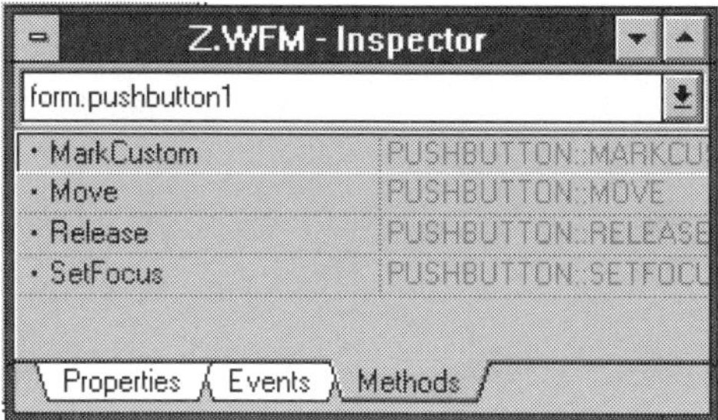

Figure 5-11. The methods of the pushbutton.

User-created methods

What happened to the method that you created, the one that was named *PUSHBUTTON1_OnClick()*? To find the method that you created, select the form object from the combo box in the Property Inspector. Figure 5-12 shows the combo box and selection of the object.

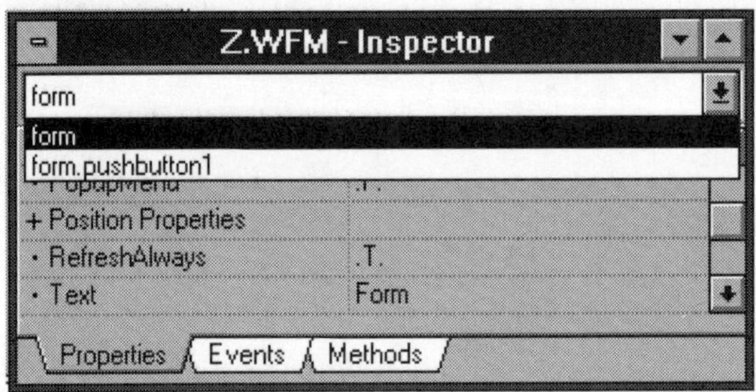

Figure 5–12. Selecting another object in the Property Inspector.

Once the form is selected, click the **Method** tab. Then click on the cell that says **+dBASE variable properties** of the Methods page. This cell will expand to display all of the dBASE created methods associated with this form class. This is the method, which is stored at the form level—technically, it is stored in the Class that created the form. Figure 5–13 shows the method highlighted.

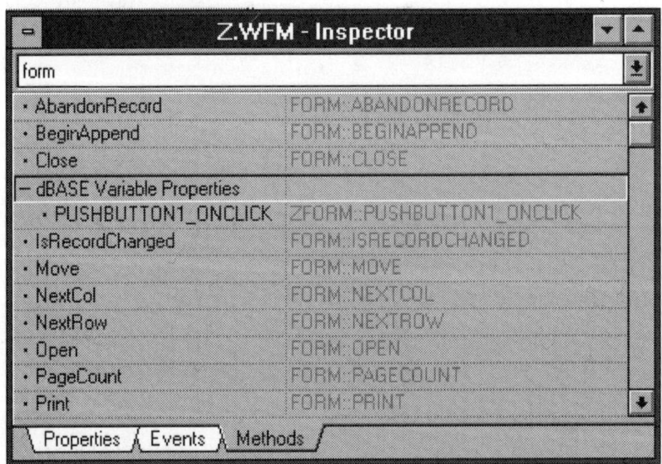

Figure 5–13. The user-created methods in the form.

Notice that user-created methods are attached at the form level rather than the control object level. There are a couple of other *built-in* methods that you should already be familiar with—the Open() and Close().

Understanding where the methods are stored. Examining Figure 5–13, you see the name of the methods in the left column of the Property Inspector. The right side shows you where the method is actually stored. For instance, all of the methods, except the dBASE created Pushbutton1_OnClick, are stored in the Class named FORM. These include the Open, Close, SetFocus, Release, Print, and others. The PushButton1_OnClick method is stored in a Class named TestEvtFORM.

Methods are normally stored inside a Class definition, although it is possible to store them outside. This subject is covered later in the book.

Working with methods

Every time you open an object using the syntax

<Object name>**.Open()**

you are using a method. In this case, it is the open method. Figure 5–13 shows several built-in methods. The following methods are the most common for a form:

Open	Opens the form object
Close	Closes the form object
Release	Releases the form object from memory
Print	Activates the printer dialog box to print the form to the printer
SetFocus	Activates the form and makes it the active (focused) object

Calling a method

When you call a method, you simply name the object and the method name that you want the object to run. To call a method you use the General format:

<Object Name>.<Method Name>([parameters])

If you need to pass any parameters to the method, you do them inside the parentheses.

Member call operator. You must place parentheses behind the name of the object, even if it is a procedure or codeblock. The parentheses [( )] are known as the *member call operator.*

Calling the Print() method of a form. To send an active form to the printer, you can simply use its Print() method. This will activate a printer dialog box like the one in Figure 5–14, which shows form named Customer. You would activate the printer routine by issuing a command like the following in your code:

```
Customer.Print().
```

Although you can call the Print() method by naming the object directly, you could also make the code more general by using the special variable operator, *form*. To activate the printer dialog box is simple.

```
form.Print()
```

This code line can be attached to a pushbutton, or placed in some other code. The keyword form will be replaced with the name of the form object when it is executed.

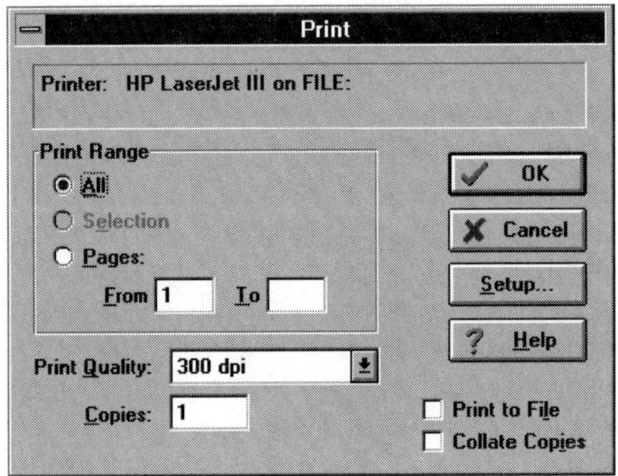

Figure 5–14. The printer dialog box for a form.

CODEBLOCKS

In addition to procedures and functions, you can create codeblocks to be used as event handlers. Codeblocks let you quickly add functionality to subroutines.

One way codeblocks can be used is to hide the routines contained within them from the rest of the code. You can assign a codeblock to a memory variable or directly to an object's properties.

What is a codeblock?

Codeblocks are small, unnamed "chunks" of code. They normally consist of one or a few commands. Using a codeblock is convenient and economical. For example, if you want to attach a few lines of code (event handler) to an event, without specifying a specific function or procedure, a codeblock is the answer. This is especially true if you don't care about reusing the code. A good example of a codeblock is one that will close a form.

```
{;form.Close()}
```

The preceding code can easily be identified as a codeblock by the braces ({ }) around the command. Notice that the preceding command *form.Close()* is preceded by a semicolon (;). The semicolon is used in a codeblock to identify a command.

Some people refer to codeblocks as anonymous functions. In part, this is because it is unnamed. Another reason is due to the nature of codeblocks—they tend to be hidden from the primary code of an application.

In addition to having a single command, like the preceding example, a codeblock can contain a group of commands or expressions. Codeblocks can be used just about anywhere—they can be used in expressions, assigned to memory variables, attached to properties, or called directly. They can even receive parameters and return values.

A codeblock actually *contains* programming code. It is simply code that is grouped into a nameless source.

Types of codeblocks

There are two different types of codeblocks.

- Statement codeblock
- Expression codeblock

The statement codeblock is similar to a procedure—it does something and may not return a value. The expression codeblock is analogous to a function—it also does something, and it always returns a value.

The braces. You can quickly identify a codeblock by the enclosing braces ({ }). A codeblock will always be between braces. It begins and ends with a brace; braces are required.

Expression codeblocks

Expression codeblocks can contain only a valid dBASE expression. They always return a dynamically evaluated value when they are executed. Although an expression codeblock can contain more than one expression, by embedding one function within another, it can only return a single value. Expression codeblocks are a way to attach event handler code to event properties like the When or Valid events.

The general syntax for an expression codeblock is

{ | <parameters> | < expression > }

Notice that the syntax uses two special sets of characters—the start/end braces

({ }) and the pipe characters (| |). The braces delimit the codeblock, whereas the pipe characters delimit any parameters being passed to the codeblock. This syntax shows that you can pass parameters to an expression codeblock as well as process an expression.

> **Parameters and Visual dBASE**
> The pipe characters must be used when creating an expression codeblock in Visual dBASE. They are not optional; if there are no parameters to pass, place the pipe characters at the beginning of the codeblock with nothing between them.

Examples of expression codeblocks

The following are examples of expression type codeblocks:

```
{|BirthDt| YEAR(Date()) - YEAR(BirthDt) >= 55}
{|a,b| a+b}
{|| (34.5 * 22.25) / 12.5}
{|a,b| INT(a+b) = INT(a)+INT(b)}
```

Each of these codeblocks perform some calculation and return a value in a single expression. The following explains the return value of each codeblock:

Table 5–4. Return Values of Expression Codeblocks.

Codeblock	Return Value
`{|BirthDt| YEAR(Date()) - YEAR(BirthDt) 7= 55}`	A number representing a person's age based on the year of birth (e.g., 2/4/50 and 12/9/50 will both return a 45 for the date 10/10/95)
`{|a,b| a+b}`	A number based on the summation of $a + b$
`{|| (34.5 * 22.25) / 12.5}`	Returns 61.41
`x={|a,b| INT(xSum) = ROUND(a,0)+ROUND(b,0)}`	Returns a logical .T. or .F. based on the values of *x*Sum, *a*, and *b*

Building on the first expression codeblock, you can attach it to the Valid event property of a field named BirthDt in a table named Retirees as in the following example:

```
CLASS MyForm of FORM()
    *
    *  additional property values and controls can be placed here
    *
    DEFINE ENTRYFIELD EntryDOB OF THIS PROPERTY;
           Top 4, Left 16, Height 1, Width 11, ;
           DataLink "Retirees->BirthDt", ;
           Valid {|BirthDt| YEAR(Date()) - YEAR(BirthDt) >= 55}
ENDCLASS
```

When a user enters a value in the BirthDt entryfield, the valid event property will trigger, and it will check to see if the age of the person, based on their birth year, is 55 or older. If yes, then the value is accepted (returning a .T.). If the answer is no, then it returns a false, and a dialog box will be activated with a message saying that the input value is not valid.

You can also use an expression codeblock associating it with a memory variable. In effect, creating a user-defined function. For instance, the following code can be entered in the Command window to assign two different codeblocks to memory variables:

```
Add2Nums = {|a,b| a+b}
xValue = {|| (34.5 * 22.25) / 12.5}
```

With the codeblocks associated with the memory variables Add2Num and xValue you can use them just as if they were functions:

```
? Add2Nums(3,4)
? xValue()
```

sidebar

What is an expression in dBASE?

An expression is one or more elements (or parts) that, when combined, will evaluate to a single value. For example, an expression is the right side of a formula

```
xName = TRIM(LTRIM(LastName))+TRIM(FirstName)
    xSqFeet = xSqMeter * 10.76391041
     xAdd = ((23.5 + 22.4) * 12) / 2.2
```

The elements that can be used are fields, constants, memory variables (including array subscripts), functions (dBASE or user defined), and mathematical operators.

The expression itself, such as the preceding three, only represents a value; thus, it is not a command itself. Expressions, like the first example, can contain functions [Trim(Ltrim())] that will convert a value [LastName] from its present value to a new value (removes all spaces before and after characters in the LastName field). It can also contain mathematical operators [+, -, *, /, etc.], such as all three examples demonstrate. All of this power when creating expressions lets you create complex expressions that can solve difficult problems.

Expression codeblocks can also contain a complete formula itself. Take the following formula, for example: xTot = xNum1 + xNum2. When performed as an expression codeblock, this will return either a .T. (true) or .F. (false) based on the values of all three variables.

Expression codeblocks only contain expressions. In each previous example, only the expression itself is enclosed between the braces. There are no display statements (SAY, ?, ??) or multiple commands. Rather, they perform some calculation and return a value based on that calculation.

If you need to have a codeblock perform more than one command, use a *command codeblock* instead. Only the expression is present.

Passing parameters to expression codeblocks

To use parameters with an expression codeblock, they must be placed at the *beginning* of the codeblock and enclosed (delimited) with the **pipe** characters (| |). This is an example of passing two parameters to a codeblock.

```
MinusIt = { |nPara1, nPara2| nPara1 - nPara2 }
```

This codeblock is assigned to a memory variable named MinusIt. It passes two parameters: nPara1, nPara2.

When you pass parameters to an *expression codeblock*, you must delimit the parameters with the *pipe* sign. If you have more than one parameter, as in the previous example, you must separate them with a comma. Notice that there is a comma between nPara1 and nPara2 in the parameter section (enclosed between the pipe characters).

Eliminating the required pipe characters in version 5.0
Visual dBASE requires that you use the pipe characters, even if you pass no parameters. This can cause a problem if you need to share code between version 5.0 and Visual dBASE. Version 5.0 requires that you use the pipe characters *only* when there are parameters to pass. If you use the pipe characters without specifying a parameter, dBASE will report an error. If you common code for Visual dBASE and dBASE for Windows 5.0, begin the codeblock with the keyword **RETURN**, converting it to a Statement codeblock. Remember to use the semicolon before the RETURN command. For example:

with Empty parameters	**with ;RETURN**
`{|| .NOT.EOF()}`	`{; RETURN.NOT.EOF()}`
`{|| (3.5 * 2.5) / 9.5}`	`{; RETURN (3.5 * 2.5) / 9.5}`

Building an expression codeblock that has parameters

Once the parameters are entered the expression immediately follows (separated by a *blank space* only). The following expression codeblock demonstrates building a codeblock with parameters:

```
{|nHours, nHrSalary| nHour * nHrSalary}
```

This codeblock receives two parameters, and then it performs a calculation. The parameter list and the actual expression are only separated by a space.

NOTE: Naming Parameters
When passing parameters to a codeblock, the name of the variable, or field, in the expression must match the name of the parameter. If you are using field names as parameters, the parameter name must match the field name exactly.

Running an expression codeblock

To run the expression codeblock, xMinus, use the following syntax:

```
? MinusIt(222.54, 123.43)
```

Notice that you called the codeblock just as you call a function. You use parentheses at the end of the name of the codeblock, just like a function, and place any parameters inside the parentheses, separating them with a comma.

Statement codeblocks

Statement codeblocks, often referred to as *command codeblocks*, are groups of dBASE commands strung together within braces, separated by semicolons. Unlike expression codeblocks, they do not directly return a value. They can contain a single command or a group of commands.

Statement codeblocks are good for attaching unnamed subroutine code consisting of one or a few commands to a memory variable or an object property. Statement codeblocks are ideal as event handlers the OnClick event property of a pushbutton.

The general syntax for a statement codeblock is

{ [| <parameters> |] ; <command1> ; <command2> ; <command3> ... }

The syntax is slightly different from a codeblock for an expression codeblock. Notice that a semicolon precedes every command. This includes placing a semicolon before the first command, regardless of using parameters. The semicolon is required. If you fail to use it, you will experience unexpected results.

Like expression codeblocks, you can pass parameters. One difference between a statement codeblock and an expression codeblock is the return of a value. The statement codeblock cannot return a value directly.

Statement codeblocks can also perform more than one command (statement). To perform more than a single statement, separate each statement by a semicolon.

Examples of statement codeblocks

The following are all examples of statement codeblocks:

```
{;form.Close()}
{;checkIt(); closeIt(cFile); closeIt(cForm)}
{|cFile,cOrd,cFind|; use (cFile) order (cOrd);
⇒xF =seek(cFind); use; return xF}
```

In these examples, the semicolon is used to separate the different commands.

Passing parameters to statement codeblocks

To use parameters with a statement codeblock, they must be placed at the *beginning* of the codeblock. In addition to being placed at the front, they must be enclosed (delimited) with the pipe characters (| |), and it must be separated from the command by using a semicolon. This is an example of passing two parameters to a statement codeblock:

```
OpenIt = {|xFILE, xORDER|; USE (xFILE) ORDER (xORDER)}
OpenIt("Customer","Cust_No")
```

The first line assigns the codeblock to the memory variable OpenIt. The second line uses the codeblock with two parameters—the file name (Customer.dbf) and the order index tag (Cust_No).

Separating commands

If the statement codeblock is to perform several commands, each command must be separated by a semicolon. The semicolon is placed in front of each command.

Building a statement codeblock that has parameters

Once the parameters are entered the expression immediately follows (separated by a semicolon). The following statement codeblock demonstrates building a codeblock with parameters:

```
EmplPay ={|nHr,nPayRt|; ? "Total pay is :"+
⇒Trans(nHr*nPayRt,"$99,999.99")}
```

This codeblock passes two parameters, and then it performs a calculation, printing the calculation to the screen. The parameter list and the actual expression are separated by a semicolon. Because a statement codeblock does not return a value, you have to use the Print command to have the calculation display. In fact, if you forget to put the ? command, the codeblock will report an error.

Statement codeblocks can use any legal dBASE command.

Running a statement codeblock

To run the statement codeblock, EmplPay(), you can type the following commands in the command window:

```
EmplPay ={|nHr,nPayRt|; ? "Total pay is :"+
⇒Trans(nHr*nPayRt,"$99,999.99")}
EmplPay(42.75, 21.724)
EmplPay(40, 12.75)
```

The first line assigns the codeblock to the variable EmplPay; the next two lines run the command codeblock with different parameters.

Notice that you did not place a question mark in front of the codeblock, nor did you use a formula like x = EmplPay(). Even though you call a statement codeblock like a function, you do not predicate it with a memory variable assignment or a print (?) command. Using a print command could cause unexpected errors in your code.

Like expression codeblocks, you use the parentheses at the end of the name of the codeblock and place any parameters inside the parentheses, separating them with a comma.

User-defined commands. The statement codeblock is a new *command* that you have created. Because of this, you do not use other dBASE commands to drive it; it drives itself. It is like creating a user-defined command (UDC) in dBASE. In fact, statement codeblocks are called UDCs in some languages.

Passing parameters to codeblocks

Parameters passed to codeblocks follow the same dBASE rules as passing them to a UDF. You can pass parameters to a codeblock in two ways.

- Reference
- Value

Having two ways to work with arrays lets you decide if you want to have memory variables that are passed to have their value updated or not.

Passed by reference. By default, all memory variables used as parameters are passed by reference to a codeblock. This simply means that the address of the actual memory variables are passed instead of the actual value in the memory variable. Because of this, the memory variable that was passed will be automatically updated. The following code will demonstrate this:

```
OldSalary = 40000
```

```
NewSalary = {|xSal|; xSal=xSal*1.2; ? xSal}
NewSalary( OldSalary )
? OldSalary        && is changed to 48000
```

Passing a memory variable by reference will change the value of the memory variable if the codeblock changes the value of the parameter name. If the preceding formula was changed to

```
NewSalary = {|xSal| ; tempSal = xSal * 1.2 ; ? tempSal}
```

the value of OldSalary will not be changed because the value of xSal was not changed. The memory variable name in the parameter list is not a new name—rather another name for the original memory variable that was passed. It is an alias name for the same variable. Therefore, changing xSal actually changes OldSalary.

Passed by value. If you need to pass a memory variable to a codeblock and have it keep its value, it is known as passing a variable by value. To pass a variable by value is to pass the actual contents of the memory variable rather than the physical memory variable. The following code exemplifies how it works:

```
OldSalary = 40000
NewSalary = {|xSal|; xSal=xSal*1.2; ? xSal}
NewSalary( (OldSalary) )
? OldSalary        && is not changed remains 40000
```

To pass a memory variable by value, simply place the name of the memory variable inside parentheses. This will force the codeblock to create a new memory variable to manipulate instead of the original memory variable.

Using codeblocks as event handlers

Codeblocks can be used as event handlers. In fact, they are ideal for use as event handlers if the code is small and doesn't have to be reused. For example, to attach code to a pushbutton that will close a form, type the following commands:

```
newForm = NEW FORM("I have a codeblock")
newForm.height = 12
newForm.width = 44
newButton = NEW PUSHBUTTON(newForm)
newButton.top = 2
newButton.left = 1
newButton.text = "Close Form"
newButton.OnClick = {;form.Close()}
newForm.Open()
```

> ! **Visual dBASE's codeblocks and semicolons**
> When creating a statement codeblock in Visual dBASE, it is essential that you place the semicolon in front of every statement of the codeblock. This includes the first statement. In version 5.0, the semicolon was not required if you only used one statement in a codeblock—so {form.Close()} would work. However, in Visual dBASE, {form.Close()} will report an error—*Variable undefined—FORM*. Although unclear, the error is telling you that it cannot understand what you are trying to do in the codeblock. Placing a semicolon preceding the command fixes the codeblock.

Once the code is created, clicking on the button will make the form close. You have just attached a codeblock to an event property. Your form should look similar to the one in Figure 5–15.

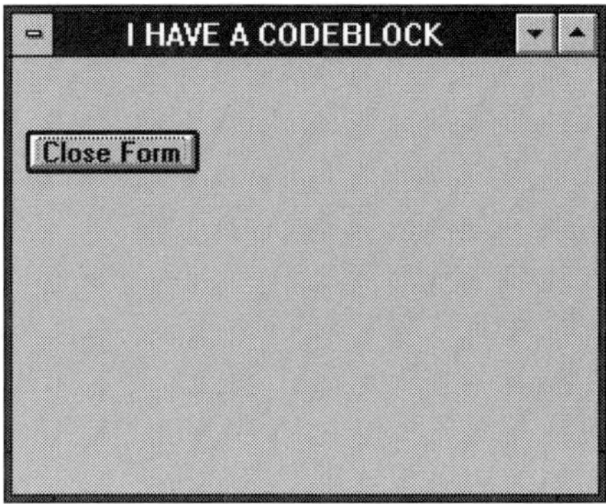

Figure 5–15. A form with a codeblock attached to the OnClick property of the button.

Attaching codeblocks to event properties

You have already created an external procedure and methods (internal procedure in a Class) and attached them to a pushbutton. Both of these methods used actual procedural code (procedure) to perform some action.

In addition to creating a procedure or function and attaching its name to the OnClick property, you can directly attach code to the OnClick event property. When you attach code to an event property, you do it through a codeblock.

The syntax to attach a codeblock to an event property is

<object name>.<event property> = {;<codeblock statement/s>}

The codeblock can have more than one command inside it. Just remember to separate all the commands by placing a semicolon in front of each command.

Advantages to using codeblocks

The advantages to using codeblocks follow:

1. Simplified functions, defined as codeblocks, can be created in a single line of code. A UDF would require several lines.
2. Codeblocks are directly associated with a specific event; therefore, their purpose and readability is easy to understand. They are directly associated with the object.
3. Codeblocks can receive a parameter by reference (default) or value, using parentheses around the memory variable name.
4. Codeblocks are easy to use as event handlers. To use them, simply assign the codeblock directly to the event property that needs the handler.

Disadvantages of codeblocks

The disadvantages of codeblocks follow:

1. They are more difficult to read and interpret than a comparative UDF.
2. They are not easily re-useable.
3. To place multiple commands in a codeblock, you must remember to separate them by placing a semicolon in front of each command.
4. A codeblock can be called from only the object itself.
5. Codeblocks are not backward compatible.

Chapter 6
The Form—The Focus

In traditional DOS-based dBASE applications, the format screen is used to view and edit records. It is the entry interface that is used to store information in the database (tables). The format screen will usually look like the paper form, which it uses to enter information into the system.

In Visual dBASE, the *form* is much more. It can be a data-entry interface for tables (databases), just like its DOS counterpart. However, the form is so much more in Windows.

Forms in Visual dBASE

In Visual dBASE, the form takes on many faces—a window, a dialog box, a menu of the window, a switching menu (graphical menu), even a full-blown application. It appears to be everything for the User Interface (UI).

The form has the ability to respond to the event-driven world of Windows as well as fully support all the graphical controls available in Windows.

Form based versus screen based

Forms begin life like a traditional DOS window—it has a border, size, position, and color. Once it begins, it can contain other objects. These objects, once placed inside the form, become an integral part of the form.

Consider the form as a parent object—the container. It contains all the other objects—text, entryfields, pushbuttons, and check boxes. These objects, the child objects, are contained inside the form.

When a form is minimized, all the child objects inside it are minimized with it. When it is closed, all the child objects inside it are closed with it. When a form is opened, all the child objects inside it are opened with it, ready to get to work. All the objects inside the form are an integral part of the form.

Containership

The concept of one object integrated inside another object is known as *containership*. This one-inside-another concept is an important difference between form-based (dBASE Windows) and screen-based (dBASE DOS) Windows.

Page orientation

In dBASE DOS, a format screen can have multiple pages. This concept is necessary because a form (screen) can only be as large as the physical screen coordinates—the visible areas of the screen. In its standard mode, this is eighty characters across by twenty-five lines. This limitation is due, in part, to the fixed-text based characters of DOS. In dBASE DOS, and some other DOS-based applications, you can increase the visible number of lines up to fifty.

In Visual dBASE, forms do not have to limit themselves to screen dimensions only. This means that a form can be any size; its boundaries can go beyond the visible areas of the screen, making it larger than the physical screen. When the form is made larger than the screen, it can have its scrollbars activated. Once active, the user can move around the form via the form's scrollbars.

➡ **Multiple pages and Visual dBASE**
Before Visual dBASE, dBASE for Windows 5.0 did not support the concept of multiple pages. Rather, all controls had to be on a single long form (with the scrollbars active) or in multiple individual forms. Visual dBASE offers several ways to work with multiple pages.

Sizing a form. A form can be any size; it can be sized to fit the existing visible area of the screen, and made smaller, longer, or wider. It can also be minimized, made normal, and maximized. The form has several properties that control these behaviors.

If you do not want the form to have the ability to be resized, you can changed the window property Sizeable. If you don't want the form to be moved, you can change its window property Moveable. There are several window properties that control the behavior of the window portion of a form—EscExit, Minimize, Maximize, WindowState, MDI, SysMenu, AutoSize, and others.

Using scrollbars. If a form is longer than the existing screen, the window boundary can display and use scrollbars to view controls beyond the physical screen view.

A scrollbar is a bar that appears at the bottom right side of a window, browse object, or list box object when its contents are not completely visible. The scrollbar contains two scroll arrows (at the ends) and a scroll box, which enable you to scroll through the contents of the window, browse object, or list box object.

These scrollbars are simply part of a form, and can be turned on, off, or made to come on automatically, by simply setting the *scrollbar* property to either 1 (On) or 2 (Auto). The default value for the *scrollbar* property is 0 (Off). Figure 6–1 shows a form with three browse tables in it. The form has scrollbars along the bottom and the right side.

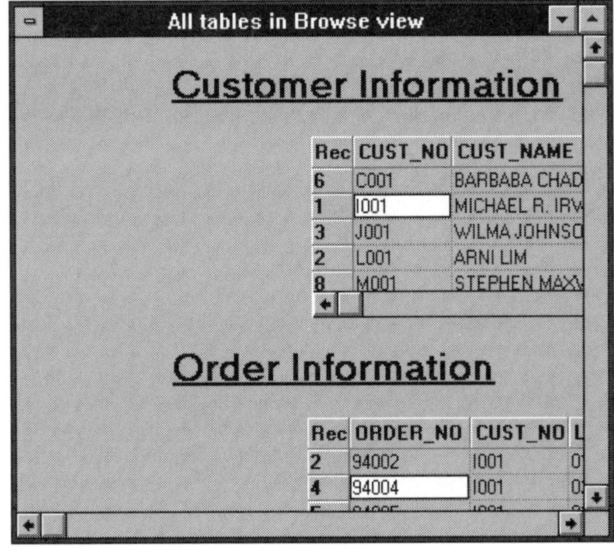

Figure 6–1. This form has three different browse tables in it.

You can only see part of the Customer Information table; the remaining part is to the right of the form boundary. Part of the Orders table is also missing (the remaining part is below the visible area of the screen and to the right). Finally, you can't see the Books table at all—it is below the screen.

Each of the browse tables have scrollbars attached, as well as the form. The form's scrollbars can be used to view different parts of the form. Figure 6–2 shows a different area of the form (bottom, right side). This part is made visible by using the form's scrollbar.

Looking at the scroll bars on the form in Figure 6–2, the *scroll box* (a small box inside the scroll bar) has moved down and across the two scroll bars. This scroll box lets you know where you are positioned in the overall form.

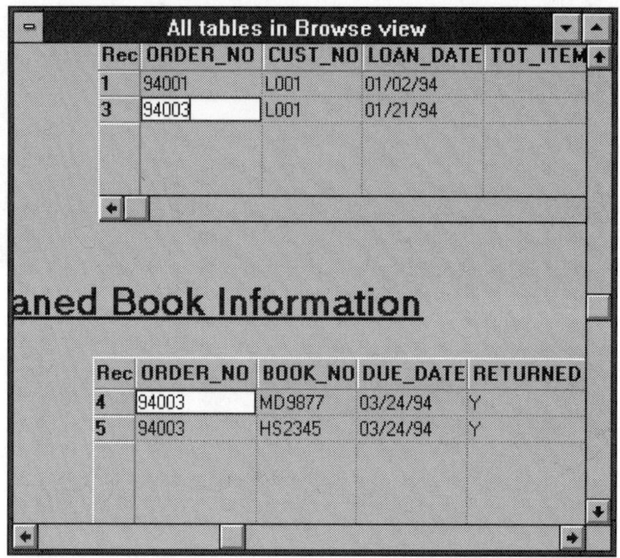

Figure 6–2. This is another part of the form with three tables.

Using the TabBox Control Object for multiple page forms

➡ Visual dBASE offers a new control object—the TabBox. It can be used to control movement between pages on a multipage form. It comprises one or more identifiable tabs located horizontally across the bottom of the control. Normally it sits at the bottom of a form. Figure 6–3 shows a multipage form with the TabBox control used to switch between pages.

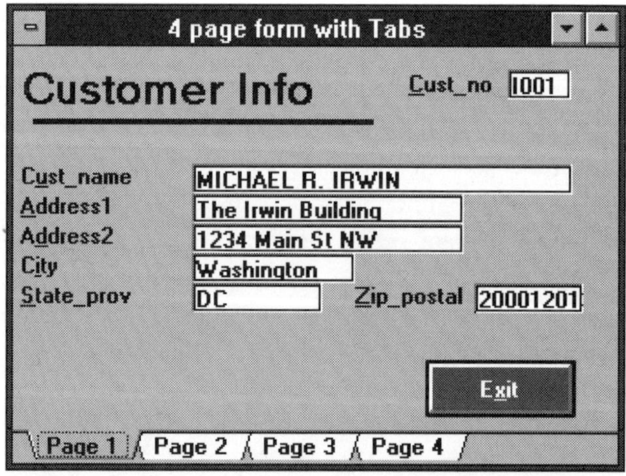

Figure 6–3. This is a multipage form using a TabBox.

Linking the TabBox to jump to the multiple pages of a form is easy. To link the two together, simply create a codeblock and attach it to the *OnSelChange* of the TabBox control. The codeblock should look like this:

```
{;form.PageNo = this.CurSel}
```

This codeblock changes the form's *PageNo* property to equal the value of the *CurSel* property (the tab number) of the TabBox.

The PageNo property

➡ To support multiple pages in Visual dBASE forms, a new property has been added to the Visual properties group of the form and its controls. This new property is named *PageNo*. Because dBASE for Windows 5.0 does not support multiple pages, it does not have or use this property.

The *PageNo* property of a form tells dBASE which page the form should be displaying in a multiple page form. By changing this property, you can control which page the form will display. The default value for a form is 1 for the PageNo property.

The *PageNo* property of the controls on a form (entryfield, text, SpinBox, pushbutton, TabBox, etc.) specifies which page each control will be located on in the form. The default value for all controls, except the TabBox, that are placed on a form is 1 for the PageNo property. The new TabBox control defaults the *PageNo* property to 0. By changing the value of this property, you can specify the page you want the control to exist on.

✔ **Setting the PageNo property to 0**
There are times that you will want to create a control, like a pushbutton, and have it appear on all pages of a form. Instead of copying the control to each page (creating a new control), you can specify a *PageNo* of **0** for the control. When the *PageNo* property is set to **0**, the control will be visible and useable on all pages of the form.

Figure 6–4 shows a multiple page form that uses two pushbuttons (Previous and Next), and a SpinBox to move from page to page or select a specific page to move to. To change to a new page, the user simply clicks on either button to move forward or backward through the pages, click on the SpinBox arrows, or enter a page value to turn to.

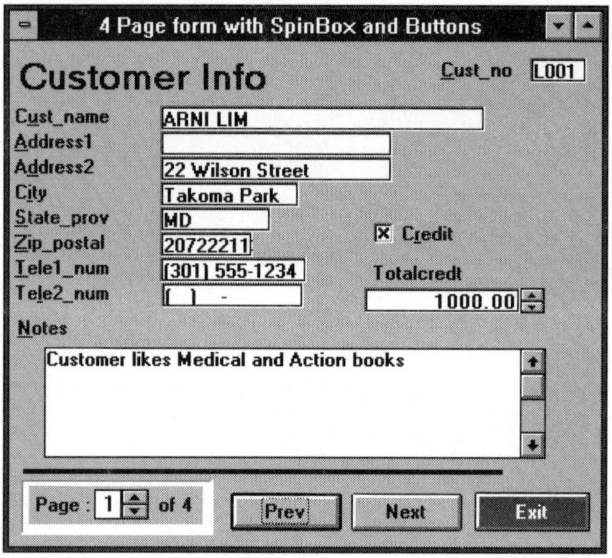

Figure 6–4. This is a multiple page form with pushbuttons.

The code attached to the OnClick property of the pushbuttons and the OnChange of the SpinBox assigns the new page number to the *PageNo* property of the form. The following shows the code for the Next Pushbutton and SpinBox that is used to change to a new page on the form:

Next Pushbutton Code	Page SpinBox Code
`Procedure NextBtn_OnClick`	`Procedure SPINPage_OnChange`
`   if form.pageno<4`	`   do case`
`      form.pageno=form.pageno+1`	`      case this.value>4`
`      form.SpinPage.value =`	`         this.value = 4`
`      form.pageno`	`      case this.value<1`
`   endif`	`         this.value=1`
	`   endcase`
	`   form.pageno=this.value`

So as the code demonstrates, the PageNo property of a form holds the value of the currently *active* page (or visible page) of the form. In contrast, the PageNo property of the other controls on the form is used to tell the control what page it is residing on.

Queries and forms

Unlike the DOS format screen, a form lets you automatically work with multiple tables (databases). You can automatically update and add information in multiple tables within a form. This means that you do not have to write any code to keep the tables in sync or to place the link field value in any field of any table—it is accomplished for you.

To use this ability, you need to create a query and specify the link field between the tables. Then you need to specify the fields in the tables that you want to use in the query. Once the query is created, you can use the query in the form by specifying the *View* property of the form.

Figure 6–5 shows a form with two tables. You can add new Customers or add new loan record information to the form in Figure 6–5. The Orders.dbf (loan information table) does not need to show the link field—CUSTNO. Nor does the user need to supply the link value for the Customer Number in the Customers table. The link field—CUSTNO will automatically be updated when you add new records to the Order.dbf from the Customer.dbf.

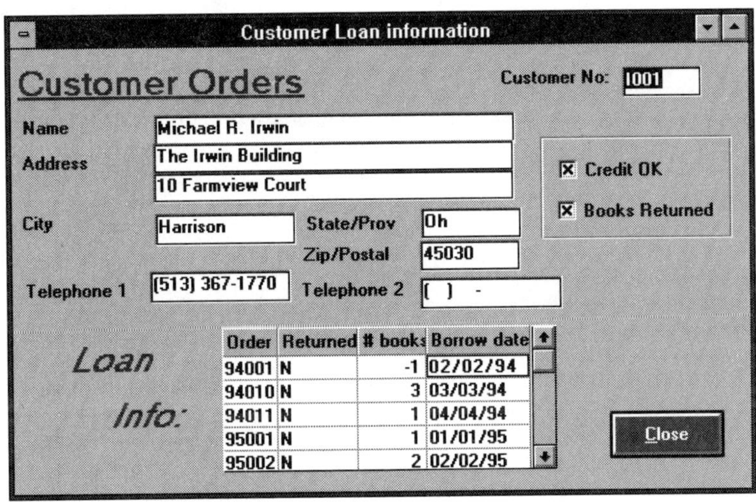

Figure 6–5. A form with two tables in it.

Query relationships. When you work with multiple tables in a form, you need to define a relationship between the tables—the link between the primary table and the secondary table (Customer and Orders). If you use the Query Design tool, you can set the relationship easily by activating the Define Relation dialog box.

To activate the Define Relation dialog box, move the mouse pointer over to the table symbol icon in the bottom left corner of the table name cell (the extreme left-most cell of the table structure). The cursor will change from an arrow to an arrow with two tables underneath the arrow (this is the relationship cursor). Hold the left mouse button down and drag the symbol to the icon in the second table. As you move the icon, a line will be drawn between the two table icons. Figure 6–6 shows how to link the two tables, using the relationship cursor and the join line. Once you move the relationship cursor to the second table's icon, release the left mouse button and the Define Relation dialog box will appear. It should look similar to the one in Figure 6–7.

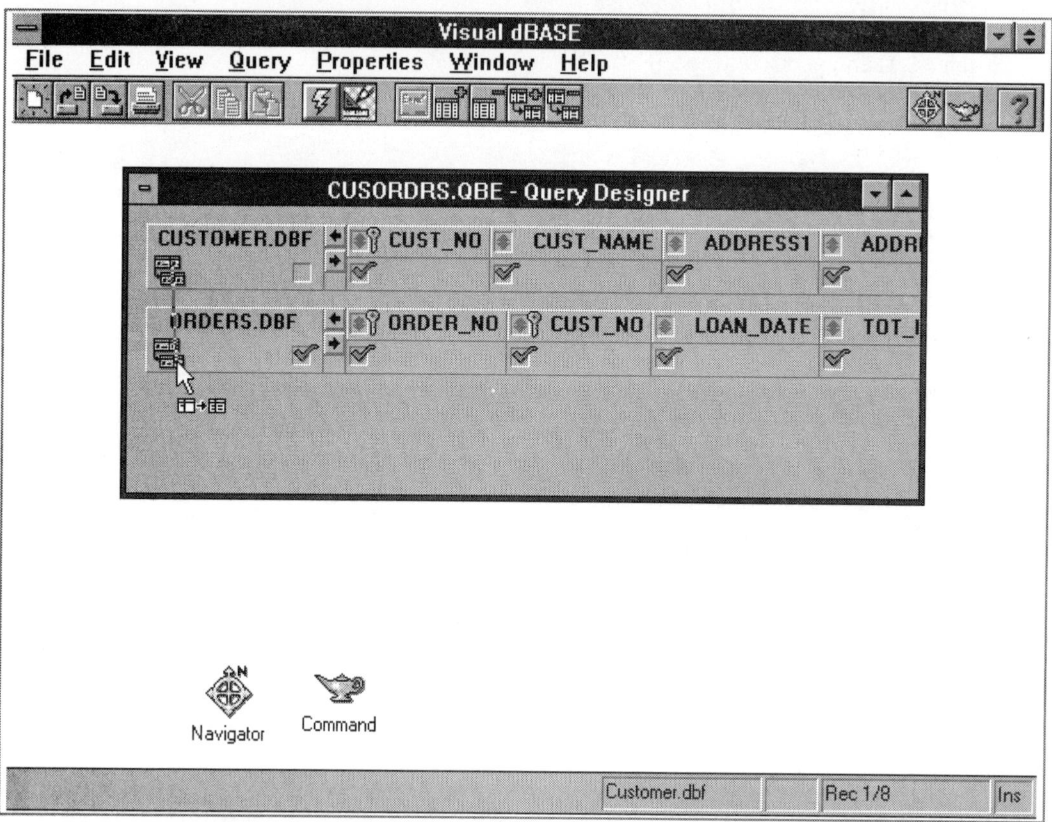

Figure 6–6. Defining a relationship graphically in the Query design tool.

With the dialog box active, you can set the relationship between the parent (Customer) table and the child (Orders). dBASE will attempt to automatically set a "best guess" relationship for you. If it is correct, simply accept it. If not correct, select a field in the parent table and link it to the correct index in the child table. You select an index instead of a field (like in dBASE DOS). Because the child table must be indexed and that index can be a single field or a concatenation of fields, you simply choose an index that has the link field at the beginning of the index.

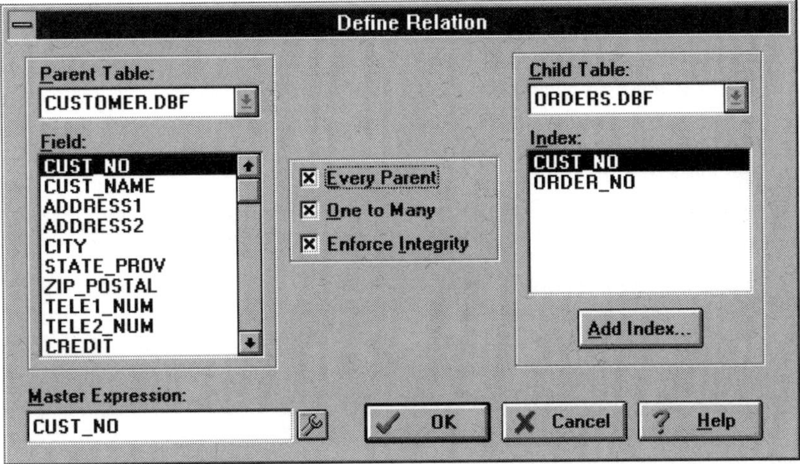

Figure 6–7. The Define Relation dialog box.

Setting one-to-many option. When you link two tables, dBASE assumes that they will have a one-to-many link. In the center of the dialog box is a check box that is labeled One to Many. If the relationship is one parent to many children make sure this box stays on (the **x** is visible). Figure 6–8 shows the one-to-many check box.

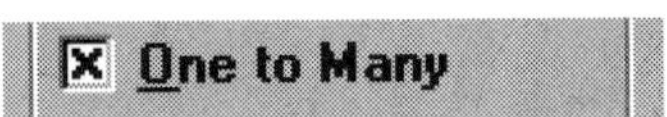

Figure 6–8. The one-to-many check box of the Define Relation dialog box.

If you turn this option off, only one child record will be shown for each parent. This option also controls how a browse of the child records will be displayed. When the check box is set, the BROWSE table will only display those records in the child table that relate to the parent record.

Setting referential integrity. While you are in the Define Relation dialog box, look at the check box labeled Enforce Integrity. It is below the one-to-many check box. Figure 6–9 shows the check box. If you are going to use this query for a form, then turn this option on (the **x** is visible).

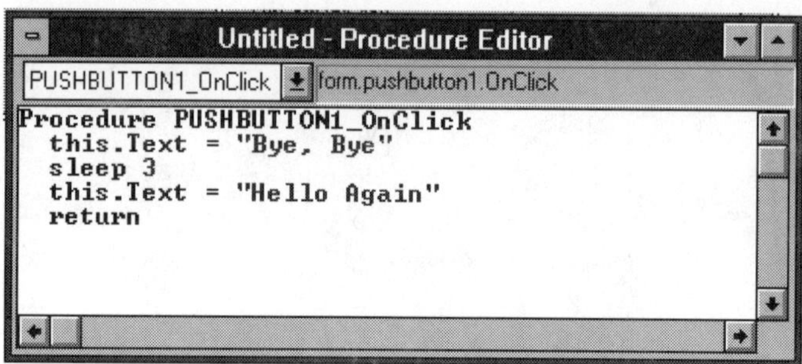

Figure 6–9. The Enforce Integrity check box.

Activating this option, which only works on dBASE tables, will help you in two ways.

1. It will automatically add the keyfield value (the link field) to a child table as you add records in a one-to-many form. It gets the value from the parent table, based on the field value in the link. The field value is made read only, so that the user cannot accidentally delete it while the new record is being added. This will ensure that you cannot add a child record that is not related to a parent record.
2. If you attempt to delete a parent record and there are still child records in the link table, dBASE will prompt you to cancel the deletion or cascade the delete. A cascade delete will erase all child records that are linked to the parent prior to erasing the parent. Because dBASE only marks dBASE records for deletion, they can always be RECALLed later.

When you work with more than one table in a form, you should get in the habit of turning this option on.

Every Parent option. If you need to see parent records that have no child records, this option should be turned on. It is located just above the one-to-many checkbox. Figure 6–10 shows this option. If the option is not set, then only those parent records that have child records will be shown; the others will be ignored.

Figure 6–10. The Every Parent option.

Modifying a relationship. If you need to modify a relationship between two tables, follow these steps.

1. Click on any field or on the cell of the table name of the **Child** table. The child table is the one with the arrow pointing to it.

2. Once selected you can choose Query >> Modify Relation . . . from the menu.

You can also use the SpeedMenu by single–right mouse clicking on the **Child** table (the one with the arrow pointing to it) and selecting the Modify Relation choice.

NOTE: The child table must have focus. If it doesn't, then the Modify Relation choice will not be available in the menu.

Types of forms

Because the form is the UI and it can be used for so many things, you should have an understanding of its multipurpose ability.

A form can be an entry/view screen as its DOS counterpart. You have already worked with many examples of this type of form in this and earlier chapters. A form can be much more than this. Forms can also be

- Dialog boxes
- Message windows
- Menus (attached to a form)
- Main driving menus—switchboards
- Complete form-based applications

The normal state of open forms is to allow a user to move from form to form. However, when opening a form you can specify that it be given total control; that is, even if other forms are open on the screen, only this form can be worked with. This ability to determine how a form will be used is controlled by the user. This means that a form can be opened in one of two states.

1. Modal
2. Nonmodal

Dialog boxes and message windows

Whenever you need to obtain additional information from a user or simply display additional information for the user, you will want to use a dialog or a message box. These two types of forms are like miniforms that are usually focused to a single purpose. Some common dialog and message boxes are

- Printer Setup dialog box
- Copy file dialog box
- User Information dialog box
- About Help message box
- Error message box

Dialog boxes. A dialog box is a form that asks for additional information from the user. It contains one or more control objects that are used to obtain information from the user. A dialog box is usually focused to a specific purpose, like the one in Figure 6–11. This shows a Print Setup dialog box used to obtain printer information from the user.

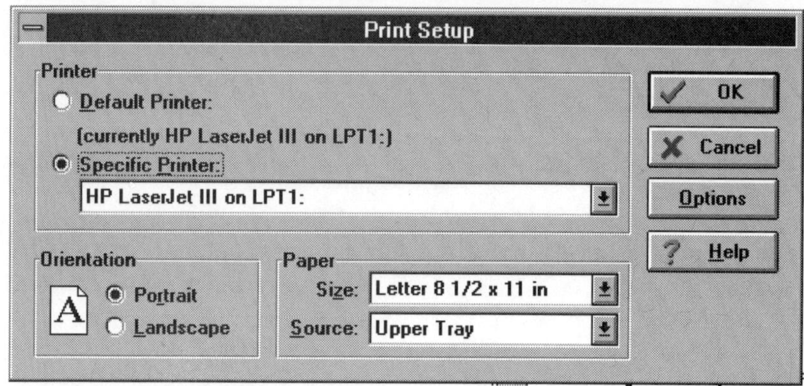

Figure 6–11. A dialog box in dBASE.

The print dialog box is used to select a printer and print options from the user. It is single purpose, although it uses several different controls to obtain information.

Message boxes. A message box is similar to a dialog box except that its sole purpose is to supply information to the user. It normally has no active control objects, other than some pushbuttons. They are used to simply display additional information. Figure 6–12 shows the Help information message box of Visual dBASE.

Figure 6–12. This is the Help information message box of Visual dBASE.

Attached menus and switchboard menus

A form can be a menu, like a switchboard, or have a menu, like a menu bar, associated with it. As a menu itself, it is a form with a series of buttons or other objects that are used to drive the application. This type of menu is referred to as a *Switchboard.* It can also be a MenuBar that is associated with a form.

Form associated Menu Class. A menu can be associated with a form. The menu, like a form, is an object that is created from a Class named MENU. The Menu Class allows you to construct Windows-type menus. The menu, once created, can be attached to the form internally (inside the form frame) or externally (on the dBASE menu bar in the dBASE window).

For instance, Figure 6–13 shows a form that has Customer information. It has a menu associated with it. The menu in Figure 6–13 is external to the Customer form. It is physically located below the Visual dBASE frame (second line of the dBASE window).

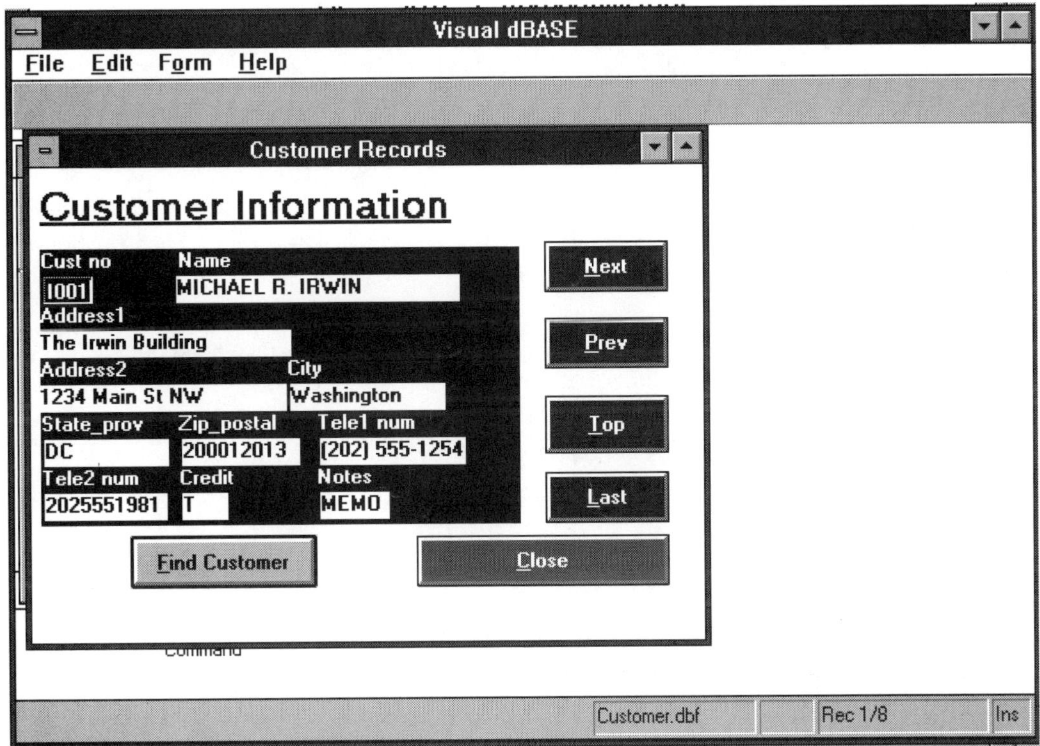

Figure 6–13. A menu attached to a form.

The menu in Figure 6–13 has four main prompts—File, Edit, Form, and Help. Under them are additional options. Notice that the menu is not inside the frame of the Customer form.

The menu itself is associated with the form by placing its name in the MenuFile property of the form. Figure 6–14 shows the menu file Customer.mnu associated with the form using the Property inspector in the form designer.

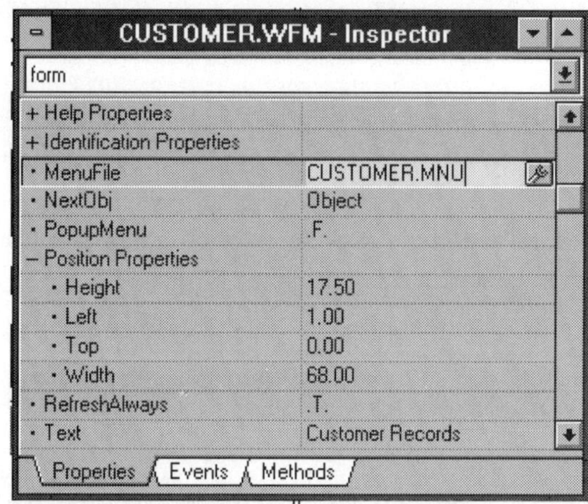

Figure 6–14. Associating a menu with a form.

Forms associated with MenuBar Class

➡ Visual dBASE has added a new menu class named MenuBar. The MenuBar class creates MenuBar objects that have properties that can be used to add the functionality of the Windows clipboard—Undo, Cut, Copy, and Paste. Because this Class does not exist in dBASE for Windows 5.0, to assign clipboard commands to a menu item you would have to create complex event procedures, based on external Windows functions.

Using the MenuBar Class in Visual dBASE, you can add the Windows clipboard functionality to menu choices by simply assigning a menu item (like Edit >> Copy) to a property of the MenuBar. This ability, to assign a menu item to a MenuBar object's property, lets you easily assign the actions of the Windows clipboard.

Using the MDI property to direct the menu location. By default, your form's menus will replace the menu bar of Visual dBASE, while the form is active. This is consistent with other Windows products. This ability to use the same space for menus and toolbars/SpeedBars is part of the Multiple Document Interface (MDI) of Windows. Windows' MDI is a standard that allows an application to manage, open, and contain more than one document/window or multiple views of the same document inside an existing window (application).

Visual dBASE supports the Windows MDI—it has several windows that can be contained within the window frame (or window) itself—the Navigator, Command Window, Form Designer Window, and your application forms. All these forms, or windows, are children of the Visual dBASE application, existing in the dBASE window.

Although the menu is normally located on the MenuBar line of Visual dBASE, there are times that you will want the menu to be on the top line of the form itself. To have the menu show up inside the actual form, like in Figure 6–15, you simply have to change a property of the form—the MDI property of the Visual grouping. By changing the MDI property to False (.F.), you are telling dBASE that the form will not be contained within the dBASE window frame. When MDI = .F., the form will exist as a Windows form, living outside of dBASE itself.

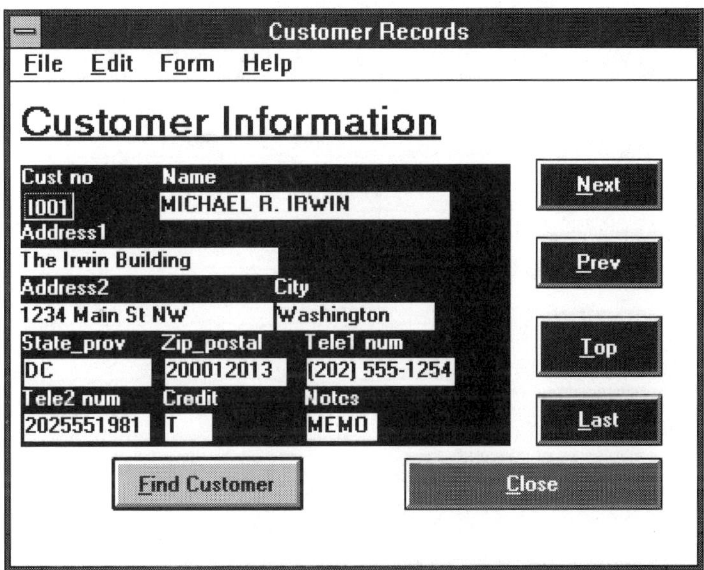

Figure 6–15. The menu inside a form.

When a forms MDI is set to .T., dBASE runs the form inside Visual dBASE's frame—making the form a child of the dBASE application. When set to .F., the form is independent of the dBASE application. Because it is no longer a part of the MDI of Visual dBASE, the menu must exist inside the form instead of inside dBASE.

A good side effect of setting the MDI to .F. is that the form that you create will become a true independent Windows application that runs at the Windows desktop surface instead of inside Visual dBASE. When minimizing dBASE, the form will still be active on the Windows desktop.

Switchboard menus. Another type of menu that can be created is a form that acts like a main driver, or menu, moving the user from one form to another. In many Windows applications this is called a *switchboard.* A switchboard is a form that is used as a front-end menu system for an application.

Figure 6–16 shows a main switchboard for an application. This form has four buttons on it: Customers, Find a Book, Reports, and Quit System. Note that the switchboard form can have a traditional menu attached to it. This form is the main driver, or main form, of an application. Its purpose is to switch users back and forth between the different tasks of the application—thus, the name switchboard. It contains a series of switches, or pushbuttons, that are used to drive the system.

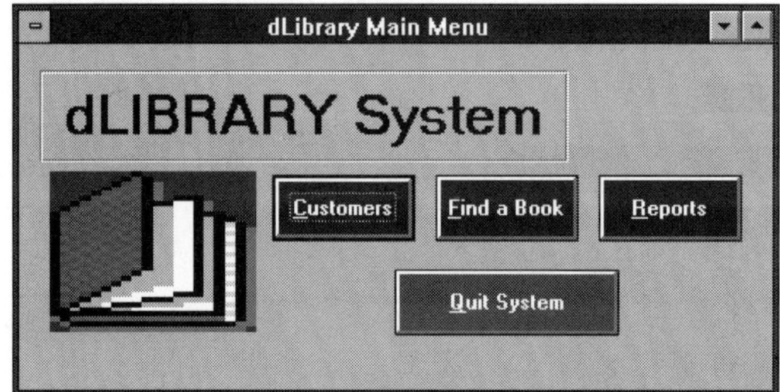

Figure 6–16. A switchboard-type menu.

Form-based applications

In Visual dBASE a form, or a series of forms, can be combined into a complete application. One form can call another form, which calls another and they are all interrelated using event handlers and event properties, tying them all together.

Figure 6–17 shows a form-based application that uses a switchboard to drive everything. It also shows the customer form that has opened the find a customer form. The complete application is a series of forms. The forms are tied together through event handlers.

In a form-based application, the program code is stored inside the form rather than external to the form. The system in Figure 6–17 contains no external programming code (*.prg). Rather, the system uses internal event handlers. This does not mean that all your code must exist in forms. In fact, you may want to have external procedure files and other programs that can be used by several applications.

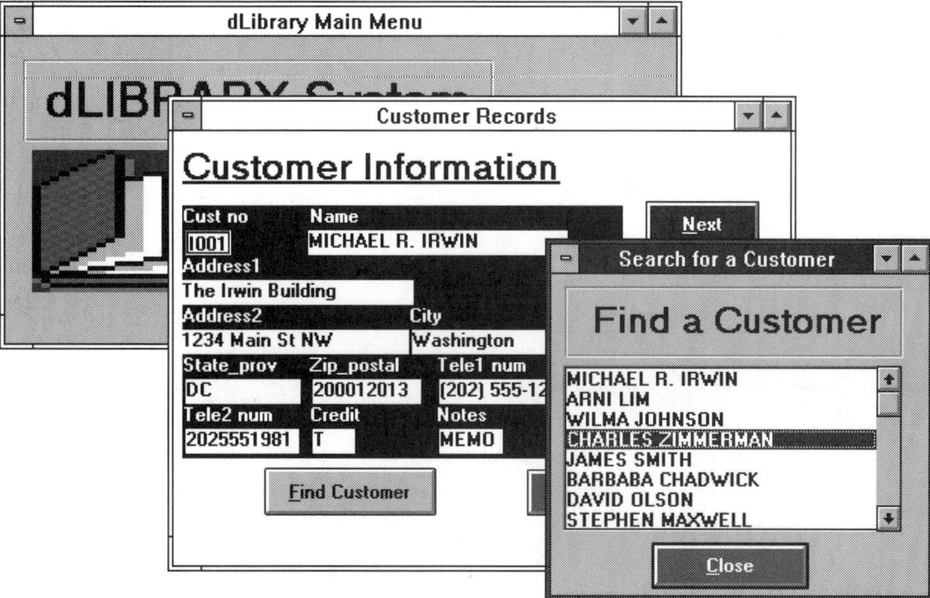

Figure 6–17. A form-based application where the switchboard form calls the customer form.

Modal versus nonmodal

There are times that you want the user to *only* enter something into a form, like in a dialog box, and not leave the form until they have typed something in. Visual dBASE lets you give a form total control of the user interface. This ability is known as making a form *modal*. When a form is modal, the user cannot switch to another window without first closing the modal window.

Nonmodal means modeless. Most of the time, a user can run several Windows applications at the same time. This is also true in Visual dBASE. You can even run the same application several times. For example, Figure 6–18 shows three customer forms active, and all three forms are showing different records.

In Windows, the default state of a window (form) is *modeless* (or *nonmodal*). A modeless window (form) is one that does not require *exclusive* interaction with a user. The user can open more than one modeless window and switch between them in an application. Figure 6–18 shows running three different customer forms at the same time. All three of these forms are modeless.

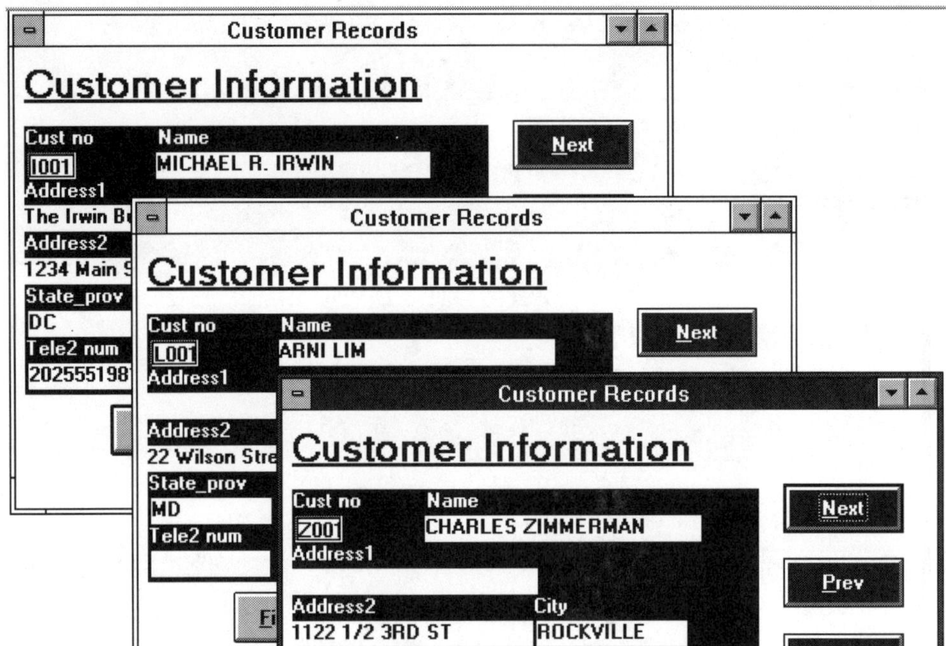

Figure 6–18. Running the same form in dBASE multiple times.

NOTE: If you need to run the same form (.wfm file) multiple times and work with different records, you need to create a different session for each form. The following code was used to run the customer form several times.

```
CREATE SESSION
DO Customer.wfm
CREATE SESSION
DO Customer.wfm
CREATE SESSION
DO Customer.wfm
```

The CREATE SESSION command lets dBASE run the same form independent from itself in another session. It creates a clean work environment (session) to perform work in. If you are going to use a common table between multiforms (like in this example), then each form should work in its own session. You could compare it with a multiuser environment where each session starts up in totally clean environment.

So modeless simply means that you do not specify a mode for the form to operate in; it becomes nonmodal by default.

The modal state. If you need to activate a form and make sure the user doesn't leave the form until they do something, you make the form *modal*. Modal simply means that when the form becomes active (gets focus) it takes complete control of the user interface.

The user can't switch to another window (form) until the modal form is exited (closed) or made nonmodal. Figure 6–19 shows a modal window (form).

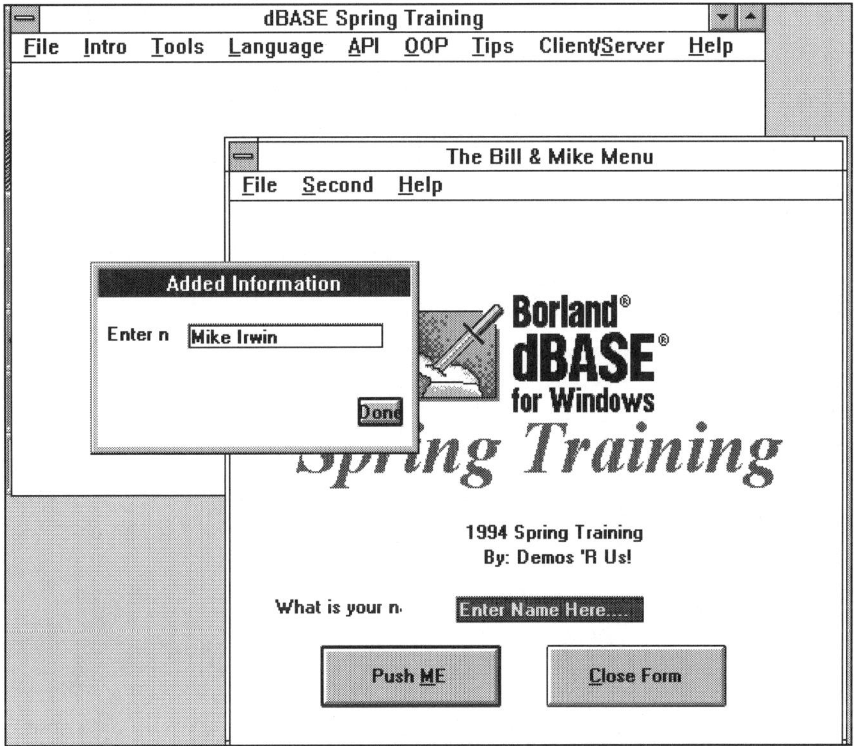

Figure 6–19. A modal window (form).

The dialog box (form) in Figure 6–19 has been made modal by using the form method ReadModal(). The form titled "Added Information" is modal. dBASE lets you know that the form is modal by changing the border to a thicker width and raises the border.

If you try to click into the form titled "dBASE Spring Training" or "The Bill & Mike Menu" form, dBASE will beep. It lets you know that you cannot do anything until you exit the modal form—"Added Information". Once you close the modal form, the others can be made active.

MOVING YOUR DOS KNOWLEDGE TO WINDOWS

Most of your dBASE DOS knowledge can be applied directly to Visual dBASE—creating dBASE tables, relating tables (databases), creating and using queries, performing database manipulation (changing data, deleting data, and recalling data), and using reports and labels. Even your procedural knowledge, the way you write one-step-after-another code, is 100 percent usable. By now, it should be obvious that the way you use your procedural knowledge has changed.

The only part that has been drastically altered is the commands that you use to work with the user—the SAYs, GETs, ?, ??, TEXT . . . ENDTEXT, and @ commands.

A new environment

The graphical world of Windows and its event driven nature offer new challenges to programmers. In Visual dBASE, the answer is use of OBJECTS. Object-oriented programming lets you create applications that can work with the user in both a graphical and event-driven environment. This new environment offers new ways to work with users—thus, a new interface, a graphical interface; and a new environment, the event-driven environment.

Remember the form, a menu, a pushbutton, a check box, and a browse are objects. In fact, everything that you would place inside the form is an object.

A new methodology

Because everything in Visual dBASE is an object, new methods were designed to let you create and work with the objects. You can use the O-O extension, NEW, to create these new objects, or you can use the dBASE-like syntax DEFINE <OBJECT TYPE> command.

Backward compatibility

Because Visual dBASE still runs most dBASE DOS applications (see Chapter 4 for more information), it needs to support the UI commands of dBASE DOS. As pointed out in Chapter 4, all DOS applications and their UI commands (@ SAY, ?, . . .) operate in the *Results pane* of the Command window.

Figure 6–20 shows a DOS application running in Visual dBASE. All DOS-based applications will run in the Results pane of the Command window.

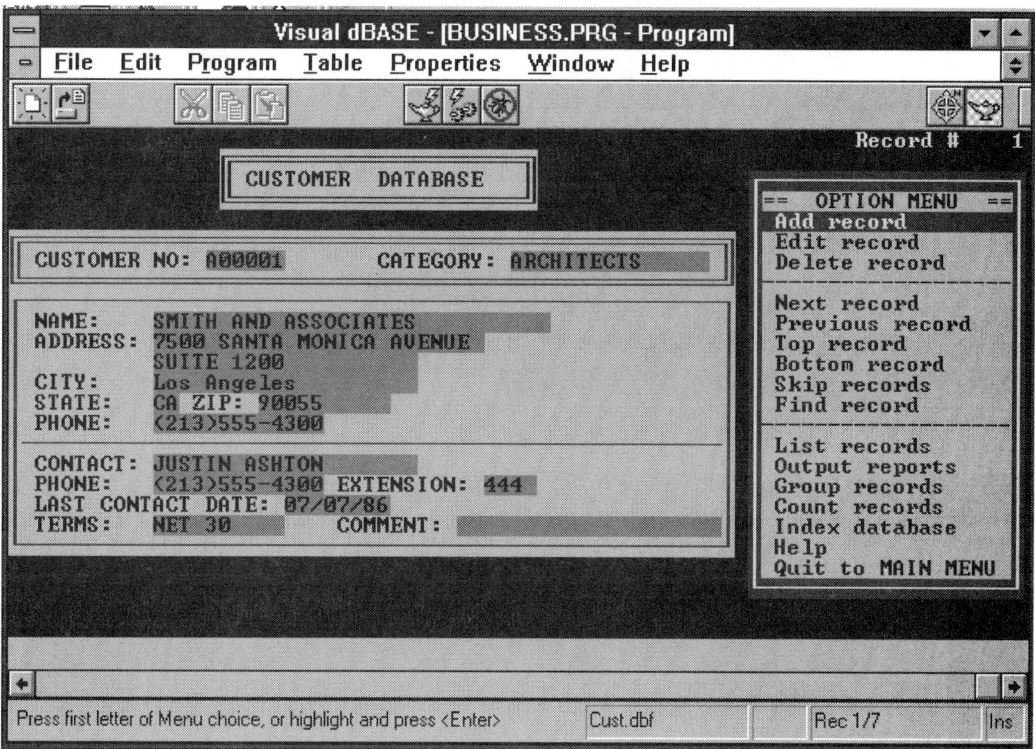

Figure 6–20. A DOS application running in Visual dBASE.

DOS user interface commands and their Windows counterparts

The following commands are DOS user interface (UI) type commands.

```
DEFINE WINDOW

DEFINE POPUP
SET FORMAT TO
READ
@ ... SAY
@ ... GET
@ ... TO ...
@ ... FILL TO ...
@ ... CLEAR [TO ...]
TEXT ... ENDTEXT
?  [AT ...]
?? [AT ...]
```

Although they will work in Visual dBASE, they will only operate in the Results pane of the Command window. They will not work with or in Visual dBASE forms. All of these commands are, in the sense of Windows forms, dead.

Because you will want to work with the new form objects and the objects that are contained in forms, you need to take your existing DOS knowledge and covert it to Windows. You need to apply the knowledge of these DOS commands into their Windows object counterparts. There are two ways to do this—a dBASE syntax-like way and an O-O way. Either way can be used to create these new Windows objects.

General dBASE-like SYNTAX

Using dBASE-like commands the syntax is

```
DEFINE <Class Name> <Object name>                                    ;
   [OF <name of Container Object]                        ;
   [ FROM <row1>, <col1> [TO <row2>,<col2> ]] |or| [AT<row>,<col>]   ;
   [PROPERTY <property name 1> <value> , <property name 2> <value>, ...] ;
   [CUSTOM <name 1> <value> , <name 2> <value>, ... ]                ;
   [WITH <para1>, <para2>, ...]
```

This syntax will let you create any of the UI objects.

The <CLASS NAME> is the name of the Class (that already exists and is in memory) that will be used to create the object.

The <Object name> is the name that you supply to the object.

The FROM ... TO option lets you set the top, left and bottom, right of an object. The AT option only lets you set the top, left of an object.

The PROPERTY keyword is required if you want to change any of the objects properties at the time of creation. When you change property values you use the property name and then the new value (do not use the equal sign in between).

The CUSTOM keyword is used if you want to create and initialize user-defined properties (memory variables).

The WITH keyword is used if you need to pass the object parameters.

General object-oriented SYNTAX

Using the O-O NEW command, the syntax is

```
<Object name> = NEW <Class Name>( <para1>, <para2>, ... )
```

Using the NEW operator, you will have to change each of the objects properties one at a time. To change an objects properties, you need to specify the name of the object, use the member access operator (dot operator), and then the name of the property. The following is the general syntax for changing property values.

<object name>.<property name> = <new value>

If you need to create your own properties (custom, or user-defined, properties) you use the same general syntax.

The DOS DEFINE WINDOW command

The equivalent to a DOS window is the form object itself. The form object, when it is initially created, is equivalent to a DOS window. It has color, dimensions, a frame (border), and event text on the title bar.

DBASE-like syntax. To create a form using dBASE-like syntax the command is

DEFINE FORM <name> [FROM <row1>, <col1> [TO <row2>,<col2>]] ;

[PROPERTY <property name 1> <value> , <property name 2> <value>, ...] ;

[CUSTOM <name 1> <value> , <name 2> <value>, ...]

For example, to create a new form

1. Named AnimalsForm
2. From 2,2 to 12, 45.5
3. Red in color
4. A title text of "Mike's Animal Form"
5. Create a new memory variable named xForm with a value of .T.

the command would be

```
DEFINE FORM AnimalsForm FROM 2,2 TO 12, 45.5 ;
  PROPERTY  ColorNormal "W/R" , Text "Mike's Animal Form" ;
  CUSTOM  xForm .T.
```

This command would actually be on a single line. If you place it in a program, you can place it on multiple lines by ending each line with the semicolon (line continuation symbol). That is what the preceding syntax does.

If you open the form [OPEN FORM AnimalsForm, or , AnimalsForm.Open()], it will look like the one in Figure 6–21.

There are a few other properties that you could set that would even give the ListBox object more power than a popup. For instance, the contents can be sorted (property name is Sorted) and it can allow multiple selections (property name is Multiple).

Instead of a listbox, you could have also used a combo box object. If you used a combo box it can be one of three types—simple, drop-down, and drop-down list.

Object-oriented syntax. To create a ListBox using the NEW operator and change properties, the SYNTAX is

<Listbox Object Name> = NEW LISTBOX(<Form Name>)

<Listbox Object Name>.<Property name> = <new value>

For example, to create the same LookUpList ListBox, the commands are

```
LookUpList = NEW LISTBOX(AnimalsForm)
LookUpList.Top = 2
LookUpList.Left = 2
LookUpList.Height = 6
LookUpList.Width = 21
LookUpList.Datasource = "File *.WFM"
```

The DOS SET FORMAT TO command

In Visual dBASE, the SET FORMAT TO command is obsolete. There is no equivalent object. Because the form object can be the equivalent of a format file and it contains other objects, when you open the form, everything else automatically opens.

The DOS READ command

Like the SET FORMAT TO command, the READ is obsolete. The READ is a procedural command that activates the @ ... GET commands of DOS.

In Visual dBASE, when you open a form, all the contents are also opened. Unless you specify that an object is not enabled (property Enabled = .F.), all the objects contained in the form are active. A user can jump from object to object using a mouse or the keyboard (tab and Shift + tab key).

You can open a form using dBASE like syntax or O-O syntax.

DBASE-like Syntax. To open a form using dBASE-like syntax, the format is

OPEN FORM <form object name> [ON <contained object name>]

The OPEN FORM will open the form object specified.

The ON option can be used to tell dBASE which contained object should gain focus first (be the highlighted object).

To open the form AnimalsForm, the command is

```
Open form AnimalsForm
```

Once the form is opened it will be modeless (nonmodal). This simply means that the user can move between this form and any other form that is active.

Object-oriented syntax. The object syntax to open a form is

<Object name (Form)>.Open()

For example, to open the form AnimalsForm, the syntax is

AnimalsForm.Open()

The form will be opened modeless. In addition to the Open() method (function inside the object), you can also open the form in a modal state. Using the Object-oriented way, you can even open a form in modal manner (while the form is opened, no other form can get focus). This can be done using the following syntax:

<Object name (form)>.ReadModal()

There is also a READMODAL() function that does the same thing but using a dBASE function. The format is

READMODAL(<Object name (form)>)

The DOS @ <row>,<col> SAY command

Like several other DOS commands, the @ ... SAY command is pretty useless in the object world. In Windows, the @ ... SAY command is similar in nature to a text object. However, a text object must be contained inside a form. This means that you must create a form first that will contain the text.

DBASE-like syntax. To create a text object using dBASE-like syntax the command is

```
DEFINE TEXT <name> [ FROM <row1>, <col1> [TO <row2>,<col2>] ;
   OF <name of Object it will be contained in>     ;
   [PROPERTY Text  < text literal> , <property name 2> <value>,
]
```

For example, to create a new text object

1. For the form AnimalsForm
2. Named cText1
3. From 2,24 to 2, 42
4. Color bright white over black
5. With text of "What is your name"

the command would be

```
DEFINE TEXT cText1 OF AnimalsForm FROM 2,24 TO 2,42   ;
```

```
PROPERTY ColorNormal "W*/N", Text "What is your name"
```

Figure 6–23 shows the text object added to the form AnimalsForm.

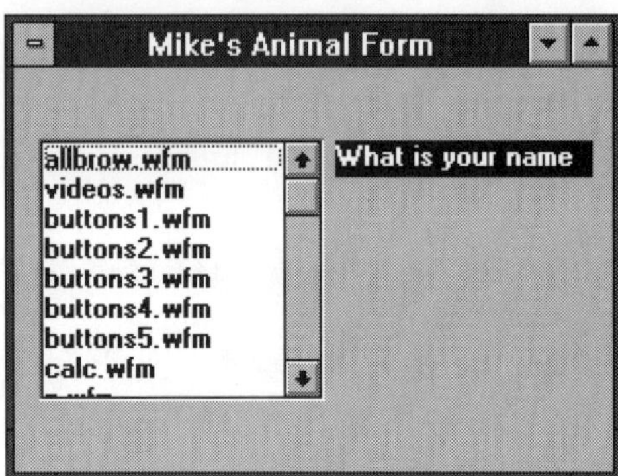

Figure 6–23. A text object added to the form.

Object-oriented syntax. To create a text object using the NEW operator and change properties, the SYNTAX is

<Text Object Name> = NEW TEXT(<Form Name>)

<Text Object Name>.<Property name> = <new value>

For example to create the same text cText1 object, the commands are

```
cText1 = NEW TEXT(AnimalsForm)
cText1.Top = 2
cText1.Left = 24
cText1.Width = 19
cText1.Text = "What is your name"
cText1.ColorNormal = "W*/N"
```

The DOS @ <row>,<col> GET command

Like the @ . . . SAY command, the @ . . . GET command is pretty useless in the object world. In Windows, the @ . . . GET command is similar in nature to an entry-field object. However, an entryfield object must be contained inside a form. This means that you must create a form first that will contain the text.

DBASE-like syntax. To create an entryfield object using dBASE-like syntax the command is

```
DEFINE ENTRYFIELD <name> [ FROM <row1>, <col1> TO <row2>,<col2>]
;
    OF <name of Object it will be contained in>            ;
```

```
    [PROPERTY MaxLength <value> ,  <property name 2> <value>,
...]
```

For example, to create a new entryfield object

1. For the form AnimalsForm
2. Named cField1
3. From 4,24 to 4, 42
4. A field entry length of 20
5. And a Color of black over bright white

the command would be

```
DEFINE ENTRYFIELD cField1 OF AnimalsFOrm FROM 4,24 TO 4,42  ;
    PROPERTY MaxLength 20, ColorNormal "N/W*"
```

The property MaxLength is needed to limit the total number of characters that can be entered in the field. The default value is MaxLength 25. The ColorNormal property is used to specify a color.

Figure 6–24 shows the entryfield object added to the form AnimalsForm.

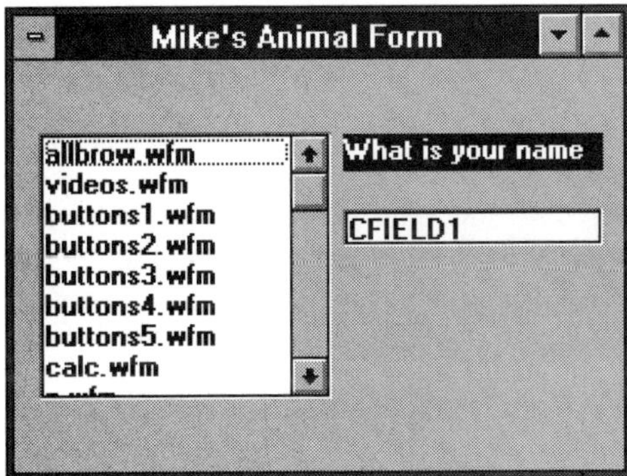

Figure 6–24. An entryfield object added to the form.

There are numerous properties that you can use when working with the entryfield object. These include the DataLink property to link the object to a field, the Function and Picture properties to specify an entry format, ValidErrorMsg and ValidRequired properties to force validity and display an error message, and ColorHighLight to specify a different color with the object (field) contents are highlighted.

Object-oriented syntax. To create an entryfield object using the NEW operator and change properties, the SYNTAX is

<Entryfield Object Name> = NEW Entryfield(<Form Name>)

<Entryfield Object Name>.<Property name> = <new value>

For example, to create the same entryfield cEntry1 object, the commands are

```
cEntry1 = NEW ENTRYFIELD(AnimalsForm)
cEntry1.Top = 4
cEntry1.Left = 24
cEntry1.Width = 18
cEntry1.MaxLength = 20
cEntry1.ColorNormal = "N/W*"
```

Additional object types for the @ . . . GET command. In addition to the entryfield object, you can use other objects that are more graphical as replacements for the @ . . . GET command. These include check boxes, combo boxes, radio buttons, and spin box. Creating them is similar in syntax to the entryfield.

The DOS ?, ??, TEXT . . . ENDTEXT commands

Like the @ . . . SAY command, all the ?, ??, and TEXT . . . ENDTEXT commands are useless in the object world. The *text* object must be used instead. For the syntax of the Text object, refer to the previous section labeled @<row1>,<col1> SAY command.

The DOS @ <row1>,<col1> TO <row2>,<col2> command

This DOS command has no direct equivalent in Visual dBASE. The closest thing to the @ . . . TO . . . command is a rectangle object.

However, an rectangle object must also be contained inside a form. This means that you must create a form first that will contain the text.

DBASE-like syntax. To create a rectangle object using dBASE-like syntax the command is

```
DEFINE RECTANGLE <name> [ FROM <row1>, <col1> TO <row2>,<col2>] ;
     OF <name of Object it will be contained in>                ;
     [PROPERTY  <property name 1> <value>, ...]
```

For example, to create a new rectangle object

1. For the form AnimalsForm
2. Named rBox1
3. From 6,24 to 9, 42
4. Background color of grey (light black)

the command would be

```
DEFINE RECTANGLE rBox1 OF AnimalsForm FROM 6,24 TO 9,42       ;
    PROPERTY ColorNormal "N*"
```

The ColorNormal property is used to specify a color.

Figure 6–25 shows the rectangle object added to the form AnimalsForm.

Figure 6–25. A rectangle object added to the form.

There are a few other properties that may be of interest—the BorderStyle can be used to the specify normal, raised, or lowered. The Text property can be used to add a title to the top, left corner of the rectangle.

Object-oriented syntax. To create a rectangle object using the NEW operator and change properties, the SYNTAX is

<Rectangle Object Name> = NEW Rectangle(<Form Name>)

<Rectangle Object Name>.<Property name> = <new value>

For example, to create the same rectangle rBox1 object, the commands are

```
rBox1 = NEW RECTANGLE(AnimalsForm)
rBox1.Top = 6
rBox1.Left = 24
rBox1.Width = 19
rBox1.Height = 4
rBox1.ColorNormal = "/N*"
```

Rectangles and text/entryfield objects. It is possible to have a rectangle in the background of text and entryfield objects. However, it means that you must define the rectangle *before* you define the text and entryfield objects that will sit in the same area. Otherwise, the rectangle will be in front of the other objects.

If this happens, you can go into the form designer and change the *z-order* of the objects. The *z-order* of an object is the *z* plane (of an *x*, *y*, *z* graph) position (front to back) of the objects. You can only do this in the form designer. There is no equivalent command in the dBASE language or property that can be set at the object level.

The DOS @ <row1>,<col1> FILL TO <row2>,<col2> command

There is no equivalent command in Visual dBASE. Because everything is an object, you will have to mimic the behavior of the FILL TO command. One way is to create a rectangle and specify the color. You will have to define the rectangle before you define any text or entryfields that will go on top of the rectangle.

The DOS @ <row1>,<col1> CLEAR [TO <row2>,<col2>] command

There is no equivalent command in Visual dBASE. This command does not support the object model—it cannot be an object. Rather, it clears an area on the screen or in a window.

If you need to clear an area of a form, you need to release the objects that are in that area. Releasing the object will clear it from memory—gone forever, having to be re-created from scratch.

There are two ways this can be done: using dBASE like syntax or O-O syntax.

Understanding contained object names. Every object has a name. In the case of the form you created and objects contained with in it, the names are

Form object	***AnimalsForm***
ListBox object	***LookUpList***
Text object	***cText1***
Entryfield object	***cEntry1***
Rectangle object	***rBox1***

These names are actually called *object reference variables*. An object reference variable is simply the name that is given to an object for referencing (calling). Depending on how you create a contained object depends on how you reference it. Although this will be covered later in the book, you need a working knowledge of how it works.

If you create a contained object using the dBASE-like syntax (DEFINE TEXT cText1 OF AnimalsForm) you must reference the contained object by the container name first.

```
AnimalsForm.cText1
AnimalsForm.cBox1
```

If you create a contained object using the object-oriented syntax (cEntry1 = NEW ENTRYFIELD(AnimalsForm), you must reference the contained object by its name only:

```
cEntry1
LookUpList
```

The reason for the difference is how each of the creation methods work. The NEW method creates an object assigning the equivalent of an alias name to the object. When NEW creates an object, it assigns another object reference variable to the object (a second name to the same object). If you take the contained cText1 object and ask it what its real name is (using a property called Name), you will see that it is really named TEXT1 (? cText1.Name). You can reference this contained text object by its real object name—*AnimalsForm.Text1* rather than the alias name of cText1.

DBASE-like syntax. To release any object, a contained object or the form, you use dBASE-like syntax.

RELEASE OBJECT <object name>

Remember, if you created the contained object with the DEFINE . . . OF . . . Command you will have to reference the name of the object [<object name>] by its full name [<container name (form)>.<object name>].

For example, to release the text object, cText, the command would be one of these:

```
RELEASE OBJECT AnimalsForm.cText1
```
(if created with DEFINE ... OF command)
```
RELEASE OBJECT cText1
```
(if created with NEW command)

Figure 6–26 shows the form AnimalsForm missing the text object, after release.

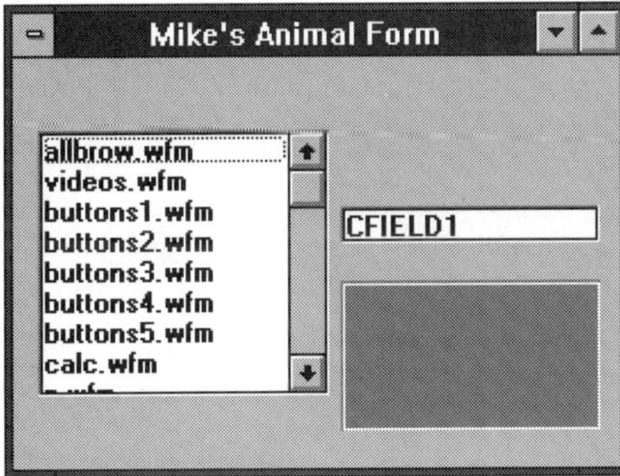

Figure 6–26. The form after releasing the text object.

Object-oriented syntax. To release an object using O-O syntax, you use the name of the object and its method named Release(). One of these would work (depending on how you created the object).

<Object Name>.Release()

<Container name (form)>.<Object Name>.Release()

For example, to release the same text object as previously, the command is one of these:

```
AnimalsForm.cText1.Release()
```
(if created using the DEFINE . . . OF . . . command)
```
cText1.Release()
```
(if created using the NEW command)

Hiding an object instead of releasing it. If all you want to do is have the object disappear from the form, you do not have to release it from memory physically. Rather, you can manipulate one of its properties—*Visible*. Every object has a property named *Visible*. This property determines if the object should be visible (.T. or .F.). The default value for the *visible* property is true.

If you change the visible property to false (.F.), you can make it visible again later by simply resetting the visible property to true (.T.).

This can only be done using object-oriented methods. The syntax is

<object name>.Visible = < value (.T. or .F.) >

How you created the object will depend on how you reference it. The following example will hide the ListBox and rectangle objects:

```
AnimalsForm.LookUpList.Visible = .F.
AnimalsForm.rBox1.Visible = .F.
```
(if the objects were created using the DEFINE . . . OF . . . command)
```
LookUpList.Visible = .F.
rBox1.Visible = .F.
```

Figure 6–27 show the same AnimalsForm with the two objects hidden (not visible).

Figure 6–27. The form with two objects hidden (not visible).

Although the ListBox and rectangle objects are not visible on the form, they do still exist. You can make them visible at any time by resetting their visible property back to true (.T.).

The DOS BROWSE command

Although the DOS BROWSE command does work in Windows, you need to understand how it works. Browse will run in its own window (form) when you run it via the BROWSE command. In addition, Browse can also be an object. As an object, it can be imbedded in any form. You can create a contained browse object, just like you created the other contained objects. It can be done with dBASE-like commands or O-O-type commands.

Changing some form properties. If you use the browse as a form object, it must be contained in a form. For the purposes of this chapter, you will need to increase the width and height of your form AnimalsForm. To change the forms properties, enter the following commands:

```
AnimalsForm.Height = 16
AnimalsForm.Width = 60
```

You will also have to specify a table or query that will be used by the browse object. To do this, you must set a form property, *View*. The form is

<Form Object Name>.View = <table name/query name>

Use any table for the demonstration. This book will use a table named Customer. The format is

```
AnimalsForm.View = "Customer"
```

dBASE-like syntax. To create a browse object using dBASE-like syntax the command is

```
DEFINE BROWSE <name> [ FROM <row1>, <col1> TO <row2>,<col2>] ;
     OF <name of Object it will be contained in>             ;
     [PROPERTY  Fields <list>, <property name 2> <value>, ...]
```

For example, to create a new browse object

1. For the form AnimalsForm (table Customer, AnimalsForm.view = Customer)
2. Named xBrowGrp
3. AnimalsForm width is changed to 60, its height is 16
4. Fields will be "CUST_NAME, ADDRESS1"

the command would be

```
DEFINE BROWSE xBrowGrp OF AnimalsForm FROM 11,2 TO 14.5,56  ;
    PROPERTY Fields "CUST_NAME, ADDRESS1"
```

To make the browse object fully visible and contain the fields Cust_name, and so on, you will have to set a few properties in the AnimalsForm before defining the Browse object. The new code would look like this.

```
animalsform.view = "Customer.dbf"
AnimalsForm.width = 60
AnimalsForm.Height = 16
define BROWSE xBrowGrp OF AnimalsForm FROM 11,2 TO 14.5,56
;
    PROPERTY Fields "CUST_NAME \22, ADDRESS1 "
```

NOTE: New Field properties for Browse fields
The Fields property is used to specify the fields to be browsed. You can use any of the options that you have used in DOS with the fields property (/R, /width, etc.) In fact, Visual dBASE has added several new options that can be used with the fields

```
\B = field range1, field range2 [ \F orce]
\P "< field picture/function clause>"
\H "<field header text>"
\V = valid condition  [ \F  orce ] [ \E = error message ]
\W = when clause condition
```

Figure 6–28 shows the Browse object added to the form AnimalsForm.

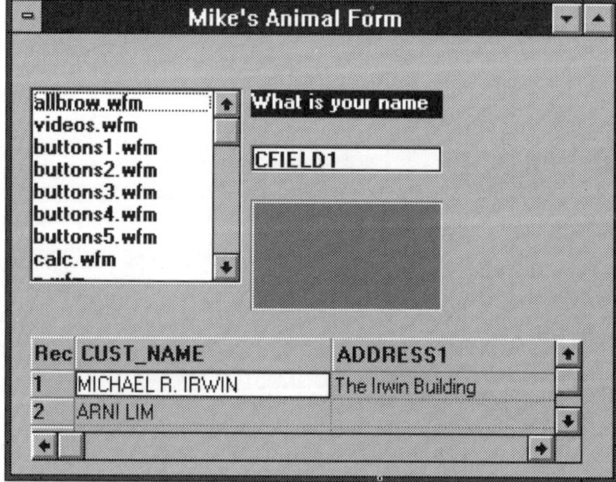

Figure 6–28. A Browse object added to the form.

There are a few other properties that may be of interest—the Alias property can be used to specify which table to browse in a query (more than one table). The Text property can be used to add a title to the top of the Browse object. There are several Edit properties—Append, Delete, Follow, Mode (BROWSE, form edit, or columnar edit), and Modify that let you set the edit options. Visual properties include ShowRecNo and ShowHeading.

All these properties can be set when defining the object, or later.

Object-oriented syntax. To create a browse object using the NEW operator and change properties, the SYNTAX is

<Browse Object Name> = NEW Browse(<Form Name>)

<Browse Object Name>.<Property name> = <new value>

For example, to create the same browse object, the commands are

```
xBrowGrp = NEW BROWSE(AnimalsForm)
xBrowGrp.top = 11
xBrowGrp.left = 2
xBrowGrp.width = 55
xBrowGrp.height = 4.5
xBrowGrp.fields = "cust_name \H="Customer" , address1,
address2"
```

A Quick Tour of the Form Designer

It isn't necessary to create all of your forms manually, by using the preceding commands. Rather, you can use a visual design tool—the *Form Designer*. Although the syntax for creating forms is relatively easy, why go through all the trouble of writing the code by hand?

Instead of writing the code by hand, use the design tool. If, after creating your form using the design tool, it is not exactly how you want it, simply modify the code by hand. Unlike its DOS counterpart, Visual dBASE's designer tools (Form, Query, etc.) allow you to create and modify code with the tool or by hand. Even if you modify your code by hand, the next time you use the design tool to modify the code, it will read and accept the changes you made by hand.

This ability, new to dBASE, is known as *two-way* tools. Using two-way tools you can create code via a tool or by hand, and it will be recognized for modification by either method.

A review of forms

A Visual dBASE form is a window. The window contains controls (objects) that are used for displaying and manipulating information. Typically, a form is associated with tables (one or more .dbfs). Through use of the form, a user can view, add, and edit information in the table(s).

A form can also be a dialog box, message box, menu system, or a complete application.

Creating and modifying forms

The form designer will let you quickly create and modify forms.

Creating a form

To create a form, using the Form Design, from the Navigator, you need to follow these steps:

1. Start the Form Designer by selecting Untitled in the Forms container.
2. Select the Form Expert or Designer (Blank Form in design surface) from the dialog box.
3. Add Controls (contained objects) to the form.
4. Modify properties and methods of the different objects (form and controls).
5. Save the form as a .WFM file (the extension will be automatic).

Following these five steps, you can create any form using the Form Designer.

Modifying a form

You can modify a form using the Form Designer or the Program Editor. When working in the Form Designer, you can make modifications to each control individually, using the Inspector, or group several objects together by selecting them using the **Ctrl** key and mouse click and change all of their common properties at one time.

Modifying a form in the Form Designer. To modify a form in the Form Designer, follow these steps.

1. Press the Form button of the Navigator to activate the forms container.
2. Select the form you want to modify by highlighting it.
3. Click on the Design button on the SpeedBar.

NOTE: You can also select a form in three other manners. For all of them, you will still need to highlight the form object name in the container. Once highlighted, you can do any of these actions to modify the form: (1) activate the SpeedMenu by single–right mouse clicking on the object name, and select the Design Form choice. (2) Press **Shift + F2** to enter the form designer. (3) You can right double–mouse click on the object name.

Modifying a form in the Program Editor. To modify a form in the Program Editor you can

1. Activate the Command window.
2. Type the Command—MODIFY COMMAND <form name>.WFM.

NOTE: You can also edit the program by right–mouse clicking on the object name, calling up the SpeedMenu, and selecting Edit as Program.

Creating a form using the Form Expert

The Form Expert is a time-saving assistant built into the Form Designer. It lets you create a quick layout of a form by answering a few questions, saving you from having to create individual controls and set their principal properties. This is because the Form Expert automatically creates, sizes, positions, and sets properties for the controls.

The Form Expert recognizes all the field types in tables (.dbfs) and assigns specific controls to each field that you select.

➡ **Enhancements to the Form Expert**

The Form Expert in Visual dBASE is even more powerful than the previous version. Using five main screens and one secondary screen, you can quickly create sophisticated forms. There are two powerful additions added to the Form Expert.

The first addition is a secondary screen activated from a pushbutton, labeled Associate Control Types with Field Types . . . on screen 3. This secondary window lets you assign a specific default control type to each field type. For instance, the default control type for *Numeric* fields is a **SpinBox**, *Memo* fields is an **Entryfield**. Perhaps you want all numeric fields to be entryfields and all memo fields; using this dialog box, you can specify what type of control types to use for each field type.

The second addition is the ability to tell dBASE how to handle multiple pages. You can specify that the Form Expert assign all fields to a single page and activate a vertical scrollbar. The other option is to select multiple pages, which will assign a TabBox control to each page of the form.

Once the form is created using the Form Expert, you can tell the Expert to run the form or take you into the design surface with the form, to work with it further. Here you can adjust the placement of controls, change the text used to identify entryfields, and add other controls—pushbuttons, and so forth.

> **!** **Changing a control type**
> If you do not change the default control types for fields, the Form Expert will assign spin boxes to all numeric fields and entryfields to memo fields. This may not be appropriate for your needs. If it isn't, and you want to change it, you will have to first delete the control and add a new one in its place.

Steps to create a one-to-many form using the Form Expert

Create a QUERY that contains both tables and link them together. The query should have all the options turned on (*every-parent, one-to-many,* and *enforce-integrity*). Save the table, and remember the name (or name it Both for this example).

Once the query is created, follow these steps to create the form.

1. Select the Form button of the Navigator, make sure that the [Untitled] choice is highlighted, and start the New form dialog box by double-clicking or pressing the Design button on the SpeedBar.
2. Choose Expert, from the New Form dialog box, then click the *Next* button.
3. Select the query that you just created, from the step 1 of 5 dialog box, and click the *Next* button.
4. Select the fields that you want placed on the form, from the step 2 of 5 dialog box, and click the *Next* button.
5. Select the One-to-Many layout scheme, from the step 3 of 5 dialog box, and click the *Next* button.
6. If you have memo fields, you may want to specify the Editor for them by pressing the Associate Control Types button and selecting Editor control for the default memo field type. (If you are on step 4 of 5 dialog box, press the Previous button to return to step 3 of 5.)
7. Change any display properties that you want to adjust. For this exercise, change the background color of the form to white by selecting the tab labeled "Form" and select "WHITE" from the combo box of the *Background Color*, then click the *Next* button.
8. Select the Design Form button to enter the Form Designer with the new form.

The form is created, and you are taken into the Form Design surface. Figure 6–29 shows the Form Designer with the form created using the Form Expert.

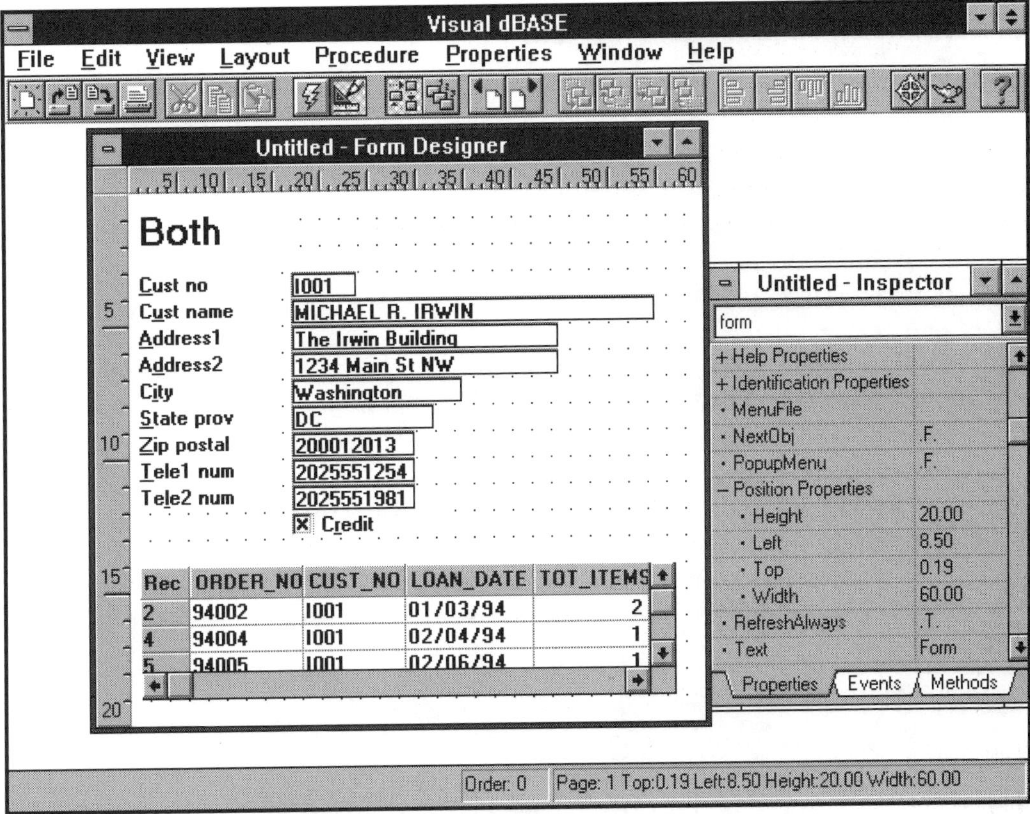

Figure 6–29. A form created using the Form Expert.

Notice that this form has BROWSE control with the fields from the child table located at the bottom of the form.

✔ **Multiple-page form**
If your form has more than one page of fields, a TabBox control will be located at the bottom of the form. To see the fields located on the second page, choose the *Next page* Button on the SpeedBar, or press the **PgDn** key. The *Next Page* button is in the middle of the speed bar and has a picture of a blank page (with the top, right corner bent down) and a blue arrow head pointing to the right.

Modifying the form created by the Form Expert

While in the form designer, you can move, add, or delete controls. The Control Palette dialog box and the Inspector dialog box help you modify existing forms. The Control Palette is used to add additional controls to your form; the Inspector lets you modify any of the controls properties.

Both dialog boxes can be activated via the SpeedMenu (single-right mouse click) or a choice under the View menu.

The field Palette dialog box

Visual dBASE has added a new tool to help you add fields from tables in the view—the Field Palette dialog box. Figure 6–30 shows the new Field Palette dialog box and the newly designed Control Palette. Notice that the Field Palette has a tab along the bottom for each table. Both palettes can be resized and moved about the screen.

If you need to add a field from one of the tables in the query to the form, simply select it in the same manner that you select any other control that is in the Control Palette.

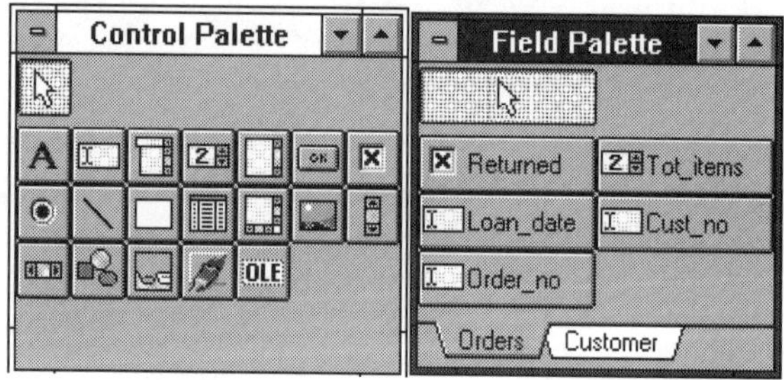

Figure 6–30. This is the new Field Palette and the newly designed Control Palette of the Form Designer.

✔ **Placement of the Field and Control Palettes**

You can place either of the palettes or both of the palettes at the top or bottom of the Form Design window by simply dragging them to the bottom or top. As you drag the palette, it will automatically change shape for placement.

Although the Form Expert is a great help, if may need a little assistance to add those final touches. Figure 6–31 shows the form after it has been modified.

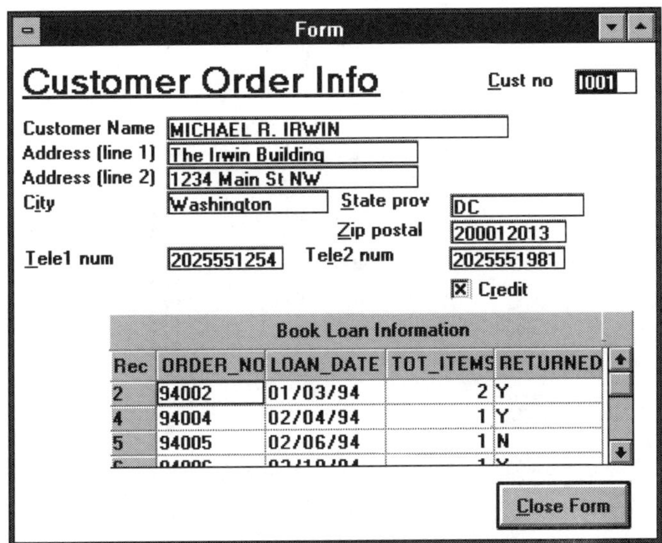

Figure 6–31. The final form after modifications.

The following changes were made to the form:

- Several text and entryfield objects were moved and given new text values (Customer Order info, Customer No, etc.).
- The BROWSE object was moved and the property Text was given the value "Book Loan Information."
- A pushbutton was added, and its event property OnClick was assigned the codeblock {;form.Close()}.

Creating a form from scratch

Remember, you do not have to use the Form Expert to create your forms—you can create a form from scratch. If you decide to create a form from scratch, you will have to create the form and all of its contained control objects and set their properties.

Starting the Form Designer

The Form Designer can be started several different ways to both create and modify a form. It can be accomplished via commands in the Command window or through the tool.

Getting to the Form Designer via the Navigator. To use the Navigator to start the Form Designer, simply activate the forms container of the Navigator by clicking on the title Forms (left column). The container will display all the existing form names.

To create a new form, double-click on the *Untitled* form icon in the forms container. The form icon is the top-most icon that looks like a form with items inside it.

To modify an existing form, select the icon and right–mouse click to modify it. A single click activates the SpeedMenu; a doubleclick takes you into the Form Designer.

Figure 6–32 shows the Navigator with the forms container active.

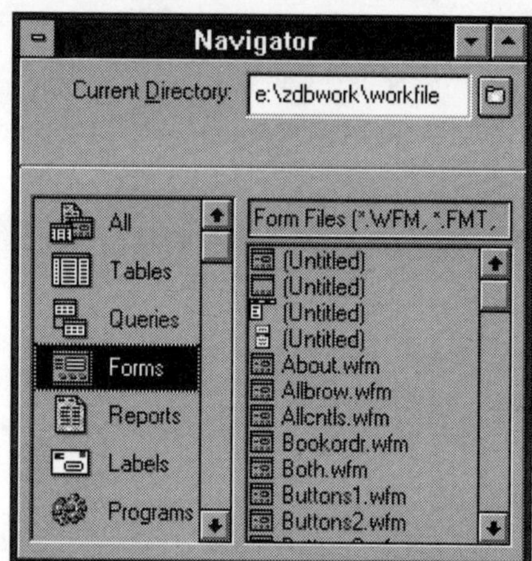

Figure 6–32. The Navigator with the forms container active.

Using the Command window to enter the Form Designer. You can create a new form or modify an existing one using any of the following commands:

```
CREATE FORM   [ <form name> ]
MODIFY FORM   [ <form name> ]
CREATE SCREEN   [ <form name> ]
MODIFY SCREEN   [ <form name> ]
CREATE APPLICATION   [ <form name> ]
MODIFY APPLICATION   [ <form name> ]
```

The name of the form is not required at creation time. If you type any of the MODIFY commands without specifying a form name, you will be taken into the Form Designer with a blank (new) form.

NOTE: If you modify a form you *must* specify the name of the form to modify. The extension .WFM is not necessary.

Typing any of these commands will immediately take you into the Form Design, passing the Form Expert.

Activating the Form Expert from the Command window. To activate the Form Designer from the Command window, add the Work Expert to the command. For instance,

```
CREATE FORM EXPERT
```

This command will immediately start the form expert on page 1 of 5, taking you through the Expert to build your form.

> ➡ **The Expert [Prompt] options**
> If you want to be prompted about using the Form Expert, you can use the Expert *Prompt* option of the Create command. The command *Create FORM EXPERT **PROMPT*** will activate the dialog box, asking you if you want to go immediately to the Form Design surface or use the Expert.

The primary form properties

If you create a form from scratch, there are fourteen form properties with which you should be concerned. The following is a list of them and their description:

Individual Properties

- View — Link a table or Query to the form
- MenuFile — Link a menu (.mnu) file to the form
- PopupMenu (new to Visual dBASE) — Link a "Speed Menu" file to the form
- Text — Give the title bar specific text

Position Properties Group

- Top — Specify a position from the top line
- Left — Specify a position from the left line
- Height — Specify how high it will be
- Width — Specify how wide it will be

Visual Properties Group

- ColorNormal — Specify the background color
- ScrollBar — Does it need scrollbars?

Windows Properties Group

- EscExit — Will the **Esc** key exit the form?
- Sizeable — Will the form be sizable?
- Moveable — Will the form be movable?
- MDI — Will the form run inside or outside of dBASE?

When you create a form, these are the main properties that you may want to set.

Steps to create a form from scratch

To create a form from scratch, follow these ten basic steps.

1. Go into the form designer (Note: If you enter using the Navigator, select Blank Form in the dialog box and press the *Next* button).
2. Activate the Controls dialog box (select View>>Controls from the menu).
3. Activate the Fields Palette dialog box (select View>>Field Palette).
4. Activate the Inspector dialog box (select View>>Inspector).
5. Specify a value for the *View* property of the form, linking it to a table or view.
6. Specify a value for the *Text* property of the form, setting a form title.
7. Resize the form to fit your needs (using the mouse or the properties).
8. Add the fields and other control objects need in the form.
9. Modify any properties for the controls using the Inspector.
10. Save and name the form.

Figure 6–33 shows a blank form (resized) with the three dialog boxes active. Notice that the Field Palette is located along the bottom of the Visual dBASE window.

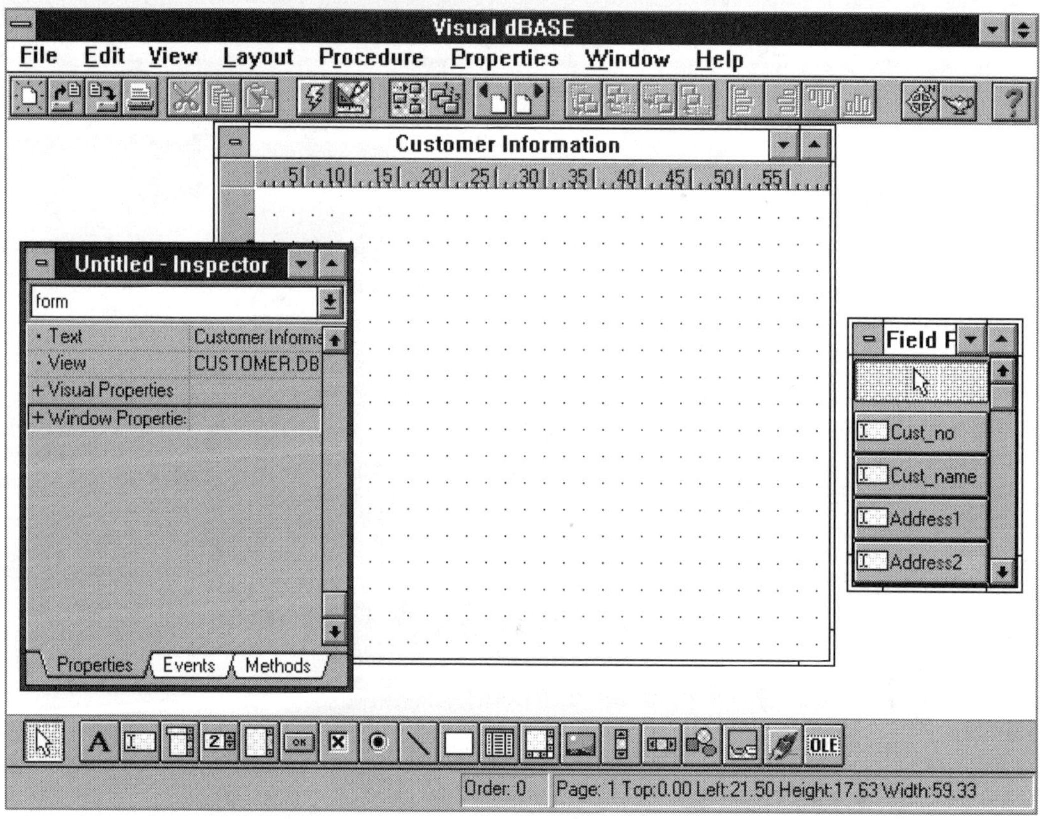

Figure 6–33. The Form Designer with an empty form object.

As you create the form and place controls inside it, you can minimize the dialog boxes—Inspector, Control Palette, and Fields Palette—giving you more visual space in which to work.

Modifying the form properties. The easiest way to change the position properties of the form (top, left, width, and height) is to move the form and resize it using the mouse. Once you move a form or resize it, the Designer will automatically update the position properties with the new values.

After you move and resize the form to what you want, you are ready to modify a few more of the form's properties. To modify a view of the form's properties, click on the Inspector dialog box. It should look similar to the one in Figure 6–34.

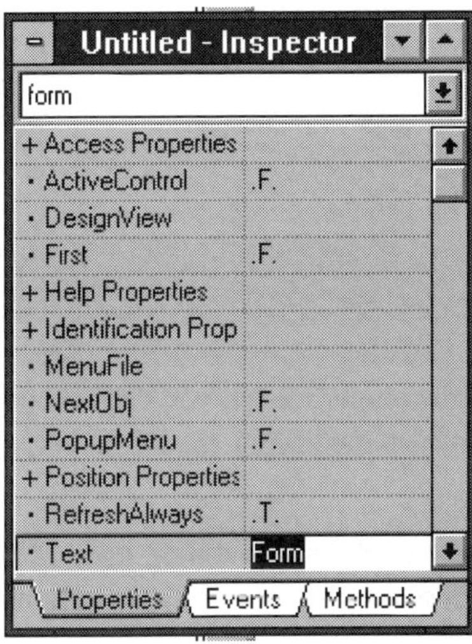

Figure 6–34. The Inspector (properties) dialog box.

The combo box at the top of the Inspector dialog box contains the name of the object whose properties you are going to change (in Figure 6–34 it says "form"). You will need to specify a table or query for the form to use (*View* property) and the text for the form title (*Text* property). Type in the name of a View and the Text to use alongside of the property names. Figure 6–35 shows some values added to the two properties.

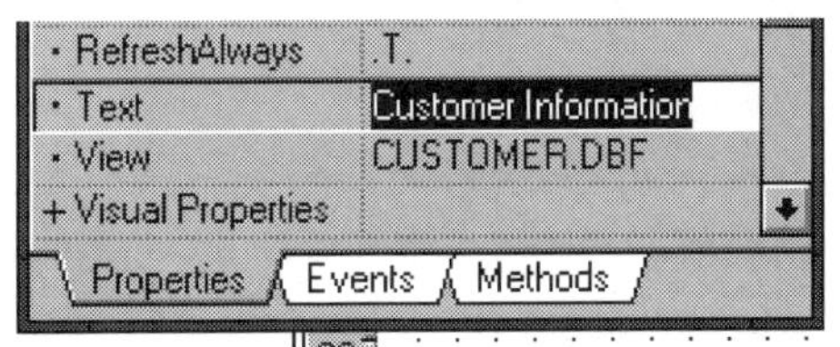

Figure 6–35. Setting the *View* and *Text* properties of a form.

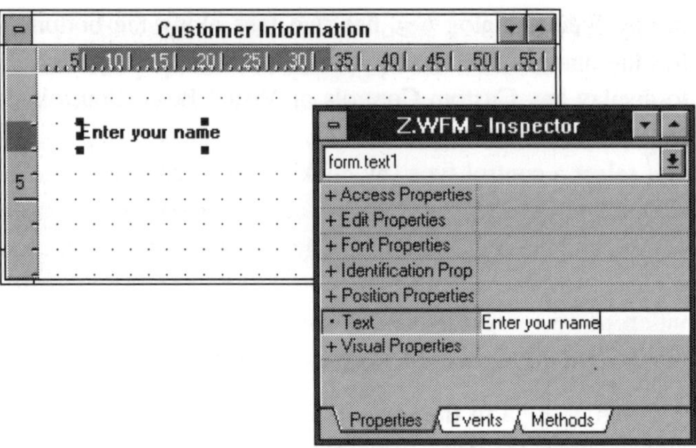

Figure 6–39. Changing the text property for the text object.

To select the text object in the property box, go to the combo box at the top and click on the down arrow to the right of the combo box. Figure 6–40 shows selecting the text object in the Inspector dialog box property page.

Figure 6–40. Selecting a different object in the Inspector dialog box.

Once the pull down is open for the combo box, select the text object.

Adding an entryfield object to the form. Now you are ready to add an entryfield object (similar to the @ . . . GET in DOS). To add an entryfield control follow these steps:

1. Select the EntryField control in the controls dialog box.
2. Place it on the form (by click and dragging the size).

Figure 6–41 shows an entryfield control added to the form.

Once the entryfield control (object) is placed in the form, you can link it to a field in the table or query. When you place the entryfield on the form, it is an object that has no value (almost like a memory variable). It can remain its own memory variable, or it can be linked to a field in the table or query. To link it to a field, change the value of the *DataLink* property of the entryfield, placing the name of the field in its cell. Figure 6–42 shows the DataLink property with a field name entered.

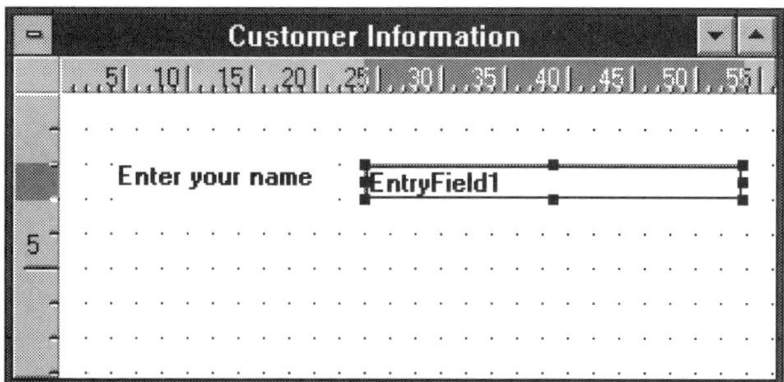

Figure 6–41. An entryfield object added to the form.

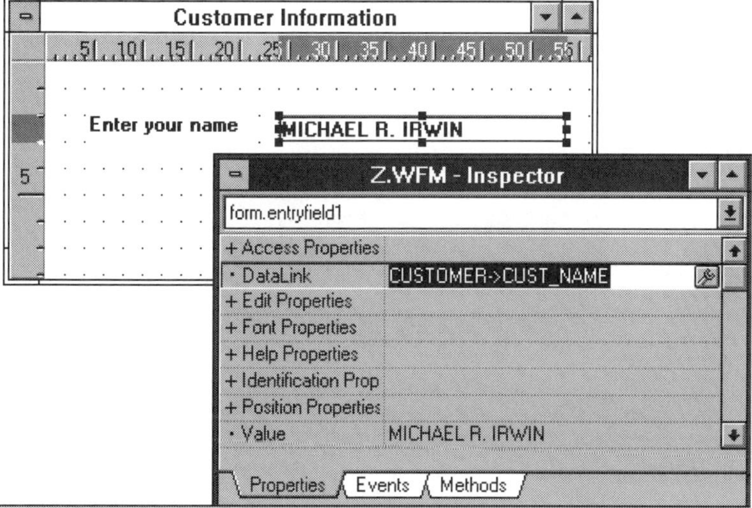

Figure 6–42. Associating an entryfield with a field.

> ➡ **Using the Field Palette**
> Visual dBASE has added a Field Palette dialog box that can assist you in adding fields from a table to a form. By selecting the field, from the Field Palette, that you want to place on the form, dBASE will automatically assign it to a control type. Once selected, you can drag the control type (linked to the field) to the form, drop it, and size it in one move. The datalink property will automatically be populated with the field name. The type of control object created will depend on the type of field being placed on the form.

With the entryfield object linked to a field, you can change other properties if you want to.

Adding a pushbutton to the form. To add a pushbutton to the form, follow these steps.

1. Select the PushButton control in the controls dialog box.
2. Place it on the form (by click and dragging the size).

Once the pushbutton is on the form, change the *Text* property to say "Close Form" by typing the following along the Text property cell of the pushbutton:

```
&Close Form
```

Placing the ampersand in front of a letter will assign the letter as a "hot key." The hot key will let you quickly move to that field on a form.

If you want to, you can change other properties as well. For instance, you may want to assign some code to the OnClick property of the pushbutton that will close the form.

Figure 6–43 shows a pushbutton control added to the form with the Text property changed. To assign a codeblock that will close the form, follow these steps:

1. Select the pushbutton control.
2. Click on the Event "tab" of the Inspector.
3. Select the OnClick property.
4. Type in the following codeblock: **{;form.Close()}** (the cell turns yellow).
5. Press the **Enter** key to accept the codeblock.

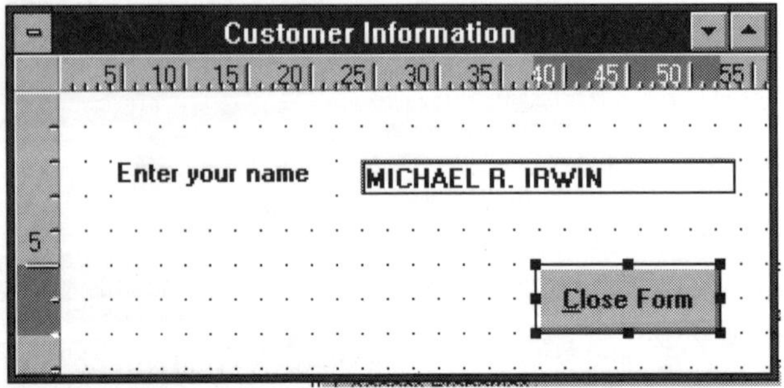

Figure 6–43. A pushbutton object added to the form.

Figure 6–44 shows the codeblock entered in the OnClick cell of the pushbutton.

Figure 6–44. Assigning a codeblock to a pushbutton.

Using Custom Controls

If you click on the "Custom" tab of the Control palette, dBASE will offer you a choice of several custom pushbutton controls that are supplied with Visual dBASE. You can select any of these pushbuttons to place on the form. They have several of the properties already set for you. For instance, the Close Button will have the text Close already on the button as well as a check mark graphic. It will also have a codeblock associated with the button to close the form.

If the custom controls are not available, it means that the BUTTONS.CC file has not been loaded by dBASE in memory.

Placing other controls on the form. You can continue to place other objects on the form and set their properties by following the same steps you did for the entryfield and text controls.

Saving the form. Once you place all the controls on the form, you should save it. You can save it by pressing the **Ctrl + S** key, or selecting File>>Save from the File menu.

NOTE: You can close the form, while in the design surface, by double-clicking on the system menu of the form window, or selecting File >> Close from the menu.

Running the form. While you are still in the Form Designer, you can click on the run button of the SpeedBar. The run button is the one in the middle that looks like a lightning bolt.

Modifying .WFM Files

With the form created and saved, you can also edit it using the Program Editor.

Two-way tools

dBASE has two-way tools. Once you have created the form using the form designer, you can modify it by hand using the Program Editor. Changing the code in the editor can be quicker than returning to the form designer and changing it there.

Once the code is changed in the Editor, you can still return to the Form Designer and work. Any changes you made in the Program Editor will be affected when you are in the Form Designer; they are not lost. This is known as two-way tools.

MODIFY COMMAND form name

You can change the forms code in the Program Editor. To change the code, type the following command:

```
MODIFY COMMAND <form name.WFM>
```

You will be taken into the Program Editor, and you can make changes to the code. Once you make changes, you can save it by pressing the **Ctrl** + **W** keys or selecting File>>Save from the menu.

Need to understand Classes. Technically, when you create a form in the Form Designer, you are actually creating a Class. To modify the code, you need to understand how Classes work. The next chapter explores objects and Classes.

Chapter 7
The Class—The Driving Force

Although there is more to explore in the Object-Oriented world, it is time to work with Classes. The Class is the controller of all objects—objects are instances of the Class that created them.

You have created forms using the Form Designer, and you have probably created some of the forms, from earlier chapters, by typing the code in directly—changing property values of the forms. These forms come from a Class named FORM.

There are two ways you can create a form. One is by creating the form from the built-in FORM Class and, once created, modifying the properties you want to change. The other method is to create your own custom Class of a form with the changes already performed.

The second way is more efficient. Remember, a form object comes from a Class, and a Class can create many objects. Usually you will want to create more than one form with the same characteristics—the same size, color, and other properties that you have determined. If you create your forms using the built-in Class FORM, you will have to reset your property preferences for each form created. Instead, creating a form from your own Customized form Class will automatically set your defaults.

Interestingly, all forms created by the Form Designer actually create a new Class of form for each one. This is also true for all menus and popups that you create in the menu designer.

This ability, to create *customized* form Classes, is powerful. For instance, you may want the name of your Company to be the title of all forms. By creating your own form Class, you can specify the Company name for the Text property of your custom form Class. Any objects that are created from your custom form Class will have your Company name already on them. If you created your own form Class, naming it CompanyFORM, you can create the form using the syntax

```
MyForm = NEW CompanyFORM()
```

When you create your own customized form Class, you do not re-create everything from scratch. Rather, you can use what is already built into the existing Class FORM, building on what it already creates.

The Class Builds the Object

All objects come from a Class. Form objects come from a FORM Class, EntryField objects come from an ENTRYFIELD Class, and so on. Each Class can create many objects and every object from the Class will have the same identical members (properties and methods).

You are already familiar with creating objects, having used one of these two constructs.

- `DEFINE <Class type> <Object Name> [PROPERTY] ...`
- `<Object Name> = NEW <Class type>()`

Either command can be used to create an object. The object came from a Class, or a template, that built the object. This Class held the definition that was used to construct the object.

Parts of a CLASS

Classes are used to create objects. The Class comprises several parts.

- Declarative boundaries
- Constructor code
- Method Declarations

The declarative boundaries

The *declarative boundaries* of a Class are simply the dBASE commands that are used to specify starting and ending points for the Class definition. Using the syntax is simple:

```
CLASS <Class Name>
 *
 * class code goes here
 *
ENDCLASS
```

The code for the Class is placed in between these two commands, declarative boundaries.

Class Constructor code

Classes hold the definitions and values needed to create the object properties and assign their initial values. The actual definitions and values for an objects properties are called the Class *Constructor* code. You create the property definitions or assign new values to existing properties by writing constructor code inside the CLASS . . . ENDCLASS.

When an object is created, Visual dBASE runs the Class like a program. The Constructor code, inside the Class, creates the object—assigning its properties and their values.

The Constructor code can contain any legal dBASE command. However, normally it only contains property names (similar to memory variable names) and their default values.

The following example creates Constructor code inside a new Class definition, named CompanyFORM. To type in this Class, create a new program named DEMOLIB.prg with the command MODIFY COMMAND DEMOLIB.PRG, then type in these lines.

```
*** DemoLib.prg
*
CLASS CompanyFORM OF FORM
 this.Top   = 2
 this.Width   = 32
 this.Height   = 8
 this.Text   = "ABC Corporation"
 this.ColorNormal   = "W+/R*"
 this.MyString = "Hello Everyone"
 this.MyNumber = 123.45
ENDCLASS
```

The preceding code creates a new Class named CompanyFORM, derived from the Class FORM. All of the code that begins with the word *this* is the Constructor code. Notice that it assigns default values to five properties, derived from the FORM Class (Top, Width, Height, ColorNormal, and Text). It also creates two **new** properties (MyString and MyNumber). Constructor code can redefine default values of properties that it inherits from other classes or create new properties.

NOTE: Understanding the CLASS Command

Notice that the first line of the Class definition uses the declarative boundary command CLASS and attaches a new, user-specified, Class name—CompanyFORM. Then the command uses the OF clause to specify that it should create the Class CompanyFORM, starting with what is already in the Class—FORM. It inherits all the properties and methods that are already created by the FORM Class.

To demonstrate how this new Class, CompanyFORM, can be used, save the preceding code to a program named DEMOLIB.prg, and type the following lines of code in the Command window:

```
SET PROCEDURE TO DEMOLIB
MyForm = NEW CompanyFORM()
MyForm.Open()
MyForm.Left = 55
YourForm = NEW CompanyFORM()
YourForm.Open()
MyForm.Close()
YourForm.Close()
```

Running this code, you will create two new forms based on the Class CompanyFORM. Notice that both forms are red in color, small, and have the same text on the title bar.

The "this" keyword of Constructor code

Throughout the new Class definition CompanyFORM, you typed ***this***. The actual word ***this*** is known as a *special object reference variable*. It is used as a reference name, which will be replaced by the object name when the object is created. It is like a place holder for the name of the object that will be created by the Class.

The *this* variable gives you a way to "soft code" the object reference variable (known as the object name). Using the special object reference variable, *this*, a Class can be generic, allowing it to create any number of objects. If you had to hard code an object name into a Class, the Class would only be able to create a single object.

Because of the *this* object reference variable, it is possible to create any number of objects from a single Class. For example, the following code creates two different forms from the CompanyFORM Class, and then changes a property value in one and looks at the same property value for each form:

```
MikeForm = NEW CompanyForm()
SueForm = NEW CompanyForm()
*
* both forms will display a 32 for their form widths
*
? MikeForm.Width
? SueForm.Width
MikeForm.Width = 50
*
* both forms will have a different value for their form widths
*
? MikeForm.Width
? SueForm.Width
```

Both forms came from the same Class—CompanyFORM. You created this Class. When the two forms were created, the *this* keyword was replaced with the actual name of the form objects—MikeForm and SueForm. By using the *this* keyword, you 'soft coded' in the name of the object in the Class. Because of this ability, many objects can be created from the same Class.

Class declaration of methods

The second thing you can do when creating your own Custom class is to declare the methods used by the objects of the Class. This section of a Class is known as the *declaration of methods* section. This method declaration is actually the code that constructs the method—a UDF, procedure, or codeblock. The following code, added to your Class CompanyFORM, adds some Class declarations:

```
*** DemoLib.prg
*
* CLASS CompanyFORM OF FORM
*
* add the following to the Class CompanyFORM
*
 PROCEDURE MyAddIt
    PARAMETER xNum
    this.MyNumber = this.MyNumber + xNum
    RETURN
 PROCEDURE BeepIt(xNum)
   FOR x = 1 TO xNum
     ?? CHR(7)
   NEXT
   RETURN
*
* ENDCLASS
```

Notice that these two method declarations are simply dBASE procedures. The difference is that they are placed inside the Class itself. They use traditional dBASE-like code.

Passing parameters to a method

The first procedure, MyAddIt, uses the traditional PARAMETER command to receive the parameter xNum. The second one, BeepIt, passes the parameter inside the parentheses alongside of the procedure name.

In Visual dBASE, you can pass parameters to a function *and* a procedure directly, by placing parentheses after the name of the procedure or function, putting the parameter name inside the parentheses. Once built, you can use the procedure or function by specifying the name of the object and the method name (procedure or function name). For instance,

```
MyForm.MyAddIt (5)
YourForm.MyAddIt(2.87)
MyForm.BeepIt(3)
```

Member call operator. Objects created from a Class call their methods by referencing the object name and the name of the method, and using the member call operator after the name. The *member call operator* is simply the parentheses [( )] after the name of the method. This is true for both procedures and functions.

The member call operator is what actually triggers the method in the Class.

The member function pointer in Objects

Although objects come from Classes and are called instances of a Class, they are not minicopies of the Class. For instance, the object does not physically contain or maintain its own methods. Rather than storing a copy of the method inside itself, it stores (holds) a reference or *function pointer* that points to where the physical method exists (in a Class). This function pointer is called the member function pointer. This means that there is only one copy of the method in memory—residing in the Class. The object only contains a pointer that tells it where to find the method.

Function pointers are like memo-field pointers. A member function pointer is a new, special type of memory variable type. It is similar to a memo-field pointer. When you create a memo field in the data structure, dBASE automatically assigns a length of 10 to the field type. This size assignment is not the size of the memo field. Rather, it is a 10-character place holder that is used to point to the actual memo that is associated with that record. The memo itself is stored in a different file (the .DBT file). So a pointer is needed to point to the correct memo for each record.

The member function pointer is similar. It only points to the correct procedure, function, or codeblock in the correct Class.

Custom Classes and procedure files

To use the Custom Class you create, you have to place it in memory. The most efficient way to create custom classes is to place their code in procedure files. Once in a procedure file, they can be placed in memory using the command:

```
SET PROCEDURE TO <procedure file name> [ADDITIVE]
```

The ADDITIVE keyword. The SET PROCEDURE TO command has a new keyword: *additive*. This keyword lets you place more than one procedure file in memory at a time. Using this keyword, you can place many procedures files in active memory. By being able to activate more than one procedure file, you will not need to create a single, large, unmanageable procedure file. Rather you can create several smaller procedure files. One may hold your Class definitions, and one may hold common procedures.

Building Custom Classes from scratch

So, Custom Classes are simply code. They can be broken into two primary parts: Constructor code and Method Declarations, both located within the boundaries of the *CLASS ... ENDCLASS* command. The following Class, named Inventory, can be added to the procedure file you have already created (DEMOLIB.prg):

```
*** DemoLib.prg
*
*   CLASS CompanyFORM OF FORM code is here
*
CLASS Invention
   this.CompanyName = "Company Name here"
   this.InvType = "Electronic"
   this.Category = ""
   this.Cost = 100.00
   this.PatentAppliedFor = .T.
   PROCEDURE ChangeCost(xValue)
      this.Cost = xValue
   RETURN
ENDCLASS
```

Unlike the CompanyFORM Class, this Class is built from scratch. It does not start based on another Class. It lacks the OF <class name> option of the CLASS command.

Visual dBASE lets you create your own Classes from scratch. This one, Invention, will build objects that have five properties (CompanyName, InvType, Category, Cost, and PatentAppliedFor) and a single method (ChangeCost).

Types of Classes

Visual dBASE has two categories of Classes.

- Stock, or built-in Classes
- Custom Classes

You can build objects from Classes already built into Visual dBASE, or you can create your own Classes. These Classes can be built from scratch or derived from a built-in Class. Why the difference?

Stock, built-in, Classes can only be used—they simply exist. Although you can use them, you can't modify them. You can't add new properties, change existing default value, or create your own methods for them.

Conversely, Custom Classes are flexible. They can be built from scratch as the Inventory Class was or built using another Class as their basis. Once created, you use them just like you use any of the built-in Classes. This ability is powerful.

Stock Classes

dBASE has twenty-eight built-in Classes. Of them, twenty-seven stock classes are documented.

AssocArray	MenuBar
Array	Object
Browse	OLE
CheckBox	OleAutoClient
ComboBox	PaintBox
DDELink	PushButton
DDETopic	RadioButton
Editor	Rectangle
EntryField	ScrollBar
Form	Shape
Image	SpinBox
Line	TabBox
ListBox	Text
Menu	

In addition to these twenty-seven classes, Visual dBASE has one undocumented class:

Timer

Every time you create a form or any of its controls (the visible objects contained in the form) using the Form Designer, you use these built-in Classes.

NOTE: Examples of the Classes

For more information on each Class, see Appendix 'A'; it covers all of the built-in Classes with coding examples, and explanations for each of their properties and methods.

Creating an object using a Stock Class

To create an object from a Stock Class, the syntax is one of these two.

<Object name> = NEW <stock class name>([parameters])

DEFINE <Stock class name> <Object name> [OF <form name>] PROPERTY ;

<property1 Property1 value> [,<property2 Property2 value> , . . .]

In previous chapters, you have created objects from Stock Classes. Some, like the control objects, are contained in a form and require parameters.

Creating a form object from the Stock FORM Class. As in an earlier chapter, to create a form object, named MyForm, you type the following in the Command window:

```
MyForm = NEW FORM()
```

Creating a control object for the form object. Control objects are the visible objects contained inside the form. If you want to create a control object that you place in a form, you must pass the form name when you create the object. For instance, to create a pushbutton, named MyButton, inside the form MyForm, you would type

```
DEFINE PUSHBUTTON MyButton OF MyForm
```

This will create a pushbutton object and place it inside the form MyForm.

User-created Custom Classes

Because built-in Classes cannot have their default values modified, you will need to assign new values to each object created by the Class. As pointed out, this can be bothersome if all of your objects need to have the same default value. Instead of using a built-in class, you can create your own Custom Classes and build your own default property values. For instance, the built-in form Class may default to the wrong size or color. Additionally, you may want all the forms you create to always have an "Exit" button in them, so you want the Custom Form Class to define the pushbutton and automatically place it in the form when the form object is created.

Remember, the premise of object-oriented development is to solve complexity *quickly*. Part of that premise suggests that coding and maintenance should be minimal.

Creating your own classes gives you the ability to quickly create new objects (for example, forms), which are personalized to your needs. You assign the default values for the properties and method of the objects that are created from your Classes. You can have a form Class automatically contain other objects when it is initially created.

The form Class is a perfect example. You may want to create your own form Class, starting with all the Constructor code and Methods Declarations that are built into the Class named FORM. Custom Classes can be built based on other Classes.

Inheritance. When you create a Class based on another Class, you *inherit* all of the Constructor code and Method Declarations that are in that class. The act of inheriting the parts of a Class is known as *inheritance*.

Using OF to create a new form Class. To build a Class based on another Class, inheriting its parts, you use the keyword OF in the CLASS command. The following example will build a Custom Class named BeepForm, starting with all the Constructor code and Method Declarations built into the stock FORM Class.

```
CLASS BeepForm OF FORM
   this.ColorNormal = "W/B"
   this.Top = 2
   this.Left = 2
ENDCLASS
```

Notice that the syntax on the first line uses the keyword OF.

```
CLASS BeepForm OF Form
```

The keyword OF tells dBASE to create the Custom Class, BeepForm, starting with (inheriting) all the existing Constructor code and Method declarations that are inside the Class FORM. You are *deriving* a new Class from another Class. In this case, you are *deriving* a new Custom form Class, named BeepForm, from the original Class form.

After you inherit all the values from another Class, you can change the ones that need to be changed. In this case, you changed the ColorNormal, Top, and Left constructor values.

Parameters and Classes

As the syntax suggests, you can pass parameters to a Class. You have already passed parameters to classes. When you create a form object, you can specify the text for the form as a parameter. When you create a pushbutton on a form, you must pass the form name to the Class as a parameter. The following exemplifies this point:

```
MyForm = NEW FORM("Mikes Form")
MyButton1 = NEW PUSHBUTTON(MyForm)
```

Checking parameters of Custom Classes that are derived. Visual dBASE will check to verify that you have passed the correct number of parameters to the CLASS declaration. For instance, if you forget to pass the name of the form to a PUSHBUTTON

Class, Visual dBASE will report an error. Retype the preceding commands in the Command window without the form name.

```
MyForm = NEW FORM("Mikes Form")
MyButton1 = NEW PUSHBUTTON()
```

Visual dBASE will report an error when you try to create the pushbutton MyButton1. This check is performed at the Class declarative level and is required.

Parameters passed to a nonderived Custom Class. Visual dBASE does not check to see that parameters are passed to nonderived Custom Classes. The following code demonstrates this point:

```
CLASS MyThing( a, b, c)
   this.x = a
   this.y = b
   this.z = c
ENDCLASS
```

If you place this Class in memory and create a new MyThing object, Visual dBASE will not report an error if you forget to pass the three parameters:

```
x1= NEW MyThing()
x2 = NEW MyThing(2, "a", .t.)
```

Both of the preceding objects will be created if you type them in the Command window.

This verification is your responsibility. You have to verify, through code, that you received the correct number and type of parameters. The two functions that help you accomplish this are

- PCOUNT()
- TYPE("<variable name>")

Parameters passed to a Class method. Visual dBASE also fails to check for parameters passed to methods inside Classes.

The PCOUNT() function. You can check for the number of parameters being passed by using the PCOUNT() function. This function will return the number of parameters being passed to the method.

The following code demonstrates how to use the PCOUNT() function:

```
PROCEDURE MyCheck
   PARAMETER xCnt, xText
   DO CASE
      CASE PCOUNT() = 0
```

```
            ? "No parameters were passed"
        CASE PCOUNT() = 1
            ? "Only 1 parameter was passed"
        CASE PCOUNT() = 2
            ? "2 parameters were passed (which is what I want)"
        OTHERWISE
            ? "More than two parameters were passed"
    ENDCASE
RETURN
```

This code simply checks the number of parameters that were passed. That is all that the function PCOUNT() does. It returns the number of parameters that were passed to the procedure.

The TYPE function. You can check the type of memory variable by using the TYPE command. It will return a string value that represents the specified data type of the variable. The following code shows how to use the TYPE function, via a dBASE procedure:

```
PROCEDURE MyCheck
   PARAMETER xCnt, xText
   IF TYPE("xCnt") <> "N"
       ? "The parameter xCnt should be numeric type"
   ENDIF
   IF TYPE("xText") <> "C"
       ? "The parameter xText should be character (string) type"
   ENDIF
RETURN
```

The TYPE() function checks to see what the data type is of the variable that was passed. This function can be used with Class methods or nonderived Class parameters.

Passing parameters to a Custom Class derived from another Class

When creating a Custom Class based on another Class that requires parameters, you must specify the same parameter on both sides of the declaration. If you create a Class based on another class (using the OF keyword) that creates control objects (pushbuttons, entryfields, etc.), you will need to pass parameters to both of the Class names. The following exemplifies passing parameters:

- `CLASS ExitButton(`*`cform`*`) OF PushButton(`*`cform`*`)`
- `CLASS UpperEntField(`*`cform`*`) OF EntryField(`*`cform`*`)`
- `CLASS SmartEdit(`*`cform`*`) OF Editor(`*`cform`*`)`

In all three examples the parameter named *cForm* is passed inside the parentheses alongside of the Class names—both the new Custom control Class name and the Stock control Class name.

Any time you create a new Class (*subclass*) that is derived (created from) another Class (*superclass*) that *requires* parameters you will pass the parameters in between parentheses after the Class name.

NOTE: Subclasses and Superclasses

A *Superclass* is the Class that you use to derive another Class (create a Class) from. The new class is known as a *Subclass*. This will be discussed more in depth later in the book.

Class parameters for FORM Classes. You can specify one parameter for Custom forms created from the Stock Class FORM, when declaring your Custom Class. The Stock Class FORM allows a single parameter: the title text for the title bar of the form. It has to be a character string that is enclosed in quotation marks. The following code demonstrates this point:

```
CLASS PassForm(xText) OF FORM(xText)
   this.top = 2
   this.left = 2
   this.width = 44
   this.height = 12
ENDCLASS
```

If you create this Class, you can create a new form using the following syntax:

xForm = NEW PassForm("Mike's FORM")

Although you did not specify the text of the form be changed (with a *this.text = xText*), dBASE automatically changes it because the default parameter of the built-in Class FORM allows you specify a Text title parameter.

If you open the form, it will look like the one in Figure 7–1.

Figure 7–1. Passing a parameter to a new form.

Forgetting Class declaration parameters. When you use a parameter with the new form code, you will be forced to pass some title text to the form when you create it. For instance, the following code will cause an error when you try to create a form:

```
xForm = NEW PassForm()
```

Because you asked for a parameter in the Custom Class definition of the form, Visual dBASE will report an error. Visual dBASE *demands* that you pass a parameter—at the form level of a Class definition.

Passing parameters to nonderived Custom Classes

If you are creating your own Custom Class (not using the OF keyword to inherit from a Superclass), you should pass the parameters using the PARAMETER keyword. The following is an example:

```
CLASS InventoryItems
    PARAMETER xType, xWt, xCst
   *  other Constructor code
   *
  this.MadeBy = "Widget Intl"
  this.Type = xType
  this.Weight = xWt
  this.Cost = xCst
ENDCLASS
```

Now that the class has been created, you can create objects from it with syntax similar to the following:

```
xItem= NEW InventoryItems("Hammer 01", 100, 45.54)
```

Passing parameters at the Class declaration level. You could have passed parameters using the following method:

```
CLASS InventoryItems(xType, xWt, xCst)
```

Both methods will let you pass parameters to a Class when you instantiate (create) the object. However, this method can cause problems when you need to verify that the parameters were passed.

The dBASE TYPE function will not work as expected if you pass parameters at the Class declaration level.

Using the TYPE( ) function with parameters

As just pointed out, the TYPE() function does not work as anticipated when working with some parameters in classes. The following section explains the problem.

Using TYPE( ) with parameters in ( ). If you create a Custom Class that uses the TYPE() function to verify the passage of parameters and those parameters are inside the parentheses, there can be a problem. The following code exemplifies the problem:

```
CLASS InventoryItems (xType, xWt, xCst)
     *
     this.MadeBy = "Widget Intl"
     this.Type = IIF(Type('xType')="C",xType,"Item Name
     Here")
     this.Weight = IIF(Type('xWt')="N",xWt,12)
     this.Cost = IIF(Type('xCst')="N",xCst,1.50)
ENDCLASS
```

When passing parameters between the parentheses at the Class declaration level, the TYPE() function will always return a **"U"** (undefined) as the data type. This means that the code will always assign the default values to properties ("Item name here," 12, 1.50). Normally, using the TYPE() function, you could check for a data type of **"U."** However, that would mean that if no parameters were passed, the value would be a logical .F. instead of the default value (because the type is always **"U"**).

Therefore, both of the following commands to create an object from the InventoryItems Class will give the same values:

```
xIt1=new inventoryitems()
xIt2=new inventoryitems("Xxx",1, 0.75)
```

If you create the preceding Class and call it using the preceding commands, the first object (xIt1) will have values of "Item name here," 12, 1.50. The second object should have values of "Xxx,"1, 0.75; however, it will also have values of "Item name here," 12, 1.50.

This is a serious problem. The bottom line is never pass values to a Class on the same line as the Class name.

Using the TYPE( ) function with the PARAMETER command. To solve the problem, always pass parameters using the PARAMETER keyword; as in the following example, the code will work.

```
CLASS InventoryItems
     PARAMETERS xType, xWt, xCst
     *
     *  the following is the Constructor code
     *
     this.MadeBy = "Widget Intl"
     this.Type = IIF(Type('xType')="C",xType,"Item Name Here")
     this.Weight = IIF(Type('xWt')="N",xWt,100)
     this.Cost = IIF(Type('xCst')="N",xCst,1.00)
ENDCLASS
```

Now if you create the same objects from the Class, they will give you the correct values.

```
xIt1=new inventoryitems()
xIt2=new inventoryitems("Xxx",1, 0.75)
```

If you create the preceding Class and call it using the preceding commands, the first object (xIt1) will have values of "Item name here," 12, 1.50. The second object will have values of "Xxx,"1, 0.75.

Using the PARAMETER command, you can make your Class declaration code generic in nature. This means that you can pass parameters or forget to pass them. The Type() function will work when using the PARAMETER command. The preceding code uses the Immediate If function, IIF(), to determine what parameters were passed and their type. This code works; the previous code gives unexpected results.

If you forget to pass the parameters, the default value will be assigned instead.

WORKING WITH THE CUSTOM FORM CLASSES

Because forms are the primary focus of all Visual dBASE application, creating your own custom form Classes is key to exploiting the power of Visual dBASE.

Why work with your own Custom Form Classes?

Now that you are creating objects, which come from Classes, you probably realize the power of the ability to program by simply changing a few properties and triggering some methods (built into the object or created for the object) based on user actions. Most of the objects you work with are the controls (visible objects) that are contained with a form. Over time, you may notice that you are constantly changing the same properties or re-creating the same methods repeatedly. The built-in default values of the Stock Class are not what you want *your* default values to be when the object is initially created (instantiated).

By creating a Custom form Class once, it won't be necessary to change the values of each form created by the stock Class—FORM. If you find yourself constantly doing the following, you need to consider creating Custom form Classes.

- Change built-in default property values
- Create your own property values (memory variables)
- Assign default actions to event properties
- Create your own methods
- Automatically create control objects

Changing built-in default property values

Custom form Classes let you assign different default property values to the object's property when it is created.

Assigning new default values to Properties

Create your Custom form Class in a procedure file. For purposes of this section, it will be placed in a procedure file named MYPROCS.prg. To create this Custom form Class, type the command MODIFY COMMAND MYPROCS in the Command window. While in the Program Editor, type in the following code:

```
*** MYPROCS.prg
*
CLASS MyForm OF FORM
   this.Top = 2.5
   this.Left = 35
   this.Width = 55
   this.Height = 12
   this.ColorNormal = "W/B"
   this.Text = "Widget Int'l"
ENDCLASS
```

This code defines a Custom form Class, named MyForm and derived from the Stock Class, FORM. It changes several of the initial values of the form properties. Save it by pressing the **Ctrl + W** key combination. Now the Class, MyForm, can be used to create Form objects that have different values from the ones created using the Class FORM.

Placing the Customized Class definition in memory

To use the Class MyForm, you must first place it in memory by loading the procedure file in memory. From the Command window, type the following:

```
SET PROCEDURE TO MYPROCS
```

Comparing your Custom form to a Stock form

To compare the forms created with your form Class, MyForm, and the built-in form Class, you can load the Class in memory and type in the following commands:

```
OldForm=NEW FORM()
OldForm.Open()
*
*   The original form is open and active;  click back into
```

```
*   the Command window and type in the following two
*   commands:
*
NewForm = NEW MyFORM()
NewForm.Open()
```

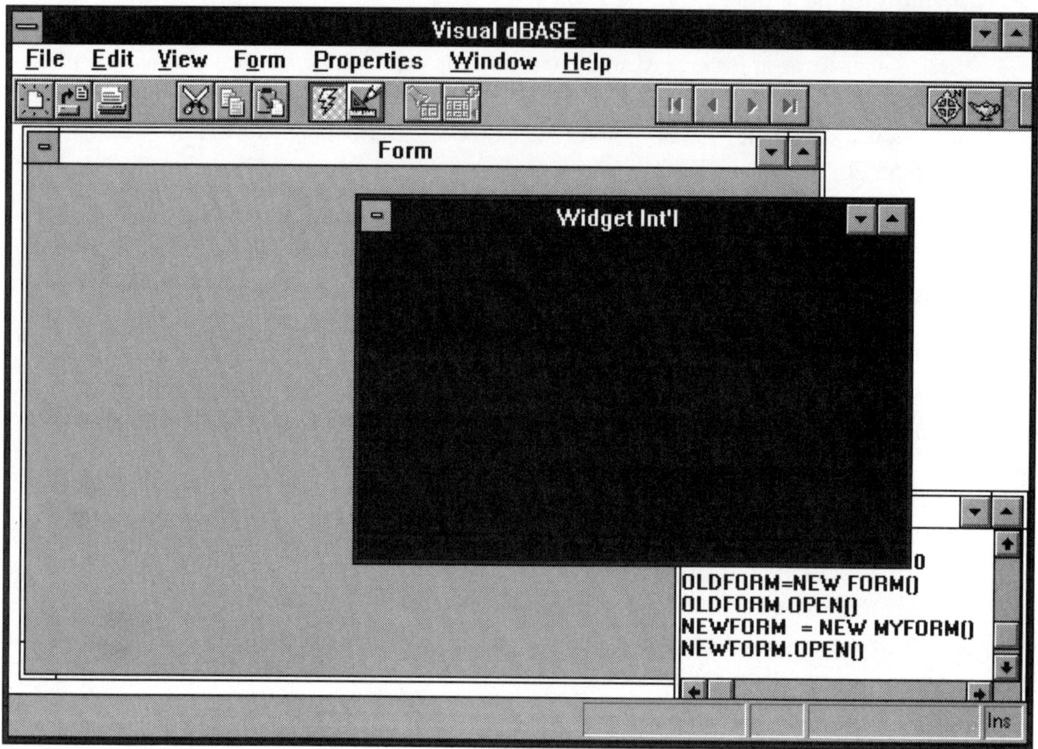

Figure 7–2. Two forms: one created from the FORM Class and another from a user-created Class.

Figure 7–2 shows both forms active in the dBASE frame. Notice that the second form (titled "Widget Int'l") has all the new properties that you assigned as the default properties. Every new form object created from the MyForm Class will have these new default values.

Creating new properties for Custom Form Classes

You can define your own properties in a Custom Class.

A property is a hidden memory variable

Because a property is really nothing more than a memory variable with a value that is hidden inside the object, you can create properties in your custom Class that become part of the objects created from the Class. The following code could be added to the CLASS MyForm earlier:

```
    ......
    * this.Text = "Widget Int'l"
    *
    *  add the next two lines
    *
    this.Color1 = "W/B"
    this.Color2 = "R/GR"
* ENDCLASS
```

This code creates two *new* properties named Color1 and Color2. Every object created from the MyForm class will have these two new properties.

Assign default actions to event properties

A Custom Class can also assign Event Handlers to event properties of the objects it will create. These Event Handlers can be codeblocks, or the name of a procedure or function.

Creating and assigning a codeblock to an event property

The following code, added to the CLASS MyForm, creates some codeblocks and associates them with the OnOpen and OnClose of a form object event properties:

```
    ......
    this.Color2 = "R/GR"
    this.OnOpen = {;public xFOpen; xFOpen ="YES"}
   this.OnClose = {;release xFopen}
ENDCLASS
```

This code has assigned codeblocks to the OnOpen and OnClose properties.

By assigning methods to event properties in the Class code, you can automatically add functionality to the form when it is created.

Understanding the Event Handler operations. In the preceding example, you have assigned code to the OnOpen and OnClose event properties of any form that is created from the Class. To see how it works, type in the following commands at the Command window:

```
SET PROC TO MYPROCS
xFORM = NEW MYFORM()
? xFOpen
*   dBASE reports an error, xFOpen has not been created YET
xForm.Open()
*   opens the form and triggers the OnOpen Event handler
? xFOpen
*   dBASE reports the value YES in the results pane
(bottom)
xForm.Close()
*   closes the form and triggers the OnClose Event handler
? xFOpen
*   dBASE reports an error, xFOpen has been released
```

Running these commands from the Command window prove that the new form object, xForm, created from the custom form Class, MyForm, attached the Event Handler codeblocks to the event properties OnOpen and OnClose.

Potential problems with public variables and objects

Using and releasing public memory variables can be a problem. If you create and open six different forms from the Class MyForm, and close any one of the open forms, the public memory variable, xFOpen, will be prematurely released. This means that the variable will no longer be available to the other five open forms.

Because of this potentially dangerous problem, you may want to hide the variables inside the object by creating a new property, instead of declaring a variable public.

Creating methods for a Custom Class

When you create your own Custom form Class, you can create your own methods for the objects. The following is a method that is added to the class MyForm:

```
this.OnClose = {;release xFopen}
PROCEDURE ChangeColor(xNum)
   IF PCOUNT()=0
       RETURN
   ENDIF
   xColor=this.ColorNormal
   FOR x = 1 to xNum
       SLEEP .1
       this.ColorNormal = iif((x/2) = int(x/2),xColor,"w/R*")
   NEXT
   this.ColorNormal = xColor
   RETURN
ENDCLASS
```

Using the method of a Custom Control Class

Once an object is instantiated (created) from the Custom Class you created, its methods can be used just like any other object method:

<Object name>.<name of method>()

For example, the method ChangeColor inside the Class MyForm can be used by typing in the following commands at the Command window:

```
SET PROC TO MYPROCS
xFORM = NEW MYFORM()
xForm.Open()
xForm.ChangeColor(11)
xForm.ChangeColor()
```

Define default controls for the form

Finally, by creating your own form Classes, you have the ability to automatically create contained objects in the form object when it is instantiated.

Defining default control objects inside the form

The following code, added to the Custom Class definition, MyForm, will create a text object and a pushbutton object in every form created by the Class. Note that it should be placed between the OnClose property and the PROCEDURE ChangeColor.

```
this.OnClose = {;release xFopen}
DEFINE TEXT TitleText OF form PROPERTY text "Title HERE" ,;
   Top 1.2, Left 1, Height 2,  Width 51 , FontSize 14, ;
   FontUnderline .t. , ColorNormal this.Color1
DEFINE PUSHBUTTON Exit OF form PROPERTY  ;
   Top (form.height-2), Left (form.width-14), Text "E&xit",;
   OnClick {;form.Close()}
PROCEDURE ChangeColor(xNum)
```

Although you added these two controls by using the DEFINE command, you could have used the NEW command. Both ways let you create objects in a Custom form Class. Borland recommends that you create contained controls using the DEFINE command, although either method works. Obviously, the DEFINE method lets you modify properties in less space and doesn't require the *this* special keyword for assigning new values.

Using the *form* keyword

The preceding DEFINE commands use both the *this* special operator keyword and the *form* special operator keyword. The *form* keyword, like the *this* word, is used as a special place holder that will be replaced with the name of the form object when it is created. In this case, the *form* keyword is used to access properties and methods of the form (form.height form.Close(), form.Width).

Any forms created from this Class will contain a text object and a pushbutton inside them.

The complete Custom Form Class—MyForm

The entire example code for the CLASS MyForm should look like this:

```
*** MYPROCS.prg
*
*
CLASS MyForm OF FORM
   this.Top = 2.5
   this.Left = 1
   this.Width = 55
   this.Height = 12
   this.ColorNormal = "W/B"
   this.Text = "Widget Int'l"
   this.Color1 = "W*/B"
   this.Color2 = "R/GR"
   this.OnOpen = {;public xFOpen; xFOpen ="YES"}
   this.OnClose = {;release xFopen}
   DEFINE TEXT TitleText OF form PROPERTY text "Title HERE" ,;
      Top 1.2, Left 1, Height 2,  Width 51 , FontSize 14, ;
      FontUnderline .t. , ColorNormal this.Color1
   DEFINE PUSHBUTTON Exit OF form PROPERTY  ;
      Top (form.height-2), Left (form.width-14), Text "E&xit",;
      OnClick {form.Close()}
   PROCEDURE ChangeColor(xNum)
      IF pCount() =0
          return
      ENDIF
      xColor=this.ColorNormal
      FOR x = 1 to xNum
          sleep .1
          this.ColorNormal = iif((x/2) = int(x/2),xColor,"w/R*")
      NEXT
      this.ColorNormal = xColor
      RETURN
ENDCLASS
```

Creating multiple form objects from the Custom Class

After placing the MyProcs procedure file in memory, you can create two different forms from the Class Myform:

```
SET PROCEDURE TO MYPROCS
OneFORM = NEW MYFORM()
OneFORM.OPEN()
*
*    refocus on the Command window and continue typing
*
AnotherFORM = NEW MYFORM()
AnotherFORM.OPEN()
```

You have just created two identical forms, one on top of the other. If you move one of the forms, you will see that they are both identical. They are the same size, and color—the same everything. The only different factor is their names: OneForm and AnotherForm. Figure 7–3 shows two forms created from the Class MyForm. (One of the forms has been moved after opening it to show you two.)

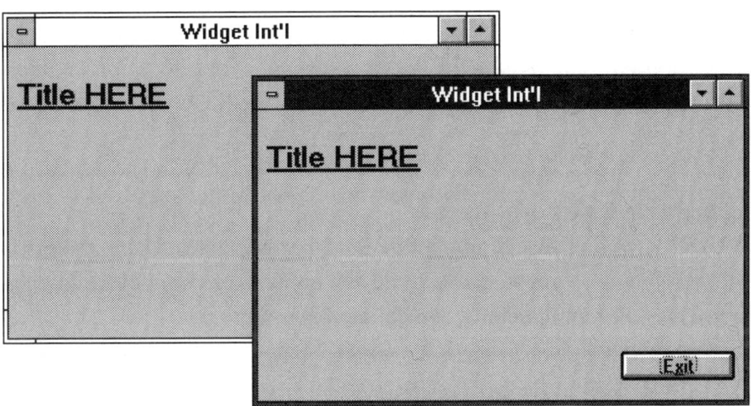

Figure 7–3. Two forms created from the class MyForm.

Specifying a Custom Form Class for the Form Design surface

➡ Visual dBASE has added the ability to create a Custom Form Class and use this Custom Class as the default class for the Form Designer. This means that you can create a Custom Form Class, setting default properties and adding control objects (pushbuttons, text, etc.) that you want in every form created. Once you create this custom Class, you can tell Visual dBASE to use this new Custom Form Class as the Base Form Class for all forms created in the Form Designer.

4. Click on the OK button.

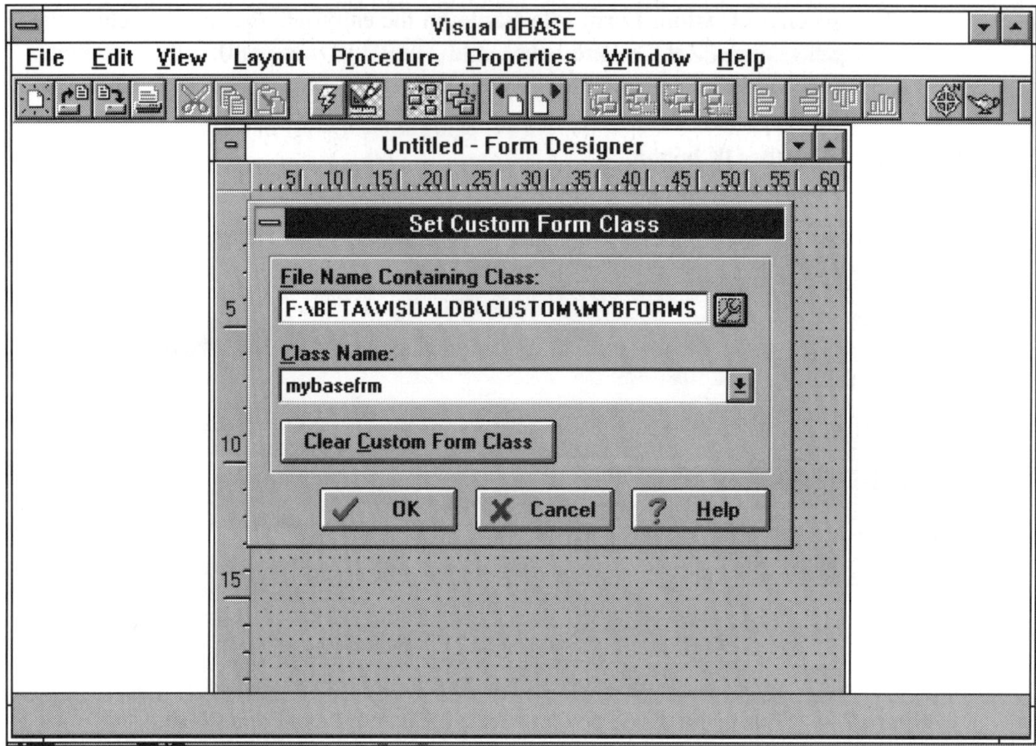

Figure 7–5. This is the Set Custom Form Class dialog box.

Figure 7–5 shows the Set Custom Form Class dialog box with the file name and Class name entered.

Once you specify the base form class, Visual dBASE will immediately return to the Design window and show the new default form. Figure 7–6 shows the new default form. Every time you create a new form, this default form will come up instead of the blank default form of dBASE.

NOTE: Resetting default values for Custom Base Form

If you need to reset the Default Base Form, simply click on the Clear Custom Form Class pushbutton of the dialog box, as shown in Figure 7–5.

Figure 7–6. This is a new default form.

[Form Designer] section of dBASEWIN.INI. The dBASEWIN.INI file maintains two settings for the Custom Base Form Class. They are located in the [Form Designer] section. They would look similar to the following:

```
[Form Designer]
BaseFormClassFileName = c:\vdbase\MyCForms.CFM
BaseFormClassName = MyBaseFrm
```

You can edit this file by using any Text Editor and manually inserting the name of the Base Form Class and the file in which it is located. Once set, every time you enter the Form Designer, creating a new form, Visual dBASE will begin with this Base Form.

Creating Classes for Control Objects

You can also create Control Object Classes. A Control Object Class is simply any of the Classes that create objects contained inside a form. Like forms, you may want to make Control Object Classes that can be used to assign *your* default properties and methods to the object at the time they are created.

You can create Classes from any existing (built-in) control object; however, the following eight Control Classes are probably the most common ones that you will want to make into Custom Control Classes:

Browse	List Boxes
Combo Boxes	Pushbuttons
Editors	Radio Buttons
Entryfields	Text

The remainder of this chapter discusses the creation of three Custom Control Classes.

Why create your own Control Classes?

By creating your own Custom Control Object Classes, you can assign new default property values and actions to event properties for the controls. In fact, you can even specify that these controls should be available in the Form Designer, just as you did with a Base Form.

User Customized Control Classes

Like creating Custom Form Classes, you create Custom Controls to change the default appearance and behavior of its objects. Perhaps you have a standard for styles that must be used for fonts and colors of text and entryfields. Instead of setting these values in every form, one field at a time, you can create a Custom Class that does the work for you.

SET PROCEDURE TO MyProcs.PRG ADDITIVE command. Again, any Custom Control Classes must be in memory to use them. You will have to load a procedure file of your custom Control Classes before you build the objects for the form. To load the file, you use the command SET PROCEDURE TO <procedure file name> **ADDITIVE**.

Custom Controls in the Form Designer

One of the primary reasons you may want to create your own Customize Control Classes is to use them in the Form Designer as you build your forms. Visual dBASE already includes several Custom Controls (Buttons.cc, TabBox.cc, etc.) that make creating forms easier. You can add your own Custom Control Classes to these.

These Custom Control objects can be selected and used just like any other control in the **Controls** dialog box (object type selector box). Figure 7–7 shows the Controls dialog box and some Custom Controls.

You activate the custom controls in the Control Palette dialog box by selecting the **Custom** tab seen at the bottom of Figure 7–7.

CUSTOM Classes. Although Custom Controls (both dBASE and Visual Basic) are covered later in the book, dBASE custom controls are simply *Custom* Control Object Classes that are placed in a special procedure file ending in the extension CC (for Custom Controls). The following code shows a CUSTOM Control Class being defined:

```
CLASS CancelButton(fn,cn) of Pushbutton(fn,cn) CUSTOM
   this.height = 1.5
   this.width = 15
```

```
    this.upbitmap = "Resource #28"
    this.disabledbitmap = "Resource #29"
    this.text = "&Cancel"
    this.OnClick = {;form.Close()}
ENDCLASS
```

The difference between this Class definition and the ones you have worked with up until now is the inclusion of the keyword CUSTOM at the end of the CLASS constraint line. By adding the keyword CUSTOM, you are telling dBASE that this control Class will be a Custom Control.

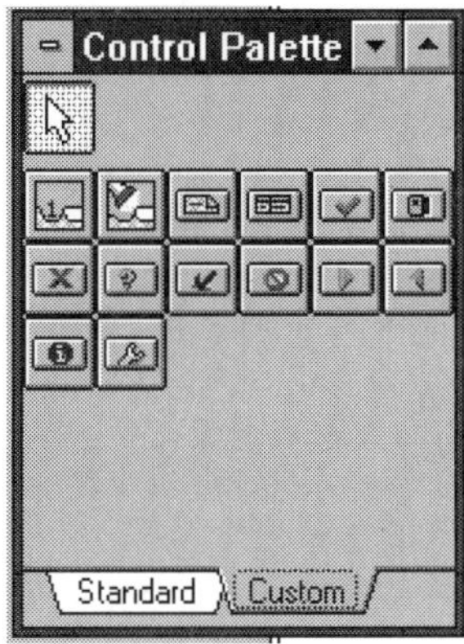

Figure 7–7. The Controls dialog box showing several custom pushbuttons.

Custom Controls: Programmed versus Form Designer. As stated, Custom Control Classes can be created for use in the form designer. If you want to create them for the form designer you simply change the extension of the procedure file holding the custom controls from .PRG to .CC.

However, you can create Custom Control Classes and place them in procedure files to be used by programs.

Parameters for a total of two parameters

Custom-created Control Classes can have two parameters.

1. The form's name (Object Reference Variable) that will hold the control object
2. The value for the **Name** property of the object

The first one, form's name, is *required*, the name property for the object is not.

The form's name = Object Reference Variables. The first parameter, the form's name, is required. You must specify the form object that will hold the control object. This form name is technically known as the *Object Reference Variable*. It is the object reference name you give it when you instantiate it. For instance,

```
MyForm = NEW FORM()
f = NEW FORM()
```

The names **MyForm** and **f** are the Object Reference Variables for the two form objects. The Object Reference Variable is what you use to identify the object.

Like form objects, control objects contained inside the form (controls) also have an Object Reference Variable (object name) that you assign. The following demonstrates this point:

```
CustomerLastName = NEW ENTRYFIELD(MyForm)
CustomerState = NEW COMBOBOX(MyForm)
```

The object reference variables for the control objects are **CustomerLastName** and **CustomerState**. The Object Reference Variable for their form is **MyForm** and **PetFrm**. In other words, an Object Reference Variable is simply the name that is used to identify the objects—forms or controls.

The NAME property of Control objects. In addition to the Object Reference Variables, control objects have an internal *NAME* property. According to the Visual dBASE documentation, this name is a read-only property. However, you can change this property like any other property in the object.

Every object contained in a form must have a unique name assigned to the Name property. Visual dBASE will assign a default name for any object based on the type of object, followed by a number TEXT1, TEXT2, ENTRYFIELD1, ...

You can change this name at the time that you create the object by passing a second parameter to the object Class. The following example will assign a **Name** property for an entryfield object:

```
MyEnt1 = NEW ENTRYFIELD(MyForm,"Ent1")
```

The name must be character type; thus, literals must be enclosed in quotation marks.

Chapter 10 explores the relationship between the Object Reference Variable, the Name property, containership, and ways to access control object property values.

Working with memory variables and user-defined form properties. Because Custom Control Classes only have two parameters, you may want to use memory variables or UDF properties to control the actions or behaviors of Custom Control Classes.

You already know how to declare your own properties and memory variables in the form by creating them in a customized form Class. You can use these custom form properties or memory variables as values in Custom Control Classes.

Creating a Custom FORM CLASS named MyForm

To work with the Custom Control Classes in the remainder of this chapter, the following Custom Form Class should exist. It should be placed in a procedure file named MYCUSTOM.prg. Type in the following program:

```
*** MYCUSTOM.prg
*
*
CLASS MyForm OF FORM
   this.text = "This Form is a CUSTOM form"
   this.Top = 2
   this.Left = 5
   this.Width = 90
   this.Height = 16
   this.ColorNormal = "W/APPWORKSPACE"
   *
   this.Color1 = "gr+/b"
   this.AliasName = ""

   DEFINE PUSHBUTTON Exit OF form PROPERTY   ;
      Top (form.height -2), Left (form.width-14), Height 1.5,
Width 12, ;
      Text "E&xit", OnClick {;form.Close()}
ENDCLASS
```

The form Class can now be used by typing in these commands:

```
SET PROCEDURE TO MYCUSTOM
fForm = NEW MyForm()
fForm.Open()
```

The form object fForm should look like the one in Figure 7–8. It has an “Exit” pushbutton already on the form.

Once the form is created, you are ready to create a few Custom Control Classes.

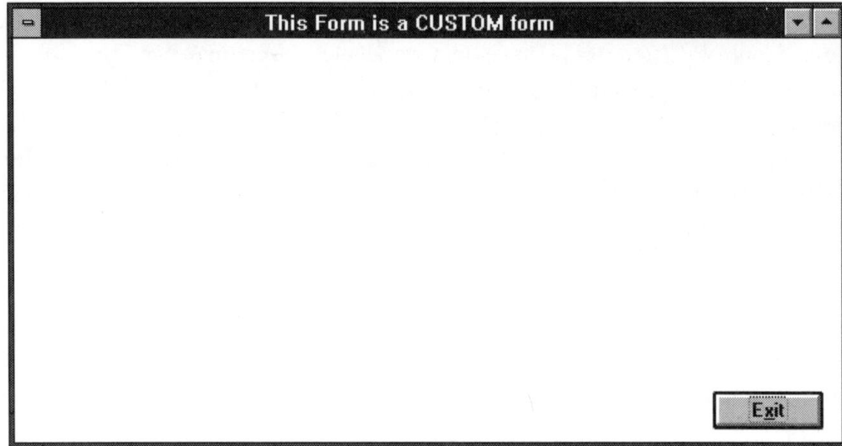

Figure 7–8. The default form for Custom Control Classes.

Creating a Custom BROWSE Control

The BROWSE Class is a BROWSE window inside a form that can display records. The Browse object has its own frame (Top, Left, Width, and Height properties).

The control objects created from a BROWSE Class must be contained inside a form. Therefore, you must pass it at least one parameter—the form name.

The Syntax for a new BROWSE Class

The general syntax for creating a new BROWSE Class is

CLASS <NewClName>(param1, [param2]) OF BROWSE(param1, [param2])

[CUSTOM]

<constructor code>

<declaration code>

ENDCLASS

This syntax is similar to the syntax you used to create a Custom Form Class. The difference is the parameters (param1 must be passed).

Naming Custom Control Class parameters. You must pass one parameter to a Custom Control Class—the one that will hold the form name. The name of the parameter (variable) must be the same for the New Class Name and the BROWSE Class name—but the name is not important. The following are both valid examples of defining a new BROWSE class with one parameter:

```
CLASS MyBrowse(f) OF BROWSE(f)
CLASS TheNewBrws(fname) OF BROWSE(fname)
```

The key to using parameters is that both names have to be the same. The parameter variable name *f* or ***fname*** is used for both parts of the Class declaration.

You can specify a second parameter as follows:

CLASS MyBrowse(fName,brwName) OF BROWSE(fName,brwName)

If you specify two parameters in the CLASS declaration, you will have to pass two parameters when you create the new Class. The first parameter will always be used to pass the container name (form); the second parameter is used to specify the value for the name property of the control object. Because dBASE automatically assigns a value to this property, you will probably not want to pass a second parameter.

✔ **The keyword CUSTOM**

The keyword CUSTOM should be added to the Class declaration line when you create your own CUSTOM Classes from built-in Classes. The manuals specify that you should use it when creating Custom Control Classes that will be used in the Form Designer. However, it appears to be optional. The keyword CUSTOM can be optionally omitted or used. It appears to have no effect on how Custom Classes are created.

A Custom BROWSE Class

The following BROWSE CLASS code will create a new class called MyBrowse and place it in the form near the bottom with a width automatically set. It should be added to the procedure file named MyCustom.prg.

```
*** MyCustom.prg
*
CLASS MyBrowse(fn) OF Browse(fn) CUSTOM
   LOCAL xAlias, xCnt, xFields, x
   *
   xAlias=""
   DO CASE
      CASE UPPER(RIGHT(form.view, 4)) = ".DBF"
         xAlias = LEFT(form.view, AT(".", form.view)-1)
      CASE UPPER(RIGHT(form.view, 4)) = ".QBE"
         IF TYPE(form.AliasName)="C"
            xAlias = form.AliasName
         ENDIF
       CASE TYPE("form.AliasName")="C" .and.
LEN(form.AliasName)>0
           xAlias = form.AliasName
    ENDCASE
   *
   xCnt=0
   xFields=""
   IF LEN(xAlias)>0
     for x= 1 to fldcount(xAlias)
```

```
        x1=flength(x,xAlias)
        x2=len(field(x,xAlias))
        xCnt = xCnt+iif(x1>x2,x1,x2)+5
        xFields=xFields+iif(len(xfields)>0,",  ","")+;
        xAlias+"->"+field(x,xAlias)
      next
    ENDIF
    *
    this.Alias = xAlias
    this.Fields = xFields
    this.Text = Upper(xAlias)+ "Information"
    this.width = iif((form.width-2)>xCnt .and. xCnt<>0,;
    xCnt,form.width-4)
    this.top = form.height-14
    this.left = 2
    Store .F. to this.Toggle, this.Append, this.Delete, ;
            this.Modify, this.ShowRecNo
ENDCLASS
```

Placing code inside a CLASS definition. Although the general syntax does not specifically show that you can add *any* procedural dBASE code inside a Class, you can. You may need to write some procedural code that will determine the values of properties based on property values of the form or public memory variables. This can be useful when building general Custom Control Classes.

Understanding the new BROWSE Class code

The following sections dissect the code in the preceding BROWSE Class. The code is broken into two sections.

- Defining an environment
- Reassigning default values

Setting up the environment for Custom BROWSE Class. The first part of the code sets up the environment so that the BROWSE Class can be used with the form Class MyForm or any other form Class. It comprises traditional procedural-type code. The first part of the code declares several memory variables as local.

```
LOCAL xAlias, xCnt, xFields, x
*
```

After the memory variables are declared, a memory variable named **xAlias** will be given a value based on several conditions. The xAlias variable will be used to set the **Alias** property of BROWSE.

```
xAlias=""
DO CASE
      CASE UPPER(RIGHT(form.view, 4)) = ".DBF"
```

```
            xAlias = LEFT(form.view, AT(".", form.view)—1)
         CASE UPPER(RIGHT(form.view, 4)) = ".QBE"
            IF TYPE(form.AliasName)="C"
               xAlias = form.AliasName
            ENDIF
          CASE TYPE("form.AliasName")="C" .and.
LEN(form.AliasName)>0
              xAlias = form.AliasName
    ENDCASE
    *
```

Notice that the code considers the possibility of using a .DBF or a .QBE. It also accounts for no view being set by the form. Once xAlias's value has been determined, two new memory variables are declared xCnt and xFields.

xCnt will be used to hold the maximum width of the BROWSE object. The width of the BROWSE object will depend on the length of the fields in the table being browsed and the total width of the form. It will be no greater than the form width. xFields is used to hold the names of the fields that will be browsed.

```
xCnt=0
   xFields=""
   IF LEN(xAlias)>0
     for x= 1 to fldcount(xAlias)
        x1=flength(x,xAlias)
        x2=len(field(x,xAlias))
        xCnt = xCnt+iif(x1>x2,x1,x2)+5
        xFields=xFields+iif(len(xfields)>0,",;
          ","")+xAlias+"->"+field(x,xAlias)
     next
   ENDIF
   *
```

The code steps through the structure of the table (xAlias) using three new functions in Visual dBASE: FLDCOUNT(), FLENGTH() and FIELD().

- FldCount() returns the total number of fields in the table.
- Flength() returns the length of a specific field.
- Field() returns the name of a specific field.

Once the environment has been set up, the Class definition changes several of the default values for any BROWSE objects that will be created by the Class.

Changing default property values. If an alias name is available, the Class will assign it to the *Alias* property. If fields are specified for the Alias, they will be assigned to the *Fields* property. Several of the position properties will also be set based on the form width and height. Finally, several of the Edit properties will be set.

The code to accomplish this is

```
   this.Alias = xAlias
```

```
this.Fields = xFields
this.Text = Upper(xAlias)+ "Information"
this.width = iif((form.width-2)>xCnt .and. xCnt<>0,;
xCnt,form.width-4)
this.top = form.height-14
this.left = 2
Store .F. to this.Toggle, this.Append, this.Delete, ;
        this.Modify, this.ShowRecNo
```

Notice the last line uses the **STORE** command to store a false (.f.) value to several properties at once.

Exploring the keywords *this* versus *form*. The Class definition uses both of the special object reference variables—*this* and *form*. The main difference between them is when they are used.

The *this* reference variable is used as a place holder for the name of the object that will be assigned when the object is instantiated. It can only be used at the same level that it is referenced. This means that if you create a new Class for some object, say, a BROWSE class, the *this* can be used at the BROWSE object level only. It cannot be used to reference a property in the form where it will be contained.

If you need to reference a property in the container form that will hold the object, you use the *form* Object Reference Variable.

The following code demonstrates this.

```
CLASS MyBROWSE(fn) OF BROWSE(fn)
    this.Top = 2
    this.Width = form.Width-4
ENDCLASS
```

The special reference variable name *this* will be replaced later by the name of the BROWSE object that is instantiated by the class MyBROWSE. The special reference variable name *form* will be replaced later by the name of the FORM object that the Browse object is placed inside of.

In the preceding example, you could have used the parameter variable *fn* instead of the name *form*., and *fn* would hold the form name at the time the form is created.

The following code could be used to show how *this* and *form* will be replaced:

```
SET PROC TO <procedure file with Class MyBROWSE in it>
f = NEW FORM()
b = NEW MYBROWSE(f)
? f.width
? b.width
```

The *this* variable will be replaced with the name **"B"** and the *form* variable will be replaced with the name **"F"** when the form object and Browse object are created.

Using the Custom Browse Control

Once the Custom Browse Control named MyBrowse is created, you can use it to create Custom Browse objects inside the Custom form MyForm. The following code uses both Custom Classes for some forms.

```
SET PROCEDURE TO MYCUSTOM
f1= NEW MyFORM()
*
creates an empty Browse object inside the form with an Exit
button
*
b1 = NEW MYBROWSE(f1)
f1.Open()
*
f = NEW MyForm()
f.view = "CUSTOMER.dbf"
*
*  creates a Browse object with a table displayed
*
b1= NEW MyBrowse(f)
f.Open()
```

Figure 7–9 shows the form, *f*, opened with the Custom Browse, *b*1, using the table Customer. Underneath this form is another form named *f*1 that has a Browse object with no table associated with it. If you move the form *f*, you can see both forms.

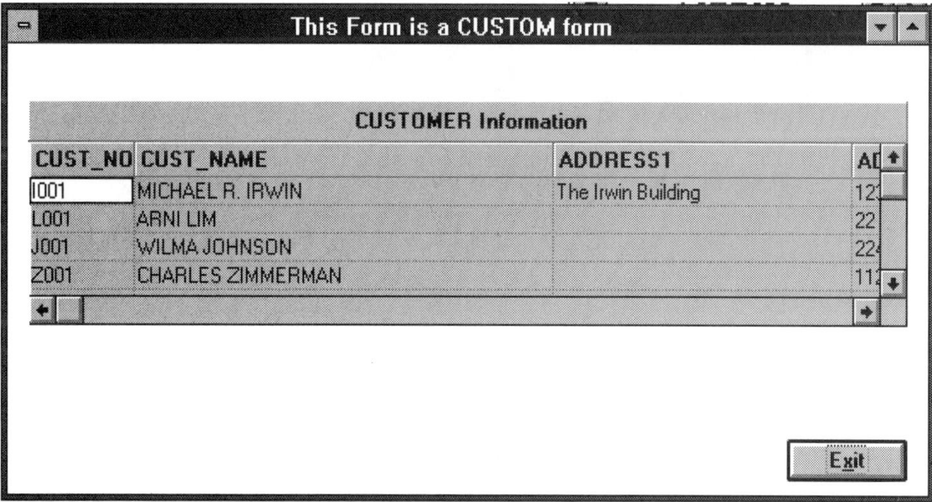

Figure 7–9. A Custom form with a Custom Browse object contained inside it.

Because you specified a .DBF view for the form, the Custom BROWSE Class MyBrowse automatically assigned the Alias and all the field names for the table to the Browse object.

Creating a custom EDITOR Class

The EDITOR class is used to view and edit text files or memo fields. It is the tool of choice for editing memo fields inside their own frame contained in a form.

Memo fields and forms

If you do not create an Editor control object for the memo field, the memo field will be a MEMO MARKER on the form. If the use activates the memo marker by double-clicking in it or pressing the **F9** key, a separate window (form) will be opened inside Visual dBASE with the memo-field contents displayed.

Figure 7–10 shows a Customer form with a memo-field window active.

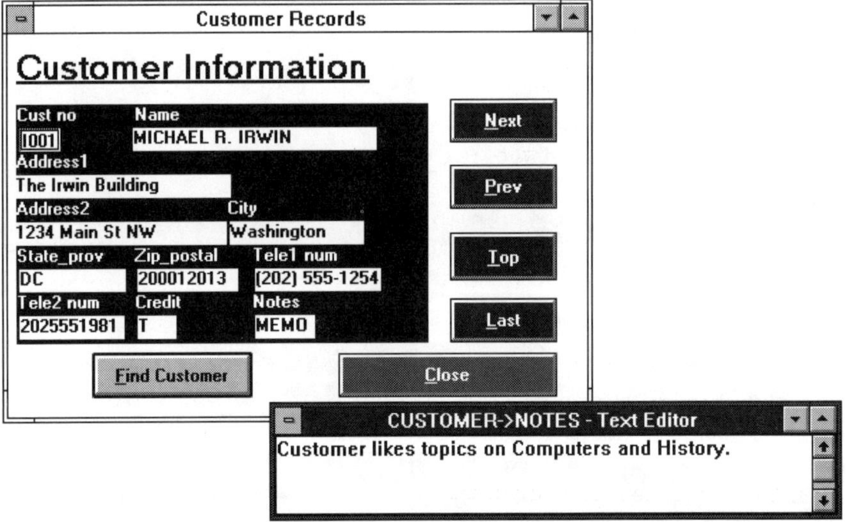

Figure 7–10. A memo field active in a separate window.

Notice that the window (form) for the memo in Figure 7–10 is separate from the form window. It was automatically created by dBASE when the user double-clicked in the MEMO marker in the form.

The MDI property. If you set the MDI property of your form to .F., the memo window (form) will be inside the dBASE frame, and your form will run outside of it, in Windows proper. This can be a problem. Your form will be running on the Windows desktop, and dBASE for Windows may be minimized. However, the memo-field window will be in the minimized dBASE. You will not be able to see your memo-field contents.

The Editor and the memo field

When you use an Editor object for the memo field, the memo field will be displayed as text in the form. Figure 7–11 shows a different Customer form that has an Editor object linked to a memo field. Notice that the Editor object is in the center of Figure 7–11. The Editor is the window alongside of the word "Notes." An Editor object can be set to any size and placed anywhere on the form.

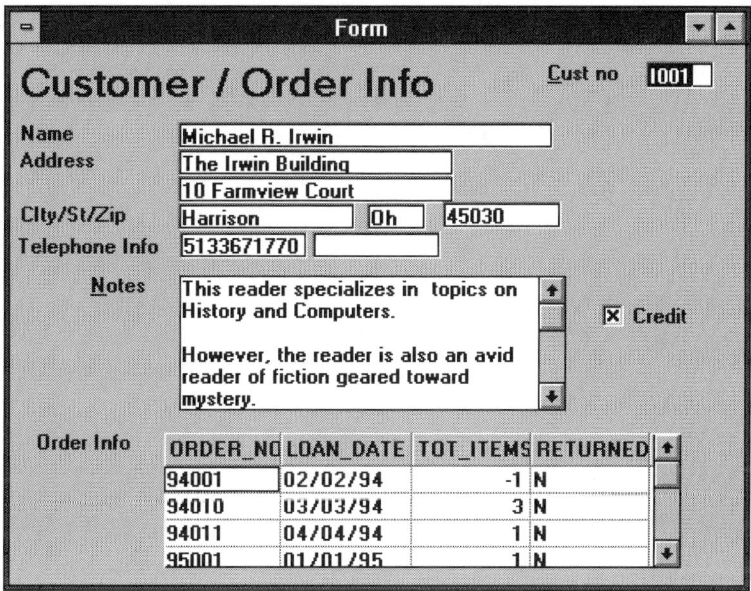

Figure 7–11. A form with an Editor object linked to a memo field.

The syntax for a new Editor Class

The general syntax for creating a new Editor class is

```
CLASS <NewClName>(param1, [param2]) OF EDITOR(param1, [param2])
   [CUSTOM]
   <constructor code>
   <declaration code>
ENDCLASS
```

This syntax is identical to the syntax you used to create a Custom BROWSE Class. (You use the Class name EDITOR instead of BROWSE.) Like BROWSE, it also requires one parameter and can use the keyword CUSTOM.

Parameters for Custom Editor Classes. You must pass one parameter to a Custom Editor class—the one that will hold the form name. The name of the parameter (variable) must be the same for the New Class Name and the EDITOR class name—but the name is not important. The following are all valid examples of defining a new Editor Class with one parameter:

```
CLASS MyEditor(f) OF EDITOR(f)
CLASS TheMemoEditor(fname) OF EDITOR(fname)
```

Placing code inside a CLASS definition. You are not limited to creating new properties, values for properties, and new methods inside an Editor class; you can also add procedural code like you did in the BROWSE Control class.

A Custom EDITOR Class

You may want to create a general EDITOR Class that will create a small Editor window in the bottom, left corner of a form and set the Wrap property to .t.

The following Editor CLASS code will create a new class called MyEditor and place it in the form near the bottom and have the Wrap property set to .t. It should be added to the procedure file named MyCustom.prg:

```
CLASS MyEditor(fn) OF EDITOR(fn)
     LOCAL xLink,xAlias
     xLink = ""
     IF TYPE("form.AliasName")="C" .and. LEN(form.AliasName)>0
        xAlias=form.AliasName
        for x= 1 to fldcount(xAlias)
           IF TYPE(field(x))= "M"
               xLink=Field(x)
           ENDIF
        next
   ENDIF
     this.datalink = xLink
     this.Top = form.height-5
     this.left = 2
     this.width = 42
     this.height = 4
     this.Wrap = .t.
ENDCLASS
```

Using the Custom Editor Control

Once the custom editor Class named MyEditor is created, you can use it to create Custom Editor objects inside the custom form MyForm or any form. The following code uses the Editor class in two different forms.

```
SET PROCEDURE TO MYCUSTOM
f1 = NEW MyFORM()
*    creates an empty editor object inside a blank form
(unlinked)
*
*
e1 = NEW MYEDITOR(f1)
f1.Open()
*
f = NEW MyForm()
f.view = "customer.dbf"
f.AliasName = "Customer"
*        creates an editor linked to a field in the table
customer
*        and placed inside the form
*
e1 = NEW MYEDITOR(f)
f.Open()
```

Figure 7–12 shows the two forms, *f*1 and *f*, one on top of the other, opened with the custom editor, *e*1. Notice that the bottom form (*f*) is using the table Customer and linked to the field NOTES, whereas the other does not (*f*1).

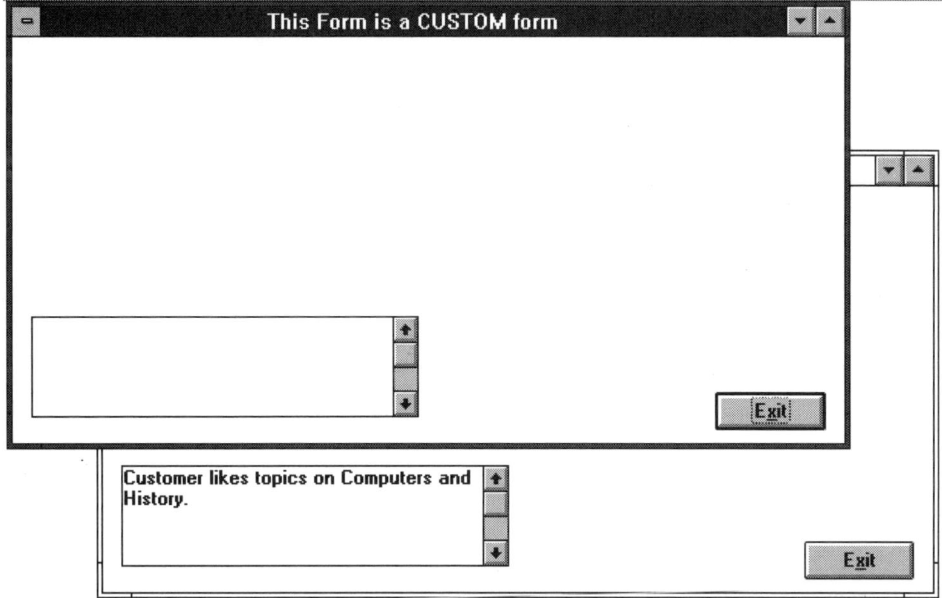

Figure 7–12. Two custom forms with a custom Editor object contained inside it.

Creating a custom ENTRYFIELD Class

The ENTRYFIELD Class is used to get information. Entryfield objects are similar to memory variables that are associated with the @ . . . GET command. They can be linked to a field in a table and are always contained in a form.

The EntryField and database fields

When you use an EntryField object in a form, it can be linked to a database (table) field by setting a property of the entryfield named DataLink.

The Syntax for a new EntryField Class

The general syntax for creating a new EntryField Class is

CLASS <ClName>(param1, [param2]) OF ENTRYFIELD(param1, [param2])

[CUSTOM]

<constructor code>

<declaration code>

ENDCLASS

This syntax is identical to the syntax you used to create a Custom Browse and Editor Class. (You named it EDITOR or BROWSE instead.) Like the previous Classes, it requires one parameter for the form name and can use the keyword CUSTOM.

A Custom ENTRYFIELD Class to convert uppercase

You may want to create a general ENTRYFIELD class that will assign different default values from the ones used by the standard ENTRYFIELD Class.

In addition, you may want to create your own ENTRYFIELD Class and define a method that can be used on the entryfield object. For instance, you may want to create an entryfield that will convert all the text inside the object to uppercase or proper case (first initial uppercase, with the remainder lowercase).

The following Entryfield Class code will create a new Class called MyEntUpper and change a couple of the default properties. It will also create a method called FixText that will convert all the code to uppercase. It should be placed in your procedure file named MYCUSTOM.

```
CLASS MyEntUpper(fn) OF ENTRYFIELD(fn)
   this.width = 45
   this.OnChange = CLASS::Fixtext

   PROCEDURE Fixtext
     this.value = UPPER(this.value)
```

```
   RETURN ""
ENDCLASS
```

This is the first Class code that you have created where a method (FixText) has been declared (written) inside the Class.

Using the Custom Entryfield Control

Once the Custom Entryfield Class named MyEntUpper is created, you can use it to create custom entryfield objects inside the custom form MyForm or any form. The following code uses the entryfield from the MyEntUpper Class:

```
SET PROC TO MYCUSTOM
f=NEW MyForm()
g1=NEW MyEntUpper(f)
g1.Top = 10.5
g1.Left = 48
g1.Width = 30
f.Open()
```

Notice that you still have to set the Top, Left, and Width properties of the new entryfield. Now that the form is open, it should look like the one in Figure 7–13.

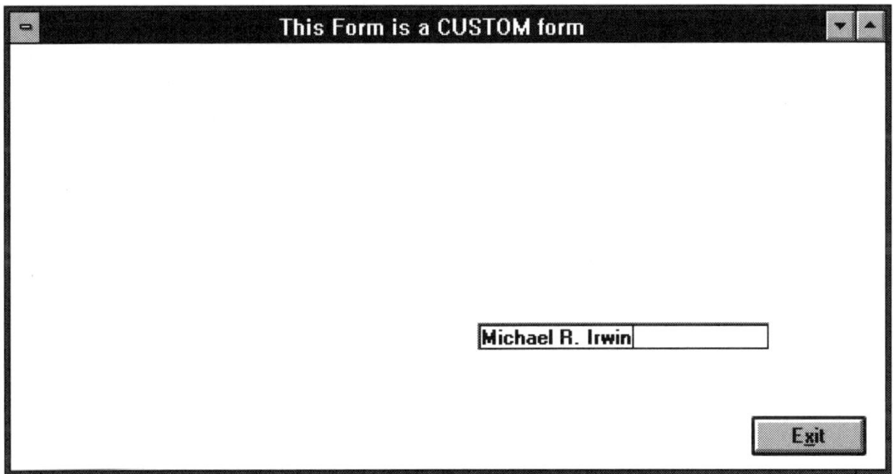

Figure 7–13. An entryfield created from a Custom Entryfield Class.

Activating the OnChange Event Handler. To activate the internal FixText() method, go to the field by tapping the **Tab** key. Once in the field, type in your name, in mixed case (uppercase and lowercase), and press the **Tab** key to go to the Exit button. The text will immediately change to uppercase.

Creating a custom TEXT class

The TEXT Class is used to create text objects with your own default property values. For instance, you may want to have a Text Class that will create Title-type text. Entryfield objects are always contained in a form.

The syntax for a new Text class

The general syntax for creating a new Text Class is

```
CLASS <ClName>(param1, [param2]) OF TEXT(param1, [param2])
   [CUSTOM]
   <constructor code>
   <declaration code>
ENDCLASS
```

This syntax is identical to the syntax you've used for all the other Custom Control Classes. (You named it TEXT instead.) Like the other Custom Classes, it requires one parameter for the form name and can use the keyword CUSTOM.

Creating a new Text Class

You may want to create a new Text Class for creating Title-type text. The following code will create a class for specifying titles. It should be placed in your procedure file named MYCUSTOM:

```
CLASS MyTitleText(fn) OF TEXT(fn)
   this.ColorNormal =  ;

IIF(TYPE("form.Color1")="C",form.Color1,form.ColorNormal)
   this.text = UPPER(form.View)+" Information"
   this.top = .2
   this.left = 1
   this.height = 2
   this.width = 71
   this.FontSize = 14
   this.FontUnderline = .t.
ENDCLASS
```

Using the Custom Text Control

The following code uses the Text from the MyTitleText Class:

```
SET PROC TO MYCUSTOM
f=NEW MyForm()
```

```
t=NEW MyTitleText(f)
f.Open()
```

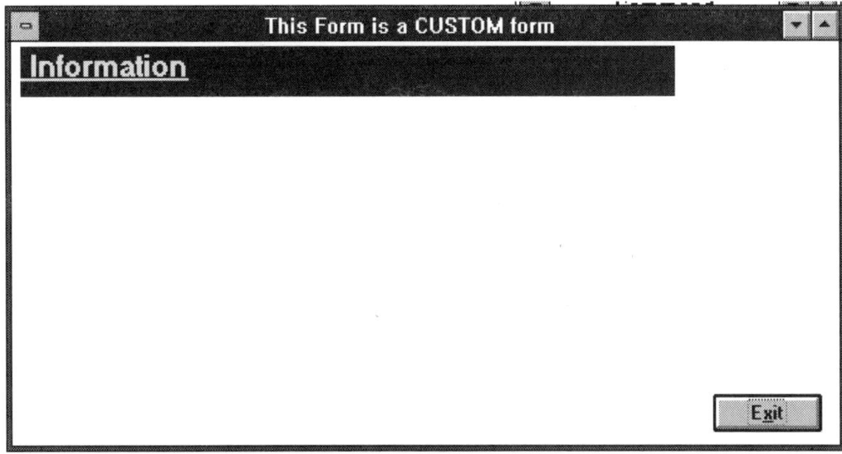

Figure 7–14. A Text object created from a custom Text Class.

Figure 7–14 shows the Text object (*t*) created by the custom Text Class named MyTitleText.

Putting all the classes to work

After you create all of your Custom Classes, to create forms and control objects, you can use them to create any number of objects. Remember, your Custom-created Classes must be available in memory if you want to use them. You can place them in memory by creating them in one or more procedure files and loading the procedure files in memory.

Once they are in memory, you can use a few lines of code to create powerful forms. The following twelve lines of code can create a form with all the special Classes that you made:

```
SET PROCEDURE TO MyCustom
f = NEW MyForm()
f.view = "Customer.dbf"
t = NEW MyTitleText(f)
b1= NEW MyBrowse(f)
f.AliasName = "Customer"
e= NEW MyEditor(f)
g1= NEW MyEntUpper(f)
g1.top = 10.5
g1.left = 48
g1.width = 30
f.open()
```

With only twelve lines of code, you can quickly create a functional program that lets you work with the information stored in the Customer table. Notice that the only two objects that are not connected to fields are the two entryfield objects created from MyEntUpper and MyEntProper classes. However, if you type some information into these two fields, and tab out of them, they will correct the text—one will turn everything upper case and the other proper case.

Figure 7–15 shows the form with all the new objects created and functional from the twelve lines of code.

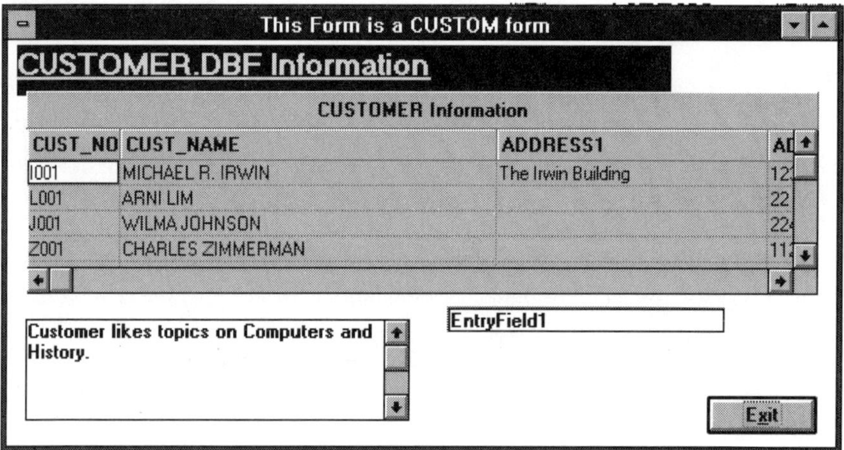

Figure 7–15. The form and its contained control objects created from twelve lines of code.

Part III Advanced Programming Techniques

Chapter 8
Preprocessor, Memory Variables, Sessions, and Compiling

This chapter explores the use of preprocessor directives, the scope and use of memory variables, naming conventions, and using sessions for running your applications in. Finally, it explores compiling your code and building Windows-based applications with the *optional* Visual dBASE Compiler.

Visual dBASE Preprocessor Directives (Commands)

Visual dBASE has a preprocessor built in. Using preprocessor commands, or directives, you can write your programs using words like "mainColor" instead of "w+/B." You can add code that will work in two different versions of dBASE, and have Visual dBASE compile the correct code for each version—for instance, a UNIX version or a Windows version. Then, at the time you compile your code, Visual dBASE will run the built-in preprocessor and replace those user-specified words with the correct literal wording or eliminate any unnecessary code based on the current version. It will require that you identify the wording or code that needs to be changed or eliminated.

The compiler and the preprocessor

According to Borland, dBASE uses a compiler that performs a single pass for compiling the code, with a built-in preprocessor. Actually, the compiler does three steps.

1. Looks through the code for preprocessor directives
2. If any exist, performs the preprocessor directives and creates an intermediate program file
3. Compiles the program file (intermediate one, if preprocessor directives exist)

When dBASE begins to compile a program (.prg, .qbe, .wfm, . . .), it first scans all of the code in the program for preprocessor directives (commands). If it finds any directives (which always begin with the pound sign—#), it evaluates them, does what they specify, and generates a temporary or intermediate program file. This intermediate file is a modified version of the original program file. Then it takes this modified .PRG and actually compiles it (from the .PRG to .PRO program, etc.).

The actual compiler only goes through the program one time (single pass). However, dBASE first runs the application program through a filtering system (preprocessor).

Pseudocompiled code

When Visual dBASE runs a program, it runs the .PRO file (or .WFO, . . .), not the .PRG file (or .WFM, . . .). This means that it must first convert the source code in a .PRG to the compiled code in a .PRO, called the object code.

Many people refer to object code, code in the .PRO, as pseudocompiled code, or p-code. This object code, *.PRO, is not a self-executable program—it still requires Visual dBASE to execute it. It is not a true, independent, self-standing program. Visual dBASE simply converts the code form source text to "tokenized" code. Tokenized code is closer to machine language, but it still requires an application program or a runtime module to read and process it.

➡ **Compiled Visual dBASE code**
Before Visual dBASE, you could only compile your code into object code. These object files end in *.??O—WFO, PRO, and so on. Visual dBASE, with the *optional* Visual dBASE Compiler, can even link these p-code objects into a Windows executable file (*.EXE), using the new BUILD command.

What are preprocessor directives?

A preprocessor directive is a command that is used by dBASE to perform some action prior to compiling the program. The type of actions preprocessors can perform are

- Global "search and replace" operations for variables (symbols) that are constant
- Global "search and replace" operations to expand formulas and functions
- Declare memory variables for the preprocessor (flags)
- Direct conditional compilation
- Specify compiler options

Preprocessor directives can be quickly identified by their names. They always begin with a pound sign (#). Table 8–1 shows the seven preprocessor directives that dBASE recognizes and their purpose.

Table 8–1. The seven dBASE Preprocessor Directives.

Directive	Purpose
`#define`	Defines a symbol or a flag
`#undef`	Undefines a symbol
`#if ... #endif`	Compiles code inside the directives if the condition is true
`#ifdef ... #endif`	Compiles code inside the directives if the symbol (identifier) is true (#define)
`#ifndef ... #endif`	Compiles code inside the directives if the symbol (identifier) is not true (no #define)
`#include`	Inserts code from a file (commonly called a *header file*) at this position
`#pragma`	Specifies the compiler option COVERAGE on | off

How preprocessor directives can help

The preprocessor directives are used by Visual dBASE to prepare your program code for compilation. The preprocessor goes through all the code looking for any commands that it recognizes and performs them on the source code. This modified code is then processed.

A preprocessor can help performance

Many say that using a preprocessor can improve the performance of your application. Depending on how you write code, a preprocessor can, indeed, improve performance.

If you use memory variables to define constants ("soft code"), like color values, a preprocessor can change the memory variable content to "hard-coded" values before the code is compiled. If you tend to use macros to "soft code" conditions that will not change during run time, a preprocessor can change the macro into "hard code" before the code is compiled.

The compiled program has less code. When you use conditional directives (#if, #ifdef, #ifndef), you will actually have less code in the compiled program. Only the conditional code that is true will be compiled; the remainder will be removed from the compiled program.

Preprocessor can aid in maintenance

The best part of using the seven preprocessor directives isn't necessarily performance; rather, preprocessor directives can help make your code more manageable. Statistics show that 90 percent of all programming time is dedicated to the maintenance of applications programs. A big portion of maintenance is adding new routines, and fixing or modifying old routines. This means you need to maintain and review a lot of documentation. Any memory variable usage will need to be documented and traced, their values need to be checked, formulas need to be verified, and interactions between applications need to be considered.

Even with use of object orientation methodologies, checking of formulas, object interactions and relations, and memory variable usage needs to be understood and considered when maintaining programs. Object-oriented programming is not 100 percent fail safe. You still need to create and maintain procedural code that performs the actual data manipulation (replaces, transactions, etc.).

A preprocessor can make code more readable

When you use a preprocessor, you can write code that tends to be self-documenting. Instead of using unrecognizable commands like **"IF n = 27"**, you can write code like **"IF n = Escape_Key_Press"**. This serves two purposes: it makes code more readable (or understandable) and self-documenting at the same time.

Where do you use directives?

Preprocessor directives can be used to help make maintenance and support of your application easier. There are three general types of preprocessor directives.

1. Defining and including
2. Conditional
3. Options

Most people who create defining preprocessor directives place them at the beginning of the main program. However, defining directives (commands) can be placed anywhere in a program.

Conditional directives (#if . . . #endif, #ifdef . . . #endif, and #ifndef . . . #endif) are switches similar to IF . . . ENDIF commands in dBASE; therefore, these types of directives may be sparsely placed throughout the code, although they tend to be at the beginning of a program. The reason for placing them at the beginning is they tend to be used for making decisions concerning what will and won't be compiled into an application.

Like the other directives, the directive #pragma is also found at the beginning of a program because its sole purpose is to set switches for the compiler.

Where to place #define directives

Because preprocessor defining directives (#define) are commands that will be processed prior to compiling the code, it seems to make sense to place them at the beginning of a program. By consistently placing them at the beginning of your code, you can determine if you have used them and know what additional files were included in your code. The goal is to make maintenance of preprocessor code easier.

Assigning #define directives to their own file. You could place all of your #define directives in their own program. Once the #define directives are in their own program, you can #include this program as the first line of any program that needs to use the #define directives. This makes maintenance of the #define directives easier—going to one source program to change or add information to them.

Using the #include directive. When compiling a program, the preprocessor will look for a #include command to include the referenced program in the current one. When Visual dBASE begins to compile a program, it looks for a #include directive (usually the first line of a program). If it finds one, it locates the program that the #include points to and physically places the program, line by line, into the existing program at the location where the #include exists. It actually replaces the #include line with the included program.

The Header file (*.h). The file that is referenced by the #include is usually used for all the define preprocessor directives. This program is commonly referred to as a *header file.* This name, *header file*, originates from the fact that programmers specify use of this file (program) on the first line of the requesting program (the program's head). The header file normally limits itself to preprocessor directives (commands).

For identification purposes, it is identified by use of the simple extension *h* (the letter ***h***), instead of .prg. By naming the header file with an extension of *h*, you can quickly identify it visually. The extension *.**h** is not required, it has just become the de-facto standard among programmers.

! **The #include directive should be used in every program**
Visual dBASE, like most languages, requires the #include directive be placed in all programs that require processing. You cannot simply use the #include directive in the main program and have the preprocessor change all #defines in all programs called by the main program. This is even true when you use the new keyword **AUTO** with the Compile command.

Programs and preprocessor directives

Programs will be easier to understand and work with once you become accustomed to reading and using preprocessor directives. The remainder of this section will use examples to demonstrate use of preprocessor directives.

Traditional code without preprocessor directives

The following code is a traditional program that can be used to run in different versions of Windows dBASE based on a public memory variable xVer50. If xVer50 is true (.t.), then it will run programs that can work in dBASE for Windows 5.0. If it is false (.f.), it will use code built for Visual dBASE and may cause errors in dBASE for Windows 5.0. Both sets of programs (Windows 5.0 and Visual dBASE) do the same thing. The main driver program could be the following code (and anything else you would want to add):

```
*** MYDEMO.prg
*
*  The xVer50 line must be changed depending on where it is run
*            True if the code is run in Version 5.0
*            False if run in Visual dBASE
*
PUBLIC xVer50, xColor1, xColor2
xVer50 = .T.
SET PROCEDURE TO dBPROCS ADDI
IF xVer50
   DO dB5SetUp
ELSE
   DO VdBSetUp
ENDIF
*
*         remainder of the code goes here
*
*** End of MYDEMO.prg
*
```

As you can see, these lines of code become the main driver. They act like a switching station, telling dBASE which programs will be run. When the code is compiled, whether it is for version 5.0 or Visual dBASE, all of the code, except the remarks, will remain in it. This means that both procedure files will also be compiled, although only one is actually used. It also means that every time you run the code, it will have to check and see if xVer50 exists and what it is set to.

This example is simplistic. A real application would probably have hundreds of lines of code for each version.

In traditional code, conditional setting must always be checked. For example, the following procedure file can be used to run programs for both conditions of xVer50:

```
***  DBPROCS.prg
```

```
*
PROCEDURE dB5SetUp
    xColor1 = "W*/B"
    xColor2 =  "GR+/R"
RETURN
*
PROCEDURE VdBSetUp
    xColor1 = "BTNTEXT/APPWORKSPACE"
    xColor2 =  "BTNTEXT/BTNFACE"
RETURN
*
FUNCTION Kilometers_number(xNum)
RETURN xNum*1.6093
FUNCTION ATRIMSTR(xNum)
RETURN TRIM(LTRIM(STR(xNum)))
```

The preceding code identifies setup code specific for dBASE for Windows 5.0 (dB5SetUp) and Visual dBASE (VdBSetUp). It also creates two functions that will be called by the main driver program (or one of the procedures in the procedure file). Because Visual dBASE can use color strings associated with the Windows color scheme, the code can be made more generic and user oriented using color schemes.

All the code in a program is compiled into the .DBO. If all the procedures, even those that aren't necessary, are compiled into one physical program, the .DBO could become unreasonably large, making a larger, more complex compiled program.

The programs running will contain all of the macros, functions, and conditional switches needed for both versions of dBASE. The switches to run the code will be constantly processed even though the actual program is only running in one environment.

Using a preprocessor can eliminate the unneeded code and variable checking.

Traditional code can be confusing. Trying to follow the logic of a program can become confusing. For instance, what does the number 27 mean in the following lines of code?

```
I = INKEY(5)
IF I = 27
   *** do code
ENDIF
```

If, instead, the program line reads: IF I = Escape_key_pressed, you would probably quickly understand that the code is looking for the pressing of the **Esc** key.

Although the example doesn't use the inkey(), readkey(), or lastkey() functions, you probably use them in your applications. When writing code that looks for key presses or scan key values in traditional code, you would look for a number to process. By using a preprocessor, you can write your code using pneumonic words that can be replaced later with their numeric equivalents. This powerful ability to "search and replace" at compile time makes it possible to write this type of code (I = Escape_key_pressed).

Traditional code may use macros. Traditional code may also use macros. Macros, by how they work, slow down the system. A macro must be expanded during runtime, validated, and, finally, processed. For example, in dBASE IV for DOS, when you want to make your colors generic you assign a macro to specify the color at runtime.

Using the preprocessor, you can specify constants using the #define and their color values. Then at compile time, the preprocessor will hard code the colors into the code. This eliminates the need for processing the lines each time they are processed.

Traditional code may repetitively call functions. The two functions ATRIMSTR() and KILOMETERS_NUMBER() must be externally called each time they are used. Then dBASE must process the functions, converting the memory variables or literals into the hard-coded process. Each time a procedure is run, it is located (found), validated, and then run. This process occurs every time the procedure is run. Given all of this occurs in a short period—but it does take unnecessary time.

Using a preprocessor, the literal value of the UDF can be placed in the code at the point where the function is, eliminating the need to call any external procedures.

Main program code with preprocessor directives

The following code is the same MYDEMO.prg, converted, using preprocessor directives. It has ***#include, #ifdef,*** and ***#ifndef*** directives (commands).

```
*** MYDEMO.prg
*     Program : myheader.h is a separate program with  #defines in
      it.
*
#include myheader.h
*
#ifdef xVer50
   *
   *  DO dB5Start program can be run based on xVer50
   *
   *   Because dBASE for Windows 5.0 has no security built in,
this
   *   startup program may be different than the Visual dBASE one
   *
#endif
#ifndef xVer50
   *
   * DO VdBStart program can be run based on NO xVer50
   *
#endif
*
*   xColor1 and BigFont need to be replaced by values in header
*   file
*
fMain = NEW FORM()
DEFINE TEXT Message OF fMain FROM 1.5, 1 TO 3.5, 35 ;
    PROPERTY ColorNormal xColor1, BigFont, Text "100 Miles are"
DEFINE TEXT ConvertIt OF fMain FROM 5,9 TO 5,35 ;
```

```
    PROPERTY ColorNormal xColor2, TEXT " 100 miles = "+ ;
    ATRIMSTR(Kilometers_number(100)) + " kilometers"
fMain.Open()
*
*** End of MYDEMO.prg
```

Comparing this code to the original code, there are no PUBLIC declarations. This eliminates the possibility of some program destroying or changing the values of the public variables.

Once compiled, it will have less code that needs to be evaluated. When the # directives are evaluated, only the code that is true will be placed in the compiled program; the remaining code will be removed.

The header file is used to define the variables and values that will be replaced in the programs.

#IFDEF . . . #ENDIF directive. #ifdef simply means ***if*** something is *defined*, ***ifdef***, then take action. The general syntax is

```
#ifdef <symbol>
   code here . . .
#endif
```

If it isn't defined, simply ignore the code inside it.

The #ifdef . . . #endif directive in the code is used to check and see if a compiler symbol, named xVer50, exists. If it does, then the code inside the condition will be compiled. If it isn't, the code inside the condition will be ignored or thrown out of the compiled program.

The compiler symbol, xVer50, is used like a flag. If it is .t. (exists), then the code is compiled. If it doesn't exist (.f.), then it is not compiled. This compiler symbol is actually known as an *identifier*. An identifier is a preprocessor word that you can create using the #define directive. It is similar to a memory variable name; however, it only exists during the preprocessor precheck for the compiler. It does not even have to exist for the #ifdef to work. In fact, if it isn't defined, the code is simply skipped.

#IFNDEF . . . #ENDIF directive. #ifndef simply means ***if*** something is *not defined*, ***ifndef***, then take action. The general syntax is

```
#ifndef <symbol>
   code here . . .
#endif
```

If the symbol is defined, the #ifndef simply ignores the code that is inside it.

The #ifndef is the exact opposite of the #ifdef directive. In this case, you checked to see if xVer50 did not exist, and if it didn't, then that code would be compiled into the program.

#INCLUDE directive. This directive is actually the easiest. It simply says go out and look for a program that is named after the #include directive and if it does exist, **include** it inside the code. The general syntax is

#include <program name>

In this case you told the program to go out and find a program named MYHEADER.h and once found, place it at the exact spot where the #include directive is. The #include line will actually be replaced with the code inside the myheader.h file.

The #include goes out and gets the *header* file. Once it gets it, it replaces the #include line of the program with the contents of the header file.

The following demonstrates how the #include works:

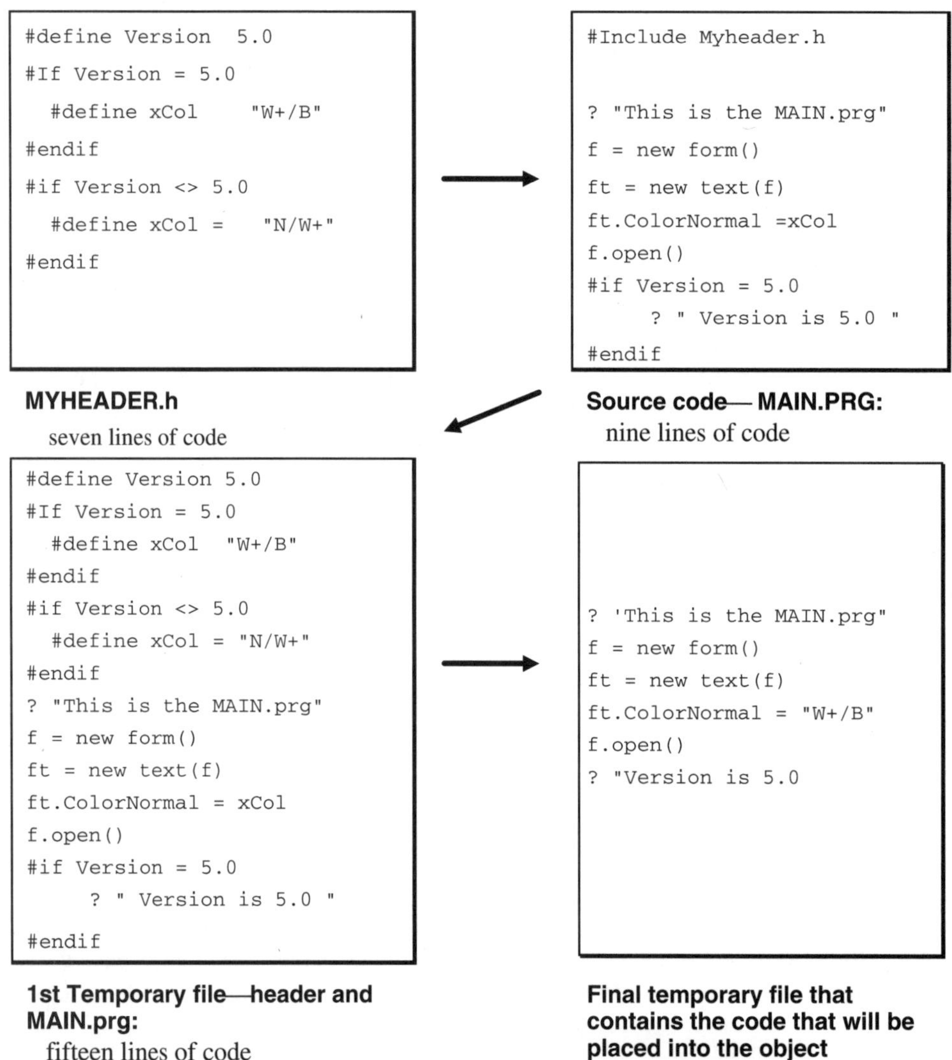

MYHEADER.h
seven lines of code

Source code— MAIN.PRG:
nine lines of code

1st Temporary file—header and MAIN.prg:
fifteen lines of code

Final temporary file that contains the code that will be placed into the object file—MAIN.PRO:
six lines of code

As the preceding programs demonstrate, when you compile the program named MAIN.prg, the following occurs:

1. The compiler looks at the program MAIN.prg (nine lines of code) and checks to see if there are any preprocessor directives in it—# commands.
2. Then the line with the #include MyHeader.h is read and the preprocessor is activated. It goes out, finds the header file (seven lines of code), and places it where the #include line is currently located in the Main.prg.
3. During this process, the preprocessor creates a temporary file, in memory, replacing the #include line with the entire contents of the include file (Myheader.h), adding all of the code from the Main.prg program to the same file (now the temporary program has fifteen lines of code).
4. Then the preprocessor goes through the # directives and processes them. In the preceding case, it
   a) Creates a constant named Version and assigns the value of "5.0" to it.
   b) Then it assigns the value "W+/B" to the constant xCol.
   c) Then it replaces the xCol references with the literal value "W+/B."
5. The code remaining (in this case, six lines) is then sent to the compiler to be compiled into the .PRO file.

Once the final program is compiled, it contains no preprocessor directives or unnecessary code. Notice that the #include directive included the header file into the Main.prg, processed all of the # directives, and sent only those lines of code that must be compiled to the compiler.

The header file for the #include in the main program

The header file has a series of definitions in it. The header file MYHEADER.h that the main program MYDEMO.prg uses is the following:

```
*** MYHEADER.h
*
*    Define a flag named xVer50
*
*  use the following directive create an identifier that will
*  be used by the #ifdef and #ifndef directives
*
*           #define xVer50
*
*  Constant identifier (symbol) color set will replace actual
```

```
*  values
*
# define BigFont Fontname "Arial", FontSize 16
*
#ifdef xVer50
    #define xCOLOR1  "W+/B"
    #define xCOLOR2  "GR+/R"
#endif
*
#ifndef xVer50
    #define xColor1 "BTNTEXT/APPWORKSPACE"
    #define xColor2 "BTNTEXT/BTNFACE"
#endif
*
*   Puts the formula in place of the UDF
*   ATRIMSTR(). In this case it converts a numeric to string and
*   trims it (both sides)
*
#define ATRIMSTR(nNumber)  trim(ltrim(str(nNumber)))
*
*  Places the actual formula in place of the UDF
*  In this case, it converts miles to kilometers
*
#define Kilometers_Number(nMiles)  nMiles * 1.6093
```

This file has a series of #define directives in it. As you see, they can be used to define a symbol, formula, or any identifying constant.

> **!** **Including header files**
> If you have #defines for constants throughout your Visual dBASE programs. Visual dBASE requires that you place the #include file that holds the #defines in *every* program that will need to be fixed.

Constants and #define directives. A constant is something that will not change values during its life. It can be a symbol, memory variable, or a UDF. For instance, most programs that use memory variables to set color, never change the variables values during the program. The variable is used to hold a color that can be changed before the execution of the program.

The #define directive can simply declare a name for an identifier or assign a value to the identifier. The value can be a single value or a formula.

#DEFINE < identifier (symbol or flag) > directive. You can use the #define directive simply to create an identifier name or flag name. The general syntax to create an identifier name is

```
#define <identifier name>
```

The <identifier name> is the name of a constant (like a variable) that you specify. It can be any valid name up to 32 characters long in Visual dBASE. For instance, you created an identifier name in the MYHEADER.h file:

```
#define xVer50
```

The <identifier name> is simply a flag that can be used by the preprocessor's conditional directives to take action on. This was done in the main program with the **#ifdef** and **#ifndef** directives.

sidebar

The __DBASEWIN__ symbol

Both dBASE for Windows 5.0 and Visual dBASE automatically define a compiler symbol named __DBASEWIN__. The name comprises two underscores: the text "DBASEWIN" and two more underscores. You can use this symbol to determine if the code being compiled is one of these versions. This can be helpful if you are writing for platform-specific code DOS versus Windows or UNIX versus Windows.

Although the __DBASEWIN__ constant exists, it will type to unknown if you test for it using the TYPE() function. This is because preprocessor symbols inside quotation marks are not substituted.

Even though the type is unknown, it can be checked to determine if it has a numeric value, using the #IF __dBASEWIN__ = <value>. The value it holds depends on the version of dBASE in Windows.

In Visual dBASE, the #IF __dBASEWIN__ = will be true if you test for values between 5.00 and 6.40, inclusive. In dBASE for Windows 5.0 it will test true for any value greater than 4.0 and less than 6.0. The following code demonstrates this.

sidebar, continued

```
        #IF __dBASEWIN__ = 4.1
* only version 5.0 will have a value less than 5.0
         #DEFINE xColor1 "N/W+"
        #ENDIF
```

As you can see from the preceding code, you can test for version 5.0 and Visual dBASE using this method. A better way to test for version 5.0 or Visual dBASE is to create your own preprocessor symbol based on the string value of __dBASEWIN__ and test for it. In version 5.0 the literal string value for __dBASEWIN__ is 5.0, Visual dBASE is 5.5. The following code demonstrates:

```
        #define MySymbol [__dBASEWIN__ ]
*  defines a constant mysymbol based on the string
*  value of __dbasewin__
        #IF mysymbol = [5.0]
         * version 5.0
         #DEFINE xColor1 "N/W+"
        #ENDIF
        #IF mysymbol = [5.5]
         * Visual dBASE
         #Define xColor1 "WINDOWTEXT/WINDOW"
        #ENDIF
```

Although this method is a little more work, it is more accurate and will let you create code that can be used in both dBASE for Windows 5.0 and Visual dBASE using the preprocessor directives.

#DEFINE < identifier (symbol) name > < replacement text > directive. In addition to using the #define directive to identify a flag (identifier name), you can also use it to assign a meaning to some constant that you create. The general syntax is

#define <identifier name> <replacement text>

The <identifier name> can be any symbol—simple text, a function name, or anything. The <replacement text> is what you want to replace the symbol with when the preprocessor is run. For instance,

```
#define MyName "Michael R. Irwin"
```

If the code has a line like

```
this.name = Myname
```

the compiler will change the line to read

```
this.name = "Michael R. Irwin"
```

In other words, the #define directive will be used by the preprocessor at the time the program is compiled to perform a *global search and replace* in your program. It will look through the code for the <identifier text>. If it finds the <identifier text>, it will replace it with the <replacement text>.

There are five definitions given in the header file that do this.

```
# define BigFont Fontname "Arial", FontSize 16
#define xCOLOR1   "W+/B"
#define xCOLOR2   "GR+/R"
#define xColor1   "BTNTEXT/APPWORKSPACE"
#define xColor2   "BTNTEXT/BTNFACE"
```

Anywhere the words BigFont, xColor1, and xColor2 are found, they will be replaced with their associated values.

Notice that the word BigFont will be replaced with the string value—**Fontname "Arial", FontSize 16**. Every place the word BigFont is located in code, it will be replaced with the entire string. The color identifier xColor1 will be replaced with the literal "**W+/B**" or the literal "**BTNTEXT/APPWORKSPACE**" depending on the xVer50 switch (version 5.0 or Visual dBASE). This process of replacing the symbol with its literal value also occurs with the second identifier (xColor2). When the codes are compiled, the preprocessor will find all occurrences of xColor1, xColor2, and BigFont, and replace them with their literal value. In other words, a preprocessor is a true global search and replace.

The following demonstrates how the #define constant will be replaced:

```
BEFORE replacement        this.ColorNormal = xColor2
```

After the preprocessor #define is processed the line will now read

```
AFTER replacement         this.ColorNormal = "GR+/R"
```

sidebar

Using preprocessor to replace text in quotations

The preprocessor will not replace text that is found in quotations, in your code. For instance, the following demonstrates

```
#define BTNFACE R+
f = new form()
f.ColorNormal = "/BTNFACE"
f.open()
```

The identifier text BTNFACE specified in the #define will not be recognized and changed in the preceding code at the line f.ColorNormal = "/BTNFACE" from its current value to "/R+". This can be a real problem when attempting to work with forms created in Visual dBASE with dBASE for Windows 5.0. You will be required to go into each form and manually remove the color references of any objects that use the new dBASE color scheme keywords.

In addition to this, the preprocessor will not support a #define directive like this:

```
#define "/BTNFACE" "/R+"
```

The preceding code will report an error at runtime. When defining < identifier text >, you cannot place the *identifier* text in quotations. So, the preprocessor doesn't go inside quotation marks to change text, nor can you specify the <identifier text> using quotations.

This can be problematic when writing code for both dBASE for Windows 5.0 and Visual dBASE. In the examples of this chapter, the code uses constants (like a memory variable) to set colors: xColor1 and xColor2. By using constants like xColor1 you can assign values that do include quotations in the #define:

```
#define xColor3 "GB+/N"
```

As this example demonstrates, you can use quotations in the replacement text ("GB+/N"), just not the <identifier text> (xColor3).

#DEFINE < user declared function > ([parameters]) < replacement text > directive. The #define directive can be used to perform *global search and replace* missions in your programs. For instance, it can go through code and look for a user-declared function, replacing it with the <replacement text>. The <replacement text> could be a "hard-coded" formula, another function, or simply anything.

A UDF is one that you reference throughout your code, but do not actually build it into a procedure file or program code. Instead, the function will be placed in the header file using the #define directive. You have a couple of them in the header file.

```
#define ATRIMSTR(nNumber)  trim(ltrim(str(nNumber)))
#define Kilometers_Number(nMiles)  nMiles * 1.6093
```

In the example of the ATRIMSTR() function, it looks for a single parameter, nNumber. The actual function ATRIMSTR() does not exist. Rather, it is the combined functions of Trim(), Ltrim(), and STR() functions. Because it is created with the #define directive, the preprocessor will go through all the code that references the function ATRIMSTR() and physically replace it with the functions TRIM(LTRIM(STR())). For instance, the program code could have the following line:

```
BEFORE replacement              ? ATRIMSTR(100)
```

The preprocessor will go out to that line, using the #define directive and replace it with

```
AFTER replacement               ? TRIM(Ltrim(STR(100)))
```

Code that will use all of the #define directives

The actual code in the program that will use all of these #defines, in the header file, is the following:

```
fMain = NEW FORM()
DEFINE TEXT Message OF fMain FROM 1.5, 1 TO 3.5, 35 ;
    PROPERTY ColorNormal xColor1, BigFont, Text "100 Miles are"
DEFINE TEXT ConvertIt OF fMain FROM 5,9 TO 5,35 ;
    PROPERTY ColorNormal xColor2, TEXT " 100 miles = "+ ;
    ATRIMSTR(Kilometers_number(100)) + " kilometers"
fMain.Open()
```

The global search and replace. The #defines of the header file will be used by the compiler to go through the code and replace the #define references with their actual values. Table 8–2 shows the identifier and what it will be replaced with based on the preceding code:

Table 8–2. Using Global Search and Replace with #define Identifiers.

Identifier (Symbol)	Replacement text
#ifdef xVer50 (xVer50 exists) PROPERTY ColorNormal xColor1	PROPERTY ColorNormal "W+/B"
#ifdef xVer50 PROPERTY ColorNormal xColor2	PROPERTY ColorNormal "GR+/R"
#ifndef xVer50 (xVer50 isn't there) PROPERTY ColorNormal xColor1	PROPERTY ColorNormal "BTNTEXT/APPWORKSPACE"
#ifndef xVer50 PROPERTY ColorNormal xColor2	PROPERTY ColorNormal "BTNTEXT/BTNFACE"
ATRIMSTR(nNumber)	TRIM(LTRIM(STR(nNumber)))
Kilometers_Number(nMiles)	nMiles * 1.6093

As Table 8–2 shows, the symbols (left column) that are used in the code from above will be replaced with the text (right column) before the program is actually compiled.

Putting it all together

To demonstrate how this works, make sure that the main program MYDEMO.prg references the #include header file MyHeader.h as the first line of the program. Then look at the header file and make sure that you haven't defined xVer50. If you have, as in the header file above, make sure that it is remarked off—* #DEFINE xVer50. Compile the MYDEMO.prg and run it, following these steps.

```
COMPILE MYDEMO
DO MYDEMO
```

Figure 8–1 shows the form created from the MyDemo program. This form uses the colors specified by Windows, based on the button colors and the application background color. It uses them because the define constant xVer50 did not exist at the time the program was compiled. In the case of the form in Figure 8–1, the top text is black on white, and the bottom text is black on gray.

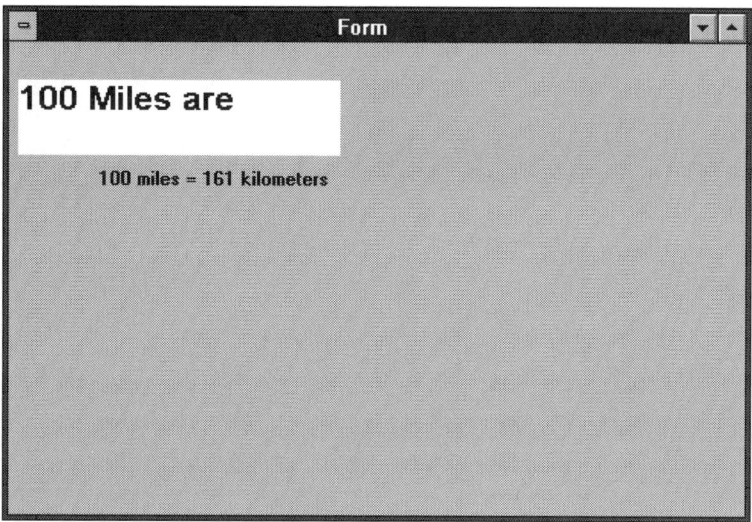

Figure 8–1. This is the form from the compiled program MyDemo.prg.

To prove that the form is running and using the Windows color palette, start the Windows Control Panel; select the Color dialog box; and change the colors of the button text, button face, and application background. Figure 8–2 shows changing colors in Windows. Notice that the Color Palette button has been pressed displaying the color palette for selecting new colors.

When you press the OK button of the Color setting dialog box, the new colors will be set. These new colors will take effect in your compiled program.

The application created by the compiler has removed all of the code associated with the #ifdef, changed xColor1, xColor2, and BigFont to their actual values, and assigned the actual function values to the user-declared functions, Kilometers_Number() and ATRIMSTR().

Now modify the header file MYHEADER.h, and add or uncomment the line to the top of the program.

```
#define xVer50
```

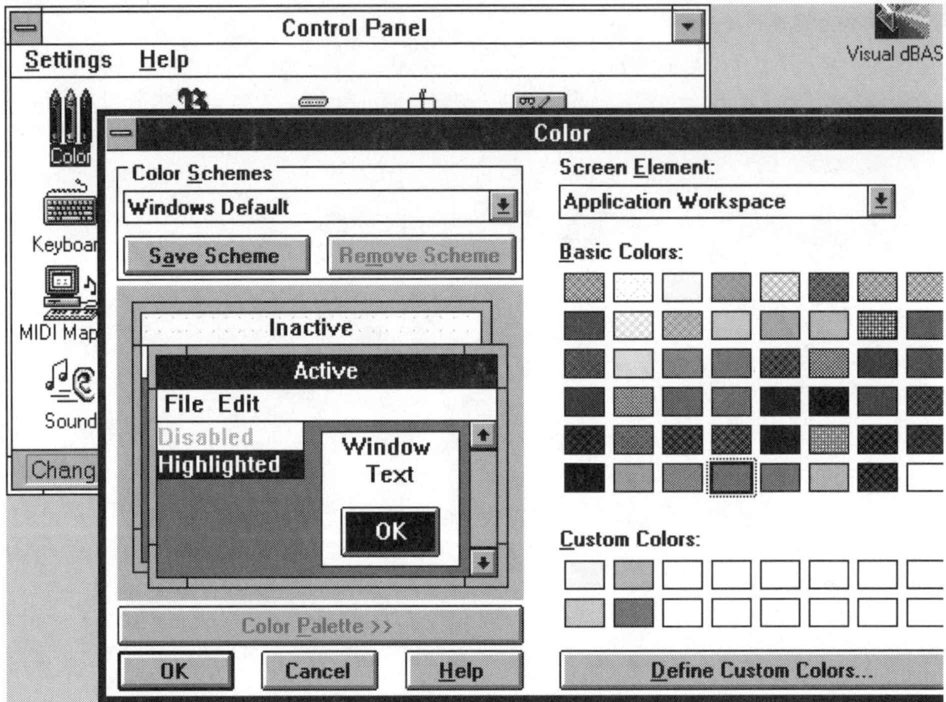

Figure 8–2. This is the Control Panel program changing Windows colors.

Now save the file and retype in the following commands:

```
COMPILE MYDEMO
DO MYDEMO
```

Because xVer50 is defined, the .pro created will create a form based on the colors white over blue and yellow over red. Changing the Windows color will not affect the form from the program MyDemo.prg because you are no longer using the dBASE color scheme keywords.

Memory Variables in Visual dBASE

Although Visual dBASE is object oriented, and a big chunk of your code can be placed in objects, thus hiding it, you will still find yourself using memory variables to manipulate some calculations, actions, or objects.

dBASE has increased the flexibility of memory variables in dBASE by giving you two new types.

What are memory variables?

A memory variable is simply a location in memory that has a value stored in it. This location is referred to by a name—the memory variable name. The value stored can be a number, a date, a logical, a string, or even an array of variables.

Memory variables are created for a wide range of purposes. However, they are mainly used to store temporary values for things like the following:

- Constant values, like global configuration settings (color, talk on, etc.)
- Calculations, for performing and storing the results
- Determine the flow of a program (IF xVariable, DO WHILE xVar ...

Creating a memory variable

You can create a memory variable in two ways:

- Using the equal sign (=)
- Using the STORE command

The = sign for setting values. If you need to set a different value for each variable, use the equal sign to set it. The following are examples of setting memory variable values:

nDtOfBirth = {01/02/65}

nAge = 43

nName = “James Johnson”

The STORE command. If you need to assign the same value to several variables, you can assign each one separately using the equal sign, or use the STORE command to assign the value to several at one time.

The following code demonstrates storing a single value to many variables.

```
STORE 5 TO nCnt, nTotal, nStep
STORE "" TO cName, cAddress, cCity, cSt_Prov
STORE 5.5 TO this.Top, this.Left, this.Height
```

When you assign a value to more than one variable, separate each variable name with a comma.

NOTE: Assigning a single value to multiple properties

Notice that the last line uses the STORE command to assign a value to several properties (Top, Left, and Height). Because a property behaves the same as a simple memory variable, the STORE command can be used to assign the same value to multiple properties at the same time.

Naming memory variables

Visual dBASE lets you name memory variables following these rules:

1. It can consist of characters, numbers, and the underscore.
2. It can also contain a space if you delimit the name with colons.
3. It must begin with an alphabetic character (*A* to *Z*).
4. It can be up to thirty-two characters long.

All of the following are valid memory variable names:

```
xCnt = 1
d1stBirthDate = {02/03/66}
My_Full_Name_Is = "Michael Richard Irwin"
:The Address is: = "The Irwin Building"
```

Notice the last one has spaces in the name. If you use spaces, the name of the variable must be delimited with colons (**:**).

Declaring memory variables

Usually you will *declare* a memory variable before you use it. Declaring a variable gives it a *scope*. The scope is simply its availability (which programs can use it) and its life span (how long it stays alive).

dBASE has always supported two variable types.

- Public
- Private

Now it has two new variable types.

- Local
- Static

Using these four types, you have focused power over how and when the variable will be used.

Although dBASE does not require that you declare variable types, it is usually a good idea to do so. To declare a variable type, you can use one of four commands: PUBLIC, PRIVATE, LOCAL, and STATIC. When you declare a variable as PUBLIC or STATIC, dBASE will automatically declare it and initialize it with a value of false (.f.).

Declaring versus initializing

When you use one of the four commands, PUBLIC, PRIVATE, LOCAL, and STATIC, you are declaring the name of a variable to be a certain type. When you assign a value to a variable for the first time, you are initializing it.

Declaring variables

The following are all examples of declaring variables:

```
PUBLIC nCNT, lOpen, cName
PRIVATE xName, dDtOfBirth
LOCAL lClose, cAddress
STATIC nTotal, cOldAddress
```

Using the scope command you declare the variables as a certain type. The variables *nCnt, lOpen,* and *cName* have been **declared** PUBLIC; *lClose, cAddress* have been **declared** LOCAL.

Initialize a variable. The first time you give a variable a value, you are initializing it. The following are all examples:

```
STORE 0 to nTotal, nCnt, nAge
lClose = .T.
lOpen = .F.
cOldAddress = "1600 Pennsylvania Ave. NW"
```

Default variable types. If you use a variable, by initializing it without specifying a scope, dBASE automatically makes the variable a PRIVATE type.

Understanding memory variable scopes

The *scope* of a memory variable determines it behavior (both its life span and its availability). Each variable type (PUBLIC, PRIVATE, LOCAL, and STATIC) has different rules concerning its life and availability.

Table 8–3 shows the rules for each type:

Table 8–3. Rules for Each Variable Type.

Type (Scope)	Life Span	Availability
PUBLIC	Released with RELEASE or CLEAR ALL commands	All subroutines, whether they are at a higher or lower level in the calling order
PRIVATE	Released when the subroutine that created it is finished	Subroutine that created it and any lower routine
LOCAL	Released when the subroutine that created it is finished	Only the subroutine that created it
STATIC	Released with RELEASE or CLEAR ALL commands	Only the subroutine that created it

Public variables

Public variables, also called *global* variables, have the widest scope. They are available to all programs at all times. They are best used for holding environment settings (forms open, talk on, default path names, login names, etc.).

Public variables offer no protection against changing the value or overwriting its contents. Although programs may use PUBLIC variables, there will be few of them.

Public availability. If you declare a variable named cNAME PUBLIC in a subprogram, all programs in the application can use it. It can be seen by all programs. The following example demonstrates its use.

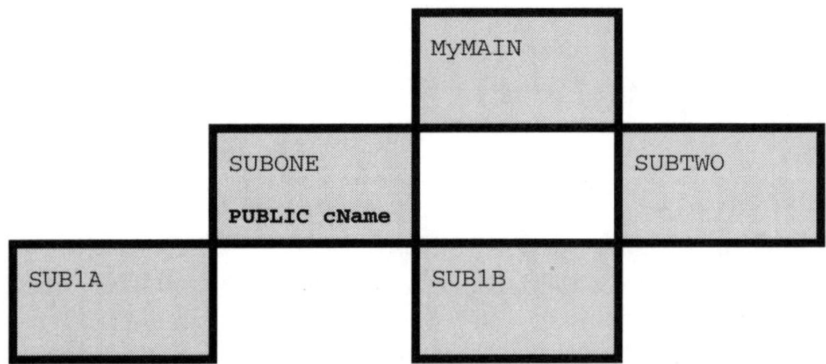

All grayed programs can see, use, and change the value of the PUBLIC variable cName.

Public life span. Public variables are available until a RELEASE or CLEAR ALL command is issued.

Private variables

Private variables are available in the program that declares them and any program lower than them in the chain.

Private availability. If you declare a variable named cNAME PRIVATE in a subprogram, all programs below the program that created it can use it. It can only be seen by programs in the chain below the declaring program. The following example demonstrates its use:

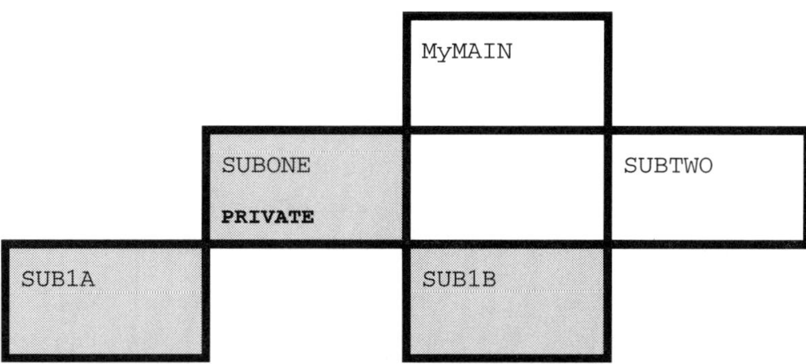

All grayed programs can see, use, and change the value of the PRIVATE variable cName. SUBONE creates it, so SUB1A and SUB2A called by SUBONE can use and change it.

Private Life Span. Private variables are released when SUBONE finishes running and returns control to MYMAIN.

Local variables

Local variables are only available in the program that declares them. No other program (procedure or function) can use or see them.

Local availability. If you declare a variable named cNAME LOCAL in a subprogram, only that program can see—nothing above or below it can see it. Some people call this single procedure availability, *data hiding*, because the variable only has a local scope. The following example demonstrates its use:

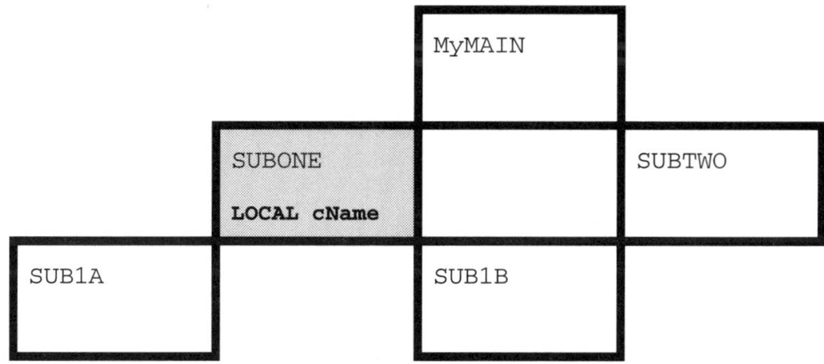

Only the single, grayed program can see, use, and change the value of the LOCAL variable cName. SUBONE creates it, so only SUBONE can see and work with it.

Local life span. Local variables are released when SUBONE finishes running and returns control to MYMAIN.

Static variables

Static variables are only available in the program that declares them. No other program (procedure or function) can use or see them.

Static availability. If you declare a variable named cNAME STATIC in a subprogram, only that program can see—nothing above or below it can see it. However, it will not lose its value when the program is exited. When you return to the program it will have the value it had when you left it. The following example demonstrates its use:

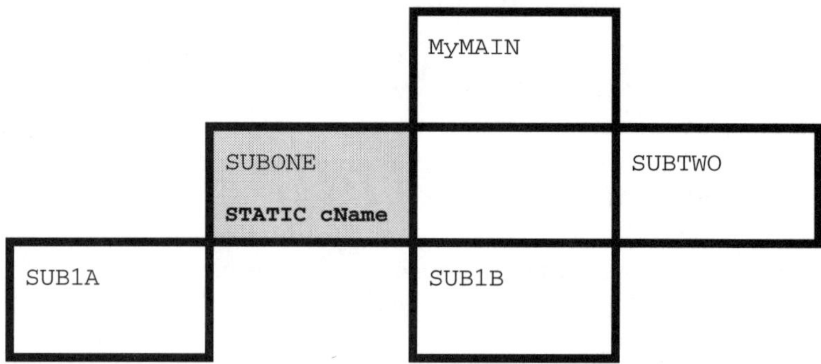

Only the single, grayed program can see, use, and change the value of the STATIC variable cName. SUBONE creates it, so only SUBONE can see and work with it.

Static life span. Static variables in SUBONE will only be released when the user issues a RELEASE or CLEAR ALL command. Static variables are local in availability, but public in memory duration.

Declaring and initializing a STATIC variable. Unlike other variables, STATIC variables can be declared and initialized on the same line:

```
STATIC nAGE = 42
```

By initializing the variable at the time of declaration, dBASE will only activate this command the first time the routine is entered. Every time it enters after that, the variable will NOT be reinitialized. For example,

```
FUNCTION AgeIt
STATIC nAGE = 42
nAge = nAge + 1
RETURN nAGE
```

If you run this function, the following will occur:

```
? AgeIt()
*  returns 43
? AgeIt()
* returns 44
? AgeIt()
* returns 45
```

The memory variable nAGE was only declared and initialized one time.

Comparing all four variable types

Table 8–4 compares all four variable types when they are declared: PUBLIC, PRIVATE, LOCAL, and STATIC. It shows which programs can use them, if they are initialized when created, and how they are released.

Table 8–4. Comparison of Memory Variable Types.

Characteristics	Public	Private	Local	Static
Is the variable type created and initialized to a value of false (.f.) when it is declared?	Y	N	N	Y
Can it be used and changed in the program that declared it (Public, Local, etc.)?	Y	Y	Y	Y
Can it be used and changed in a lower-level subroutine called by the program?	Y	Y	N	N
Can it be used and changed in a higher-level subroutine called by the program?	Y	N	N	N
Is it automatically released when the program that created it ends?	N	Y	Y	N
Is it only released via a RELEASE or CLEAR ALL command?	Y	N	N	Y

When you suspend a program, dBASE automatically assigns the PRIVATE status to memory variables that you initialized in other programs and in the Command window. This includes arrays, which behave just like any other variable type.

If a program is not suspended, dBASE will assign the PUBLIC status to all variables that you created (initialized) in the Command window.

Naming and Working with Tables, Functions, and Procedures

When working with Visual dBASE, you are not limited to creating dBASE tables; you can also create Paradox tables and a wide range of SQL tables. Nor are you limited to 10 or 40 work areas; there are now 225 work areas available per *session*. Finally, naming conventions for functions and procedures has been improved.

Local tables/databases

dBASE can be used against local tables or server tables. The local tables can be dBASE type or Paradox type. There are a few enhancements to using local tables; for instance, you can specify a default table type, even automatically move all the fields from a record to memory variables.

Naming local tables

Because local tables, dBASE, and Paradox, are stored in DOS, you are limited to the standard **8,3** naming convention, if you are running Visual dBASE in Windows 3.1. The general format is

<Table Name>**.**<ext>

where the <table name> can be any legal DOS name up to eight characters long, and the table can have an extension up to three characters long.

sidebar

Naming tables in Windows 95

If the specific disk volume supports long filenames, like in Windows 95, a table name can be assigned up to 255 characters. If the disk volume does not support long filenames, Windows 3.1x, you are still limited to 12 (8 dot 3) characters. You can use the new Visual dBASE function FNAMEMAX(<path\filename>) to determine the support. This new function will return a 12 in Windows 3.1x and 255 in Windows 95.

For more information on Visual dBASE additions for Windows 95, see Appendix D: Windows 95 and Visual dBASE.

Paradox table names. By default Paradox tables have an *extension* of **.db**. If the table has binary, memo, OLE, or graphic fields, the data for these field types will be stored in another file with the same name but an extension of **.mb**.

Paradox will not create backup files when you change the structure of the table.

dBASE table names. By default, dBASE tables have an *extension* of **.dbf**. If the table has binary, memo, or OLE fields, the data for these field types will be stored in another file with the same table name but an extension of **.DBT**.

If you change the structure of the table, dBASE will create a backup file of both files (.dbf, and .dbt) with the extension **.DBK** and **.TBK**. If you decide to change the structure of a dBASE table, you must have exclusive use of the table. The USE <table> EXCLUSIVE command is to use the table exclusively.

Although dBASE tables do not have to have the extension .dbf, the memo field must be the same name and have the extension .dbt. The table name can have any extension. For instance, catalog files are actually .dbfs with an extension of .cat.

Naming fields in tables

Depending on the type of table, names can generally be alpha or numeric.

Paradox field names. Field names in Paradox can be uppercase or lowercase, alpha or numbers, special characters (# @ $ % ^ _), or even spaces. It can be up to twenty-five characters long.

If you use spaces in the field names, you must delimit it with colons to reference it. For instance, if the name of the field is **My Last Name**, you reference it by typing **:My Last Name:**.

dBASE field names. Field names in dBASE tables can be alpha, numbers, or the underscore. It can be a maximum of ten characters long. The name must begin with an alphabetic character (*A* to *Z*).

Naming alias for local tables

When you use a table, you can specify an alias name that can be used to reference the table instead of the actual name. The name can be up to thirty-two characters long, and can contain alpha, number, or underscore. It cannot contain spaces and must begin with an alphabetic character. Any of the following can be legal alias names:

```
USE Customer ALIAS MyFirstDatabase
USE Orders ALIAS TheOrderInformation
USE PETS ALIAS Critters
USE Child ALIAS K
```

As the name suggests, it can be anywhere from one up to thirty-two characters in length.

NOTE: You can not use the names **A, B, C, D, E, F, G, H, I,** and **J** for alias names. These names are already assigned to work areas 1 to 10.

Once you create an alias for a table, you can select it by using the SELECT command with the alias name.

> ***sidebar***
>
> **The ALIAS and Windows 95**
>
> If you are running Visual dBASE in Windows 95 and use the ALIAS clause of the USE command, the *short name* of the table filename is used for the Alias. Because all files in Windows 95 have both a file name and an alias name, if you pass the table file name to another application in a program using dBASE as a DDE server, you must use the short name. The new function FSHORTNAME(<filename>) can be used to determine the file's short name. This function will return the Windows 95 short name. If you use the command in Windows 3.1x, it will return the actual file name. This command will also support the SET FULLPATH ON/OFF command in both Windows 95 and Windows 3.1x.

Work areas and names. dBASE uses work areas in which to place tables. You can have more than one table open at a time. To use more than one table, each one needs to be placed in its own work area. The dBASE documentation suggests that there are 255 work areas. However, it appears that you can only select 225 of them.

Work areas can be selected by the name of the table in them, the alias name for the table, or the work area name. Work areas can be selected by using their number. The command

```
SELECT <work area number>
```

work area can be any valid number (1 to 225). Work areas 1 to 10 can also be selected using the first ten alphabetic letters (*A* to *J*). SELECT C and SELECT 3 will both select the third work area.

TYPE [dBASE | Paradox]

Because you can use both dBASE and Paradox tables, dBASE offers a new keyword with several commands—TYPE [dbase|paradox].

USE <table> TYPE. dBASE lets you use dBASE and Paradox tables separately or together; you can set a relationship between them and obtain data from them simultaneously. To be able to "mix and match" tables, you need to specify the table type.

Adding the keyword TYPE and the table type to the USE command lets you accomplish this.

```
USE Customer TYPE dBASE IN 1
USE Pets TYPE Paradox IN 2
```

USE <tablename.ext>. In addition to using a table by specifying the type, you can simply use it and specify the extension if the extension is .dbf or .db. The following demonstrates this.

```
USE Customer.dbf IN 1
USE Pets.db IN 2
```

COPY <scope> TYPE . You can use either table and copy the records or fields in it to the other type by using the TYPE option. For instance, the following code will copy a dBASE table to a Paradox table.

```
USE Customer TYPE dBASE IN 1
COPY FOR LASTNAME < "C" TO ABCUST TYPE PARADOX
```

SET DBTYPE TO[dBASE I Paradox]

You can set the default type of table dBASE will use (.dbf or .db) by using the new command SET DBTYPE TO. Normally when you use the command USE, you do not specify the file extension (.dbf or .db). By default, dBASE tables (**.dbf**) can be used without specifying their extension or the TYPE option in the USE command.

If you will be using primarily Paradox tables, you can change the default to Paradox (**.db**) tables. To change the default, issue this command:

```
SET DBTYPE TO PARADOX
```

Procedures and functions

Procedures and functions have been enhanced. If you use a procedure or function inside a class definition, it is now referred to as a "method." The primary improvements are in the naming and calling methods.

Naming a procedure or function

If the procedure or function is stored in a class or procedure file, it can have a name as long as thirty-two characters.

Passing parameters to procedures and functions

You can pass parameters to procedures and functions in two ways.

```
PROCEDURE/FUNCTION  Test
     PARAMETER < parameter list >
PROCEDURE/FUNCTION Test({parameter list})
```

Both methods work for passing parameters. For instance, the following two procedure headings are identical:

```
PROCEDURE TestIt
    Parameter xCnt, cName
PROCEDURE TestIt(xCnt, cName)
```

The primary difference is recognition of the type of parameter being passed.

Testing with the TYPE( ) function. If you use the PARAMETER keyword, like in the following code, the TYPE( ) function will recognize the type of parameters being sent. This code is saved to a procedure file named TypeProc.prg.

```
*** TypeProc.prg
*
PROCEDURE Test
    PARAMETERS Param1, Param2
    ? "Parameter 1 is TYPE : "+Type('param1')
    ?  "its value is "
    ?? param1
    ? "Parameter 2 is TYPE : "+Type('param2')
    ?  "its value is "
    ?? param2
RETURN
```

To use the TEST procedure, type in the following lines:

```
SET PROCEDURE TO TypeProc ADDI
DO Test with 1, 2
Test ("abc" , .T.)
```

Running the procedure TEST the first time, DO TEST WITH 1,2 will result in the procedure reporting both parameters as numeric type. The TEST("ABC", .T.) line will report one parameter as Character, the other as Logical. Figure 8–3 shows the Command window with the preceding commands and the resulting answers.

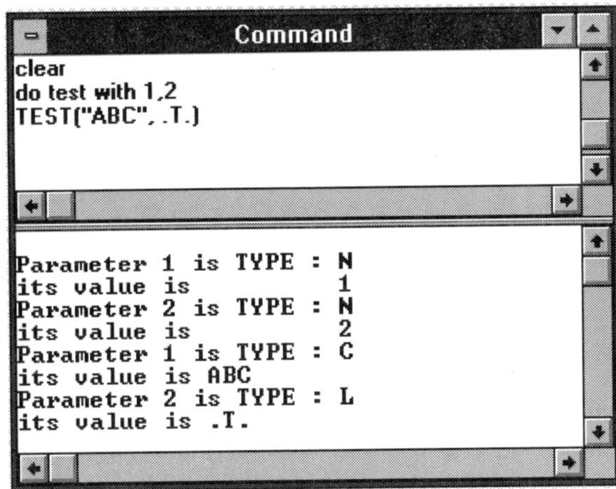

Figure 8–3. This is the Command window showing the results of a program.

If you modify the code by changing the first line to the following one, and removing the parameter line, the parameter will be passed, but its type will be Undefined ("U"):

```
PROCEDURE Test(Param1, Param2)
```

So the TYPE() function cannot be used to test the parameter type if you pass the parameters between the parentheses of a procedure or function. If you rerun the code for the Procedure test (after loading its procedure file in memory), the program's TYPE() function will always return the value *U* for unidentified.

Calling functions and procedures

When you call a function, you have traditionally used some code methodology to activate the function:

```
dummy = MyUDF()
? MyUDF()
```

Now dBASE will let you call a function without having to assign it to the print statement (?) or as a value to a variable (x=UDF()). Now you can simply activate the function directly:

```
MyUDF()
Date()
```

If you do not tell Visual dBASE to display the return value of the function—"date()" instead of "? date()", it will execute the function but *not* display the value.

Work Sessions

Visual dBASE has added the concept of work sessions. A *session* is an environmental setting that controls how dBASE works with tables, settings, and certain operations. Setting sessions on or off will determine how you can work with multiple open files or tables in forms.

Setting sessions on/off

When working with tables, queries, forms, and reports in the Navigator, you can control how Visual dBASE will work with them.

Standard dBASE DOS methodology

When you worked with these objects, using the Control Center of dBASE DOS, opening a table would leave the table open until you specifically told it to close. When you run a query from the control center, it will run until you close it; however, when you close it and are returned to the control center, the files remain open. If you BROWSE a table and try to BROWSE the same table in the same window, you will receive an error. The window is already in use for the BROWSE. This is standard dBASE DOS behavior. If Sessions is set off in Visual dBASE, this is the type of behavior dBASE will follow. A query can only be displayed in one window at a time. The table will remain open until you specifically close it.

Windows methodology

If you want Visual dBASE to follow the standard Windows conventions, you will need to make sure that Sessions is on (which is the default value). For instance, Windows conventions allow tables to be viewed in multiple windows—one a BROWSE, another an edit, and maybe another a form. When Sessions is set on, Visual dBASE will follow standard Windows conventions when working with the Navigator.

Setting the sessions settings. The Sessions status can only be set or changed via the Desktop Properties dialog box. To turn sessions on or off, follow these steps:

1. Select Properties >> Desktop from the menu bar.
2. Click on the Files tab to select the Files page.
3. Click the sessions checkbox (on or off).

There is no equivalent SET command that can be used to set sessions on or off. Every time you run a form or open a table or query, Visual dBASE will run or open them in their own Sessions. Figure 8–4 shows the actual commands that Visual dBASE issues when you double-click on a query named BOTH.qbe in the Navigator.

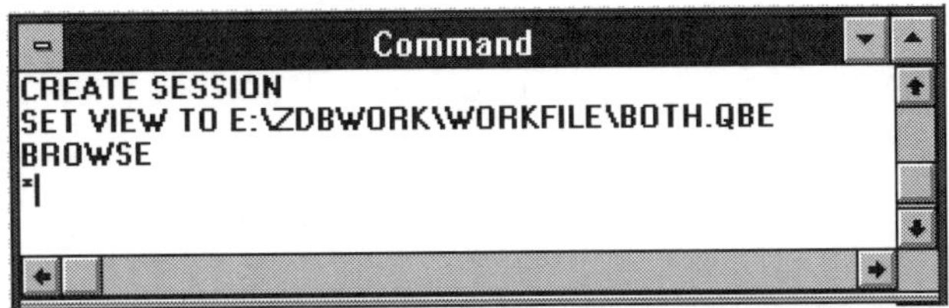

Figure 8–4. The commands issued via use of the Navigator.

Notice that with Sessions on, Visual dBASE issues three commands to display a query.

```
CREATE SESSION
SET VIEW TO <view name>
BROWSE
```

When you close the Browse window, Visual dBASE will close the query and the underlying tables. This is because Sessions is set on. If Sessions were off, the underlying tables would remain open.

The CREATE SESSION command

To create a new session, simply use the command

```
CREATE SESSION
```

The command has no arguments.

> ! **CREATE SESSIONS**
> If you type CREATE SESSIONS (plural), dBASE will assume you want to create a table named Sessions and open the Create Table window.

Once you create a session, it begins a new, clean, work session within dBASE. It can be compared with running in a multiuser environment on a single machine, in a single session of dBASE. Specifically CREATE SESSION does the following:

- Makes all 225 work areas available, in the new session, even when other programs have tables open. Even if another session has the same table open, this session will move through the table independent of the other sessions.

For instance, each session can be pointing to different records in the same table and performing different actions against the same table. When updates to a table are performed in one session, the changes are reflected in the same table opened in another session (just like multiuser).

- Sets the value of most SET commands to their default value; there is a listing of all the SET commands affected later in this chapter.
- Works with existing memory variables. It does not affect the access or status of existing memory variables. The access to the variables is controlled by their scope (public, local, etc.).

Sessions

Creating a session affects most of the environment; how and what it affects, depends on the uses in the Session.

Sessions and memory variables

Sessions do not affect memory variables at all. A public memory variable is available across all sessions.

Sessions and objects

Like memory variables, Sessions does not affect objects and references to objects. The following code can be used to demonstrate.

```
*** CH08TEMP.PRG
*
CREATE SESSION
f1 = NEW FORM("Form 1")
  STORE 5 TO f1.Height, f1.Top, f1.Left
  f1.Width = 35
CREATE SESSION
f2 = NEW FORM("2ND Form")
  STORE 2 TO f2.Top, f2.Left
  f2.Height = 8
  f2.Width = 20
CREATE SESSION
f1.Open()
F2.Open()
```

Although form F1 and F2 were both created in their own Sessions, they can be opened and worked with anywhere. Sessions does not affect the objects themselves.

Sessions and tables

When Session is on and a table is opened in multiple sessions, the table is treated the same as if it were opened in multiuser. Locks are supported the same as multiuser.

Opening and closing a table with a window. If the Desktop property Sessions is on and the table is displayed in a window, the table is closed when the window is closed. If Sessions is off and a window is closed, the table is left open.

This is the Sessions property of the desktop versus the CREATE SESSION command.

Multiple views of the same table in a single SESSION. If Sessions is on, you can view a table in more than one window. You do not have to create a separate Session for each view. The following commands demonstrate this:

```
USE CUSTOMER
BROWSE
EDIT COLUMNAR
EDIT FORMAT
```

Figure 8–5 shows the results of the preceding commands.

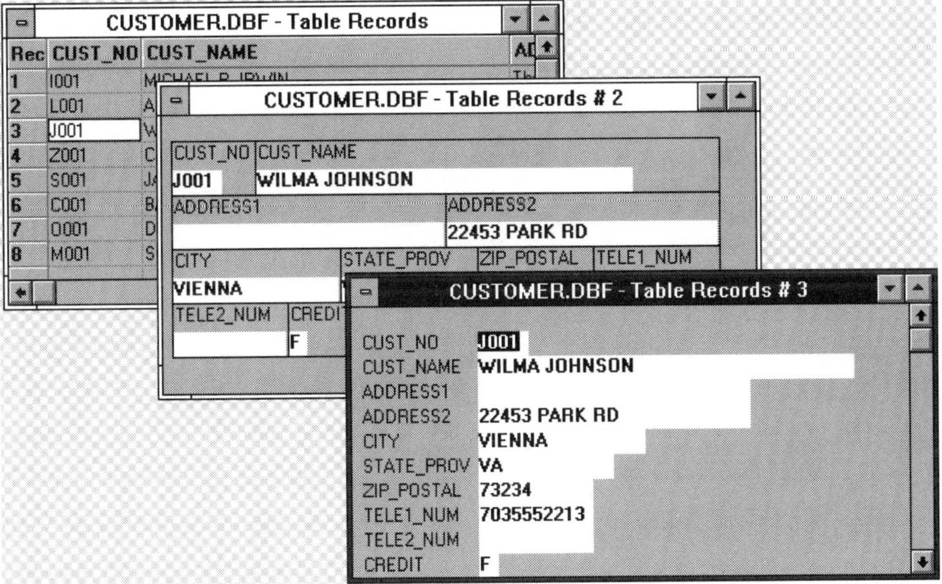

Figure 8–5. Opening three windows for the same table.

Notice that the same table is displayed in three different views. Yet they are all pointing to the same record. If you are working in one Session with multiple views of the same table or query, dBASE will automatically synchronize all of the windows. As you move through the records in one window, the others will automatically move.

When a table is displayed in more than one window, the table will not close until all the windows that use it are closed.

EDIT COLUMNAR versus EDIT FORMAT command

Visual dBASE lets you edit records in two formats: columnar or format. Figure 8–5 shows both. The format display is in the center; columnar is at the bottom, right side of the figure. If you simply type EDIT by itself, whichever view you have specified in the Desktop properties dialog box will be viewed. If you want to specify a specific type of view, use the COLUMNAR or FORMAT clauses of the EDIT command.

Different Sessions allows viewing different records of a table. To display different records of the same table, you need to create a new Session for each view of the table. The following commands demonstrate this:

```
CREATE SESSION
USE CUSTOMER
BROWSE
CREATE SESSION
USE CUSTOMER
EDIT COLUMNAR
```

Notice that you need to reuse the Customer file for each Session. Because each session has its own work areas and its own environment, you need to specify which file(s) to use in each session.

Figure 8–6 shows the results of the preceding commands. Notice that the BROWSE view is showing Charles Zimmerman's record while the edit view is showing Wilma Johnson's record.

Sessions, open files, and closing windows

When you close the window of a session, like the BROWSE and EDIT windows from the preceding code, the Session automatically closes the underlying tables.

Sessions and work areas

When you create a new session with the CREATE SESSION command, each new session will have its own 255 work areas available to it. This lets you open multiple files in multiple sessions without having to worry about work area usage by another session. Each session has its own area, 1, and so on.

If Session is turned off from the Desktop Properties dialog box, there is only one set of work areas.

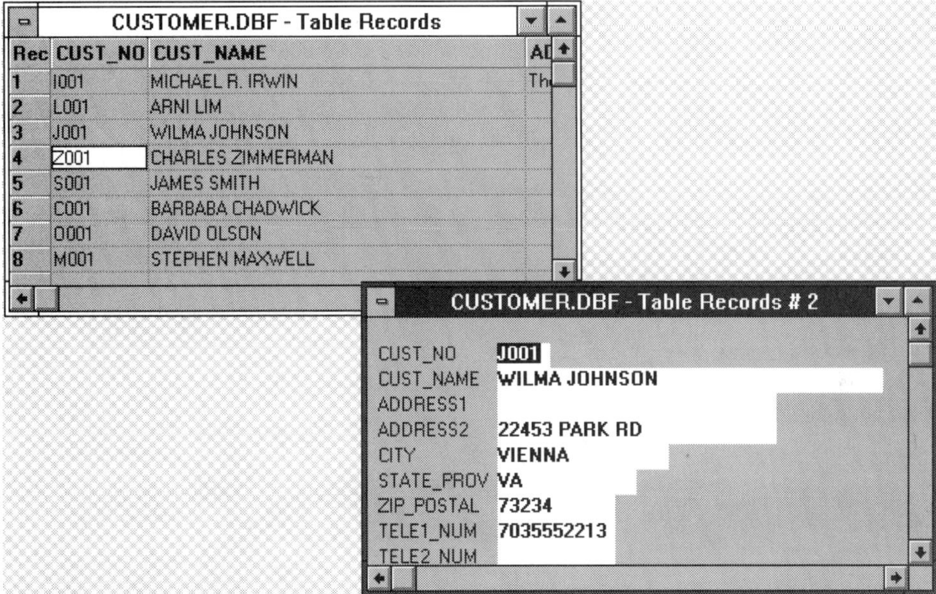

Figure 8–6. Two views of the same table showing different records.

Sessions and the Command window

The Command window always exists in its own session. If you run the code displayed in Figure 8–6 and activate the Command window, the function ? DBF() will report no database is in memory.

Sessions and queries

Queries use sessions the same way that a table does. You can have multiple views of the same query in a single session—they will always point to the same record. If you want the same query to be used and pointing to different records, you need to open the query for each view in its own Session.

Sessions and forms

Forms that use the same table(s) as other forms (that are open) need to be opened in their own session. If you do not open them in their own Session, only the last one opened will be able to move through the records of a table or query. The other form, the first one opened, will freeze on either the last record displayed or a blank record. The following code demonstrates this:

```
DO CUSTOMER.WFM
DO CUSTOMER.WFM
```

Figure 8–7 demonstrates the problem that can occur. Once the forms are opened, the top one has been moved to the bottom, right corner.

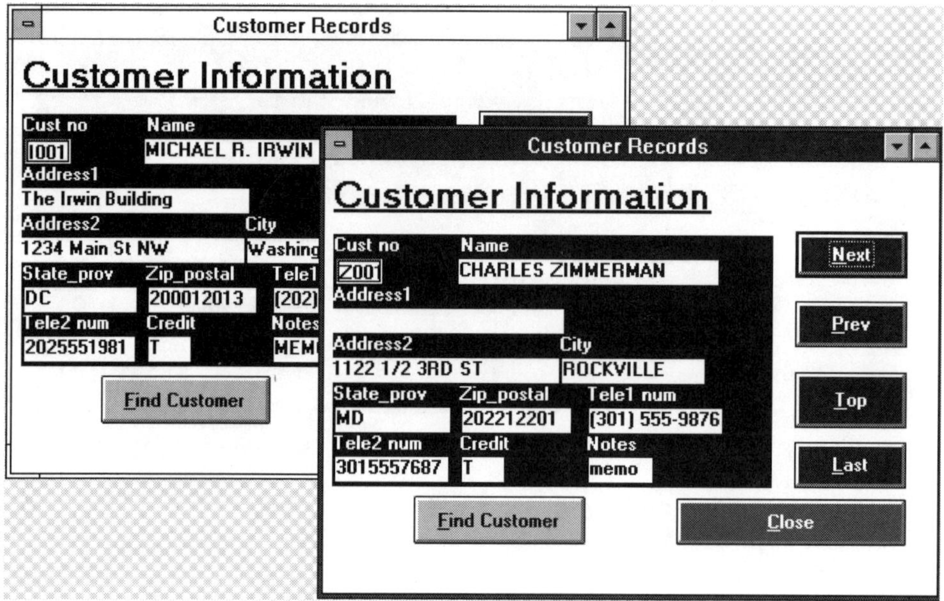

Figure 8–7. Opening the same form twice.

With both forms open, click on the next button of the top form. Notice that it continues to display the Michael Irwin record. However, as you click on the buttons, the second form does update to the new records correctly. The problem is you aren't pressing the second one's buttons. In dBASE for Windows 5.0, the problem was even worse: The first form would not display any field information for the table; rather, all the fields were empty.

You can quickly fix this problem by running each form in its own Session. Running the same form in different Sessions will have both forms display records correctly and independently:

```
CREATE SESSION
DO CUSTOMER.WFM
CREATE SESSION
DO CUSTOMER.WFM
```

By opening each form that uses a common table in their own session, actions performed on the table in the active form will not affect the table used in another form. So you can use the same form to display different records from the same tables by simply running the form twice—each in its own Session space.

Sessions and reports/labels

All reports and labels always open in their own sessions. Because of this, you can run multiple reports simultaneously that may use the same tables.

Sessions and SET commands

The following SET commands only work with the current session. They will be reset for each session:

```
AUTOSAVE      BLOCKSIZE     CARRY
CENTURY       CONFIRM       CUAENTER
CURRENCY      DATABASE      DATE
DBTYPE        DECIMALS      DEFAULT
DELETED       DELIMITERS    DIRECTORY
EXACT         EXCLUSIVE     FIELDS
FILTER        IBLOCK        INDEX
KEY           LOCK          MARK
MBLOCK        MEMOWIDTH     NEAR
ORDER         PATH          POINT
PRECISION     REFRESH       RELATION
REPROCESS     SAFETY        SEPARATOR
SKIP          TALK          UNIQUE
```

These SET commands can hold different values in each session. Every time you create a new Session, these SET commands are set to their default values for the individual Session.

Compiling Visual dBASE Programs

Once your code is written, you need to compile the program file into an object code file that can be run by Visual dBASE.

Compiled object files

By default, Visual dBASE creates compiled object files in the same directory as the source code. The compiled object files, those that have *o* as the last letter of the extension, are what Visual dBASE actually runs. Once compiled, the source code (*.prg, *.wfm, etc.) can be removed from the directory.

File extensions for source and object files

Table 8–5 shows the default extensions that Visual dBASE assigns to the source files it compiles.

Table 8–5. Files Compiled by Visual dBASE.

File Type to Compile	Source File Extensions	Compiled File Extensions
Program files	.PRG	.PRO
Form files	.WFM	.WFO
Query files	.QBE	.QBO
Menu files	.MNU	.MNO
Popup files (new)	.POP	.POO
Custom form file	.CFM	.CFO
DOS format file	.FMT	.FMO
DOS report file	.FRG	.FRO
DOS label file	.LBG	.LBO

Visual dBASE will not create DOS files; however, it does support them and will compile them for backward compatibility.

!

Naming files

Visual dBASE compiles all programs, ending them with a file extension that has an *o* as the last letter. It is important that you do not use any filename extension that ends with the letter *o* for your program source code file names. If you do, Visual dBASE may automatically overwrite your source file. The compiled object file uses a binary format that cannot be viewed or modified.

Commands that compile programs

Visual dBASE has several commands that will compile program files. The following is a list of commands that will compile a program:

- DO will compile a program and run it if no errors are found.
- SET PROCEDURE TO <file> will compile the program file if a .PRO doesn't already exist and load it into memory if no errors are found.
- SET LIBRARY TO <file> works just like Set procedure to.
- COMPILE will compile programs without executing the object code.

Automatic compiling

The DO command will depend on the status of the SET DEVELOPMENT environment setting. If you have SET DEVELOPMENT ON (default setting), Visual dBASE will automatically compile your code when you use the DO <program name> command. Actually, what the SET DEVELOPMENT ON command does is have dBASE look for a .PRO file of the same name as the program, or WFO for a form (WFM). If there is one, it checks the date and time to see if they are the same. If the date/time stamp is different, or the file does not exit, it recompiles the program for you.

Using the COMPILE command

The COMPILE command has several advantages over compiling program files using the DO or SET PROCEDURE TO commands.

The COMPILE command lets you

- COMPILE more than one source file at a time.
- It does not execute (*.prg) or open (*.wfm) the object file, once it is compiled.
- It can use *wildcards* in the filenames and compile unrelated files.

➡ **New features of compile command**

In addition to this, Visual dBASE has added three more features to the COMPILE command.

- Use the AUTO option to compile program files (*.prg) *called* by the specified compile program.
- Create a response file (*.RSP) for the *Optional Visual dBASE Compiler* kit.
- Create a log file (*.log) of warnings or errors.

How the COMPILE command works

The general syntax of the COMPILE command is

```
COMPILE <filename>|<file skeleton list> ;
    [AUTO] [LOG <filename>] [TO <response filename>]
```

COMPILE creates object code from files specified in the <filename> or <file skeleton list>.

The AUTO switch. If you specify the AUTO option, the compiler will compile all source code files called from any files in the <file skeleton list>. This includes any calls made by DO, SET PROCEDURE TO, and SET LIBRARY TO commands. If a User-Defined Function is encountered, the compiler will look for a program file that has the same name.

The AUTO switch does not recognize files that are included as properties of objects; for instance, the view property of a form that specifies a QBE file, or the menu property that specifies an MNU file. The QBE and MNU will not be compiled via the AUTO switch. They must be explicitly named in the <file skeleton list>.

Compiling non-AUTO recognized objects
If you want to have the program AUTO compile all objects, any that cannot be recognized by the AUTO switch can be placed in a dummy IF statement, like the following:

```
IF .f.          && will never be executed
  DO AllCust.QBE
  DO MyCust.MNU
ENDIF
```

Although the preceding code will never be executed when the form or program executes, the AUTO switch of the COMPILE command will see the DO command and automatically compile the code.

The LOG switch. The LOG option will create a text file with any warning and errors generated by the compiler. The extension of this file will be .TXT.

The TO switch. The TO option will create a text file with a list of all the output object code files that were generated by the COMPILE command. This file will be used by the BUILD command of the optional *Visual dBASE Compiler* kit. The extension of this response file is .RSP.

When you use the COMPILE command to compile a program, a Compilation Status dialog box is activated, like the one in Figure 8–8.

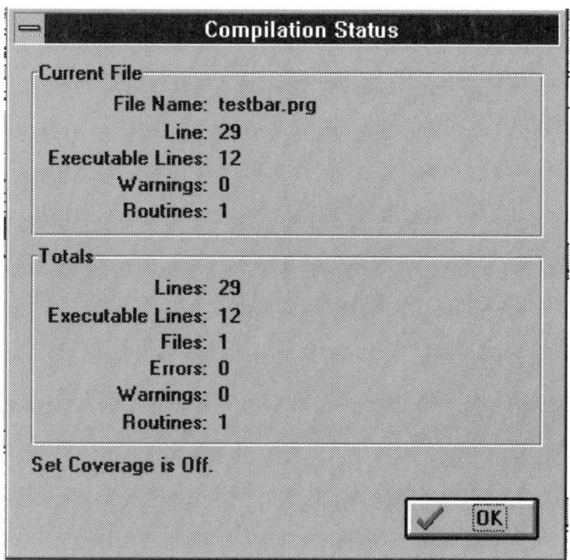

Figure 8–8. The COMPILE dialog box.

✔ **Recompiling all programs**
To recompile all programs in a subdirectory, use the command COMPILE * in the Command window.

The menu choice Program >> Compile . . .

➡ Visual dBASE has added a new menu choice to the Program menu—Compile. . . . This menu choice will activate a dialog box, similar to the one in Figure 8–9. It can be used to specify all the options of the COMPILE command.

The BUILD options. The BUILD options of the Compiler dialog box will do nothing if you do not have the optional *Visual dBASE Compiler* kit. The optional Compiler kit installs a file named DBWSTUB.INI to the same directory as dBASEWIN.BIN. If this file is found, the Build options will allow you to automatically call the builder to link your compiled programs into an .EXE.

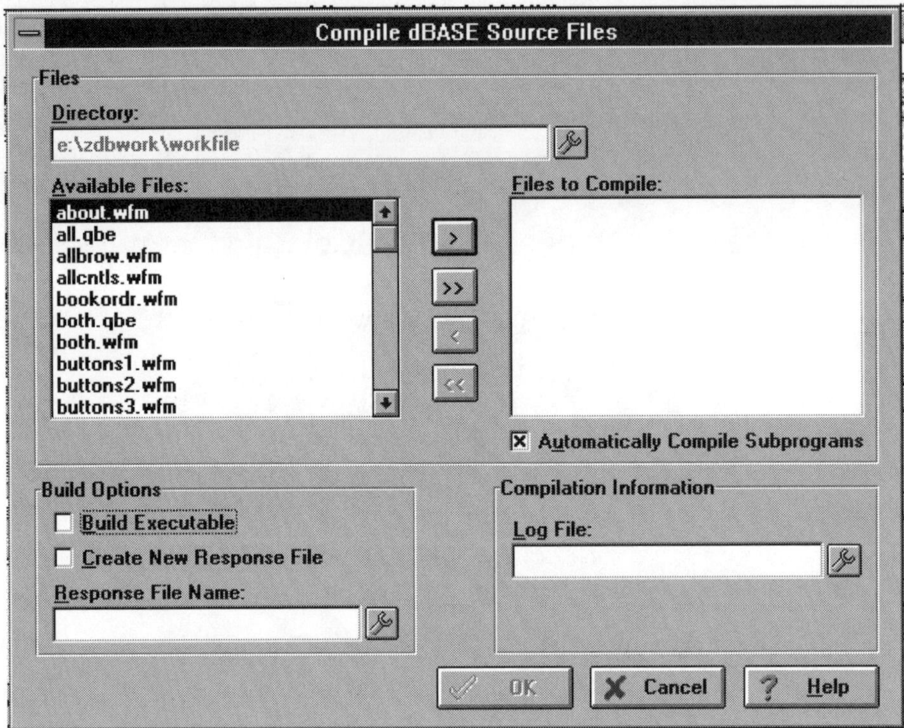

Figure 8–9. This is the Compile dBASE source files dialog box .

The optional compiler kit

Visual dBASE has an optional compiler kit that can be used to provide the developer with the tools necessary to create stand-alone Windows executable programs from their Visual dBASE source code. These programs can then be distributed to users royalty free, eliminating the need to purchase Visual dBASE.

Built into Visual dBASE

When you install the compiler kit, it will become part of the base Visual dBASE product, adding the BUILD command and two new menu choices under the Program menu.

The BUILD command

The general syntax for the BUILD command is

BUILD <filename list> | FROM <response filename> ;
[TO <Exe filename>] [SPLASH <bitmap name>] [ICON <icon name>]

BUILD will create an executable program that can run under Windows independent of Visual dBASE. It creates it from a file list or from a response file (*.rsp) created by the COMPILE command.

The FROM option. If the FROM option is used, the response file created by the COMPILE option can be used to BUILD the executable. The response file holds the names of all the compiled programs.

The TO option. If the TO option is used, BUILD will create the executable naming it based on the filename specified by this option. If the TO option is omitted, BUILD will assign the executable the same name as the first file in the <filename list> or the <response file>.

The SPLASH option. If you specify the SPLASH option with a bitmap file name (*.bmp), the BUILD command will link the bitmap into the executable. Then, when the executable file is loading, it will use the bitmap file for displaying during the load process.

The ICON option. If you specify the ICON option, the BUILD command will link the icon file into the executable. This icon will be used as the program icon for the desktop and when the application is minimized.

The new Program menu choices

In addition to the BUILD command, Visual dBASE will have two new commands added to the Program menu. Figure 8–10 shows the new menu options added to the program menu.

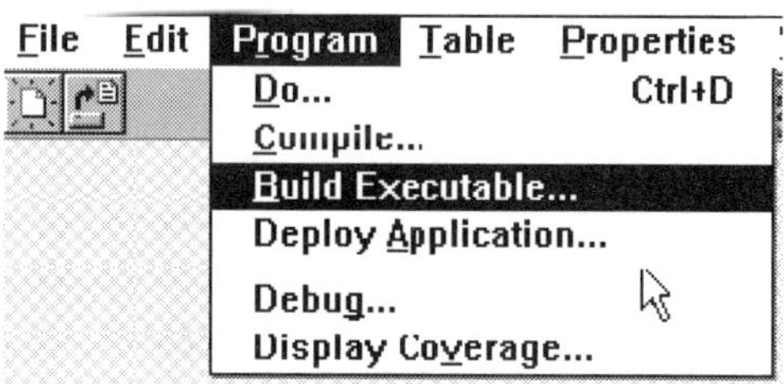

Figure 8–10. The Compiler menu choices.

The two menu choices added are

- Build Executable . . .
- Deploy Application . . .

Build Executable choice. The Build Executable choice will let you build a stand-alone Windows executable via a dialog box. Selecting this choice, you will be presented with a dialog box similar to the one in Figure 8–11.

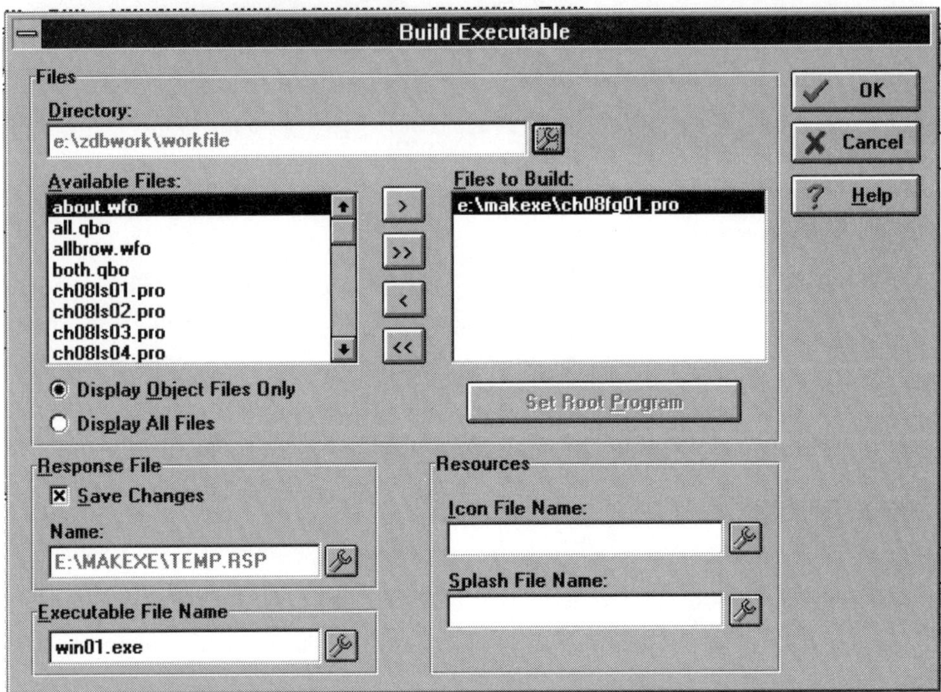

Figure 8–11. The Build Executable dialog box.

Using this dialog box, you can easily build a Windows executable.

Deploy Application choice. The second choice added to the Program menu is the Deploy Application choice. This choice will assist you in building an install set for your application. The install set is a set of subdirectories that will contain all the files necessary to install your program on your customers' computers. It will create the INSTALL.exe and the installation diskettes for you. The number of diskettes and options that will be installed depend on your applications needs. Figure 8–12 shows the Deploy Application dialog box.

When you use this choice, it will build a standard Borland-like install with installation diskettes that you can use for your customers. It will compress all the files into .PAK files and store them on installation diskettes. This lets you distribute your application to your customer in a professional environment. When the customer installs your diskettes they will install using the same familiar Borland vehicle on the road "Speedometer" screen that they have seen with Borland products.

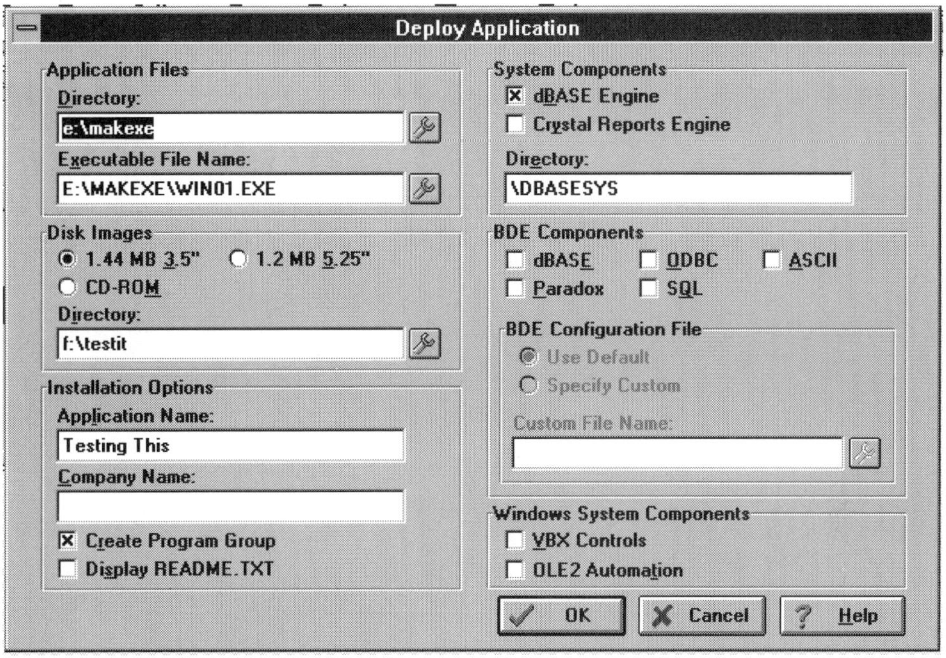

Figure 8–12. This is the Deploy Application dialog box.

Because the time necessary to build the Deploy Application diskettes can be time-consuming, you will be presented with a dialog box that keeps you informed, like the one in Figure 8–13.

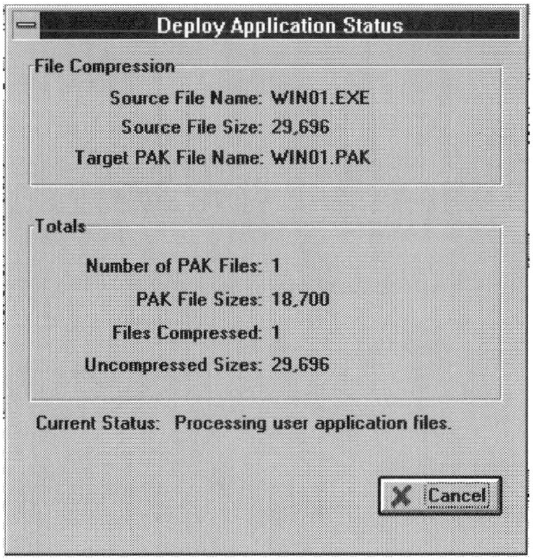

Figure 8–13. The Deploy Application status dialog box.

Commands not supported by the Visual Compiler

There are a few Visual dBASE commands that are not supported by your compiled applications. You should be aware of these and avoid them in the code that you create. They are

```
BUILD                                 MODIFY STRUCTURE
CREATE < * objects >                  SET
COMPILE                               SET DESIGN
DEBUG                                 SET DEVELOPMENT
INSPECT                               SET ECHO
MODIFY < * objects >                  SET STEP
```

```
  * objects = Catalog, Command, Form, Label, Menu, Query,
⇒* Report, and Screen
```

Chapter 9
Testing Your Programs

After creating your programs, you will probably want to test them. You test programs both for bugs (or errors) and user satisfaction/performance.

Although testing for user satisfaction and performance are important, they are subjective in nature. This type of testing is very subjective. Conversely, there is a tool and a couple of commands available in Visual dBASE that can truly help you find those "pesky bugs" that creep up in your code.

Testing Methodologies

Testing can be done in several ways.

- Running the Compiler (or simply doing the program)
- Visually reviewing (stepping through) the code
- Running all portions of the application
- Observing others running the program
- Using tools to check for runtime and logic errors

Most programmers tend to test their applications for "bugs," or errors, and let others test their applications for performance and user acceptance.

Compiling the code

The easiest, and usually the first, way to test for application errors is to simply execute the code. The code will run if you issue any of these commands.

- `DO <program name>`
- `SET PROCEDURE TO`
- `SET LIBRARY TO`
- `SET FORMAT TO [DOS-based commands]`

dBASE will run the code and even recompile it if it has changed since the last time it was run (assuming that SET DEVELOPMENT is set ON).

If Visual dBASE encounters any *syntax errors* in the program, the compiler will notify you of an error and give you the option to fix it. Figure 9–1 shows the Program Alert dialog box that will come up if an error is encountered.

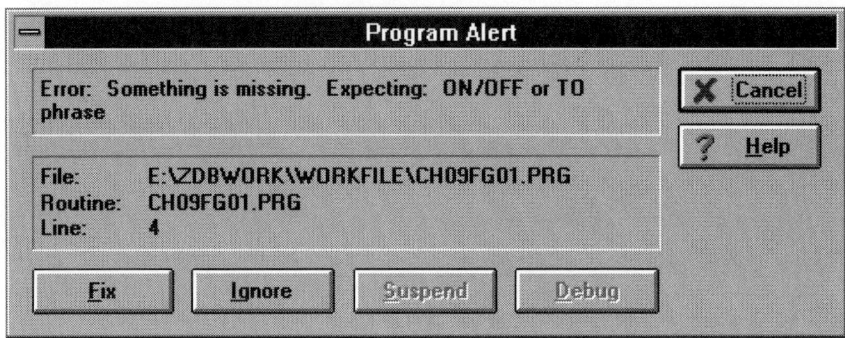

Figure 9–1. The error box when doing a program.

If you select the Fix choice, dBASE will take you automatically into the Program Editor to the line that caused the error. In this case, it will take you into the Editor and point to line 4. Figure 9–2 shows the program editor set to line 4.

CH09FG01.PRG - Program Editor

```
*
*
SET CUAENTER FOF
SET TALK OFF
CLEAR
DEFINE WINDOW MyWin from 5,5 to 18, 25   && create and open form
ACTIVATE WINDOW MyWin
DO WHILE .T.                                         && driver to get ch
  mChoice = " "                                            && starts h
  @ 0,2 TO 2, 14
  @ 1,4 SAY "Main Menu"
  @ 4,2 SAY "1. Add Records"
  @ 5,2 SAY "2. Edit Records"
  @ 6,2 SAY "3. Quit"
  @ 8,2 GET mChoice
  READ
 @9,2 CLEAR TO 10,14
```

Figure 9–2. The Program Editor sitting on line 4.

Notice that line 4 has an error; it says SET CUAENTER FOF instead of OFF. Once you fix the error, the program will be recomplied and run automatically. You will not be returned to the Command Window and have to retype in the command.

Using SET CUAENTER switch

The SET CUAENTER (on/off) switch controls how the **Enter** key works while in forms. In most Windows applications, pressing the **Enter** key submits the form. This means that when the user presses the **Enter** key in an Entryfield object, nothing happens—they will not be taken to the next field. To move to the next field you use the **Tab** and **Shift-Tab** keys. In DOS versions of dBASE, pressing the **Enter** key in a field moves the cursor to the next field. If you want the user to move to the next control object (field) in a form when they press the **Enter** key, set CUAENTER OFF (on is the default). By setting CUAENTER off, the user can still use the **Tab** key and now the **Enter** key to move from field to field.

You can turn CUAENTER OFF by using the SET command or by selecting Properties >> Desktop . . . >> Data Entry (tab) >> CUA Enter, via the menu.

SET DEVELOPMENT ON

The default value for development is on. If development is on, dBASE will automatically recompile an application.

Using the COMPILE command

You can also compile a program file by using the command COMPILE. *Compile* will compile source code—program files (*.PRG, *.WFM, *.MNU, *.QBE), creating object files (*.PRO, *.WFO, *.MNO, *.QBO).

The following are all valid examples of using the Compile command:

- `COMPILE MyPrg`
- `COMPILE *.WFM`
- `COMPILE DemoMenu.mnu`

When you use the Compile command, and SET TALK is ON, dBASE will display the Compile Status window. It is similar to the one in Figure 9–3.

The Compilation Status window shows you any errors it found, warnings, and the number of routines in the program that it compiled. In this case, it compiled 893 lines, of which 282 were executable (the others are remarks or blanks). It also has fifteen routines in one file.

- GENERATE
- SET COVERAGE On/OFF

The GENERATE command

If you ever need to populate a database quickly (add dummy records to the table), the GENERATE command can be beneficial. It will add the number of records that you specify with totally random values.

The general syntax for using this command is

GENERATE <number of records>

The <number of records> can be a number between 1 and 1,000,000,000 or until the table is full. The only limitation on the number of records is limited by the maximum size of the table. The table itself cannot be greater than 2,000 megabytes in size.

GENERATE will fill a table with random sample data so you can use it for testing and debugging. If the table contains existing records, GENERATE does not destroy them; rather, it appends the number of records that you specify to the table.

When you use the GENERATE command with a table containing a memo field, dBASE creates an empty memo field for each record (it will show MEMO—uppercase—in the marker), but it does not fill the associated memo file with data.

WORKING WITH COVERAGE

Visual dBASE offers a tool, called Coverage, that can be used to determine if logical blocks of a program will run (execute). The commands that let you work with Coverage are

- SET COVERAGE ON/OFF
- DISPLAY / LIST COVERAGE

These commands are used to test your code and then analyze the results.

It does this by reading all the blocks of code that are in a program when it is executed. It counts the number of times each block is processed and if a block is missed. Then it creates a report of what was processed. This analysis can help identify areas where routines are never processed. You can then decide to test further (using the debugger) to see if the condition that would have called the block ever exists.

Using Coverage

To use Coverage, you need to do three things.

1. Turn Coverage ON.
2. Compile and run the program.
3. View the results of running the program (in the .COV file).

dBASE will create a file with the results of the Coverage analysis. The file created will have an extension of .COV and a name the same as the program that ran.

Turning Coverage ON

The fastest way to turn Coverage ON is using the command:

```
SET COVERAGE ON
```

However, you can also set it on by performing these steps:

1. Select Properties >> Desktop . . . from the menu.
2. Click the **Programming** tab in the Desktop Properties dialog box.
3. Click the checkbox labeled **Coverage** in the section labeled Program Development (top, center of page).

You can also specify that Coverage be placed on using the preprocessor directive:

```
#pragma COVERAGE(ON)
```

Once Coverage is ON, dBASE will create or update a coverage file (.COV).

The .COV file. The coverage file (.COV) is a binary file that contains cumulative statistical information on how many times dBASE enters and exits each *logical block* of a program. When you call a program, procedure, or UDF that is located in a program file (*.prg) or form (*.wfm), dBASE will automatically create a new .COV file for that program while it is running. The coverage file will have the same name as the program and the extension .COV.

> ! **Coverage and Form files**
> If you work with .wfm files and one .wfm calls another one, dBASE will not create a new .cov file for the .wfm. You will have to run the other .wfm seperately to test it.

Logical blocks. A logical block of code is any code that lies within any flow-of-control commands, like IF . . . ENDIF, FOR . . . NEXT, DO CASE . . . , and so on. If a program has no flow-of-control commands, then the entire program is a single logical block.

A Demonstration of the coverage file

The following code can be used to demonstrate logical blocks and how the coverage file works:

```
 1  *** DEMOCOVG.PRG
 2  PUBLIC xTest
 3  do COVSTART    && calls an external program that makes OOP
form
 4  do USTART      && calls the internal procedure
 5  RELEASE ALL
 6  CLEAR ALL
 7  CLOSE ALL
 8  RETURN
 9  *
10  PROCEDURE UStart
11      SET TALK OFF
12      CLEAR
13      DEFINE WINDOW MyWin FROM 2,2 TO 18,60 COLOR W/B
14      ACTIVATE WINDOW MyWin
15      @2,2 SAY "Hello People"
16      @5,10 SAY "THIS IS another SAY line"
17      @13,30 SAY "Press escape to exit"
18      DO WHILE .T.
19          i = inkey(2)
20         @14,10 SAY space(40)
21         IF i = 27
22             EXIT
23         ELSE
24           @14,10 SAY "Only the ESCAPE key will stop this"
⇒            COLOR W/R
25         ENDIF
26      ENDDO
27      DEACTIVATE WINDOW MyWin
28  RETURN
```

This program has twenty-eight lines of code, including remarks. The fourth line calls a Procedure file that is inside the DEMOCOVG.prg. The third line calls an external program named COVSTART.prg. The contents of COVSTART.prg are

```
*** COVSTART.prg
*
SET STATUS OFF
F=NEW FORM()
f.height = 12
f.width = 35
B=NEW PUSHBUTTON(F)
B.ONCLICK = {;form.Close()}
b.top = 8
b.left = 22
```

```
b.height = 1.5
b.text = "E&xit"
IF TYPE ('xTest')= "L"
   F.OPEN()
ENDIF
RETURN
```

It has sixteen lines of code, including remarks. With the two programs created, you can type the following commands to create a Coverage file about the program, DemoCovg:

```
SET COVERAGE ON
DO DEMOCOVG
SET COVERAGE OFF
```

The DemoCovg program will call the CovStart program, which will create a Visual dBASE form and then call the internal Procedure, Ustart, which will create a DOS-based window that will run in the Results pane of the Command window with traditional DOS commands. The COVSTART program creates a new form with a Close button and opens it. The Ustart procedure will create and open a window in the Results pane of the Command window—waiting for you to press the **Esc** key to close the window.

Coverage files of called programs. If a program that is being executed calls another program, that program will have a coverage file created for it also. Its coverage file will have its name and the extension of .COV. In our example, you will have two coverage files after running the DEMOCOVG program.

```
DEMOCOVG.COV
COVSTART.COV
```

It created two coverage files because democovg.prg called covstart.prg.

> ! **DIR *.COV display bug**
>
> If you attempt to see if the Coverage files exist using the DIR command, you may experience what you believe is a display bug in Visual dBASE. It may report 0 bytes in 0 files. Visual dBASE does not initially write the COV files to disk. Rather, it maintains them in memory until you need them. If this happens, don't be concerned; your coverage files are there. If you use the command DISPLAY COVERAGE?, it will write them to disk so that you can use them. In fact, if you use any other Visual dBASE command that may change the environment, such as changing directories, reusing the SET COVERAGE ON command, dBASE will refresh its memory and write the files to disk.

Turning COVERAGE OFF. If you forget to turn Coverage OFF with the SET COVERAGE OFF command, dBASE will create a .COV file for every program (*.prg) and form (*.FRM) that you run. Although this will not hurt anything, it will clutter your subdirectory with a lot of .cov files.

Displaying the .COV file

Once the Coverage file has been created, you are ready to display or list the Coverage file. Because the name of the program was DEMOCOVG.prg, the Coverage file will be named DEMOCOVG.COV.

LIST or DISPLAY coverage

Once a coverage file is created, you can display it using the command DISPLAY COVERAGE. The general syntax for displaying coverage is

DISPLAY COVERAGE <COV file name> | <wildcards in COV filename>| ?

[ALL] [SUMMARY] [TO FILE <filename> | ? [TO PRINTER]

or

LIST COVERAGE <COV file name> | <wildcards in COV filename>| ?

[ALL] [SUMMARY] [TO FILE <filename> | ? [TO PRINTER]

To display the coverage file for the program DEMOCOVG, the command would be

```
DISPLAY COVERAGE DEMOCOVG
```

The coverage will look something like this.

```
E:\ZDBWORK\WORKFILE\DEMOCOVG.COV
Block 1, line 2 to 7, was exercised 1 times.
Block 2, line 11 to 17, was exercised 1 times.
Block 3, line 19 to 20, was exercised 1 times.
Block 4, line 24 to 24, was exercised 0 times.
Block 5, line 27 to 27, was exercised 1 times.
4 blocks out of 5 blocks tested.
Test coverage is 80.00% complete.
```

NOTE: Interpreting this report

Notice that the Coverage file reports that only 80 percent of the blocks were processed (four out of five). The fourth block, "line 24 to line 24," was not processed. If you go back to the source code, you can see that this line wouldn't be processed if the user presses the **Esc** key in fewer than two seconds. If you let the program run longer than two seconds, this block should be processed.

LIST versus DISPLAY. Like the LIST and DISPLAY commands in dBASE DOS, DISPLAY will display one window of informaton at a time. Then it will prompt you to continue. LIST will display all of the contents at one time, without prompting you to continue.

NOTE: Redirecting the Coverage report

The display coverage commands can also direct the Coverage report to a file or to the printer. If you send it to a file, you can specify the filename to send it to, or use the question mark option to bring up the Windows file create file dialog box. The syntax would look something like this.

DISPLAY COVERAGE DEMOCOVG [TO FILE<filename>] | ? | TO PRINTER

The ALL option. If you specify the ALL option after naming the Coverage file you want to look at, Visual dBASE will display the following information:

1. The contents of the main Coverage file named on the command line
2. The coverage file for each program or procedure file called by the main Coverage file
3. The total number of logical blocks for all program files that were entered and exited
4. The percentage of logical blocks that were entered and exited for all programs

In the case of our example, you can see all of the Coverage information by typing in this command:

```
LIST COVERAGE DEMOCOVG ALL
```

dBASE displays the coverage file for the main program and the called program, CovStart. The results will look something like this.

```
E:\ZDBWORK\WORKFILE\DEMOCOVG.COV
Block 1, line 2 to 7, was exercised 1 times.
Block 2, line 11 to 17, was exercised 1 times.
Block 3, line 19 to 20, was exercised 1 times.
Block 4, line 24 to 24, was exercised 0 times.
Block 5, line 27 to 27, was exercised 1 times.
4 blocks out of 5 blocks tested.
Test coverage is 80.00% complete.
E:\ZDBWORK\WORKFILE\COVSTART.COV
Block 1, line 3 to 12, was exercised 1 times.
Block 2, line 14 to 14, was exercised 1 times.
2 blocks out of 2 blocks tested.
Test coverage is 100.00% complete.
*** Total: 6 blocks out of 7 blocks tested.
*** Total: test coverage is 85.71% complete.
```

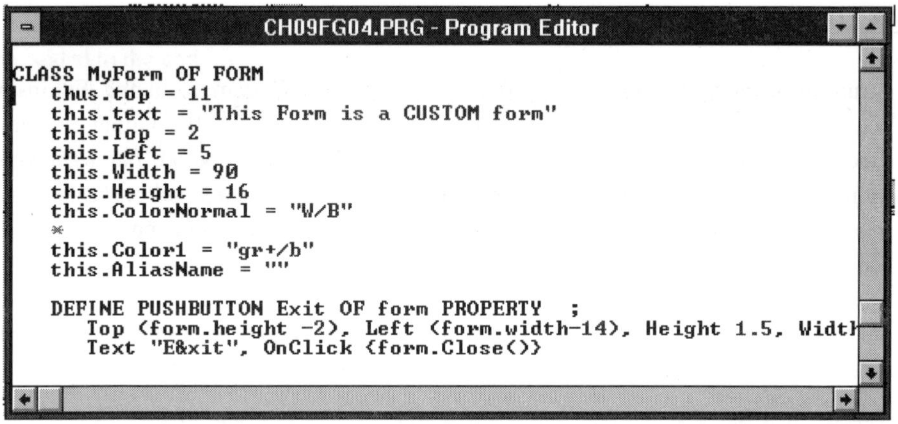

CH09FG04.PRG - Program Editor

```
CLASS MyForm OF FORM
   thus.top = 11
   this.text = "This Form is a CUSTOM form"
   this.Top = 2
   this.Left = 5
   this.Width = 90
   this.Height = 16
   this.ColorNormal = "W/B"
   *
   this.Color1 = "gr+/b"
   this.AliasName = ""

   DEFINE PUSHBUTTON Exit OF form PROPERTY  ;
      Top (form.height -2), Left (form.width-14), Height 1.5, Widt
      Text "E&xit", OnClick {form.Close()}
```

Figure 9–5. The Text Editor active with the pointer sitting on the offending error line.

When you enter the Text Editor, dBASE immediately takes you to the line of code that caused the runtime error. In this case, the line has "thus.top" instead of "this.top." Now you can change the code and save it with **Ctrl-W**. Once you save it, Visual dBASE will attempt to continue running the program (with the changes effected).

Debugging your runtime errors. You can also choose to debug your runtime errors. If you choose *debug*, dBASE will activate the graphical debugger (a separate Windows application), load your program, and stop at the offending line. Figure 9–6 shows the debugger active.

Notice that the debugger is a separate program. When it loads, it initially displays four windows. The top, left window has your program (MYCUSTOM.PRG) loaded; it is known as the Module window. It has highlighted the offending line, "thus.top = 11" The bottom, right window, named the Stack window, tells you which line of code is the offending line "Line 138 in file. . . ."

Modifying code in the debugger. When working in the debugger, the first thing you will observe is that you *cannot* change code in the debugger itself. Rather, you select Program >> Fix from the menu, and you are returned to Visual dBASE with the code placed in the Program Editor. The debugger will be closed, and you fix the code in dBASE itself. The debugger only lets you work with the program code, not change it.

Logical Errors

In addition to compile errors and runtime errors, your code may have *errors in logic*. The program can be syntactically correct and have no apparent runtime errors, yet still produce incorrect results. For example, you may have code that is suppose to run when an event occurs (like opening a form or double-clicking on an object), but the event never occurs. You have looked at the code, and the method is attached to the event. Why doesn't it work? Does the event ever occur? This type of error is known as a logic error.

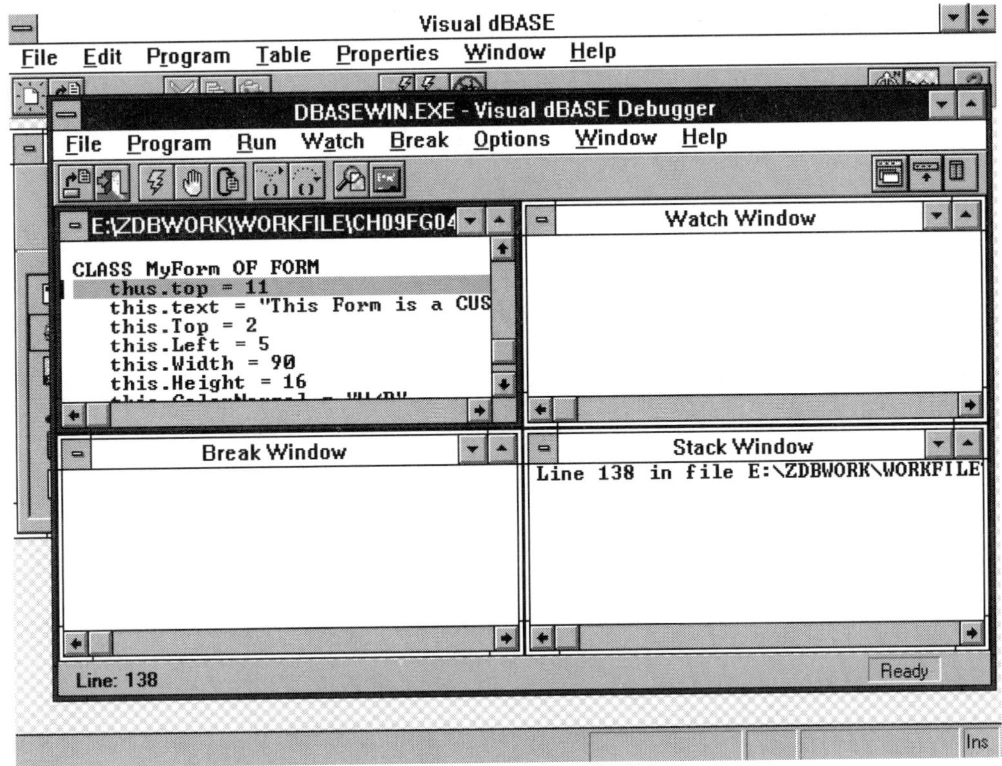

Figure 9–6. The debugger loaded from a runtime error.

You may have a memory variable that was declared PUBLIC and is initialized by all forms instantiated (created) by a certain class. That same variable is RELEASEd when one of the forms is closed; all it takes is the closing of a single form. If you create two forms from the same Class and close one of the forms, the PUBLIC variable will be released with the issuance of the RELEASE command. If the variable still needs to be used in code of the other open form, it will cause an error. This is another type of logic error.

Logic errors will not be trapped at runtime because they are errors created during the planning and implementation of the automation process. These types of errors are the most difficult to ferret out.

SET TRAP, ECHO, and STEP commands. In previous DOS versions of dBASE, you have three commands that can help you in solving these types of problems. If they are switched ON, they can activate the debugger or perform other debugging tasks. These commands are

- SET ECHO On/OFF
- SET TRAP On/OFF

- SET STEP On/OFF

None of these commands will work in Visual dBASE. Because all debugging is performed in the separate dBASE debugger, these three commands are obsolete. If you place them in your code, Visual dBASE will do the following:

- SET TRAP ON is simply ignored.
- SET ECHO ON will open the debugger.
- SET STEP ON will open the debugger.
- SET < any of them > OFF will be ignored.

Using the debugger

The debugger is good for finding logic errors in your code—those errors that just seem to happen with no explanation.

Starting the debugger

The debugger can be started inside or outside of Visual dBASE. You have already started it by clicking on the debug button of the Alert box while inside dBASE.

Starting the debugger from Windows. Because the debugger is a separate Windows-based application, you can start by clicking on the debugger icon from the Program Manager (or whatever Windows shell you are using). The icon looks like the one in Figure 9–7.

Figure 9–7. The debugger icon in Windows.

When starting the debugger outside of dBASE, you must load the program, using the menu; to be debugged, it will not automatically load the program.

Starting the debugger from Visual dBASE. The debugger can be started from inside Visual dBASE. It can be started using the tools or via a command. The command DEBUG will start it. The general syntax is

```
DEBUG [<filename> | ? | <wild cards in filename > | <procedure/UDF name> ;
```

[WITH <parameter list>]]

The <filename> can be any program, form, procedure, or UDF. You can also pass parameters to the file at the time you debug it.

NOTE: Loading an Empty Debugger

You do not have to specify a <filename> when starting the debugger; you can simply issue the Command DEBUG. You will be prompted for a filename; if you click Cancel, the debugger will be loaded with no file active.

Using menus, you start the debugger following these steps:

1. Click in the Command window (make it the point of focus).
2. Select Programs >> Debug . . . from the menu choice.
3. Specify a program or form name in the Open File dialog box.

The six windows of the debugger

Once the debugger is activated, you will see a screen similar to the one in Figure 9–8.

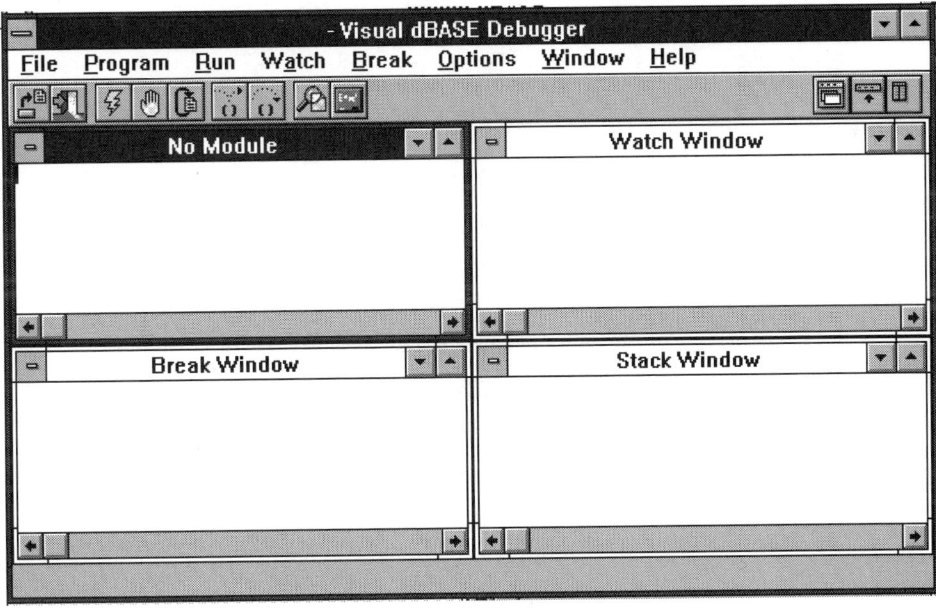

Figure 9–8. The debugger.

Notice that when the debugger first opens, it shows four windows. Starting from the top left, moving clockwise (left to right, down, left, up), the windows are

- Module window
- Watch window
- Stack window
- Break window

The debugger has two other windows that can also be opened.

- Open Text file window (from the File menu)
- Inspect window (from the Program menu)

The Module window. This window is where your source code will be displayed. If you haven't loaded a program to debug, follow these steps:

1. Select File >> New from the menu.
2. Select a program file to debug and press the OK button.

Once the source code is loaded, the debugger will highlight the current line of the program. It will look similar to Figure 9–9. Notice that the Module window displays in its title the name of the current program being debugged.

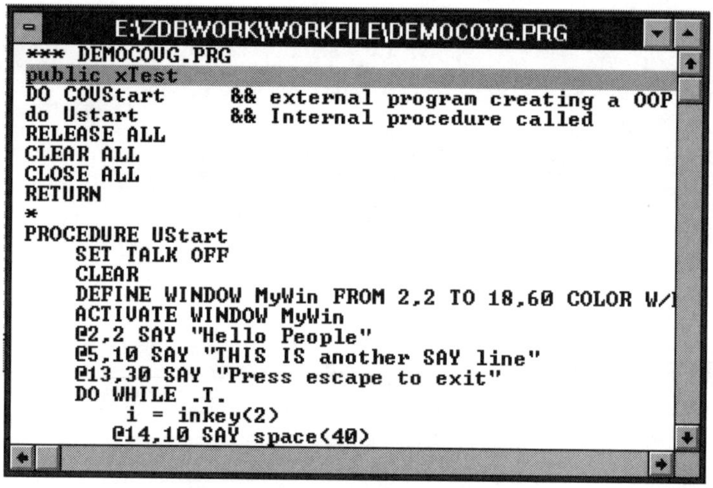

```
E:\ZDBWORK\WORKFILE\DEMOCOVG.PRG
*** DEMOCOUG.PRG
public xTest
DO COUStart        && external program creating a OOP
do Ustart          && Internal procedure called
RELEASE ALL
CLEAR ALL
CLOSE ALL
RETURN
*
PROCEDURE UStart
     SET TALK OFF
     CLEAR
     DEFINE WINDOW MyWin FROM 2,2 TO 18,60 COLOR W/
     ACTIVATE WINDOW MyWin
     @2,2 SAY "Hello People"
     @5,10 SAY "THIS IS another SAY line"
     @13,30 SAY "Press escape to exit"
     DO WHILE .T.
         i = inkey(2)
        @14,10 SAY space(40)
```

Figure 9–9. The Module window.

The debugger will only work with one program in the Module window at a time. The file that appears in the Module window is the module that you are currently debugging. When the application calls another program, it will be moved into the Module window automatically.

The Watch window. The Watch window is where you can specify names of expressions and variables that you want to watch or view their values. They do not have to exist at the time that you specify them. Figure 9–10 shows the Watch window, located top, left corner of the debugger, with some variables specified. Notice that all of the variables are undefined.

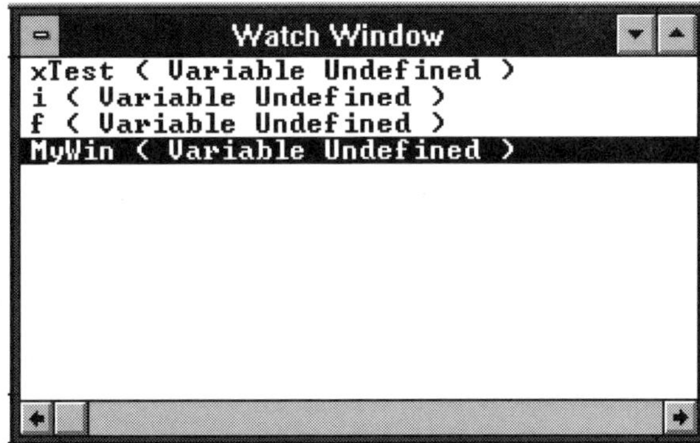

Figure 9–10. The Watch window.

You can quickly set a watch point by pressing **Ctrl-W** and then add the name of the variable you want to display.

The Break window. The Break window shows all the breakpoints set in the current program and lets you add, edit, or remove breakpoints. Figure 9–11 shows the Break window, located bottom, left corner of the debugger, with one breakpoint set.

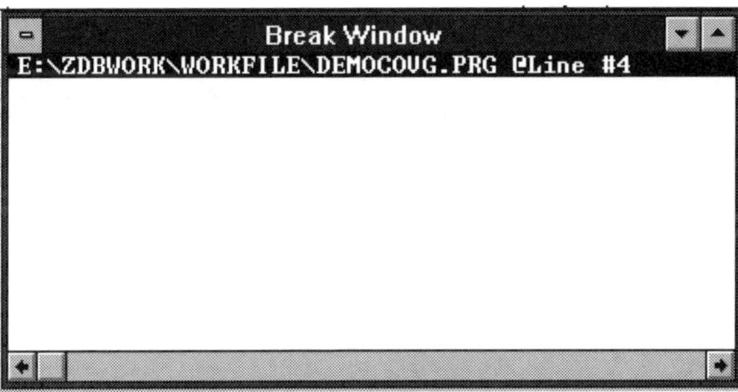

Figure 9–11. The Break window.

You can quickly set a breakpoint by going to the beginning of any line and clicking the mouse when a Stop sign becomes visible. The line will turn red.

The Stack window. The final window that is initially opened is the Stack window. It shows you any calls made in the debugged program to other modules (programs, procedures, and UDFs). Figure 9–12 shows the Stack window, located bottom, right of the debugger.

It can be broken into two groups—left and right sides. The left side has nine buttons. Each one corresponds to a menu choice. From left to right, they are:

- Load New program to debug (File>>New of the menu)
- Exit the debugger (File>>Exit menu)
- Run the program at full speed (Run>>Run menu)
- Pause the program execution (Run>>Stop menu)
- Reload the program from disk (Run>>Reset menu choice)
- Run a single source line of code, stepping into (Run>>Trace Into menu)
- Execute a line of code skipping calls (Run>>Step over menu)
- Inspect a variable or expression (Program >> Inspect . . . menu)
- Evaluate/change an expression (Program >>Evaluate/Modify . . . menu)

The right side of the speedbar has three additional buttons. These buttons are used to:

- Restore debugger to normal size
- Reduce debugger to menu and speedbar
- Change the speedbar to a popup

These three buttons have no corresponding menu choices. They let you change the appearance of the Debugger window. The second button—reduce debugger to menu and speedbar—will minimize the debugger to look like the one in Figure 9–16. Using the debugger in this small window lets you view forms and windows in Visual dBASE as they are being debugged.

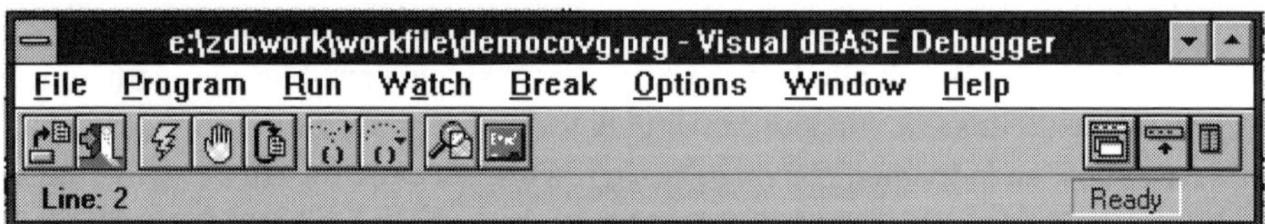

Figure 9–16.

Loading programs to debug

You can load a program file as you open the debugger or load it after the debugger is running. You can also load subroutines while in the debugger.

Loading a program file when starting the debugger. To load a program file when starting the debugger, simply specify the name of the program after the word DEBUG.

```
DEBUG MYDEMO
```

This will debug a program named MYDEMO.

Loading a program inside the debugger. To load a file after starting the debugger, select File >> New . . . from the debugger menu or click on the first button of the speedbar and specify the name of the program file to Debug.

Loading subroutines. If you run a main program that calls other programs, the debugger will automatically load the subroutine when the main program calls it. You can also load a subroutine before the program calls it. You can load a called module (external program) from the menu or while in the Module window.

To load another program module from inside the debugger, follow these steps:

1. Select File >> Load Module from the menu.
2. Enter the name of the module in the dialog box.

To load another module from the Module window:

1. Right click in the Module window (to activate the speedmenu).
2. Select the Load Module option.
3. Select the name of the procedure to load.

The loaded module will now be displayed in the Module window. This module will not run when you click on the Run button. It is simply being displayed so that you can examine it.

NOTE: Returning to the main program from a loaded module

If you need to move back to the original program, select the name of the program Module from the Stack window.

Controlling program execution

Once a program is in the debugger, you can do several things that control the execution of the program.

- Run
- Animate
- Trace
- Step
- Set breakpoints
- Stop

Running the program. While you are in the debugger, you can choose the run option, clicking the speedbar button or selecting the menu choice. The application will run inside dBASE. Before running, you may want to set breakpoints to halt execution temporarily and return you to the Debugger window.

Animate. You can run the program in animation mode from the debugger. When you animate a program, the debugger continuously runs the program, pausing at each command line and updating the information in all the Debugger windows (Watch, Inspect, etc.).

The program is actually running in Visual dBASE; however, it runs at a speed determined by you. While running, the source code will scroll through the Module window.

To animate a program, select Run >> Animate from the menu.

To set the speed of the animation, choose Options >> Animation Speed . . . from the menu and set the speed (by moving the scrollbox of the scrollbar). You can set the speed from slow to fast.

Tracing. You can run a program by running it one line at a time in the debugger, or *tracing* it. When tracing a program the debugger will run each line. There are two methods that can be used to trace through a program. One visually shows each line of the program as it is being executed. When it reaches a line that calls another program or UDF (DO . . .), it can treat the line as a single statement or move you into the called program and begin to trace through it.

Trace into. To trace the module and continue tracing into the subroutines, choose the *trace into* speedbar button or the menu choice.

Step over/skip. To trace the displayed module only, treating each call as a single step, select the *step over/skip* speedbar button or Step Over menu choice. Selecting this option will trace through the module, skipping over any subroutines (for the tracing). It still runs the subroutine, simply treat it as a single step.

Breakpoints. A breakpoint will stop program execution so that you can examine variables, fields objects, and expressions; change their values; and examine what subroutines the program is currently in.

This is probably the most powerful tool of the debugger. If you suspect that your code has a bug in it, you can set breakpoints where you believe the bug is located. Once set, the program will halt execution when it reaches the breakpoint and return to the debugger. Once back to the debugger, you can examine the values and, if necessary, begin tracing through the code one line at a time.

You can set breakpoints based on a condition or a specific program line.

Stopping. You can also stop a program that is running, being animated, or stepping by selecting the Stop choice in the Run menu prompt. Stopping execution of a program is like pausing it while stepping through it. You only stop at the current line, which is highlighted in the Module window.

Working with breakpoints

Setting breakpoints and viewing information in the debugger is the best way to determine problems in your code. You can set two different types of breakpoints:

- Program line
- Conditional

Setting a program line breakpoint

A program line breakpoint is set based on reaching a specific line of code being executed. When the program gets to the line, it stops execution and returns to the Debugger.

Three ways to set a line breakpoint. You can set a breakpoint at any line of code in the program. This can be accomplished in three ways. All three ways require that you first move the cursor to the line where you want to set a breakpoint. Once on the line, you set it by

- Pressing the **F2** key to toggle a breakpoint on/off
- Selecting Break>>Toggle ON/OFF from the menu
- Moving the cursor to the left of the command. When you see the stop sign, click the left mouse button.

Figure 9–17 shows the cursor becoming a stop sign when moved to the left side of a command line in the Module window.

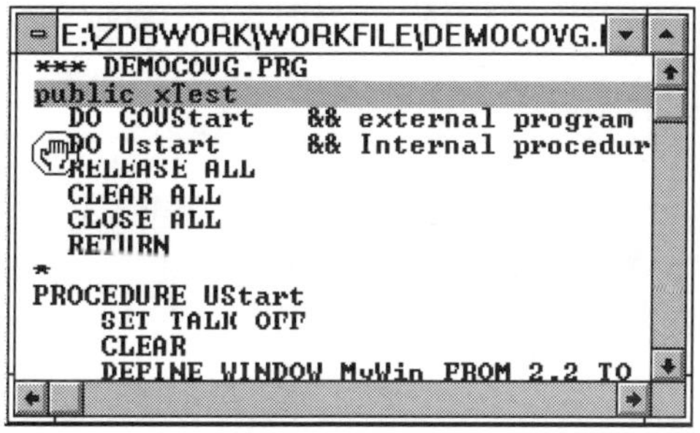

```
E:\ZDBWORK\WORKFILE\DEMOCOVG.I
*** DEMOCOVG.PRG
public xTest
  DO COVStart      && external program
  DO Ustart        && Internal procedur
  RELEASE ALL
  CLEAR ALL
  CLOSE ALL
  RETURN
*
PROCEDURE UStart
    SET TALK OFF
    CLEAR
    DEFINE WINDOW MyWin FROM 2.2 TO
```

Figure 9–17. The stop sign cursor for setting breakpoints.

Figure 9–17 shows the stop sign cursor. Move the mouse to the line where you want to place a breakpoint. While at the beginning of the line, the pointer changes to a Stop sign with a hand inside it. Click on the mouse and the line will be highlighed, setting the breakpoint. Figure 9–18 shows the module and break window with a line breakpoint set.

The line will turn red to let you visually know that a breakpoint has been set. Once set, the line breakpoint information is added to the Break window.

Notice that Figure 9–18 shows the breakpoint line is highlighted (turned to red) in the Module window, while the breakpoint information is displayed in the Break window. The breakpoint is highlighted in red, while the current line is highlighted in light blue (two lines above the breakpoint).

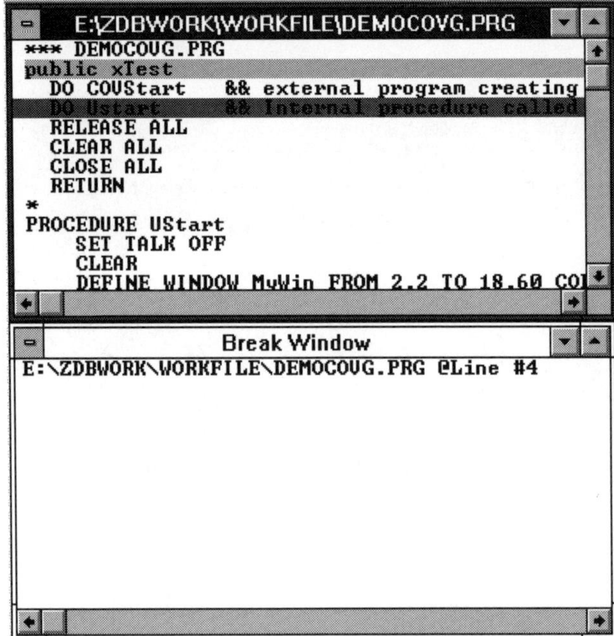

Figure 9–18. The Module and Break windows.

Setting a conditional breakpoint

A conditional breakpoint can be set based on any condition. The condition can be a line number in a program (like the previous example) or when a variable has a certain value. It can even be based on a number of passes through a DO WHILE, SCAN, or FOR looping command. It can be any legal dBASE condition.

Unlike setting line breakpoints, you can specify what action should be taken when the breakpoint is reached.

Creating a conditional breakpoint. To set a conditional breakpoint, move to the Break window and activate it by clicking in it. Once it is the active window (has focus), you can set a breakpoint by doing any of these actions:

- Select Break >> Add from the menu.
- Right click to activate the speedmenu and select Add.
- Double click (left mouse) the mouse inside the Break window.

Once you select Add, or double-click, an Add Breakpoint dialog box will appear. It should look like the one in Figure 9–19.

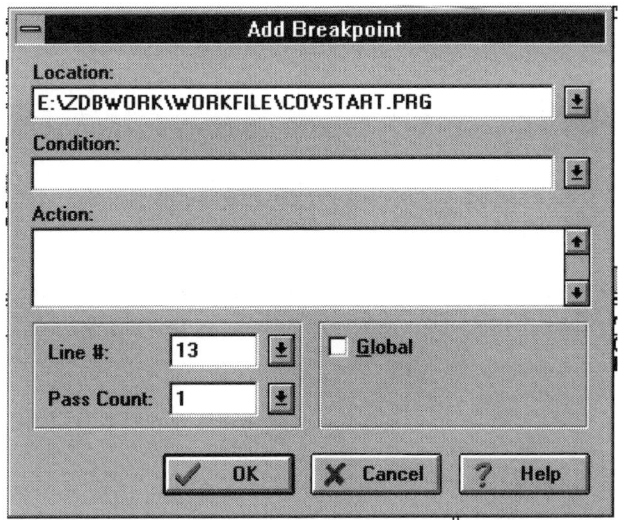

Figure 9–19. The Add Breakpoint dialog box.

By default, the Add Breakpoint will automatically add the current program name. The Add Breakpoint dialog box lets you specify:

- Location
- Condition
- Action
- Line number
- Pass count
- Set a global status

Most of these choices are self-explanatory:

- The location is the name of the module (program) to set the breakpoint in.
- The line number is the number of the line in the location program that will be used to trigger the breakpoint.
- The condition is a valid dBASE expression that will be used as the condition to trigger the breakpoint.
- The action is what command you want to execute when the breakpoint condition is met.

Specifying a pass count. You can specify a pass count for looping programs. To specify a pass count you need to specify a condition and then set the number of passes. The condition can be something that resides inside a DO WHILE loop. It can be set globally or specific to a progam.

Specifying a global status. If you check the global checkbox in the Add Breakpoint dialog box, two new options appear as shown in Figure 9–20.

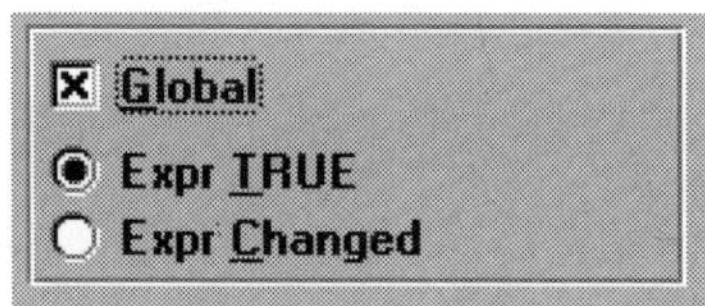

Figure 9–20. The global checkbox of the Add Breakpoint dialog box.

The location and line number choices are disabled when you select this choice. Actually, they disappear from the dialog box. A global breakpoint deals with conditions across all programs.

Once you decide to create a global breakpoint you can select one of two conditions. The first radio button lets you define the *condition* for an **expression** that is **true** (.t.); the second lets you define the *expression* for an **expression** that has **changed**.

Setting breakpoints in event handlers

You can debug an event handler by setting a breakpoint in the event handler (method). Once set, run the program that contains the form or object which has the event handler associated with it.

While the form is active, interact with the object to trigger the Event Handler. You will be taken into the debugger. At this point you can trace or animate the code.

Working with Watch expressions

A Watch expression is any valid expression—field, memory variable, object property, and so on. You may want to watch the values of expressions during the execution of the program. You use the Watch window to view expressions.

You can set *watchpoints*, before expressions are initialized (declared with PUBLIC, LOCAL, . . . or assigned a value x=10).

Once set, you view their value in the Watch window. Every time the program pauses (returns to the debugger), the Watch expressions will be updated.

In addition to viewing Watch points, you can also change a watch point value, controlling execution of a program.

Setting a watchpoint

The easiest way to set a watchpoint is to highlight the expression or variable in the Control window and press **Ctrl-W**. Visual dBASE moves the specified watchpoint to the Watch window.

You can also set watchpoints by right mouse clicking in the Watch window and selecting Add from the speedmenu or left double clicking in the Watch window. Figure 9–21 shows the Add Watchpoint dialog box.

Figure 9–21. The Add Watchpoint dialog box.

Once activated the Add Watchpoint dialog box can be used to type in a watch point—a field name, a variable name, object, and one of its property names, and an array element.

Changing a watchpoints value

Besides watching the values of a variable, field, and so on, you can change its value. This can be extremely important for testing routines. For instance, you may need to change the value of a variable to force an IF condition to operate the ELSE portion. The easiest way to change a watchpoint value is to click in the Watch window. Once in the Watch window

1. Highlight the watchpoint you want to change.
2. Right mouse click and select **Change . . .** from the speedmenu.
3. Type in the new value.

Changing undefined variables. If the variable in the Watch window shows that it has not been defined in the program yet, you will not be able to change its value. The value can only be changed after the variable is initialized and typed (character, numeric, etc.).

Changing values in methods. Be cautious when changing values for methods, procedures, and UDFs; you may get unexpected results. You may be unexpectedly returned to a called program or disable an Event Handler.

Remember: When changing values in the watch window, unexpected things can occur.

Watching arrays and objects. When you need to examine an array or object, the Watch window will only let you examine a single value of the array or object (property). Instead of watching an array or object you can inspect them to see all the values of the arrays elements or the properties of the object.

Inspecting expressions (variables, etc.)

In addition to watching expressions, you can activate the Inspection window and inspect expressions. Inspecting expressions is similar to watching them.

Inspecting versus watching

The big difference between watching an expression and inspecting it can be determined by the name of the operation.

To watch is to wait and look. When you watch something, you can look for it. It may not exist yet, but when it does, you will recognize it and know that it is there. You anticipate looking for it (watching for it). Once it arrives, you continue to watch it, and see what happens to it.

Inspecting something. If you need to inspect something, it must already exist. You can't wait for something to appear if you are inspecting it. It already exists and is in front of you to inspect or look at it. So to inspect an object, array, memory variable, or field, it must already be established and have some value in it (exist).

Inspecting arrays and objects

Unlike watching, you can inspect the array or object as a whole. You see all the elements or properties at one time.

Inspecting an expression

The fastest way to inspect an expression, while stepping through a program is to highlight the expression after it is created and press **Ctrl-I** (or select Program >> Inspect from the menu). Visual dBASE will open an Inspect dialog box where you can place the name of the variable (or expression) you want to inspect. Then it will open the Inspect window and display the current value for the expression. Figure 9–22 shows the Inspect window open for a memory variable named *xTest*.

Multiple Inspect windows. Every time you request an inspection of an expression, Visual dBASE will put the expression in its own Inspection window.

The Inspection window

Each Inspect window has its own SpeedMenu, which can be opened by right mouse clicking. You can do any of the following to the expression that you are inspecting:

Range. You can set a range (lower and upper limit) for the expression.

Change. You can change the value of the selected item.

Inspect again. Lets you reinspect the expression.

Descend. Is used to go down layers of an object.

Hex expand. View the hexidecimal value of binary strings variables.

Inspect new expression . . . . Clear the current value and place a new one to examine.

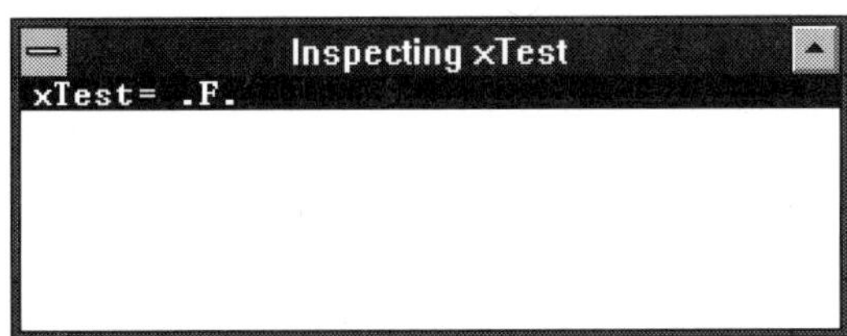

Figure 9–22. The Inspection window.

Modifying and evaluating expressions

You do not have to create a watch point to modify or evaluate an expression. If you need simply to check the value of an expression or want to modify it, right mouse click while in the Module window and select Evaluate/Modify from the SpeedMenu. Visual dBASE will activate a dialog box similar to the one in Figure 9–23.

Figure 9–23. The Evaluate/Modify dialog box.

You can use this box to evaluate the value of any expression or modify the expression value to alter program logic.

Debugging Event Handlers

You can debug an Event Handler (method, or codeblock), the same way you debug any procedural code—setting breakpoints, tracing, stepping, and animating. Breakpoints become critical aid when debugging Event Handlers.

The type of Event Handler that is assigned to the event will determine how you will debug the Event Handler code. In general to debug Event Handler code, you set the breakpoint in the Event Handler, and then trace the code as it is processed in the Event Handler.

The code to demonstrate debugging an Event Handlers

Because an Event Handler can be as small as a single line of code (like a codeblock), where you set the breakpoint becomes critcal. The following code can be used to examplify the problem:

```
*** CUSTDbug.wfm
*
LOCAL f
f = NEW CUSTOMERFORM()
f.Open()
CLASS CUSTOMERFORM OF FORM
   this.Width =          68
   this.Height =         12
   this.View = "customer.dbf"
   this.Text = "Customer Records"
   this.OnOpen = {;Public xFind; xFind = Recno()}
   this.OnGotFocus = {;go xFind}
   DEFINE TEXT TEXT1 OF THIS PROPERTY ;
         Top 0.5, Left 1, Width 43.5, Height 2.0, FontSize 18, ;
         Text "Customer Information"
   DEFINE TEXT TEXT2 OF THIS PROPERTY ;
         Top 3, Left 15, Width  34.5, Height 2.3, Text "Name", ;
         Border .T., ColorNormal "w*/n"
```

```
   DEFINE ENTRYFIELD ENTRYFIELD1 OF THIS PROPERTY ;
         Top 4, left 18, Width 30, Height 1, OldStyle .t. , ;
         DataLink "CUSTOMER->CUST_NAME", ColorNormal "n/w*"

   DEFINE PUSHBUTTON PUSHBUTTON1 OF THIS PROPERTY ;
         Top 8, Left 10, Width 18, Height 2.0 ,;
         OnClick CLASS::PUSHBUTTON1_ONCLICK,;
         Text "&Find Customer", ColorNormal "N/W"
   DEFINE PUSHBUTTON PUSHBUTTON2 OF THIS PROPERTY;
         Top 8, Left 40, Width 18, Height 2.0, ;
         Text "&Close", ColorNormal "W*/R*" ,;
         OnClick {;form.close()}
   Procedure PUSHBUTTON1_OnClick
   create session
   do findcust.wfm
ENDCLASS
```

Typing in the above code and running it, you will see a screen similar to the one in Figure 9–24.

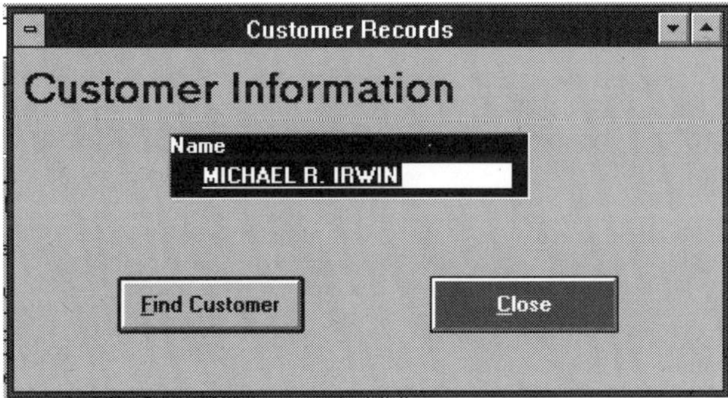

Figure 9–24. A form to be debugged.

Debugging Event Handler codeblocks

To set a breakpoint on a codeblock associated with an event, you set it at the define level or based on a condition within the codeblock. For instance, Figure 9–25 demonstrates setting a breakpoint on the OnClick event of the pushbutton.

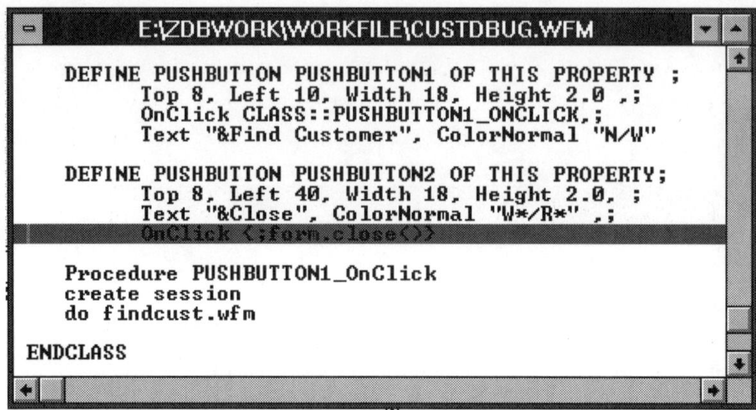

Figure 9–25. Setting a breakpoint on a codeblock Event Handler.

Using the preceding code, load it into the debugger, go to the line with the OnClick property for the pushbutton, and place a breakpoint at the line.

Setting breakpoints at the define level of codeblocks. The breakpoint can be set at the DEFINE level for a codeblock Event Handler. That is what you did for the breakpoint in Figure 9–25. If you run the code inside the debugger, it will stop execution during the defining of the pushbutton (PUSHBUTTON2) at the OnClick line.

At this point you can perform two steps—set a watchpoint and trace the code from this point on.

To set a watchpoint, do the following two steps:

1. Select Watch >> Add from the menu (or speedmenu in the Watch window).
2. Type in—***form.PushButton2.OnClick*** in the Add Watchpoint dialog box (Figure 9–26).

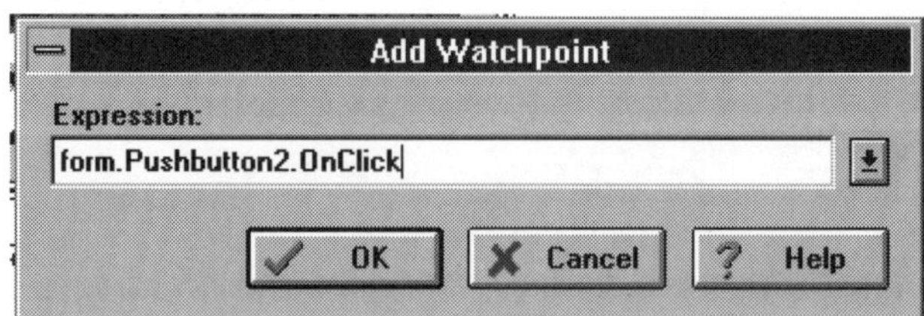

Figure 9–26. Adding the watchpoint for OnClick of the pushbutton.

The reason you used the special variable *form* is because the form can be given any name when it is created from the Class. The point you will see its value is when it is assigned. Notice that the name of the pushbutton is PushBUTTON2. The name was specificially assigned when you defined the pushbutton with the *DEFINE PUSHBUTTON PushButton2 OF this* command inside the class definition.

With the watchpoint set, the Watch window shows the expression and informs you that the expression is currently Undefined. Because you set a breakpoint at this line, it stopped before processing the line. Now press the skip into button and the line will be processed. The moment it is processed, the expression will show a value like in Figure 9–27.

Figure 9–27. The Watch window showing the Onclick property.

When you clicked on the trace into button, Visual dBASE executed the next line of code, which assigned a codeblock to the OnClick property. That is why the value changed in the Watch window.

As Figure 9–27 demonstrates, the codeblock has been assigned to the onClick property of the pushbutton named PushButton2. Once you click on the Close button in the active form, the debugger will end its session because you have no other breakpoints set.

Setting a breakpoint inside a codeblock. If you have a codeblock that performs more than one step, you can set a global condition based on a value within the codeblock. In the preceding code, there is a multiple command assignment in the OnOpen event of the form:

```
this.OnOpen = {;Public xFind;xFind=Recno()}
```

This event handler codeblock performs two steps—first it declares a variable xFind as Public, then it makes xFind equal to the record number (type numeric). You can build a breakpoint on this code by adding a new breakpoint based on a condition of xFind = Recno(), or when it turns to a numeric type. To set (add) a breakpoint for xFind, follow these steps:

1. Click in the Break window.
2. Double-click to activate the Add Breakpoint dialog box.
3. Click the **Global** check box on.
4. Make sure the Expr TRUE button is active under the Global checkbox.
5. Go to the Condition box.
6. Enter in **TYPE("xFIND")="N"** to the Condition box.

The Condition box should look similar to the one in Figure 9–28.

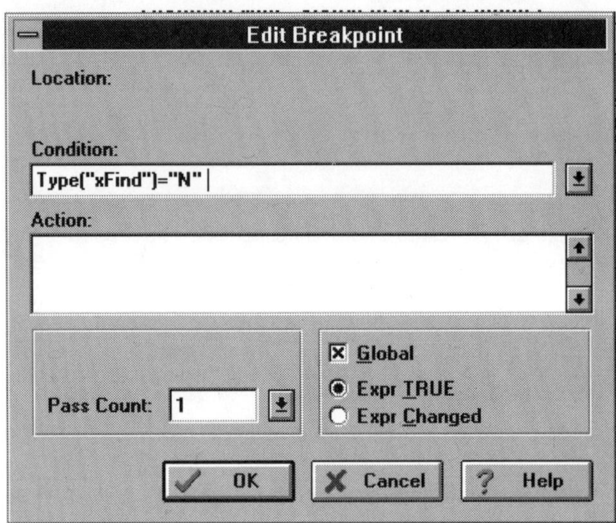

Figure 9–28. Setting a condition based on something inside a codeblock.

Once you have typed in the new breakpoint condition, the Break window should look similar to the one in Figure 9–29.

To set a breakpoint based on some action inside the codeblock, it must be a global condition that is not associated with a line number. If you assign it with a line number, the assignment will be based on the DEFINE object, rather than the action within the codeblock.

> **!** **Use caution when setting conditional breakpoints**
> Setting breakpoints on conditions within a codeblock can give you unexpected results. Because you are setting them based on something in an unnamed function or procedure (a codeblock) that simply sits in memory, dBASE may do unexpected things during the debugging of the code. Remember, you cannot change code in the debugger; rather, it is done in the Text Editor. Therefore, setting breakpoints with a codeblock may be a bad way to do it.

Instead of setting conditions inside a multi-statement (command) codeblock, consider converting the codeblock to a procedure or function that can be embedded into the Class itself (as a method) and debugging the method instead. This is safer and more readable for modifying later.

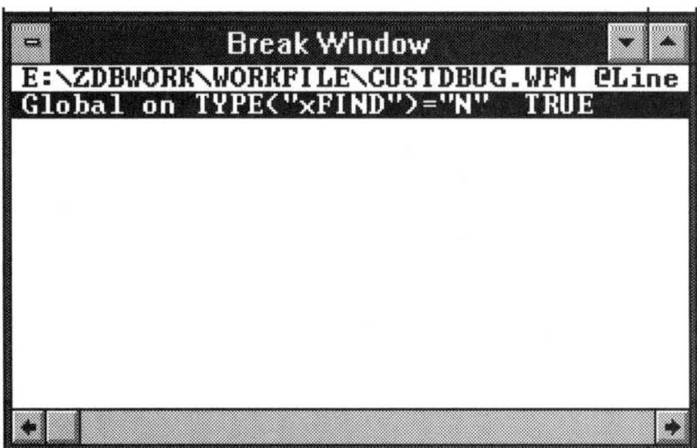

Figure 9–29. The Break window with a global condition set based on an action inside a codeblock.

Debugging Event Handler methods

To set a breakpoint on a method associated with an event, you can also do it at the define level or at the method (procedure/function) level. Ideally, you want to set it at the method level so that you can trace or step through the code as it is being executed to verify that it works correctly. In the example code, you have an internal event handler named PUSHBUTTON1_OnClick. The code looks like this (it is inside the class definition):

```
. . . . .
   Procedure PUSHBUTTON1_OnClick
   create session
   do findcust.wfm
ENDCLASS
```

Setting a breakpoint at the method level. To set a breakpoint at the method level, simply go to the method and set the breakpoint where you want the code to stop executing. For example, you may want to see a breakpoint at the very beginning of the procedure PUSHBUTTON1_OnClick—the first line of code.

Figure 9–30 shows setting a breakpoint on the first line of the procedure. Notice that Figure 9–30 shows the breakpoint is set inside the method.

Setting a breakpoint for the procedure name line. You cannot directly set a breakpoint on the procedure name line. Because you must set breakpoints on valid expressions, the procedure (method) name line is not a valid expression. If you need to set a breakpoint based on the name of the procedure, follow these steps:

1. Click in the Break window.
2. Right mouse click to call up the SpeedMenu.
3. Select Add from the menu . . . the Add Breakpoint dialog box appears.
4. Click the **Global** checkbox on.
5. Go to the Condition box.
6. Enter in **PROGRAM()="PUSHBUTTON1_OnClick"** to the Condition box.

This lets you set a breakpoint based on a program name.

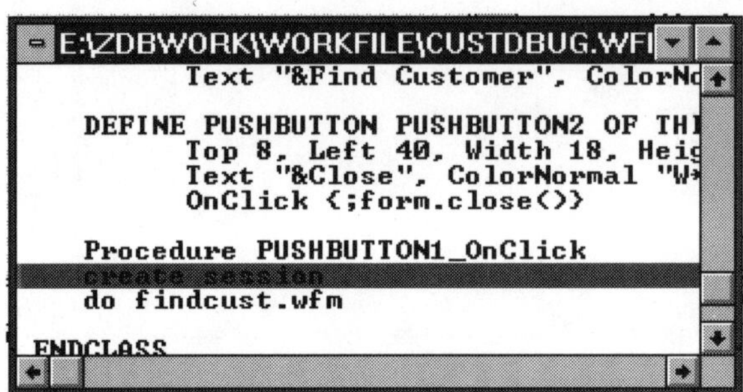

Figure 9–30. Setting a beakpoint inside a procedure method.

Configuring the debugger

When you use the debugger, you can choose options from the menu to set up the environment for the debugger. Once you have set up the environment the way you want it, you can save these options in a configuration file (.CFG).

The .CFG file

The configuration file does not have to reside in the \dBASEWIN\BIN directory. Rather it should be placed in the directory where you are debugging the programs. You can name it whatever you want (the default name is *default.cfg*). You can have more than one configuration file.

Saving a configuration file. After you adjust your environment, you can save the debug configuration file by selecting Options >> Save Options . . . from the menu. The debugger will activate a Save File dialog box similar to the one in Figure 9–31. You give the configuration file a name and save it.

Loading a debug configuration file. If the debugger finds a file named DEFAULT.CFG, it will automatically load the configuration file. If it does, the debugger uses the Windows system font, the current directory, and the fastest animation speed. It also opens with all four of the main windows open—Module, Watch, Break, and Stack.

If you want to load a different configuration file select Options >> Restore Options . . . from the menu, then select the configuration file you want to restore from.

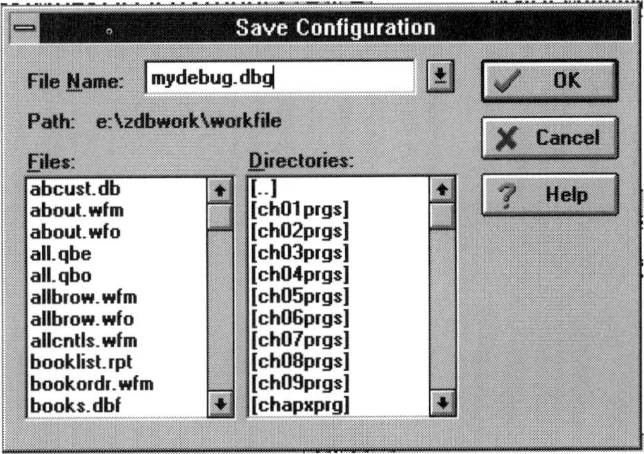

Figure 9–31. The Save Configuration dialog box.

NOTE: If you start the debugger from the Program Manager (Windows), it will look for the configuration file in the \DBASEWIN\BIN directory. After you load the debugger, you can load another configuration file using the Options menu choice.

Setting configuration defaults

The following options can be set and saved to a .CFG file:

- *Desktop.* The arrangement of the four debugger windows.
- *Application.* The default application to debug.
- *Breakpoints.* Specify any breakpoints in default application.
- *Watchpoints.* Specify any watchpoints for the default application.
- *Speedbar.* Placement (Normal, Popup, Reduced, and Vertical).

Once you set up the environment the way that you want it (moving windows around, etc.), check on those options that you want set (default is all set).

Setting the animation speed

You can also set the animation speed, from the Options menu. You move the slider between the two ranges of the horizontal scrollbar to set the speed.

Setting fonts

You can also set the default display fonts for the text in the windows by choosing Options >> Display Fonts. ...

Setting default source path

You can also choose Options >> Source File Path . . . to specify which path the debugger should use to load files from. This is used to set the default path.

Attaching the debugger to different instances of Visual dBASE

➡ You can run more than one instance of Visual dBASE and link them to a single instance of the debugger. If you start the debugger from within one of the instances of Visual dBASE, the debugger will attach to that instance.

If you run different applications in each instance of Visual dBASE, you can attach to any instance from inside the debugger by following these steps:

1. Choose File >> Attach from the Debugger menu.
2. Select which instance of dBASE you want the debugger to attach to, from the Attach to Active Application dialog box.

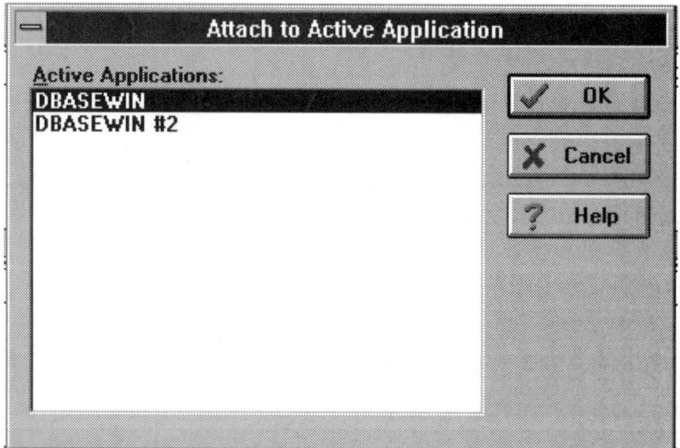

Figure 9–32. Selecting a Visual dBASE instance to attach to.

Figure 9–32 shows the dialog box. Once attached, the debugger will work with that instance of Visual dBASE.

Chapter 10
Intense Workout of Objects and Classes

So far you have worked with objects and classes to create forms, place controls (visual objects) inside forms, change object properties, and attach code (methods) to property events.

You have worked with objects by changing their properties and triggering their methods. You have created your own Classes, assigning new values to properties, creating new properties, and even new methods. Now you will fully exploit all the power of both objects and classes.

WORKING WITH OBJECTS

Objects are instances of the class that creates (instantiates) them. Once instantiated, they live independently. If you create two objects from the same class, they are independent objects. One can be moved, and the other remains where it is.

All the objects you have created so far are from the form class or from one of the control object classes. Remember, a control object is simply a visual control inside a form—a pushbutton, entryfield, and text.

Creating objects from the stock OBJECT( ) class

In addition to creating objects from the form or control classes, you can also create objects from the OBJECT class. The object class is simply a Class that has Constructor code that creates an ***empty*** object.

The stock object has no properties or methods. Once created, you can create all of its properties and methods.

User-defined object definitions

You create user-defined objects from the empty class named OBJECT, and customize them by creating their own properties and methods. Once the object is created, it is its own entity. It can be manipulated; it can be worked with.

Creating a user-defined object. To create your own empty object named ObjStudent, type in the following from the Command window:

```
ObjStudent = NEW OBJECT()
```

Now the object exists.

Creating properties for the empty user-defined object

This object is empty—it has *no* properties or methods. Now add some properties to the object. For instance, the following code will assign eight new properties to the object named ObjStudent. Each line starting with the NEW command can be entered in the Command window, one at time, or you can place them into a program. The example below is placed in a program named OBJTEST2.prg (then it is run with the DO OBJTEST2 command):

```
*** OBJTEST2.prg
*
PUBLIC OjbStudent
*
*  Set the procedure to itself to work with the methods
that
*  will be created later
*
SET PROCEDURE TO OBJTEST2
ObjStudent = new OBJECT()
ObjStudent.Name = "Joan Waters"
ObjStudent.DateOfBirth = {02/02/72}
ObjStudent.Course1="English Lit 401"
ObjStudent.Course2="History - World 404"
ObjStudent.Course1GradeQtr1 = 4.0
ObjStudent.Course2GradeQtr1 = 3.5
ObjStudent.Course1GradeQtr2 = 3.0
ObjStudent.Course2GradeQtr2 = 3.0
```

If you place this code inside a program, you will need to declare the object ObjStudent public, or you won't be able to work with it in the Command window. Remember, dBASE defaults all variable types to private, unless you specify otherwise.

Placing this code in a program will make it easier to use repeatedly in the next section. Notice that the SET PROCEDURE TO line has been added to make this procedure file automatically when you run the program.

Once the program has been run, or the preceding lines have been entered in the Command window, you can work with the property, changing its values, or just looking at its values. The following commands can be entered in the Command window to prove that you have an object with properties:

```
? ObjStudent.Name
```

```
? ObjStudent.Course1
? ObjStudent.Course1GradeQtr1
ObjStudent.Course1GradeQtr1 = 3.75
? ObjStudent.Course1GradeQtr1
                    . . . . .
```

After you entered the commands, dBASE displayed the correct values for each. You even changed the value for the property Course1GradeQtr1 from 4.0 to 3.75.

This object is unique. Once created, it will exist on its own. What you can't do with the object is create another object exactly like it, based on the object.

Objects *cannot* create other objects. An object cannot be used to create a new object. Objects, in Visual dBASE, must come from CLASSes. Because an object is an instance of the class, it is a creation of the class. The class holds most, if not all, of the objects methods.

Can I use a formula like MyObject = ObjStudent? At this point, you are probably wondering about using the object (ObjStudent) to assign all of the values to another object using a simple formula **x=y**. If you try to create a new object by saying

```
MyObject = ObjStudent
```

you will be creating an alias name for the same object. Although this will be covered later in this chapter, you need to know that if you assign MyObject = ObjStudent, all you are really doing is giving the object ObjStudent a second name. It is like assigning an alias or nickname to the same object. For instance, the author's name is Michael Richard Irwin; however, most people call him Mike or Michael instead of his whole name. Some people may even refer to him as Mr. Irwin. Mike, Michael, and Mr. Irwin are all aliases (or nicknames) for the same person (Michael Richard Irwin).

User-defined Class definitions. If you need to create more than one object with the same properties, you need to create your own class using the **CLASS . . . ENDCLASS** construct (command). Inside the Class definition, you assign properties and methods that can be used by any object created (instantiated) from it.

Creating methods for a user-defined object

You can also create methods for the user-defined object. Methods normally reside in the Class definition that is used to create the object and the object stores a *function pointer* in itself that points back to where the method actually resides. However, you can also create methods assigning them directly to the object. For instance, you can add two methods to the object named ObjStudent in the program Objtest2 (or type them in the Command window):

```
    . . . . .
ObjStudent.Course1Avg = {; RETURN (objstudent.course1gradeqtr1 +
;
```

```
                                objstudent.course1gradeqtr2)/2 }
ObjStudent.Course2Avg = {; RETURN (objstudent.course2gradeqtr1 +
;
                                objstudent.course2gradeqtr2)/2 }
```

The preceding code will create two methods named Course1Avg and Course2Avg. They are both codeblocks (versus procedures or functions). You know that they are statement codeblocks because the formula is enclosed between curley braces (**{ }**). Notice that the formula has the object name and property name of the numeric fields that are holding the grades for the quarter.

NOTE: Using RETURN in a codeblock

Because you want to have the object's method return a value from the codeblock, you need to use the RETURN keyword to specify what you want returned. By creating a codeblock with RETURN you are creating a type of un-named function, and all functions always return a value.

Once a method has been created for the object, it can be used like any other method. To run them, you would enter commands like the following in the Command window:

```
? ObjStudent.Course1Avg()
? ObjStudent.Course2Avg()
```

When you run these two methods, they will report back the grade average for each course based on the two quarter grades. If you change the grade values for any of the quarters, these methods will return the corrected values.

Creating an external method for an object. You can also create an external method (function, procedure, or codeblock) that can used by the object. To do this, you would follow these steps:

1. Create the external procedure or function placing it in a procedure file.
2. Create a new object property and assign the name of the external method.
3. Activate the procedure file with SET PROCEDURE TO.
4. Run the method like any other method of the object.

The following code can be added to the bottom of the program OBJTEST2.prg to demonstrate this.

```
  . . . .
objstudent.GradeAvg = ClassAvg
FUNCTION ClassAvg
  Parameter Grade1, Grade2
  Return (grade1+grade2)/2
```

If you have typed all the commands in at the Command window, you will have to create a new procedure file and place the function ClassAvg in the program file.

The preceding lines create a new Function named ClassAvg that will be placed in memory using the SET PROCEDURE TO command. Above the Function declaration is a new property named *GradeAvg* that is given the value of ClassAvg (the function name). When you declare a property in this manner, dBASE assumes that you want to create a method and assigns the name of the method (ClassAvg) to the property name. When you get ready to execute the method (now called GradeAvg) it will point to ClassAvg and run the external method named ClassAvg. GradeAvg becomes the internal *Function pointer* to the external function named ClassAvg.

With the program completed, you can use the external method, ClassAvg, by typing in code like the following in the Command window:

```
DO OBJTEST2
? ObjStudent.Name
? ObjStudent.GradeAvg(ObjStudent.Course1GradeQtr1, ;
                      ObjStudent.Course1GradeQtr2)
```

Notice that the last line uses the assigned property (really a method) GradeAve to run the external program ClassAvg. The code never references the name ClassAvg. The only reference is when you assigned ClassAvg to equal the property (internal method) GradeAve. If you forget to place the function in memory, dBASE will report an error.

Why use external methods? You may want to create external methods to be used by more than one object or object type. By creating external methods, they can be assigned to any object via a property definition. This means that you can create a library of common methods (procedures and functions) that can be used by more than one object or one object type (many objects from the same class).

INSPECTing the user-defined object properties and methods

You can use the Inspect() function to view all of the user-defined properties and methods. To inspect the object ObjStudent, run the program, make it an active procedure file and then inspect it.

The complete program should now look like this.

```
*** OBJTEST2.prg
*
PUBLIC OBJSTUDENT
SET PROCEDURE TO OBJTEST2
ObjStudent = new object()
objstudent.Name = "Joan Waters"
objstudent.DateOfBirth = {02/02/72}
objstudent.course1="English Lit 401"
objstudent.course2="History - World 404"
```

```
objstudent.course1gradeQtr1 = 4.0
objstudent.course2gradeQtr1 = 3.5
objstudent.course1gradeQtr2 = 3.0
objstudent.course2gradeQtr2 = 3.0
ObjStudent.Course1Avg={; RETURN (objstudent.course1gradeqtr1 + ;
       objstudent.course1gradeqtr2)/2}
ObjStudent.Course2Avg={; RETURN (objstudent.course2gradeqtr1 + ;
       objstudent.course2gradeqtr2)/2}
objstudent.gradeavg = ClassAvg
FUNCTION ClassAvg
  Parameter Grade1, Grade2
  Return (grade1+grade2)/2
```

With the program complete, you can run it and inspect the properties and methods of the object ObjStudent by typing in the following commands from the Command window:

```
CLEAR ALL
DO OBJTEST2
INSPECT(OBJSTUDENT)
```

The Inspect() function will activate the Property Inspector. It should look similar to the one in Figure 10–1.

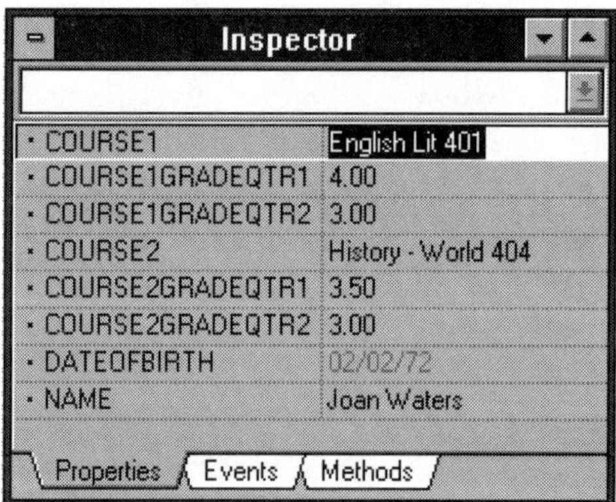

Figure 10–1. The Property Inspector showing the properties of the object ObjStudent.

When you click on the **Properties** tab (bottom) of the Property Inspector, you will see all the properties that you created for the object. Figure 10–1 shows all of them. Notice that the ones you created named Course1Avg, Course2Avg, and GradeAvg are not displayed in the properties page of the Property Inspector. These three can be found in the methods page, since they are methods. If you click on the tab marked **Methods**, you should see the three of them. If you expand the size of the dialog box to look like the one in Figure 10–2, you will see the formulas for Course1Avg and Course2Avg methods.

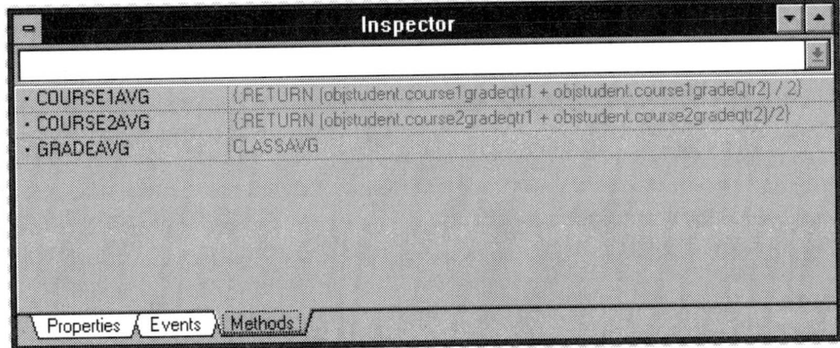

Figure 10–2. The methods of the object ObjStudent.

Notice that the method named GradeAvg does not show the formula; rather, it shows the name of the function, ClassAvg. This tells you that it is looking for a function named ClassAvg in a procedure file in memory. It does not tell you that the procedure is loaded, just that it is the one that will be run when the method GradAvg is executed.

Working with object reference variables

When you create an object, you specify a user-supplied name for the object. This command will create an object named TheForm:

```
TheForm = NEW FORM()
```

The user-supplied name for the object is **TheForm**. This user-supplied name is really known as the *object reference variable*. The object reference variable is simply the name that you assign to the **object** that will be used to **reference** the object **variable**.

Every time you use the NEW operator to create any object, you are assigning a user-supplied name to the object, known as the *object reference variable*.

The object's property Name versus an object reference variable

In addition to the user-supplied *object reference variable* (name), all of the Stock (built in) control objects (pushbuttons, checkboxes, etc.) have a property called *Name*.

The form object does not have a property titled Name; nor do the Array, DDELink, and DDETopic objects. All the remaining stock objects do. In fact, any object that is contained in the form, called a control object, will have a *Name* property.

The Name property. The property, *Name*, is the actual name assigned to the control object. This name is the name that is used by dBASE, internally, when it works with the control object on the form.

This is the complete opposite of using the NEW command. When creating a control object with NEW you assign an object reference variable and dBASE assigns the name property.

Containership and accessing controls
If you are totally confused at this point, you may want to jump ahead a few pages and read through Object Containership Revisited. Then return here to continue.

Assigning an object reference variable to a control object. A control object created with the DEFINE command assigns a new value to the *Name* property of the object. To access the properties of the control object, you specify the name of the form, then the object name (created with the DEFINE command), and finally the property name.

If you type any portion of the name wrong (form, object, property), an error will occur. To avoid this problem you can assign an object reference variable name to the control object after it is created using the DEFINE command. By assigning an object reference variable you can use it *or* the actual name.

The following code will assign aliases (object reference variables) to the Pushbutton and the Text objects contained in the form xFORM:

```
MyButton = xForm.xButton
MyText = xForm.xText
```

Having created object reference variables for the Pushbutton and Text objects, you can reference the control objects using the actual object name (<form>.<control>) or the object reference name. The following code demonstrates this:

```
? MyButton.Name
? xForm.xButton.Name
? MyButton.Text
? MyText.Name
? xForm.xText.Text
```

This code displays property values by using the object reference name or the actual name of the object.

Understanding object reference variables

An object reference variable is simply a name, that is specified by you, that you use to reference an object. They are slightly different than traditional memory variable names because of how they are used. To understand better how object reference variables work, you can compare them to memory variables.

Assigning values to memory variables. When you asssign values to memory variables, they contain the actual value. For instance, a date memory variable will contain a specific date; a character memory variable, a specific piece of text. The variable name points to the specific date or text value. The variable contains the actual value. The following code assigns values to two variables:

```
dBirth = {02/04/52}
cName = "Michael Irwin"
```

The variable dBirth contains the date value for February 4, 1952, and the variable cName contains the text name Michael Irwin.

Once you declare a memory variable and assign it a value, it physically contains that value. For instance, you can now assign another memory variable based on one already created:

```
xBirthDate= dBirth
xNewName = cName
```

Now the new variable xBirthDate and the old variable dBirth both hold values equal to the date February 4, 1952. This is also true for the two variables, xNewName and cName, containing the text "Michael Irwin."

If you change the value of dBirth it will *not* affect the value in xBirthDate; they are both independent variables with their own values. This is also true for xNewName versus cName. All four variables contain their own physical values.

The following code can demonstrate traditional memory variables:

```
xNum = 10              && store the number 10 to variable named xNum
yNum = xNum            && store the number 10 to variable named yNum
xNum = 20              && store the number 20 to variable named xNum
         && overrides the previous value stored in xNum
? xNum                 && displays the number 20
? yNum                 && displays the number 10
```

The preceding code shows that when each variable is created, it is individually assigned a physical value. Even when you assign one by using another xNewName = cName.

Assigning values to object reference variables. Object reference variables work differently, they only reference (or point) to an object, they are not the object itself. Although you can use the object reference variable with a member name (property or method) to have the object do something—display a value, change a value, or run a method. The object is independent. The following code can be used to demonstrate this:

```
MyObj = NEW OBJECT()      && Creates an object named MyObj
MyObj.yNum = 10           && assign the value 10 to yNum
```

```
YourObj = MyObj            && assign a new object reference
                           && variable to
                           && object pointed to by MyObj
? MyObj.yNum               && returns the number 10
? YourObj.yNum             && returns the number 10
YourObj.yNum = 20          && assign the value 20 to yNum
? MyObj.yNum               && returns the number 20
YourObj.xText = "YES"      && assign the value YES to xText
? MyObj.xText              && returns YES
```

When you created the object named MyObj, you created a physical object. The name MyObj, the object reference variable, only points to the object.

When you said YourObj = MyObj, you did not create another physical object; rather, you gave the same object another object reference variable (an alias name). When you change values using MyObj, you change values in the object that is pointed to by both names (MyObj and YourObj). Adding a new property and its value (xText) using YourObj is the same as adding it with MyObj. Both object reference variables point to the same physical object.

Any object can have any number of object reference variables (names) pointing to it. Because the object reference only references the object, you can specify any number of references for the object.

The life span of an object. If you assign several object reference variables to an object, the object will continue to exist until all of the object reference variables are released. Continuing with the same code using MyObj and YourObj reference variables, the following will demonstrate the life span of an object:

```
? MyObj                   && returns the type OBJECT
? MyObj.xText             && returns YES
? YourObj.xText           && also returns YES
RELEASE MyObj             && releases the varible MyObj
? MyObj                   && reports an error-variable undefined
? YourObj.yNum            && returns 20
? YourObj                 && returns the type OBJECT
```

Even though you released the variable named MyObj, the object still exists. This is because the object reference variable, YourObj, still exists.

You work with object reference variables the same way that you work with other memory variables. They can be given new values, passed as variables, returned from user-defined functions, and released.

Object containership revisited

Because a control object is contained in a form, there has to be a way to reference it. Because it is contained in the form, you reference it by the form name, then the control object *Name* (property). This means that you reference any contained object's property or method using the following syntax:

<Form name>.<Control Object>.<Property|Method name>

You must use the *member access operator* (dot) between the form object, object name, and member name. This is known as dot notation.

Objects contained inside objects

The following code creates a simple form and places a pushbutton inside the form. Then it will manipulate the pushbutton in the form.

```
** CONTEXAM.prg
*
Public xform
xForm = NEW FORM()
xForm.Height = 12
DEFINE PUSHBUTTON Exit OF xFORM PROPERTY ;
     Top 10, Left 45
xForm.Open()
xForm.Exit.Height = 1.5
xForm.Exit.OnClick = {;form.Close()}
xForm.Text = "A contained Object"
xForm.Exit.Text = "Bye Bye"
```

Once the preceding code is typed in (the PUBLIC is only necessary for a program), the form should look similar to the one in Figure 10–3.

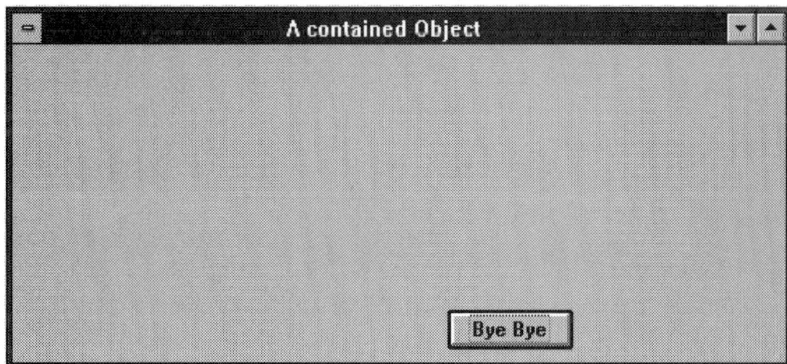

Figure 10–3. A form with a control object contained inside it.

Parent and child. Because the pushbutton, named Exit, is contained in the form, you reference the pushbutton by naming the form first. The form is considered the *parent* of all objects contained within it. The pushbutton is a *child* of the parent.

By naming the complete chain (parent, and then child) you can tell dBASE which object you want to work with. For instance, to change the text of the form, xForm, you specified **xForm.Text="A contained Form"**. To reference the text of the pushbutton, Exit, you specified **xForm.Exit.Text="Bye Bye"**.

Because the child is contained within the object, you need to reference the parent then the child and finally the objects property name if you want to change a property value, like in the example above (xForm.Exit.Text versus xForm.Text).

Taking advantage of the object reference variable

When you create a control object, like a pushbutton, using the DEFINE command, you specify the name that will be given to the *Name* property of the contained object. For instance, DEFINE PUSHBUTTON Exit OF xForm creates a new pushbutton inside the form and changes the *name* property to Exit.

Once you create a control object inside a form, you can assign an object reference variable to the object by following this simple formula:

<Object reference Variable> = <form name>.<Object Name>

To assign an alias name (object reference variable) of xPB to the Exit button, the command is

```
xPB = xForm.Exit
```

Once you create an object reference variable, you can manipulate the objects properties and methods by using the object reference variable instead of the entire object name (form, object, then member). The following two lines of code will change the width and text of the Exit object:

```
xPB.Text = "Close Form"
xPB.Width = 15
```

The NEW operator, object reference variable, and Name property. When you create a contained object using the NEW operator (command) you automatically create an object reference variable for the object. To create another button on the form using the NEW operator, type in the following:

```
xPB2 = NEW PUSHBUTTON(xForm)
xPB2.Text = "Help"
xPB2.Top = 10
xPB2.Left = 30
xForm.PUSHBUTTON1.height = 1.5
```

The object reference variable name of the pushbutton is xPB2, the actual name (*Name* property) is PUSHBUTTON1, which was assigned by Visual dBASE. If you create a second pushbutton, Visual dBASE will name it PUSHBUTTON2. You can access any of the properties using the real name—xForm.PushButton1.<property> or the object reference variable name—xPB2.

When you create a control object using the NEW operator you can specify a value for the *Name* property at the time you create it. For example, to create a third button on the form, you can type in the following commands:

```
xPB3 = NEW PUSHBUTTON(xForm,"MyButton")
xPB3.Text = "Open"
xPB3.Top = 10
xPB3.Left = 15
xForm.MyButton.Height = 1.5
```

Having manipulated the control objects by their object reference variables and their names, the form should now look like the one in Figure 10–4.

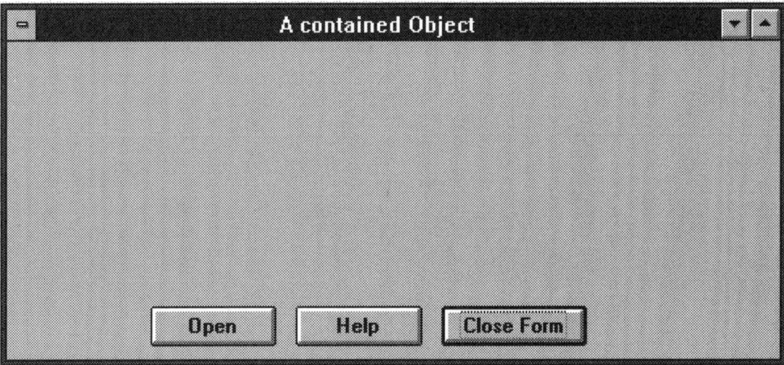

Figure 10–4. The form with three buttons.

So you can use the object reference variable to assign a user-specified alias to the name of the object. By doing this, you can change the object's properties or trigger their methods by using the alias name instead of the complete chain name (form, object, and property).

Objects and encapsulation

The properties and methods of an object are contained in that object. Their values are hidden from other objects. This act of hiding values inside an object is known as *encapsulation.* Encapsulation is the act of encasing (enclosing) something in another as if in a capsule. The properties and methods, members, of the object are encased within the object.

This act of encapsulation is an important tenet of object-oriented programming. It gives you the ability to hide the values of the properties (memory variables) from other properties, in other objects, with the same name.

Because of encapsulation, all objects can have the same named property (memory variable), like *text*, yet the value for each property will be unique to each object.

Using objects as parameters

Objects and their properties can be used as parameters. You can pass them and use them for returning values.

Passing object reference variables (names)

You can pass an object reference variable to a procedure. For example, you may want to create a procedure that can center any contained object on a form from top to bottom or from left to right. The procedure will be placed in a procedure file named PARAPROC.prg and it could look something like this.

```
*** PARAPROC.PRG
*
PROCEDURE CenterIt
   Parameter xObj, xWay
   IF PCOUNT()=2 .and. xWay =2
      xObj.Top = ((xObj.Parent.Height - xObj.Height)-1)/2
   ELSE
      xObj.Left = (xObj.Parent.Width - xObj.Width) /2
   ENDIF
RETURN
```

This code uses the objects property *Parent* to obtain the width of the parent (form) without knowing the name of the form. It cannot use the special variable name *form* to accomplish the same thing. The *form* variable cannot be used because it can only be used at the level of the object creation in a Class. Therefore, you need to use the object property *Parent* to accomplish much the same thing as the special variable *form*.

Now that the procedure CenterIt is created, you can use it to center any object on a form. The following code will demostrate use of the procedure CenterIt:

```
SET PROC TO PARAPROC
xFrm = NEW FORM()
xFrm.Height = 12
xFrm.Open()
xBtn1 = NEW PushButton(xFrm)
DO CenterIt with xBtn1          && centers from left-to-right
DO CenterIt with xBtn1, 2       && centers from top-to-bottom
```

This code will create a form that looks similar to the one in Figure 10–5.

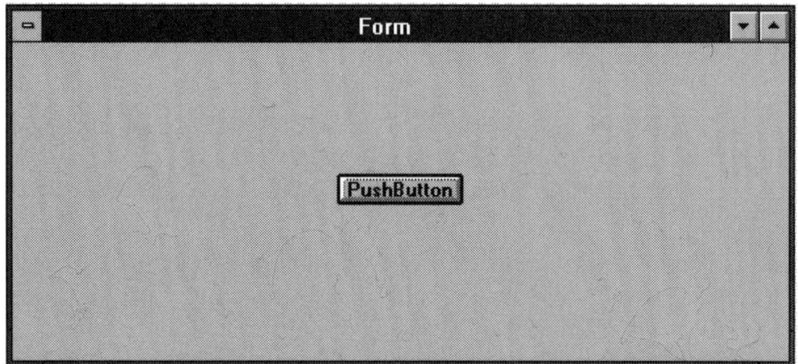

Figure 10–5. A form with a pushbutton object centered using a procedure.

Passing an object's property

You can also pass an object's properties as parameters. For instance, you may want to align an entryfield object either alongside of a text object or immediately below the text object. You can do this by using a procedure that will obtain the name of the entryfield object, the Top, Left, Width, and Height properties of the text object, and a number to specify where it should be aligned. The procedure can be added to the PARAPROC.prg. It would look something like this.

```
   . . .
PROCEDURE NextTo
   Parameter xEntObj, xTop, xLeft, xWidHght, xType
   IF xType = 1
      xEntObj.top = xTop
      xEntObj.Left = (xLeft+xWidHght +1)
   ELSE
      xEntObj.Left = xLeft
      xEntObj.Top = (xTop+xWidHght)
   ENDIF
RETURN
```

This procedure will align an entryfield alongside of or below a text object. Once it is created, you can use code like this to demonstrate its use.

```
SET PROC TO PARAPROC
xFrm=NEW FORM()
xFrm.Height = 9
xFrm.Open()                 && return to the command window
xText = NEW TEXT(xFrm)
xText.Top = 2
xText.Text = "Customer Name:"
xText.Width = 15
xEnt=NEW ENTRYFIELD(xFrm)
*
```

```
*  this one moves an entryfield below the text field
*
DO NEXTTO WITH xEnt, xText.Top, xText.Left, xText.Height, 2
*
* this one moves the entryfield alongside the text field
*
DO NEXTTO WITH xEnt, xText.Top, xText.Left, xText.Width, 1
```

If you type in these lines of code, the entryfield will be placed, first in the top left-hand corner of the form, then moved to below the text, and finally moved alongside of the text object (Customer Name:). The final move should make the form look similar to the one in Figure 10–6.

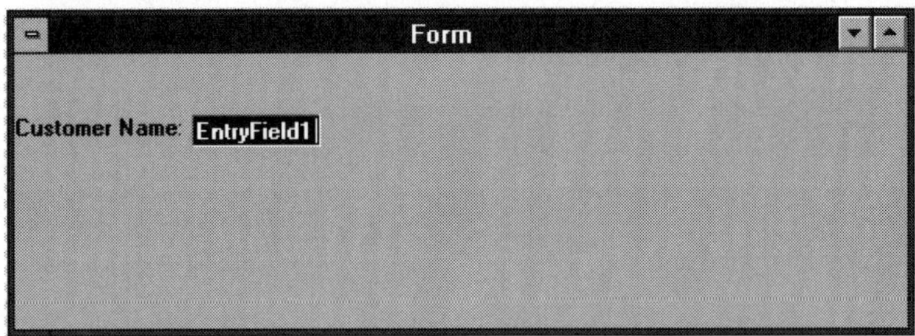

Figure 10–6. A form that places the entryfield using an object's properties as its parameter.

The procedure NextTo used three properties from the text field. If the entryfield is to be placed below the text field, the properties passed were the text objects Top, Left, and Height. If it was placed alongside of the text object, the properties passed were the Top, Left, and Width.

Returning an object from a function

You can return an object reference variable as well as use it for parameters. The following function will create a new pushbutton and return the new object to the object reference variable name. It can also be included in the procedure file PARAPROC.prg:

```
  . . .
FUNCTION NewButton
   Parameter xFrmName,xText, xTop, xLeft, xWidth
   xBtn = NEW PUSHBUTTON(xFrmName)
   xBtn.Top = xTop
   xBtn.Left = xLeft
   xBtn.Width = xWidth
   xBtn.Text = xText
RETURN xBtn
```

The Function will create a new pushbutton on a form at the location specified by the parameters. For instance, the following code will create a form and then create a pushbutton on the form using this function:

```
SET PROCEDURE TO PARAPROC
xFrm = NEW FORM()
xFrm.Height = 12
xBT = NewButton(xFrm, "HOT Button", 10, 35, 22)
xFrm.Open()
```

Your form should look like the one in Figure 10–7.

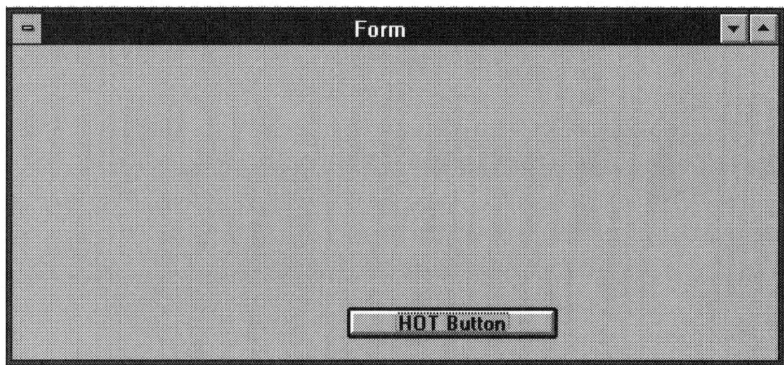

Figure 10–7. A pushbutton created using a function.

Making objects go away

Once an object is created, you can release it from memory in three ways:

```
RELEASE <object reference variable>
RELEASE OBJECT <object reference variable>
<object reference variable>.Release()
```

The last two methods will release the object, freeing up memory and resources to be used by other objects. However, the first one will only release the object reference variable if the form or the object contained in the form is open/visible. If the form or object is closed/invisible, it will also release the form or contained object.

RELEASE <object reference variable>

You can release any object reference variable from memory by using the RELEASE command followed by the object reference name. The following demonstrates use of the RELEASE command:

```
xF = NEW FORM()
xF.Height = 10
xF.Top = 3
xF.Open()              && opens the form xF
? xF                   && returns the value OBJECT
RELEASE xF             && releases object reference variable xF,
                       && Only the object reference is released—
                       && not the object
? xF                   && error -- undefined variable
```

If you type in the preceding code, your screen should look similar to the one in Figure 10–8.

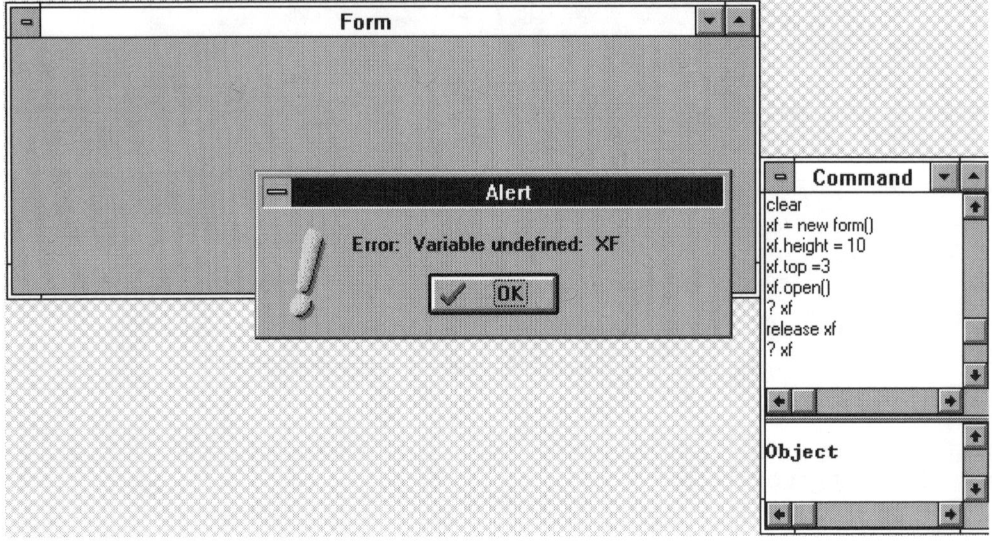

Figure 10–8. Releasing an open form object.

Notice that the object (form in this case) still exists because it is open. Only the object reference variable was released—not the object; therefore, the Alert box with the error message.

Releasing open objects. If the form or a contained object is open, it is not released from memory when using the RELEASE command—only the object reference variable name. To release the form from memory, it must be closed first. Figure 10–8 shows the form still open. Once an object is created and opened, the RELEASE command will only release the object reference variable name from memory.

Releasing closed objects with more than one object reference variable. If you give an object more than one object reference variable (name), and release one of the names, only that name is released from memory. If the object is closed or open, the object will not be released until all of the object reference variables are released from memory using the RELEASE command. The following code demonstrates this:

```
xF = NEW FORM()
xF.Height = 10
xF.Top = 3
xF.Open()              && opens the form xF
aForm = xF             && assigns another reference variable to
                       && the object
RELEASE xF             && releases the xF variable name
aForm.Top = 5          && changes the Top property of the object
aForm.Close()          && closes the form object
RELEASE aForm          && releases the aForm variable name and
                       && releases the closed OBJECT
```

Even though you released the xF object reference variable (name) for the object, the object has a second object reference variable name, aForm. When the form is closed and aForm is released, the object is finally released from memory.

RELEASE OBJECT <object reference variable>

This command, *RELEASE OBJECT*, will explicitly release the object from memory. This will be true even if you use more than one object reference variable name. The RELEASE OBJECT command will close an open object and physically release it from memory. The following code will demonstrate this:

```
MyFrm = NEW FORM()           && create a form object
YourFrm = MyFrm              && assign a 2nd name (obj. ref.
                             && variable)
MyFrm.Open()                 && Open the form
RELEASE OBJECT MyFrm         && release the object itself
YourFrm.Text = "HELLO"       && results in an error -- the
object
                             && is gone
? MyFrm                      && the variable still exists, and
                             && reports type OBJECT. It just
                             && doesn't point to any object in
                             && memory (it was released)
```

The RELEASE command releases the object reference variable name only. The object may still remain (if it is open).

The RELEASE OBJECT releases the physical object. The object reference variables will still exist; however, they will not point to the object any longer, because the object was removed from memory with a RELEASE OBJECT command. If the object is a form and it is open, it disappears because the object is released from memory.

> **!** **Running the sample code**
> If you run this code from a program, the form will not disappear when it encounters the two lines that cause the errors.

<Object reference variable>.Release()

You can release an object from memory by using its RELEASE method. The form and all control objects in the form have a Release() method. It works identical to the RELEASE OBJECT command. The following code demonstrates this:

```
MyFrm = NEW FORM()           && create a form object
YourFrm = MyFrm              && assign a 2nd name (obj. ref.
                             && variable)
MyFrm.Open()                 && Open the form
YourForm.Release()           && release the object itself
MyFrm.Text = "HELLO"         && results in an error—the object
                             && is gone
? YourForm                   && the variable still exists, and
                             && reports type OBJECT. It just
                             && doesn't point to any object in
                             && memory (it was released)
```

The release() method of an object works exactly like the RELEASE OBJECT command. Although the object is released, the object reference variables assigned to the object still exist.

To release the object reference variables, use the RELEASE command.

Releasing parent and child objects

You can release any child object inside a parent, like text objects, entryfield objects, and pushbuttons in a form. To release them, use their individual Release() methods.

If you release the form object itself, all of the child objects will automatically be released when the form is released.

WORKING WITH CLASSES

The CLASS is a template that is used to create objects, instantiating (creating) any number of objects—all objects identical. They will have the same default properties and methods.

You have already created your own classes using the CLASS ... ENDCLASS constructs. To create objects from your own Classes, they must be in memory (like a procedure file).

Creating Classes

You can create a new Class from scratch, building all of the properties and methods to be used by the objects instantiated from the class, or build it based on another Class definition.

As you recall, the class consists of two primary parts: the Constructor code and the Method Declaration.

Constructor code

The Constructor code is the property declarations and assignment of its default values. The following code is typical Constructor code:

```
this.Top = 2.5
this.Left = 3
this.Text = "Demonstration"
```

When declaring the properties and default values in a Class, you use the special variable *this*—to be used as a place holder for the name of the object that will be created.

Creating controls in form Classes

When creating your own Class of form, the Constructor code may include definitions of other objects that will be contained with the form created from the CLASS. For instance, if you are creating your own form Class, you may want all form objects created from the Class to have a pushbutton inside it that will close the form. This definition of the contained object is also Constructor code. The following could be an example that will create a pushbutton inside a new form Class definition:

```
DEFINE PUSHBUTTON Exit OF form PROPERTY ;
      Top 1, Left 1, Text "Close", OnClick {;form.Close()}
```

When defining objects that will be contained inside a new form Class, they will normally use the special variable *form*. Like the special variable *this*, the *form* variable is a place holder that will be replaced with the actual form name when the form is instatiated (created).

Method Declaration

You can also create your own methods from the objects created by the Class. The method can be a procedure, function, or even a codeblock. The following code could be an example of a method that is declared inside the Class definition:

```
PROCEDURE FixUpper
    this.value = UPPER(this.value)
RETURN
```

A method is simply a procedure or user-defined function that is associated with a Class. It is normally enclosed inside the CLASS ... ENDCLASS constraint; however, it doesn't have to be placed inside the Class. It can be referenced inside the class instead.

Create a class from other classes

You have already created new classes from classes. The advantage of creating a class from another class lies in setting your own default values for the object's properties and methods.

When you create a class from another class, you inherit all the properties and methods from the other class. Then you can change only the ones that suit your needs.

To create a new class based on another class you must use the keyword ***OF*** in the CLASS construct. The following code exemplifies this:

```
CLASS HelpForm OF FORM()
  this.top = 2
  this.height = 12
  this.text = "On Line Help System"
  this.ColorNormal = "W/R"
ENDCLASS
```

Once you create your own Class based on another Class, you can load it in memory and then use it to create any number of objects. In this case, all object forms created from the HelpForm Class will be red in color and have a height of 12. The syntax to use the class HelpForm is the same as the syntax for using the class Form:

<object reference variable> = NEW HelpForm()

Using the FROM <filename> option with Classes

➡ Visual dBASE has added a new clause to the CLASS construct:
CLASS <new class name> OF <Base class name> FROM <path\program>

Using this option you can create new Classes from existing classes that are not in memory. For example, you have a procedure file named MyClass.prg that has a new Class definition named MainHelpForm. You can derive (create) new form sub-Classes from the base Class MainHelpForm even if the procedure file it is in (MyClass.prg) is not loaded in memory.

This is discussed in detail later in this chapter.

Create a new, empty class

You can also create your own Class from scratch. If you create your own class you will have to build all of the properties and methods from scratch. There is nothing that will be inherited from another class. The following code exemplifies building your own class:

```
CLASS Video
   this.Title = ""
   this.Length = 2.0
   this.Format = "VHS"
   this.Year = Year(date())
   this.Director = ""
   PROCEDURE NewTitle
       parameter xName, xBy
       this.title = xName
       this.Director = xby
    RETURN
ENDCLASS
```

This Class could be used to create individual objects for each video tape and video compact disk. It has several properties and one method (NewTitle) that each object will be given when they are instantiated from the Class using the command:

```
<object reference variable> = NEW Video()
```

CLASS hierarchies

When you create a Class based on another Class, you are creating an infrastructure of a hierarchy, or the foundation of a ranked ordering of Classes. This hierarchy you are building is like a pyramid. There is a single Class at the top that can be used to create several lower Classes. Those lower Classes can be used to create new Classes. The top is a single Class, and the lower levels widen as you go down through the hierarchy.

The hierarchy is simply the building of a Class off of another Class. That Class can then be used to build new Classes.

There are two basic types of Classes:

- Base Class
- Sub-Class

Base Classes

The *base Class* is the class that is used to create other Classes. When you create a new form Class (like HelpForm earlier) from the Class, FORM, the FORM Class is the base Class. You can quickly identify a base Class by looking at the syntax that was used to create the new Class. For example:

```
CLASS HelpForm OF FORM
```

Any Class name after the OF keyword is the base Class for that new Class.

Sub-Classes

The sub-Class is derived from a base Class. In the example above, you derived the new Class HelpForm from the base Class Form. The HelpForm Class is derived from the Form class. This means that the HelpForm doesn't have to re-create (duplicate) all of the properties and methods that already exist in the base Class (Form). Rather, it accepts all of them and changes only the ones that you want to change.

Once a sub-Class is created, it can change any of the property values or methods that it received from the base Class. It can even make new properties and methods.

Deriving a sub-Class from another sub-Class. You can create sub-Classes based off of other Classes that were derived from other Classes. The following code will be used to demonstrate this. It is stored in a procedure file named CLSPYRMD.prg:

```
*** CLSPYRMD.prg
*
CLASS MainForm OF FORM
   this.ColorNormal = "W/N"
   this.height = 10
   this.width = 40
   Store 2 to this.Top, this.Left
   DEFINE PUSHBUTTON Exit OF form PROPERTY Top 8.5, Left 2, ;
                    Text "&Close", OnClick {;form.Close()}
ENDCLASS
CLASS SecondForm OF MainForm
   this.ColorNormal = "W/W"
   Store 7 to this.Top, this.Left
   this.width = 60
ENDCLASS
CLASS ThirdForm OF SecondForm
   this.ColorNormal = "N/W*"
```

```
   this.Left = 20
   this.Top = 5
ENDCLASS
```

There are three classes in this code—MainForm, SecondForm, and ThirdForm. MainForm is derived from the base class Form. SecondForm is derived from MainForm. MainForm is SecondForm's based form; yet, MainForm is a subform of Form. Finally, ThirdForm is derived from SecondForm.

Once you create this code, you can use it by typing in the following commands, in the Command window:

```
SET PROCEDURE TO CLSPYRMD
xF = NEW MainForm()
xF.Text = "1st Form"
yF = NEW SecondForm()
yF.Text = "2nd Form"
zF = NEW ThirdForm()
zF.Text = "3rd Form"
xF.Open() ; yF.Open() ; zF.Open()
```

✔ **Using semicolons with commas**
Notice that the last line has three commands seperated with semicolons (;). Using semicolons between commands, you can enter more than one command at a time in the Command window.

Running the code, your screen should look like the one in Figure 10–9.

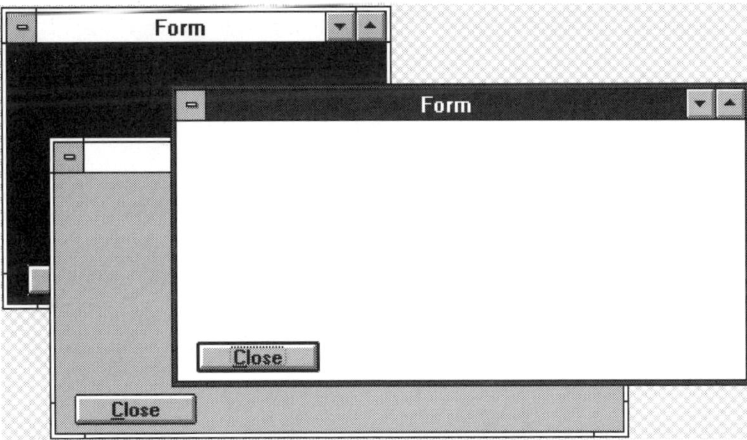

Figure 10–9. Three forms, with two created from Classes derived from sub-Classes.

Inheritance revisited

The CLASS MainForm defines a pushbutton and places it on all forms created from it. The other two Classes, SecondForm and ThirdForm, never define the pushbutton. Yet all forms created from these two Classes also have pushbuttons on them.

Each form Class inherits all of the properties and methods from the Class it is derived from.

The act of inheriting the base Class properties and methods in known as *inheritiance.* Inheritance, although easy to understand, is the second tenet of object orientation. It works at the Class level (versus encapsulation that works at the object level). This tenet makes it possible to reuse existing properties and methods from one object to another based on the Class definitions in the hierarchy of Classes.

By reusing existing properties and methods, new Classes can be created with minimal code and will be relatively simple to maintain.

Working with the properties

When you work with classes that are derived from another class, you will probably change the default values of those properties that you want your objects to have. This is known as reinitializing property values.

Reinitializing the property values

The code in the CLASS MainForm of the procedure file CLSPYRMD.prg reinitializes several property values. The code that reinitialized the values was the following:

```
CLASS MainForm OF FORM
   this.ColorNormal = "W/N"
   this.height = 10
   this.width = 40
   Store 2 to this.Top, this.Left
```

When MainForm was derived from the Form class, it received all of the properties and their values in the FORM class. Because all of them are correct except the above five (ColorNormal, Height, Width, Top, and Left), only those five have to be reinitialized.

Working with the methods

When you create your own Classes, you can also create new methods or change the behavior of existing methods; for example, modify the Class definitions in the code of the procedure file CLSPYRMD.prg.

```
*** CLSPYRMD.prg
*
CLASS MainForm OF FORM
   . . .
*   Note the changes to the Text and OnClick properties of the
*   Define pushbutton Exit command
*
   DEFINE PUSHBUTTON Exit OF form PROPERTY Top 8.5, Left 2, ;
                  Text "&Move", OnClick CLASS::MoveForm
*
*   Add this procedure to the Class MainForm
*
   PROCEDURE MoveForm
      form.Text = "I moved LEFT to "+STR(form.Top,4,2)+", ";
              +STR(form.Left+20,4,2)
      form.left = form.left+20
      RETURN
ENDCLASS
CLASS SecondForm OF MainForm
  . . .
*
*  Assign a new value to the Exit pushbutton's OnClick of the
form
*
   form.Exit.OnClick = CLASS::MoveForm
*
*  Create a new function, also named MoveForm inside the
*  Class SecondClass
*
   PROCEDURE MoveForm
      form.Text = "Moved UP to:  "+STR(form.TOP-3,4,2) + ", " + ;
                           STR(form.LEFT,4,2)
      form.top = form.top -3
      RETURN
ENDCLASS
CLASS ThirdForm OF SecondForm
*
*  No changes are made to the Class ThirdForm
*
ENDCLASS
```

This code creates a new method named MoveForm() in the MainForm Class. It also creates a new method also named MoveForm() in the SecondForm Class.

NOTE: Two Classes, two MoveForm methods

The second Class named SecondClass derived the method MoveForm from the Class MainForm. Then it created its own MoveForm, changing the behavior of the MoveForm method that it got from the Class MainForm. It moves up instead of left. This is known as polymorphism. There is more on Polymorphism later in this chapter.

Creating a new Method in a Class

In the preceding code, you create a new method in the MainForm Class. The code to create this method is

```
PROCEDURE MoveForm
      form.Text = "I moved LEFT to "+STR(form.Top,4,2)+",
";
              +STR(form.Left+20,4,2)
      form.left = form.left+20
      RETURN
```

This method, procedure, will move the form to the LEFT 20 characters. To trigger the method, the user presses the pushbutton, Exit. The code was modified to reflect that the button will move the form. The new code reads

```
DEFINE PUSHBUTTON Exit OF form PROPERTY Top 8.5, Left 2, ;
                   Text "&Move", OnClick CLASS::MoveForm
```

Notice that the OnClick property has been assigned the method MoveForm in the Class definition.

The special variable CLASS. When you use the special variable CLASS, it will be replace with the actual Class Name when the object is instantiated. Because objects do not create copies of any methods in their class, they use a function pointer that tells them where to find the method. The function pointer uses the name of the Class and the method name if the method is stored in the Class definition.

Using a new class method. To use the new class method, type in the following command and then press the pushbutton labeled Move:

```
SET PROC TO CLSPYRMD
xF = NEW MainForm()
xF.Open()
```

Every time you Click the move button, the OnClick property event will activate the procedure MoveForm inside the Class MainForm, moving the form to the left, by 20 positions. You can still grab the form and move it by clicking and dragging on the title bar.

Overriding a method

The new code in the Classs SecondForm OF Mainform in CLSPYRMD.prg, *overrides* a derived method (inherited method). To override an existing, inherited method, simply redefine the method in the new class and call it instead of the method in the base class. The following code is new code for a method that has the same name; however, it is created in the SecondForm Class.

```
PROCEDURE MoveForm
  form.Text = "Moved UP to:   "+STR(form.TOP-3,4,2)+",  "+ ;
                         STR(form.LEFT,4,2)
      form.top = form.top -3
      RETURN
```

The procedure has the same name as the method inside the MainForm Class—MoveForm. Although the Class SecondForm derives the Procedure MoveForm from the MainForm Class, you have created a new one in SecondForm with the same name. Once it is created, you need to tell the objects created from this Class to use this MoveForm instead of the MoveForm in the MainForm Class.

When you created the Class SecondForm, it inherited all of the Constructor code and Methods Declarations from the base class. This means that the OnClick property for the pushbutton Exit was assigned the code in the MoveForm method that is found in the MainForm Class. The CLASS::MoveForm assignment tells the OnClick to run the MoveForm that is in the first class where it encounterd the CLASS:: keyword, MainForm.

You can change this assignment by reinitializing the OnClick property to use the MoveForm in the new Class SecondForm. The command to do this is

```
form.Exit.OnClick = CLASS::MoveForm
```

The command is the same as in the MainForm Class, OnClick = CLASS::MoveForm. However, now, the special variable CLASS will be replaced with the Class name, SecondForm, when the form objects are instantiated instead of MainForm.

Notice, you didn't have to re-create the pushbutton, Exit. Because the pushbutton, Exit, was inherited from the MainForm, all you had to do was redefine a value for the OnClick property of the pushbutton, Exit, on the *form*.

NOTE: Testing inherited properties

You can test to see which method the OnClick property of the pushbutton will run. To see if this is true, go back into the code from the program CLSPYRMD.prg and re-mark off the line of code that reads *form.Exit.OnClick* = . . . If you run the programs and click on the form from the SecondForm Class, it will still move to the left. When you remove the remark from the line and retry, the new form will move up.

Different methods—same name

Notice that the Methods in both Class defintions have the same name, MoveForm. The second method actually inherits the first method named MoveForm. Then it overrides the behavior of that Method by creating its own MoveForm.

When two methods, procedures or functions, have the same name in memory, it is known as polymorphism. One method will be used over another, based on where the object is instantiated from and the behavior it has been assigned.

Any objects created from MainForm will use the method MoveOver, located in the Class MainForm. Any objects created from the SecondForm or ThirdForm, will use the method stored in the Class SecondForm. ThirdForm Class inherited all of the members in SecondForm, including the overriding behavior of the OnClick and the new method, MoveOver.

Polymorphism visited

Polymorphism can be understood by examining the word itself. It has two main parts to the name—Poly and Morph.

Poly simply means many. *Morph* simply means to change, or in modern-day terms, to have many forms. So combined it means to take on many forms. This is a loose definition of polymorphism.

When you created the subclass SecondForm from the MainForm, you changed the behavior of the inherited method MoveOver. By changing the behavior you have used polymorphism. You created two different methods with exactly the same name.

Polymorphism in the O-O world simply means to "have many shapes." It is the ability to implement an action (method) that has a common name to all objects within the Class hierarchy, in the way that is approriate for *that* object.

Same name—different behavior

Polymorphism is the last tenet of object orientation. It is the most difficult to understand, yet its simplicity is so powerful. Implementing polymorphism in your applications gives you the ability to create a common subroutine name, across all Classes in the hierarchy. Even though the subroutine (method) has the same name, it can have different behaviors based on your overriding the inherited behavior of the method in the new Class.

In Visual dBASE, Polymorphism only deals with methods at the Class level. You can create a method in one class and redefine its behavior in a sub-Class within the hierarchy of the derived Classes.

Understanding the theory

To better understand the theory of polymorphism, consider the Print function in Windows or the plus operator in dBASE.

The Windows print function. When you work with the Print function in Windows, it can do several different things based on what is sent to it:

If you send plain text to the Print function, it will print text to the printer.

If you send binary data to the Print function (pictures), it will print pictures on the printer.

If you send formatted text to the Print function, it will print formatted text on the printer.

If you send a combination of formatted text and binary data to the Print function, it will print that information on the printer.

You may actually have four different print functions in memory—depending on what type of information that is sent to the Print function. The type of information being sent will determine which Print function will be used to print the information to the printer.

Polymorphism is when you have more than one function or procedure with the same name, and the correct one will be executed based on what is passed to it.

dBASE's add operator. Another example of polymorphism could be the plus operator. If you pass the plus operator two numbers, it will add them together and give you their sum. If you pass the plus operator two text strings, it will concatenate them and give you a string value of both text strings placed side by side.

If there are two different plus functions in memory with the same name and you pass them either two numbers or two strings, you don't want to remember which one to use. You just want the program to take both of these things (numbers or strings) and do the right thing with them (add them or concatenate them).

This ability is the premise of polymorphism.

Advantages of polymorphism. When a language supports polymorphism, you can name a single action, like FixText, and based on what you send it (object and property) it will act differently. One FixText will make text all UPPERCASE, another will make text all Proper Case, yet another may reverse text (niwrI .R leahciM will be converted to Michael R. Irwin).

By using the same name for an action, you will not have to remember different names for similar actions—Fixing Text.

Protecting members of a Class

➡ Visual dBASE has added a new clause to the CLASS declarative—PROTECT. The *PROTECT* clause lets you protect specific members (properties and methods) of objects instantiated from Classes. By protecting specific properties and methods of an object, you make them inaccessible to someone using the object.

Making an object's property inaccessible

Normally, when an object is created, the user can immediately change the values or access the methods of the object by directly manipulating them. Using the PROTECT clause you can make the properties unavailable to the user.

This can be extremely useful when creating your own Classes. For instance, you may want all forms created by your company to have the company name on the titlebar and the Color of Purple. Once set, you do not want it changed by the user. The following code will define a Class that will do just this:

```
*** ALLFORMS.prg
*
SET PROC TO ALLFORMS
CLASS CompanyForm OF FORM()
   PROTECT text, ColorNormal
   this.Text = "My ABC Company, Inc"
   this.ColorNormal = "/RB"
   this.Width = 45
   this.Height = 10
ENDCLASS
```

If you run this code, using the following commands, you should see a form similar to the one in Figure 10–10.

```
DO ALLFORMS
xForm = NEW CompanyForm()
xForm.Open()
```

Figure 10–10. This is a form with two properties protected—text and ColorNormal.

Protected properties can be directly changed. Now that the form is open, return to the Command window and try to access the properties, *text* and *ColorNormal* for the form named xForm:

```
xForm.Text = "New FORM"
```

```
? xForm.Text
xForm.ColorNormal = "/W+"
? xForm.ColorNormal
```

All of these commands will issue the same error—

```
Error:  Property not accessible:  <Property name>
```

You can't change the properties, in fact, you can't even look at the Protected properties!

Protected properties are removed from the Inspector. Now examine the form, xForm, using the Inspect() function:

```
INSPECT (xForm)
```

Looking at the properties of the form, xForm, you will see that both *Text* and *ColorNormal* have been removed from the Inspector. Figure 10–11 shows the form xForm, created from the Class CompanyForm and a second form, based on the standard Class FORM. It also shows the Inspector active for both forms.

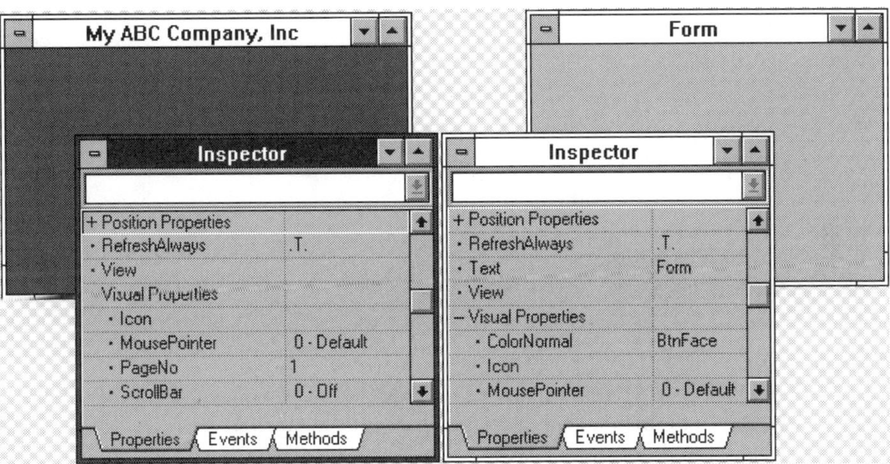

Figure 10–11. The Inspector for two forms.

The left inspector is for the form named xForm (the Company form). Notice that it doesn't have either property—*text* or *ColorNormal* available. The *Text* property is usually between RefreshAlways (below the – Position Properties) and View properties. The ColorNormal can be found below the –Visual Properties line and Icon. Notice they are both visible in the Inspector for the other form, located on the right side of Figure 10–11.

Internal functionality of Classes become invisible. By protecting properties and methods in this way, the user of the Class can only interact with nonprotected members.

The internal functionality of the Class can be made invisible to them using the PROTECT clause.

This means that the user can still use the Class; however, the actual implementation of the Constructor code and the Methods Declarations becomes inaccessible to them. By identifying members to be protected by the Class, you can still allow the user to access the *interface* into a Class, while protecting the *implementation* of how the Class works and what the user can access.

Separation of the Class interface from its implementation offers several advantages to the designer of the Class. Use of protected members insures the integrity of the Class by eliminating the ability to make undesired changes to them. By protecting members of the objects created by the Class (properties and methods), the designer can change the implementation knowning that he or she will not break any code written by users based on the class. Of course, this assumes that the interface of the Class remains constant.

From the users' perspective, they will have less members to be concerned with. If the users learn that they will need to work with protected properties, they will be required to turn to the designer to give them the ability.

If protected properties or methods need to be directly accessed, it will be the designer's responsibility to program that ability into the Class.

Accessing protected members

Once protected, the user cannot *directly* change the value or even access a protected property. If the user needs the ability to modify or access values in Protected properties or methods, you will have to build methods, in the same Class, that allow you to change them.

Class methods can access protected members. Although the protected member is unavailable to the user, it is still there. It can be modify, *indirectly*, by creating a method at the Class level to change it.

A Class level method can change a protected property of any object instantiated by the Class. However, it means that you must create the method at the Class level.

A method to change protected text. For instance, the following two methods can be constructed in the Class, CompanyForm, placing them after the Constructor code (this.Height = 10):

```
 this.Height = 10
*
* Place these two procedures after the this.Height line
* in the Class CompanyForm in the procedure file ALLFORMs.prg
*
 PROCEDURE NewColor(nColor)
   this.ColorNormal = nColor
 PROCEDURE NewTitle(nTitle)
   this.Text = nTitle
```

```
    *
    * These two procedures need to be placed before ENDCLASS
    *
*   ENDCLASS
```

With the two methods created, rerun the program and change the properties using them.

Using Class methods to modify protected property values. The following code can be used in the Command window to demonstrate changing a protected property's value:

```
CLEAR ALL
DO ALLFORMS
xForm = NEW CustomerForm()
xForm.Open()
*   the next line will report an error
xForm.Text = "This will not work"
*   the previous line will report an error
xForm.NewColor("/W")
xForm.NewTitle("How about that?")
```

As you can see from the preceding lines of code, the property, *text*, cannot be directly changed (xForm.Text = "This will not work"). However, using the function *NewTitle()* in the Class, CompanyForm, does let you change the text. The function *NewColor* will let you change the color of the form.

Users still can't examine either property, nor can they directly change their values. If you want to give users the ability to change protected properties, you will have to create methods that they can use to change them. Even though the property is protected from them directly, using the functions you built, they can *indirectly* modify or even view them. It is up to you to decide what they can and cannot do.

Class level members can be protected

When protecting members, you can only protect actual properties and methods of the object instantiated from the Class. This seems obvious; however, it can seem confusing when you begin working with contained objects in the Class. For instance, create another Form Class in the ALLFORMS program that looks like this:

```
CLASS My2ndForm OF Form()
  PROTECT height, width, text, this.xButn.Top,
form.xButn.Left
  this.height = 12
  this.width = 45
  this.Text = "My Other Company, INC."
  Define PUSHBUTTON xButn OF form PROPERTY ;
```

```
        Top form.Height - 2, Left form.Width - 15, Width 12,
;
        Height 1.5, Text "Exit", OnClick {;form.close()}
ENDCLASS
```

This code suggests that it will protect the properties *Height, Width,* and *Text* of all objects instantiated from the Class My2ndForm. It also suggests that it will protect the *Top* and *Left* properties of the PushButton, xButn, inside the form. The code uses both the *this* and the *form* keyword to test if either one of these references can work.

Class level members only. However, the properties of the pushbutton xButn are NOT protected. Do the following lines of code:

```
DO ALLFORMS                    && loads procedure file
yForm = NEW My2ndForm()
yForm.Text = "This won't work"      && Text is protected
yForm.xButn.Top = 1.0            && should be protected - but ISN'T
```

As the code demonstrates, the properties of the Class My2ndForm are protected. However, the control object properties are not protected. This is true if you use the *this* or the *form* keyword to identify the property. In fact, you can't protect the pushbutton at all inside the Class definition My2ndForm.

Protecting members of the Class only protects the physical properties and methods of a given object instantiated by the Class. It will not protect members of contained objects created in the Class.

Protecting contained Form Class object members. If you need to protect members of objects created in a Form Class, you will need to create new Classes for each control object that you want to place in the form and protect its members. Once created, this new Control Class can then protect its own properties.

You can then use this new control Class to protect its own properties.

Accessing contained Class protected properties. So, you can create custom Classes of controls and protect their values. Then you can protect the values of the form Class. Protected properties of contained Classes will need procedures created to let you change their values also. For instance, let's tie the two protected Classes together. You want to create a form Class that will place an Exit button at the bottom right corner of the form. Then you want to guarantee that if the user resizes the form, the pushbutton will be moved to the bottom right corner of the resized form. Finally, you want to make sure that the user doesn't move the pushbutton themselves or change the title of the form.

The following code will let you build and protect a form and its pushbutton.

```
*** TWOCLASS.PRG
*
Public xF
SET PROC TO TWOCLASS
```

```
xF=NEW My2ndForm()
xF.Open()
CLASS My2ndForm OF Form()
  PROTECT text
    this.height = 12
    this.width = 45
    this.Text = "My Other Company, INC."
    this.OnSize = {;this.Exit.FixIt()}
    Dummy = NEW ExitButton(this)
ENDCLASS
CLASS ExitButton(fName) of PUSHBUTTON(fName)
   PROTECT Top, Left, Height, Width, Text, Name
     this.Top = form.height - 2
     this.Left = form.width - 15
     this.Width = 12
     this.Height = 1.5
     this.Text = "E&xit"
     this.Name = "Exit"
     this.OnClick = {;this.parent.Close()}
   PROC FixIt
     this.Top = form.height - 2
     this.Left = form.width - 15
ENDCLASS
```

Once you type in the above code, run it and resize the form using the mouse or by typing in new values for the form (xF) width and height properties—xF.Height = 6.5. The Exit button will stay along the bottom right side of the form.

However, if you attempt to access the protected properties of either the form, *xF*, or the Exit button, *Dummy*, you will not have access.

Referencing methods in Classes

When you create Classes, from scratch or from other Classes, you can build sophisticated systems quickly and efficiently. Because you inherit members of the previous Class (base Class), you only have to reinitialize those properties and methods that you want to change for the derived class. All of the other properties and methods will remain intact, unchanged, and available to the objects that are created by the Class.

When you create Classes from Classes you are building a Class hierarchy. Each sub-Class is derived from a base Class. The base Class passes all of its properties and methods to the sub-Class.

Technically, the sub-Class does not receive copies of all the base Classes Constructor code and Method Declaration. Rather it maintains pointers back to the base Class that maintains the physical copies of the members. The only members that reside in the sub-Class are those that are reinitialized or created from scratch at that level.

So when a Class needs the method for the object that it instantiated (created), it points to the correct Class that has the method. Thus the method runs.

The Class and the CLASS scope resolution operator (::)

To access a method in the current Class, you need to use the Class *scope resolution operator* (::) with the method name.

The following code will create a new Class of pushbutton named GrandFatherButton and create a method (procedure) in the class named SizeIt:

```
*** CLASMEMB.prg
*
CLASS GrandFatherButton(fN) OF PUSHBUTTON(fN)
    this.Text = "One Big Button"
    this.Width = 24
    this.Top = 2
    this.Left = 4
    this.FontSize = 13
    this.Height = 2
    this.OnClick = CLASS::SizeIt
    PROCEDURE SizeIt
      this.width = IIF(this.width>39, 24, this.width+2)
      this.fontSize = IIF(this.fontSize> 20, 13, this.fontSize + 1)
      this.height = IIF(this.height>3.75, 2, this.height + .25)
    RETURN
ENDCLASS
```

Once the code is created (in this case in a procedure file named CLASMEMB.prg), it can be used to create pushbuttons in a form.

Assigning a Class method to an event property. Any pushbutton created with the Class GrandFatherButton will run the procedure (method) name **SizeIt** in the Class. The line that tells the pushbutton to run the method SizeIt is the following:

```
this.OnClick = CLASS::SizeIt
```

This line assigns the method in the CLASS (named GrandFatherButton) to the OnClick button of the pushbutton created from the Class.

To specify the method inside the class, you must use the name of the Class (or the special variable name CLASS) and the scope resolution operator, double colons between the name of the object and method name.

Using the class Name or the special variable—CLASS. Instead of using the special variable named CLASS, you could have specified the class name:

```
this.OnClick = CLASS::SizeIt
this.OnClick = GrandFatherButton::SizeIt
```

Either of these two commands will tell the object to go to the Class SizeIt and run the method. CLASS is simply used as a placeholder to be replaced with the name of the Class when the objects are instantiated.

Using a method in the Class. To use the method in the Class, you can create a form and then create the pushbutton for the form. Once the form is opened you can click on the pushbutton to activate the SizeIt method. The following code can be typed in to demonstrate the use of the pushbutton SizeIt method:

```
SET PROCEDURE TO CLASMEMB
xForm = NEW FORM()
xForm.Height = 12
xBT = NEW GRANDFATHERBUTTON(xForm)
xForm.Open()
```

Once the form is opened, you can click on the button, and it will grow in size. Pressing the button will make the button get wider, heigher, and the text larger. Figure 10–12 shows the form with the button larger (clicked several times).

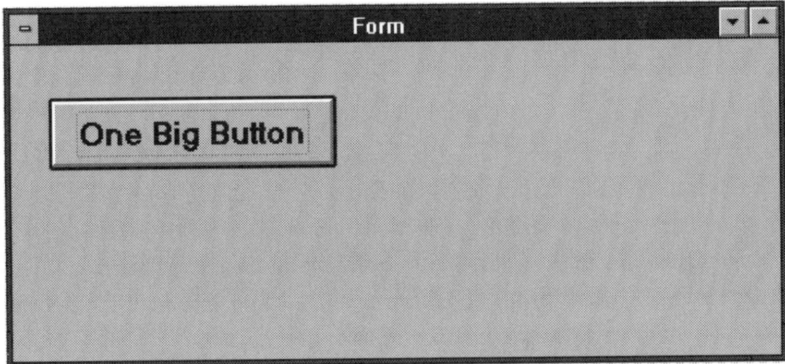

Figure 10–12. A form with a large pushbutton on it.

Accessing methods in classes of the hierarchy

Besides accessing methods inside a class, you can also access methods in another Class within the hierarchy. To demonstrate this, add the following code (two more button Class definitions) to the procedure file CLASMEMB.prg.

```
CLASS FatherButton(fn) OF GrandFatherButton(fn)
    this.top = 8
    this.text = "and Smaller"
    this.OnClick = CLASS::SizeIt

    PROCEDURE SizeIt
        this.width = IIF(this.width<17, 24, this.width - 2)
        this.fontSize = IIF(this.fontSize<10,13,this.fontSize -
1)
        this.height = IIF(this.height<1.25, 2, this.height - .25)
    RETURN
```

```
ENDCLASS

CLASS ChildButton(fn) OF FatherButton(fn)
    this.top = 14
    this.text = "??????"
ENDCLASS
```

This code will create two additional button classes—FatherButton and ChildButton.

Accessing its own method

The FatherButton will use its own SizeIt method, based on the line of code.

```
this.OnClick = CLASS::SizeIt
```

It will look inside itself (FatherButton) to size the button. The Sizeit method in the Father Class will make the button smaller. Any objects created from the FatherButton will have the button get smaller when it is clicked.

Automatically accessing a derived method

Finally, the third button (ChildButton) inherits everything from the FatherButton and simply changes the top and text properties for all objects created from it. Therefore, any objects created from the ChildButton class will have the same behavior and appearance as any objects created from the FatherButton, except the text and top position will be different. The following code can be used to demonstrate this:

```
SET PROC TO CLASMEMB
xF=NEW FORM()
xBt1 = NEW GrandFatherButton(xF)
xBt2 = NEW FatherButton(xF)
xBt3 = NEW ChildButton(xf)
xF.Open()
```

With the form created and opened you can press the three buttons. All three start the same size. If you click on them, they do different things. The top one (grandfather) will get larger, and the other two will become smaller. Figure 10–13 shows the form with the three buttons after they have been clicked several times.

Notice that the button created from the ChildButton (bottom of the form) also gets smaller, even though no OnClick property was specified telling it which method to use from which Class. It inherited the value for the OnClick property from the ParentButton. That OnClick said to use the SizeIt in the ParentButton (CLASS::SizeIt).

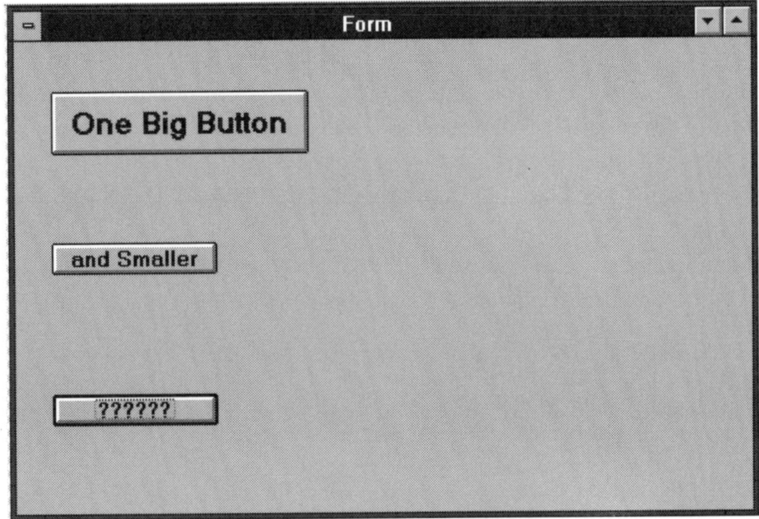

Figure 10–13. Working with different methods.

Using the special variable name SUPER

In addition to the special variable CLASS, there is a second special variable named *SUPER*. The SUPER variable can be used to reference a method in the base Class that was used to create the derived Class. For instance, go into the Class FatherButton and change the OnClick line to the following:

```
CLASS FatherButton(fn) OF GrandFatherBUTTON(fn)
   . . .
   this.OnClick = SUPER::SizeIt
```

Now save the code and rerun the same commands you ran before.

```
SET PROC TO CLASMEMB
xF=NEW FORM()
xBt1 = NEW GrandFatherButton(xF)
xBt2 = NEW FatherButton(xF)
xBt3 = NEW ChildButton(xf)
xF.Open()
```

SUPER = Base class. Now when you press all three of the buttons, they will all get larger. The second button uses the SizeIt in its super-Class (the base Class named GrandFatherButton).

When you use SUPER, it will reference the base Class that was used to derive all of the properties and methods. Notice that the second Class, FatherButton, still has a method inside it called SizeIt. However, none of the objects created from it or ChildButton uses this method. They all use the SizeIt method in the class GrandFatherButton.

Because the FatherButton class has assigned the SUPER::SizeIt to the OnClick and the FatherButton is the Class used to derive the ChildButton, the ChildButton will also use the same Method. You can tell the ChildButton objects to use the Method in the FatherButton by again using the SUPER::SizeIt method and attaching it to the OnClick property of the ChildButton. To do this, you would add a line to the ChildButton Class:

```
CLASS ChildButton(fn) OF FatherButton(fn)
   this.top = 14
   this.text = "??????"
   this.OnClick = SUPER::SizeIt
```

Adding this line to the code, when you rerun the same commands as before, the top two buttons will grow larger when they are pressed but the bottom one will get smaller. Now the one created from ChildButton will get smaller. It looks to its BASE class (SUPER), which is FatherButton, for the method SizeIt.

Using the Class name with the scope resolution operator

Besides using the special variables CLASS:: and SUPER::, you can also use the Class name directly. For instance, go back into the FatherButton Class and change it back to:

```
CLASS FatherButton(fn) OF GrandFatherButton(fn)
   . . .
   this.OnClick = CLASS::SizeIt
```

Now objects created from the FatherButton and ChildButton will both get smaller when they are clicked. However, you aren't finished yet. Now go back into the ChildButton Class and change its OnClick from SUPER:: to the following:

```
Class ChildButton(fn) OF FatherButton(fn)
   . . .
   this.OnClick = GrandFatherButton::SizeIt
```

Now run the same lines of code that you created before:

```
SET PROC TO CLASMEMB
xF=NEW FORM()
xBt1 = NEW GrandFatherButton(xF)
xBt2 = NEW FatherButton(xF)
xBt3 = NEW ChildButton(xf)
xF.Open()
```

Running this code, and pressing the three buttons, will result in a form similar to the one in Figure 10–14. Notice that only the button created from the FatherButton Class gets smaller. The one created from the ChildButton gets larger, like the

GrandFatherButton object. This is because the code specifically named the GrandFatherButton Class as the Class to use for the method SizeIt.

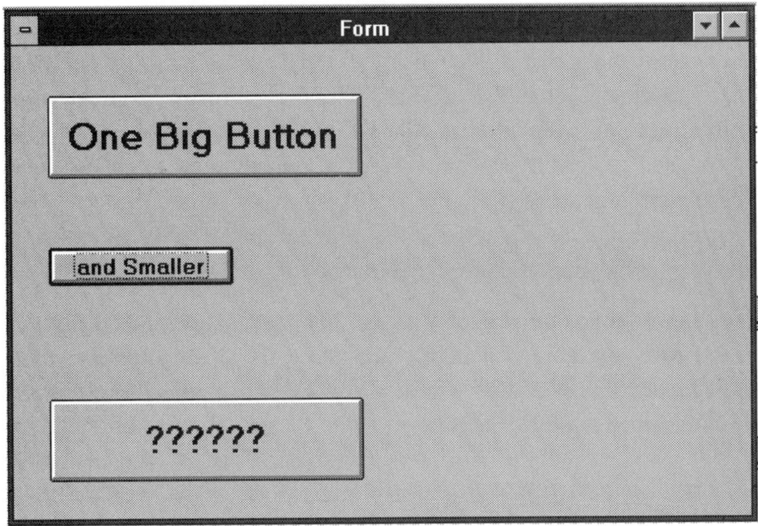

Figure 10–14. The three pushbuttons with new behaviors.

Creating methods

Up until now, you have been creating all of your class methods inside the Class. That is normally where you will create methods. However, you can also create them externally in procedure files and access them from the Class.

Methods inside a Class

Declaring a user-defined function, procedure, or codeblock inside the Class makes the method available only to those objects created by the Class or by Classes below it in the Class hierarchy.

Each object will contain a function pointer back to the method. By using this method, you can define a function in one place (in a Class) that can only be seen and used by the objects created from the Class (or from the hierarchy of the Class). These methods are hidden from any other objects that were not created by the Class (or a sub-Class of the Class).

Accessing a method inside the Class. To access or run a method inside the Class, simply use the object reference variable (name) with the method name, followed by the parentheses. For example,

```
xForm.Close()
```

```
xBt1.SizeIt()
```

Building methods outside of the Class

You can create methods that reside outside of the Class definition. This can be beneficial if you need to create a method that can be used by many different types of objects (created from several different Classes). To build a method (procedure or user-defined function) that can be used by several Classes, you need to create the method and place it in an independent procedure file (outside of the Class definition). For instance, you may want to create a couple of procedures that will increase a property value or decrease a property value for any numeric property of any object.

Creating methods outside of a Class. To create a method outside of a Class, you simply need to create a procedure file and place the procedures and functions in the procedure file, just like you always have. The following three procedures are placed in a procedure file named EXTRMEMB.prg:

```
*** EXTRMEMB.prg
*
PROCEDURE LessBy
    Parameter xObjProp, xQnty
    xObjProp = xObjProp - xQnty
    RETURN

PROCEDURE MoreBy
    Parameter xObjProp, xQnty
    xObjProp = xObjProp + xQnty
    RETURN
PROCEDURE BeepIt
  ?? CHR(7) + CHR(7)
  RETURN
```

This code creates three procedures that can be used by many different Class definitions for many objects. By moving the methods outside of the class, they can be used by many different Classes.

Using a property assignment to activate it. With the external methods created and placed in a procedure file, you need to assign them to a method inside the Class. To create a method that will use the external procedure LessBy, MoreBy, and BeepIt, you need to assign the name of the external procedure or function to a constructor (property) inside the Class definition. The following form, Class HelpForm, can be added to the same procedure file as the procedures:

```
CLASS HelpForm OF FORM
   this.Less = LessBy
   this.More = MoreBy
   this.Beep = Beepit
```

```
ENDCLASS
```

When you created the Class HelpForm, you created three new property names (Less, More, and Beep) and given them a value of the name of the Procedures in the procedure file.

By assigning an external procedure file to a property, the property is changed to a method. To access the methods, type in the following commands:

```
SET PROC TO EXTRMEMB
xF = NEW HelpForm()
xF.Open()
*
* return to the command window
*
xF.Less(xF.Height , 10) && makes the height 10 less
xF.Beep()               && beeps
xF.More(xF.Top,3.5)     && makes the top 3.5 larger
xBt=NEW PushButton(xF)  && creates a button on the form
xF.More(xBt.Top, 6)     && makes the top of button 6 more
xF.More(xBt.Left, 22)   && makes the left of button 22 more
```

Once you assign a property name to an external procedure or UDF, it becomes the method of declaration for the Class. Therefore, to access the external LessBy, MoreBy, and BeepIt procedures you use the internal methods—Beep(), Less(), and More().

Using the special variable *this* in an external method

You can use the *this* and *form* variables in an external method. However, they can only be used when associated with a property value or a method name. For instance, add the following two PROCEDURES, (DownBy1, UpBy1), and CLASS definition, (MyInventory), to the procedure file named EXTRMEMB.prg:

```
*** EXTRMEMB.prg
     . . .
PROCEDURE DownBy1
  Parameter xNum
  xNum = IIF(Type("xNum")<>"N",1,xNum)
  this.Qnty = this.Qnty - xNum
  RETURN
PROCEDURE UpBy1
  Parameter xNum
  xNum = IIF(Type("xNum")<>"N",1,xNum)
  this.Qnty = this.Qnty + xNum
  RETURN

CLASS MyInventory
   this.Company = "AmComp Parts"
   this.Type = ""
   this.Qnty = 100
```

```
    this.Down = DownBy1
    this.Up = UpBy1
ENDCLASS
```

Once you have added these procedures, notice that they both use the special variable *this* to assign a new value to the Qnty property of any object created by it.

Now you can run the code to see how it works, typing in these commands:

```
SET PROC TO EXTRMEMB
Hammer01 = NEW MyInventory()
? Hammer01.Qnty           && returns a value of 100
hammer01.Down()
? hammer01.Qnty           && returns a value of 99
Hammer01.Up(40)
? hammer01.Qnty           && returns a value of 139
Hammer01.Down(55)
? hammer01.Qnty           && returns a value of 84
```

Method declarations inside versus outside a Class

The primary difference between putting the method internal or external to the Class is its availability to Classes. If a method is internal, it can only be used by objects created from that Class or in a sub-Class from the Class hierarchy. An internal method is hidden from all other classes. Therefore, any objects that are not created from the class where the method exists will not be able to use the method. In fact, they won't even know that the method exists.

By storing methods internally, each Class can have their own methods. In fact, if they are created in a hierarchy, they can overload the behaviors of the method by re-creating the method in a sub-Class.

If you create a function or procedure external to the class, it can be used by several different Classes. Each class will need to assign the name of the external procedure or function to a Constructor (property). This Constructor will become a Method Declaration and point to the external function or procedure.

Part Four Working with the Outside World

Chapter 11
Visual dBASE, DDE, OLE, OLE2, and Multimedia

Visual dBASE is capable of working with sound, images, and video. It can store and manipulate pictures and sound in Visual dBASE OLE fields. It has multimedia language extensions that can help you develop multimedia applications.

CLIPBOARD, DDE, AND OLE

Using Windows and dBASE, you can integrate data from different applications. One of the easiest ways to exchange and integrate information is by using the Windows *Clipboard.* The Clipboard is only one way available to exchange information in Windows. Windows can exchange information through three basic methods.

- Clipboard
- Dynamic Data Exchange
- Object Linking and Embedding

Using these methods, you can use exchange information between Windows application. In fact, you can work with different data types, different data formats, and different applications using these methods—sharing and using information between sources.

The Clipboard

Information—data and pictures—can be transferred between applications through the Clipboard. Data transferred in this manner is *static.* If the data changes, you must manually recopy the changes to the document to remain up to date.

The application that receives the data from the Clipboard must know and understand how to work with the format structure of the data being transferred. If you send a set of cells from a spreadsheet to a word-processing application, the word-processing application must understand how to work with the spreadsheet cells.

Temporary data blocks

The Clipboard in Windows is simply a movable, temporary block of data taken from the Windows global memory heap. It acts like a viewer in this small block of memory. It is a liaison between two Windows applications, or Windows and a DOS application (running under Windows). It can be used to transfer information between two documents in the same application, or as a temporary storage area for an application.

The Windows application that places the data in the Clipboard is known as the *Clipboard Owner.*

Automatic format recognition

Depending on the data type, the Clipboard offers automatic format support. If it understands the data type, it will display it. It recognizes text and pictures; the types of text and pictures it can display are

- ASCII text
- OEM text
- Rich text format
- PC Paint (PCX)
- Bit Map pictures (BMP)
- Clipboard files (CLP)

If CLIPBRD.exe, the Clipboard program, recognizes the format (indicated earlier), it will attempt to display the data in a window. However, it can be used to copy almost any type of binary data.

Using the Clipboard

The Clipboard is the easiest way to exchange data. Most, if not all, Windows applications offer support for the ***Cut, Copy,*** and ***Paste*** functions of the Clipboard. Just about any part of a window can be highlighted and then cut or copied to the Clipboard.

Cutting text and pictures. Once you highlight some text or a picture on the screen, you can select a choice from the applications menu or press the keyboard combination **Ctrl-X.** Once selected, the application removes the highlighted text or picture from the screen. It is copied into the Windows clipboard, where it will reside, temporarily, until another cut or a copy operation is performed.

Copying text and pictures. You can also copy highlighted text. It works similar to cutting highlighted regions of the screen. Only you use the key combination **Ctrl-C.** Once you press the key combination or select the menu choice, Windows makes a copy of the highlighted region and places it in the Clipboard area of memory. It will remain there until another cut or copy operation occurs.

Pasting text and pictures. If a receiving application recognizes the type of data stored in the clipboard region, you can paste it into the current application. To paste data from the Clipboard region of memory, simply select the menu choice to paste, or press the key combination **Ctrl + V.** The text or picture will be pasted into your application.

Dynamic Data Exchange (DDE)

Windows has another method for sharing data between applications known as *Dynamic Data Exchange* or simply DDE. It provides immediate *real-time* updating of data. DDE complements the static data exchange capabilities of the Clipboard by creating a link between the source document and the target document. The linked applications do not have to be similar in purpose or function (two spreadsheets, two Borland products, etc.). However, both applications have to support and use DDE to exchange data using this method.

In addition to sharing data, DDE can be used to send run (execute) commands from the Client to the Server program. This can be an extremely useful feature when used in event-driven applications like Visual dBASE.

The target document will use the link to dynamically retrieve data whenever the source document (the controller of the data) updates it. Using DDE, you do not have to remember to update the target file every time the data is changed in the source document. This is a distinct improvement over the Clipboard.

The Windows message system

Windows is a *message-driven architecture*. The operating system (Windows) handles the details of window sizing and moving logic—not the application. The application simply responds to the system function of sizing and moving. This same messaging system is how applications exchange date among themselves.

The Windows messaging system is an agreed-on system of messages that all Windows applications agree to use. It is made up of commands, requests, and acknowledgments that are posted from one application to another. Every keystroke, mouse movement, and window action is actually controlled by these messages. This information includes things like the relative time a key or the mouse button is pressed, if it is released, if the keystroke was long enough to display repeat keys, and which key or button was actually pressed.

Windows in Windows. The visual foundation of Windows are *windows*. Each of these objects, windows are the central focus of Windows. They are simply rectangular objects on a screen. The window is the point that receives the user input from a mouse or keyboard and where the output is graphically displayed.

The user interacts with these windows by using control objects (pushbuttons, scrollbars, etc.). The window receives the user input through "messages" to the window.

The messaging system relies heavily on the window and communication between a window, other windows, the user (mouse/keyboard), and other peripheral devices (printers, scanners, etc.).

Message types. These messages include program functions like

- CreateWindow(Classname, . . .)
- ShowWindow(hwnd, nCmdShow)
- UpdateWindow(hwnd)
- GetMessage(. . .)
- TranslateMessage(. . .)
- DispatchMessage(. . .)

All applications created for Windows have agreed to use this messaging system as the way to work in Windows.

DDE uses the message system. DDE uses this same messaging system to exchange and share data. The requesting application, called the *Client*, requests information from some other application, known as the *Server*. This request is done through the Windows messaging system.

How DDE works

DDE lets you exchange instructions and information between Visual dBASE and another Windows application. Visual dBASE does this through a channel known as DDELink. This is Visual dBASE's built-in support for Windows DDE.

When a DDE Client requests information from a DDE Server, a series of messages are sent back and forth between the Client, Windows, and the Server.

If the Server program is not running, Windows will start it. If the Server recognizes the type of information being requested and can access the information, it opens a hidden window (called a child window) that is used to maintain and track the messages. Once this is accomplished, a DDE conversation takes place between the applications.

Once initiated, the two applications will communicate with each other until one of them sends a DDE_Terminate message. At this point, the DDE conversation is ended and the Server closes the child window.

What is needed to activate a DDE conversation. To launch a DDE conversation you need to send three separate pieces of data—the *application,* the *topic*, and the *item*. These three items must be supplied by the Client applications and sent to the Server program. Although these items are required, the Client must also send a request to start DDE conversation.

Most Windows applications support DDE, with most of them supporting more than one method of creating a DDE link. There are three basic ways to create a link.

1. Using the Clipboard to create the initial link
2. Using program level Link tools
3. Using an embedded command language

Types of DDE links

DDE links can be accomplished through three different methods.

- Cold
- Warm
- Hot

The main difference between these three linking methods is how the data are updated. Most client applications can only support cold and hot links. Visual dBASE can support all three methods of linking, as a Client or Server.

Cold links. In a *cold link*, the Client application explicitly requests new data be sent. This type of link isn't smart. It doesn't have any information about the current status of the data, whether it has changed or not.

Warm links. In a *warm link*, the Server application notifies the client whenever it makes changes to the data. The Client acknowledges the message, then it decides if it, the client, will request the new data, or just acknowledge the message.

Hot links. In a *hot link*, every time the data is updated, the Server application automatically sends the new data to the Client program and Client acknowledges the message, accepting the new changes.

Object linking and embedding (OLE)

The final method of exchanging data among Windows applications is *object linking and embedding*, or simply OLE. OLE complements the Clipboard and DDE by providing additional functionality when working with compound documents.

It is useful for those times when DDE and the Clipboard cannot perform the services necessary for exchanging compound data. Through OLE, Visual dBASE can control external applications or parts of them, allowing Visual dBASE to maintain the direction of services from external applications.

OLE complements DDE and Clipboard

OLE uses the Clipboard's and DDE's linking mechanisms. It supports the *Copy, Paste* and *Paste link* commands. It can be used to select data from a source, Server (like the Clipboard), and paste (or paste link) the data in the destination application, the Client.

It defines a series of common rules that client programs use to determine if the data should be imported (pasted) as an object or as converted data. It also lets you paste different user-controlled formats, by using the *Paste Special* command.

Compound documents. OLE lets the user store a document that was created by one application in another document of a different application. The data are stored in what is known as compound documents. This ability is an important tenet in Windows. It lets the user store and present data from a single document, when the source of the data can be many different applications and formats.

Embedded versus linked

An *embedded* object is a document that is stored inside the OLE field of a table. A *linked* object is a document that is stored in a separate file (versus in a table). The OLE field containing a linked object only contains pointer information, which is used to find the object on the disk.

Visual dBASE and OLE

Visual dBASE uses OLE for embedded sound, pictures, and even videos. These binary data types can be stored externally or in tables.

It can store documents from any OLE Server (program that creates sound, pictures, and video) in a BLOB field. A BLOB field is simply a field that can hold any type of Binary Large OBject (BLOB). dBASE can store OLE Server data in both Paradox and dBASE tables in an OLE field type. The field is labeled a General field ("G" type) when you look at the structure extended data type.

NOTE: The general data type

If you list the structure, dBASE reports a type OLE. However, if you copy the structure extended to another database you will observe that dBASE labels this as a type G. Use the command COPY STRUCTURE EXTENDED TO command to see the actual data type.

The OLE field type is one of the most important field types that dBASE uses for multimedia applications.

OLE2 automation support in Visual dBASE

➡ Although Visual dBASE offers full OLE support, it offers limited OLE2 support. It has added the OLE2 ability to use Visual dBASE as an OLE Automation Controller. As an OLE Automation Controller, Visual dBASE can call methods and access properties of any OLE Automation Object that is installed and registered in the Windows System Registry.

Visual dBASE accomplishes this through a new Class OLEAutoClient. Using objects from this Class, you can use methods and properties in Visual dBASE, as they are imported into dBASE, directly manipulating them.

Initialization of OLE2 libraries

OLE2 libraries are automatically initialized when Visual dBASE starts up. If an error occurs during startup, OLE automation will be disabled. If this happens, you will need to look at the installation methodology of each of the OLE2 libraries. Usually the problem proves to be an incompatibility of an application's OLE2 library. If the OLE2 library appears OK, you will need to explore incompatibility of down-level versions of some or all of the OLE2 libraries.

OLEAutoClient Class

Visual dBASE offers the new Class OLEAutoClient. It lets you link to other OLE2 compliant applications, like the new versions of Microsoft Excel 5.0 and Access 2.0.

Incompatibility issues. Because OLE—and OLE2, specifically—is an evolving standard, older versions of applications like Microsoft's Word for Windows 6.0x, may not fully support options like collection objects. Even newer applications, like Excel 5.0, won't fully support OLE2 options, like the Index option.

NOTE: What is a collection object

A collection object is a group of related objects that are placed together in a single grouping for access of their individual methods and properties. It is similar to moving all the subscripts of several single-dimensional arrays into a new array of two dimensions.

WORKING WITH DDE IN VISUAL DBASE

Visual dBASE offers two Classes for working with DDE: DDELink and DDETopic. If you need to use Visual dBASE as a client, you will create a DDELink object. If you need to work with DDE as a server, you will create a DDETopic object.

Visual dBASE as a DDE Client

Using DDE, Visual dBASE can connect to any other Windows application that supports DDE as a Server. Once connected, dBASE can obtain information from the other program or even write information into the other program. For instance, using DDE as a Client you can perform these types of actions.

Connect to Quattro Pro for Windows and manipulate information in a work sheet. You can add new values based on existing conditions in both a Visual dBASE application and cells of the work sheet.

Connect to a Word for Windows form letter, supply the appropriate information from a table, and then have Word for Windows print the letter out. Or start Word for Windows, create a complete document, and print it in Word for Windows—all from within Visual dBASE using DDE.

A DDELink object will start a session in the Server applications and establish the link. Once established, you can communicate with the Server using the methods of the DDELink object.

Creating a DDELink object

To use Visual dBASE as a DDE Client you need to create a DDELink object. To create a DDELink object, simply enter the command:

```
MyLinkObj = NEW DDELink()
```

Once you instantiate a DDELink object, you need to tell it to *initiate* a link with another DDE-aware Windows application. To initiate a DDE link, use the *Initiate* method of the object you have created. The following is the syntax used to connect to a Server:

```
MyLinkObj.INITIATE("<EXE Program name>", "<program file
name>")
```

The Initiate() methods requires two parameters

Initiate("<EXE program name>", "<program file name>")

where "<EXE program name>" is the name of the Windows program to run, and "<program file name>" is the name of a file that the EXE program works with. If you fail to supply a program filename as a second parameter, you will receive an error.

Both parameters passed in the Initiate function are character based; therefore, they both require quotation marks be placed around them.

NOTE: Supplying a false <program file name>

If you supply a nonexistent file name to a program when trying to activate a DDELink with the program, it is up to the program to decide what to do. For instance, Word for Windows will simply refuse to run. Quattro Pro will run, load a new work sheet by the name you have specified, and report an error. It is up to the DDELink program to decide what to do with the error.

Connecting to a spreadsheet program. For instance, if you want to connect to Quattro Pro for Windows and open a work sheet named IRWIN01.WB1, you would enter the following commands:

```
MyLinkObj = NEW DDELink()
MyLinkObj.INITIATE("QPW", "c:\workfiles\Irwin01.Wb1")
```

Notice that the command passes both the file name and its path for QPW.exe. If you do not specify the full path of the file name, the Server, Quattro Pro, may not find the file and create a new blank work sheet.

Connecting to a word-processor program. If you want to connect to Word for Windows 6.0 and open a form letter named ThankU.doc, you would enter commands like this:

```
MyLinkObj = NEW DDELink()
MyLinkObj.INITIATE("WINWORD", "d:\MyDocFiles\ThankU.doc")
```

As in the spreadsheet example, the full file name and path were supplied to Word for Windows to initiate the DDELink.

Working with a DDELink object

Once you have initiated a DDELink, dBASE, the Client can talk with the Server, Quattro Pro for Windows, or Word for Windows 6.0. There are three basic DDELink methods that you can work with in conjunction with the Server.

- PEEK()
- POKE()
- EXECUTE()

The PEEK() method. The PEEK() method of a DDELink object lets Visual dBASE examine the contents of a particular location in the Server. In other words, it lets you retrieve information from the Server application. For example, you may want to look at the contents of the work sheet cell A1 on page A of the work sheet, IRWIN01.wb1. The following command is how you would do it:

```
xVal = MyLinkObj.Peek("A:A1")
```

xVal will receive the value of the contents in cell A1 of page A in the QPW work sheet.

NOTE: The return value of a Peek() is always character

In the preceding example, xVal will hold a value that is character based. If the spreadsheet cell has the numeric value 50, it will be received by dBASE as the character value 50. You will need to convert the value to numeric if you want to perform some calculation with it.

The POKE() method. The POKE() method does exactly the opposite of the PEEK() method. It sends a value to a specific location within the Server application (work sheet, letter, etc.). If a value already exists at the location it is sending it to, it will overwrite the existing information.

For instance, to send a new value in the Cell A:B8, if the current value is less than 100, you would write the following lines of code:

```
IF VAL(MyLinkObj.Peek("A:B8")) < 100
    MyLinkObj.Poke("A:B8", 125)
ENDIF
```

Notice that poke requires two parameters:

POKE(<where to go>, <what value to put there>)

In this example, you used poke to go to cell A:B8 and placed the numeric value 125. Unlike the Peek() method, the POKE() function can pass any type of data as the second parameter, <what value to place there>, as long as the Server recognizes it. However, the first parameter, <where to go> must be character based.

Another example would be passing a value to Word for Windows that would be placed at a specific *Bookmark* within Word for Windows.

```
MyLinkObj.poke("Name", "James C. Doe")
```

This code will look for a Bookmark location named *Name* in the Word for Windows document and place the name “James C. Doe” at that location.

The EXECUTE() method. The other method you will probably work with from the DDELink object is the Execute() method. This method lets you pass through a script or macro command that the Server can use. The script or macro command must be in the language used by the Server application—QPW macro language or Word Basic for Word for Windows. The following demonstrates sending some Word Basic commands to Word for Windows to place a signature block at a Bookmark location and print the current document.

```
MyLinkObj.Poke("Salutation" ,"Thanking You,")
MyLinkObj.Execute('[InsertPara]')
MyLinkObj.Execute('[InsertPara]')
MyLinkObj.Execute('[InsertPara]')
MyLinkObj.Execute('[Insert "Michael R. Irwin"]')
MyLinkObj.Execute('[FilePrint]')
```

The Execute() method passes Word Basic commands to Word for Windows.

InsertPara sends a CR/LF (new line statement).

Insert sends the text specified to the existing location of the pointer.

FilePrint sends the message to have Word for Windows print the document.

DDE Linking to a Quattro Pro file

Visual dBASE can easily link to a Quattro Pro work sheet, interactively reading and writing information.

The Quattro Pro work sheet

Figure 11–1 shows a simple work sheet. Notice that most of the cells contain numeric values. It uses a series of formulas to perform calculations.

IRWIN01.WB1

	A	B	C	D	E	F	G
1	Cost Sheet 1995						
2							
3		Jan.	Feb	Mar	Apr	May	Jun
4	Salaries						
5	James K.	200	200	200	200	200	200
6	Susan P.	50	50	50	50	50	50
7	Vivian S.	125	125	125	125	125	125
8	Michael R.	50	50	50	50	50	50
9							
10	*Sub - Total*	425	425	425	425	425	425
11	**Qtr sub-Total**			**1275**			**1275**
12							
13							

A B C D E F G H I G

Figure 11–1. This is a QPW work sheet.

The Visual dBASE program will open QPW with this spreadsheet; make sure it is the correct sheet by looking at the value in cell A:A1. Then it will go to the B8 cell, check the value (50), and if it is < 100, change the value. Once the value is changed, the spreadsheet will perform all of the ripple calculations, and the spreadsheet will now look like Figure 11–2.

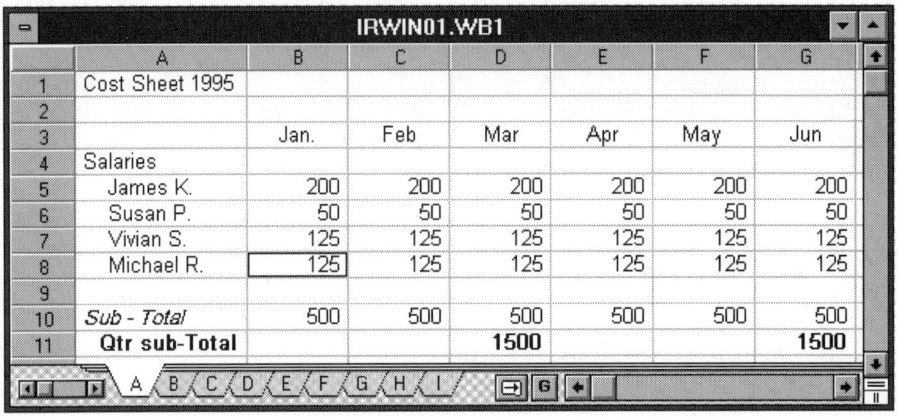

IRWIN01.WB1

	A	B	C	D	E	F	G
1	Cost Sheet 1995						
2							
3		Jan.	Feb	Mar	Apr	May	Jun
4	Salaries						
5	James K.	200	200	200	200	200	200
6	Susan P.	50	50	50	50	50	50
7	Vivian S.	125	125	125	125	125	125
8	Michael R.	125	125	125	125	125	125
9							
10	*Sub - Total*	500	500	500	500	500	500
11	**Qtr sub-Total**			**1500**			**1500**

A B C D E F G H I

Figure 11–2. This is the new spreadsheet with the values changed by a DDELink.

The Visual dBASE DDELink program

The following program listing will link to QPW and make the changes to cell A:B8:

```
*** DDELKQPW.prg
*
*  Link to QPW, calling in a work sheet and changing
*  values to one of the cells, based on its value
*
xLinkObj = NEW DDELink()
*
IF xLinkObj.Initiate("QPW", "C:\WorkFile\Irwin01.WB1")
  IF val(xLinkObj.Peek("A:B8")) < 100
     xLinkObj.Poke("A:B8",125)
     ? "CHANGED to " + xLinkObj.Peek("A:B8")
  ELSE
     ? "Value was NOT changed, already over 100 "
  ENDIF
ELSE
   ? chr(7)
   ? "FAIL to Link to QPW sheet IRWIN01.WB1"
ENDIF
RETURN
```

This program uses the Initiate() method to start QPW and load the work sheet. Then it uses the Peek() and Poke() methods to examine and change information in the spreadsheet. Notice that the Initiate() method returns a logical value—.T. if the Initiate() method worked, and .F. if it doesn't work.

DDE linking to a Word for Windows 6.0 or 7.0 document

Visual dBASE can work with a Word for Windows document. It can direct Word for Windows to create new text, print a letter, or place text at specific locations within the document using Word Basic.

The Word for Windows document

If you need to have Visual dBASE place some field data in a specific location of a Word document, you need to identify the location by placing a *Bookmark* at the location you want to supply information at. For instance, Figure 11–3 shows a form letter that will be used to place information into Visual dBASE.

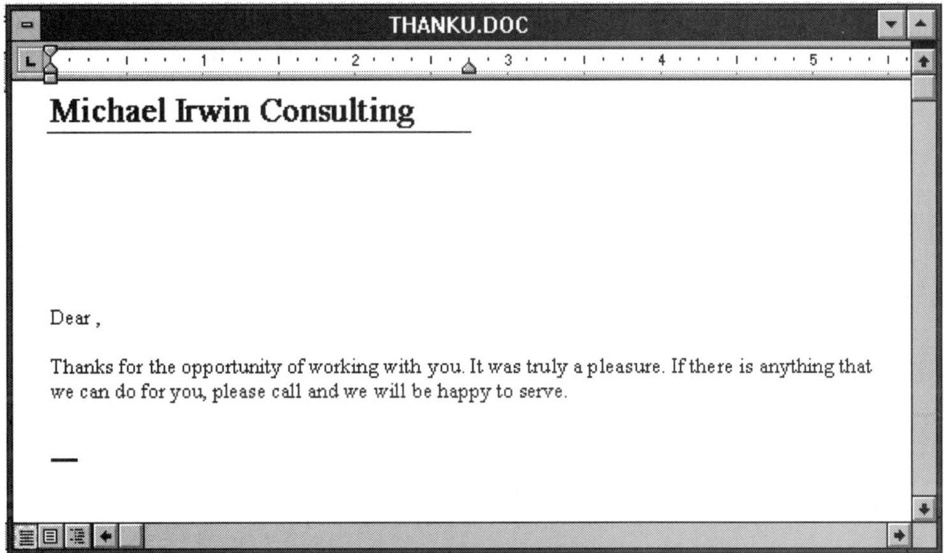

Figure 11–3. This is a form letter in Word for Windows.

The preformatted letter in Figure 11–3 can be used by Visual dBASE. However, before dBASE can poke data, like name of addressee, date, and signature block, into the form letter, you will need to create some bookmarks at the point of insertion.

Creating a bookmark in Word for Windows. To create a bookmark in Word for Windows, go to the point where you want to insert it and choose **B**ookmark from the **E**dit menu. For example, go to line 3 in the form letter. Then select bookmark from the edit menu. A dialog box will appear like in Figure 11–4. Type **Name** to name the bookmark at line 3, then click on the Add button.

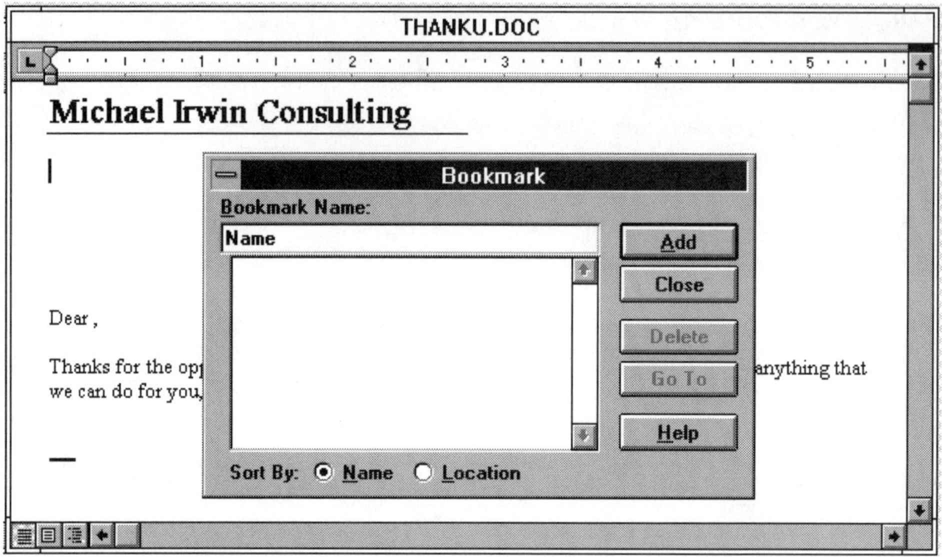

Figure 11–4. Creating a bookmark in Word for Windows.

Now that you have added the first bookmark, place four more in the document using Figure 11–5 as a guide. The "I" bar and the names will not appear in your document (they have been added to stress the location of the bookmarks). Once the bookmarks have been created, save the form letter, naming it THANKU.doc. You are ready to work with the document.

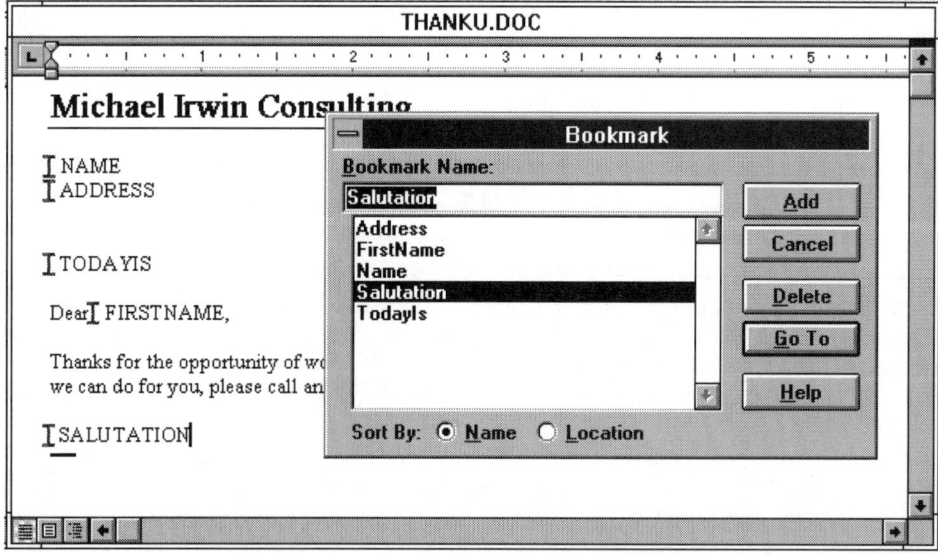

Figure 11–5. Five bookmarks in a form letter.

Using a Word form letter from Visual dBASE

Once the form letter has been created, you are ready to use it. You will tell dBASE to Poke text into the locations where the bookmarks have been created.

The following code will create a DDELink to Word for Windows, populate the form letter, print it, and abandon the changes.

```
*** DDEfrmLt.prg
*
*  Link to existing Word for Windows document to
*  Supply form letter info and then print the new
*  letter, closing the link -- not saving changes
*
xFormLtr=new ddelink()
*
IF xFormLtr.initiate("WINWORD",
"E:\zdBWork\WorkFile\ThankU.doc")
  xFormLtr.Poke("name", "James C. Doe")
  xFormLtr.Poke("address", "1 Circle Drive")
  xFormLtr.Poke("TodayIs", date())
  xFormLtr.Poke("FirstName", "Charlie")
  xFormLtr.Poke("Salutation", "Thanking You")
  xFormLtr.Execute('[PageDown 1]')
  xFormLtr.Execute('[InsertPara]')
  xFormLtr.Execute('[InsertPara]')
  xFormLtr.Execute('[Insert "Michael Irwin"]')
  xFormLtr.Execute('[InsertPara]')
  xFormLtr.Execute('[Insert "Consultant"]')
  xFormLtr.Execute("[FilePrint]")
  xFormLtr.Execute("[FileClose 2]")
  xFormLtr.Terminate()
ELSE
  ? CHR(7)+CHR(7)
  ? "Fail to Link to Word for Windows document
'DDEClnt.doc'"
ENDIF
RETURN
```

Running this program will activate Word for Windows, fill in the bookmarks with the text specified, print the form letter, and abandon the changes to the file. Figure 11–6 shows the form letter, filled in and printed via DDELink commands from Visual dBASE.

Using Visual dBASE as a DDE Server

Visual dBASE can also be used as a DDE Server. To use Visual dBASE as a DDE Server, you need to instantiate a DDETopic object. Using the DDETopic object, another Windows application can attach to Visual dBASE as a Client, and read and write data in a Visual dBASE document (table or query file). It can even send dBASE programming commands to the DDETopic session.

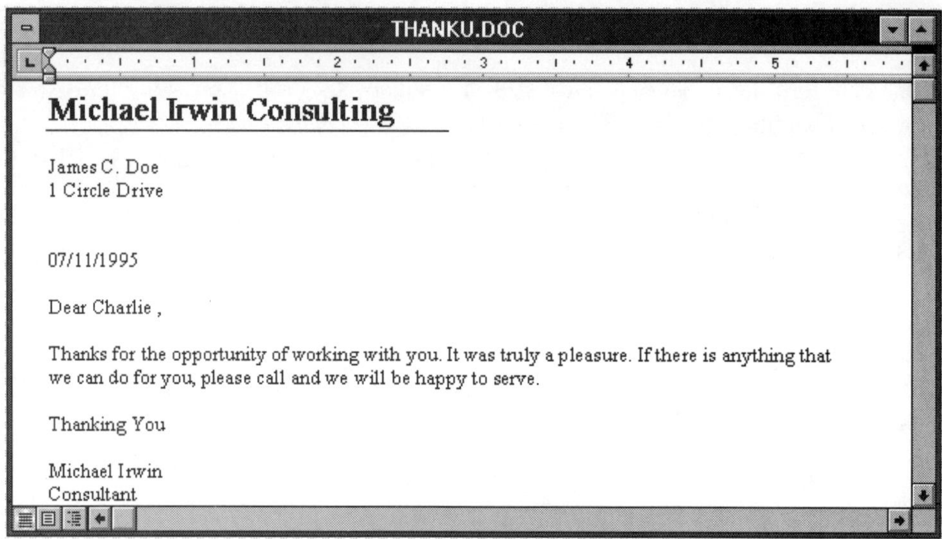

Figure 11–6. This is the form letter filled in.

To have another application start Visual dBASE as a DDE Server, the DDETopic object must already reside in memory. This means that dBASE (the server application) must execute a startup program before the DDELink can be established.

The following actions must occur to use dBASE as a Server:

1. The Windows application that is the DDE Client must start a dBASE session.
2. The Client must instruct dBASE to immediately run an intialization program that will create the DDETopic object in dBASE.
3. The Client must then initiate the DDE link with a dBASE document (table or query).

These three steps are surprisingly easy to do.

An Initialization Handler for the Server

First you must write a small dBASE program that will be used as the *Initialization Handler*. This special program makes a specific session of Visual dBASE appear as a DDE Server.

To accomplish this, it will need to assign a name to the *DDEServiceName* property of the Visual dBASE object (_app) itself. Then it has to assign an event handler (function name) that will be used to instantiate the DDETopic object. This is accomplished by assigning the name of the function to the *OnInitiate* Event property of Visual dBASE.

The following sections clarify this point.

Visual dBASE is an object named _APP. Visual dBASE is itself an object. It has the object name of **_APP**. That name is a single underscore (_) and the letters "APP." This object can be inspected like any other object of Visual dBASE. Inspecting it—INSPECT(_app)—reveals that it has six general properties, one event property, and zero methods.

The Initialization Handler code. The two you need to be concerned with for using dBASE as a DDE Server are

- DdeServiceName
- OnInitiate

The default value for DDEServiceName is **DBASEWIN**. However, you will probably want to specify a different value for this property, allowing you to run more than one session of dBASE. The OnInitiate property has no Event Handler assigned to it.

When you want to make Visual dBASE a Server, the Client must start Visual dBASE and run a startup program called the *Initialization Handler*. This program only needs two lines:

```
_app.DDEServiceName = "<user assigned name>"
_app.OnInitiate = <name of function to create DDETopic object>
```

The DDETopic object code

Because the Event Handler program that will create the DDETopic object must be in memory, you will probably want to create a little more code for the Initialization Handler. You need to create the initialization function that will actually create the DDETopic object. It will be triggered when the Client attempts to Initiate a DDELink with dBASE.

The following is an example that will be used by Quattro Pro:

```
*** DDETopic.Prg
*
SET PROC TO DDETopic.PRG
********************
******   Part A   ******
********************
*  Following is the Initialization code for Server
*  It assigns a name to the _app.DDEServiceName
*  property and a function name to the OnInitiate property
*  DDEServiceName is property that holds DDE session name
*  OnInitiate event property will run the function
specified
*  when the Client attempts to initiate a DDELink
*
_app.DDEServiceName = "VdBServer"
_app.OnInitiate = StartHandler
*
```

```
*  End of Intialization code
*
*******************
******   Part B  ******
*******************
*   The following function will be started when the Client
*   initiates a DDE Link with this session of dBASE
*   (VdBServer)
*
*   The parameter TopicName is passed to the StartHandler
*   function by the Client program—NOT dBASE
*
FUNCTION StartHandler (TopicName)
  *       Create a custom DDETopic object
  xDDESrv1 = NEW SpdShtDDETopic(TopicName)
  ? "Server is ACTIVE"
  ? "The Topic is ", xDDESrv1.Topic
RETURN xDDESrv1
*******************
******   Part C  ******
*******************
*
CLASS SpdShtDDETopic(cTopic) OF DDETopic(cTopic)
  *
  *   Code goes here for the new topic server and its
  *   functions. Depending on the type of actions the
  *   Client will be doing you will have to specify code
  *   for the OnPeek, OnPoke, OnExecute methods of
  *   the new object instantiated from this CLASS.
  *
ENDCLASS
```

This code is filled with remarks attempting to explain what it does. It is broken into three primary areas.

Part A. The Initialization Handler

Part B. The Event Handler to create the DDETopic object

Part C. The Class definition to specify actions for the DDELink events

The Initialization Handler code (Part A) is the only thing that is originally run when starting dBASE with the program name. This is done by the Client by issuing a command to start dBASEWIN and run this program.

Once the program is running, the Client then attempts to initialize a DDELink with this session of dBASE which triggers the (Part B) Event Handler (Function StartHandler). The Function StartHandler creates the DDETopic object from the Class definition that you specify in the Class SpdShtDDETopic() code (Part C).

Using Quattro Pro as a Client to Visual dBASE

Figure 11–7 shows the spread sheet DDETOPIC.WB1 that has a macro starting at Cell A:A1. It is made up of two different Macro commands—EXEC and INIT. There are three cells of interest: A:A1, A:A2, and A:C5.

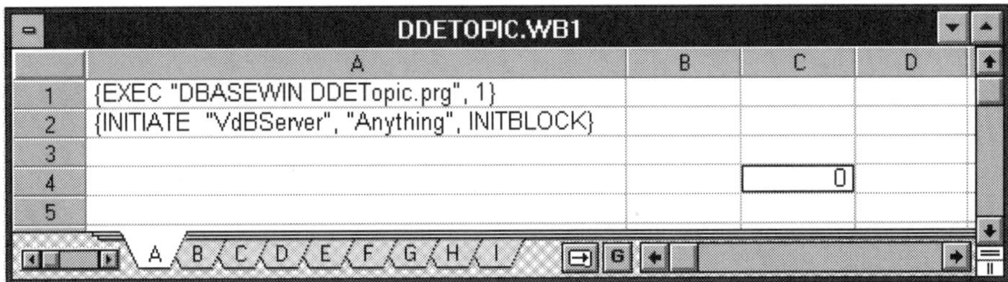

Figure 11–7. This is the Client DDELink macros for Quattro Pro.

Start Visual dBASE and activate the Initialization Handler. The first Cell, A:A1, has an EXEC macro command:

```
{EXEC "DBASEWIN D:\MyPRGS\DDETopic.PRG", 1}
```

This Quattro Pro macro command tells it to start dBASE and pass the program named DDETopic.prg to dBASE. It also specifies that the dBASE window should be opened in its normal restore size (2 = minimize; 3 = maximize).

Attempt to initialize a DDELink with Visual dBASE. The second Cell A:A2 has an INIT macro command:

```
{INIT  "VdBServer", "AnyThing", INITBLOCK}
```

This command tells Quattro Pro to attempt to Initiate a DDELink with the Visual dBASE DDE Server having the name “VdBServer.” It also tells it to pass the name “AnyThing” to the DDE Server as the Topic name. dBASE will use this name as the parameter TopicName in the FUNCTION StartHandler. Remember, the Function StartHandler has been assigned in the Initialization Handler as the program to be executed with a Client attempts to initiate a DDE session. Finally, the INIT macro command specifies a cell by BlockName as the cell that will hold an internal number that specifies the DDELink created by this INIT command.

The block name in the INIT command, INITBLOCK, simply points to the cell A:C5. This cell must be empty. It will hold the generated identification number of the DDELink created from Cells A:A1 and A:A2.

Now, the Client would issue poke, peek, and execute commands to this Visual dBASE Server (DDETopic object), obtaining data and passing data to it.

Running the DDE Client macro. If you run this macro in Quattro Pro for Windows, it will start a separate session of dBASE and initialize a DDE Link with it. Once these two macro commands are completed, a DDELink will be established in the "VdBServer" session of Visual dBASE. Figure 11–8 shows the Command window for the DDE Server session of dBASE. Notice that the Command window in Figure 11–8 shows that Quattro Pro started dBASE and ran the program DDETopic.prg (the EXEC macro) as seen in the Entry pane of the Command window. The Results pane of the Command window shows that the Initialization Handler was executed and it assigned the values "VdBServer" and "Function: STARTHANDLER." Then the Quattro Pro INIT macro started the DDELink, passing the value "AnyThing" as the parameter of the StartHandler function.

Figure 11–8. This is the DDE Server Command window.

If you inspect (_app) of this session of dBASE, you will see that it is, indeed, the VdBServer session.

An active DDELink exists between Quattro Pro and Visual dBASE. Visual dBASE is the Server of this DDELink.

Overview of Multimedia in dBASE

dBASE offers support for Multimedia. When you create a table and specify a field type of Binary or OLE, you are given automatic support for the Binary or OLE data type.

To do multimedia in dBASE for Windows, your hardware will need to support multimedia—a sound card with drivers (or the speaker driver software), and any applications that are needed to support the multimedia functions you want to perform. For instance, Video for Windows or some other video driver if you want to display and work with videos.

Binary fields

dBASE can store pictures and sound in Binary fields. Once stored, it can display the pictures or play the sound file. It will not support editing of the picture or sound file.

Picture formats

➨ Visual dBASE has added four additional graphics formats to its automatic display and recognition support. Now dBASE will automatically display these graphic formats—Windows Bit Map (BMP), PC Paint (PCX), Icon (ICO), Tag Image File Format (TIF), Windows Meta File (WMF), and Encapsulated PostScript (EPS). They will automatically be supported when you Edit or BROWSE the table or query using the binary field. Figure 11–9 shows a BROWSE table with the Image Viewer window active. As you move through the records in the table, the Image Viewer window will automatically update the display with the next picture from the database.

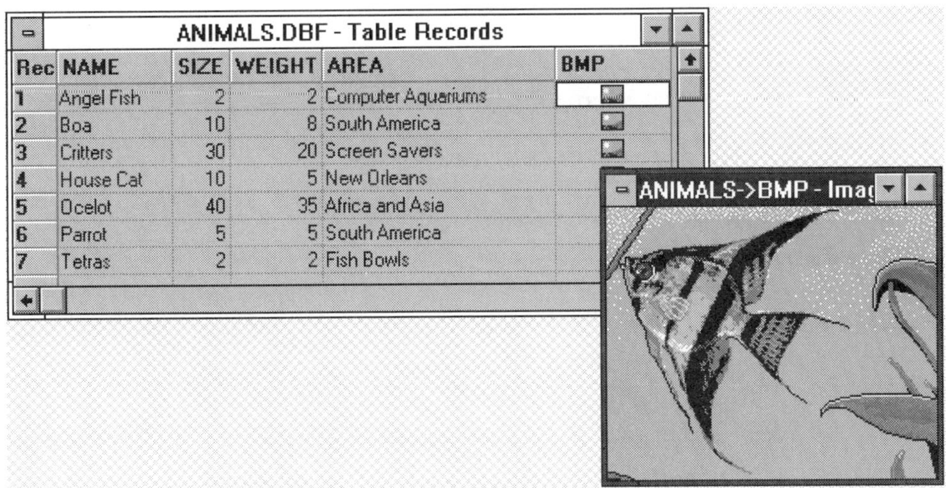

Figure 11–9. A binary field with pictures in it.

The file used in Figure 11–9 comes with dBASE and is located in the SAMPLES subdirectory under the \VisualDB directory on your disk. It is named ANIMALS.dbf.

When you first BROWSE a file with a Binary field, dBASE displays it like it does the Memo field—as a small icon in the field. You can identify the field as a binary type based on the picture. If the field is holding picture data, it displays a scenery picture.

To activate the Image Viewer window, you can double-click on the field picture icon, press F9, or select View >> Field Contents from the menu.

Sound formats

dBASE can also display and store sound in the same binary field as it uses for displaying graphics. It automatically recognizes and plays Windows audio files (*.WAV). Figure 11–10 shows a PICTURES.dbf with the Sound Player window active. It can be activated clicking on the field picture icon, pressing F9, or selecting View >> Field Contents from the menu.

As you move through the records in the table, the Sound Player window will automatically update the display with the next sound from the database. Clicking on the Play button activates the sound.

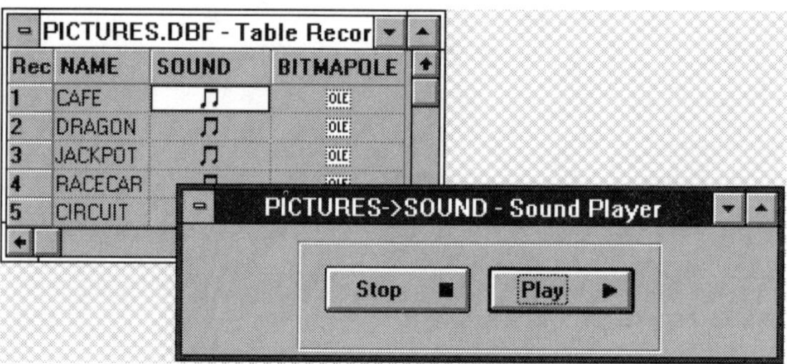

Figure 11–10. A binary field with sound in it.

The file used in Figure 11–10 also comes with Visual dBASE and is located in the SAMPLES subdirectory.

You can quickly determine that the binary field holds a sound file by the picture of the musical note as a small icon in the field. This is distinctly different from the picture of the scenery of graphics stored in the binary field.

Store any type of data

A binary field is not limited to storing these six graphic and one sound file types; these are the binary types that Visual dBASE can automatically detect and store. However, it can store any type of data in a binary field type.

OLE fields

An OLE field, like a binary field, can store picture and sound fields. The difference between it and a binary field is the editability of the data stored in an OLE field.

An OLE field stores the document or a disk location pointer. This pointer tells dBASE where the document can be found. Binary files that are stored in an OLE field are linked to an OLE Server in Windows. All this means is that the picture, sound, or other binary data that is in the OLE field was created by some Windows application that can be used by dBASE to Edit the stored data.

An OLE field can even be used to store Video clips, such as .AVI and .MOV files.

Single pictures

dBASE can display and store pictures in an OLE field. It automatically recognizes and displays any type of picture that can be linked to a Server application. Figure 11–11 shows the OLE field viewer active with a Paintbrush Picture object being displayed.

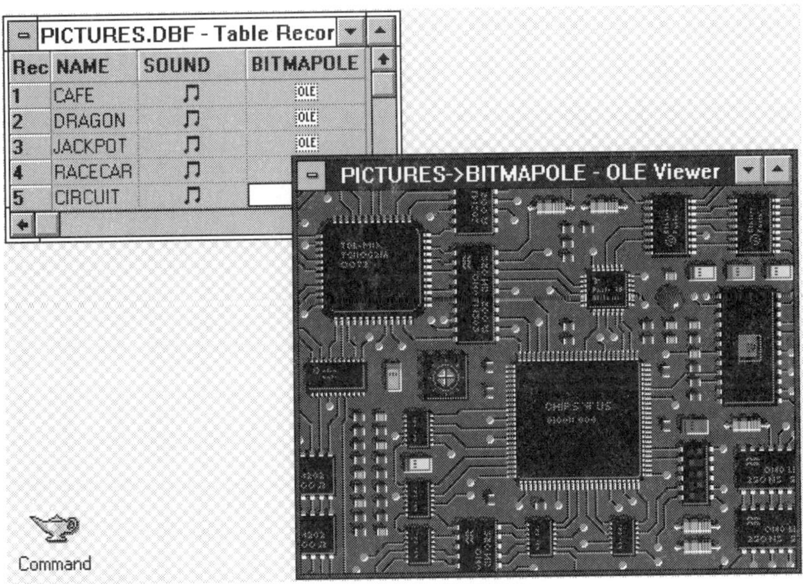

Figure 11–11. OLE field viewer with Paintbrush Picture object.

You can quickly determine that the field is OLE type by the word OLE in a small icon in the field. If the field is empty, it will show an empty rectangular icon.

The OLE Viewer window. Once the OLE Viewer window is active, you can use it for displaying the picture or use it to launch the Server application that created (or can work with) the OLE object. Like the Image Viewer and Sound Player windows, the OLE Viewer window will automatically point to the correct field contents remaining in synch with the current record in the Browse window. Every time you skip to a new record in Browse, the OLE Viewer will be updated with the new OLE object.

While in the OLE Viewer window, you can automatically launch (run) the Server application by double clicking on the picture or by selecting the proper choice from the Edit menu. You can also activate a SpeedMenu by right mouse clicking in the OLE Viewer. The SpeedMenu can be used to

- Insert new Objects in the OLE field
- Cut existing objects to the Clipboard
- Paste a link in the OLE field
- Set the single OLE Viewer property—size to Object

Inserting objects is based on the system registry of OLE object applications in Windows. When you select Insert Object into OLE field, you will be given a dialog box, similar to the one in Figure 11–12, with all the available object types that you can bring into the OLE field. The object types are based on your system and what OLE Servers you have available in Windows.

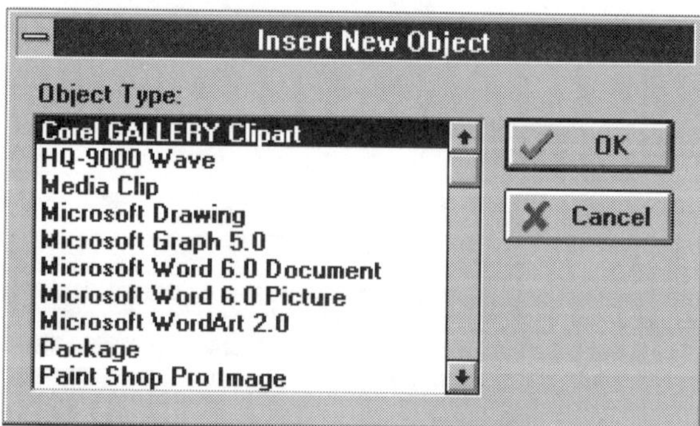

Figure 11–12. The Insert New Object dialog box for OLE fields.

Instead of inserting the actual object, you can also paste a link to the OLE object. Pasting a link lets you store the filename of the linked object and a picture to display in the OLE viewer. That way you can still access the file without invoking the database table.

Video files

If your system supports video files, you can have an OLE object store an audio visual (video) file. For example, the table in Figure 11–13 has an OLE field with .AVI (Intel-based audio visual files) records and MOV (Macintosh, Motorola-based Videos).

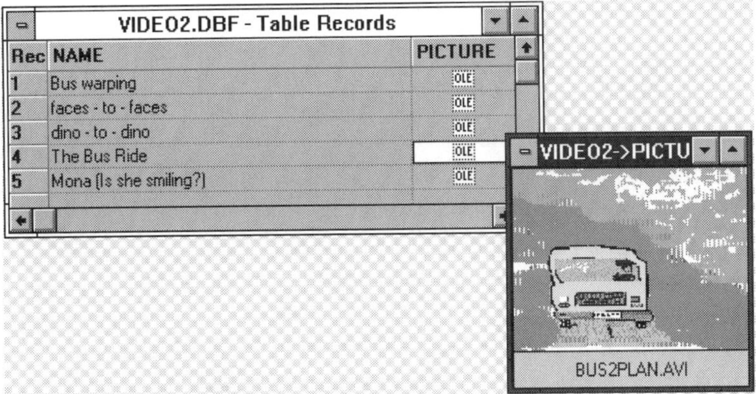

Figure 11–13. Using .AVI files in dBASE.

If you double-click on the OLE viewer window, dBASE will automatically activate Video for Windows (or whatever viewer you have) and run the .AVI file in a Video for Windows window. Figure 11–14 shows the same .AVI running in a Video for Windows window.

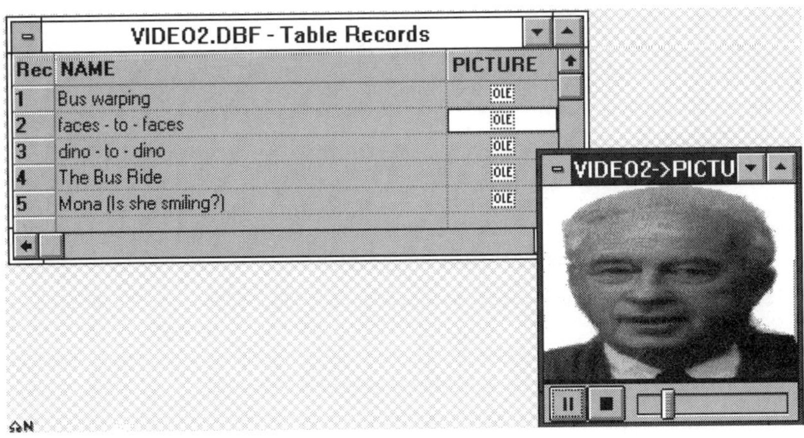

Figure 11–14. Running an .AVI file inside dBASE.

dBASE automatically ran the video file, simply by double clicking on it. You don't have to create a program to get this type of multimedia support. It is already built in through the OLE field.

When you store an OLE object, you are asked what type of OLE server will be linked to. The server can be one that simply plays the object, or one that can be used to create it.

OLE field versus Binary field

Both field types, OLE and Binary, are actually memo fields. They, like regular memo fields, have a 10-byte block number in the record, and blocks in the .DBT file. Unlike the memo field commands, which are only aimed at text-based manipulation, OLE and binary data can use new commands that are geared to binary data (sound and pictures). You can use both types in the same database. In fact, you can use memo fields, OLE and Binary, in the same database.

The primary difference between these two data types is the editing capabilities of OLE fields. Both fields can store similar types of data. They both have their own strengths.

- A binary field contains data stored in binary format—it can be bitmap images, sound, or any type of binary data.
- OLE fields tend to contain documents inserted in a dBASE/Paradox table from another Windows application that also supports OLE. The document can either be linked by reference or actually embedded in the field.

Binary field advantages

1. Any type of binary data can be stored in the field.
2. The data stored does not require a connection to another Windows program.
3. Storage space for binary fields is smaller than embedded OLE documents.
4. The time to insert and view data to/from a binary field is faster than an embedded OLE document.
5. You can assign a user-specified binary data type number when you add data to a binary field.

OLE field advantages

1. You can link to an OLE document rather than embed it.
2. A link requires less disk space than inserting binary data or embedding the OLE document.
3. OLE field data can be edited once it is embedded or linked by using the external link application (which created it).

4. Stored OLE data can be automatically updated with the data changes in the original file.

Working with Binary Data and Fields

Binary fields can be used to store any type of binary data. Once you store the data in this field type, it can be used in forms and reports. The data stored in binary fields will be static; once stored, it cannot be edited. A binary field is used to store and view binary data.

Storing data in a binary field type

You can assign a custom data type number to the data when you add it to a binary field via the command language. You supply a user type number between 1 and 32K-1. Numbers between 32K and 64K-1 are reserved for Visual dBASE.

Technically, dBASE stores binary data in a memo file (.DBT file) and assigns the record a predefined number. The numbers dBASE recognizes are found in Table 11–1.

Table 11–1. Binary-Type Numbers.

Number (Type)	Purpose
1 to 32K-1	User-defined file type
32K (32768)	.WAV file
32K+1 (32769)	PCX, BMP, ICO, TIF, WMF, and EPS graphic file types
32K+2 - 64K -1	Reserved by dBASE

Determining the type of data stored in a binary field
You can determine the type number by using the function BINTYPE(). If the number returned is 32768, it is a WAV file; 32769 one of the recognized graphic files. If it returns a 0, it means that the field data was not understood by dBASE or the field is empty. To determine if the field is empty, you can use the EMPTY() function.

Determining the content of a binary field

You can tell what the status of a binary field is by the type of icon displayed in the binary field cell. Figure 11–15 shows all four different icons that can be displayed in the binary field.

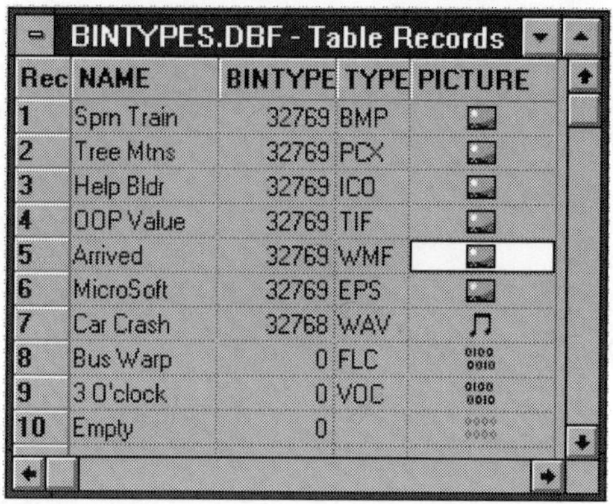

Figure 11–15. The four icons that can be displayed in a binary field.

The four icon types depend on the type of data being stored. Table 11–2 associates the icon type with the type of binary data stored in the field.

Table 11–2. Binary Types and Icons.

Icon	Binary type
Scenery	dBASE recognized graphic file
Musical note	.WAV sound file
Offset 0s and 1s	User-specified type
Gray box of 0s	Empty cell

Putting a picture/sound in a binary field

To append or replace a binary field's contents you use the REPLACE BINARY command. The general syntax for the command is

```
REPLACE BINARY <binary field name> FROM <filename.ext>
              [TYPE <binary type user number>]
```

This command places the contents of a binary file into a binary field, replacing whatever was already in the binary field. It is equivalent to the REPLACE MEMO command that stores text in a memo field. You must specify the filenames extension. If the extension is one that dBASE automatically recognizes (.WAV, .PCX, .TIF, .BMP, etc.), it will automatically store the correct binary type number (sound 32K, graphic 32K+1). This field type, binary field, is ideal for storing images, sound, and other user-defined binary type information.

The following will place a .BMP picture in record 4 and a .WAV sound in record 5:

```
USE MISCBINS
```

```
GO 4
REPLACE BINARY PictSnd FROM SIGN.BMP
GO 5
REPLACE BINARY PictSnd FROM CARCRASH.WAV
```

The REPLACE BINARY scope. The REPLACE BINARY command can only be used to copy a binary file to the **current** record's binary field. You must be sitting at the correct record before you issue the command. There is no other scoping that is allowed.

The TYPE specifier. If you place a binary file type in a binary field that dBASE does not recognize, you can specify a TYPE. The number must be between 1 and 32K-1 (32767). It is user-supplied and can be used in a program later. To determine the binary type of data stored in the field, you can use the BINTYPE() function. To use this function you must specify the field name. For example,

```
xType = BINTYPE(PictSnd)
```

```
GO 6
REPLACE BINARY PictSnd FROM FLYBY.VOC TYPE 3
```

Storing different binary types in the same field. When you create a binary field, you do not have to store the same type of data in the field. You can store a sound file in record 2, a picture file in record 3, and another sound file in record 4. Any type of binary data can be stored in the same field. Each record can only have one type of binary data in a single field. If you need to store a sound file and a picture file for each record, you will need two different binary fields. For instance, a single record (like 32) has a binary field, PictSnd field. It cannot hold a PCX, and a WAV file in the same field. This one field can only hold one binary file either the PCX or the WAV.

Storing text information. A binary field can also be used to store text-type data. This data can be formatted text, like a word-processing document or simple ASCII text. If you need to store simple, nonformatted text, a MEMO field is a better place. Any binary data can be stored in a binary field.

Getting information from a binary field

After the data are in a binary field, there are a few commands that will let you work with the data. You can copy the field contents to a file, display a picture, or play a sound.

Copying a binary field to an external file

You can copy the contents of a specific binary field to a file using the COPY BINARY command. The general syntax of the command is

```
COPY BINARY <binary field name> TO <filename.ext>
[ADDITIVE]
```

You use this command to export data from the binary field of the current record to a file.

The ADDITIVE option. The ADDITIVE option will append the contents of the field to the end of whatever is already in the named file (if it exists). This is useful if you need to combine the contents of several binary fields into a single external file.

> ! **Overwriting existing files**
> When you do not use the ADDITIVE option, and you have SAFETY ON, using COPY BINARY to an existing file will force dBASE to display a warning message before overwriting the file. If SAFETY is OFF, it will overwrite the file without warning you.

Using filename extensions. If you do not specify an extension, dBASE will automatically supply one for you. If the data type is a sound file that Visual dBASE knows, it will supply the extension .WAV. If the data type is one of the graphic files that it knows, it will supply the extension .BMP. Otherwise, dBASE will give it the extension .TXT.

> ! **Supplying improper extensions**
> Although Visual dBASE has built in support for .PCX, .ICO, .TIF, .WFM, and .EPS graphic file types, it will not append the correct extension to the file if you forget to pass it an extension. Visual dBASE assumes all pictures that it recognizes are .BMP type.

Displaying a picture from a binary field

You can display a graphic (.BMP, .PCX, .TIF, ICO, . . .) that is stored in a binary field using the command RESTORE IMAGE FROM. In fact this same command can be used to display any dBASE-recognized graphic file (external or internal). The general syntax of the command is

```
RESTORE IMAGE FROM < BINARY <binary field name> >|
<filename>  ;
                    [TIMEOUT <number of seconds>] ;
                    [TO PRINTER]
```

When you display an image using this command, it will be displayed in its own window inside the dBASE frame. Figure 11–16 shows a picture named TREEMTN.bmp displayed inside its own window. The command used was

```
RESTORE IMAGE FROM TREEMTN
```

Figure 11–16. A picture file displayed with the command RESTORE IMAGE FROM.

> ! **Specifying an extension**
> If an extension is not supplied, Visual dBASE will look for a file with the extension of .BMP. If it doesn't find one, it will automatically report an error.

The TIMEOUT option. The Timeout option lets you specify a number of seconds to display the image on the screen. For instance, you many only want to display a picture for two seconds then go on to the next one. The following code would go through a database and display all the records pictures, changing the picture every two seconds:

```
*** SHOWPICS.prg
*
USE MIKEPETS
GO TOP
DO WHILE .NOT. EOF()
   RESTORE IMAGE FROM BINARY Picture TIMEOUT 2
   SLEEP
   SKIP
ENDDO
RETURN
```

This code will display each image in its own open window for two seconds, then close the window.

> ✔ **Using the SLEEP command**
> This code uses the command SLEEP. It waits the designated number of seconds before returning control to the program. It is similar to the INKEY(number) function; however, unlike the Inkey() function, pressing a key does nothing. It is used to halt temporarily execution of the program because the restore image command immediately returns control to the program after executing. If the Sleep command were not there, there would be several pictures on the screen, each in their own window, waiting for two seconds and then closing.

Specifying the BINARY keyword. Notice that this code restores images from a BINARY field named Picture. If you are going to restore images from a field, you must specify the keyword BINARY before the name of the field.

Scoping a Restore Image from BINARY. If you specify the BINARY keyword with a field, you will only display the picture in the current record being pointed to. This command does not support any further scoping capabilities.

Playing a sound from a binary field

You can also play sounds (.WAV) stored in a binary field using the command PLAY SOUND. In fact this same command can be used to play any .WAV file (external or internal). The general syntax of the command is

```
PLAY SOUND <BINARY <binary field name>> | < FILENAME <filename> >
```

The following examples play a couple of external .WAV files and the sounds from a field named MusicDemo:

```
*** PLAYSNDS.prg
*
PLAY SOUND FILENAME CarCrash
SLEEP 1
PLAY SOUND FILENAME Laser
*
*  Music.dbf found in directory below samples:
*  \VisualDB\SAMPLES\MUSIC
*
USE Music
GO TOP
LOCATE FOR .NOT. EMPTY(SOUND)
*    only play 5 sound files
FOR x = 1 to 5
  PLAY SOUND BINARY Sound
  sleep 4
  SKIP
NEXT
RETURN
```

✔ **Finding an external file**
When looking for external files, Visual dBASE uses the current path set with SET PATH to find the file specified.

The keywords BINARY and FILENAME. When working with PLAY SOUND, you must specify one of the two keywords—FILENAME or BINARY—to tell Visual dBASE where to find the file that it will play.

Specifying an extension. The preceding code played two external .WAV files. Notice that it did not specify the extension .WAV; it is assumed to be .WAV.

Scoping the PLAY SOUND BINARY command. The PLAY SOUND BINARY <field name> command will only play the current record being pointed to. It has no other scoping capabilities.

Object-oriented Image commands

dBASE has a Class type IMAGE that can be used to create image objects. These objects are control objects that are placed inside a form for displaying images in a form. Like other control objects, you can create image objects using the NEW command or the DEFINE command.

DEFINE IMAGE command

You can create an image object using the DEFINE IMAGE command. The general syntax for creating an image object is:

```
DEFINE IMAGE <object name> OF <form name> PROPERTY ;

    Top <xNum>, Left <xNum> , Height <xNum>, Width <xNum> ;
    DataSource "FILENAME <name of image> |    ;
                  RESOURCE <#xNum  [name of DLL file] > | ;
                  BINARY <field name> "
      <other properties ... >
      CUSTOM <custom property list, ... >
```

DataSource property. Using this syntax, you can create an image object and link it to a picture. To link to a picture, you use the property named *DataSource*. There are three different sources you can use for an image—a FILENAME, a BINARY field name, or a RESOURCE in a .DLL.

The following code will create a form and place three different pictures on the form. The pictures come from three different sources.

```
*** MYPICS.WFM
*
f= NEW PicForm()
f.open()
CLASS PicForm of FORM
  this.height = 13
  this.view = "Animals"
  this.text = "Pictures"
  this.ColorNormal = "n/W*"

  DEFINE IMAGE iPic1 OF this PROPERTY;
     top 1, left 1, height 2, width 4, ;
```

```
      datasource "RESOURCE #108"
   DEFINE IMAGE iPic2 OF this PROPERTY;
      top 4, left 1, height 4, width 18, ;
      datasource "FILENAME TREEMTN.BMP"
   DEFINE IMAGE iPic3 OF this PROPERTY;
      top 2, left 24, height 8, width 32, ;
      datasource "BINARY BMP"
   DEFINE TEXT tWord1 OF this PROPERTY;
      top 11, left 12, width 45, height 1.8, ;
      fontsize 16, fontunderline .T. , ;
      text "Images from 3 Sources"
ENDCLASS
```

The only difference between the three commands (other than placement) is the data source assigned to the DataSource property. When you specify a data source, you must use one of the keywords—BINARY, RESOURCE, or FILENAME.

Once the file is created, you can run it by typing DO MYPICS.WFM. It will create a screen that looks similar to the one in Figure 11–17.

Figure 11–17. A form with three different images on it.

CLASS IMAGE

You can also create an image object by using the CLASS . . . IMAGE command. The general syntax for using the CLASS construct is:

CLASS <object reference variable>(form name) OF IMAGE(form name)

this.DataSource = "<Source type> <field/file/resource #>"

The DataSource is key. Like the DEFINE IMAGE command, the key to attaching an image to an object is using the DataSource property. You must specify one of the keywords—RESOURCE, BINARY, or FILENAME—and the name of the field, or the file, or the resource number.

The following code demonstrates use of the CLASS ... IMAGE command:

```
*** MYCIMAGE.PRG
*
CLASS PicImage(fn) OF IMAGE(fn)
   this.top = 2
   this.left = 2
   this.height = 8
   this.width = 32
   this.DataSource = "FILENAME treemtn.bmp"
*   this.DataSource = "BINARY BMP"
*   this.DataSource = "RESOURCE #108"
ENDCLASS
```

Once you create this code, placing it in a procedure file, you can use the class like any other class. The following code demonstrates use of an image class:

```
SET PROC TO MYCIMAGE
f = NEW FORM()
*   If data source is BINARY, you need to specify a table
*    Unremark the next line
*    f.view = "Animals"
*
xPic = NEW PicImage(f)
f.Open()
```

If you run this code, the form will look something like the one in Figure 11–18.

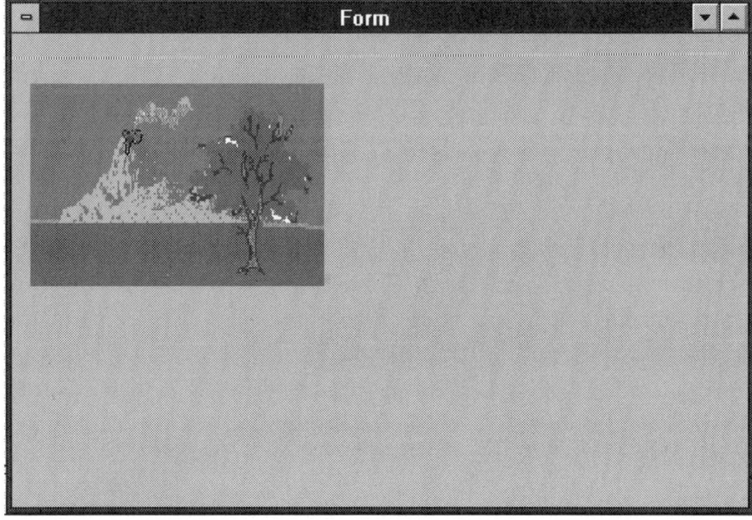

Figure 11–18. A form with an image created from the Image CLASS.

In this case, the DataSource was an external file named TREEMTN.BMP. The other two datasources have been remarked off in the code. If you specify a Resource, then all you need is the keyword RESOURCE and the number of the resource. If you specify a field, you must use the keyword BINARY and the name of the field. Before you can use a field, you must specify a database or query name in the form's *View* property.

WORKING WITH OLE DATA AND FIELDS

An OLE object, also called an OLE document, can be any type of binary data—like a spreadsheet, word-processing document, graphic image, video file, or any other document created by another Windows application that is known as the OLE Server. The OLE server is the application (.EXE or .DLL) that will be used to edit the OLE document that is embedded or linked in an OLE field of Visual dBASE.

Once an OLE document is stored in an OLE field, it can be used for forms and reports. Unlike data stored in binary fields, OLE field data can be modified and updated. Once stored, it can be edited by the Server application it is linked to.

Storing data in an OLE field type

You can have one or more OLE fields in a table. You can even store different types of OLE Documents in different records (same field Name—different records).

Technically, dBASE stores OLE data in a memo file (.DBT file), just like binary data.

Putting an OLE document in an OLE field

To append or replace an OLE field's contents, you use the REPLACE OLE command. The general syntax for the command is

REPLACE OLE <OLE field name> FROM <filename.ext>

[LINK]

The REPLACE OLE command is used to insert the contents of an OLE document into the current record's OLE field. You can add a new OLE document or replace an existing one. If an OLE document is already in the field, it will be replaced with the new one.

You can embed the actual OLE document in the OLE field or access the OLE document by linking it to the OLE field. The default is to embed the OLE document into the field.

The following code would be an example of storing Word for Windows documents in a Visual dBASE for tracking documents. It will physically place a copy of the document into an OLE field named Document.

```
*** ADDOLE.prg
```

```
*
USE DOCTRAKR
GO BOTTOM
APPEND BLANK
REPLACE FileName with "FOODSea2.doc", ;
        KeyWords with "Fish, Food, Cold"
REPLACE OLE Document FROM "FoodSea2.doc"
```

The last command will insert the Word for Windows document "FoodSea2.doc" in the OLE field Document.

Browsing through the table and displaying the OLE field will look something like Figure 11–19.

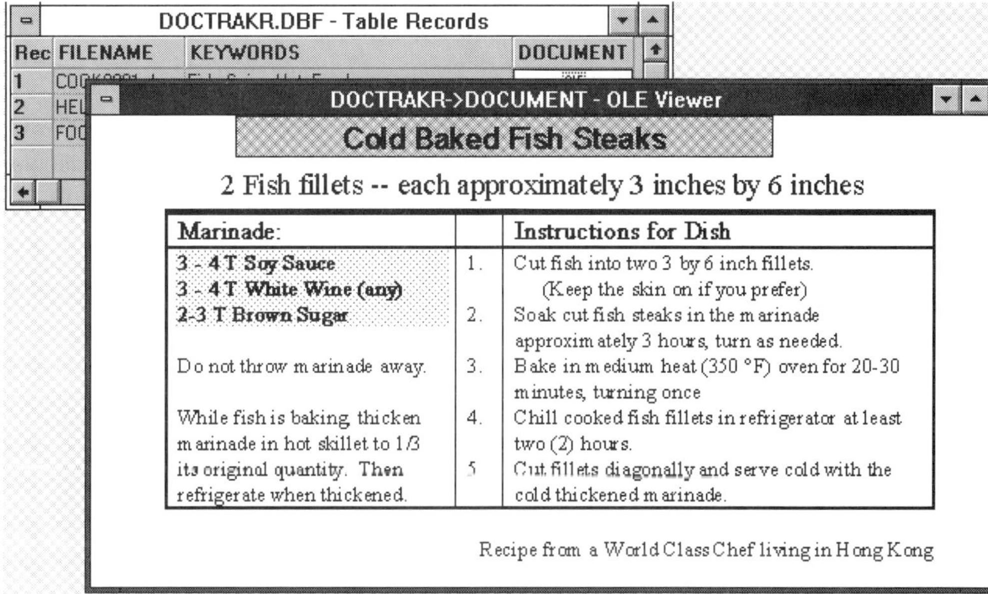

Figure 11–19. This is an OLE field.

Specifying the filename. When you use the REPLACE OLE command, you must specify the extension of the file that will be embedded or linked. The extension is used by Windows to determine if there is a Server registered that can work with the OLE document.

Scoping the REPLACE OLE command. The Replace OLE command only works with the current record and field being referenced. You can only replace one OLE field at a time. If you have several OLE fields in the record, you must REPLACE OLE each field individually.

You cannot replace OLE in more than the current record. There is no other scoping ability associated with this command.

The [Extensions] section of the Win.Ini. The **[extensions]** section will look something like this.

```
[extensions]
pcx = pbrush.exe ^.pcx
rec = recorder.exe ^.rec
```

The [Embedding] section of the Win.Ini. The **[embedding]** section will look something like this.

```
[embedding]
PBRUSH = Paintbrush Picture, Paintbrush Picture,
pbrush.exe,
⇒ picture
SoundRec = Sound, Sound, SoundRec.exe, picture
```

Displaying a picture from an OLE field

You can display an OLE document when you are in a BROWSE or an EDIT window by pressing the F9 key, selecting View >> Field Contents from the menu, or double-clicking the OLE field. dBASE will open the OLE Viewer. It will stay synchronized with the records as you move through the browse table or the edit records.

Commands to display an OLE field document. There are no commands available that will let you display an OLE field document from the Command window or in dBASE code. If you need to display an OLE field document, you should create a form object and place an OLE object in the form.

OLE Viewer tasks

Once the OLE viewer is active, and it is in focus (you are sitting in the Viewer window), you have several things you can do with the object. What you can do with the object will depend on the type of OLE object (document) that you are working with. The main choices are

- Cut
- Copy
- Paste
- Paste Link
- Insert Object . . .
- Links . . .
- Delete
- <Server Object> choices (Edit and Play, if appropriate)

All except the last two tasks (delete and <Server Object>) are available via both the Edit menu and the SpeedMenu (right mouse click). The Delete and <Server Object> choices tasks are only available via the Edit menu.

Cut, copy, and paste. You can cut, copy, and paste an OLE document, just like you do with the Clipboard. You can remove it from the field by cutting it. You can copy it. Finally, you can paste whatever is in the document reference of the Clipboard memory region to the OLE field.

Paste link. You can also paste link an OLE document reference on the Clipboard to the OLE field of the current record. The command will link data that was previously placed in the Clipboard by another application. The OLE document (or a visual representation of it—like a small audio tape for sound) will appear in the OLE Viewer.

When you paste the contents of the Clipboard, they are not deleted from the Clipboard, so you could paste the same document into several different OLE fields. The contents are removed from the Clipboard when you perform another Cut or Copy command.

Insert Object .... You can embed the object, using the Insert Object ... choice from the SpeedMenu or the Edit menu. This is the same as using the REPLACE OLE command.

Links .... If you paste link an OLE object into an OLE field, the Links ... option will be activated. If the OLE field is embedded, the Links ... choice will not be available (grayed out).

To paste link an OLE object, simply use the keyword LINK with the REPLACE OLE command:

```
REPLACE OLE BITMAPOLE FROM "COOK0001.DOC" LINK
```

This command will replace the OLE field BitMapOle with a reference pointer to the document file "Cook0001.doc" instead of actually embedding it.

If you select Links ..., you will activate a dialog box similar to the one in Figure 11–22, which shows the Server name (Microsoft Word for Windows 6.0), the name of the OLE object (COOK.0001.DOC), and the type of update (Automatic). You can change the Update from Automatic to Manual, force an update now, change the link, and cancel the link. Finally, you can use the Links ... choice to Edit the object.

If you leave the OLE object set to automatic updates, it will operate extremely slowly because it has to constantly check to see if the object has been updated by the Server application.

Delete. You can delete the OLE document by selecting the Delete option of the Edit menu.

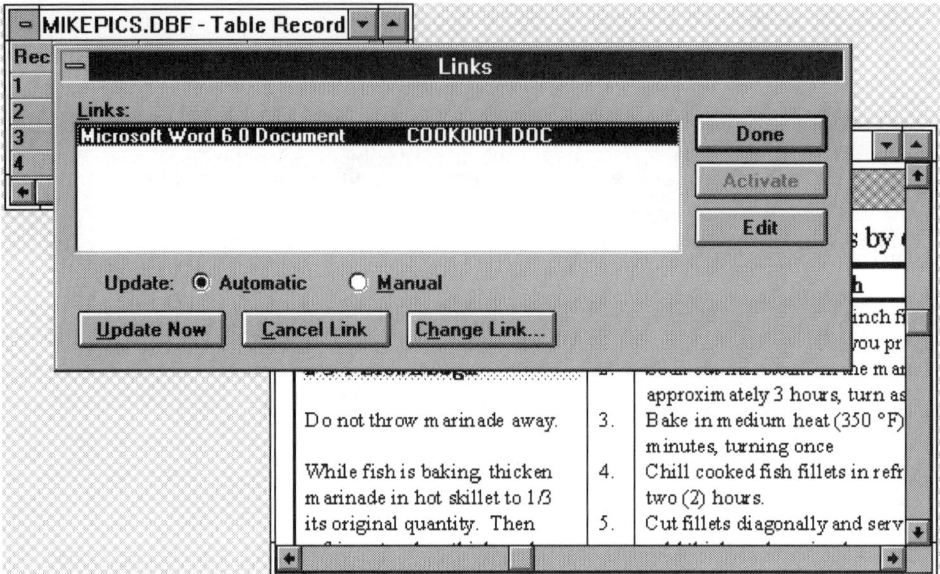

Figure 11–22. The Links dialog box.

<Server Object > choices. The Edit menu will include a Server choice at the bottom of the Edit menu. For instance, Figure 11–23 shows the Edit menu. At the bottom of the menu is the choice Sound Object. It has two choices in a cascading menu—Play and Edit.

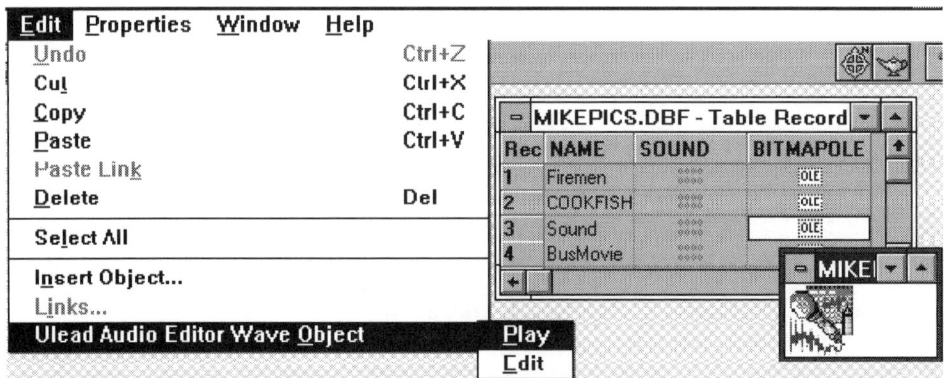

Figure 11–23. The Sound Choices prompt of the edit menu for an OLE object.

The last prompt of the Edit menu will always be the Server application. Its cascade menu will offer available choices for the Server application—edit or, if appropriate, play the object.

Object-oriented OLE commands

dBASE has a Class type OLE that can be used to create OLE objects. These objects are control objects that are placed inside a form for displaying OLE documents in a form. Like other control objects, you can create an OLE object using the NEW command or the DEFINE command.

DEFINE OLE command

You can create an image object using the DEFINE OLE command. The general syntax for creating an image object is

DEFINE OLE <object name> OF <form name> PROPERTY ;

Top <xNum>, Left <xNum> , Height <xNum>, Width <xNum> ;

DataLink "<field name>"

DataLink property. Using this syntax you can create an OLE object and link the object to an OLE field. Unlike the Image object, an OLE object can only be linked to an OLE field. Because the field can contain documents that are embedded or linked, you can view documents that are physically in the table or external to the table. However, the OLE object will only link to the field.

The following code will create a form and place an OLE object on the form. The Objects (sound, video, and pictures) come from the same source—the Picture field:

```
*** MYOLE.wfm
*
f = NEW MYOLE()
f.Open()
CLASS MYOLE OF FORM
   this.Height = 14
   this.Left = 1
   this.Top =  0
   this.Width = 40
   this.ColorNormal = "N/W*"
   this.View = "Video2.dbf"
   DEFINE OLE oObjs1 OF THIS PROPERTY ;
        Top 2, Left 6, Width 27, Height 9.2,;
        DataLink "VIDEO2->PICTURE"
ENDCLASS
```

When you run this form, you will see the OLE object viewed in the form. If the object cannot be viewed in the form, then a representation icon will be displayed. Figure 11–24 shows the OLE object displaying a short cartoon video.

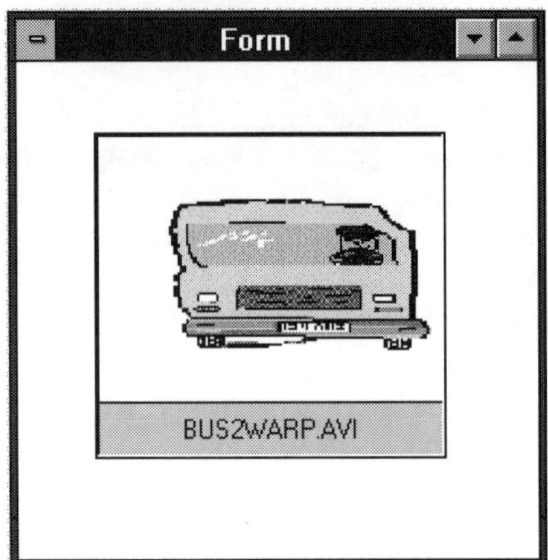

Figure 11-24. An OLE object in a form.

Playing a sound or video. Although you can create a pushbutton to play the sound or the video, you can also play them by simply double clicking on the OLE object in the form.

CLASS OLE

You can also create an OLE object by using the CLASS . . . IMAGE command. The general syntax for using the CLASS construct is

CLASS <object reference variable>(form name) OF OLE(form name)

this.DataLink = "<field name>"

The DataLink is the key. Like the DEFINE OLE command, the key to using an OLE field for a form is the DataLink property.

```
*** MYCOLE.PRG
*
CLASS DocOle(fn) OF OLE(fn)
   this.top = 2
   this.left = 6
   this.height = 9.2
   this.width = 27
   this.DataLink = "Video2->Picture"
ENDCLASS
```

Once you create this code, place it in a procedure file. Then you can use the class like any other class. The following code demonstrates use of an OLE class:

```
SET PROC TO MYCOLE
f = NEW FORM()
```

```
f.view = "Video2.dbf"
xDoc = NEW DocOle(f)
f.Open()
```

This code will open a form similar to the one that was displayed in Figure 11–24.

Some important members of the OLE object

The *DataLink* property is the most important property that you can set. However, there are several read-only properties that you should be aware of and one method that you may find very useful:

- ServerName
- LinkFileName
- OLEType
- DOVerb

The ServerName and LinkFileName properties. These two properties, *ServerName* and *LinkFileName,* hold the name of the Server application that can edit and play (if appropriate) the OLE document.

The OLEType property. The *OLEType* property holds a value from 0 to 2, which can be used to tell you if the OLE field is empty, or has an embedded or a linked document. Table 11–3 shows the values and what they represent.

Table 11–3. The OLEType Property.

Property Value	Binary Type
0	OLE field empty
1	OLE object is embedded
2	OLE object is linked

The DOVerb method. The *DoVerb* method of an OLE object is used to start an OLE Server session. It can have two parameters. The actual use is

<form name>.<OLE object name>.DoVerb(xNum,cTitle)

xNum is a number used to specify Play or Edit mode.

cTitle is a text string.

The first parameter of the DoVerb() method can be

0 (Play) to play a video or sound file stored in or linked to an OLE field

1 (Edit) to edit a video or sound file stored in or linked to an OLE field

The second parameter, according to the dBASE documentation can be used to display a string of text in the title bar of the Server window, if a Server window appears. However, it appears to have no effect when working with videos. So you can simply ignore the second parameter.

The following code is the primary portions of code necessary to play an OLE object in a form. It will create a pushbutton and assign the DoVerb() method to the button labeled "PLAY."

```
*** SHOWMOVI.WFM
*
f = NEW SHOWMOVI()
f.Open()
CLASS SHOWMOVI OF FORM
   this.Height =  14
   this.Width =   55
   this.ColorNormal = "/W*"
   this.View = "VIDEO2.DBF"
   DEFINE OLE oDoc1 OF THIS PROPERTY ;
     Top 3, Left 4.6, Height 9.2, Width 27, ;
     DataLink "VIDEO2->PICTURE"
   DEFINE PUSHBUTTON pBt1 OF THIS PROPERTY ;
     Top 6.5, Left 38, Height 1.5, Width 15, ColorNormal "N/W", ;
     Text "Play", OnClick CLASS::PlayIt
   DEFINE PUSHBUTTON pBt4 OF THIS PROPERTY  ;
     Top 11, Left 38, Height 2, Width 15, ColorNormal "W*/R*", ;
     Text "E&xit", OnClick {;form.Close()}
   Procedure PlayIt
     form.oDoc1.DoVerb(0)
ENDCLASS
```

When you run this code, it will open a form that looks similar to the one in Figure 11–25. The form in Figure 11–25 has additional objects added to the code—two more buttons and some text. It shows the Server application running in the space assigned to the OLE object in the form. The Server application was activated by pressing the Play button. The OnClick event property of the Play button executes some code that uses the DoVerb() method of the OLE object.

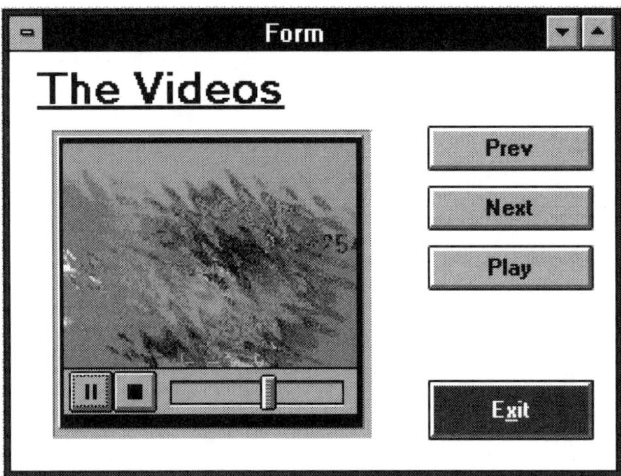

Figure 11–25. A form with an OLE object and the Server application running

Chapter 12
The Windows API and DLLs

Visual dBASE is capable of working with third-party tools like Dynamic Link Libraries (DLLs) and Visual Basic Controls (VBXs) discussed in the next chapter. It works with and understands the Windows Application Programming Interface (API) and can use resources in the API.

Best of all, it can all be accomplished without having to learn "traditional" languages like Assembler, C, C++, or Pascal to access these abilities.

Windows Environment

The Windows environment is a graphical environment that allows the user to execute multiple programs concurrently. It supports high-quality graphics and has a standard set of tools and user interface (UI) objects built in. All Windows compliant applications use these standard set of tools and UI objects to give applications a common "look and feel" between programs. This is especially true with windows, menus, dialog and information boxes, and icons.

Windows API

Windows has its own Application Programming Interface (API). This interface is a series of programs that contain libraries of C functions. It is contained in several DLLs. Some of the more common Windows files that are part of the Windows API library are USER.EXE, KRNL386.EXE, GDL.EXE, COMMDLG.DLL, VER.DLL, TOOLHELP.DLL, and most font files (*.FON) and driver files (*.DRV).

Windows resources

A *resource* is a data entity that is a portion (defined object) of the visible part of a Windows program. When you open a form or a dialog box and click on a button to perform a task in a program, you are interacting with the application's resources. These visual buttons, dialog boxes, and forms are only one type of resource. Other types include icons, bitmaps, menus, charter strings, and cursors.

These resources can exist in an independent application or inside a program's .EXE. However, they do not actually reside in the program's normal running portion of the code (the data segment). All this means is that they are not loaded into memory when the .EXE is executed. Rather, they are loaded into memory only when Windows or the application needs them.

Resources are not loaded in memory at run time; they are stored in separate application code—.EXEs and .DLLs. They normally reside separate from the application code, letting you modify them without changing the actual program source code.

Because the resources reside independent from the application code, you can share these resources among many Windows applications.

Accessing resources in a DLL

To use a resource, a Windows application requests the resource through the Windows operating system. Each resource has a unique identifier associated with it. This identifier can be a number or a name that is unique for each resource. For instance, Figure 12–1 shows a resource numbered #108 (the pound sign is required) on a pushbutton labeled "What" in a small form.

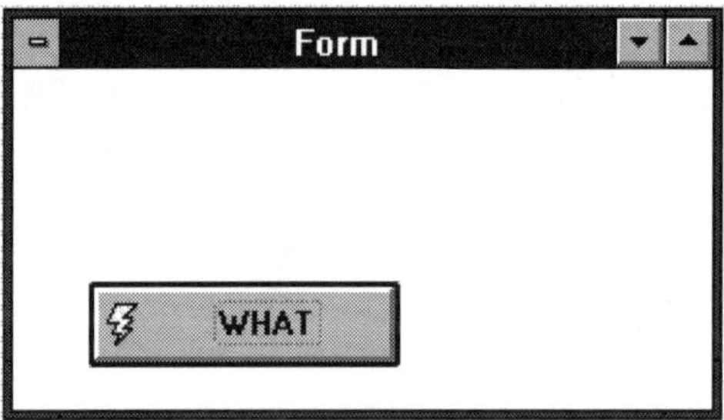

Figure 12–1. A pushbutton with a resource from the dBASE resource file.

The resource on the pushbutton object in Figure 12–1 is the lightning bolt. It is found in a file named. The pushbutton has a property named *UpBitMap* that was used to specify the resource and the number for the pushbutton. The code that accesses this resource is

```
DEFINE PUSHBUTTON PUSHBUTTON2 OF THIS PROPERTY ;
     Top 5, Left 5, Height 2, Width 20, ColorNormal "n/w",
;
     Text "WHAT", UpBitmap "RESOURCE #108   RESOURCE.DLL"
```

Dropping the Resource.DLL reference

Resource.DLL is the standard DLL used by Visual dBASE for forms. It is automatically loaded when dBASE is run. Therefore, you do not have to specify this DLL. However, if you need to pull a resource out of another DLL, you will have to reference it.

The Resource.DLL file

Visual dBASE uses the file named Resource.DLL, and the equivalent file in dBASE for Windows is DBAS0009.DLL. To run this demonstration in the older version, use this file instead. The file Resource.DLL is included with dBASE although it cannot be distributed with your Visual dBASE compiler or distribution kit programs. Instead, it will use the dB550009.DLL file. This file is lacking some of the same resources or assigns different numbers to the same resource. For instance, #108, does not exist; however, new ones do, like #36 (a checkmark above a line).

Working with DLLs

DLLs are simply programs (files) that contain compiled program code that Windows applications can load and run. Many times you can identify a DLL file by the extension DLL. However, a DLL can be an .EXE, a .DLL, or even a .VBX program. They are written in a wide range of languages (like C, C++, Pascal, etc.) and use strict specifications that allow them to be used by other Windows applications.

DLLs can contain resources that can be used by other Windows applications. These resources include dialog boxes, menus, icons, string tables, and bitmaps. Accessing and using DLLs lets a Windows program call and use preexisting functions or resources. These functions and resources do not have to exist in the program that calls them. This means that your dBASE applications can use existing resources that are built into other Windows programs.

Why use DLLs?

The concept of libraries and linking do not have the same meaning in Windows as they do in dBASE IV. To dBASE IV users, a library is a file that is maintained and used that consists of common routines (procedures and UDFs) that are incorporated into your application. Linking, using DBLINK, is the process of compiling programs and library routines into one large object file of pseudocode (.DBO). This type of linking can be considered "static linking." The library is directly linked to the application.

In Windows, a Dynamic Link Library contains functions or resources that can be called from *any* other application that is running in the Windows environment. It can be created in any language that follows strict specifications and uses a common calling method (convention).

In Windows, applications perform *dynamic linking* for routines and resources. That is, the link is done at runtime. This ability means that an application can perform linking many times while it is operating (running). The only condition is: If the resource or function exists in a DLL, the DLL must be available (on disk) when the application calls the function or resource.

Advantages to DLLs

By maintaining the functions and resources in separate files (as opposed to compiled with the applications routines),

1. Functions and resources in a DLL can be shared among applications.
2. Application programs are smaller in size (shared code is not compiled in).
3. When the application is changed, only the application needs to be recompiled.
4. When changes are made in the DLL, only it needs to be compiled.
5. Changes made in a DLL will be effective through all applications that use them.

Accessing DLL functions in Visual dBASE

Using a DLL is similar to using any procedure file. You load the DLL into memory (it must be available). Once loaded in memory you use any of its functions or resources. When you are done using them you release the DLL from memory. The DLL is loaded at runtime, so it must be available when the routine or resource is called inside it.

You can load a DLL using the Windows API function LoadLibrary(). LoadLibrary is a Windows function that will return the *Instance Handle* of the DLL. This Instance Handle is needed to access and load the resources.

Prototyping functions

Before you can access a DLL function, you will need to prototype the function. Once it is prototyped, it will be available to dBASE just as if it were an internal dBASE function.

First use the EXTERN command. dBASE uses a new command, *EXTERN*, to prototype each non-dBASE function. You can remember the name of the function by both its name and its purpose—EXTERNal preparation of non-dBASE functions/ resources.

The EXTERN command needs to be placed at the beginning of your code (or before the function or resource is called). Normally, people will place the EXTERN statement in their header file (*.h) and include it using the the pre-processor #include command.

The EXTERN statement is required, in dBASE, to prototype the non-dBASE function.

Why prototype external functions? The primary reason for declaring a prototype of a non-dBASE functions deals with the passing of parameters. Because a DLL can be written in any language, C, C++, Pascal, etc. you need to be able to pass parameters back and forth between the DLL and dBASE. The function will probably need some information from dBASE to know what to do. The data types may be different between dBASE and the language that the DLL is written in. C and C++ do not have a datatype "N" (dBASE numeric); rather, they have data types like *int* and *double float*. Pascal and Assembler have even different ones.

When dBASE sends and receives parameters to DLLs, it needs to know how to convert the parameters and return values to/from Windows data types. The prototype specifies to dBASE how it will convert its arguments to the data types the external function can use, and convert the value of the return values (from the external function) back into data types dBASE can use. Before you can call a DLL function, it must be prototyped with EXTERN.

The EXTERN command

The general syntax for this command can be in two formats.

```
EXTERN [CDECL] <return type> <function name> ;
   ( [ <parameter type 1> , [ <parameter type 2>, . . . ]] ) ;
   [<path>] < filename >

EXTERN [CDECL] <return type> <User Defined Function name> ;
   [ <parameter type 1> ,  [ <parameter type 2>, . . . ]] ) ;
   [<path>] < filename > FROM < export name > | <ordinal number>
```

There are three required parts of the EXTERN statement.

1. <return Type>
2. <Function name|UDF name>
3. <Filename>

The [CDECL] option

The [CDECL] option tells dBASE to use the C language calling convention versus the default Pascal calling convention. Using the C language convention lets you pass additional parameters beyond the ones specified in the declaration for this function. The default is Pascal because it is the most frequently used convention.

The <return type> parameter

This specifies the data type of the value returned by the function. This is a required parameter of the EXTERN statement. This value is a predefined type (CDOUBLE, CINT, etc). If the function needs to, it can simply return a void value using the type CVOID. This and <parameter type #> are important ones to dBASE. dBASE will have a different data type than the external program so you need to specify the correct value here.

The <function name> parameter

This is the name of the external fucntion. It is also a required part of the EXTERN statement. Technically, it is the *export* name of the external function that is contained in a .REF (reference) file associated with the .DLL file holding the function.

The <user-defined function name> option. If you use the <user-defined function name> option instead of the <function name>, it will hold the name you give the external function instead of the *export* name. If you specify it, you must use the FROM <expC > |<expN> clause to identify the function in the DLL.

The FROM <expC>|<expN> option. The FROM <export name> | <ordinal number> is the name or number of the actual function inside the DLL file. This name (character based, expC) or number (#<expN>) is stored in the .REF file that is associated with the DLL file.

The <parameter type > parameters

Like the <return type> this specifies the data type of the value passed to the function. It is only required if the external function requires parameters.

The <file name> parameter

This is the name of the DLL file that holds the external function. It is a required part of the EXTERN command. This name must include the extension of the DLL filename. The filename of each DLL loaded in memory must be unique (not the extension). For instance, you cannot load DBASE01.FON and DBASE01.DLL into memory at the same time, even though they have different file extensions.

Using the EXTERN command to prototype and load an external function

You can load functions from Windows API files or any other DLLs created by someone. You use the EXTERN to load the *external* function, making it available to dBASE.

Loading a function in a Windows API file

The following code example uses the EXTERN command to load a function in the Windows API file USER.EXE:

```
*** MYEXTERN
*
EXTERN CWord ;
          MessageBox(CHandle, Cstring, Cstring, CWord)
USER.EXE
RETURN
```

Notice that the EXTERN statement specifies three parameters.

1. <return type> (CWord)
2. <function name> (MessageBox)
3. <filename> (USER.EXE)

The command also declares four parameter types for the function MessageBox. The Windows function MessageBox requires four parameters; therefore, you must declare all four variable types that will be passed.

When you prototype a function using the EXTERN command, the function will be registered in dBASE. It is automatically available for use as if it were any other dBASE function, once it is prototyped.

Loading a non-Windows API function from a DLL

You can also prototype a function that is not in a Windows API. To load a non-Windows API function, you use the same EXTERN statement. In this example, you will prototype a function named ComputerAverage that can be found in the DLL named DBEXTERN.dll. This DLL ships with dBASE and can be found in a subdirectory under the directory where dBASE was placed on your machine. If you loaded dBASE using the default, the command is

```
*** MYEXTERN
*
*     . . .
EXTERN CDECL CDOUBLE ComputeAverage()     ;
                   D:\VisualdB\Samples\Extern\dbextern.dll
RETURN
```

This command will make the function ComputeAverage() available to dBASE, just like it was a function built into dBASE.

NOTE: Specifying the path

Notice that it used the entire path to specify the DLL file. If the file is in the dBASE path (SET PATH TO), you do not have to specify the full path. If it isn't, you must specify the full path to locate the file.

When you prototype a function, the function becomes immediately available to dBASE. The DLL itself (which may contain additional functions and resources) is not directly available, only the function that was externed inside the DLL. If you need to load the DLL itself, you use the LOAD DLL command discussed later in this chapter.

Supplying the correct data types

When you specify data types in the EXTERN statement, you must use keywords that represent the data type being passed. In the preceding EXTERN statement, you used several keywords for data types—CWord, CHandle, and Cstring.

Which data type is which? The data type keywords you pass depend on what data type the external function needs. The data type is dependent on which language in which the function was written.

Table 12–1 shows the common data types for several languages:

Table 12–1. Data Types for EXTERN.

Windows Keyword	Parameter, Return Value, or Both	dBASE Data Type	C Data Type	Pascal Data Type	Assembler Data Type
CDOUBLE	Both	Numeric	Long double (80 bit)	Double	N/A
CHANDLE	Both	Numeric	Handles like HWIND, HDC, HANDLE	Handles like HWind, HDC, HFont	dw
CINT	Both	Numeric	int	Integer	dw (16 bit)

Table 12–1. Data Types for EXTERN, continued.

Windows Keyword	**Parameter, Return Value, or Both**	**dBASE Data Type**	**C Data Type**	**Pascal Data Type**	**Assembler Data Type**
CLOGICAL	Both	Logical	Short int	Integer	dw (16 bit)
CLONG	Both	Numeric	Long int (32 bit)	Long Int	dd (32 bit)
CSTRING	Both	Character	char far * (zero terminated)	PChar	dw (16 bit)
CVOID	Both	N/A	Void	Procedure	N/A
CWORD	Both	Numeric	Short int (16 bit)	WORD	dw (16 bit)
CVAR	Both	Any type	dBASEVar	N/A	N/A
CPTR	Parameter	N/A	Void *	Pointer	dd (32 bit)
...	Parameter	Any type	Count, DBaseVar *	N/A	N/A

The CVAR data type is only used when calling DLLs written in C (or C++) specifically for dBASE taking advantage of the callback capabilities. The elipse option (three periods) only works when you use the C calling convention by including the CDECL command.

Using the data types. Using this table, you can determine the correct data type to pass to the external function. If the function is written in C and requires a *short int (16 bit)*–type parameter, you would specify CWORD as the Windows calling type in the EXTERN statement. Then, when you attempt to use the external function inside dBASE, you would pass it a Numeric data type.

For instance, our EXTERN statement, used earlier, for the function MessageBox is

```
EXTERN CWord ;
      MessageBox(CHandle, Cstring, Cstring, CWord)
USER.EXE
```

This statement will return a numeric value. The function MessageBox() needs four parameters—Chandle (dBASE numeric), two Cstring (character in dBASE), and CWord.

Looking at the table, the function will return a numeric data type back to dBASE (CWord is numeric in dBASE, short int [16 bit] in C). The MessageBox() function will be sent a dBASE number, two strings and another dBASE number. It will receive them in the format that it recognizes—HWIND, char far (terminated with a 0), and short int (16 bit).

So the EXTERN statement uses a common keyword type to convert data types from one language to another. When it prototypes a function, it specifies how Windows is to convert the data types.

Loading and using the DLL function

Once you prototype a function using the EXTERN command, you do not need to do anything else. Simply use the function as if it were part of dBASE. This is true for Windows API functions as well as any other function in other DLLs.

After you have prototyped an external function, it is automatically loaded for you when you use it in dBASE.

Using the DLL functions

Now that you have prototyped the two functions, MessageBox() and ComputeAverage(), you are ready to use them. The following is the complete code for prototyping both functions. It is placed in a file named MYEXTERN:

```
*** MYEXTERN
*
EXTERN CWord ;
      MessageBox(CHandle, Cstring, Cstring, CWord) USER.EXE
EXTERN CDECL CDOUBLE ComputeAverage() ;
      D:\VisualdB\Samples\Extern\dbextern.dll
RETURN
```

When you run this program using the DO MYEXTERN command, the two functions are automatically available to you in dBASE.

NOTE: You have both of these DLLs—USER.EXE is part of Windows and DBEXTERN.DLL ships with Visual dBASE.

Calling the DLL functions. With the functions prototyped, you are ready to use them. The following code can be typed into another program that will call the extern functions in MyExtern.

```
*** TRYEXTN.prg
*
*    run the EXTERN code program
DO MYEXTERN
*    using the MessageBox() function
*
```

```
xVoid = MessageBox(_app.framewin.hwnd, "Do you want to Quit" ,;
      "Exit Message Box", 4)
CLEAR
IF xVoid = 6
   @2,2 SAY "Now you could quit"
ELSE
    @2,2 SAY "You pressed the NO key"
ENDIF
SLEEP 2
CLEAR
*
* using the ComputerAverage() function
aGrades = NEW ARRAY(4)
   aGrades.Average = ComputeAverage
   aGrades[1] = 4.0
   aGrades[2] = 3.5
   aGrades[3] = 3.0
? "Computed average Grade for "
? " three classes is:", TRIM(LTRIM(STR(aGrades.Average())))
SLEEP 2
RETURN
```

The code uses both functions. First it calls the MessageBox() function and displays a message based on what key was pressed. Then it uses the ComputerAverage() function to compute the average grade for the three classes.

Loading a DLL in memory

To access external functions in a DLL, you must use the EXTERN command to make the DLLs function available. In addition to prototyping and accessing external functions, you can also use resources that are in DLLs, like bitmaps.

LOAD DLL Command

When you use the EXTERN command and specify a DLL name, the DLL is automatically loaded the first time the EXTERN function is run (prototyped). This is the most common way to load a DLL.

You can also load a DLL in memory—you can use the Windows API call LoadLibrary() or the dBASE command LOAD DLL. They both appear to do the same thing—explicitly load the DLL into memory (with the exception that LoadLibrary() returns the handle to the DLL).

The general syntax to load a DLL is

LOAD DLL [<path>] <DLL filename.ext>

The following example loads the DLL named BCBTDBWL.DLL located in the dBASE directory:

```
LOAD DLL BCBTDBWL.DLL
```

Load DLL versus memory residence. Even though you initialize a DLL with LOAD DLL, it doesn't physically become resident in memory. dBASE can access its resources; however, to access a function within the DLL you must use the EXTERN statement discussed earlier. Because of this, a DLL only needs a small amount of memory, regardless of the DLL file size.

Memory management is handled automatically, keeping track of all DLL files in memory and using a *reference counter* each time another application loads a specific DLL.

The [<path>] option. If you omit the path option when calling the file, dBASE will look in the following directories for the DLL:

1. The current directory
2. The Windows directory (where WIN.COM is located)
3. The Windows System directory (where the GDI.EXE is located)
4. The dBASE directory (where dBASEWIN.EXE is located)
5. The directories in the DOS environment (PATH =)
6. Any network directories that are mapped

It does *not* use the dBASE path (SET PATH TO) to find the DLL file.

Accessing resources in DLLs. Once the DLL is loaded, its resources can be accessed. The following code demonstrates how to use an image resource in the DLL file named BCBTDBWL.DLL located in the dBASE subdirectory for an image object on a form:

```
*** MYDLLEX.prg
*
*  The load DLL appears to be optional
*
LOAD DLL BCBTDBWL.DLL
*
f = NEW FORM("Demo of DLLs")
DEFINE IMAGE iPic1 OF f PROPERTY;
   top 3, left 3, height 3, width 10,  ;
   DataSource "RESOURCE F2 BCBTDBWL.DLL"
DEFINE IMAGE iPic2 OF f PROPERTY ;
   top 3, left 20, height 3, width 25, ;
   DataSource "RESOURCE SCC_KEYS BCBTDBWL.DLL"
DEFINE IMAGE iPic3 OF f PROPERTY ;
   top 8, left 10, height 8.5, width 35, ;
   DataSource "RESOURCE BAS_TLNK BCBTDBWL.DLL"
f.Open()
```

NOTE: Where is BCBTDBWL.DLL located?

The file BCBTDBWL.DLL is located in the same dBASE subdirectory as the main program file, dBASEWIN.EXE.

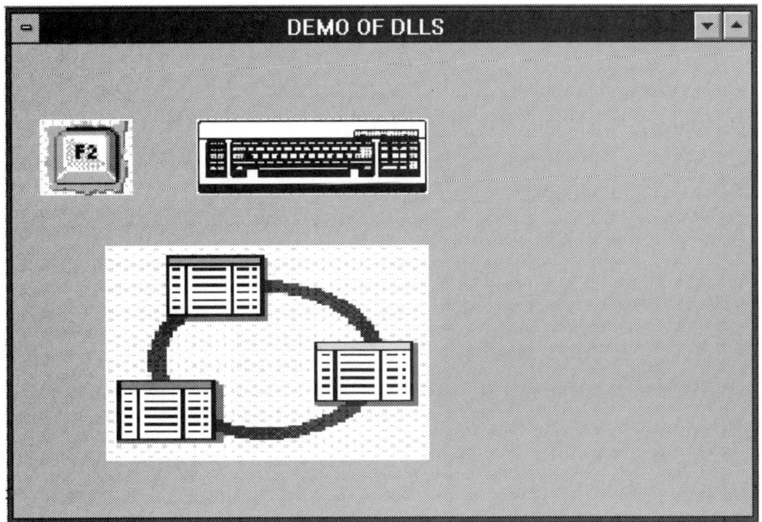

Figure 12–2. A form with three resources loaded from a DLL.

If you run this code, it should display a form similar to the one in Figure 12–2.

Notice that you did not specify a number as you have in earlier examples. Rather, you assigned a resource name from the DLL. DLLs can have numbers to reference resources or names. You must specify the handle that is appropriate for each resource. In this case, it was names BAS_TLNK, SCC_KEYS, and F2.

Specifying the DLL name. If you assign a resource that is located in a DLL other than DBAS0009.DLL, you must specify the name in the command "RESOURCE <name|#number> <DLL filename>". The <DLL filename> must also specify the extension for the DLL.

✔ **LOAD DLL need not apply.**
The LOAD DLL command is actually optional. According to the dBASE documentation, you need to LOAD a DLL to make the file's resources available to your application. However, if you are assigning a resource to a property of the IMAGE object, or one of the BitMaps for pushbuttons, like in Figure 12–2, you do not need to load the DLL first. If you LOAD a DLL and do not specifically reference where an image (BMP) can be located for the IMAGE object, an error will occur—"not found." This command appears to be useless. So in the preceding code, you could have removed the line LOAD DLL BCBTDBWL.dll.

Loading VBX controls. The next chapter discusses Visual Basic Controls (VBX); however, the LOAD DLL command is necessary to load .VBX files in memory.

Releasing a DLL from memory

If you load a DLL in memory, and you are finished with it, you should release it from memory when you are done, using the command

```
RELEASE DLL <DLL filename>
```

This command releases and deactivates the DLL in memory. It works the same as the Windows function FreeLibrary(), except that it doesn't require the handle of the DLL (like the FreeLibrary() function does).

Unloading a DLL that was loaded more than one time. DLLs are only physically loaded in memory one time. If a library is loaded several times using LOAD LIBRARY, Windows keeps track of the number of loads requested and increments a *reference counter*. The DLL is only loaded one time. When you issue a RELEASE DLL command and the DLL's reference counter is greater than 1, then Windows decrements the counter by 1. It will not release the DLL from memory until the reference counter for the DLL is decremented to 1.

CALLING WINDOWS API FUNCTIONS

Once you EXTERN a function located in the API, you are automatically ready to use it. API calls are identical to other DLL calls with two major exceptions: All API libraries are loaded when Windows is started, and they can't be released because they must always remain in memory.

You can prototype an API function using the EXTERN command. One of the most common Windows API functions is the MessageBox() function. Although you have already seen a demonstration of the MessageBox() function, it will be covered in detail in the next section of the chapter.

Calling the EXTERNal function MessageBox

After you specify the prototype for the function in a program using the EXTERN command, you can run it. The EXTERN command must be executed before you can use the function.

Prototyping the EXTERN MessageBox

You specified an EXTERN statement for the Windows MessageBox function, earlier. It was placed in the MYEXTERN.PRG. It looked like this:

```
*** MYEXTERN
*
EXTERN CWord ;
      MessageBox(CHandle, Cstring, Cstring, CWord) USER.EXE
```

Now that you have the prototype of the external function, you can specify the prototype by running the program with the EXTERN statement in it.

```
DO MYEXTERN
```

This command will load the EXTERN statement into memory. Once it is loaded in memory, you can access the MessageBox function, just like any other dBASE function.

NOTE: For the remainder of this exercise you may want to delete everything else in the program MYEXTERN except the EXTERN statement. You will add more code to the program later.

Normally you would have more than one EXTERN statement, and it will be placed either in a header file (*.h) or at the beginning of the program.

Calling Windows MessageBox() function

With the MessageBox() function prototyped, you are ready to use it. From the Command window, type in the following command (as one single line of code):

```
xVal=MessageBox(_app.framewin.hwnd,"Do you Want to
⇒continue?", "My Message Box", 36)
```

After you do this, dBASE will display a message box similar to the one in Figure 12–3.

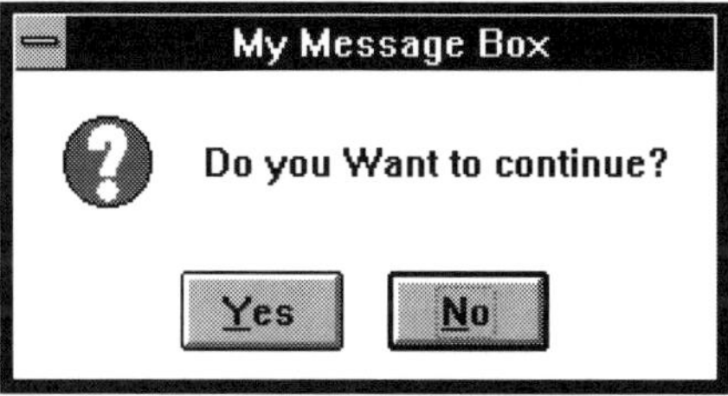

Figure 12–3. A message box created by the Windows MessageBox() function.

Notice that the message box displays your Message and Title that you passed it. It also displays two buttons—YES and NO—as well as a graphic picture (question mark). The number and type of buttons and the graphic are determined by the last number that you pass the function (36).

The MessageBox parameters

The MessageBox function requires four parameters, and all of them perform different functions. They are

1. The handle of the program calling it (will use hwnd property)
2. The message to be displayed in the box
3. The title to be displayed for the box
4. The type of MessageBox to display

The first parameter will always be the same.

```
_app.framewin.hwnd
```

The other three will change based on the title you want, the message, and the type of box to be displayed.

Creating a function to call MessageBox

Having to constantly type in this megaline to access the built-in Windows MessageBox function can prove impractical—you will always have to pass four parameters, and the first one remains constant.

Calling Windows functions from dBASE procedures and UDFs. Instead of typing this in all the time, you could create a procedure or UDF in dBASE that will call the MessageBox function. The following code demonstrates this; it creates a procedure file named MYEXPROC.PRG and a function inside it called MyWinMsg:

```
*** MYEXPROC.prg
*
FUNCTION MyWinMsg
PARAMETER xMessage, xTitle, xCnt
IF pcount() <3
  xMessage = "Is everything OK?"
  xTitle = "Information Box"
  xCnt = 1
ENDIF
*
*  The MessageBox() function accepts four functions
*      1st—the handle of the program calling it (will use
*      hwnd property)
*      2nd—the message to be displayed in the box
*      3rd—the title to be displayed for the box
*      4th—the type of MessageBox to display
*
*                 the fourth option cannot be any remaining
*                 number of 6, 7, 13, or 15 when divided by
*                 16 (Modulo 16)
*
xVoid=0
```

```
IF at(STR(Mod(xCnt,16),2)," 6, 7,13,15")=0
    xVoid = MessageBox(_app.framewin.hwnd,  xMessage, xTitle,
xCnt)
ENDIF
RETURN xVoid
```

The user-defined function MyWinMsg() needs three parameters as shown in the preceding code. If it doesn't get three, it will supply default values. Then it will pass the three parameters to the Windows function, MessageBox(), and run the MessageBox() function.

Remember, the MessageBox() function uses the fourth parameter (very last one) to determine what type of box and the number of buttons that should be displayed.

Make your functions generic. This program is made generic so that you can pass any title text, message text, and box number type to it. The <box number type> will be used by MessageBox to determine the type of box to display.

Because the MessageBox function returns a value, a UDF was created to pass the value back to any program using the dBASE function MyWinMsg().

MessageBox returns a value. When MessageBox() runs, it will return a numeric value to dBASE. In the preceding code, it will be in the variable xVoid.

The value returned will be determined by which button was pressed in the MessageBox. It will always be the same for the type of button that was pressed. For instance, the OK button will always return a 1, Cancel a 2, Yes a 6, No a 7, etc. When dBASE receives the number, it can use it to perform some action (like in an IF ... or DO CASE ... statement).

Running the function that calls MessageBox()

With the two programs created (MYEXTERN and MYEXPROC), you are ready to use them. The following code will load the EXTERN statement and run the function MyWinMsg giving you a message box with two buttons—Retry, Cancel:

```
*** USEMYMSSG.prg
*
DO MYEXTERN
SET PROC TO MYEXPROC
MyWinMsg("What do you want to do","My HELP",5)
```

Understanding the MessageBox() function

The Windows MessageBox() is one of the common external functions that can prove useful for you. You can activate the box from any dBASE code and, when the user presses one of its buttons, take the appropriate action based on the return value. You won't have to create standard MessageBox objects in dBASE. Rather, use what already exists in Windows.

You control the type of message box that will be displayed. For instance, Figure 12–4 shows a message box with a single button in it, and Figure 12–5 shows one with eight buttons in it.

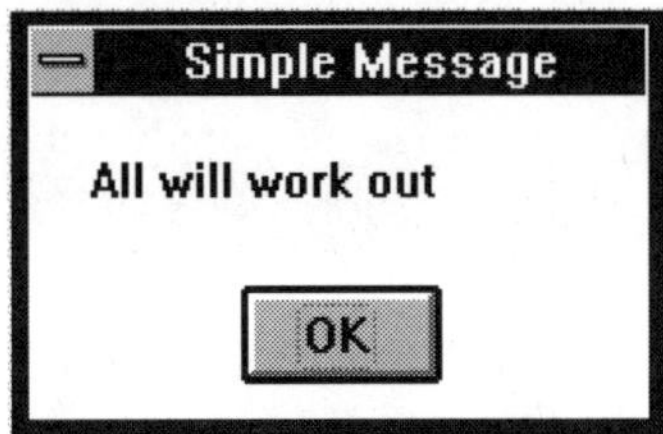

Figure 12–4. A message box with one button.

This message box, Figure 12–4, is the result of this command:

```
MyWinMsg("All will work out","Simple Message",0)
```

Figure 12–5. A message box with many buttons in it.

And this, Figure 12–5, is a result of the following:

```
MyWinMsg("I am truly confused","WHAAAAAT",59)
```

The Windows MessageBox() can display sixty different message boxes. Each box will have different buttons and pictures inside them. You can add your own title and text in the window giving you the ability to make an unlimited number of different message boxes.

There are twelve basic boxes (each box contains one or more buttons). The remaining forty-eight use the same twelve basic boxes and add a graphic displayed.

A few deadly box-type numbers

Several numbers will create a message box without any buttons and no ability to be closed. This means that if you pass one of these box type numbers to the MessageBox() function, you will have to quit Windows and restart.

Never 6, 7, 13, or 15. These numbers are 6, 7, 13, 15, . . . Any number that gives you a remainder of 6, 7, 13, or 15 after being divided by 16. For example, 22/16 = 1 with a remainder of **6**, 55/16 = 3 with a remainder of **7**. If you create a message box with a number that roots to 6, 7, 13, or 15 as a remainder, you will receive a message box like the one in Figure 12–6.

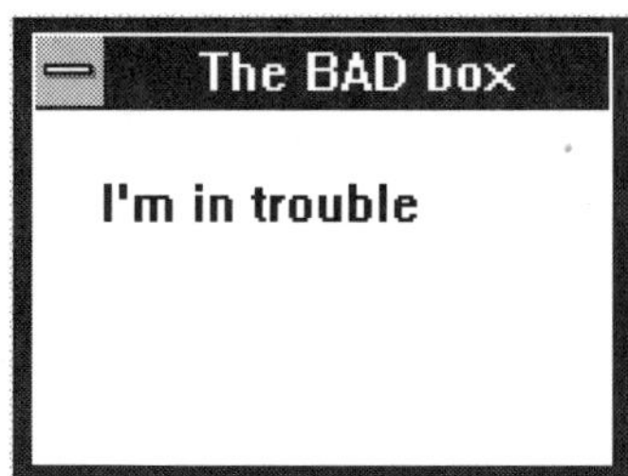

Figure 12–6. A message box with no buttons and no way out.

If you receive a message box like the one in Figure 12–6, you will have to quit Windows by going to the Program Manager and quitting, or, worse, **Ctrl+Alt+Del** (the three-finger Vulcan salute).

The seven button types used in the MessageBox() boxes

Although there are twelve basic boxes that the MessageBox() function can create, each of the boxes can only display and use seven different buttons. Remember the message box in Figure 12–5? It had eight buttons; the Cancel button was displayed two times.

The Windows MessageBox() function only supports seven basic buttons. The order, and which buttons used, is determined by the <box type number> that you pass to it. These seven buttons include the OK button, Cancel button, and so on.

Seven buttons and their purpose. Figure 12–7 shows the seven basic buttons that the MessageBox() function uses and what they can be used for.

The return value of the seven buttons. When a user presses one of the seven buttons, it will always return the same value to dBASE. For instance, if the user pressed the OK button, it will return a 1, Cancel a 2, and so forth. Figure 12–7 shows the number that will be returned if the user presses that button. The value will always be the same based on the button type pressed.

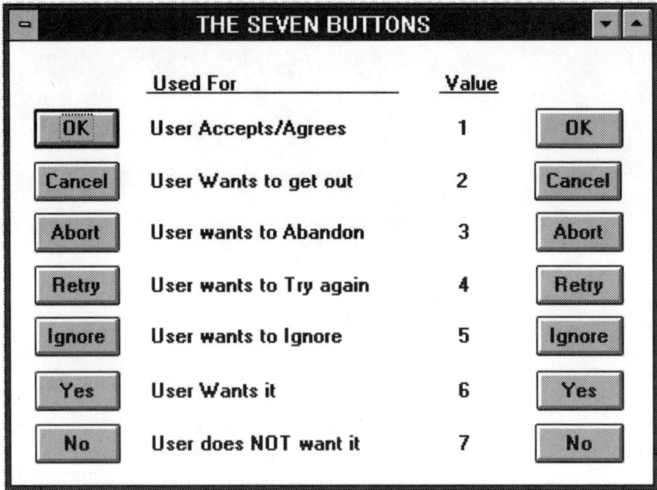

Figure 12–7. The buttons used by the MessageBox() function.

The boxes of MessageBox()

The MessageBox() function can display twelve basic boxes. Each box can have from one to eight buttons in it. When you pass the MessageBox() a box number, it takes that number and creates a specific box with a specific number of buttons. Table 12–2 shows the <box number> that you can pass and which buttons will be in the message box.

If you pass 10 to the MessageBox(), it will place five buttons on the box. However, the fifth button will display **IT =,** and it is inactive. No matter how many times you press it, it won't do anything.

Understanding Table 12–2. Table 12–2 has ten columns. The first column has the number that you would pass to the MessageBox() function. The second column shows the number of buttons that will be displayed in the box for that type of message box. The third to ninth columns are the actual button types that will be displayed. It also shows the return value. The last column will tell you if the **Esc** key is active and if it does work, and what number will be returned when the user presses the **Esc** key.

Using Table 12–2, you can determine which buttons will be in the box based on the number you pass to it. For example, if you pass the MessageBox the number 14, it will display a box with the Cancel and Retry buttons on it. If you pass it the number 4, it will display the Yes and No buttons.

Table 12–2. MessageBox Box Types.

<box #>	No. of Buttons	OK 1	Cancel 2	Abort 3	Retry 4	Ignore 5	Yes 6	No 7	Esc Key Value
0	1	x							1
1	2	x	x						2
2	3			x	x	x			—
3	3		x				x	x	2
4	2						x	x	—
5	2		x		x				2
8	2			x	x				—
9	5	x	x	x	x	x			2
10	5		x(2)		x			x	2
11	8	x	x(2)	x	x	x	x	x	2
12	1						x		—
14	2		x		x				2

The other 48 boxes. In addition to the twelve basic boxes, Windows can display forty-eight additional boxes. These other forty-eight boxes use the same default buttons of the twelve basic boxes. The difference is the graphic that it will display.

The Windows message box can display four graphics:

- Stop Sign (STOP)
- Question Mark (?)
- Exclamation Point (!)
- Information Letter (i)

To display the Stop Sign in any of the twelve basic boxes, select the box you want to have the Stop Sign in, and add sixteen to the number. For instance if you want the box to display the abort, retry, and ignore buttons with the Stop Sign, you will pass 18 to the function (2 + 16).

To display the Question Mark in any of the twelve basic boxes, select the box you want to have the Question Mark in, and add 32 to the number. For instance, if you want to display the Question Mark with the OK and Cancel buttons, pass 33 to the function (1 + 32).

To display the Exclamation Point in any of the twelve basic boxes, select the box you want to have the Exclamation Point in, and add 48 to the number. For instance, if you want to display the Exclamation Point with the Yes button only, pass the number 60 (12 + 48).

Finally, to display the Information Letter in any of the twelve basic boxes, select the box you want to have the Information Letter in, and add 64 to the number. For instance, if you want the box to display the OK button only, with the Information Letter, pass 64 (0 + 64).

Using the Windows API function GetPrivateProfileString()

Another external function that you can use is the GetPrivateProfileString() function located in the KRNL386.EXE file of the Windows API. As the name implies, this function will get information from somewhere.

Prototyping the GetPrivateProfileString() function

To prototype the GetPrivateProfileString() function, you need to use the EXTERN command. The format for this function is

```
*** MYINFO.PRG
*
EXTERN CWord GetIt(CString, CString, CString, CString, ;
       CInt, CString) KRNL386.EXE FROM "GetPrivateProfileString"
EXTERN CWord MessageBox(CHandle, Cstring, Cstring, CWord)
USER.EXE
STORE SPACE(50) TO cUserName, cCompanyName
nUserLen = GetIt("Install", "Username", "None Specified", ;
                    cUserName, 50,
"D:\VisualDB\BIN\DBASEWIN.INI" )
nCompanyLen = GetIt("Install", "Company", "None Specified", ;
                    cCompanyName, 50,
"D:\VisualDB\BIN\dBASEWin.ini" )
cUserName = LEFT(cUserName, nUserLen)
cCompanyName = LEFT(cCompanyName, nCompanyLen)
MessageBox(0, "This copy of dBASE is registered to" ;
            + CHR(13) + CHR(13) + CHR(10) + ;
           "    Customer :"+CHR(9)+cUserName+CHR(13)+CHR(10)+ ;
           "    Company :"+CHR(9)+cCompanyName, ;
           "Info from DBASEWIN.INI", 0)
```

This program will use the GetPrivateProfileString() function to obtain the information in the dBASEWIN.INI file. You will have to specify the correct location for your dBASEWIN.INI file (D:\VisualDB\BIN\). The original file should be located in the BIN directory of Visual dBASE.

Setting an alias (UDF) name. Notice that the program does not use the function name GetPrivateProfileString(); rather, it uses the function name GetIt(). When you EXTERN an external function, you can specify your own function name (user-supplied name). If you do this, then you must use the FROM <function name> option of the EXTERN command.

If you run this program (MYINFO.prg), you will see a message box similar to the one in Figure 12–8.

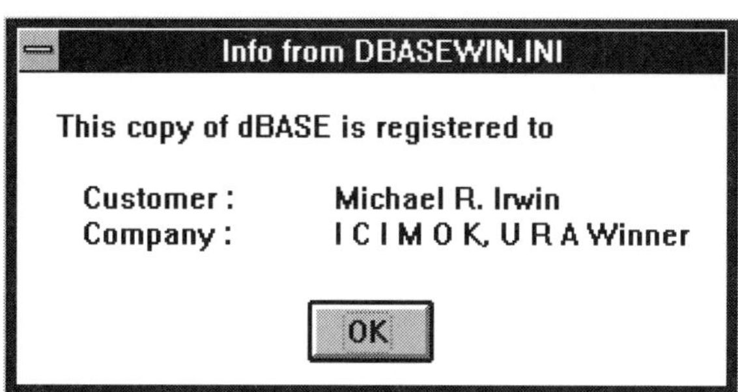

Figure 12–8. Information extracted from the DBASEWIN.INI file.

Formatting text for the message box. If you need to format text to display more than one line in the message box, you must send a carriage return/line feed (CR/LF) after each line. To send a CR/LF use the CHR() function in the following manner:

```
CHR(13)+CHR(10)
```

You can send multiple line carriage returns by passing the carriage return, CHR(13), several times or the linefeed, CHR(10), several times. If you need to send a tab, use the CHR(9) command.

THE RESOURCE() FUNCTION

In addition to the EXTERN command, dBASE offers you a new function that can be used to obtain character type information (string resources) from DLLs directly.

The function RESOURCE() can help you obtain string text from a DLL file. It can be used to obtain a character string from a resource in a DLL file, as long as the text is less than 64K in size. Anything beyond 64K is simply truncated, and ignored.

> ✔ **Limitations**
> The dBASE documentation states that the size limitation is 32K; however, when testing the resource() function, it appears that the text string returned will be up to 64K-1 bytes.

Using the resource() function

The resource() function can be useful for extracting character string information from a DLL. The general syntax for this command is

RESOURCE(<resource id number>, <DLL filename.ext>)

<resource id number>

The <resource ID number> is the numeric value that identifies the character string resource inside the DLL.

<DLL filename.ext>

The <DLL filename.ext> is the name of the DLL file that has the string inside it.

Getting Windows user information

You can use the resource() function to obtain Windows user information without having to EXTERN a Windows API DLL. The following code will extract the username and company name:

```
*** MyRscIN.prg
*
cWinUserName = Resource(514, "USER.EXE")
cWinCompanyName = Resource(515, "USER.EXE")
? cWinUserName
? cWinCompanyName
```

This code will obtain the username (string # 514) from the USER.EXE program and the company name (string # 515) from the USER.EXE. Then it will print the names to the screen. You could fancy up the code by placing the information in a message box as you did when you obtained the name of the user and company for the dBASEWIN.INI file.

If you wanted to display the returned information in a message box you should add the following lines of code:

```
*** MyRscIn.prg
*
EXTERN CWord MessageBox(CHandle, Cstring, Cstring, CWord) ;
                USER.EXE
cWinUserName = Resource(514, "USER.EXE")
cWinCompanyName = Resource(515, "USER.EXE")
MessageBox(0, "This copy of Windows is registered to" ;
            + CHR(13) + CHR(13) + CHR(10) + ;
```

```
            "    Customer
:"+CHR(9)+cWinUserName+CHR(13)+CHR(10)+ ;
            "    Company :"+CHR(9)+cWinCompanyName, ;
            "Info Obtained from Windows ", 0)
```

Running this modified code will give you a window similar to the one in Figure 12–9. The information that was obtained in Figure 12–9 actually came from Windows (USER.EXE). It actually looked at the WIN.INI file and obtained the informtion. To prove that it got the information from Windows, you can **Alt-Tab** through the Windows applications while the message box is active until you see a task switch box like the one in Figure 12–10. This lets you know that the information and the message box are actually from Windows. Notice the Windows icon of the flag on the left side.

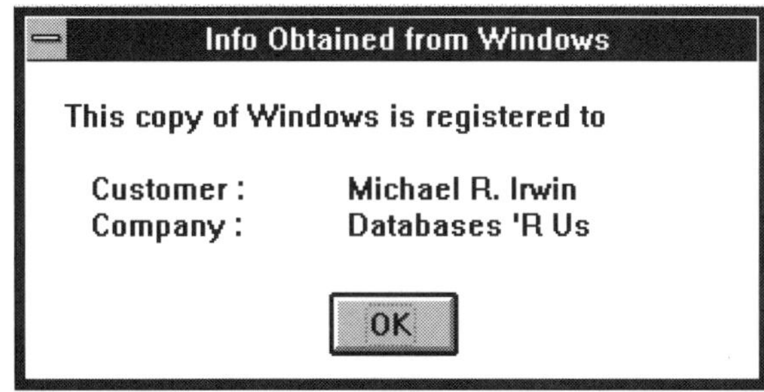

Figure 12–9. Putting information from Resource() into a message box.

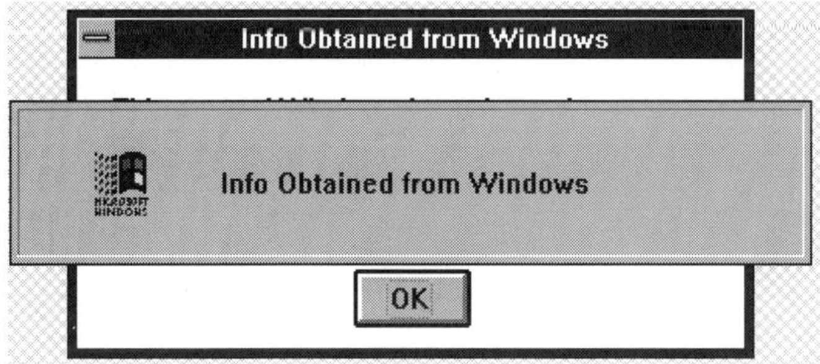

Figure 12–10. Information obtained from Windows.

Using resource() for international translations

The resource( ) function can be very useful for internationalizing applications. You can accomplish language changes without changing program code.

If you store all of your message and display text, that will need to be translated in a DLL file, the application can retrieve all the messages at runtime using the resource() function.

When you need to modify the application, you can go into the DLL, translate all the strings into the new language, and save the DLL under a different name. Then you simply reference the new DLL for all display text and messages.

Maintain resource IDs. If you decide to use the resource() function for access to all string text for international use, make sure that you maintain the same order and resource IDs for all of the text in the DLLs.

Chapter 13
Working with Custom Controls

Visual dBASE lets you create and work with user-defined interface objects. These user-defined interface objects, *custom controls*, are simply custom Classes for control objects like pushbuttons, entryfields, and text objects. Once customized, redefining their appearance or behavior, you can use them in the form designer when creating forms.

WHAT ARE CUSTOM CONTROLS?

Custom controls are usable control objects that can come from two sources.

- dBASE custom controls
- Visual Basic controls (.VBX)

These custom controls are used in forms *and* when *building* forms using the Form Designer. Using custom controls can simplify and shorten the process of building forms. These custom controls are preexisting, reusable objects with their characteristic properties, Event properties, and methods preset to your specified values.

They are simply predefined Classes (you build from stock controls) or Visual Basic controls. A Visual Basic control, written in C, C++, or Pascal, is a special type of DLL.

What is a control (Object)?

A *control* is the visual interface object that is contained in a form object. Visual dBASE has many types of control objects—Text, Entryfields, Pushbuttons, Checkboxes, Listboxes, and others. When creating a form, you select these controls from the *Control Palette* in the Form Designer. Figure 13–1 shows the Control Palette containing the built-in controls of Visual dBASE.

The control palette shows the nineteen stock (built-in) control objects available to dBASE.

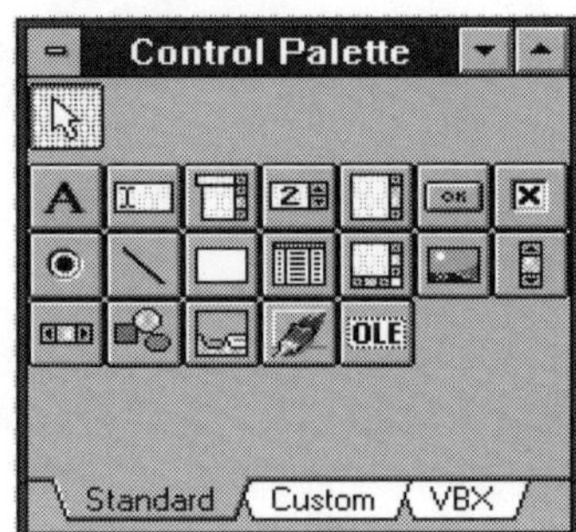

Figure 13–1. The Control Palette of the Form Designer.

> **Stock control objects**
> Visual dBASE has added three new control objects—Shape, Paintbox, and TabBox; the other sixteen are available in both versions of dBASE.

Why use custom controls?

Custom controls can be used for a wide range of purposes.

1. Maintain appearance standards
2. Build in additional functionality
3. Offer additional visual controls for the user
4. Specify new default property values for controls

Maintain appearance standards

Custom controls can be used to set standard interface object appearances. You may have developed a standard style convention for your company or your clients. It may include specific font sizes and colors for different types of objects. You may have standards for three different types of text objects. For example, you may want all Title type text objects to have a font type of Times New Roman, a size of 18 point, color bright white on gray, always bold, and underlined. You may want all of your standard type text to be Arial, black on light gray, and 12-point font size.

Build in additional functionality

You can create custom controls that automatically support validation processing rules. For instance, you may want to create a custom Entryfield control that will automatically convert all text entered to uppercase and have no initialized value. Or you may want another Entryfield control that will automatically convert text in the field to proper case when something is entered.

Another example could be a custom listbox that automatically allows for multiple selections.

Offer new visual controls for the user

You can create new visual controls like clocks, calendars, VCR controls, and other graphic devices that can make your forms more functional. They can be created using dBASE code accessing Windows API controls or using Visual Basic controls.

Specifying new default properties for controls

You can simply create controls that change the behavior and appearance of built-in controls. The BUTTONS.CC library that ships with dBASE does this. It is a series of pushbuttons that have a graphic and text already associated with the button—some even have procedural code attached. Some of the buttons included are NextButton, PrevButton, CloseButton, ReportButton, and OKButton.

By precreating your own controls, you can create forms quicker and more efficiently.

WORKING WITH dBASE CUSTOM CONTROLS

You can create your own dBASE custom controls using the CLASS construct with which you are already familiar. Once created, they need to be placed in a special procedure file, called a *custom control library*, and loaded into memory. Once your custom Classes are loaded in memory, you can use them in forms just like they are built-in control objects. They will be available in the Control Palette on a page labeled Custom.

Loading dBASE custom controls

To have your custom controls appear on the *Custom* page of the Control Palette in the Form Designer, you need to install them. You can install them permanently (whenever you use Visual dBASE, they are available) or just for the current work session. By making them permanent, they will automatically install when you start up dBASE, making them always available in the Form Designer.

Loading controls for the current session only

If you want to load your custom controls for the current session only, simply place the procedure file in memory. For instance, assume that you have a procedure file named MyCCVbx.CC (you will create this procedure file in the upcoming pages). This file contains several custom controls. To load it in memory, you simply type

```
SET PROC TO MYCCVBX.CC ADDITIVE
```

Once loaded, they are available in the Form Designer, via the Control Palette, on the Custom page.

The keyword ADDITIVE. The SET PROCEDURE TO command has a new keyword—ADDITIVE. Using this keyword lets you put more than one procedure file in memory at a time.

When adding procedure files to memory, you should use the new keyword, ADDITIVE, at the end of the command. If you omit the keyword, ADDITIVE, dBASE will remove any existing procedure files already loaded, as it places the new one in memory.

> **!** **The ADDITIVE keyword is essential**
> If you forget to use the additive keyword and you have additional custom control files loaded, they will be unloaded, just as if they were any procedure file. This simply means that you will need to reload all of them, again using the keyword ADDITIVE.

The .CC extension. Although the dBASE documentation states that you must specify the extension **.CC**, *custom control*, dBASE will load any CLASS definitions of control objects that are in memory. This means that the procedure file does *not* have to end in the extension .CC; it can end in .PRG or .ANY (or anything you want it to).

All control objects that are loaded in memory will be made available in the Form Designer. This is true if they end in .CC, .PRG, or .ANY. It is also true if they use the keyword CUSTOM, or CUSTOM is ignored.

Loading a control library from the Navigator. If the procedure file (custom control library) ends in the extension .CC, you can automatically load it from the navigator. To load it from the Navigator, you can specify the file skeleton ***.CC** in the *Custom* panel of the Navigator. Once you specify the file skeleton, you can load the .CC file as a procedure file by double-clicking on the filename or dragging the filename into the Command window and releasing it.

Figure 13–2 shows the custom control library in the Navigator. Notice that the Custom panel of the Navigator in Figure 13–2 is displaying both custom control libraries and visual basic controls (.VBX).

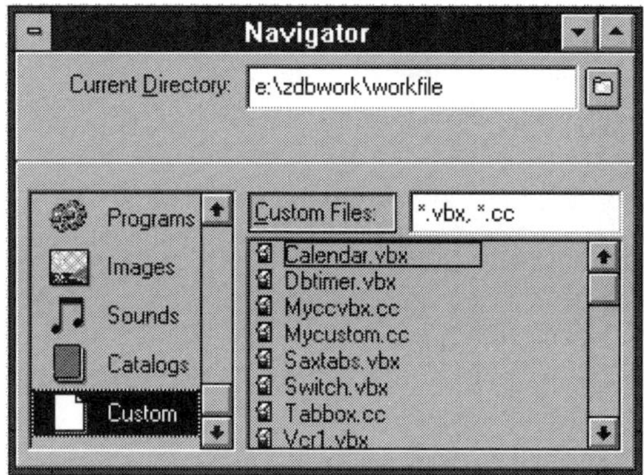

Figure 13–2. Displaying and using control libraries in the Navigator.

✔ **Loading .CC and .VBX files**
This same trick works for Visual Basic Controls. Simply specify *.VBX, *.CC in the custom container of the Navigator, and then double-click on the ones that you want to run.

Problem/advantage of session-only loading. If you load a custom control library automatically, dBASE will add a SET PROC TO <custom control library> command in all the forms that it creates in the Form Designer. If you load your custom control library for the current session, Visual dBASE will only place the SET PROC TO command in the form created during that session.

Some people consider this a problem; others view it as an advantage. The point is that in Visual dBASE if you SET PROC TO in a custom control library it will be available only until you release the procedure file or quit dBASE. Next time the same procedure file will not automatically be available to the Form Designer.

➠ **SET PROC TO and Form Designer**
This behavior of adding the SET PROC TO in the .WFM is new. The dBASE for Windows 5.0 version will NOT add the procedure file to your form. This means that, in Version 5.0, you will have to do one of two things: either type in the SET PROC TO command before you use the form that has custom control objects in it, or modify the form code (.WFM) and add the SET PROC TO command to the code.

Automatically loading control libraries

You can also load custom control libraries one time and have them automatically loaded every time you start dBASE. Once installed, dBASE will place them in the initialization file—dBASEWIN.INI. Visual dBASE has made this easy.

To accomplish this, you will need to *Set Up* the Custom Control procedure file one time from within the Form Designer. Once you specify one or more Custom Control files via a SET UP menu choice (File >> Set Up Custom Control . . .), it will automatically be available to you every time you use the Form Designer.

Setting up custom control libraries. To set up custom control libraries and place them in the DBASEWIN.INI file, follow these steps:

1. Create your custom controls in a procedure file, name it with the extension .CC.
2. Open the Form Designer with any form active or a blank form.
3. In the Form Designer select File >> Set Up Custom Controls . . . menu.
4. Select the ADD button from the Set Up Custom Controls dialog box.
5. Select the custom control file (*.CC) that you want to set up from. Choose Custom Controls dialog box (or change directory to the location of the control file that you want to load).

If you follow these steps, you will load the new Custom Control file and be returned to the Set Up Custom Control dialog box. This dialog box should look similar to the one in Figure 13–3.

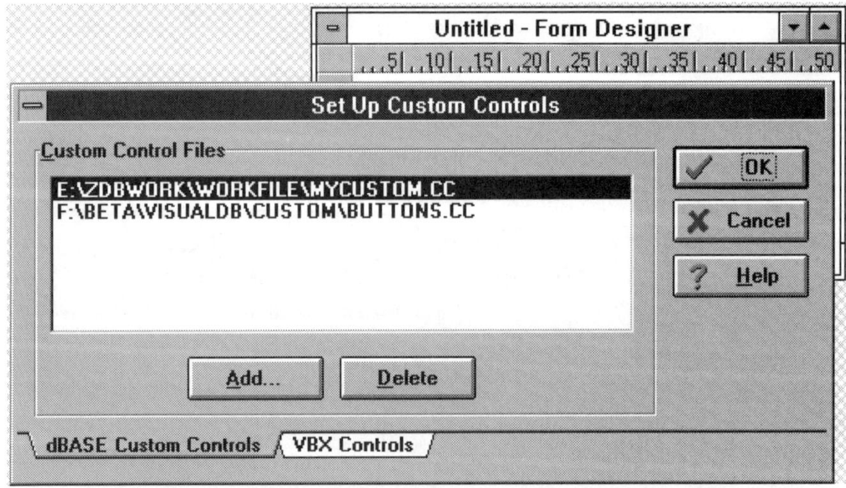

Figure 13–3. The Set Up option for custom controls.

As you can see from Figure 13–3, the Set Up Custom Controls dialog box is available when you are in the Form Designer. In this case, a new file named MYCUSTOM.cc was loaded.

When you install a custom control library, dBASE will automatically add a line to the DBASEWIN.INI file. Once added, every time you begin dBASE it will automatically load this custom control file into memory.

Custom controls and the DBASEWIN.INI file. When dBASE installs a custom control library in the DBASEWIN.INI file, it adds a line to the section labeled **[CustomClasses]**. This section of the configuration file is used to specify which custom control libraries should automatically be loaded when dBASE is started.

If you edit your dBASEWIN.INI file, you can examine this section [CustomClasses] of the file. It should look something like the following:

```
[CustomClasses]
CC0=E:\ZDBWORK\WORKFILE\MYCUSTOM.CC
CC1=F:\BETA\VISUALDB\CUSTOM\BUTTONS.CC
```

You can also install custom control libraries manually, by editing the DBASEWIN.INI file using any ASCII type (plain text) text editor. Go to the section titled [CustomClasses] (if you do not have one, create one). Once at the section, add a line using the following format:

```
CC<nNum> = < .CC filename>
```

You must supply two pieces of information. CC<nNum> must be supplied with an integer number between 1 and 99. The number <nNum> can be any number. This number has no significant meaning; it is used by dBASE as an internal number. It must be unique; you cannot have two CC1s (CC1 = and CC1 =). The second piece of information that you must supply is the custom control filename.

Code generation and custom control libraries

Forms created by the dBASE Form Designer that use custom controls from libraries will add them to the source code.

Advantage to setting up custom control libraries. Once you add a custom control library, via the Form Designer menu or manually, Visual dBASE will automatically add a line of code specifying the custom control library to load if you use one of its custom controls in the form. The following code is used to demonstrate; it was taken from the top of a form file named Z.WFM:

```
** END HEADER—do not remove this line*
* Generated on 07/14/95
*
```

```
parameter bModal
local f
f = new ZFORM()
if (bModal)
   f.mdi = .F. && ensure not MDI
   f.ReadModal()
else
   f.Open()
endif
CLASS ZFORM OF FORM
Set Procedure To MYCUSTOM.CC additive
   this.text = "Demonstration"
```

dBASE will load any necessary procedure files at the beginning of the Class declaration (CLASS ZFORM OF FORM). The Form Designer will automatically load any needed custom control libraries, whether they are in the dBASEWIN.INI file under the [CustomClasses] section, or load with SET PROC TO command.

> ➡ **Only needed files are loaded**
> Visual dBASE will only specify procedure files that are actually used. If you load a *.CC file but do not use any of its Custom classes, it will not be added to the WFM file. This behavior is different in dBASE for Windows version 5.0. The older version will reference every custom control file that is found in the dBASEWIN.INI file.

Never move a referenced custom control file. Notice that dBASE specifies the entire path and filename when it loads the procedure file. This means that you must keep the procedure file in the same directory or change the form (*.WFM) code manually.

If you attempt to run or modify a form that has references to a control library that has been moved, dBASE will report an error like the one in Figure 13–4.

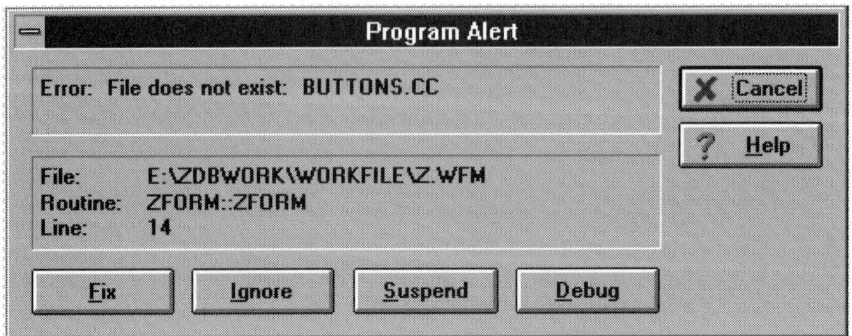

Figure 13–4. The error reported when dBASE cannot find a custom control library.

Notice that the message does *not* reference the full path for the file Buttons.cc. Rather, it simply informs you that the file does not exist, instead of its not being found. This rather ambiguous message can be bothersome.

NOTE: Understanding the Alert box

The Alert box gives you four options. If you select Fix, you will be taken into the Program Editor. If you attempt to Ignore and you have any controls that were created by some Class in the library, dBASE will remove them from the form, after supplying a second Alert box if the control references a method in the same missing control file. If you Cancel, dBASE will return you to the Command window. This same error will occur if you attempt to Modify the form.

Unloading dBASE custom controls

Once a custom control library is loaded, it can be unloaded using any of these commands.

- `CLOSE PROCEDURE`
- `CLOSE ALL`
- `SET PROCEDURE TO`

Any of these commands can remove custom control libraries from memory—one at a time or all of them at once. You can remove custom control libraries that were loaded automatically by dBASE or loaded using the SET PROCEDURE TO command.

CLOSE PROCEDURE <procedure filename.ext>

You can remove a dBASE custom control library from memory using the CLOSE PROCEDURE command. The general syntax is

CLOSE PROCEDURE < .CC filename.cc >

Using this command, you can close a procedure file currently active in memory. If you need to remove more than one procedure file, you will have to use the command for each one that you need to close. For example, to remove the library named BUTTONS.CC, the command would be

```
CLOSE PROCEDURE BUTTONS.CC
```

Only the Buttons.cc file will be removed from memory.

CLOSE ALL

You can also use the CLOSE ALL command to remove procedure files from memory. Using this command will close ***all*** local tables, databases, indexes, procedure files, format files, low level files (Fcreate(), Fopen()), and alternate files (.txt).

It does not close DLLs loaded with LOAD DLL, files opened using the SET DEVICE / PRINTER TO, and SQL databases (Server databases).

SET PROC TO

If you forget to use the keyword ADDITIVE when adding a new procedure into memory, any existing control libraries and other procedure files will automatically be closed.

Creating your own custom controls

By creating your own custom text objects (or any other control type object), you can preset all of those properties in the custom controls that you create. Then these custom controls can be used in all of your forms.

Five Class Definitions of custom controls

The following custom control Class definitions can offer several new dBASE custom controls in the Form Designer. To create a Custom Control Class, you can manually type in a new Class definition based on an existing stock control Class. When creating Custom Control Classes, place them in a procedure file that ends with an extension of .CC (for custom control).

The .CC extension
Although you could have used the extension .PRG, you may want to specify .CC to remind you of the contents—Custom Control Classes.

Perhaps you want to specify a new text type control that can be used for title type text on your forms. Instead of selecting a text control and changing the properties every time, you could create a Custom Text Control Class, name it Title, and select the Title control from the Control Palette when creating your forms. The following code will create a Custom Title Text Class and four additional custom controls. You should save all of these controls in a procedure file named MYCCVBX.CC.

```
*** MYCCVBX.cc
*
```

```
CLASS Title(fn) OF TEXT(fn) CUSTOM
    this.Font = "Times New Roman"
    this.FontSize = 18
    this.FontBold = .t.
    this.FontUnderline = .t.
    this.ColorNormal = "W*/w"
    this.Height = 1.6
ENDCLASS
CLASS Standard(fn) OF TEXT(fn) CUSTOM
    this.Font = "Arial"
    this.FontSize = 12
    this.ColorNormal = "N/w"
    this.Height = 1.1
ENDCLASS
CLASS Upper(fn) OF ENTRYFIELD(fn) CUSTOM
    this.Function = "@!"
    this.value = ""
ENDCLASS
CLASS Proper(fn) OF ENTRYFIELD(fn) CUSTOM
    this.value = ""
    this.OnChange = CLASS::MakeProper
    PROCEDURE MakeProper
      PARAMETER xName
       this.value = Proper(this.value)
    RETURN

ENDCLASS
CLASS Multi(fn) OF LISTBOX(fn) CUSTOM
    this.Sorted = .t.
    this.Multiple = .t.
ENDCLASS
```

This code creates five new custom control classes that can be used in the Form Designer. There are two text type, two entryfields, and one listbox. Once created and saved in the file named MyCCVbx.cc, you can work with them.

The CUSTOM in the CLASS definition

Examing the new code for any of the Classes, you will notice the keyword CUSTOM added to each of the CLASSES in the code. The following shows its use:

```
CLASS Multi(fn) OF LISTBOX(fn) CUSTOM
```

According to the dBASE documentation, you must supply the keyword CUSTOM when you create a custom control. However, the keyword appears to be an optional word. The Class will be available in the Custom page of the Control Palette even if you omit the keyword CUSTOM.

> !
> **The CUSTOM keyword**
> The CUSTOM option does appear to be used to specify which properties of the Constructor code to stream to the object. For instance, if a custom control is a subclass of another Class that originates from a stock class (twice removed), using CUSTOM does appear to force the Control Palette to show base Classes of the Custom Classes. It also seems to affect any Custom controls derived from VBX controls. In dBASE for Windows 5.0, it also made sure that the Class level methods were found and used. This is not a problem in Visual dBASE.

Loading and working with a custom control library

Once your Control Classes are created and placed in a procedure file, you can load the library and use it to create your own custom controls.

Loading a custom control library. With the Custom code in a procedure (library) file named MyCCVbx.cc, you can now activate the procedure file, making the controls available to you in your Control Palette. Loading it can be done two ways.

1. SET PROC TO MyCCVbx.cc ADDITIVE
2. Adding it to the Set Up Custom Control dialog box of the Form Designer.

Verifying a custom control library is present. To verify that it is in memory and usable in the Form Designer, perform the following steps:

1. Create a new form with the CREATE FORM command.
2. While in the Form Designer, activate the Control Palette, if it isn't open. (Use the SpeedMenu—right click and select Control Palette.)
3. Click on the tab (bottom of Control Palette) labeled *Custom.*

You should see your five new custom controls added to the Control Palette. It should look like the one in Figure 13–5.

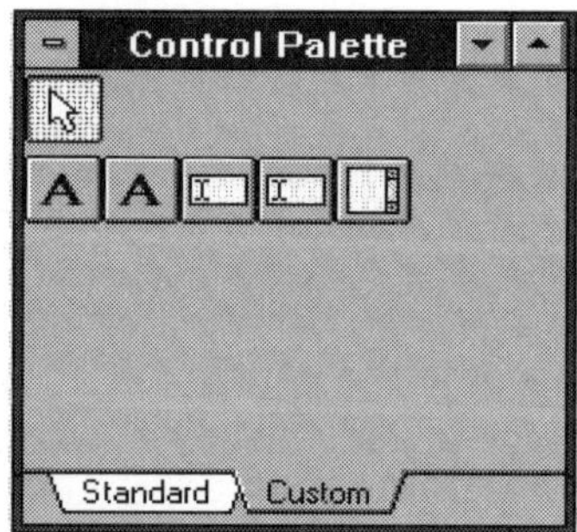

Figure 13–5. Your custom controls added to the Control Palette.

When you click on the Custom tab, you may have other custom controls already available (normally a series of control buttons that ship with dBASE).

Using a custom control. Now that your new custom controls are available, you can use them like any other control. Simply select them and place them on your form. Once on the form, you can modify any of the properties that you need to change by using the Property Inspector.

Figure 13–6 shows the form designed with all five of the new custom objects placed on it and running. Although the form in Figure 13–6 is not effective, the point of it is that it has all five new custom control objects. The top is a title that is a specific size and color (white on gray). The name field will automatically convert all entered names into proper case. The city field converts all text to uppercase. Finally the listbox automatically sorts the book order numbers. When creating this form, you use the default values of each custom control and change the text for the custom text fields (Title, NormalText) and linking the other custom controls to fields in the tables (Customer or Book Orders). Using the custom control objects that you created in the Form Designer can save you hours of work.

Figure 13–6. A form with your five new custom controls.

Creating and saving custom controls in the Form Designer

➡ You can also create custom controls in the Form Designer. Visual dBASE has added the ability to create a custom control directly in the Form Designer and save them to a Custom Class definition. This means that you do not have to manually create your Control Classes and then load them into the Form Designer.

Once you create one or more controls and assign the property values and methods that you want them to have, you can specify that one or more of them be saved as custom controls.

Creating a custom control using the Form Designer

To create a custom control in the Form Designer, you need to do four things:

1. Get into the Form Designer.
2. Select a base control (a control to work with).
3. Modify the properties and add any methods that you want in this new control.
4. Save the control as a custom control using the File>>Save as Custom . . . menu.

Selecting a base control. A base control is simply any control that is in the Control Palette. Once you select one and place it on the screen, you are ready to work with it.

Modifying the properties and adding methods to a control

➡ For instance, follow these steps to create a four-page custom tab control based on the new stock TabBox control.

1. Activate the Control Palette and Inspector for the form.
2. Select the TabBox control from the Control Palette by double-clicking on it.
3. While the TabBox is highlighted, click in the Inspector dialog box.
4. Select the DataSource property, under the Data Linkage Properties section, and click on the Builder button (the wrench on the right side).
5. When the *Data Source Property Builder* dialog box appears, click on the wrench button alongside of the Data Source entry box.
6. Go to the String entryfield of the *Build Array* dialog box (Figure 13–7).
7. Type in and press **Enter** or click on the Add button the four words—One [click Add button], Two [Add button], Three, Four.
8. With the four Array elements added to the Array Element listbox, highlight the default value TABBOX1 and click on the Remove button to remove it from the list.
9. Click the OK button to return to the DataSource Property Builder.
10. Click on the OK button to return to the Inspector.

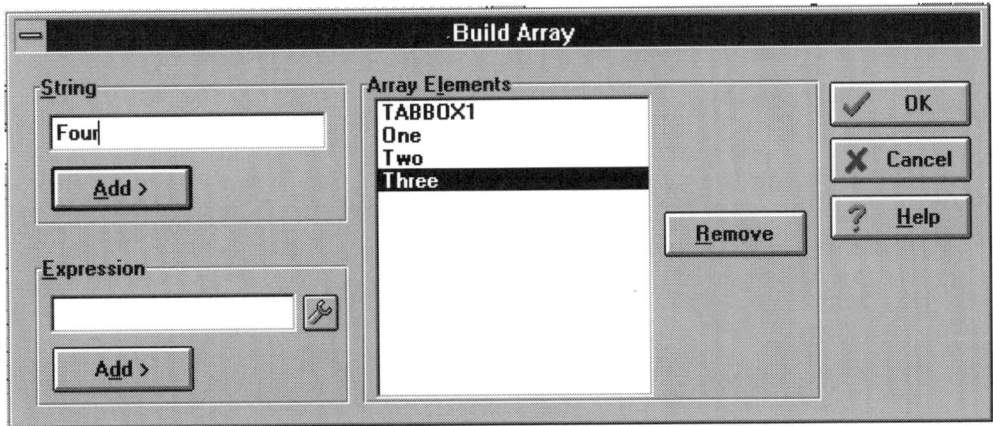

Figure 13–7. This is the Build Array dialog box.

Once you have specified the four tab tags in an array and returned to the Inspector, the form will look something like the one in Figure 13–8. Notice that four named tabs have been added to the form.

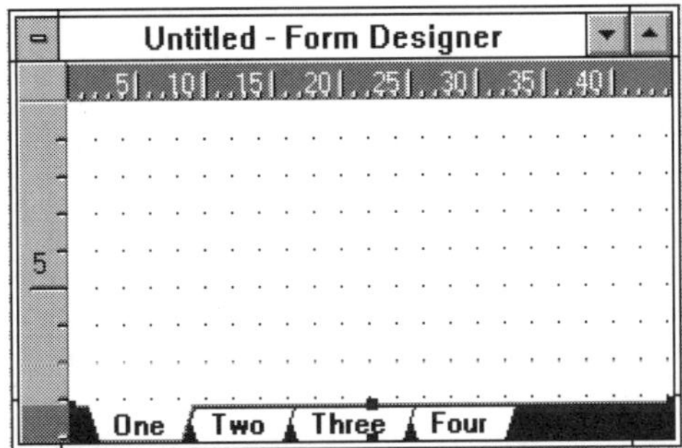

Figure 13–8. This is the four tab form.

With the DataSource property set, you are ready to assign an action to the OnSelChange event property. Click on the Events tab of the Inspector and go to the OnSelChange cell. Type in the following codeblock:

```
{;form.PageNo = this.CurSel}
```

This codeblock will synchronize the tabs to the pages of the form. The cell should look like the one in Figure 13–9.

Figure 13–9. This is the OnSelChange cell of a TabBox.

CRITICAL: Rename the control object. Now that you have created this control for the form, you *must* change the **Name** property of the object under the Identification Properties section of the Inspector. Click on the Properties tab of the Inspector, go to the Name property cell, and type in the following new value:

```
FourPageTAB
```

The Name cell should now look like the one in Figure 13–10.

Figure 13–10. This is the new Name value.

Renaming the object is *critical*; if you forget to rename it, Visual dBASE will name it the same as the original control—TabBox—and ignore it when you create a new control Class.

Saving a control object as a Custom Control Class. With the custom control object renamed, its other properties set, you are ready to save it as a custom control. To save it as a custom control, follow these steps:

1. Make sure the TabBox control is highlighted in the form.
2. Select File >> Save as Custom . . . menu choice to activate the Save as Custom dialog box.
3. The *Save Selected Controls as Class* button (top left) is selected. The Place in Control Palette check box (bottom left) should be checked on. Verify that the new Class name *FOURPAGETAB* is shown in the Class Name entryfield. (If not, go back and select it in the Form Designer.)
4. Go to the Custom Control File Name entryfield and type in **MYNEW.CC** to save the selected control to a new custom control file (Figure 13–11).
5. Click the OK button, or press the **Enter** key to save the control to the custom control file MyNew.cc.

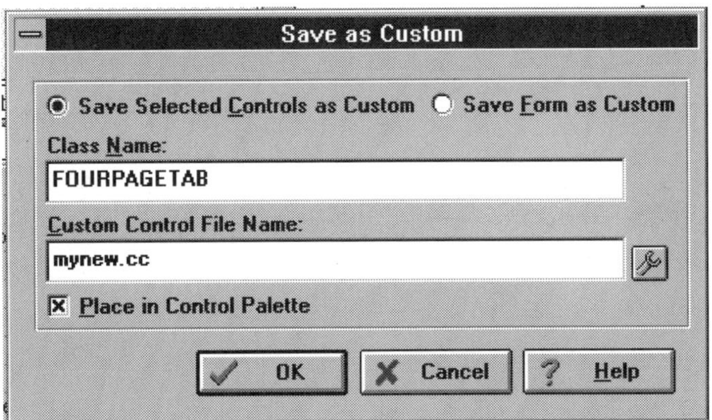

Figure 13–11. This is the Save as Custom dialog box.

Visual dBASE creates a new Custom Control Class named FOURPAGETAB, and then saves it to a file named MYNew.cc. It also makes it active and places it in the Control Palette to be used.

NOTE: New Custom Control Classes

Visual dBASE does not add the newly created custom control file as a permanent custom control file. You will need to select File >> Set Up Custom Controls . . . menu choice and add the new file MyNew.cc to the list.

Working with multiple custom controls in the Form Designer

You are not limited to creating a single custom control. Rather you can create any number of them and save them to a new Custom Control file or an existing Custom Control file.

Create a custom control that creates another control. With the MyNew.cc file, create, another custom class—a rectangle that will be located at the top of the form and hold a single Exit button. This is equivalent to "faking" a SpeedBar at the top of your form.

Follow these steps to create a new class of rectangle—SpdBarRectangle. Select a rectangle from the Control Palette, and change these properties, assigning their new values.

Text	""
Left	0
Top	0
Height	1.7
Width	50
BorderStyle	1—Raised
ColorNormal	"/W"
Name	**SpdBarRectangle**
PageNo	0

With the properties changed, click on the Event tab, select the OnOpen event, click on the wrench button to open the Procedure Editor, and type in the following event.

```
Procedure RECTANGLE1_OnOpen
   DEFINE PUSHBUTTON ExitBtn OF form PROPERTY ;
   Top 0.08, Left 0.5, Width 4.2, Height 1.55, ;
   SpeedBar .T., UpBitMap "Resource #28", ;
   Text "", PageNo 0, OnClick {;form.Close()}
```

Saving a custom control to an existing file. Now that the custom control is created, you can have the Form Designer save this control as a Custom Control Class to the existing file MyNew.cc. Follow these steps to save it to an existing file:

1. While the rectangle is highlighted, select File >> Save as Custom . . . menu choice.
2. Make sure that the Classname is SpdBarRectangle in the entryfield.
3. The file MyNew.cc should already be selected in the Custom Control File Name entryfield. If not, select it or type in the name.
4. Press the OK button.

Now you have two custom controls in the custom control file MyNew.cc. Notice that both of them are available in the Custom page of the Control Palette.

WORKING WITH VISUAL BASIC CUSTOM CONTROLS

Visual Basic controls are user-interface objects (control objects) that are written in C or Pascal and compiled into a special type of DLL having an extension of .VBX. VBXs, like dBASE custom controls, appear in a form object (contained within it).

They usually have their own visual appearance and offer their own functionality. They have properties and methods that can be used to change their appearance.

There are a lot of third-party vendors and shareware sources that supply or offer libraries of VBX controls. Visual dBASE supports version 1 Visual Basic controls. It does not support the new .OCXs or older Visual Basic controls.

Installing/loading VBX controls

Like dBASE custom controls, you can install Visual Basic controls two ways:

- LOAD DLL
- Add them to the DBASEWIN.INI file

LOAD DLL <VBX name.exe>

You can load a .VBX control by using the LOAD DLL command. A VBX is a DLL, and like other DLLs, it can be loaded in memory using the LOAD DLL command. The general syntax is

LOAD DLL [<path>] <DLL filename.ext>

When you use this command, you must specify the file extension (.VBX).

This command will let you load one DLL at a time. For instance, dBASE ships with two DLLs that you can load—VCR1.VBX and SWITCH.VBX. To load these two DLLs, type in the following commands:

```
LOAD DLL \VisualdB\SAMPLES\VCR1.VBX
LOAD DLL \ VisualdB\SAMPLES\SWITCH.VBX
```

This will load both DLLs into memory. Remember, Visual Basic Controls (VBX) are a special type of DLL.

Installing in the DBASEWIN.INI file

You can also install the .VBX controls by placing them in the DBASEWIN.INI file. You can install them following the same steps you did when installing the dBASE custom controls. They can be installed using the menu choice File >> Set Up Custom Controls . . . from the Form Designer menu or manually placing them in the Set Up file under the section heading [DLLs].

```
[DLLs]
DLL0=D:\ VisualdB\SAMPLES\VCR1.VBX
DLL1= D:\ VisualdB\SAMPLES\SWITCH.VBX
```

To install VBXs by hand, go into the DBASEWIN.INI file using any ASCII type (plain text) Text Editor. Go to the section titled [DDLs] (if you do not have one, create one). Once at the section, add a line using the following format:

DLL<nNum> = < .VBX filename.ext>

You must supply two pieces of information. DLL<nNum> must be supplied with an integer between 1 and 99. The number <nNum> can be any number. This number has no significant meaning; it is used by dBASE as an internal number. It must be unique; you cannot have two DLL1s (DLL1 = and DLL1 =). The second piece of information that you must supply is the DLL filename.

Releasing a VBX control

Unlike traditional DLLs, a Visual Basic control cannot be released from memory once it is loaded. This is true if you load it from the configuration file or use the LOAD DLL command. If you attempt to release the VBX control using the RELEASE DLL command, you will receive an error message in an Alert box, like the one in Figure 13–12.

Figure 13–12. The error message when you try to release a Visual Basic control.

VBXs use memory. Because you cannot release Visual Basic Controls, you should use them sparingly. They take up both memory and resources that cannot be reclaimed until you leave dBASE. Because of this, you may not want to load .VBXs from your configuration file (DBASEWIN.INI).

Using VBX controls

A VBX can be added to a form just like any built-in control using the Form Designer. Once a VBX has been added to the form, the form is executed just like any other form.

Creating a form with .VBX controls

To create a form with VBX controls, enter the Form Designer and select the VBX control you want to use from the Control Palette. They can be found on the VBX page by clicking the VBX tab at the bottom of the palette. Figure 13–13 shows the VBX page and three VBXs.

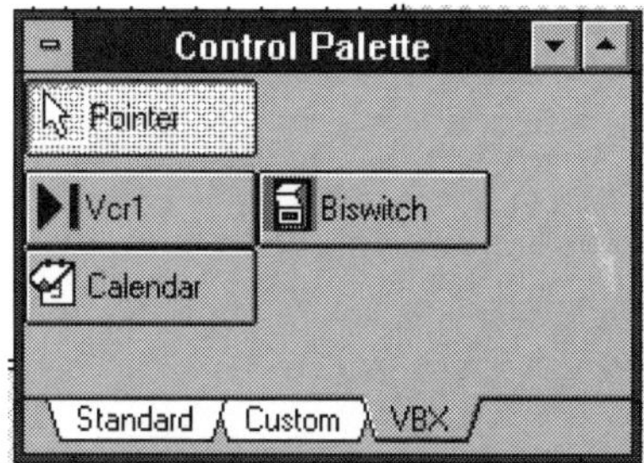

Figure 13–13. Selecting a VBX from the Control Palette.

Two of the controls in Figure 13–13 are shipped with dBASE—VCR1 and BISWITCH. The third one, CALENDAR, is an independent third-part control. It and many others can be found on the CompuServe ©® electronic bulletin board.

➡ **The VBX page**
Notice that Figure 13–13 shows a VBX page tab in the Control Palette, which is a new feature; dBASE for Windows 5.0 combined both dBASE custom controls and VBXs on the same Custom tab. Also notice that the Control Palette in Figure 13–13 shows both the VBX name and the bitmap (graphic). This is an optional switch that can be set by setting Control Palette properties . . . from the SpeedMenu (right mouse button) or the Properties menu. This Properties dialog box is also new to Visual dBASE. The default is BitMap only.

Now you can select them and place them on a form. Figure 13–14 shows a form being created with four Visual Basic controls. The new one is SAXTabs (a third-party VBX). Instead of using SAXTabs, you could use the new TabBox control of Visual dBASE.

As you build the form, like the one in Figure 13–14, you can change property values of the VBX controls, using the Property Inspector. It is no different than changing properties for the built-in controls.

Assigning property values. Each VBX will have its own properties, event properties, and methods. They are created and assigned by the creator of the Visual Basic control. In addition to the ones supplied by the vendor, dBASE adds several properties to each VBX control. Figure 13–15 shows the Property Inspector for a VBX control.

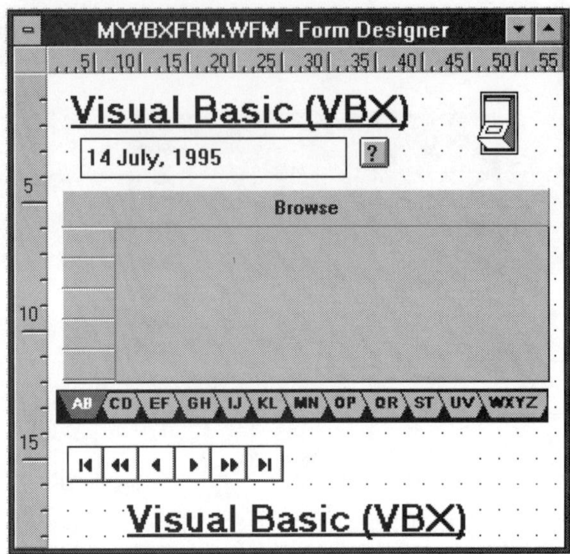

Figure 13–14. Building a form with several VBX controls.

Figure 13–15 shows the Properties for the VCR1 Visual Basic control. It also has several Event properties and Methods that can be used to set event handlers and perform actions against the VCR1 control.

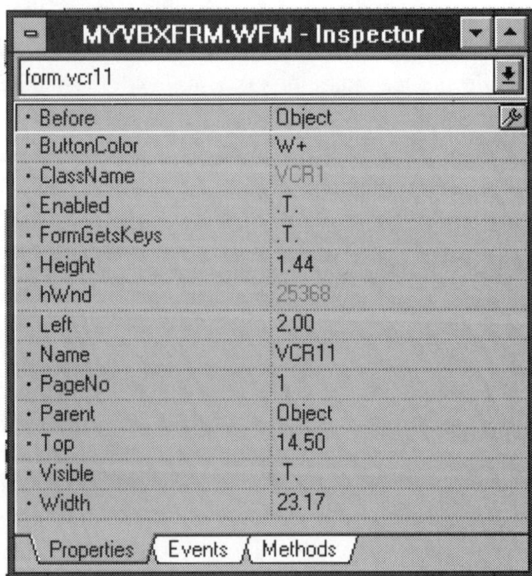

Figure 13–15. The Property Inspector for a VBX control.

dBASE added properties. In addition to the properties supplied by the vendor of thc VBX, dBASE automatically adds the following properties to each VBX:

- *Parent* is a property used to reference the form window in which the control is placed. It is a redirector-type property. When you click in the cell of this property and click on the tool icon, you will be moved to the parent object (form) in the Property Inspector.
- *HWnd* is used to assign a read-only handle to the form window where the VBX control is placed. This handle is a numeric value that is unique for each control and is assigned by Windows.
- *Before* is used to hold the reference to the object that precedes the VBX control in the tabbing order. When you click on the tool icon of the Before property, you will be taken to the object that precedes the .VBX control in the Property Inspector.
- *FormGetKeys* is a logical property that defaults to true (.t.). It is used to specify whether the form or the .VBX control will receive several keystrokes. Specifically, the key strokes are **Esc**, **Tab**, **Shift-Tab**, **Ctrl+End**, and **Ctrl+W**. If you set this value to false (.f.), the VBX control will receive the key combinations instead of the form (FormGetKeys).
- *VBStream* is used to store information used by the VBX control to read the .BFM file (created by the Form Designer). This is a property that is added when the WFM file is generated. You will not see it on the Property Inspector.

The .BFM file

When the Form Designer generates a form that contains Visual Basic controls, it generates a file that has the same name as the form with the extension of *.BFM*. This file is a binary form manager file that contains binary information about the initial state of all the VBX controls in the form.

! **The .BFM file must exist**
The .BFM file must be present when you run a form that contains VBX controls. If the file is not present when you attempt to run the form, you will receive an error message similar to the one in Figure 13–16.

When you get the error box message like in Figure 13–16, check to make sure that you are in the correct subdirectory first—that is, the subdirectory where the form is located. This error message will appear if it cannot find the .BFM file even though you specify the .WFM file by the path. The .BFM file must be in the current directory for the .WFM file to work.

Figure 13–16. The error box for a missing VBStream file (.BFM file).

The LOAD DLL and VBStream property. When the Form Designer saves a form with VBX controls, it will place a LOAD DLL command before the DEFINE statement of the VBX control and then assign the property VBStream to the VBX control DEFINE statement. The following code illustrates this:

```
load dll VCR1.VBX
   DEFINE VCR1 VCR11 OF THIS PROPERTY ;
     VBStream "MYVBXFRM.BFM 56",;
     Top 12.8, Left 2, Width 23, Height 1.4 ,;
```

Notice that dBASE loads the VBX just before it DEFINEs it and it assigns a new property, VBStream, with information about the .BFM file and a number for internal information. If you rename the .WFM and .BFM files you will have to go into the WFM file and change the reference name of the .BFM file in the VBSteam property for each VBX control.

Renaming a form. If you rename a form created by the Form Designer, that contains VBX controls, you will have to also rename the .BFM file. If you forget to also rename this file, the form will not run.

If you rename the form (*.WFM) and .BFM file, don't forget to go into the WFM file with the command modify command <wfm file> and change the .BFM name for each of the VBStream properties of each VBX control.

Help for VBX controls

Help for the specific properties and methods of a VBX control is not provided by dBASE. Because the control is provided outside of dBASE, Help is the responsibility of the creator of the control. Many of the .VBX controls that can be found on CompuServe©® and other electronic bulletin boards lack good Help and documentation.

Understanding the code

Once the form is complete, dBASE will generate the code and a .BFM file for the form containing the VBX controls in it. The .BFM file is simply a binary data file that is used by the WFM. The form developed for this example with the four VBX controls has the following code. The code was shortened by combining several lines of properties together in all the DEFINE statements, but all the code was created by the Form Designer.

```
*** MyVbxFrm.wfm
*
parameter bModal
local f
f = new MYVBXFRMFORM()
if (bModal)
   f.mdi = .F. && ensure not MDI
   f.ReadModal()
else
   f.Open()
endif
CLASS MYVBXFRMFORM OF FORM
   this.Top = 0.5
   this.Height = 18.5
   this.Width = 55
   this.Text = "VBX Custom Controls form"
   this.OnClose = {;close database}
   DEFINE TEXT TSAY1 OF THIS PROPERTY;
    Top 0.5, Left 2.5, Width 36, Height 1.8, FontSize 18, ;
    FontUnderline .T., Text "Visual Basic (VBX)"
   DEFINE BROWSE B OF THIS PROPERTY;
    Top 4.5, Left 1.5, width 53, Height 7.5, Visible .F., ;
    ColorNormal "N/W", ScrollBar 2
   load dll f:\beta\visualdb\samples\vcr1.vbx
   DEFINE VCR1 VCR11 OF THIS PROPERTY;
    VBStream "MYVBXFRM.BFM 56", Top 14.5, Left 2, Width 23, ;
    Height 1.2, OnOpen CLASS::VCR11_ONOPEN,;
    OnFastForward CLASS::VCR11_ONFASTFORWARD,;
    OnBegin CLASS::VCR11_ONBEGIN, ;
    OnEnd CLASS::VCR11_ONEND, ;
    OnFastBackward CLASS::VCR11_ONFASTBACKWARD,;
    OnBackward CLASS::VCR11_ONBACKWARD,;
    OnForward CLASS::VCR11_ONFORWARD
   load dll f:\beta\visualdb\samples\switch.vbx
   DEFINE BISWITCH BISW1 OF THIS PROPERTY;
    VBStream "MYVBXFRM.BFM 87", Top 0.5, Left 45.5, Width 5.5, ;
    Height 3, OnOn CLASS::BISW1_ON, OnOff CLASS::BISW1_OFF
   load dll E:\ZDBWORK\WORKFILE\VBXS\CALENDAR.VBX
   DEFINE CALENDAR CLDR1 OF THIS PROPERTY;
    VBStream "MYVBXFRM.BFM 179", Top 2.5, Left 3.5,;
    Width 33, Height 1.5625
   load dll vbxs\saxtabs.vbx
   DEFINE SAXTAB TAB OF THIS PROPERTY;
    VBStream "MYVBXFRM.BFM 284", Top 12.2979, Left 0.8, ;
```

```
 Width 52.5352, Height 1.3271, OnClick CLASS::MOVERECORD
DEFINE TEXT TEXT1 OF THIS PROPERTY;
 Top 16.4, Left 8.5, Width 36, Height 1.8, ;
 FontSize 18, FontUnderline .T., Text "Visual Basic (VBX)"
Procedure BISw1_On
  form.view = "vbxCustm.qbe"
  form.vcr11.ButtonColor = "W+"
  form.tab.visible = .t.
  form.b.visible = .t.
  form.b.Alias = "Customer"
RETURN

Procedure BISw1_Off
  form.vcr11.ButtonColor = "N"
  form.tab.visible = .f.
  form.b.visible = .f.
  form.view = ""
  form.b.alias=""
RETURN

Procedure VCR11_OnBegin
  IF Len(form.view)>0
    GO TOP
  ENDIF
RETURN

Procedure VCR11_OnEnd
  IF Len(form.view)>0
    GO BOTTOM
  ENDIF
RETURN

Procedure VCR11_OnForward
  IF Len(form.view)>0
    SKIP
    IF EOF()
      form.Message.text="Bottom"
      SLEEP 1
      form.Message.text = ""
      GO BOTTOM
    ENDIF
  ENDIF
RETURN

Procedure VCR11_OnBackward
  IF Len(form.view)>0
    SKIP -1
    IF BOF()
      form.Message.text="T O P"
      SLEEP 1
      form.Message.text = ""
      GO TOP
    ENDIF
  ENDIF
```

```
RETURN

Procedure VCR11_OnFastForward
  IF Len(form.view)>0
    SKIP +2
    IF EOF()
      form.Message.text="Bottom"
      SLEEP 1
      form.Message.text = ""
      GO BOTTOM
    ENDIF
  ENDIF
RETURN

Procedure VCR11_OnFastBackward
  IF Len(form.view)>0
    SKIP -2
    IF BOF()
      form.Message.text="T O P"
      SLEEP 1
      form.Message.text = ""
      GO TOP
    ENDIF
  ENDIF
RETURN

*********

PROCEDURE MoveRecord
SET NEAR ON
DO CASE
  CASE form.tab.Activetab=0
   SEEK 'A'
  CASE form.tab.Activetab=1
    SEEK 'C'
  CASE form.tab.Activetab=2
    SEEK 'E'
  CASE form.tab.Activetab=3
    SEEK 'G'
  CASE form.tab.Activetab=4
    SEEK 'I'
  CASE form.tab.Activetab=5
    SEEK 'K'
  CASE form.tab.Activetab=6
    SEEK 'M'
  CASE form.tab.Activetab=7
    SEEK 'O'
  CASE form.tab.Activetab=8
    SEEK 'Q'
  CASE form.tab.Activetab=9
    SEEK 'S'
  CASE form.tab.Activetab=10
    SEEK 'U'
  CASE form.tab.Activetab=11
```

```
        SEEK 'W'
    ENDCASE
    RETURN

    *********

    Procedure VCR11_OnOpen
      form.vcr11.ButtonColor = "N"

    Procedure Form_OnOpen

    Procedure DBTIMER1_OnTimer
    form.text1.text="Time is "+time()

ENDCLASS
```

This code has several control objects and methods built inside it. They are:

Two Text Objects

One BROWSE Object

Four Visual Basic Control Objects (VBX)

Ten Event Handlers (methods stored in the CLASS)

All of the control objects were created graphically. While the Event Handlers were created in the Form Designer by writing code in the Procedure Editor.

The Procedure Editor. When you create your forms, like the one created previously, you will place control objects on the form and set new values for some of the properties (either by moving the objects with the mouse or by typing in new values in the Property Inspector).

However, once the controls are where you want them, you will have to write small procedures (methods) and attach them to any events that you want to have take action. To write your Event Handlers (methods) you will use the Procedure Editor built into the Form Designer.

To activate the Procedure Editor, you can select it using the SpeedMenu. An even better way is to select the Event property that you want to attach the method to and double-click on the small tool icon on the right side of the event property. When you do this, the Procedure Editor will open. If you opened it from the Event properties page dBASE will automatically give the procedure a name. While in the Procedure Editor, you simply have to type in the code necessary to perform the task. Notice that the code is extremely short in Figure 13–17. This is typical of method code in an O-O environment. The method in the Procedure Editor is the one that will be run when the BISWITCH is clicked and turned on. It is named BISw1_On.

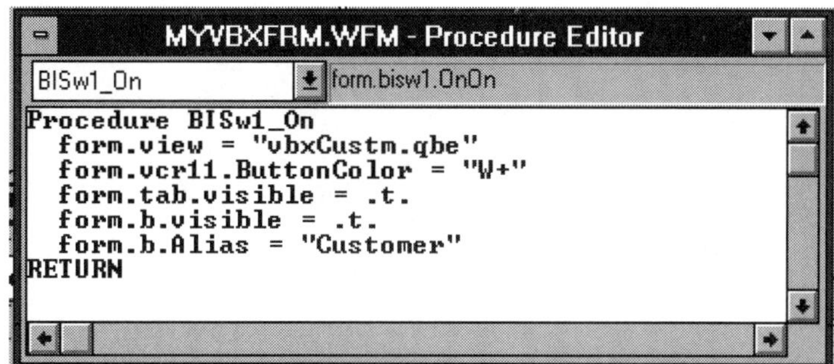

Figure 13–17. The Procedure Editor inside the Form Designer.

Examining the code in Figure 13–17, notice that all it does is set properties for other objects on the form. It specifies a query to be used by the form, a table alias to be used by the browse object, and makes two controls visible (the SAXTAB and the browse objects).

As you continue to work in the O-O environment, you will learn to code small routines like this and attach them to events of objects.

Running the form file with VBX controls

Once the code is completed, you can run the program the same way you run any other form or program, with the DO command. To run this program, type in the following command from the Command window:

```
DO MYVBXFRM.WFM
```

When the form is opened it will look like the one in Figure 13–18. Notice that it does not display the Browse window.

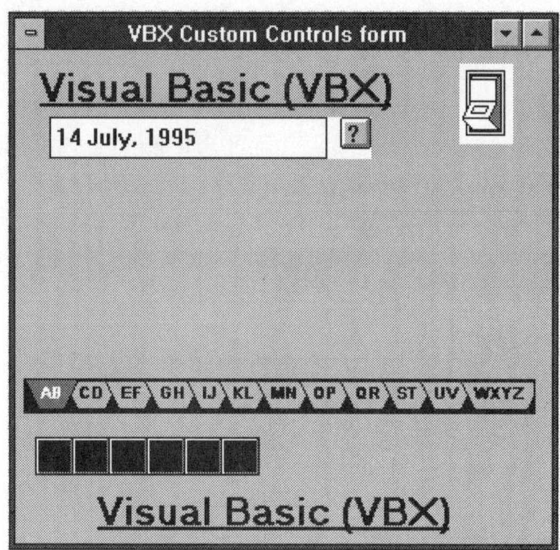

Figure 13–18. The program running with several VBX controls.

Notice the Switch VBX control in the top right corner. It has two conditions—on and off. When you click on it, the state of the control will change (a different picture will appear). Also across the top (on the left side) is a the Calendar control. It has a date in it and a small icon (question mark is on the icon) to the right side of it. If you click on the small icon ? button, it will activate a Calendar dialog box that can be used to select a new date for the object graphically. Figure 13–19 shows the Calendar active.

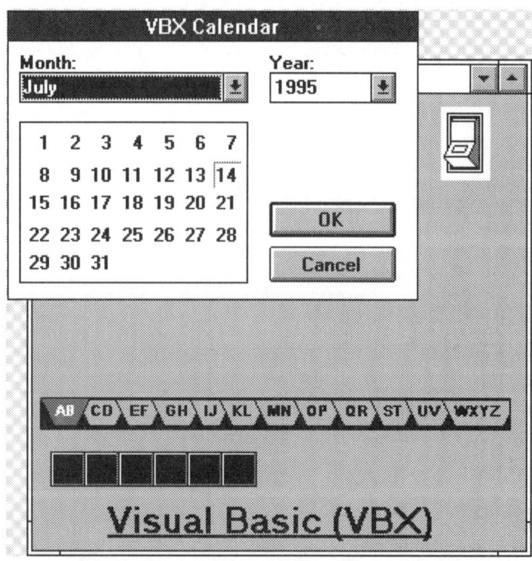

Figure 13–19. The Calendar VBX control active.

All of the functionality of the Calendar control is built into the control. No code had to be written to use it or select dates using the graphical calendar.

Now the real power. When you click on the BISWITCH in the left top corner, the form will appear like the one in Figure 13–20. Notice that the Browse window is now visible, the VCR controls at the bottom are active and visible, and there is a small tabbing control active below the Browse window. The tabbing control works like the tabs in your school binders when you were in school. If you press the ST tab, the Browse window will immediately move to the first *S* record, and so forth.

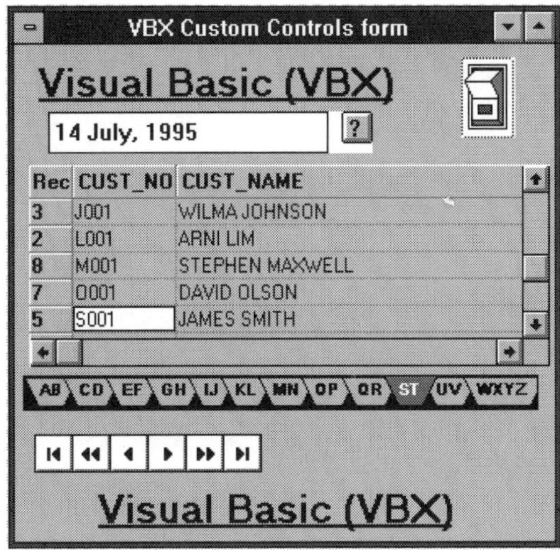

Figure 13–20. The complete form.

Although the last two-and-a-half pages of code seems like a lot, half of it involves small routines. For example, thirty lines are used to seek through the browse table when the user clicks on one of the tabs. Another fifty-five lines are for the six small procedures associated with the VCR buttons. If you press the left one, you will be taken to the top of the file, the one next to it will skip back by two records each time, and then the next one skips one record.

The most powerful code is the two methods associated with the BISWITCH. Between both methods there is only twelve lines of code. But this code makes objects appear, disappear, and become associated with queries (tables and sort orders).

Chapter 14
Visual dBASE, Client/Server, and SQL

Visual dBASE lets you create and work with Client/Server applications. It accomplishes this by use of a common database engine, known as the Borland Database Engine (BDE).

Understanding the dBASE implementation of Client/Server

The BDE is the central portion of the architecture for the Integrated Database Application Programming Interface (IDAPI).

IDAPI is middleware that is similar to ODBC; in fact, it complements ODBC. Unlike ODBC, it is not solely dependent on Windows. The primary vendors that established IDAPI were IBM, Borland, Novell, and WordPerfect. Since its creation, over forty vendors are now a part of it and support it. They include companies like Oracle, Informix, Gupta, and others.

Middleware solves incompatibility and complexity

When you connect a local dBASE or Paradox table to SQL tables, there are many potential problems or conflicts that need to be resolved.

- Local dBASE tables are record oriented.
- SQL tables are set oriented (they have pages, not records).
- Table formats are considerably different (dBASE, Oracle, or Sybase).
- The database may operate on different hardware platforms.
- Work in different operating systems.
- Understand different network protocols.
- Work with tables in different manners.
- Support indexes differently.
- Work with different language drivers.

These are just a few of the problems that middleware attempts to solve. It breaches the gap of hardware, operating system, network operating systems, communications, and database application methodologies between databases and their tables.

IDAPI SQL Implementation

Because dBASE and other navigational (record oriented) database systems differ significantly from SQL transaction-based systems, you need a way to have each system type talk to each other. IDAPI does this for you.

dBASE adds, edits, and deletes records directly to the physical table where the data are stored. When it is done in a multiuser environment, record and table locks are used to ensure data integrity. These locks are used to ensure that no more than one user can modify the record at the same time. SQL databases do not work against the tables directly, rather they use transaction methods to perform these actions.

In most SQL databases, the user requests a record or set of records which are "copied" and supplied to the user. These transparent copies are what are used to make additions, changes, and deletions. Once the user is finished, the transaction changes are either *committed* or *abandoned*. If they are committed, the original data will be changed to reflect the new changes.

Transactions. IDAPI reads the dBASE statements and converts them to transaction-oriented formats needed by the SQL database. You can use the new Transaction() functions to Start, Commit, and Rollback the transaction.

Error reporting. Because record and file locks are not available in SQL databases, more than one user can access the same records and make changes to them in an SQL environment. This requires that more error checking be developed for SQL databases. When this occurs, the dBASE rlock() and flock() functions break (fail or report .f.), and an error will occur.

Because of this, developers need to use ON ERROR routines that check for broken locks and perform some recovery procedure. They can use the new IDAPI DBError() function to determine if the locks are still affected when the transaction is completed.

Data types. Each database has its own data types. Interbase has field types like Number, LongRaw, Char(n), Blob, Double, and Varying. Oracle has types like Char(n), VarChar(n), Long, Float, and Raw. Sybase/SQL Server has types like Text, SmallInt, Float, Bit, Money, Image, DateTime, Real, and VarBinary(n).

dBASE types Float, Number, Character(n), Memo, Date, and Memo (OLE, Image) are equivalent to the types of other databases. However, the translation from one to another can be a chore. IDAPI can automatically assist in using each database's data type and allow dBASE to use and understand each different internal representation of the data types.

Visual dBASE and SQL tables

When working with SQL tables, Visual dBASE offers direct support through tables, queries, and forms, via the user interface. It also offers an SQL Statement Builder that can assist you in building SQL statements.

SQL tables

Visual dBASE, through its interface tools, lets you create tables, add records, edit records, read records, delete records, and create indexes. Although you can create tables, once a structure is created, you cannot modify the structure of a table.

➡ **Referential integrity support**
You can use referential integrity, at the database level, via pulldown menu choices of the File >> Database >> Define Referential Integrity.

The only way to work with referential integrity and SQL tables is via the interface menu system. No language level support is offered in Visual dBASE.

➡ **NULL support**
Visual dBASE has added NULL support. You can specify the keyword NULL in expressions built against SQL tables, and it will operate correctly.

Query support for SQL tables

You can create and use a query against SQL tables. You can join tables, filter data, and select specific fields for the view. You can also specify a sort order.

The view is usually editable. However, there are conditions that will create a read-only view. Once created, an answer set from a query can be written to a dBASE table.

! **Read-only queries**
If you check a Record Order in the Query Designer for a field that is *not* indexed, the view of the resulting records will be read-only.

Form support for SQL tables

Like using forms against local tables, you can create a form, setting its view property to an SQL table or a query based on SQL data. Depending on the underlying query or table, the form can be used to edit and add records to the database.

Report support for SQL tables

You can use the data from an SQL table or query as the basis of any report.

The SQL Statement Builder

Visual dBASE has added a utility that can assist you in creating SQL statements. It can be used to build SQL statements, teaching you the differences between an SQL query and a dBASE query statement.

The SQL Statement Builder lets you build SQL DML commands. A DML command is a command that involves data manipulation. It stands for Data Manipulation Language. SQL, although the most common language among relational databases, comprises a limited number of commands. These commands are only used to manipulate data. There are no commands in SQL to control program flow (DO, IF, . . .), define classes (DEFINE, NEW . . .), or control the user interface (@ SAY, FROM, TO, AT, . . .). SQL relies on other languages to perform these functions.

The SQL Statement Builder can perform the same operations and update tables as the Query Designer two-way tools. It can be found in the \VISUALDB\UTILS directory of Visual dBASE, if you performed a full installation.

DESIGNING CLIENT/SERVER APPLICATIONS WITH DBASE

Although this book is not focused on Client/Server directly, this chapter attempts to discuss design considerations of creating Client/Server applications using dBASE.

dBASE is Client/Server capable, out of the box. It has added language enhancements and extensions to support, access, and work with SQL data in other formats and those residing in other server databases.

When you decide to move to Client/Server, you have several more things to consider over the PC-based applications. The good news is that the amount of work needed to implement the design can be less than creating the application with local tables.

Tables and indexes

The first focus area is the creation, your tables, and indexes.

Normalizing the tables

Good table design is critical for Client/Server applications. Servers tend to be optimized for handling normalized tables (at minimum of third normal form, preferably 5NF). Using dBASE 5.0 for Windows, the Server becomes an extension of the dBASE rather than a replacement source for local tables (dBASE and Paradox). dBASE can be used to obtain data from a mix of tables that are local, in a Server, or on a local area network (LAN).

So when you create a Client/Server application, the most critical thing to consider for local and remote tables is the design of those tables.

The easiest way to remember normalization is to make sure that every field in every table is

Related to the Key, the Whole Key, and nothing but the Key.

Primary keys. Every database should have a primary key. A primary key is an index that is created that will hold a unique value that can be used to identify any record in the table. For instance, a customer table may contain a customer number. This customer number needs to be unique for every customer in the database. Every record should have a unique value in the Customer_Number field.

First normal form—eliminate repeating groups. All fields in a record of the table should be related to the key. There should be no recurring data between fields. For instance, look at this structure.

Employee.dbf
Employee_Number

Name

Address

SpouseName

Child1Name

Child2Name

All fields (attributes) of a record should be related and grouped together into their own table, relating back to another table by some key.

This table needs all of the depend fields removed from the table and placed in another table. If a field is not directly related to the purpose of the table (track unique employee information as it is related to the EMPLOYEE_NUMBER field, primary key), the field should be removed and placed in another database. In this case, this table can be broken into two new tables:

Employee	**Dependents**
Emp_No	Emp_No
Name	DependType
Address	DependName

Because some employees will not be married, some will have fewer than two children, and others more, this new table structure can be used to store exact information about each employee. Notice that the two tables have a common field (Emp_no) that can be used to relate the records between the two tables.

Second normal form—eliminate redundant data. If you have fields that are only related to part of the primary key field, these fields should be grouped in their own table and related back through some key value.

This level deals with complex primary keys. A complex primary key is one that is built based on more than a single field. Any fields related to the key must be related (or associated) with the entire key. If you have a primary key that is built by combining the Lastname field and the Firstname field, all the fields in the table must be related to the combined key of both fields. For instance, if you have a field (Lineage) that holds the lineage based on a person's surname (Irish, Japanese, German, etc.) then the field does not belong in this table because it is only related to the Lastname part of the primary key.

Third normal form—eliminate fields independent of the primary key. If a field does not contribute to or directly relate to the primary key of the record, then it belongs in its own table. This level of normalization may have to find hidden or transitive dependencies.

An good example would be a table that has a Zip or Postal Code field, a City field, and a State/Providence field. The city and state_prov field are not needed in the table. They are directly linked to the Zip_Postal field. They can be removed from the table and placed in their own table.

Server indexes

Database Servers rely on indexes for providing rapid searching, querying, and exporting of information. An index can be used as a key field (called the primary key index), as well as a sort order for extracting data based on another field in the table. When you create indexes for a server database, you do not have to design the table to make the linking field keys.

Local tables

When you create your local tables, you should name them knowing that you may have to move them later. You should not hard code in the name of the tables and their path when creating applications. Rather, place the directory that will be used to store the tables in the path.

Indexes. Only build indexes for local tables that are absolutely necessary.

Remote tables

You need to have the Data Base Administrator (DBA) create the tables and indexes that will be placed on the server and used by the client/server application. The DBA will need to know about how you will work with the data and what type of information needs to be stored it the tables.

Integrity. The DBA will also need to know about what type of integrity will need to be built into the new tables at the Server. Are fields required to have a content, which fields cannot have duplicate data, what format should certain fields be stored in (all uppercase, etc.)?

Referential integrity tools. If your server supports Referential Integrity (RI) at the database level, you can use the new dialogs of Visual dBASE to assist you in specifying RI against the *currently* active database (the database activated with SET DATABASE TO command). Using this new tool, you can add, edit, or drop individual rules for the current database.

It will establish and query various referential integrity rules on a product basis only. For instance, the following commands will be issued, depending on the type of server, to remove a Primary Key from a table named TheTable:

Interbase/Sybase

```
ALTER TABLE TheTable DROP CONSTRAINT (ID number)
```

Oracle (depends on version)

```
ALTER TABLE TheTable DROP PRIMARY KEY
```

or

```
ALTER TABLE TheTable DROP CONSTRAINT (ID number)
```

The command that will be used is already built into dBASE and stored as a resource. It can differ minimally, as in this example, or drastically—thus, build is a resource.

Indexes. Indexes in Servers do slow down the system, so you need to work with the DBA to decide which indexes should be created. They take time and require space to build and maintain. If you need an index, then build it; if it is just a nicety, do not build it.

Existing tables on a Server. If your application will use tables that already exist on the Server, but they are not in the format that you would like, request (from the DBA) that a view (a virtual table) be generated of the physical table with which you can work.

You could use a local query to build the view. However, this can be time consuming if it has to be built every time you need to use the query. Also, if you specify an order that is not already associated with an index, the view will be read-only. Therefore, if the view will constantly be used, have it build at the Server level.

It is better to use a view of a table than to build temporary indexes to be used by your application. The view is handled by the Server, so there will be no performance hit that would be associated with building temporary indexes.

Preparing to work with the Server data

When you decide to move data to, or use data in, a Server you will need to use the IDAPI configuration utility that ships with dBASE. Using this application, you will need to specify alias names, and specific physical information about the database and the Server—passwords, addresses, and so on.

Getting server information

You will need to have the DBA supply you with certain information about the database. You will need to known the actual name of the UNIX Server and the database, the Internet Protocol (IP) address for the file server itself, and for each client connected to the network. This information will be needed when you create aliases using the IDAPI configuration program that comes with dBASE.

Aliases. Before connecting to a Server database, you will need to decide on an alias name to use to reference remote objects. You will assign aliases through the IDAPICFG.EXE program located in the IDAPI subdirectory. This alias name will be used by your applications instead of table names and paths (directory names, drive names).

➡ **Null data type**
The NULL data type is fully supported by Visual dBASE. Although the .dbf file format does not support NULL as a value, it is supported by other databases, recognized, and used by Visual dBASE.

The NULL constant

NULL is a new constant that possesses a value of NULL and a type of unknown. It is not bound to any specific type of data (character, numeric, etc.). This means that it can be used by any function or command without generating a mismatch error, except the @ GET command which is looking for a specific type of data.

The following command demonstrates this point.

```
TYPE(NULL)              && returns "U", for unknown
EMPTY(NULL)             && returns .T. (It is empty)
ISBLANK(NULL)           && returns .F. (It is not blank)
LastName = NULL         && returns .T. or .F. based on value of LastName
DTOC(NULL)              && returns a blank... converted to spaces
SEEK NULL               && if a table type supports NULL this will find the first
                           primary key value of NULL
SIN(NULL)               && since a function can use NULL it remains NULL
? SIN(NULL)             && will print 0, zero, since the output must be numeric
```

Default internal values for NULL

If you use the NULL constant in functions or commands that require a display of a specific data type, the NULL constant will be converted internally to one of six data types that can be displayed—Character, Numeric, Logical, Date, BookMark, or Unknown.

Functions can use a NULL value as NULL. However, they cannot display a value as NULL. Therefore, for display purposes, NULL will be always be converted.

THIS	will display as	THIS
`? NULL`		`?" "`
`SET TYPEAHEAD TO NULL`		`SET TYPEAHEAD TO 0`
`? STR(NULL)`		`?" "`
`? COS(NULL)`		`?" "`
`? YEAR(NULL)`		`?" "`

Although most of these visually converted the display item to character, check to see if the left = the right like this.

```
? NULL = ""
```

```
? NULL = 0
? STR(NULL) = ""
? VAL(NULL) = ""     && result in data type mismatch error
? VAL(NULL) = 0
? YEAR(NULL) = ""    && result in data type mismatch error
```

The resultant answer will always be false or result in a data type mismatch. Because what is displayed (in dBASE) must be one of its recognized data types, dBASE defaults to an empty character value—“”.

However, if you use the type command to determine if the data type being displayed is a character, the answer will depend on what is needed to be passed by the function for command. For instance, the following shows the values that will be displayed with these commands:

```
? TYPE('COS(NULL)')       && display N for numeric
? TYPE('FILE(NULL)')      && display L for logical
? TYPE('DTOC(NULL)')      && display C for character
? TYPE('CTOD(NULL)')      && display D for date
```

In other words, the NULL data type is corrected for the function that will be using it.

Upsizing an Existing PC Application

Using Visual dBASE, you can move an existing dBASE application into the Client/Server world with minimal effort. You will not have to re-create all of your programs from scratch—rather move the data and modify the applications. This is known as upsizing applications.

Using Borland’s SQL Link (required for Client/Server and purchased separately) you can upsize your application into the Client/Server world. Upsizing lets you use all the invested knowledge you have in dBASE—tools and language. The end users won’t have to learn new methods of doing things; dBASE will continue to appear to work the same for them.

When upsizing, you need to follow a few basic guidelines, based on the needs already specified for the Server. Following these guidelines, you can have your database Server integrated into your business application with minimal down time.

NOTE: What is SQL Links?

When you are ready to use Visual dBASE as a front-end tool for Client/Server applications, you will be required to purchase a program that will supply the correct language drivers for the SQL server you will attach to. This product is known as *SQL Links*. It is sold separately by Borland.

The character set that you use in your desktop computer, called a code page, may be completely different from the one used by your Server. If you attempt to display data from the Server without some sort of language driver, you may receive and send incorrect characters to the SQL database.

SQL Links provides the language drivers necessary to convert the text between your desktop computer and the Server computer. This driver also contains the necessary conventions required by the particular SQL Server you are going against. These conventions include sort order and uppercase conventions required by the Server.

Changing field names

If you want to move an existing application to a database Server, you need to examine your table field names and restructure them if needed. Remove all special symbols (including spaces, #, &, etc.) from the field names if you use Paradox tables.

If you do not remove special symbols, SQL link will replace them with underscores (_). Once you fix your local table's field names you will have to modify any code that references the fields to reflect the new field names.

Assigning aliases

You will have to go into the BDECFG.EXE (dBASE for Windows 5.0 uses a file named IDAPICFG.EXE) and assign aliases that can be used to connect to your remote tables. This alias will let dBASE know where the remote tables will be located. You can create aliases for local tables (dBASE and Paradox) as well as remote tables (Oracle, Sybase, etc.).

Moving local data to the database Server

You will move your data to the database Server. The code itself will remain local.

Create all Server databases

The Server databases and tables will have to be created. Unlike dBASE, a database in an SQL-based system is a collection of tables (called databases in dBASE). One database can contain any number of tables.

The databases will have to be created by the DBA or some other system administrator that can act as the DBA on the Server.

Exporting local data

You can export your local data to a server database by using the COPY TO command.

COPY TO. The COPY TO command can be used to export data from dBASE / Paradox tables to SQL tables within a Server database. To use the command, BDE (or IDAPI in dBASE for Windows 5.0) must be configured with the alias name for the remote database.

To COPY TO a SQL table, you must specify the database name and the table name to create. The following example will create a new table in an Oracle database named (alias) ORAC_Employee:

```
USE History TYPE DBASE
COPY TO :ORAC_Employee:History
```

This command will open the history.dbf table and copy it to a new table named History in the Orac_Employee database. The name Orac_Employee was created as an *Alias* in the IDAPI configuration program.

NOTE: Using colons around database names

Notice that you have to place the database name inside colons—:Orac_Employee:. This tells dBASE to use the Server database to copy the table to.

If the database is not open, BDE (through SQL Links) will inform Visual dBASE, and it will display a dialog box in which you specify the parameters, such as a login name and password—a name that will be used to establish a connection to that database, opening it so that the new table can be created and populated with the new records.

Changing local applications

Once the new databases and tables have been moved to the Server, you will need to examine your local applications.

Changing local application code

You will, at a minimum, have to add a few new commands to your applications. The SQL databases will need to be opened to use their tables, field names may have to be changed to reflect the new field names, and so on.

OPEN DATABASE / SET DATABASE TO. You will have to add the OPEN DATABASE <Server database alias name> to your code. This command is used to establish a connection with the Server database alias as defined in the IDAPI configuration utility. Unlike local tables, the Server database must be opened before you can access the tables inside it. When you open a database you may need to specify login parameters that the database needs.

When you set up the alias configuration information in BDE.exe, you will have to specify certain database specific information that is needed to make the connection. Once the connection is made, you can use traditional dBASE commands against the remote tables.

```
APPEND FROM
COPY TO
CREATE
```

You can also use the SET DATABASE TO command to specify a default database to use for the local commands (COPY, APPEND, BROWSE, etc.). dBASE lets you open more than one remote database at a time, from different formats. Using the SET DATABASE TO command simply specifies one of the open databases as the default type. Remember, an SQL database is a collection of tables—not the tables themselves.

USE :database:table. You can also use the standard use command with the database identifier name to open and create tables. For instance, the following command will open an SQL Server table named Demographics in the database Statistics:

```
USE :STATISTICS:Demographics
```

ERROR handling for REPLACES. You will probably have to add additional error handling code for all REPLACE commands against remote tables. Remember SQL databases don't support record level locking. You can use several new functions to assist you.

DBERROR()
Used to return the IDAPI error number for the error that occurred (or the last one that occurred). The error will be generated by the table that had some action taken against it, like a replace command. This lets you know if a "broken" record or file lock occurred against the SQL table.

DBMESSAGE()
Used to return the message associated with the error that just occurred against the current table. It is returned by IDAPI.

SQLERROR()
Returns the last Server error number reported by the Server.

SQLMESSAGE()

Returns the last Server error message reported by the Server.

Blank and duplicate record handling. Normally, SQL tables do not support blank or duplicate records. If the user tries to create a new record (APPEND, EDIT, or BROWSE) that will cause a duplicate or blank record, the program will report an error.

Deleting records. SQL tables do not mark records for deletion. They physically remove them. Any code that you have in your programs that mark records for deletion must be changed. Otherwise, the delete command will physically remove the record—permanently.

Possible add transaction sequence code. Because SQL tables use transactions instead of record locks and file locks, you may want to add transaction processing sequence code to your current applications.

Remove all hard-code path names. You will have to go in and change all references to local tables, replacing them with the remote table names. If you have path names in your code, it will also have to be replaced and alias database names and tables used instead.

Changing field names. You may have to change field names if you used special characters in your local table field names. Even if you didn't change the field names when you moved your data, IDAPI may have. You can use the remote table and LIST STRUCTURE to see what the new field names are. If they are different, any code that references them will have to be changed to reflect the new field names.

REPLACE ALL RECNO() with BOOKMARK(). If your code has any RECNO() functions in it, SQL tables do not use records. Instead of recno(), you can use the bookmark() function. The bookmark() function lets you set points in your table that can be gone back to later. The following code demonstrates use of the bookmark() function:

```
xREC = Recno()           && sets mark based on record number
DO WHILE ...
     * processing code here
ENDDO
GO xREC                  && return to record
*
*
xRec = Bookmark()        && sets mark in set
DO WHILE ...
      * processing code here
ENDDO
GO xRec                  && returns to same place in set
```

Change queries and forms for remote field information

You will have to go into your queries and forms and change the reference from the local to the remote table.

Queries. The query will have to be changed to reflect the new table names, based on the table name. You do not have to specify the database alias name, it can be handled by the USE and OPEN DATABASE commands.

Forms and reports. If your form uses queries, you will not have to change the *View* property. If the form doesn't use queries, you must change the *View* property to reflect the Remote table name.

All of the forms will have to make changes to the *DataLink, DataSource, Alias,* and any other properties that reflect field, alias, and table names. They will have to reflect the new table and field names.

Setting final touches

You will probably want to revise the logic in your applications to take advantage of transactions and provide for referential integrity by coding it in dBASE or invoking it at the Server-level. Use database Server features, like triggers and data dictionaries.

Specifying the location for integrity

You should set up your integrity at the table level in the Server. There you can define triggers that will perform cascade deletes and updates. This can be accomplished by creating triggers at the Server level. Once created, dBASE applications can be created independent of the data integrity issues. Any dBASE application can then have code in that will trigger the cascade delete or update, making it trigger automatically.

Working with automatic refreshes

SQL tables do not refresh automatically when the data changes. If you need to refresh your SQL data on the screen, you can use the new command REFRESH, which will force the data link to go out and refresh the data from the SQL tables.

The REFRESH command actually forces a new request for data from the Server. You can make refreshes appear automatic by activating the REFRESH command based on some timer event in the processing. Although you could refresh based on time events, it can be very time-consuming and waste connection cycles. A better way to refresh data would be to use a pushbutton attaching code to it to refresh data. Then, if users want to see new views (current data), they can simply press on the button to refresh the data. To use the REFRESH command type in the following syntax:

REFRESH <alias area number> | "<alias name/letter>"

The *Alias* name after the command can be the physical alias or a work area reference (1 to 225; **A** to **J**). The name must be enclosed in quotations.

MODIFYING CODE TO SUPPORT SERVER DATA

There are several new commands that can be used to help you when working with remote data. These extensions and new commands are enhancements to the dBASE language.

Working with external tables

There are several commands that assist you when working with Server tables.

OPEN DATABASE

This command will open any BDE/IDAPI alias, whether it is local, on a network (Standard), or Server database (Remote . . . specific type of database—Oracle, Sybase, Interbase, SQL Server, etc.).

The syntax is simply

OPEN DATABASE <aliasname> [LOGIN <username/password>]
[WITH <options string>]

<AliasName> is the name of the alias that was created in the BDE / IDAPI configuration utility.

When you login to a database, you may be prompted for specific information that is required by the connection. Using the option LOGIN and WITH options, you can automate much of the process.

<Username/Password> are the character strings that will be passed when prompted for a Username and/or password.

<Options string> is the character string that can be used to pass Server-specific information required by the particular database server you are connecting to.

The database Server information needed can be supplied to you by the Database Administrator. You may also want to consult with the Borland SQL Links documentation for specific Server-requested information.

If you want to specify the Password and Username each time a connection is made, do not use these two options and the Server will prompt you for them.

SET DATABASE TO

This command will let you specify *focus* for a particular IDAPI alias. Once set, all access and processing commands will work against that database's fields. To use it, you simply type the command:

```
SET DATABASE TO <alias name>
```

Bookmark()

This command places a "bookmark" reference to the current record (point in the data set). It is used in place of the RecNo() function for Paradox and SQL tables, which do not support record numbers. You use it by assigning it to a variable name:

```
xVariable = BOOKMARK()
```

SQLExec()

This function can be used to issue an SQL statement/command directly against local or Server tables. It uses the following syntax:

SQLEXEC(<Character Expression 1> [<Local Table Name>])

When you use it, IDAPI will return an error code back to let you know if it worked correctly. If it returns a zero, no error occurred.

The parameter <Char Expr 1> is the SQL statement itself. The second parameter <Local Table Name> is optional. It is used to return the answer set to a local table (dBASE or Paradox).

An example could be the following:

nVoid = SQLEXEC("SELECT Name, Address FROM Personnel WHERE ;

Division = 1001", "DIV1001")

This code will create a dBASE table (or Paradox if DBType is set to Paradox) of records from a Remote Oracle table named Personnel (which is in the database OPEN DATABASE).

Embedded SQL (ESQL)

➡ Visual dBASE has added the ability to embed SQL (ESQL) directly into your code. Using SQL in this manner allows you to create live and updateable views mixing SQL statements with standard dBASE commands (DML commands).

Local or remote data. Using ESQL, you can work with local (.DB and .DBF) or remote data. To work against local data, the tables must be aliased using the SQL engine of BDE. BDE will then perform the Database Manipulation Language (DML) commands against both types of tables (local and remote.) The DBE will optimize the performance against remote tables by passing SQL statements directly to the Server (back end) that is connected via SQL Links or ODBC.

SQL commands. The SQL commands that you use will depend on the back end (Server) you are working with. Because each Server may support different variants of the same command, the SQL statement that you build will specifically depend on the type of Server.

Working with stored procedures

➡ Visual dBASE has added the ability to work with procedures that are stored in a database server, known as *stored procedures*. To take advantage of existing stored procedures, you have to prototype them as if they were any other external function.

Using EXTERN to prototype

Before using a stored procedure, it must be prototyped using EXTERN. Once EXTERNed, it can be used like any other function in dBASE.

The EXTERN SQL statement. The syntax for the EXTERN statement of a store procedure is slightly different from an EXTERN statement of a DLL:

EXTERN **SQL** [<return type>] <procedure name> ([<arguments data types>])

[<database name>] [FROM <stored procedure name>]

SQL is a *required* keyword designator for the EXTERN statement. When Visual dBASE encounters this it knows to look for the procedure in the active database or the one specified in the <database name> option.

<Return Type> is the data type for any return value. Normally no value is returned. However, if a value is returned, you must specify the type of value.

<procedure name> is the *required* Name of the stored procedure. This is the name that will be used to call the procedure from within dBASE. It does not have to be the same name as the **actual** stored procedure name. Rather you can specify any name you want and point to the correct stored procedure name via the FROM <stored procedure name> option.

<arguments data types> are required if the procedure needs parameters.

<database name> is needed if the database name is different from the database specified in the SET DATABASE TO command.

FROM <stored procedure name>. If the <procedure name> is different than the <stored procedure name>, then this option is necessary to point to the correct procedure. It is also necessary when the procedure name needs to be qualified with a user name, package name, or report server address.

Notice that the keyword SQL has been added, and that the <return type> prototyping is optional. Normally, stored procedures only operate locally; therefore, they will not return a data value. However, if they do, like an alerter in Sybase, you must specify the type of data being returned. For instance, if the stored procedure returns an integer, you would specify CINT as the return data type.

Calling a stored procedure. Once a stored procedure has been EXTERNed using the EXTERN SQL command, you can call it as if it were any other dBASE function:

<Procedure Name>(<arguments>)

The CPRT and CPRTOUT arguments. If you need to pass or use arguments in a Stored procedure you can specify two different prototype argument types—CPRT and CPRTOUT.

The CPRT data type is the same as in other EXTERN statements. This specifies that the data type is used for input and for output.

The CPRTOUT data type is new. It is used to specify that the data type being passed is simply for output.

The SQLERROR() function. To determine if a stored procedure has executed correctly, you can use the SQLERROR() function. If it reports false, the stored procedure worked correctly.

Using stored procedures. The following code can demonstrate how to extern and access a store procedure. It will use a stored procedure named AverageGrade. AverageGrade is a procedure on the server that takes three values—StudentID, Quarter, and initial value:

```
OPEN DATABASE MyOracle1
SET DATABASE TO MyOracle1
EXTERN AverageGrade(CSTRING, CINT, CPTROUT)
*
cID = "IR001"
nQrt = 1
nAvg = 0
AverageGrade(cID, nQrt, nAvg)
IF SQLERROR() = 0
  ? "Server error -- " + SQLMessage()
ELSE
   ? TRIM(Last)+", "+TRIM(First)+" average is : "+
STR(nAvg)
ENDIF
```

This code will run the server stored procedure AverageGrade() that requires two arguments—one character-based (ID number), one numeric (quarter). Then it will store a numeric value in the third argument.

Automatic declaration of stored procedures

> If you want to declare all stored procedures in a database, you can use the optional keyword AUTOEXTERN with the OPEN DATABASE command. Visual dBASE has added this option, eliminating the need to EXTERN any stored procedure calls. Once the database is open, the stored procedures are automatically and immediately available.

The AUTOEXTERN option. As stated earlier, the syntax for the OPEN DATABASE is

OPEN DATABASE <database name> [LOGIN . . .] [WITH . . .] **[autoextern]**

If the new AUTOEXTERN option is included, dBASE will internally EXTERN all stored procedures that are on the server specified by the IDAPI <database name> of the BDE.

Working with tables

Visual dBASE offers several commands that can assist you when working with local tables and remote tables, intermingling them. These commands let you specify local default data types, work with a local table and all of its associate files (.dbf, .dbt, .mdx, etc.), even use remote tables like local tables. For instance, use a Copy command to copy remote table contents to a local Paradox table.

SET DBTYPE

You can specify which type of local table will be the default file extension type using this command. The choices are dBASE (.dbf) and Paradox (.db). This can be a useful command if you tend to use one table (Paradox or dBASE) more than the other. The default table type is dBASE. If most of your tables will be Paradox, you can set the type to Paradox.

```
SET DBTYPE TO Paradox
```

USE <tablename [.ext] I TYPE <dBASE I Paradox>

When mixing table types, you can open them using the standard USE command. When using the command, you can specify the extension (.dbf or .db) when opening the file or the new keyword Type. The following commands will work the same:

```
USE Customer.db
USE Customer TYPE Paradox
```

USE [:<dbname>:]<table name>. The USE command can also be used to open remote tables. If you use the OPEN DATABASE command, and then the SET DATABASE TO command, you can simply access any remote table like you do a local table—USE tablename.

However, if you do not SET DATABASE TO or forget to use the OPEN DATABASE command first, you can add the database name (alias) to the table name when you open the table. The following code will do the same thing:

```
OPEN DATABASE SQLServAnimals
SET DATABASE TO SQLServAnimals
USE Owners
OPENDATBASE SQLSerAnimals
USE :SQLSerAnimals:Owners
USE :SQLServAnimals:Owners
```

The third example will open a Login dialog box if the database isn't currently open. The second method is the preferred method for using remote tables.

APPEND FROM

This command can be used to append records into a local or remote table from a local or remote table. All of the following are examples of using the APPEND FROM command:

```
OPEN DATABASE Oracle_Vehicles
SET DATABASE TO Oracle_Vehicles
USE Vintage
APPEND FROM OldCars.db
APPEND FROM StateCars TYPE DBASE
SET DBTYPE TO DBASE           && default
USE OldCars
OPEN DATABASE Sybase_Cars
OPEN DATABASE Oracle_Vehicles
APPEND FROM :Sybase_Cars:Vehicles FOR CarYear<{01/01/52}
APPEND FROM :Oracle_Vehicles: Oracle_Vehicles FOR Age>25
```

COPY TO. This command works the opposite of the APPEND FROM command. Instead of adding records to the current open table, it copies records from the current open table to a NEW table in some format. It can copy to local or remote tables. It creates a new table, of the specified type, and copies records to it. The following are all valid examples of usage of the command:

```
USE Customer.dbf ORDER LastOrderDt
USE Orders.db ORDER CustID in B
```

```
SET RELATION TO CustID INTO Orders
COPY TO :Oracle_Person:ActiveCust FOR LastOrderDt>DATE()-
100
COPY TO Potential TYPE Paradox
COPY TO SendCust.db
```

Working at table level

There are several new commands that will let you work with tables and their associated files as one group. For instance, a dBASE table named Customer.dbf can have all the following tables directly associated with it:

Customer.dbf

Customer.dbt

Customer.mdx

The customer.dbf can also have several .NDX files associated with it.

A Paradox table can have all of the following associated with the Customer.db table:

Customer.db

Customer.mb

Customer.val

Customer.px

Customer.Xnn (nn is a number for each single-key secondary index)

Customer.Ynn (nn is a number for each single-key secondary index)

Customer.XGn (n is a number for each multikey secondary index)

Customer.YGn (n is a number for each multikey secondary index)

If you need to copy, delete, or rename the table, all of the associated tables also have to be renamed, deleted, or copied. You can accomplish this using the new table-oriented commands . . . COPY | RENAME | DELETE TABLE <table name>.

When these commands work, they will work with the database type specified. To use these commands, the table being worked with must be **closed**.

COPY TABLE. You can use this command to COPY the table and its associated files to a new table (giving it associated files). To copy the CUSTOMER.dbf and CUSTOMER.db to new dBASE and Paradox tables, use the following commands:

```
CLOSE DATABASE    && the table must be closed
USE Customer.dbf
COPY TABLE TO NewDCust
USE CUSTOMER.db
```

```
COPY TABLE TO NewPCust
```

These commands will copy all of the associated table files to the new database and associated tables.

NOTE: When you use this command with dBASE tables it will *not* copy associated .NDX files. It only copies the files that have the same base name as the table.

DELETE TABLE. When you use this command, it will delete the table and all associated table files related to it. For instance, if you want to delete all of the Paradox table files that you just created,

NewPCust.db

NewPCust.db

NewPCust.mb

NewPCust.val

NewPCust.px

NewPCust.X1

NewPCust.XG1

issue this command:

```
DELETE TABLE NewPCust TYPE Paradox
```

RENAME TABLE. If you need to rename a table and associated table files, use this command. It will rename the table and all associated files:

```
RENAME TABLE NewDCust.dbf TO XXX
```

MULTIUSER CONSIDERATIONS

The data integrity architecture of SQL databases is radically different from the architecture of dBASE. They use an entirely different scheme. The basic premise of Client/Server is that the Server controls the data integrity centrally.

This means that dBASE (and the local programmer) has lost control of the data integrity. This is actually a plus. Because you can move all the data integrity out of the local database applications (client apps) and place it central, maintenance of the integrity becomes a simple process. Only one site has to make modifications.

If a user changes a record in Browse (interactively), the Server, not dBASE, decides if the data will be changed—thus ensuring the data integrity.

This means that client programs will not have to maintain record change error handling routines in them. If the user makes a change to the data that violates the integrity rule set at the server, dBASE will inform the user of the conflict and the change will not be posted in the table. The program can then allow the user to make changes that will be accepted and resubmit the record for acceptance.

You can trap for errors using the DBERROR() function and ON ERROR command. These can be used to watch for Server rejection of records, determine why it wasn't accepted, and perform some action based on the error.

dBASE versus SQL locking

Even though SQL databases do lock records, they do not lock them the same way that dBASE does. dBASE is designed around a record-oriented schema. This simply means that records are modified one at a time. When a program places a lock on a record, no other user can access the record for changes to that record. All other records are not affected by the record lock. Before another user can change a locked record, it must be released.

To improve performance, most SQL database servers don't actually lock records, they lock the entire data page (many records) on which the records reside. When it locks an SQL record, other users are temporarily "stopped" from using any records in that page. A copy of the page is made (virtual table) and passed to the user. Then the other users do the same thing. No one actually uses live data from the underlying tables—they use copies of the data. The database does not automatically notify the user that they have been stopped, and when users get their copy of the records, they will not be notified that changes have been made to the underlying records while they are working with their view. To see any posted changes, they have to request specifically refreshed data from the Server.

Read-before-write approach

When working with SQL data, you should change the way you approach working with the records. You need to take what is known as a read-before-write approach. This approach minimizes record locking. The Borland Database Engine automatically supports this method when accessing SQL tables.

Transactions

Visual dBASE uses a new transaction processing model that is effective for the object-oriented and event-driven world of Windows and the Client/Server model.

Dialect-based transactions

Depending on where the transaction occurs, the transaction process will be different. It can handle local transactions against dBASE and Paradox tables or Server transactions against Server databases (Sybase, SQLServer, Oracle, . . .).

Each SQL database uses different dialect to perform transactions. IDAPI will convert the transaction requests to the appropriate dialect and rules that must be followed for the dialect.

Differences from dBASE transactions

There are three new functions that perform transaction processing:

- BeginTrans([“<database name> [, <isolation level>]]”)
- Commit([“<database name>”)
- RollBack([“<database name>”)

If you specify an SQL database name, the transactions will apply as local non-Server transactions.

➡ **The new BeginTrans Isolation Level option**
Visual dBASE has added an optional <Isolation level> option to the BeginTrans function. This can be called with or without the database name. For instance, the command BeginTrans(<isolation level>) will begin a transaction against the currently open database.

BeginTrans(). This function will start a transaction. All record and file locks are held until the transaction ends. If your database is specified, the transaction will work against the current database set with the SET DATBASE TO command.

If you can being a transaction, the command will return a true (.t.). The following syntax will begin a transaction:

```
xChk = BeginTrans()
xError = .f.
ON ERROR DO ChkError
IF xChk
    * USE ...
     *  transaction processing goes here
     * this would include the COMMIT() and ROLLBACK() code
ELSE
     *  transaction not possible at this time
     * display message to user
ENDIF
PROCUDURE ChkError
* error checking code here
```

```
*       you can use DBERROR() and SQLERROR()
*       to check the type of error
xError = .t.
RETURN
```

BeginTrans(<isolation level>). Using the new <isolation level> option of the BeginTrans() function, you can specify an isolation level based on one of four values:

1. 0—Use default isolation level on Server
2. 1—Dirty Read (uncommitted changes read)
3. 2—Read Committed (committed changes)
4. 3—Repeatable Read (full read repeatability)

If no isolation level is specified, level 0 will be assumed.

> **!** **Server specific**
> Isolation level support is Server specific. If you attempt to specify a nonsupported level, IDAPI will report a "Not supported" error. Interbase only supports Read Committed and Repeatable Reads. Oracle supports Read Committed and Repeatable Reads (as read-only). Sybase only supports Read Committed.

ROLLBACK() and COMMIT(). Both of these commands will end a transaction and release existing locks. The difference is what they do after ending the transaction.

The COMMIT() function will attempt to commit all changes (make them permanent) that have occurred before the Commit() function. If it can commit the changes, it will return a true (.t.). If an error occurs during the commit(), it will return a false(.f.)

The ROLLBACK() function will cancel the transaction and restore the open files to the state that they were in before the TRANACTION() function was issued. It will return a true (.t.) if the rollback was successful, a false if there was a problem.

The following code could be added to the IF xChk . . . ELSE . . . portion of the previous transaction code:

```
IF xError
   x=ROLLBACK()
    if .not. x
      ? 'The Rollback was unsuccessful ... you are in deep do do
"
    endif
  ELSE
     * commit code here
     x= COMMIT()
     if .not. x
      ? "could not commit changes"
      x=RollBack()
```

```
    if .not. x
       ? "couldn't roll back either ... I FAILED YOU"
    endif
  endif
ENDIF
```

Using transactions in forms

To use a transaction in the form, attach the BeginTrans() function as a method in the startup code for the form or attach it to a pushbutton. Attach Commit() and Rollback() to a pushbutton to finish the changes (either commit or abandon them). You should also place a Commit() or Rollback() to the OnClose event of the form. If you attempt to close a form while a transaction is active, you will receive a dialog box informing you of the problem.

What can you do in a transaction?

Once a transaction is active, you can perform any of these commands.

- APPEND
- APPEND BLANK
- APPEND MEMO
- REPLACE
- REPLACE MEMO/BINARY/OLE
- DELETE
- RECALL
- BLANK
- INSERT (in active indexes)
- BROWSE/EDIT
- @ GET . . . READ
- RLOCK()
- FLOCK()

Commands that cannot be used in transactions. If you use any of these commands in a transaction, an error will occur.

- PACK
- ZAP
- CONVERT
- DELETE TAG
- BeginTrans()

- `MODIFY STRUCTURE`
- `CLEAR ALL`
- `CLOSE ALL`
- `CLOSE DATABASE`
- `CLOSE INDEX`
- `CREATE FROM`

USING SQL IN VISUAL DBASE

➡ Visual dBASE has added additional support for using SQL. There are now five different ways you can mix SQL and dBASE operations:

1. Using the new SQL statement builder to build and understand SQL statements. This can be used as a tutorial utility to demonstrate the differences between SQL and dBASE commands.
2. Using dBASE's SQLEXEC() function to execute local SQL statements against local dBASE and Paradox tables interactively.
3. Using dBASE's SQLEXEC() function to execute pass-through SQL statements against data stored in an SQL Server.
4. Using the EXTERN SQL function to call a procedure stored on a remote SQL database server.
5. Embedding SQL statements inside dBASE programs and using the programs against local tables (dBASE and Paradox) or remote SQL Server data.

NOTE: SQL remote servers

Accessing remote SQL servers will require installation of Borland's SQL Links (a separate package) and setting up the remove server aliases using the BDE of Visual dBASE.

What is SQL?

SQL is a child of SEQUEL (Structured English QUEry Language), which was designed over twenty-five years ago at IBM. SQL was created to construct relational database management systems on *any* hardware platform. It was first available in 1981 in a commercial package and has become the standard language for networking query requests across different software and hardware platforms.

It is not a complete language; rather, it is a sublanguage that is used as an embedded language in an existing programming language. It can be used as both a Data Definition Language (DDL) and a Data Manipulation Language (DML).

Using SQL statements

When you use an SQL statement, you specify what you want to do with the data stored in a single table, just like you would with dBASE. However, SQL can work with more than one table at a time (similar to working with Queries in dBASE). For instance, consider the following:

- SQL statements can address multiple operations against more than one table at a time.
- SQL statements are nonprocedural. They work by specifying the operation to be performed against the data, not the procedural method of accessing it. The method of performing the action is determined by the SQL server.
- SQL statements work against a set of data. They are set oriented. This means that they operate on sets of records instead of individual records. By entering a single command, SQL will operate against a set of data.

Using SQL for DDL

As a DDL language, SQL can be used to Create, Alter, and Drop tables, indexes and views, Grant and Revoke rights to tables, and even assign default values to columns.

It can accomplish these tasks by using SQL commands like the following:

```
ALTER TABLE
CREATE INDEX
CREATE TABLE
CREATE VIEW
DROP INDEX
DROP TABLE
DROP VIEW
GRANT
REVOKE
```

Specific implementations will depend on the server table, or local table being worked with. For instance, the ALTER TABLE command can have several different options.

```
ALTER TABLE <table name> ADD PRIMARY KEY <expession>
ALTER TABLE <tablename>. DROP CONSTRANT <ID number>
ALTER TABLE <tablename> ADD FOREIGN KEY <expression>. .
.
ALTER TABLE <tableName> ADD CHECK <expression>
```

Using SQL for DML

As a DML language, SQL can be used to Select information from tables, Update column data (fields) in tables, Insert new rows (records) in tables, and even Delete rows (records) from tables.

It accomplishes these tasks by using SQL commands like the following:

```
DELETE
INSERT
SELECT
UPDATE
```

Using Embedded SQL

➡ Embedded SQL (ESQL), also called procedural SQL, lets you optimize your code for use with SQL data. This means that you can use commands like UPDATE (SQL) to perform set-oriented operations against the set-oriented SQL data.

When working with ESQL in Visual dBASE, you simply enter the command directly. This is different from previous versions of dBASE where you specifically had to turn SQL on with SET SQL.

IDAPI databases must be created. To use ESQL, you must specify an alias for the databases that you want to use SQL against in the BDE/IDAPI configuration program. The database must be opened using the OPEN DATABASE command.

If you use the SET DATABASE TO commands all SQL commands will be directed to the specified database. If you do not specify the SET DATABASE TO command, you will have to specify the database name with the table name when issuing SQL commands.

ANSI 1992 SQL support. To use SQL against local tables (dBASE and Paradox), Visual dBASE supports and conforms to ANSI 1992 SQL. This means that you work with local tables following the standards set by ANSI 1992.

When working with remote tables in Server databases, you will need to conform the SQL statements to the Server's dialect.

SQL Statement Builder

➡ The SQL statement builder is a utility that is supplied with Visual dBASE for creating SQL statements and learning the differences between dBASE and SQL. The SQL statement builder (SQL.WFM) lets you build SQL DML commands.

Working with the SQL Statement Builder

The SQL Statement Builder is automatically installed in the UTILS subdirectory of Visual dBASE when you choose full installation or use the Custom setup option and include "Utilities and Custom Controls."

Running the SQL Statement Builder. The SQL.WFM program will work with the Animals table by default. It can be used to teach you the syntax differences between dBASE and SQL. Figure 14–1 shows the SQL.wfm program running.

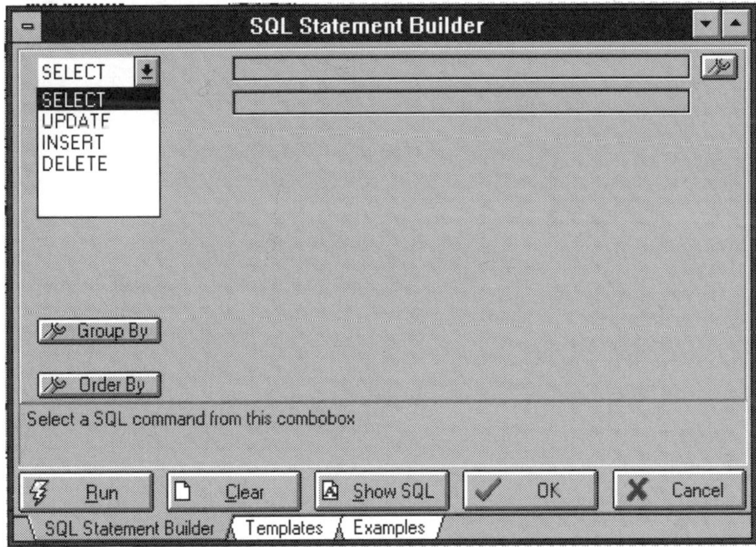

Figure 14–1. This is the SQL Statement Builder.

To run the form SQL.WFM, either change directories to the \VisualDB\UTILS directory or set the directory in the path using the SET PATH TO .; D:\VisualDB\UTILS command. Figure 14–1 shows the SQL Statement Builder running. Once active, you can use it to build SQL SELECT, UPDATE, INSERT, or DELETE commands.

Notice that the SQL Statement Builder has three tabs across the bottom. The first one gives you a page used to build SQL statements, the second offers templates, and the third uses examples to demonstrate an SQL statement versus dBASE statements.

A quick tour of the SQL Statement Builder

For example, you can select any table and build an SQL Select statement using the statement builder. Figure 14–2 uses a table named Customer. Then it looks for all records that have a Customer ID > "D," ordered by Customer ID number. If you build this statement using the builder and press the Show SQL button, your screen should look similar to the one in Figure 14–2.

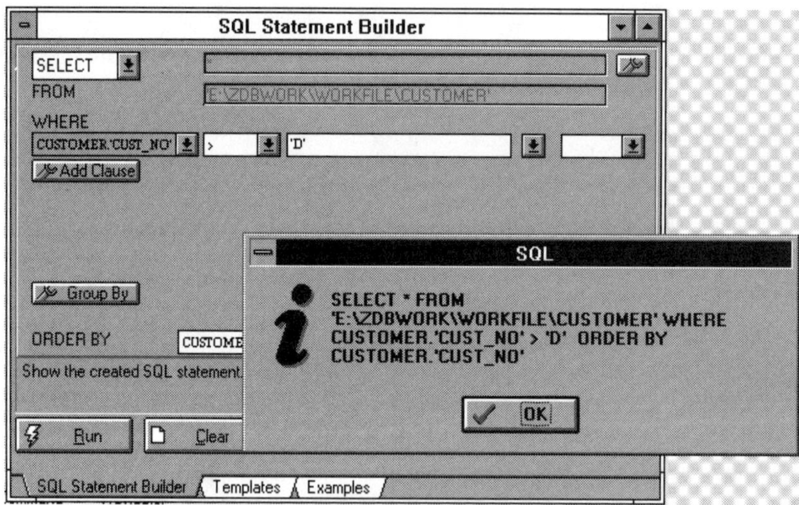

Figure 14–2. This is the SQL statement built by dBASE.

The WHERE clause. After you SELECT a table, SQL lets you specify a WHERE clause, like in the statement built in Figure 14–2. The WHERE clause lets you specify a logical constraint on the rows that will be displayed in the results table. It is similar to the SET FILTER command of dBASE.

The GROUP BY clause. You can also specify a Group By clause that will let you group aggregate functions to obtain averages, sums, and counts of any column in the data set. This clause is similar to the TOTAL ON command. Using the GROUP BY clause, dBASE will create an answer table.

The ORDER BY clause. This clause lets you specify a specific order to view the answer set in. It is similar to setting an index or using the SET ORDER command of dBASE.

The new Embedded SQL command of Visual dBASE

➡ Visual dBASE offers support for sixteen new SQL commands and functions. These commands can be used directly in dBASE code to perform DML actions.

The sixteen SQL commands of Visual dBASE

Table 14–1 shows the sixteen new commands and which types of SQL tables they work against—local SQL or pass-through SQL. Each command can be entered directly into dBASE case—thus, the name-embedded SQL:

Table 14–1. SQL Commands / Functions of Visual dBASE.

Command/Function	Local SQL	Remote SQL
`ALTER TABLE`	Yes	Yes
`COMMIT`	No	Yes
`CREATE INDEX`	Yes	No
`CREATE TABLE`	Yes	Yes
`CREATE VIEW`	No	Yes
`DELETE`	Yes	Yes
`DROP INDEX`	Yes	No
`DROP VIEW`	No	Yes
`GRANT`	No	Yes
`INSERT`	Yes	Yes
`REVOKE`	No	Yes
`ROLLBACK`	No	Yes
`SELECT`	Yes	Yes
`SET TRANSACTION`	No	Yes
`UPDATE`	Yes	Yes

Notice that several of the commands are only usable against SQL Server tables. Any of these commands can be embedded directly into your program code. Although the Table 14–1 suggests that the commands will work locally or remotely, they depend on the SQL support of each specific database Server. Therefore, the actual syntax may differ slightly between tables.

Part Five Building a Working Model

Chapter 15
Building the Application: Piece by Piece

This is the final chapter of this book. It quickly explores the Tools of dBASE and will build a complete object-oriented Windows application. It will attempt to cover all of the tools and build an application from scratch. It will accomplish this building on the knowledge you have gained throughout this book.

THE dLIBRARY SYSTEM

The purpose of the dLibrary System is to track book loans. This section builds the system, taking you through building the tables, forms, menus, and reports. It builds the major portions of this system, leaving some of the personalize portions for you to complete. Once you have finished this chapter, you will have a good working system that relies both on good database principals and object-oriented programming techniques.

The primary components

The primary components of the "dLibrary System" are

- A Switchboard (splash) screen with a graphic on
- A main menu system using pulldown menus
- Forms for viewing Customers, Orders, and books
- A popup menu (SpeedMenu) attached to the Customer form
- A form for Adding new Customers
- A form for Adding new Orders/Books
- A form for Finding a specific book by title or author
- Customer Search box
- An About box
- Two Complete Reports
- Ability to set user preferences

Now on to creating and tying the system together. It will lack any further reports that you may want to build, as well as any other forms for adding, viewing, or working with the underlying tables—for instance, statistical reporting, or easily updating existing records as books are brought back. This system can be easily modified or adjusted to use for tracking any type of sold or loaned information.

CREATING THE TABLES

Before an application can be created, you need to decide what type of information that you want to track and create your tables.

The tables needed by the system

This system will need five tables.

CUSTOMER.dbf
Holds customer specific information like name, address, credit information, and so on.

ORDERS.dbf
Holds visit-specific information, like date of visit, number of books borrowed, and if all the books were returned.

BOOKS.dbf
Holds records for each book borrowed per visit. Holds a book reference number, the due date, and if it (the single book) has been returned.

TITLES.dbf
Acts as a look-up for the BOOKs table. Holds the actual book title. Each physical book, although unique as a physical item, can be a copy of the same book. So, each physical book in the system that will be borrowed will be assigned a unique number for that book. In addition, there may be some books that have the same identical title yet are written by different authors. Again, this requires some way to identify each individual book. This table is used to assign a unique value to each physical book for reference by the Books table.

AUTHORS.dbf
Acts as a look-up for the Titles table. It holds the actual Author name(s). Because one author can write many books and the library can have multiple

copies of each author's book, you can identify each author by a unique identifier. If a book is a collective work of authors, then the collective names would be identified as a unique number, based on the collective work.

Understanding how the system works

To decide what tables will be needed, you need to consider how the actual book loaning occurs.

Customers can go to the library any number of time, generating a new order (or visit) record each time they go and borrow books.

Every time customers decide to borrow, they can borrow one or more books.

Each book can be borrowed by many different customers many different times; however, the physical book can only be borrowed by one customer at a time.

Each book is written by one or more authors. Each author can create more than one book.

Additionally, there can be any number of copies of the same book that are loaned by the library.

Finally, each book is written by a specific author or group of authors. Each author, or group of authors, can write more than one book.

Setting up the table relationships

With this understanding, the following relationship begins to materialize:

```
Each (1) Customer = Many Orders
   Each (1) Order = Many Books borrowed
      Each (1) Book borrowed = 1 specific physical book
         Each (1) Book = 1 Author
```

Now you have a working knowledge of the system. The time has come to create the tables.

The easiest way to create them is using the Table Designer. To create the Customer table, go to the Navigator and double click on the <Untitled> choice in the Tables container. Visual dBASE will display the new Table dialog box. Here you can select the Expert button or Designer button. For this exercise, simply click on the Designer button. An alternative method is to type the command CREATE in the command window. Either method will take you into the table designer that looks similar to the one in Figure 15–1.

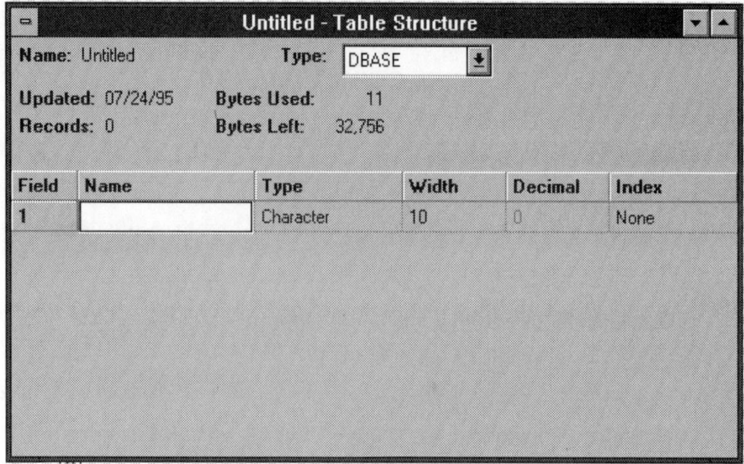

Figure 15–1. The Table Designer.

> ➡ **The Table Expert**
> Visual dBASE has added an expert that can assist you in creating tables. It lets you select from a series of sample tables and then specify the fields that you want from those tables; finally, it requests the type of local table that you want to create (dBASE or Paradox), and then it makes the table. It uses default field names and widths. Once you answer these questions, Visual dBASE lets you go into the Designer to modify the structure—add indexes, change field names, lengths and types, add additional fields.

While in the Table Designer, you can create local dBASE and Paradox tables. If you have Borland's SQL Link program, you can also create any Server tables that you have been given rights to in the database. This means that you can create tables for Server databases like Oracle, Sybase, InterBase, . . .

The Customer table

While in the Table Designer, type in the field names, types, and widths for the Customer table. The following is the structure for the Customer table:

Table 15–1. The CUSTOMER.dbf.

Structure for table CUSTOMER.DBF					
Field	**Field Name**	**Type**	**Length**	**Dec**	**Index**
1	CUST_NO	CHARACTER	4		Y
2	CUST_NAME	CHARACTER	35		N
3	ADDRESS1	CHARACTER	25		N
4	ADDRESS2	CHARACTER	25		N
5	CITY	CHARACTER	15		N
6	STATE_PROV	CHARACTER	12		N
7	ZIP_POSTAL	CHARACTER	10		N
8	TELE1_NUM	CHARACTER	10		N
9	TELE2_NUM	CHARACTER	10		N
10	CREDIT	LOGICAL	1		N
11	TOTALCREDT	NUMERIC	12	2	N
12	NOTES	MEMO	10		N
** Total **			170		

Customer.dbf indices. INDICES: The Customer table has one index on CUST_NO. If you didn't create it when you created its structure, create it now by using the command INDEX ON.

```
INDEX ON CUST_NO TAG CUST_NO
```

After creating the Customer table, you also need to create the following four tables and their indices:

The Orders table

The structure for the Orders table follows:

Table 15–2. The ORDERS.dbf.

Structure for table ORDERS.DBF					
Field	**Field Name**	**Type**	**Length**	**Dec**	**Index**
1	ORDER_NO	CHARACTER	5		Y
2	CUST_NO	CHARACTER	4		Y
3	LOAN_DATE	DATE	8		N
4	TOT_ITEMS	NUMERIC	3		N
5	RETURNED	LOGICAL	1		N
** Total **			22		

Orders.dbf indices. INDICES: The Orders table has two simple indices, indexed on ORDER_NO and CUST_NO. If you didn't create them when you created structure, create it now by using the command INDEX ON:

```
INDEX ON ORDER_NO TAG ORDER_NO
INDEX ON CUST_NO TAG CUST_NO
```

The Books table

The structure for the Books table is

Table 15–3. The BOOKS.dbf.

Structure for table BOOKS.DBF					
Field	**Field Name**	**Type**	**Length**	**Dec**	**Index**
1	ORDER_NO	CHARACTER	5		Y
2	BOOK_NO	CHARACTER	6		Y
3	DUE_DATE	DATE	8		Y
4	RETURNED	LOGICAL	1		N
** Total **			21		

The books.dbf indices. INDICES: The Books table has three indices, indexed on ORDER_NO, BOOK_NO and DUE_DATE. If you didn't create it when you created structure, create it now by using the command INDEX ON:

```
INDEX ON ORDER_NO TAG ORDER_NO
INDEX ON BOOK_NO TAG BOOK_NO
INDEX ON DUE_DATE TAG DUE_DATE
```

The Titles table

The Titles table structure is

Table 15–4. The TITLES.dbf.

Structure for table BOOKS.DBF					
Field	**Field Name**	**Type**	**Length**	**Dec**	**Index**
1	BOOKNUM	CHARACTER	6		Y
2	BOOKTITLE	CHARACTER	35		N
3	AUTHORNO	CHARACTER	5		Y
** Total **			47		

The indices of the Titles.dbf. INDICES: The Titles table has four indices. Two of them are simple and are indexed on BOOKNUM and AUTHORNO. They could have been created at the time you created the table. The other two are more complex and require building by hand. These are the BOOKORD index built on the formula—LEFT(BOOKNUM,2). The other is BOOKTITLE built on the formula—Trim(BookTitle).

If you didn't create the first two when you created structure, create it now by using the command INDEX ON. The other two will have to be created using INDEX ON.

```
INDEX ON BOOKNUM TAG BOOKNUM
INDEX ON AUTHORNO TAG AUTHORNO
INDEX ON LEFT(BOOKNUM,2) TAG BOOKORD
INDEX ON Trim(BOOKTITLE) TAG BOOKTITLE
```

The third index, BookOrd, will be used by one of the reports. The fourth index, BookTitle, will be used by a Find book form and will search on the Literal of the book title.

The Authors table

The final table for this system is the Authors table:

Table 15–5. The AUTHORS.dbf.

Structure for table AUTHORS.DBF					
Field	**Field Name**	**Type**	**Length**	**Dec**	**Index**
1	AUTHORNO	CHARACTER	5		Y
2	AUTHOR	CHARACTER	25		N
** Total **			31		

The indices of the Authors.dbf. INDICES: The Authors table has one index. It is a simple index on AUTHORNO. If you didn't create it at the time you created the table, do it now.

```
INDEX ON AUTHORNO TAG AUTHORNO
```

Adding test data to the records

Once you have created all five of the tables, you will need to add some data to each table. One way is to use the new command—GENERATE. This command will let you quickly add random data to the tables.

Generate xNum

You can add truly random data quickly to a table by using the GENERATE command. Use the following command to generate two records for the Customer.dbf:

```
USE CUSTOMER
GENERATE 2
```

You have just generated two random records for the Customer table.

Examining the random data. Now you can examine the contents of the two records added, using the GENERATE command, by editing the table. If you type EDIT you should see a screen similar to the one in Figure 15–2.

Notice that the data entered is truly random data. Each field has been assigned a value; however, there is no apparent logic to the data. It is simply random data. Using this command, you can quickly populate any table with useless data records. Even Memo file has been marked as containing data. This is the only field that is not populated with data. The Generate command simply marks the field as if it contained data. But the Memo field itself is empty.

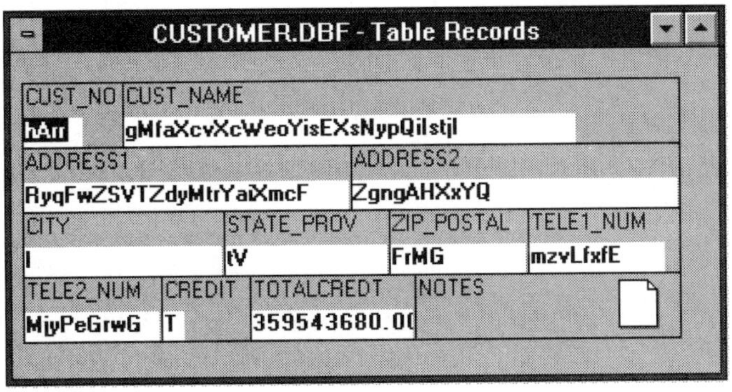

Figure 15–2. The data placed in fields with the GENERATE command.

Making the data sensible

To see some meaningful relationships, you will have to edit the Customer table and change the records to make sense. Then you will need to append records to the other four tables.

Customer.dbf. You do not have to modify all fields—only the ones listed in Table 15–6. The following fields should be changed to the values displayed:

Table 15–6. The Customer Data.

FieldName	First Record	Second Record
CUST_NO	I001	L001
CUST_NAME	Michael R. Irwin	Arni Brown
ADDRESS1	The Irwin Building	Evangelista Hospital
ADDRESS2	300 Indiana Ave	1020 West 40th St
CITY	Washington	Toronto
STATE_PROV	DC	ON
ZIP_POSTAL	20009	M2N 6P6
NOTES	This reader likes topics on history and computers	This reader likes topics on history and medicine

Orders.dbf. Now you need to create at least three records in the Orders table. Use Table 15–7 to place values in the fields of the first three records of the Orders.dbf.

Table 15–7. The Orders Data.

FieldName	First Record	Second Record	Third Record
ORDER_NO	95001	95002	95003
CUST_NO	I001	L001	L001
LOAN_DATE	02/02/95	06/01/95	08/03/95
TOTAL_ITEMS	2	1	2

Books.dbf. Working with the books table, add five records, placing the values in the fields specified in Table 15–8.

Table 15–8. The Books data.

FieldName	First Record	Second Record	Third Record	Fourth Record	Fifth Record
ORDER_NO	95001	95001	95002	95003	95003
BOOK_NO	HS2345	CP2112	MD9876	MD9877	HS2345
DUE_DATE	02/23/95	02/23/95	06/22/95	08/22/95	08/22/95

Titles.dbf. The titles table needs at least four records added. Table 15–9 shows the changes you should make to the titles.dbf.

Table 15–9. The Titles Data.

FieldName	First Record	Second Record	Third Record	Fourth Record
BOOKNUM	HS2345	CP2112	MD9876	MD9877
BOOKTITLE	The History of the World	The dBASE Book	Ear Surgery Procedures	Art of Colon Surgery
AUTHORNO	LB01B	IB01A	IE01A	ES01A

Notice that there are only four records here, although there are five records in the Books table. The fifth record in the Books table references is the same book as record 1 of the Books table.

Authors.dbf. The final table (authors.dbf) needs at least four records added. One for each new title in Table 15–9. Table 15–10 shows the first four records that should be placed the Authors table.

Table 15–10. The Authors data.

FieldName	First Record	Second Record	Third Record	Fourth Record
AUTHORNO	LB01B	IB01A	IE01A	ES01A
AUTHOR	Lim, Broken and Sorrow	I. M. Bad	I. B. Ent	Eu B. Slippery

MAKING THE QUERIES FOR THE SYSTEM

Many database application systems will use queries. A query is simply a view of information that is obtained from one or more tables.

If you are going to create forms that will display and edit fields from more than one table, you will need to create a query for the form to use. All reports also require a query if you are going to obtain data from more than one table. So you will probably want to create a few queries for the system.

You will need to create three queries for your system.

- BOOKAUTH.QBE
- ALL.QBE
- TITLEORD.QBE

The first two will be used for some of the forms; the last one will be used for one of the reports.

To create the queries, you can use the query design tool in dBASE. To start the Query Designer, click on the <untitled> name in the Query panel of the Navigator or type in the Command:

```
CREATE QUERY <query name>
```

As you enter the Query designer, you will be prompted for a table or query to open and use in the query design surface. The screen will look similar to the one in Figure 15–3.

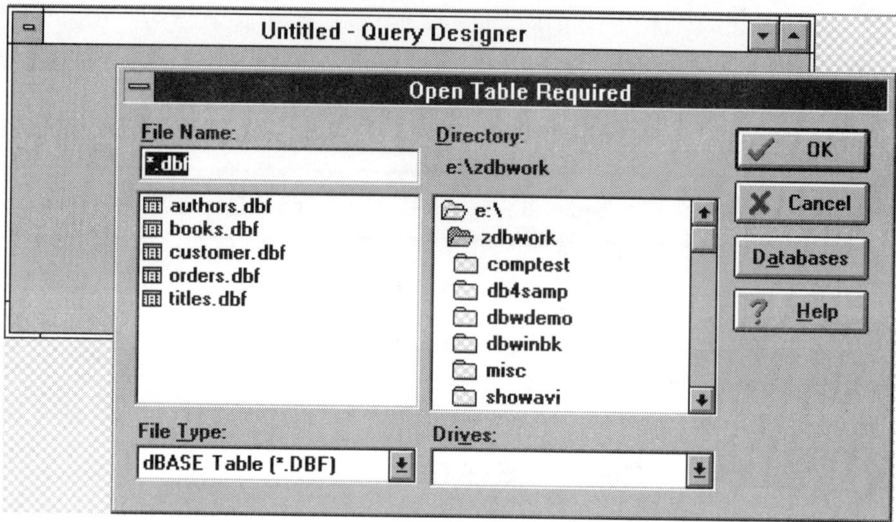

Figure 15–3. Entering the Query designer tool.

Select the Customer.dbf (table) and press the OK button. You will enter the query design surface and the table Customer.dbf will be brought in. Now you are ready to create the first query—ALL.qbe.

The ALL.QBE

This query will use all five tables and set one-to-many relationships between all of them. This query will be used by one of the forms that you will create. The screen should now look like the one in Figure 15–4.

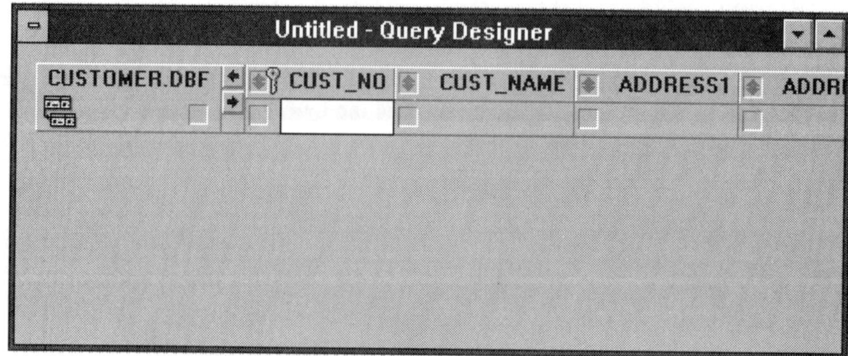

Figure 15–4. The query design surface.

The query design surface should be showing you the Customer table loaded in the Query Designer. If you added the wrong table, you can select the remove pushbutton on the speedbar. Figure 15–5 shows the add table button and the remove table button.

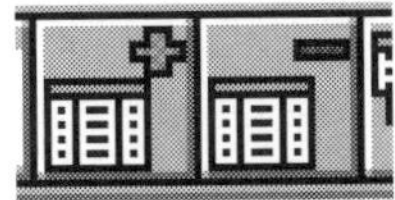

Figure 15–5. The add and remove table buttons.

Selecting and de-selecting tables

You will need to bring all the tables into the query. The order you want to bring the tables in will be

1. CUSTOMER
2. ORDERS
3. BOOKS
4. TITLES
5. AUTHORS

To add or remove a table, you use the add or remove buttons shown in Figure 15–5. These buttons are located in the middle of the speedbar. The one on the left (with the green plus sign) will activate the Add Table dialog box to select another table. The one on the right (with the red negative sign) will remove a table that you have clicked on in the design surface.

Add the Orders.dbf by selecting it from the Add Table dialog box. (Click on the add table button.) Now that the Orders table has been added, and it is located below the customer table in the Query Design surface.

Add the remaining three tables in the order needed—Books, Titles, and authors. The Query design surface should now look like Figure 15–6.

Selecting fields for the query

With all the tables selected and added, you are ready to pick the fields for the query. Go to the Customer table (the table on top) and click on the check box under the name of the table (the table name is on the left side of the structure). All of the fields should show checkmarks in them. The table name check box is used to select all fields.

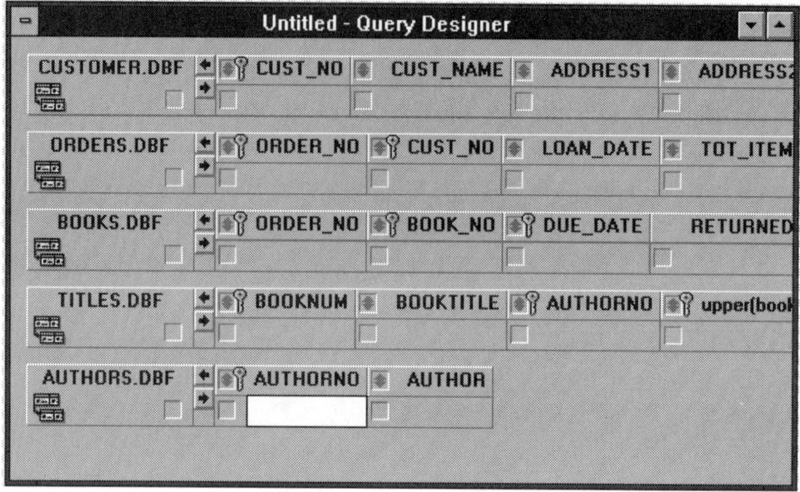

Figure 15–6. This is the query design surface with all five tables loaded.

With all the fields selected for the Customer table, you need to also select all the fields for the remaining tables. Once selected, your screen should look like the one in Figure 15–7.

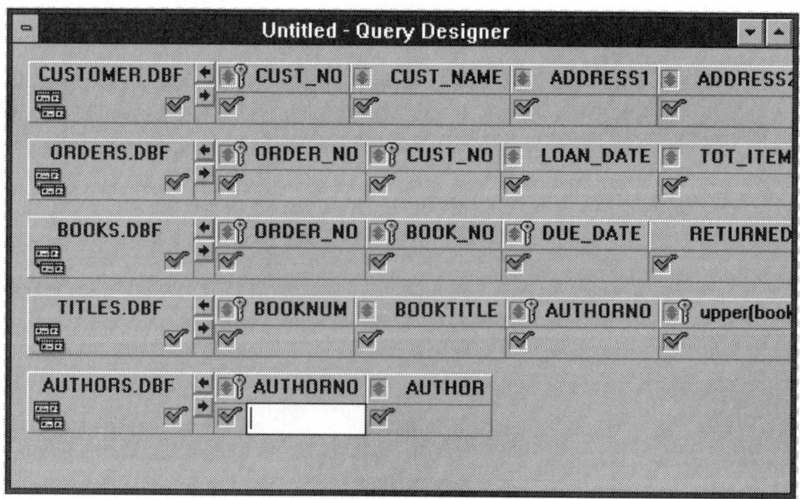

Figure 15–7. Selecting fields in a table for the query.

NOTE: Where are all the fields?

Notice that you do not see all of the fields for each table. You can click on the small arrows alongside of the table name to display more of the fields in the table. The two arrows (one pointing left—atop of the other one pointing right) can be used the same as the **Tab**, **Shift-Tab** key combination. The F3 and F4 keys will move you between tables, and the F5 key will select/de-select a field. These key combinations are the same as the dBASE DOS query tool.

Setting an index order

Looking at the Customer.dbf table skeleton, look at the first field CUST_NO. Alongside of the field name (left side) is a key. The key lets you know that there is an index that uses this field.

Next to it (left side) is a small box with what looks like a light gray directional arrow (going both up and down). Click in this box, and you will see a pulldown appear that looks similar to the one in Figure 15–8.

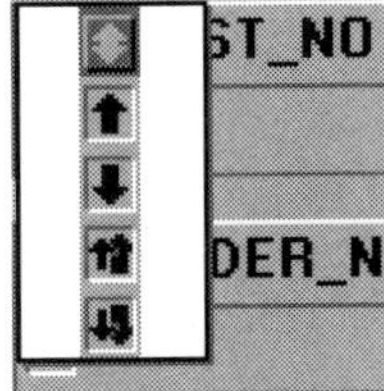

Figure 15–8. The index pulldown box.

This pulldown shows five different graphic arrow choices. The top one is a large arrow pointing up. These five arrows represent how you want to sort the data for the view:

Single up arrow	ASCII ascending sort (A - Z, a - z)
Single down arrow	ASCII descending sort (Z-A, z-a)
Two up arrows	Dictionary ascending sort (Aa - Za)
Two down arrows	Dictionary descending sort (Zz - Aa)
Up-down arrow	No sort order

With the pulldown active, select the first arrow (Single Up Arrow). This sets the query in order by the CUST_NO of the Customer.dbf.

Setting Customer-Orders relationship

Now you are ready to set the relationship between the tables. To set all the relationships between tables, you will set each relationship individually. In other words, you will set the relationship between the Customer and Orders table. Then you will set the relationship between the Orders and the Books table.

The mechanics of the Customer-Orders relationship. To set a relationship between the Customer and Orders table, go to the *table icon* under the name of the Customer.dbf (on the left side of the table skeleton). The mouse pointer will visually change to an arrow with a table icon under it. Click and drag the arrow to the *table icon* of the Orders.dbf. The table icon is the one that looks similar to the one in Figure 15–9.

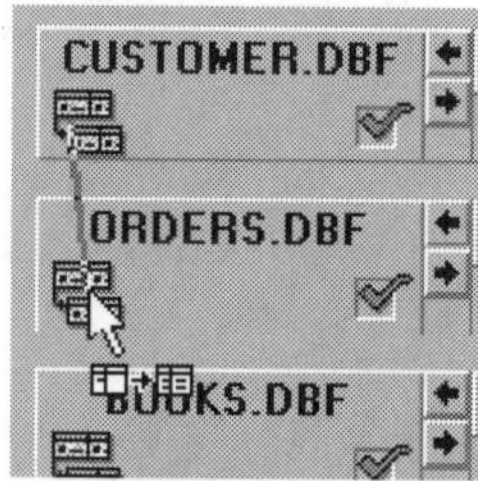

Figure 15–9. The table icon.

Notice that the pointer in Figure 15–9 has changed from a simple pointing arrow to an arrow with a table icon immediately below it. The table icon can be seen at the top, left corner of the Books table skeleton, covering the Books.dbf name. Figure 15–9 also shows the line that is dragged between the two tables when you click and drag the mouse pointer. When you release the mouse button, a Define Relation dialog box will appear. While in the dialog box, do the following:

1. Double-click on the field CUST_NO under the Customer table.
2. Double-click on the index name CUST_NO under the Order table.
3. Click the Every Parent check box on.
4. Click the Enforce Integrity check box on.

The dialog box should look similar to the one in Figure 15–10.

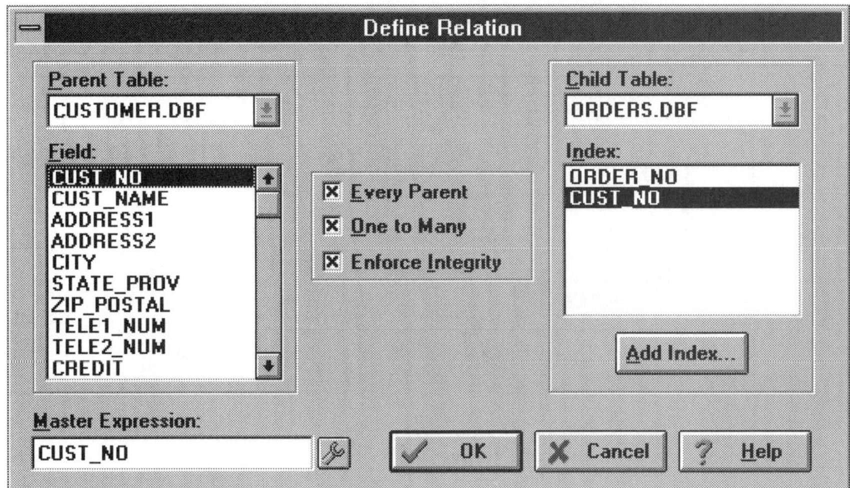

Figure 15–10. The Define relation dialog box.

Every Parent. This box is used to specify that every record in the parent table will appear in the view, whether or not it matches any records in the child table. If the box is left unchecked, only records in the parent table that match a record in the child record will be displayed.

One to Many. The box is checked by default. If you will have the potential for more than one child record against each parent record, leave this box on. In other words, will one customer probably go to the library and borrow books more than one time?

Enforce Integrity. This option applies only to queries that will be used as a *view* for a form. If the box is checked on, the Browse display will update automatically as you add records to the child table or the parent table. It will also ensure that you will not delete a parent record in a form if there are corresponding child records. It helps enforce data validation between the two tables (for both cascading deletes and updates).

Saving the relationship. With the relationship set, you click on the OK button to save it and return to the query design surface. Once complete, it should look like the one in Figure 15–11. As Figure 15–11 shows, you have only set the relationship between the Customer and Orders tables.

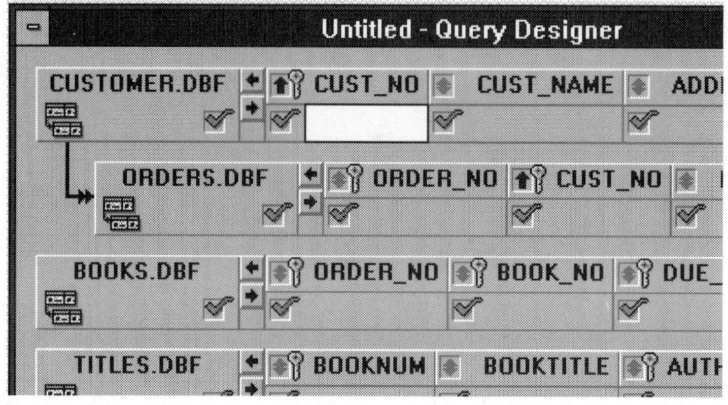

Figure 15–11. The relationship between Customer and Orders completed.

> ✔ **One-to-many indicator**
> Notice in Figure 15–11 that the Orders table has been indented from the Customer table and a linking arrow has been added between them. The arrow is a two headed arrow—it has two pointers on the end. This lets you know that you have checked the one-to-many option. If the relationship is a one to one, you will only see one head.

Setting the remaining relations

You now need to re-activate the Define Relation dialog box and set relations between the remaining four tables. When the dialog box appears you need to select all check boxes and set them on (Every Parent, One-to-Many, Enforce Integrity).

The relations are between these tables.

Orders to Books	Linked by ORDER_NO to ORDER_NO
Books to Titles	Linked by BOOK_NO to BOOKNUM
Titles to Authors	Linked by AUTHORNO to AUTHORNO

To set the relationship between Orders and Books, follow the steps you did above for the Customer to Orders. The difference is that you will go to the *table icon* under the name of the ORDERS.dbf (on the left side of the table skeleton). The mouse pointer will visually change to an arrow with a table icon under it. Click and drag the arrow to the *table icon* of the BOOKS.dbf.

Then once you are in the Relationship Builder dialog box, set the relationship and check all three check boxes on.

Perform these same steps between the other three tables. After you have completed the relationships, the query should look like the one in Figure 15–12.

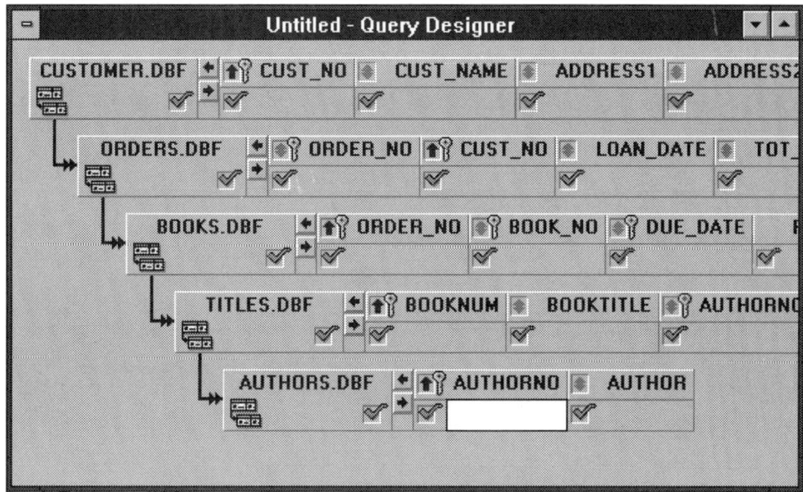

Figure 15–12. The relations for the ALL.qbe.

Saving the ALL.qbe query. To save the query, you can double-click on the system menu and answer yes to the query has changed dialog box, Save current changes. Another way is to press **Ctrl+S** or select File >> Save from the query design surface menu. Save the query and name it ALL.QBE.

The first query is complete. You are ready to create the BOOKAUTH query.

The BOOKAUTH.QBE

This query will be used by one of the forms. The form will let you search for a book by the author name or the title of the book. This query will use two tables—Titles and Authors. It will also exploit a powerful feature of dBASE—the ability to open a table more than once. It will actually use the AUTHORS table twice. The first instance of AUTHORS will be linked to the TITLES table for use in a Browse object and for setting filters. The second instance will be used by the form to select an author name in a list box. This second instance of AUTHORS will NOT be linked to the TITLES table.

Selecting tables for the BookAuth query

To create the Bookauth query you will need to open the Titles table first. Then, with the Titles table on the query work surface, add the Authors table two times. Then select all the fields from all three tables. The query should now look like the one in Figure 15–13.

Figure 15–13. This is the BookAuth.qbe with three tables selected.

> **!** **Tables automatically load with CREATE QUERY command**
> If you issue the Create Query command and the Design Surface shows a series of tables already loaded, you have just taken advantage of a feature of the CREATE QUERY command. When you type the command, Visual dBASE will look to see if there are any tables already in use in the current work session. If there are, dBASE automatically loads them into the Query Designer. If there is any relations between tables, it will also read them and automatically set them. Should this happen by mistake, you can abandon the query and use the command CLOSE ALL to close all the tables. You can also click on the Delete table button of the Speedbar, and the table being pointed to will be removed from the query. If a relation is set to another table, the relation will also be destroyed.

Setting relations between Titles and Authors

Once the tables have been added and all of their fields checked on, you are ready to set relations between the Titles table and the first instance of the Authors table.

Go to the *table icon* under the name of the TITLES.dbf (on the left side of the table skeleton). The mouse pointer will visually change to an arrow with a table icon under it. Click and drag the arrow to the *table icon* of the AUTHORS.dbf.

In the Define Relation dialog box, set the relationship between the two tables based on the AUTHORNO. Then make sure all three of the check boxes are checked. The Define Relation dialog box should look like the one in Figure 15–14.

With the relations set, save the relationship by clicking on the OK button. You will be returned to the Query Designer window.

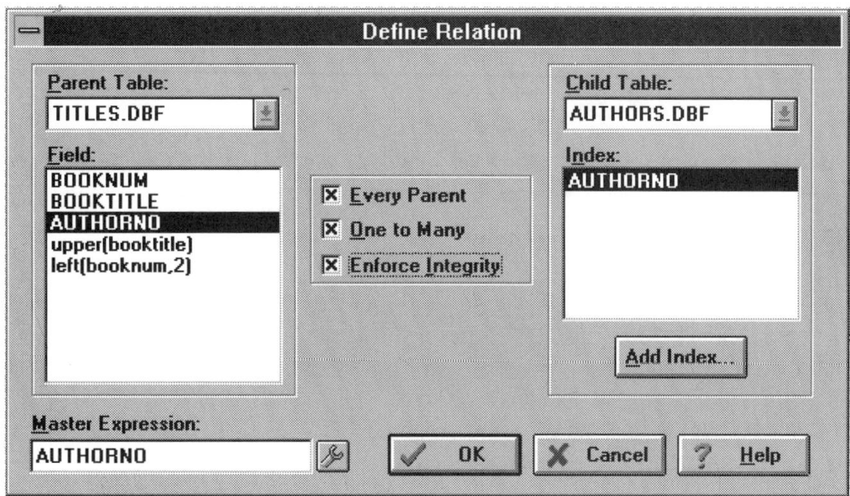

Figure 15–14. The relations between Title and Authors.

Using the second copy of Authors. The BOOKAUTH query should have a single relation between the Titles table and one copy of the Authors table. Figure 15–15 shows the completed BOOKAUTH query.

Figure 15–15. This is the complete BookAuth.qbe.

Notice that the second copy of Authors.dbf is in the query; however, it is not linked to either of the other two tables. The Authors table will be opened two times when the query is run. With the query complete you are ready to save the query, naming it BOOKAUTH.qbe.

The BOOKAUITH.qbe code

Once the query is saved, you should be aware of the alias names that will be used in the query. To determine the alias names you can use the query (SET VIEW TO BOOKAUTH) and then check using the function ALIAS() by moving to each work area, like this:

```
SET VIEW TO BOOKAUTH
SELECT A            && move to area 1 or a
? alias()           && displays TITLES
? alias(2)          && displays ATHORS
? alias(3)          && displays _3
```

Notice that the third alias has been named "_3". You will use this alias name in the form later.

You can examine the code to see how the query was created, but it will not reveal the alias names for each table. The following is the listing from the BookAuth.qbe:

```
* Visual dBASE .QBE file 9
CLOSE DATABASES
SET EXACT ON
*
* Opens the titles table in area 1
*
SELECT 1
USE TITLES.DBF ORDER TAG AUTHORNO
*
* Opens the authors table in area 2
*
SELECT 2
USE AUTHORS.DBF ORDER TAG AUTHORNO
*
*   sets relations between titles and authors
*
SELECT 1
SET RELATION TO AUTHORNO INTO AUTHORS CONSTRAIN INTEGRITY
SET SKIP TO AUTHORS
SET FIELDS TO BOOKNUM, BOOKTITLE, AUTHORNO, ;
                        BOOKORD=LEFT(TITLES->BOOKNUM,2), ;
TAG01=UPPER(TITLES->BOOKTITLE)
SELECT 2
SET FIELDS TO AUTHORNO, AUTHOR
*
*  Reopens the authors table (AGAIN) in another work area (3)
*
SELECT 3
USE AUTHORS.DBF AGAIN
SET SKIP TO AUTHORS
SET FIELDS TO AUTHORNO, AUTHOR
*
```

```
SELECT 1
GO TOP
```

As the code shows, there is no reference to the alias names for each table. This means that Visual dBASE will use default alias names.

Alias names of Query tables
Notice that the code does not tell you the alias name. You could modify the code to specify a specific alias for each table when it is opened—USE <table> ALIAS <aliasName>; however, it isn't necessary. Visual dBASE will automatically use the table name as the alias, unless the table is opened AGAIN. The second instance of the open table will be automatically assigned the underscore and the work area number—"_3"— as an alias name.

THE TITLEORD.QBE

This is the last query you will need to create. It will be used by one of the reports. It has two tables in it—TITLES.dbf and Authors.dbf. The two tables are linked by the AuthorNo field. You need to create it and go to the last field in the query.

The last field in the query is actually an index expression—*LEFT(BookNum,2)*. This expression is the index that you created when you created the table. It was named bookord. Go to the field and select the index order ASCII Ascending (Up arrow).

The query is now done. It should look like the one in Figure 15–16.

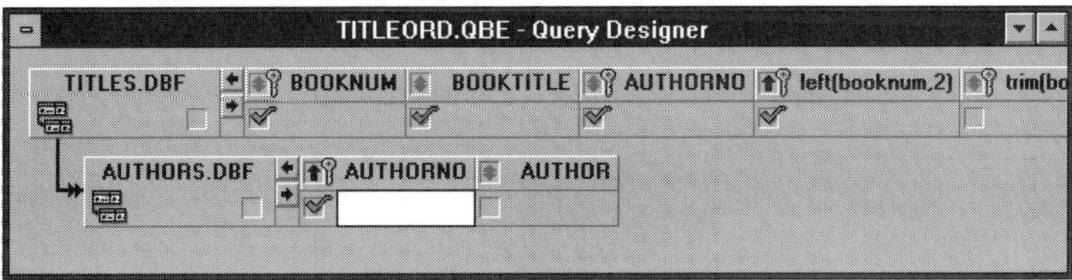

Figure 15–16. The TITLEORD query.

WORKING WITH THE FORMS

The form designer will be used to visually create all of the forms of the system. You will need to create seven forms:

```
MAINMENU.WFM        && main switchboard form
CUSTOMER.WFM        && used to display and add customers
FINDCUST.WFM        && used to locate an existing customer
FINDBOOK.WFM        && form used to locate a book
ORDERS.WFM          && main program for visits and books info
PICKBOOK.WFM        && used to select new books
ABOUT.WFM           && form used to display Help information
```

These forms will work together and become the primary application. The first form will be used to select the other forms. It will act like a *SwitchBoard*. It will drive all of the other forms.

All of the forms will contain, within themselves, all the procedures they need (methods) and will execute the code based on certain events occurring. Some of the code will affect tables that are displayed in other forms.

You can easily create these types of forms using the graphical tools of Visual dBASE.

The MAINMENU.wfm

This menu will have a simple graphic on it and several pushbuttons. Later you will create a menu bar that can be attached to this main menu form. It should look like the one in Figure 15–17 when it is completed.

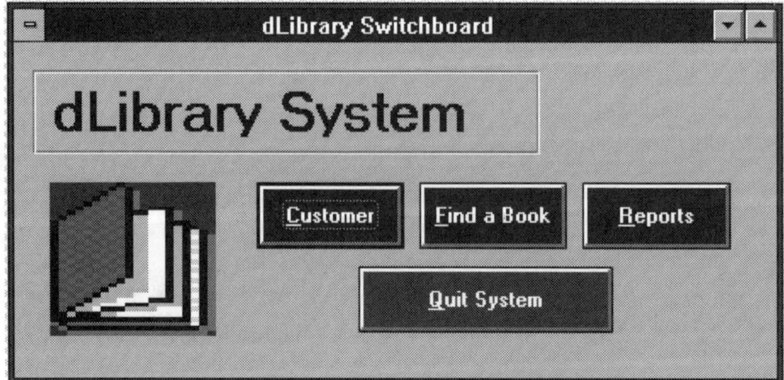

Figure 15–17. The main switchboard.

Creating the basic form and control objects contained in it

Go into the Form Designer and resize the form to about the relationship you see in Figure 15–17. Then add the following control objects to the form, setting their properties (through the property inspector) following these nine steps:

1. Select a rectangle and place it toward the top—stretching it (about 4 inches by 1 inch) to look like the one in Figure 15–17. Set its properties—Text + "" to nothing (empty this property).
2. Select a text object and place it inside the rectangle you just created. Then set its properties—Text dLibrary System, FontSize 25, Width (stretch the box long enough to see the full text).
3. Select an image object and place it below and left of the rectangle (the book picture in Figure 15–17). Then set its DataSource property to RESOURCE #641. When setting the DataSource you can click on the tool (wrench) button on the right side and use the Choose bitmap dialog box. (Select RESOURCE and click on the new wrench button, going to #641.)
4. Select a pushbutton and place it on the form making it proportionate to the Customer button as in Figure 15–17. Set these properties—Text &Customer, ColorNormal W*/B*.
5. Copy the Customer button by pressing **Ctrl+C** while the button is highlighted. Then paste the button back by pressing **Ctrl+V**. One button will be placed on top of the other one.
6. Move the pasted button to the right of the Customer button. Change the property, Text, to &Find a Book.
7. Copy either button and paste it again.
8. Move the new pasted button to the right of the Find a Book button. Change the Text property to &Reports.
9. Finally, create one more button and make it longer than the other three, and place it below and center of the other three. Change these properties—Text &Quit System and ColorNormal W*/R*.

Setting several event properties

Now that the visual portions of the form have been created, you are ready to create a few event handlers (object methods, functions/procedures). You will need to assign event handlers to the OnClick event properties of the buttons. You will also need to create the methods (event handlers) that will be assigned to the OnClick properties.

The OnClick of the Exit button. While in the form designer, follow these steps:

1. Set focus (click on) to the Close button, activating it.
2. Once active, activate the Property Inspector.
3. Click on the Events tab.
4. Select the OnClick property of the Exit button.
5. Type in the following codeblock:

```
{;form.Release(); release fMain}
```

Notice that there are two semicolons in the codeblock—one leading (at the first position) and the second one between the two commands. This codeblock will close and release the form from memory. Then it will release the memory variable *fMain* from memory.

NOTE: The fMain memory variable

The variable fMain will be manually inserted into the program MAINMENU.WFM after you have completed creating the form in the Form Designer.

The OnClick of the Customer button. Like the Exit button, select the Customer button in the form and then select the OnClick property for it.

Selecting objects in the Inspector
Although you can continue to switch back and forth between the Form Designer and the Inspector, if you know the name of the object (control of the form), you can directly select the object name from the combo box of the Inspector.

To create a method for the Customer button, follow these steps:

1. Click on the wrench button of the OnClick property.
2. Visual dBASE opens the Procedure Editor.
3. Type the following four lines of code into the editor:

(Do *not* add the first line of the procedure; it will automatically be added by Visual dBASE. If the customer button was not created first, it may have a different number after the word PUSHBUTTON; do not worry about it.)

```
Procedure PUSHBUTTON1_OnClick
   form.visible = .f.
   create session
   do customer.wfm
   return
```

When the user clicks on the Customer button, the form will be made invisible (not closed) and a second form named Customer.wfm will be run in its own session.

NOTE: Using RETURN for procedures

Although you are not required to use the Return command when creating procedures, it is a good idea to get in the habit of using it. By always using RETURN as the last command, you will visually recognize the end of the procedure. It also makes use of the command consistant with Functions. You are required to use the RETURN command with functions, specifying a value.

The Find a Book button. Like the Customer button, click on the OnClick property of the Find a Book button (PUSHBUTTON2), activate the procedure editor, and type in the following method (the top line should already be there):

```
Procedure PUSHBUTTON2_OnClick
    form.visible = .f.
   create session
   do findbook.wfm
  return
```

Like the Customer button, this procedure will hide the MainMenu form and run another form, named FindBook.wfm.

Saving the form

The form is now fairly complete. You haven't added an event property to the Reports button; however, it can be added to the form later. Save the form, and return to the Command window.

Modifying the code for the MainMenu.wfm form

Now that you have created the event handlers (codeblocks and procedures) for the buttons on the form, you need to make a few minor changes to the code generated by Visual dBASE's form designer. Use the command MODIFY COMMAND MAINMENU.WFM to enter the program editor. An alternative method is to highlight the form name in the Navigator and select Edit as Program from the SpeedMenu (right mouse click). Visual dBASE will load the form program into the Editor.

Adding some code to the form MainMenu.wfm. To work with all the forms of the dLibrary system interactively, you will need to modify the code to do two things:

1. Make the name of the form available to all other running forms.
2. Make the form name unique.

To accomplish this, you will need to specify a unique form name for the MainMenu form when creating the form object with the NEW Operator. You will also need to specify that this name is declared PUBLIC.

The code changes of the MainMenu.wfm form. When you examine the code created by the form designer, you will notice that all forms, created by Visual dBASE, have the same first nine lines of code. These nine lines of code (between the top remark lines and the CLASS declaration command) should look similar to the following:

```
*
parameter bModal
local f
f = new MAINMENUFORM()
if (bModal)
   f.mdi = .F. && ensure not MDI
   f.ReadModal()
else
   f.Open()
endif
CLASS MAINMENUFORM OF FORM
```

It declares a variable ***f*** as local, and uses ***f*** for the name assigned to the form object reference variable (f = NEW <MyClass formname>().

➡ **The bModal parameter**

Visual dBASE has added code that will let you open a form as modal or nonmodal. If you want to open a form as modal, you can run the code passing a logical true (.t.) to the code, using a command like this.

```
DO Customer.WFM with .T.
```

Visual dBASE will change the Multiple Document Interface (MDI) property to false (.f.) and then open the form as modal, READMODAL(). Only non–MDI forms can be opened in a modal state. This code is not present in dBASE for Windows 5.0 forms.

All nine of these lines between the remarks and the Class declaration will need to be removed and the following three lines of code added.

```
*
PUBLIC fMain
fMain = new MAINMENUFORM()
fMain.Open()
CLASS MAINMENUFORM OF FORM
```

This code will declare a Public variable fMain that can be used by any open forms. It will be used when returning to the MainMenu form from the Customer and Find a Book form. They will check to see if there is a form object named fMain alive in memory. If it is, it will change the fMain form object's visible property to .t., making the MainMenu form re-active.

Once added, you can save the form, pressing **Ctrl+W**, or selecting File>>Save from the menu.

The CUSTOMER.wfm

This form will be used to capture customer information. You can use the Form Expert to help you create the basic form and then modify it, changing a few colors and adding the pushbuttons to it. When created, the form should look similar to the one in Figure 15–18.

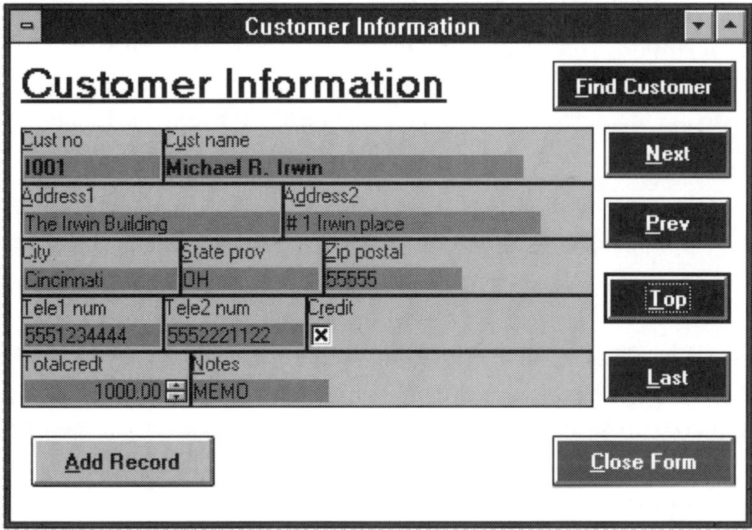

Figure 15–18. The complete Customer form.

This form will be used to display customer information and add new customers to the Customer.dbf. If the user clicks on the Add Record button, two new buttons will appear and the user will be able to add new records. Figure 15–19 shows the two new buttons, added between the Add Record and Close Form buttons. They are added when the user clicks on the Add Record button and lets them save a record or abandon the record when it is typed in.

Figure 15–19. These are the two buttons used for adding records.

Three new form objects

The form will take advantage of three new form level methods that Visual dBASE has added to form objects—BeginAppend(), SaveRecord(), and AbandonRecord(). Using these three methods, you can add records to a table using the tables phantom EOF() record (an empty record buffer). By adding records, one at a time, to this phantom record, you can abandon the new record without, physically, adding an empty or bad record to the table.

Creating the basic form and its control objects

To create this form, you need to use the Form Expert. You can start by selecting the [Untitled] form from the Navigator and then clicking on the Expert button. An alternative method is to use the command CREATE FORM EXPERT from the Command window.

Once the Form expert has begun, follow these steps to create the basic Customer form:

1. Select the Customer.dbf from the first screen, then click on the Next button.
2. Select all fields, then clicking on the All fields right button (>>) click the Next button to move to screen 3 of 5.
3. Select the Layout Style of Form Layout (top right picture in Layout section).
4. Click on the Associate Control types button to activate the dialog box.
5. Click on the Reset button to reset field associations to default, then click on the OK button to return to screen 3. Click the next button to move to screen 4 of 5.
6. Select the Scheme GRAY from the combo box in the center of the dialog box, then click on the next button.
7. With the form complete, click on the Design button to take the completed form into the design surface to finish working on it.

The form should now look like the one in Figure 15–20.

Finishing the Customer form

With the basic form in place, you are ready to make some minor changes to the existing objects and then add several pushbuttons. Finally, write some methods that will be used to form the form. Remember, the Customer form should look like the one in Figure 15–18.

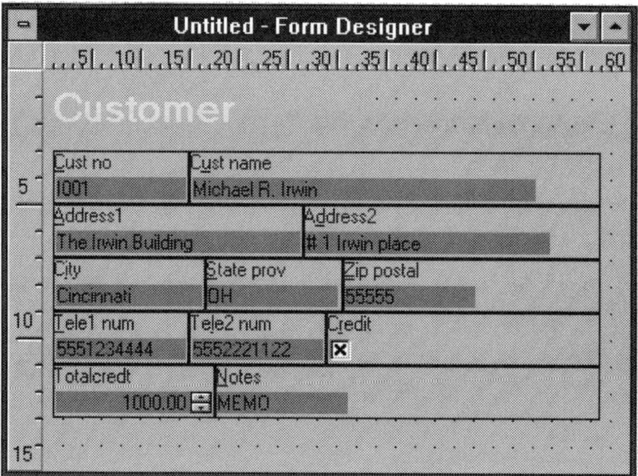

Figure 15–20. The partially created Customer form.

The following steps will modify the existing objects and add the new pushbuttons to the form, Customer.wfm:

1. Select the form object and change its ColorNormal property from "W" to **W+** or **W*** to make the form background bright white (versus light gray). Stretch the form to a sufficient width to add buttons along the right side and length to add buttons across the bottom.
2. Select the object Form.title (the Yellow title of the form), then change its Text property to "Customer Information." Stretch the width to fit the text. Change the Underline property to True (.T.). Finally, change the ColorNormal property to N/W* (black on white).
3. Place a pushbutton on the form to the right of the Cust name field.
4. With the pushbutton on the form, change these properties: ColorNormal **W*/B**, Text **&Next**, TabStop **.f.**, FontBold **.T.**, Height **1.8**, and Width **12**.
5. Copy the Next button by highlighting it and pressing **Ctrl+C**.
6. Paste the copied Next button and move it below the Next button (alongside of the Address2 field).
7. With the second button active, change the Text property to **&Prev**.
8. Now repeat the process of copying and pasting one of the blue buttons. Place this button to the right of the Credit field, below the Prev button. Once placed, change its Text property to **&Top**.
9. Again copy one of the blue buttons and paste it below the Top button, alongside of the Notes field and change its Text property to **&Last**.

At this point, the form should look like Figure 15–21. Notice that the four directional buttons are alongside of the main display portion of the Customer information.

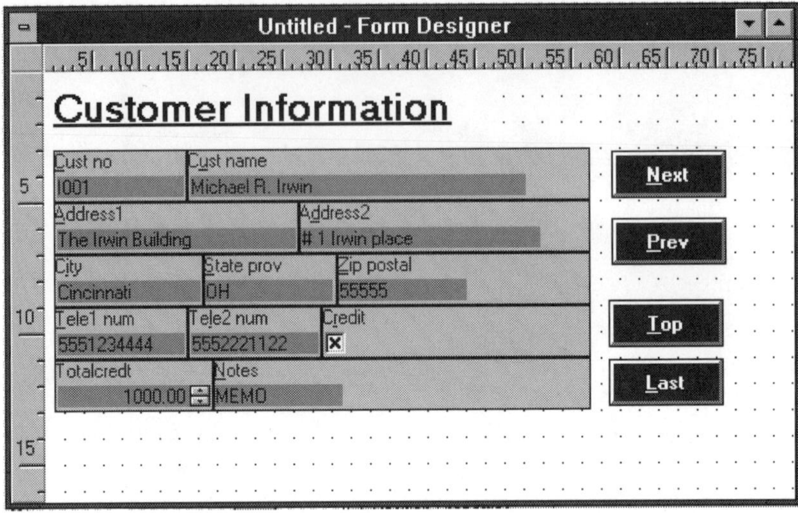

Figure 15–21. This is the Customer form being created.

Now you are ready to place the remaining five buttons on the form.

10. Select one of the blue buttons and copy and paste it above the Next button, at the top of the form. Then change these properties of the button: Text **&Find Customer**, ColorNormal **W*/N**, and Width **18**. Finally, visually move it so that the right side of the button aligns with the right side of the other four blue buttons.

11. Copy this Find Customer Button and paste it below the Last button, at the bottom right corner of the form. Change these properties: Text **&Close Form** and ColorNormal **W*/R***.

12. Copy the Close form button and paste it to the left bottom corner, under the TotalCredit field. Then change these properties:Text **&Add Records** and ColorNormal **N/W**.

13. Create a rectangle between the Add Records and Close Form buttons along the bottom and change these properties: Text (empty—no text), ColorNormal **W*/N**, BorderStyle **2- Lowered**, PatternStyle **1-BDiagonal**.

14. Copy any of the blue buttons and move it inside the rectangle between the Add Records and Close Form. Then change these properties: Visible **.F.**, Height **1.5**, Text **&Save**, and ColorNormal **N/W**.

15. Copy the Save button and paste the new Save button to the right of it, in the rectangle (next to the Close button). Change its Text Property to **A&bandon**.

The visual parts of the form are now complete and the form should look like the one in Figure 15–22. Notice that this is still an unnamed form and you are still in the Form Designer.

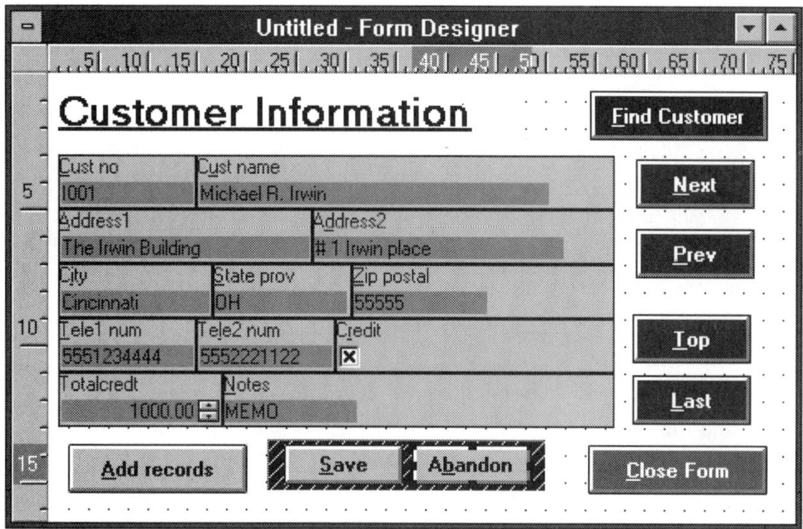

Figure 15–22. This is the complete visual portions of the Customer form.

Now, you are ready to add the methods to the event properties.

Setting the event properties for the Customer form

This form will need several methods for some of the form events and a codeblock or method for each pushbutton. The form has five basic groups of events handlers (codeblocks or procedures) that must be created.

- Form level
- Closing form button
- Navigational buttons
- Finding customer button
- Adding new records button

The form-level event procedures. You will need to create methods for three properties—OnOpen, OnClose, and OnGotFocus.

The OnOpen will be used to set up the initial environment for the form. This will include creating a few new form properties and externing the Windows MessageBox function.

To create the procedure for the OnOpen event property, click on the OnOpen event property cell of the form and click on the wrench button to open the Procedure Editor. Once in the Editor, the first line should already be present (Procedure FORM_ONOPEN), type in the following procedure for the OnOpen property:

```
Procedure Form_OnOpen
    form.RecNo = RECNO()
    form.CUAEnter = SET("CUAE")
    form.outside = .f.
    EXTERN CWord ;
         MessageBox(CHandle, Cstring, Cstring, CWord) USER.EXE
```

This event creates three new form properties—RecNo, CUAEnter, and Outside. Each of these are assigned an initial value. The Outside property will be used to determine if the user has left the form to run the FindCust form. The CUAEnter property will be used when adding records. The RecNo property will be used to determine if the form needs to be refreshed (viewing the correct record).

With the OnOpen event procedure created, you need to create an event procedure assigned to the OnClose event of the Customer form. This procedure will close the database, release the form, and then release the variable reference for the form. Finally, it will determine if the main menu is active and, if so, make the main menu visible. Create the OnClose procedure by clicking on the OnClose event cell, then typing in the following event procedure:

```
Procedure Form_OnClose
   close database
   form.release()
   Release fCust
   if type('fMain') = 'O'
     fMain.visible = .t.
   endif
```

Notice that this event checks to see if the *fMain* is an object (form). It sets its visible property to true. It also closes the database and releases the form.

Finally, the OnGotFocus event needs to have an event procedure created that will be used to update the record pointer if the user leaves the form and selects a new customer to view. The procedure for the OnGotFocus event property is

```
Procedure Form_OnGotFocus
    if form.outside
      form.outside = .f.
      go form.RecNo
    endif
```

This procedure simply checks to see if the form's Outside property has been set to true (.t.). If it has, it goes to the new record in the table, updating the form.

The Close Form button. This group comprises a single button—the Close Form button. The purpose of this button is to close the form. This can easily be accomplished by assigning a codeblock to the OnClick property of the button. You can set the codeblock directly in the Property inspector. Go to the OnClick cell and type in the following codeblock:

```
{;form.Close()}
```

The Find Customer button. The OnClick property of the Find Customer button is another procedure. The procedure looks like this.

```
Procedure PUSHBUTTON5_OnClick
     form.outside = .t.
     Create Session
     DO FindCust.wfm
```

This procedure sets the Outside property of the form to true (.t.). Then, it runs the FindCust form allowing the user to select a new customer from a list.

The navigational buttons. There are four basic navigational buttons—Next, Prev, Top, and Last. The Next and Previous buttons will let the user move through the records, forward and backward, one record at a time. The Top and Last buttons take the user to the first and last record of the table.

The Next button will need to skip to the next record of the table. After skipping, it needs to determine if it has moved to the end of the file; if yes, go back to the last record of the table. The event procedure is

```
Procedure PUSHBUTTON1_OnClick
     SKIP
     IF EOF()
       go bottom
       form.Recno=Recno()
       ?? CHR(7)
       MessageBox(_app.framewin.hWnd,;
            "This is the Last Record","Alert",0)
     ENDIF
```

The name of the procedure may be different if you have not created this button first, earlier in this section. Notice that the procedure will activate the MessageBox of Windows and inform the user that they have reached the last record.

The next procedure that needs to be created is for the Prev button. This button will skip back one record at a time. The procedure is

```
Procedure PUSHBUTTON2_OnClick
   *
   * The first BOF() is to check if already at BOF()
```

```
* from the VCR buttons built into the Speed BAR
*
 IF BOF()
   GO TOP
 ENDIF
 skip -1
 IF BOF()
   GO TOP
   ?? CHR(7)
   MessageBox(_app.framewin.hWnd,;
          "This is the first record","Alert",0)
 ENDIF
```

Notice that this button will also display the MessageBox, informing the user that they have reached the first record of the table. It immediately checks for the beginning of the file, in case the user uses the navigational buttons on the SpeedBar. When the user goes to the first record using the Navigator and then clicks on the back button, the record pointer will point to the beginning of the file marker (BOF). Clicking on the Prev button will attempt to move the pointer beyond the BOF marker, creating an error. Therefore, it is necessary to immediately check for the BOF() status.

The next two buttons, Top and Last, can be set using a codeblock. Going to the Top button and clicking on the OnClick property of the top button, enter the following codeblock:

```
{;go top;form.recno = RECNO()}
```

Notice that this codeblock has two commands—Go Top and form.RecNo = RecNo(). They are seperated by semicolons. You also need to place a semicolon at the beginning of the codeblock.

The final navigational button is the Last button. It also uses a codeblock assigned to its OnClick event property.

```
{;go bottom; form.recno=Recno()}
```

The Add Records buttons. Adding records uses three buttons—Add Records, Save, and Abandon.

The Add Records button will make the Save and Abandon buttons visible (and the box they are found in). It will go to the bottom of the table and use the new Visual dBASE, BeginAppend(), method of the form.

```
Procedure PUSHBUTTON6_OnClick
     set cuaenter OFF
     form.rectangle1.visible = .t.
     form.pushbutton8.visible = .t.
     form.pushbutton9.visible = .t.
     GOTO BOTTOM
     SKIP
```

```
        form.BeginAppend()
```

This code sets the CUAEnter value to OFF. When set to Off, pressing the **Enter** key will move to the next field of the form, like it does in dBASE DOS. The code also makes the two buttons visible and then begins to add records to the Customer form.

> ➡ **The BeginAppend() method**
> This method is new to Visual dBASE. It lets you progammatically begin adding records to the existing table using the current form. The dBASE for Windows 5.0 could only duplicate this ability by using the menu choice Form >> Add Records (Ctrl+A). The BeginAppend() method of a form will go to the phantom record (pointer to end of file) and begin adding information to this phantom record. Then, using the new SaveRecord() method of a form, the current record can be saved. Visual dBASE has also added an AbandonRecord() method that can be used to abandon the changes.

With the Add buttons method created, you need to create a method for the Save button. This is the event procedure that you will create.

```
Procedure PUSHBUTTON8_OnClick
    IF form.IsRecordChanged()
      form.SaveRecord()
      GO BOTTOM
      SKIP
      form.BeginAppend()
    ENDIF
```

> ➡ **The IsRecordChanged() method**
> This procedure uses the new IsRecordChanged() form method to determine if there have been any changes to the current record. If there have been changes, the record is saved and the BeginAppend() is performed again to add another record.

The last procedure needed for the Add records is the procedure for the Abandon button:

```
Procedure PUSHBUTTON9_OnClick
   xAns = messagebox(_app.framewin.hWnd,;
        "Are you sure you want to abandon this Record" ,;
         "Abandon Record", 4)
   IF xAns = 6
     form.AbandonRecord()
     form.rectangle1.visible = .f.
     form.pushbutton8.visible = .f.
     form.pushbutton9.visible = .f.
     go bottom
```

```
    if type('form.CUAEnter')="C" .and. form.CUAEnter =
"ON"
       set CUAEnter ON
    endif
  ENDIF
```

This procedure will run the MessageBox function to verify that the user wants to quit adding records and abandon this record. If the user answers Yes, the record is abandoned and the Save and Abandon buttons are hidden. It also returns to the last record of the form and if the CUAEnter switch was originally on, it resets the switch to on. If the user answers No, the procedure returns to the record to continue adding information.

The procedures are now complete for the Customer form. It can be saved and tested.

Modifying the Customer form

Like the Main menu form, you need to make a few minor changes to the code generated by Visual dBASE's form designer to the Customer.wfm. Use the command MODIFY COMMAND CUSTOMER.WFM to enter the Program Editor. An alternative method is to highlight the form name in the Navigator and select Edit as Program from the SpeedMenu (right mouse click). Visual dBASE will load the form program into the Editor.

Adding some code to the form MainMenu.wfm. To work with all the forms of the dLibrary system interactively, you will need to modify the code to do two things:

1. Make the name of the form available to all other running forms.
2. Make the form name unique.

To accomplish this, you will need to specify a unique form name for the Customer form when creating the form object with the NEW Operator. You will also need to specify that this name is declared PUBLIC.

The code changes of the MainMenu.wfm form. When you examine the code created by the form designer, you will notice that all forms, created by Visual dBASE, have the same first nine lines of code. These nine lines of code (between the top remark lines and the CLASS declaration command) should look similar to the following:

```
*
parameter bModal
local f
f = new CUSTOMERFORM()
if (bModal)
   f.mdi = .F. && ensure not MDI
   f.ReadModal()
else
   f.Open()
```

```
endif
CLASS CUSTOMERFORM OF FORM
```

It declares a variable *f* as local, and uses *f* for the name assigned to the form object reference variable (f = NEW <MyClass formname>().

All nine of these lines between the remarks and the Class declaration will need to be removed and the following three lines of code added.

```
*
PUBLIC fCust
fCust = new CUSTOMERFORM()
fCust.Open()
CLASS CUSTOMERFORM OF FORM
```

This code will declare a Public variable fCust that can be used by any open forms. It will be used when returning to the Customer form from the Find Customer form. It will check to see if there is a form object named fCust in memory.

Once added you can save the form, pressing **Ctrl+W**, or selecting File>>Save from the menu.

FINDCUST.WFM

This form uses a single table—Customer. The form's *view* property needs to be set to CUSTOMER.DBF. Once completed, it should look like Figure 15–23.

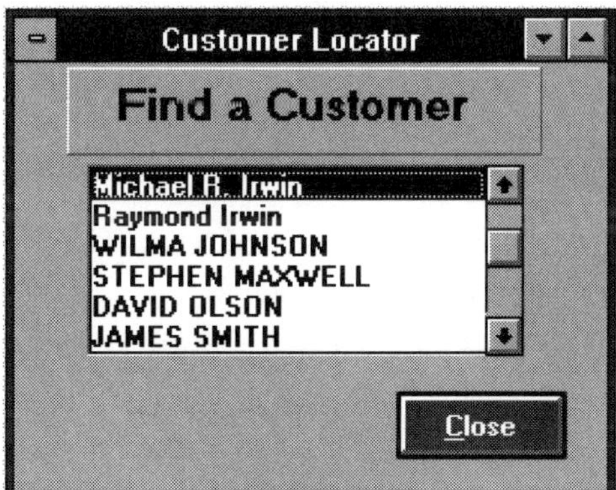

Figure 15–23. The completed FINDCUST form.

Notice that the FindCust form uses four control objects.

- Rectangle
- Text
- Pushbutton
- Listbox

Building the FindCust form

Create the visual portions of this form, including the Close button.

Setting the form properties. The form itself should have the following properties set—Text **Customer Locator**, Top **8**, Left **45**, Width **43.5**, Height **11.5**, and View **Customer.dbf**.

It should also have the OnOpen event property set using a codeblock. It should be set to

```
{;SET ORDER TO CUST_NO}
```

Once the form properties are set, you need to create the four control objects of the form.

The Rectangle of the FindCust form. At the top of the form, create a rectangle and set the following properties—Top **0.125**, Left **3.8**, Width **34.8**, Height **2.4**, Text **""**, Border **.T.**, and BorderStyle **1**.

With the rectangle created and its properties set, you should create the text object that will exist on the rectangle.

The Text object of the FindCust form. Inside the rectangle you need to place a text object and set these properties—Top **0.4**, Left **7.5**, Width **27**, Height **1.7**, FontSize **14**, and Text **Find a Customer**.

The Close pushbutton of the FindCust form. Now you can add the Close pushbutton and set these properties—Top **8.8**, Left **28**, Width **12.5**, Height **1.8**, Text **&Close**, and ColorNormal **w*/r***.

The Listbox object of the FindCust form. The last object you need to create is a listbox object. It should have the following properties set—Top **2.8**, Left **5.5**, Width **32**, Height **5**, ColorNormal **N/W***, ColorHighlight **W*/N**, and DataSource **FIELD CUSTOMER->CUST_NAME**.

Notice that you had to set the DataSource for the listbox. Although the form's *view* property is set to Customer.wfm, you still need to set the *DataSource* property of the listbox. This property is given the value

```
FIELD CUSTOMER->CUST_NAME
```

It uses the keyword FIELD to tell dBASE that it wants to build the list from a field. The other options are Array, File, Structure, and Tables.

You can use the built-in tool to fill this field or type in the value.

Saving the FindCust form. Once the four control objects are created, save the form naming it FindCust.wfm.

Creating a single method for the FindCust form in Editor

You only need one method for this form, attached to the Close button's OnClick property. However, because this is a Windows application, it would be nice to create a method on the *OnLeftDblClick* property of the listbox that lets the user leave the form either way. The method needs to reset the *RecNo* property of the fCust form if it is open. Then it needs to close this form. Once the RecNo property is set to the new record in the fCust form, when the user is returned to the fCust form (Customer form), the form will point to the new record.

You could create two identical event properties using the form designer by typing in the same procedure two times, attaching it to each event property—OnLeftDblClick of the listbox and OnClick of the pushbutton. However, it would mean that you have the same procedure typed in twice.

There is no easy way to assign a single Class level procedure to event procedures using the form designer. However, once a form is saved, you can manually insert the event procedure into the Class definition and then assign it to the two control objects. To add an event procedure named PickDone, type in the following command from the command window:

```
MODI COMM FINDCUST.WFM
```

Once in the Editor, locate the DEFINE LISTBOX LISTBOX1 command and place a comma and a semicolon after the last property of the listbox LISTBOX1, then add the following new line of code to the command:

```
ColorHighLight "w*/n" , ;
OnLeftDblClick CLASS::PickDone
```

Notice that the comma and semicolon are added to the line above the new line added. The ColorHighlight "W*/N" should be the last line of the listbox DEFINE command. If it isn't in your form, simply add the comma and semicolon to the last property and then add the new line of code.

> ! **Using the CLASS:: command**
> You must specify the DOUBLE set of colons when assigning the CLASS procedure PickDone to an event property. If you fail to use the double set of colons, Visual dBASE will report an error.

With the OnLeftDblClick property set for the the listbox, you now need to do the same thing for the Close pushbutton (named PUSHBUTTON1) of the form. Add the same basic command and the comma, semicolon to the pushbutton Define statement. This time, set the procedure against the OnClick property:

```
ColorNormal "w*/r*" , ;
OnClick CLASS::PickDone
```

If ColorNormal is not the last property, simply assign a comma and semicolon to the last command, then add the new line of code OnClick CLASS::PickDone.

Now that the PickDone event procedure has been assigned to both the OnClick of the pushbutton and the OnLeftDblClick of the listbox, you need to create the Class procedure named PickDone. Go to the bottom of the Class definition, just above the ENDCLASS construct, and type in the following procedure code:

```
    OnLeftDblClick CLASS::PickDone
  Procedure PickDone
   if Type("fCust") = "O"
     fCust.RecNo = RECNO()
   endif
   form.Close()
ENDCLASS
```

With the procedure added, you can save your work and test the program.

The FindBook.wfm form

The FindBook form can be used to find any book in the system. You can find a book by entering an author name or the name of the book title. You can also find an author by selecting from a list of books, or selecting an author and seeing all of the books written by the author.

The three pages of the FindBook form

This form has three pages; each page can be accessed via a tabbox control located along the bottom of the form.

The first page of Findbook.wfm. Figure 15–24 shows the first page of the FindBook form.

Notice that the form in Figure 15–24 has a TabBox object across the bottom. These tabs let you choose any of the three pages of the form—Locate, By Author, or By Title. It shows the first page (locate) of the form. This page can be used to find books or authors by typing in a complete or partial name of the author or book. If there are any books or authors matching the request, they will be displayed in a browse object at the bottom of the first page.

Figure 15–24. This is the FindBook form.

The second page of Findbook.wfm. If the user clicks on the By Author tab, they are taken to the second page of the form. Figure 15–25 shows the second page of the form.

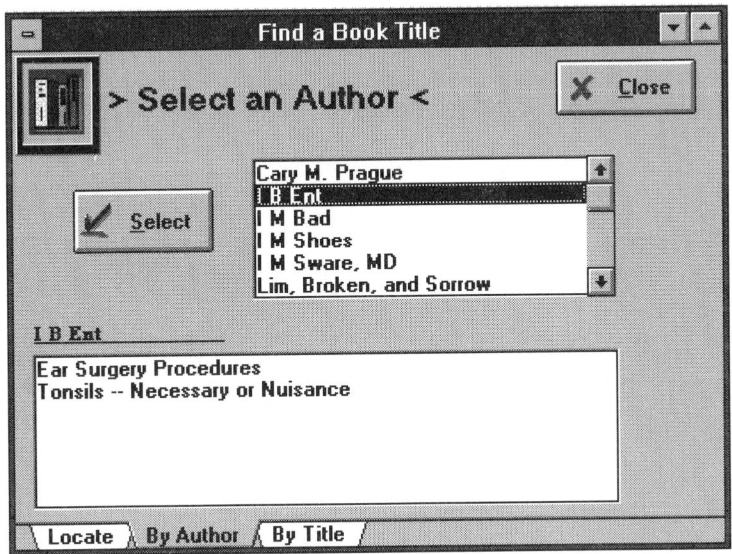

Figure 15–25. This is the second page of the FindBook form.

Notice that the second page, as shown in Figure 15–25, uses two listboxes. The top one is used to select an author. The second one will display all works of the author.

The third page of Findbook.wfm. Finally, if the user clicks on the third tab, they are taken to page 3 of the form. Figure 15–26 shows the last page of the form.

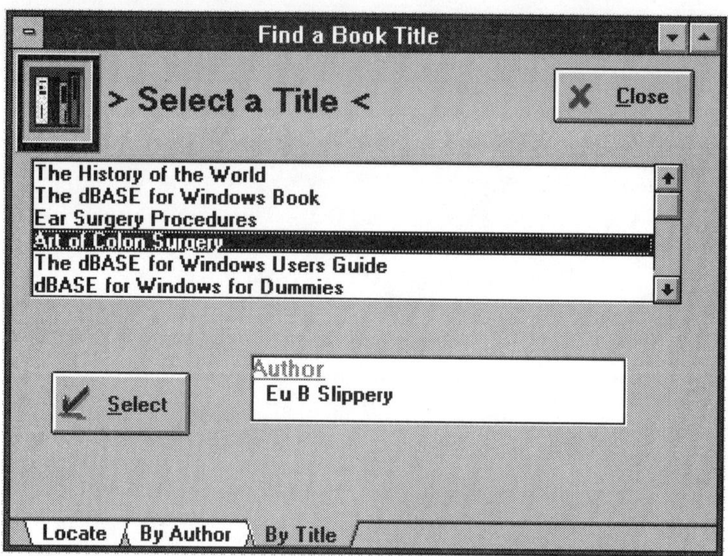

Figure 15–26. This is the last page of the FindBook form.

This third page uses one listbox, displaying all the book titles and one text object to display the author's name. Each physical book has only one author (the author can be one or more persons).

Common elements of all pages in Findbook.wfm.

➡ Notice that all three pages have a couple of objects the same—the TabBox, the Close button, and the graphic in the top left corner. When working with multiple pages in forms in Visual dBASE, you can specify a value of 0 for the pageno property of a control object. By assigning the value 0, Visual dBASE will place this control on all pages.

This simply means that you do not have to re-create the same control over and over for each page.

The Findbook form and PageNo 0 objects

The Findbook form has two event procedures attached to the OnOpen and OnClose of the form. It also has several objects that are contained within it and assigned a PageNo of 0.

The FindBook form view property. This form uses the BookAuth query. This is the one that has two copies of the Authors table in memory. The second copy is in area 3, and has an alias of "_3". The second copy of the Authors table will be used by the listbox of author names on the second page.

The two form event handlers. The OnOpen procedure of the form will have to perform three actions—set the order of the tables to natural, set the CUAEnter switch ON, and create a new array object for the form. This array object will be used by the second listbox of page two in the form. The following is the code for the OnOpen event procedure:

```
Procedure Form_OnOpen
     set order to
     SET CUAEnter ON
     form.BookList = new array()
```

The OnClose procedure will need to perform just like the OnClose of the Customer form. It will release the current form, release the form variable name (fFind), and make the main menu form visible, if it exists. The code is:

```
Procedure Form_OnClose
   close database
   form.Release()
   release fFind
   if type('fMain') = 'O'
     fMain.visible = .t.
   endif
```

The control objects of PageNo 0 in the form. The form has five control objects that have their PageNo property set to 0. They include the Close button, two rectangles and an image object (top, left corner), and the TabBox along the bottom of the form. The visual portions of the five objects are self-explanatory. Once created you need to attach a few event handlers to some of the objects.

The Close button event handler. The Close button has a single codeblock attached to the OnClick property:

```
{;form.close()}
```

The TabBox event handlers. Two event handlers need to be created for the TabBox along the bottom of the form. The first one is attached to the OnOpen property. It can be a simple codeblock that passes the value stored in the CurSel property of the TabBox to the PageNo property of the form:

```
{;this.cursel = form.pageno}
```

This codeblock is used in case the form opens on a page other than the first page.

In addition to the OnOpen property, you need to create an event procedure and attach it to the OnSelChange property of the TabBox.

```
Procedure TABBOX1_OnSelChange
     form.pageno = this.cursel
     SET FILTER TO
     DO CASE
       CASE form.Pageno = 1
          form.radiobutton1.setfocus()
       CASE form.pageno = 2
          form.browse1.visible = .f.
          form.listbox1.setfocus()
ENDCASE
```

This event procedure sets the form.pageno property to the value of the selected tab. It then turns any filter off and checks to see what page it is currently on. Depending on the page, it sets focus to one of the objects on the page.

The first page of the FindBook form

Of the three pages, this one probably has the most complex event procedures attached to it. It contains all of the objects specified with a PageNo of 0, plus nine additional objects:

- Two rectangles and a text object associated with the title across the top
- One text object for the match section
- One browse object to display the user's request
- Two radiobuttons for selecting a category
- One entryfield for the user to enter information
- One find pushbutton to find the user's choice

All of the new controls on page 1 have their PageNo property set to 1.

The Default property of the Find pushbutton. The pushbutton has one interesting property set—the Default property is set to true (.T.). The close button, also on the form, is set to .f.. By setting the default property value of one pushbutton to .T., when the user presses the **Enter** key (and CUAENTER is ON), Visual dBASE will default the action associated with the pushbutton that has a true value. In this case, it will be the Find button on page 1.

The two radio buttons and the single entryfield have a procedure attached to their OnGotFocus properties. The pushbutton has an event procedure attached to its OnClick event property.

The procedures of the radiobuttons. The two radiobuttons have similar event procedures—they move the entryfield so that it aligns next to the selected radiobutton and then sets the focus to the entryfield.

The radiobutton that has the text of Author has the following procedure associated with its OnGotFocus event property:

```
Procedure RADIOBUTTON1_OnGotFocus
     form.entryfield1.top = 5
     form.entryfield1.setfocus()
```

The radiobutton that has the text of Titles has the following procedure associated with its OnGotFocus event property:

```
Procedure RADIOBUTTON2_OnGotFocus
     form.entryfield1.top = 6.5
     form.entryfield1.setfocus()
```

Notice that they both move the control object ENTRYFIELD1, then they set focus to the entryfield.

The procedure of the entryfield. The entryfield, EntryField1, also has a procedure associated with its OnGotFocus, which is

```
   Procedure ENTRYFIELD1_OnGotFocus
     form.browse1.visible = .f.
     set filter to
```

It hides the browse object and clears any filter that might be set.

The procedure of the Find pushbutton. This is clearly the most complex event procedure of the form. It creates a new property for the browse object in the form named FindName, based on the value of the entryfield value. Then it creates a second property for the form browse object that holds the length of the FindName value.

After creating these two properties, it checks to see where the Entryfield is currently located, based on its Top value. If it is a five, the user has typed an author name; otherwise, the user has typed in a title.

Finally, it sets a filter based on what the user has typed into the entryfield. If the user enters an asterisk, it uses the asterisk as a wildcard. Once the filter is set, it activates the browse object, setting its fields to the titles and the author name. Then it makes the browse object visible.

The following code is the event procedure attached to the Find button:

```
Procedure PUSHBUTTON3_OnClick
  form.Browse1.FindName = ;
     LTRIM(TRIM(UPPER(form.Entryfield1.value)))
  form.Browse1.LenFind = LEN(form.Browse1.FindName)
  *
  IF form.entryfield1.top = 5
   DO CASE
    Case AT("*",fFind.Browse1.FindName) = 0
     SET FILTER TO fFind.Browse1.FindName $ ;
     LEFT(UPPER(AUTHORS->Author),fFind.Browse1.LenFind)

   Case AT("*",fFind.Browse1.FindName) = 1 .and. ;
                      form.Browse1.LenFind> 1
     fFind.Browse1.FindName =  SUBS(fFind.Browse1.FindName,2, ;
         form.Browse1.LenFind-1)
     SET filter to fFind.Browse1.FindName $ UPPER(authors-
>Author)

     Case AT("*",fFind.Browse1.FindName)> 1 .AND. ;
                         RIGHT(fFind.Browse1FindName,1) = "*"
       SET filter to LEFT(fFind.Browse1.FindName, ;
                           at("*",fFind.Browse1.FindName)-1) $
;
                           LEFT(UPPER(authors->Author),  ;
                           at("*",fFind.Browse1.FindName)-1)

     Case AT("*",fFind.Browse1.FindName)> 1
      SET filter to LEFT(fFind.Browse1.FindName, ;
                    at("*",fFind.Browse1.FindName)-1) $ ;
                    LEFT(UPPER(authors->Author),  ;
                    at("*",fFind.Browse1.FindName)-1) ;
              .and. RIGHT(fFind.Browse1.FindName, ;
                    fFind.Browse1.LenFind - ;
                    at("*",fFind.Browse1.FindName)) $ ;
                    SUBS(UPPER(authors->Author), ;
                    AT("*",fFind.Browse1.FindName),30)
    ENDCASE
  ELSE
    DO CASE
     Case AT("*",fFind.Browse1.FindName) = 0
      SET FILTER TO fFind.Browse1.FindName $ ;
      LEFT(UPPER(BOOKTITLE),fFind.Browse1.LenFind)
```

```
   Case AT("*",fFind.Browse1.FindName) = 1 .and. ;
                          form.Browse1.LenFind > 1
    fFind.Browse1.FindName =  SUBS(fFind.Browse1.FindName,2, ;
                             form.Browse1.LenFind-1)
    SET filter to fFind.Browse1.FindName $ UPPER(BOOKTITLE)

   Case AT("*",fFind.Browse1.FindName)> 1 .AND. ;
                           RIGHT(fFind.Browse1.FindName,1) = "*"
     SET filter to LEFT(fFind.Browse1.FindName,;
                            at("*",fFind.Browse1.FindName)-1) $ ;
                            LEFT(UPPER(BOOKTITLE), ;
                            at("*",fFind.Browse1.FindName)-1)

   Case AT("*",fFind.Browse1.FindName)> 1
     SET filter to LEFT(fFind.Browse1.FindName,;
                             at("*",fFind.Browse1.FindName)-1) $ ;
                             LEFT(UPPER(BOOKTITLE), ;
                             at("*",fFind.Browse1.FindName)-1) ;
             .and. RIGHT(fFind.Browse1.FindName, ;
                             fFind.Browse1.LenFind - ;
                             at("*",fFind.Browse1.FindName)) $;
                             SUBS(UPPER(BOOKTITLE), ;
                             AT("*",fFind.Browse1.FindName),30)
   ENDCASE
 ENDIF
 form.browse1.fields = 'titles->BOOKTITLE\H="Title of Book"\35,
;
                   authors->AUTHOR\H="Name of Author"\20'
 GO TOP
 form.browse1.visible = .t.
```

The second page of the FindBook form

This page uses five new controls, in addition to those that are placed on PageNo 0. It has two text objects, one Select pushbutton and two listboxes. The top listbox is used to display the author names, the second one is used to display all books published by them.

All of the new controls on page 2 have their PageNo property set to 2.

The event procedure of page 2. There is only one event procedure for page 2 of the FindBook form. Both the Select pushbutton and the listbox (located at the right top of page 2) run the same event procedure. This procedure, called LISTBOX1_OnLeftDblClick, is inside the form. Its purpose is to assign the name of the author selected by the user to one of the text fields on page 2 and create a new property for the listbox1, named xAuth. This new property will hold the name of the author selected by the user. Then it sets a filter based on the authorno selected from the second copy of the Authors table. Finally, it moves the user's titles to the form array Booklist created when the form was opened. Once the titles have been moved into the array, the array is set as the value for the datasource of the second listbox on page 2. The code for the procedure is

```
Procedure LISTBOX1_OnLeftDblClick(flags, col, row)
     form.text3.text = _3->author
     form.listbox1.xAuth = _3->authorno
     set filter to fFind.listbox1.xAuth = titles->authorno
     go top
     form.BookList.size = 0
     do while Titles->authorno = fFind.listbox1.xAuth
       form.BookList.add(titles->BOOKTITLE)
       skip
     ENDDO
     SET FILTER TO
     form.Listbox2.datasource = "ARRAY form.BookList"
```

The third page of the FindBook form

The last page of the form also has five additional controls—three text objects, one listbox, and one pushbutton. The listbox is used to display the titles of the books. One of the text fields is used to display the name of the author. When a user selects a title, he or she can either double click on the choice in the listbox or click the pushbutton.

All of the new controls on page 3 have their PageNo property set to 3.

The event procedure of page 3. Like page 2, there is only one event procedure for page 3 of the FindBook form. Both the Select pushbutton and the listbox run the same event procedure. The procedure is

```
Procedure PUSHBUTTON4_OnClick
     form.text5.text = authors->author
```

This form simply changes the text value of the text field to the name of the author that the user selects.

Manually changing the first few lines of code

Like the Customer and Mainmenu form, you need to change the first several lines of code and give this form a unique public name. The name is fFind. This name is used by all of the filters within the form. The new code for the top of the form is

```
public fFind
fFind = new FINDTITLFORM()
fFind.Open()
CLASS FINDTITLFORM OF FORM
```

> **!** **Setting filters and public variables**
> The SET FILTER TO command requires use of a public variable or a property of a public object. It will not support or allow the use of the *this* or *form* special variable operators. If the variable is not public, the filter will not be able to be set and Visual dBASE will report an error. However, as all the codes demonstrate on all the pages of this form, you can use a custom property of the object, as long as the form is declared public. This is the purpose of declaring the variable fFind public.

The Orders.wfm

This form is the main form for displaying and adding visit and book information. It is the form that is used to add new visits and books for each visit. It can also be used to update returned books. The form looks like the one in Figure 15–27. It uses the ALL query that has all of the tables needed by the system.

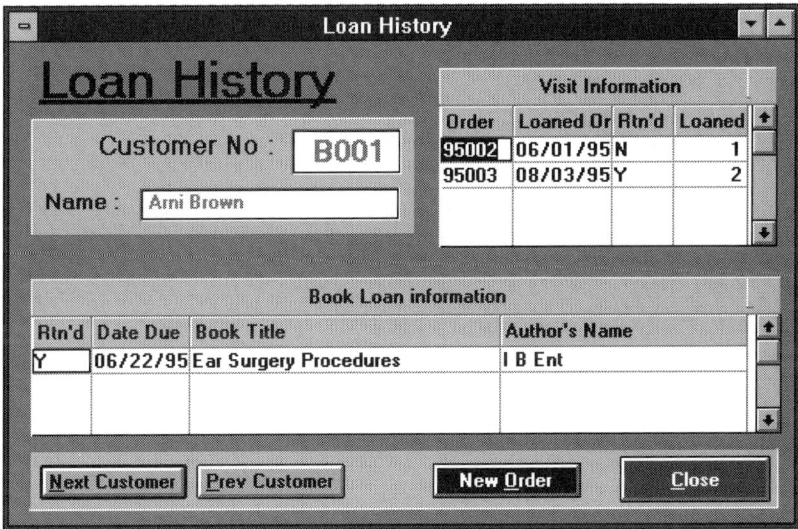

Figure 15–27. This is the BookOrdr form.

Notice that the form has two browse objects. The browse object located on the right side has the visit information concerning the order number, the load date, and the number of books loaned. The second browse object holds the name of the books and author names that are borrowed and their due dates.

When the user clicks through the Visit records, the books loaned Browse table changes to reflect the books borrowed for that visit.

When the user needs to add a new record, several things happen.

1. A method builds a new order number.
2. The PickBook form is activated for selecting the books.
3. If the user selects no books, nothing is done.
4. If the user selects some books, a new record is added to the Orders table, and new records are added to the Books table for each book borrowed.
5. The number of books selected is automatically added to the Orders table, and all Returned fields are set to False.

Although the form is included on the disk with this book, there is some interesting code that needs to be understood.

Building a new order number

The following code, placed in the Orders form, is the core code necessary to create a new order number:

```
Procedure NextOrdr
    local xNo,xNewNo
    create session
    use orders order order_no
    go bottom
    xNo = order_no
    form.xNo = order_no
    xLeft2 = RIGHT(STR(YEAR(date())),2)
    *
    IF xLeft2 <> LEFT(xNo,2)
        xNewNo = xLeft2+"001"
    ELSE
        xNextNo = val(right(xNo,3))+1
        xNewNo = left(xNo,2)+iif(xNextNo<100,"0","") +;
            iif(xNextNo<10,"0","") +
ltrim(trim(str(xNextNo)))
    ENDIF
    *
    form.NextNo = xNewNo
    use
```

This code uses standard dBASE-like code to build a new order number, automatically. Once created, the number is stored in a new property of the form.

Important event procedures

There are two additional event procedures in the Orders form that are important. One is the driver that is used to select the borrowed books; the other is for updating the screen, with the new records added, on returning from the PickBook form.

The procedure for getting new orders. The New Order pushbutton is used to trigger the NextOrder procedure and also run the PickBook form, used to select the books, is controlled by another method of the form object:

```
Procedure PUSHBUTTON3_OnCLICK
   *      New Order button
    form.CustNo = Customer->Cust_No
    form.NextOrdr()
    create session
    do pickbook.wfm
```

By the time the PickBook form is run, the current Orders form will have two properties existing—the CustNo property (with the current customer number) and the NextNo property (with the next available number for adding an Order). The NextNo property was created by the NextOrder method of the form.

The procedure for updating the current form. When the FindBook form ends, it adds a new Orders record for the user and new Book records for all the books selected. Then it returns to the Orders form.

When returning to the Orders form, the two browse objects need to be updated. Using the new Visual dBASE Refresh() method of the form will not update the records being displayed in the browse object. The user could page down until he or she moves to the new record and Visual dBASE will immediately update the browse object with the new record added. However, this could be problematic for the user. If they don't see the new record, they will assume that it hasn't been added.

➡ **How Visual dBASE refreshes browse objects**
Visual dBASE does not automatically refresh the browse control object until the user is inside the object and moves to the point where it must update the object. Although this greatly improves the performance of the overall program, it can be frustrating when the user adds records to the underlying tables via a separate form running in a different session. You can programmatically force the browse object to update its contents by moving to the last record of the browse object and then back to the first record.

When the user returns to the Orders form, from the PickBook form, the OnGotFocus event property is used to trigger an update to the browse object. The following code demonstrates how the form can update the browse objects using the browse object's Keyboard() method:

```
Procedure FORM_OnGotFocus
   IF TYPE("form.CustNo") <> "U"
       form.browse1.setfocus()
       form.Browse1.Keyboard("{CTRL+PgDn} + {Ctrl+PgUp}")
   ENDIF
```

Notice that the Keyboard() method of the browse object passes the keystrokes to go to last record in browse (Ctrl+PgDn) and then to the first record (Ctrl+PgUp). This forces the browse object to update its contents, displaying the new record(s) in the object.

The PickBook.wfm

This form is used to select the books to be borrowed by the user. It is a simple form with a listbox that displays all of the books. It looks like Figure 15–28. The form appears atop of the Orders form.

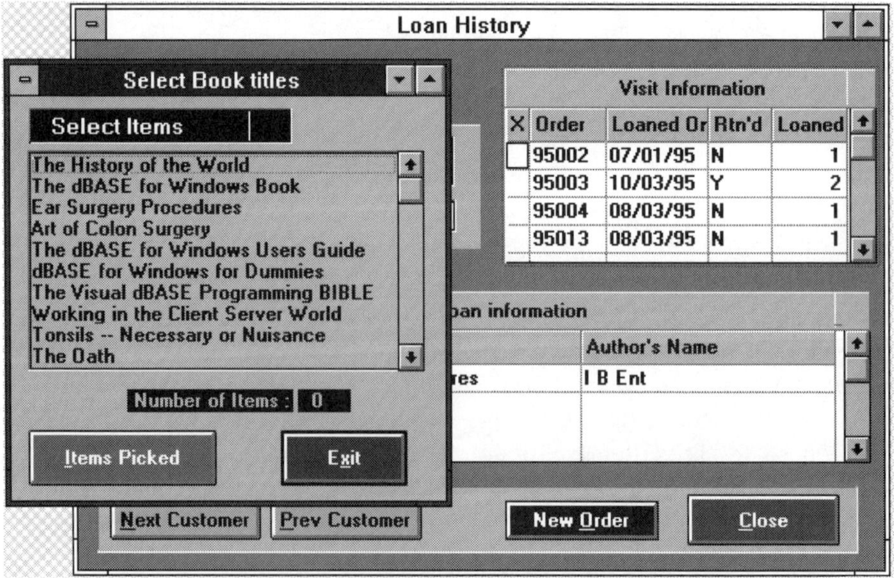

Figure 15–28. This is the PickBook form used to selected books.

Notice that the form in Figure 15–28 has a single listbox and two buttons. The listbox is used to select the books—supporting the Windows **Ctrl + Shift** key combination for selecting items.

Again, this form is included on the enclosed disk with this book.

The primary procedures of the FindBook form

This form has seven procedures that are triggered by five event properties—two for the form, one for the listbox, and one for each button on the form. Of primary interest are

- The OnOpen property of the form
- The OnSelChange property of the listbox
- The OnClick of the Close button

The OnOpen event procedure. This procedure simply declares an array named TempArray in the form. It will be used to hold the items selected by the user in the listbox. The code for the method against this event, OnOpen, is:

```
Procedure FORM_ONOPEN
    form.TempArray = new array()
```

This procedure will create an array in the Pickbook form when the form is opened.

The OnSelChange event property. When the user selects items in the listbox of the form, the total number of books selected is displayed at the bottom of the form. The method is

```
Procedure COUNTSEL
    xNum=0
    FOR xCnt = 1 to LISTCOUNT(form.PickerBox)
      IF .NOT. ISBLANK(LISTSELECTED(form.PickerBox,xCnt))
        xNum=xNum+1
      ENDIF
    NEXT
    form.text2.text = STR(xNum,3)
```

This procedure uses two dBASE functions, ListCount() and ListSelected(), to determine how many items were selected by the user. When the user changes his or her selection in the listbox, the OnSelChange event is triggered, running this code.

The ListCount() function is used to determine how many items are in the listbox. The ListSelected() function looks at the current Listbox line being pointed to and determines if the user has selected this line. By using these two commands, the program can count all of the items selected in the listbox.

The OnClick event property. This property calls three procedures—AddPics(), GetPicks, and NewRecord().

The AddPics() method is used as the driver for getting the user's selections (GetPicks) and then adding new records to the Orders and books tables (NewRecord). The code of the method is

```
Procedure AddPicks
    form.GetPicks()
    IF form.TempArray.size>0 .and. TYPE("fOrdr") = "O"
      create session
      form.NewRecord()
    ENDIF
    form.Close()
```

The code will run the GetPicks() method to determine if the user has selected any records. It will only run the other method when the form is called from the Orders form and has selected items. It always closes the form.

The GetPicks() method is similar to the CountSel method of the OnSelChange property. However, it moves the selections of the user into the array, TempArray, created when the form was opened.

```
Procedure GetPicks
    form.TempArray.size = 0
    FOR xCnt = 1 to LISTCOUNT(form.PickerBox)
      IF .NOT. ISBLANK(LISTSELECTED(form.PickerBox,xCnt))
         form.TempArray.add(LISTSELECTED(form.PickerBox,xCnt))
      ENDIF
    NEXT
```

Notice that this code sets the size of the array to 0. Then it uses the ListCount() and ListSelected() functions of dBASE to move selections made by the user to the array using the add() method of the array, TempArray.

The final method called by the AddPicks is the NewRecord() method. This method is used to update the Orders and Books tables with the selections made by the user:

```
PROCEDURE NewRecord
  CREATE SESSION
  use books in a
  use titles order booktitle in b
  use Orders in c
  xCnt = 1
  do while .t.
    IF TYPE("form.TempArray[xCnt]")<> "C"
       exit
    ENDIF
    append blank
    seek(form.temparray[xCnt],"B")
```

```
    replace order_no with form.NewOrdNo, book_no with B-
>BookNum,;
                Due_date with date()+21,  returned with .f.
     xCnt=xCnt+1
  enddo
  sele c
  go bottom
  append blank
  replace  cust_no with form.OldCustNo, order_no with
⇒form.NewOrdNo, ;
              loan_date with date(), tot_items with xCnt-1,
⇒             returned with .f.
  SELE A
```

This code simply adds the new records to the Orders and Books tables.

Although this form is not activated via the MainMenu, you could add a fourth button to the Switchboard form (MainMenu) running this Orders form. It will be driven via one of the menu prompts added to the MainMenu of the system.

ABOUT.wfm

This form will use no tables. It is simply an information box that displays information about the system. Once completed it should look like Figure 15–29.

Figure 15–29. The completed ABOUT form.

It will be activated by a menu choice associated with the MainMenu form.

The two procedures that it runs are attached to the OnLostFocus and OnGotFocus of the form. The code is

```
Procedure Form_OnGotFocus
     cMem=LTRIM(STR(MEMORY()))+" KB"
     form.entryfield1.value = cMem

Procedure Form_OnLostFocus
    form.Release()
```

The second procedure immediately destroys the form when the user moves to another form outside of dBASE to another Windows application. This makes the form totally self-cleaning—whether the user presses the button or not, the form disappears when it losses focus.

THE MENUS

This application has two menus and one popup associated with it—one menu with the switchboard (Main menu) and a menu and popup with the Customer form. Although any of the forms can and should have a menu associated with it, this system only has two associated.

> ➡ **Popups and Visual dBASE**
> Popups are new to Visual dBASE. You can create a popup, just like creating a menu, using the CREATE POPUP command. A popup is a SpeedMenu that is activated via the right mouse click.

The easiest way to create a menu or popup is to use the dBASE menu Designer.

Creating a menu for the Customer form

To create a menu, you can go to the Command window and type in the following command:

```
CREATE MENU
```

You will be taken into the Menu Designer. It should bring up a window with an empty menu bar across the top. It will look similar to Figure 15–30.

You can use the Menu Designer to create menu prompts, examine properties for each prompt, and attach methods (procedures) to events of the menu objects.

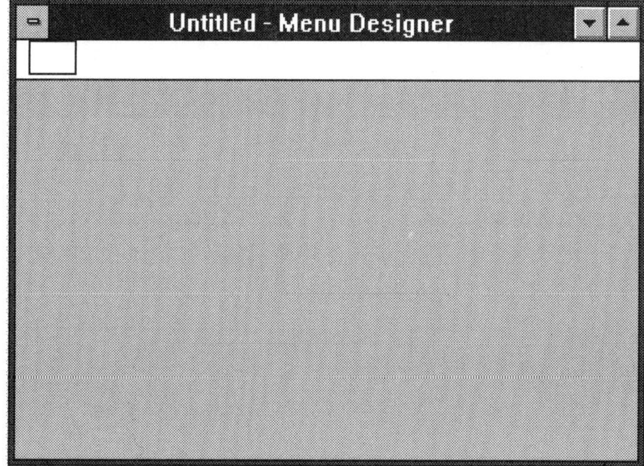

Figure 15–30. The Menu Designer.

Creating prompts for a menu

To create a File prompt for the first position of the menu and make the **"F"** key "hot." Then make a Data prompt for the first position and make the **"D"** hot, do the following steps:

1. Type **&File** in the prompt box.
2. Press the **Tab** key or right arrow (at the end of the prompt).
3. Type **&Data** in the new prompt box.

NOTE: You can go back to the File prompt at any time by pressing the **Shift+Tab** key combination until you return.

Creating a submenu prompt called a menu item. Once you have created the menu prompts for the bar, you are ready to create the submenus, called menu items. Table 15–11 shows what the completed menu and the submenu prompts should be created in the Menu Designer:

Table 15–11. The Customer Menu.

Menu Prompt	File	Edit	Data
Submenus:	Print	Undo	Add Customer
	—	Cut	Find Customer
	Quit	Copy	
		Paste	

Notice that each menu prompt has at least one menu item. You create a submenu prompt, called a menu item, the same way you created the menu bar prompt. Notice also that Table 15–11 shows an Edit menu. You will add this menu and its menu items later.

➡ **The automatically created Edit menu**
Visual dBASE has added the ability to add an Edit menu and its four prompts automatically to a menu that you are creating. To have Visual dBASE add the Edit menu, you select Menu >> Insert "Edit" Menu from the menu bar.

To create the Add Customer and Find Customer prompts of the bar prompt, Data, follow these steps:

1. Move to the Data prompt using the **Tab** key.
2. Press the Down Arrow once.
3. Type **&Add Customer** in the empty cell.
4. Press the Down Arrow once.
5. Type **Find C&ustomer** in the empy cell.

With the two submenu prompts, called commands or menu items, added, you are ready to add the other six prompts for the File and Edit menus. To add the menu items for the File prompt, simply repeat the steps just performed to add the menu items for the Data menu.

NOTE: Moving between menu prompts

You can move back and forth between menu prompts and menu items (commands) using the **Arrow** keys or **Tab** keys.

Inserting a separator. Notice that you inserted a separator in one of the prompts. To insert a separator bar, you press the **Ctrl+T** key combination or type in some text (like underscore) and fix it later, changing the Property *separator* to .T.

Having added all of the prompts, your menu should now look similar to the one in Figure 15–31.

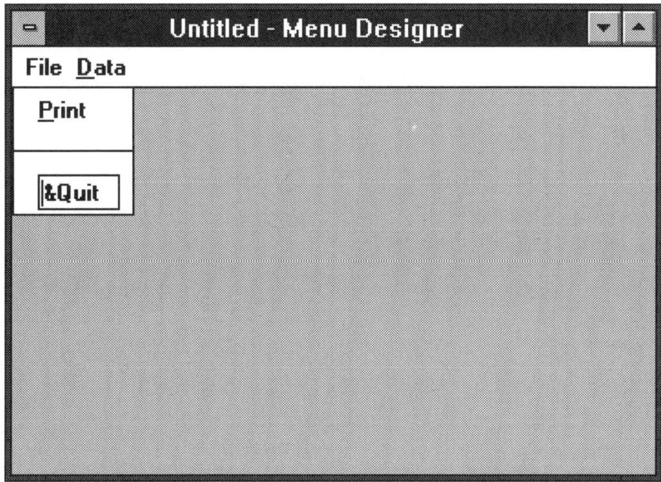

Figure 15–31. The menu prompts added.

Although all of the prompts are assigned, you only see the submenu prompts associated with the File bar prompt. If you move to the Data prompt, its submenu prompts will appear.

Assigning properties for the prompts

After placing all of the prompts on the menu, you may want to change a few of the identification properties. To change them, simply highlight an item and select Inspect from the SpeedMenu or View >> Inspect menu choice.

The following two properties are the primary ones with which you will work:

Separator
Used to make a prompt line a separator line. The line will be skipped as the user goes through the prompts. If there is any text in the *Text* property, it will not be displayed. Rather, a solid bar will be placed in the text portion of the screen. If you need to convert a prompt to a separator, simply set the separator property to .t.

ShortCut
This property is used to assign a key combination ("hot") key that will perform the same actions as selecting the menu bar and prompt. If you assign a hot key to a menu prompt, the menu will display it in a prompt cell when the menu is active.

Assigning a ShortCut key to a menu item. To assign a ShortCut key to the File >> Print item, follow these steps:

1. Select the Print prompt under the File menu.
2. Activate the Inspector (SpeedMenu, right mouse, select Inspector).
3. Select the ShortCut key cell.
4. Type **Ctrl+P** in the cell.

You can add additional shortcut values to the other menu items.

NOTE: Shortcut keys and Menus

A Shortcut key can only be assigned to Menu items. The Menu prompts on the menu bar cannot have shortcut keys associated with them.

Figure 15–32 shows the menu with two prompts—File and Data and their menu items. Notice that it shows hot keys for some of the prompts.

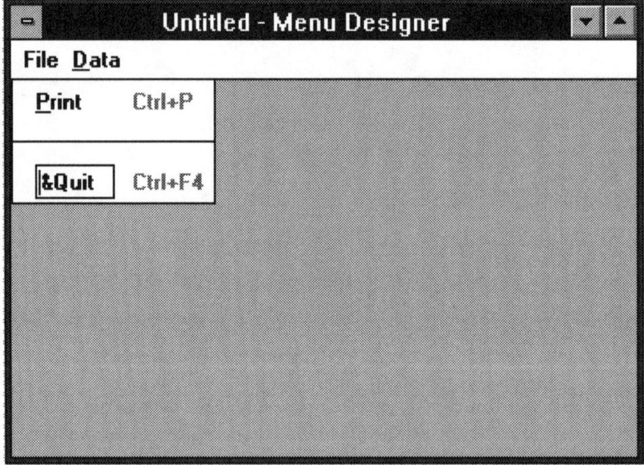

Figure 15–32. The hot keys associated with a menu.

The **Ctrl+F4** key combination is associated with the Exit prompt and **Ctrl+P** associated with the Print prompt.

➡ **The hot key assignment**
In the dBASE for Windows 5.0, the menu designer would not display the hot key in the prompt. However, Visual dBASE displays the hot key, grayed out, letting you know that the key combination is a hot key assignment.

Automatically adding the "Edit" menu and its menu items

➡ Visual dBASE has added the ability to create an "Edit" menu for menu bars. This "Edit" menu will be used to perform standard windows actions. Before Visual dBASE, this ability was not available. To add an edit menu and its associated menu items, follow these steps:

1. Move the cursor to the Data menu item.
2. While on the Data menu item, select the **Menu >> Insert "Edit" Menu** choice.

Visual dBASE automatically inserts an Edit menu, at the point where the cursor was sitting. It moves the Data menu and its items to the right.

Understanding the Edit menu. In addition to creating the "Edit" menu and associated menu items (Undo, Cut, . . .), Visual dBASE automatically assigns hot keys to each prompt. It also automatically assigns values to several properties of the new MenuBar object. When the code is saved, it will have code similar to the following assigned to the menu:

```
this.editUndoMenu = this.edit.undo
this.editCutmenu = this.edit.cut
this.editCopymenu = this.edit.copy
this.editpastemenu = this.edit.paste
```

The properties EditUndoMenu, EditCutMenu, . . . are part of the new Class MenuBar. This class lets you specify menu items that will be associated with the Windows editing actions (Undo, Cut, . . .).

If you fail to automatically create an Edit menu, you will have to manually insert the preceding code into your new menu code.

Assigning actions to the menu items

Although the "Edit" menu already has actions assigned to it, the other menu items have no actions associated with them so far. You need to add procedures for each menu item in your menu.

Every prompt of a menu and the menu's items have two properties that can be used to perform some actions—*OnClick* and *OnHelp*. The OnClick property is the one that you will want to use to attach code for when the user selects the item. For instance, the Exit menu item, Print menu item, Customer menu item, Find Book menu item, and the others.

Creating a procedure for a menu item. To create a menu prompt method, you perform the same steps that you do when creating a method for any other event property:

1. Set focus to the menu prompt you want to assign code to
2. Activate the property inspector (SpeedMenu, Object inspector choice)
3. Click the *Event* tab in the property inspector
4. Go to the OnClick event property
5. Type in the codeblock or activate the procedures window and type the code in the Procedures window

To print a form from a menu item. The easiest way to print a form is simply to attach a codeblock to the OnClick property of the menu prompt or a pushbutton. The codeblock is

```
{;form.print()}
```

The form has a built-in method called print that will activate the printer dialog box and let you print the form.

Adding a new Customer form from a menu item. To have the menu item, Data >> Add Customer, start the append routine, you will want to assign the same code that you have attached to the New Customer button of the Customer form:

```
Procedure ADD_CUSTOMER_OnClick
 set cuaenter OFF
 form.rectangle1.visible = .t.
 form.pushbutton8.visible = .t.
 form.pushbutton9.visible = .t.
 GOTO BOTTOM
 SKIP
 form.BeginAppend()
```

This code will automatically start the add routine for the Customer form.

With the code assigned to the Data >> Add Customer menu item, you can now add code to the other menu items. This menu is include on the enclosed disk, it can be examined to see all of its procedures attached to the menu items.

Saving the Customer menu

Once you have created the menu and assigned all the procedures or codeblocks to the menu items, you need to save the menu and name it Customer.mnu.

Assigning the Customer menu to the Customer form

Once created, you can manually insert the Customer.MNU into the Customer.wfm by assigning the name of the menu to the MenuFile property of the Class definition. The line to add to the Class definition is

```
CLASS CUSTOMERFORM OF FORM
   this.MenuFile = "Customer.mnu"
       . . .
```

Adding the Customer.mnu to the MenuFile property will let the Customer form automatically use the menu when the Customer form is running.

Figure 15–33 shows the Customer form running with the Customer menu active and the File menu open with the two prompts available for use.

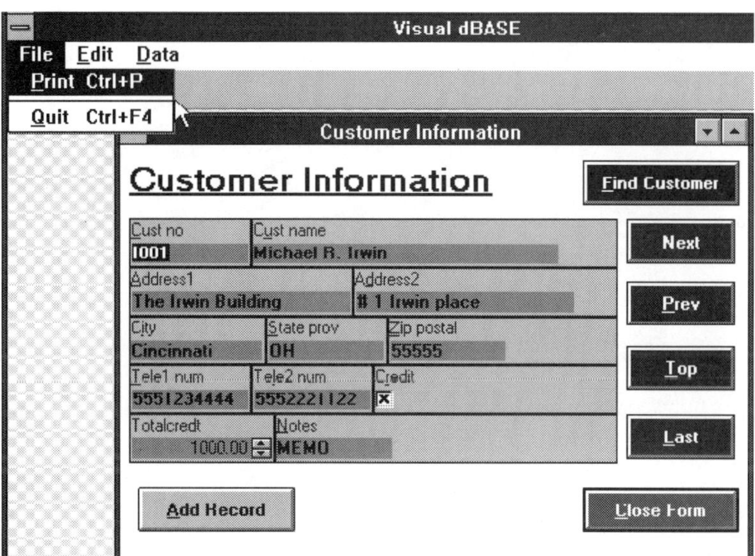

Figure 15–33. This is the customer menu for the Customer form.

The menu for the MAINMenu form

The second menu used by the system can be created exactly the same as the Customer menu. It has menu prompts and submenu prompts. The menu items should be similar to the one in Table 15–12.

Table 15–12. The Main Menu.

Menu Prompt	File	Data	Find	Reports	Help
Submenus	Exit	Customer	Customer	Customer	About
		Orders	Book	Books	

This menu will be attached to the MAINMENU.wfm through the Menu property. Once set, when you run the form the menu will look similar to the one in Figure 15–34.

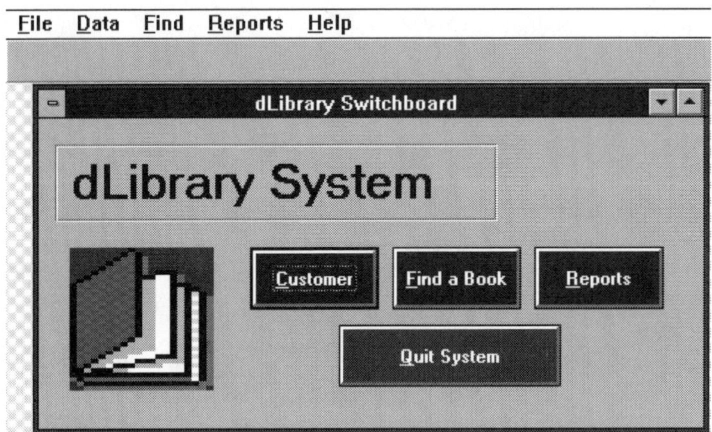

Figure 15–34. This is the MainMenu forms menu.

This menu is easy to create. Notice that the Data menu has the Orders choice. This choice will run the Orders form.

Creating a popup for the Customer form

➡ Visual dBASE has added the ability to create and work with popups. A popup menu, called a SpeedMenu by Borland, is activated when the user right mouse clicks in the form with which the SpeedMenu is associated.

Popups versus menu bars. A popup is created just like a menu. However, the code is slightly different. A menu explicitly uses a keyword *root* as a parameter when instantiating the menu. This means that it can be associated with any form by simply using a property of the form. Unlike a menu, a popup's name must be explicitly passed when activating it. The method used to attach and activate a popup is slightly different.

A popup will normally contain those menu bar items that are most commonly used. It can have more than one column; however, it usually only has a single column. In addition, all the prompts of a popup are usually available and take some action. Of course, a popup can have separators to group actions within it.

Creating the Customer popup menu

To create a popup menu for the customer, you can use the command

```
CREATE POPUP
```

Visual dBASE takes you into the menu/popup builder. Once in the builder, you build the SpeedMenu, Popup, just like you would a menu bar.

The prompts of the Customer popup. Once in the Popup Menu Designer, you want to create four prompts that perform the actions specified in Table 15–13.

Table 15–13. The Customer Popup.

Prompts	Action
&Find Customer	Will run the FindCust form
&Add Customer	Will begin the add customer routine
&View Orders	Will run the Orders table to work with orders
&Close Form	Will close the form

You need to attach the same actions that were attached to any buttons or menu items that perform the same actions.

Once created, the completed popup should look similar to Figure 15–35.

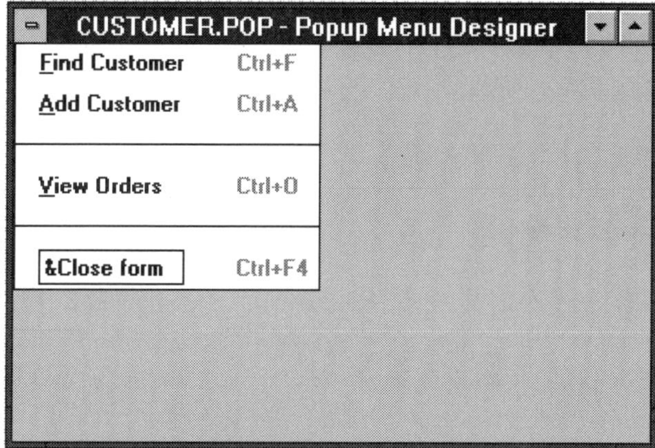

Figure 15–35. This is the Customer popup.

The methods of the popup

When you assign methods to a popup you can assign methods in two ways—using codeblocks or by writing new procedures in the popup definition. You can use procedures that already exist in the form or create new ones in the popup class.

Using popup class-level procedures. If you create new procedures and attach them to the OnClick property, they will be built in the popup definition (CLASS POPUP). Once created, you will need to place the Popup class in memory to make them accessible when you need to run them.

This will require that you specify the command SET PROCEDURE TO <Popup name> in your code.

Using codeblocks for methods. Codeblocks can be used to assign multiple commands, even to run methods that exist in the form which it will be associated with.

If you want to reference an existing method of the form, you can use a codeblock. The following codeblock, placed in the OnClick cell of the Find Customer menu item, will run the form method for finding a customer:

```
{;form.PUSHBUTTON1_OnClick()}
```

Notice that it supports use of the *form* special reference variable.

You can also create a codeblock that will perform several steps. For instance, the Customer form has no methods in it that will run the Orders form, the following code attached to the OnClick property of the View Orders menu item will do the trick:

```
{;create session;do orders.wfm}
```

This codeblock will perform two actions—create a session and run the Orders form.

Advantages to popup codeblocks. Using codeblocks for all of your event procedures eliminates the need to place the popup code in memory using the SET PROCEDURE TO command. Codeblocks also let you work with existing methods—placing the code in one place makes maintenance easier.

The popup should be saved and named Customer.pop. Then you are ready to attach the popup menu to the Customer form.

Attaching a popup menu

Attaching a popup to a form is *not* accomplished via a form property. There is a new property named *PopupMenu* for forms. However, this property appears to be a logical value—its default value is False. When you attach a popup object to a form, this property holds the pointer to the popup associated with the form and places the word *Object* in the cell.

To associate a popup with a form you must perform at lease two steps (steps 2 and 3):

1. If the popup has any methods created inside it, place it in memory using the command—SET PROCEDURE TO popup name.
2. Run the popup, and assign it to a form and assign a name to it.
3. Assign this newly named popup to the form object.

Step 1 only needs to be done if the popup you created uses its own event procedures.

Running the popup program to activate it. The PopupMenu property of a form is not given a value in the traditional manner. It cannot be set inside the Inspector.

Unlike other control objects, the popup object must be explicitly set via code. The easiest way is to set it in a procedure associate with the OnOpen of the form.

The following code has been added to the customer form's OnOpen event procedure:

```
Procedure Form_OnOpen
   DO Customer.pop with form, "MyPop"
   form.PopupMenu = form.MyPop
    form.RecNo = RECNO()
    form.CUAEnter = SET("CUAE")
```

The two bold lines have been inserted into the OnOpen procedure. They run the popup, naming it and associating it with the Customer form. Then they assign the popup, based on the passed name, to the PopupMenu property of the form.

The Property Inspector. When you inspect the form, you will see that the PopupMenu property does not hold the name of the popup, rather the word *Object*. It points to the object reference that lets you inspect the popup.

Using the Customer popup. Figure 15–36 shows the completed popup opened atop of the Customer form. When the user right mouse clicks anywhere on the form, the popup will appear at the point he or she clicked. In Figure 15–36 that is between the Next button and the Name field.

THE REPORTS

dBASE uses Crystal Reports as the report writer that ships with Visual dBASE. It is a third-party tool that is integrated with the IDE of dBASE. All reports require that a query be used. Your system has two reports.

```
CUSTINFO.rpt
BOOKLIST.rpt
```

The CustInfo report prints information about all of the customers for the library. The Booklist is a detailed report that shows the book titles and authors for all books in the library.

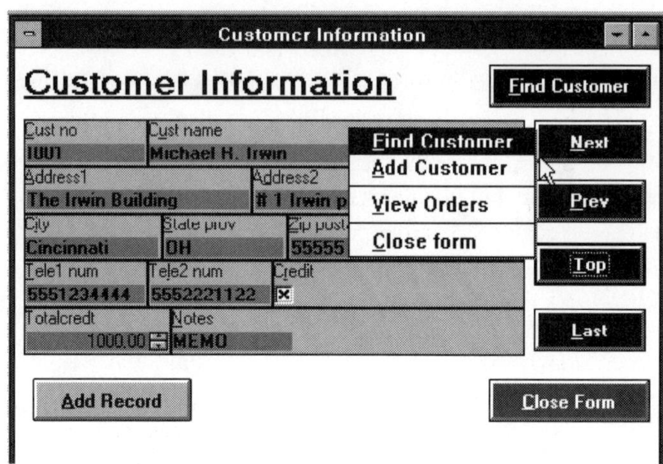

Figure 15–36. This is a popup menu.

Overview of Crystal Reports

Crystal Reports is a separate Windows report writer that works with dBASE, integrating the memory heap space for sharing parameters and using the expression builder of dBASE. It can be started outside of dBASE (in Windows) by clicking on the Crystal Reports icon in the Visual dBASE group or by typing CREATE REPORT from the Command window within dBASE.

Some of the features of Crystal Reports

Crystal Reports is closely integrated with Visual dBASE. Some of the features are

Live Editing
You can format reports while it is running and displaying the actual report in a print window. This lets you quickly and visually align the text of your report.

Banded Design
It is a banded report writer like dBASE IV, yet even more powerful. It can build reports quickly using band-oriented technology—Headers, Footers, Detail, Group (By), and Page bands.

Store report data
The data can be stored in the report itself, letting you change the format of the report as it is running without waiting long times for re-execute commands to take effect.

Integration of dBASE memory variables
The heap space of dBASE can be read and used by Crystal Reports. This means that you can pass expressions and variables to Crystal Reports to print a report. The Expression Builder in dBASE is also used by Crystal Reports directly. Thus you can use point-and-click to create expressions.

Once launched, you will be prompted for a Query or Table name. After specifying a query, you will be taken into Crystal Reports.

One negative to the reports

The biggest report drawback is that you must use a Crystal Reports runtime module when you run the report. To some programmers, the biggest report drawback is the fact that it does not create source code that can be modified by the programmer. However, you can take a created report back into Crystal Reports and modify it using the tools.

What if Crystal Reports does not run? You may install dBASE and Crystal Reports, run dBASE, and everything works perfectly. The minute you go to run Crystal Reports, it starts and then you get a message that informs you that the version of BWCC.DLL you have on the machine is invalid or missing.

Don't be concerned. It simply means that you probably have an older version of BWCC.DLL sitting in your SYSTEM directory under the Windows directory. When dBASE installs and there is an existing copy of BWCC.DLL in the system directory, it will not overwrite the existing copy when it installs Visual dBASE. dBASE itself does not use the Borland Windows Custom Control (BWCC) DLL; however, Crystal Reports does.

If this happens, simply rename the BWCC.DLL in the c:\Windows\SYSTEM subdirectory or whereever it is, and reinstall dBASE, using Custom Setup and specifying Crystal Reports only.

CUSTINFO.rpt

The custinfo report uses the Customer table and will look something like the one in Figure 15–37 when it is run from within your application.

Notice that Figure 15–37 only shows you the top, left corner of the report. It displays the same record information for all the records in the table customer.

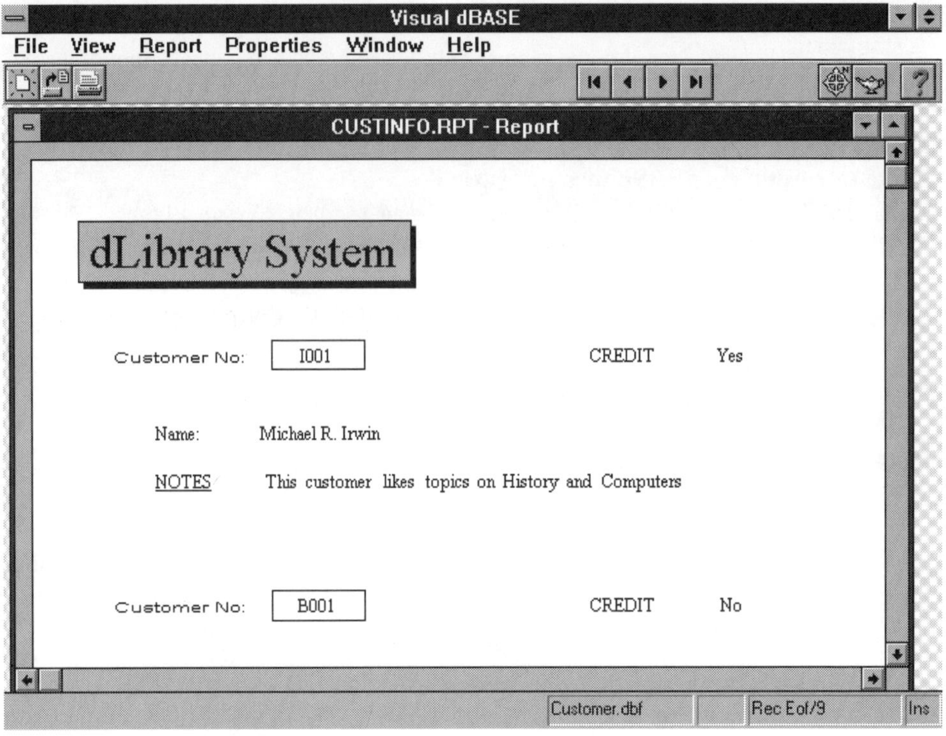

Figure 15–37. The main menu for the system.

> **The report expert**
> Visual dBASE has added a report expert that will help you create a detail or summary report. However, it has several limitations; the most important is lack of support for any memo fields, OLE fields, and Binary fields. This means that you cannot create a report that contains Memo field text or pictures.

To create the CUSTINFO report, type the following commands in the Command window:

```
CLEAR ALL
CLOSE ALL
CREATE REPORT CUSTINFO
```

dBASE will open a dialog box (Open Table required) and prompt you for a table or query name—specify the **CUSTOMER.dbf** and click the OK button.

> **!** **Using open table/query**
> If a table or query is open, you will not receive the open Table dialog box. Rather, Crystal Reports will run with the existing view.

The Crystal Reports entry screen. dBASE will launch Crystal Reports. It displays an Insert Database fields dialog box at the bottom, right corner and the report window across the center of the screen.

You will need to work with both areas of the Report designer—the Insert Database Fields dialog box and the Report window (titled: CUSTINFO.rpt).

A couple of buttons on the toolbar. The two main buttons you will work with on the toolbar are in the center; they should look like the ones in Figure 15–38. These two buttons, from left to right, let you insert a new database field, and edit or insert a new text field.

Figure 15–38. The insert database / insert text field buttons.

The SpeedMenu. Most of the work that you want to do with the entryfields and text objects on the report can be accomplished by clicking the right mouse button to activate the *SpeedMenu*. Figure 15–39 shows a SpeedMenu for a text object (called a text field in Crystal Reports).

dLibrary S
Name: dLibrary System
Change Font...
Change Format...
Change Border and Colors...
Edit Text Field...
Send Behind Others
Delete Field
Cancel Menu

Figure 15–39. The SpeedMenu for a text object in Crystal Reports.

Creating and working with a text field (text object). To create the title, **dLibrary System**, for your report, follow these steps:

1. Click on the Edit text button on the toolbar (right one in Figure 15–38).
2. Crystal Reports activates an Edit Text Field dialog box.
3. Type in the text **dLibrary System** and click on the *Accept button.*
4. Crystal Reports places a small rectangular (empty) icon on the screen. Move the icon to the top, left corner of the page header section (top band).
5. Click to place the text field (object) at the top, left corner.

Once the text object is placed on the report, you can modify its appearance by working with the speedmenu choices:

- Change font . . .
- Change format . . .
- Change border and colors . . .

First change the size of the font by selecting the font dialog box and changing the font size to 24. Then change the format alignment to center by selecting the Format dialog box and changing the alignment field to centered. Finally, change the border and color information by doing the following inside the Format Color and Borders dialog box:

1. Click the border check box on (second from the top of window).
2. Crystal Reports activates all the check boxes for the sides (left, top, right, and bottom).
3. Click the fill check box on, and select the light grey color (silver).
4. Go to the sides area, and click the Drop Shadow check box on.
5. Click on the OK button.

With these appearance additions completed the text field (object) should look similar to the one in Figure 15–40.

dLibrary System

Figure 15–40. The new text field title in Crystal Reports.

If you need to edit the text, activate the SpeedMenu and choose the Edit Text field . . . prompt.

Creating and working with a table field object. Once the title is placed on the form, you are ready to place fields in the Details band of the report. To place the CUST_NO field (and an associated fieldname) on the report surface, follow these steps:

1. Open the Details area so that it is about 2 inches high.
2. Go to the Insert database field dialog box.
3. Double click on the field CUST_NO. (Crystal Reports will place a rectangle [empty] on the screen.)
4. Move the rectangle to an area in the Details region and click the button (you can position it afterward). (Crystal Reports will place both the field in the details band and an associated title of the field [a text object] in the page header area.)

You can change the appearance of the entryfields, just as you did with the text fields in the previous section.

Moving text and fields around. Once the text and fields are placed on the form, they can be moved around by clicking on the field (which will highlight it) and moving it by dragging it to the new position.

The completed report. You can select, modify, and move the objects on the form following the above steps. You should now make your completed report look similar to the one in Figure 15–41.

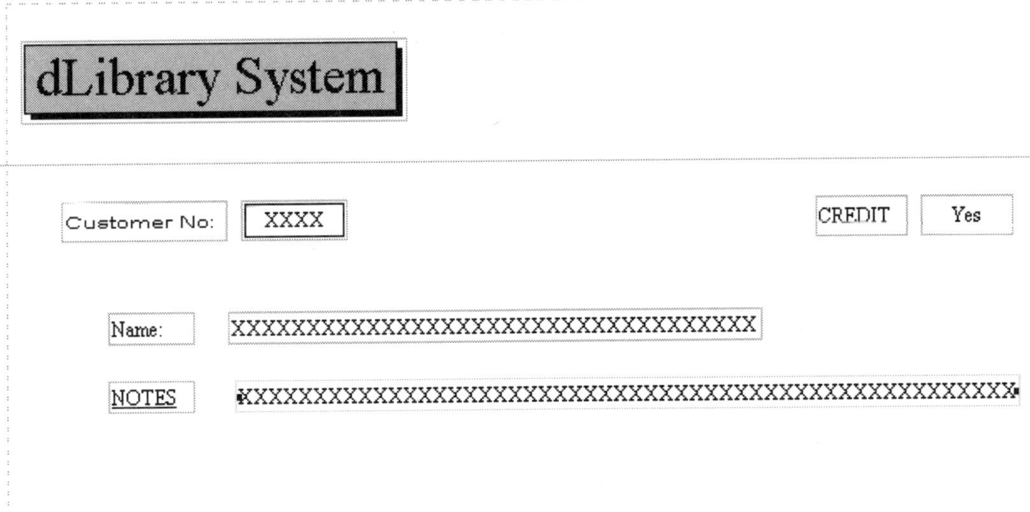

Figure 15–41. The completed report in Crystal Reports.

Once the report is done, save it. There is no source code that can be examined or changed for the report.

BookList.RPT

Once you have created the report CUSTINFO.rpt, you should create the second report BOOKLIST.rpt. This report will use the query named TITLEORD.QBE. You can create it using the same steps you did to create CUSTINFO.rpt.

Once you have completed creating it, it should look the screen inside Crystal Reports seen in Figure 15–42.

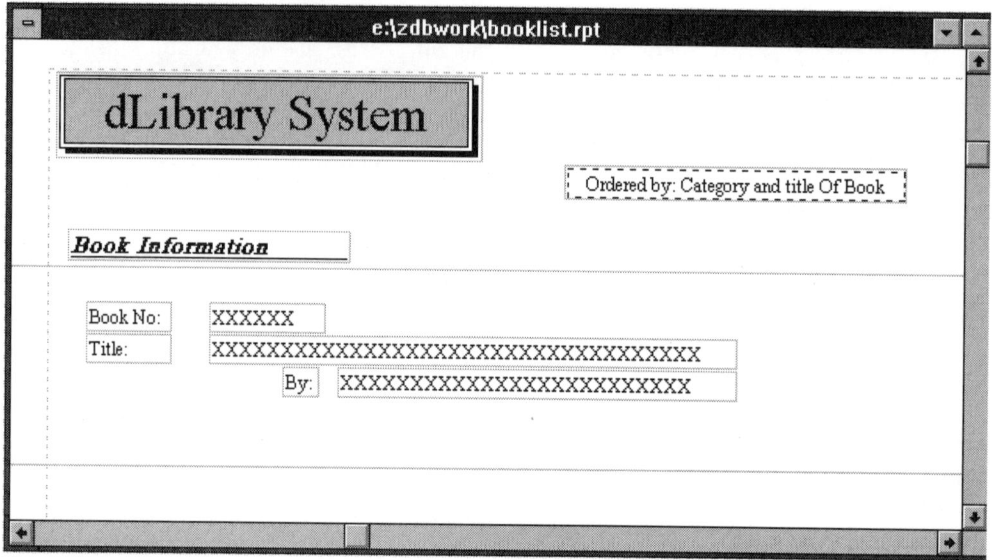

Figure 15–42. The booklist report.

Notice that you do not see the titles of the bands in Figure 15–42. If you look down at the bottom of the figure, you will see that the form has been moved to the right to show all of the information that is in the report.

THE END

This is the complete application created in Visual dBASE. It could have additional functionality and power added to it with minimum effort. For instance, the Report button on the MainMenu form could be activated running another (new) form that lets users select which report they want to run.

Windows help could be easily integrated into the system, as well as any of the multimedia type objects you have worked within this book.

The Visual dBASE compiler

All of the coding techniques and code used in this book have been compiled (at press time) in the final shipping version of both Visual dBASE and the Visual dBASE compiler and they work as expected. The Compiler can be purchased separately from Borland to create and run true Windows programs that do not rely upon Visual dBASE.

The author's special thank you

You've come this far. This is only the beginning of programming in the Object-oriented world using Visual dBASE.

This book only scratches the surface of the power in Visual dBASE. I wish I had the time to continue to write; alas, if I do not stop writing this book, it will be five thousand pages long and never get printed.

So instead of writing more, when you work with this product, you may want to explore using this product to

- Build Windows help files into your dBASE applications.
- Link your dBASE applications to the outside world—scanners, camera, VCRs, modems, and voice recognition systems. Link them in real time to these external I/O devices to extract and input information into your system.
- Link your dBASE applications to other Windows applications to explore and exploit the power of OLE and DDE fully.
- Use the Open Architecture with Windows and Windows resources. The Open Architecture of this product is powerful. As such, you can use some powerful external functions and other resources with minimal effort. Of course, to use them, you need to be aware of them.

Fully exploit the Client/Server model. The Client/Server model in this product, IDAPI, and SQL Links lets you really explore the world of Client/Server with minimal effort.

Thank you for taking the time to read and use this book. I truly hope that it has helped you better understand and explore developing dBASE applications through programming in Visual dBASE.

Appendix: Part One

The following is a complete listing of all the Stock CLASSES (built-in Classes) that are included with Visual dBASE. It offers you an in-depth view of all the properties and methods.

- Properties—General
- Properties—Event
- Methods

In addition, an example is supplied that will help show you how to use each of the Class types.

There are twenty-eight Classes that are built into Visual dBASE. They are

- ARRAY
- ASSOCARRAY
- BROWSE
- CHECKBOX
- COMBOBOX
- DDELINK
- DDETOPIC
- EDITOR
- ENTRYFIELD
- FORM
- IMAGE
- LINE
- LISTBOX
- MENU
- MENUBAR
- OBJECT
- OLE
- OLEAUTOCLIENT
- PAINTBOX
- POPUP

- PUSHBUTTON
- RADIOBUTTON
- RECTANGLE
- SCROLLBAR
- SHAPE
- SPINBOX
- TABBOX
- TEXT

Again, each Class is explained and has a short example supplied.

In addition to these documented Classes, there is also another class that is not documented:

- TIMER

THE ARRAY CLASS

Objects created from the Class Array can be used to store multiple memory variables. The Class Array lets you group memory variables into locations that you can access individually using their subscripts.

An object created from an Array Class does not have to be contained in a form. It can stand on its own in memory.

Array example

The example creates a form containing a pushbutton for each field in a table. The field-names are stored in an array object named **aFieldNames**:

```
LOCAL xFieldForm
xFieldForm = NEW ArrayForm()
xFieldForm.OPEN()
CLASS ArrayForm OF FORM
  this.width = 44
  this.view = "CUSTOMER.DBF"
  AFieldNames = NEW ARRAY(1)
    FOR i = 1 TO FCOUNT()
      aFieldNames.ADD(1)
      aFieldNames[i] = NEW Pushbutton(this)
      aFieldNames[i].text = FIELD(i)
      aFieldNames[i].top = i * 1.2
      aFieldNames[i].left = 2
      aFieldNames[i].width = 18
    NEXT
ENDCLASS
```

Figure A1–1 shows the form and Array subscript (buttons) from the preceding code.

The properties and methods of an Array Class

Table A1–1 shows all of the properties, their default values, and a short description.

Table A1–1. The Array Class.

Property/Method	Default	Description
Add()	N/A	Adds elements to an Array object
ClassName	ARRAY	Identifies the Array object class
Delete()	N/A	Deletes an element from a one-dimensional array object. Can also delete a *row* or *column* from a two-dimensional array object
Dimensions	0	Holds the number of dimensions in the array object
Dir()	N/A	Stores the DOS name, size, date and time, and file attribute(s) of files to an Array object
DirExt()	N/A	Stores the extended DOS name info for Windows 95's long filenames
Element()	N/A	Holds the number of a specified element in the Array object
Fields()	N/A	Holds structure information on the current table in the Array object
Fill()	N/A	Puts a user-specified value into one or more cells of the Array object
Insert()	N/A	Inserts a new element into a one-dimensional array object. Can also insert a row or column of elements into a two-dimensional Array object
Resize()	N/A	Increases or decreases the number of elements in the Array object
Scan()	N/A	Scans an array object for a user-supplied value
Size	N/A	Increases or decreases the number of elements in an Array object
Sort()	N/A	Sorts the cell contents (elements) in a one-dimensional Array object. It can also sort the rows in a two-dimensional Array object
Subscript()	N/A	Holds the row number or the column number of a specified element in an Array object

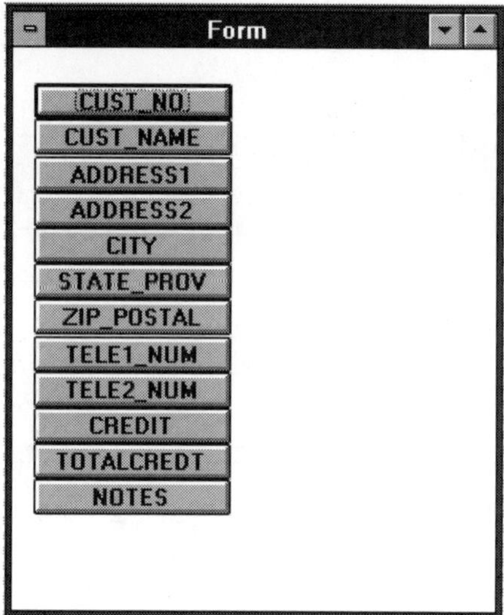

Figure A1–1. Using an Array Class.

THE BROWSE CLASS

Objects created from the Class BROWSE can be used to display a BROWSE format (or single record edit) in a form. It can be used as an editing tool for displaying and changing multiple records in a row format.

Objects created from a BROWSE Class must be contained in a form.

Browse example

The example creates a form containing a Browse object for the **Customer** table.

```
LOCAL xForm
xForm = NEW BrowseForm()
xForm.OPEN()
CLASS BrowseForm OF FORM
  this.width = 44
  this.view = "CUSTOMER.DBF"
  DEFINE BROWSE bTablBrw OF this PROPERTY;
      Alias "Customer", Fields "Cust_No, ADDRESS1, ADDRESS2", ;
      TOP 2, left 2, width 40, height 8, Text "Customer Info"
ENDCLASS
```

Figure A1–2 shows the form and a Browse object from the preceding code.

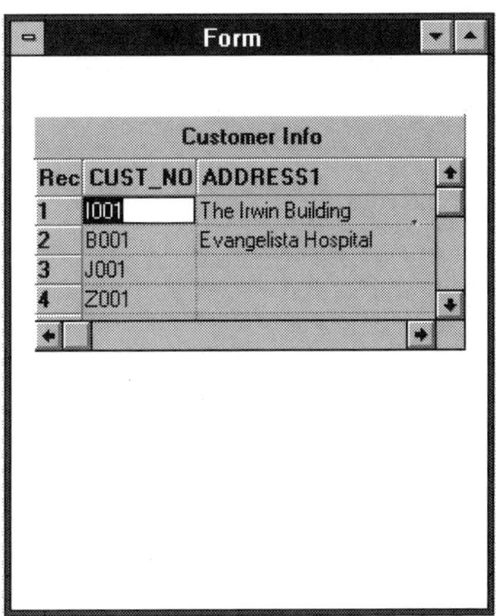

Figure A1–2. Using a Browse Class.

The properties and methods of a Browse Class

Table A1–2 shows all of the properties, their default values, and a short description.

Table A1–2. The Browse Class,

Property/Method	Default	Description
Alias	""	Assigns a table name from a query for the object to browse
Append	.T.	Allows adding of records
Before	N/A	Names that object the Browse object precedes in the tabbing order of the parent form
ClassName	BROWSE	Identifies the Browse object's class
ColorHighlight*	WindowText/Window	Holds the color of the highlight of object
ColorNormal*	BtnText/BtnFace	Holds the color of the object
COPY()*	N/A	Copies from the selected item to Clipboard
CUATAB*	.T.	Tells browse how to use the **Enter** key
CUT()*	N/A	Cuts the currently selected item in Browse object

Table A1–2. The Browse Class.

Property/Method	Default	Description
Delete	.T.	Allows records to be marked for deletion
Enabled	.T.	Holds the status of the selectability of the object
Fields	""	Specifies the names of the fields to display, and any field options to apply to each field
FieldWidth	N/A	Holds the width of a character field in the object
Follow	.T.	Determines if the object will allow updating of the display following the record as it moves to its new index order when a key field value is changed
FontBold	.F.	Holds the bold type attribute value (.t. or .f.)
FontItalic	.F.	Holds the italic type attribute value (.t. or .f.)
FontName	MS Sans Serif	Holds the font name used for displayed characters
FontSize	8.00	Holds the size of the font in points
Header3D*	.T.	Makes the headings display in 3D (raised)
Height	8.00	Holds the height value
HelpFile	""	Holds the name of the Windows Help file (.HLP) that contains context-sensitive Help topics
HelpID	""	Holds the context string or context number of a Help topic in a Windows Help file (.HLP)
HWND	N/A	Holds the Browse object handle
ID	-1	Holds the Browse object's numeric value
Keyboard()*	N/A	Lets the user supply keystrokes to object
Left	0	Holds the position of the left border
MarkCustom()*	N/A	
Mode	0	Holds the display format mode
Modify	.T.	Holds the value for the user altering records
MousePointer	0	Holds the mouse pointer type when the pointer is over the Browse object

Table A1–2. The Browse Class.

Property/Method	Default	Description
Move()	N/A	Lets the Browse object be moved or sized
Name	BROWSE1	Holds the Browse object's name
OnAppend	N/A	Runs a program when a record is added to the table
OnChange	N/A	Runs a routine when the user changes a value
OnGotFocus	N/A	Runs a program when the object receives focus
OnHelp	N/A	Runs a routine when the user presses F1
OnLeftDblClk	N/A	Runs a program when the user double-clicks the object
OnLeftMouseDown	N/A	Runs a program when the user clicks the object with the left mouse button
OnLeftMouseUp	N/A	Runs a program when the user releases the left mouse button while the pointer is over the object
OnLostFocus	N/A	Runs a program when focus is removed
OnMiddleDblClk	N/A	Runs a program when the user double-clicks the object with the middle mouse button
OnMiddleMouseDown	N/A	Runs a routine when the user clicks the object with the middle mouse button
OnMiddleMouseUp	N/A	Runs a program when the user releases the middle mouse button while the pointer is on the object
OnMouseMove	N/A	Runs a program when the user moves the mouse over the object
OnNavigate	N/A	Runs a program when the user moves to a different record
OnOpen	N/A	Runs a program when the parent form is opened
OnRightDblClk	N/A	Runs a program when the user double-clicks the object with the right mouse button
OnRightMouseDown	N/A	Runs a program when the user clicks the object with the right mouse button

Table A1–2. The Browse Class.

Property/Method	Default	Description
OnRightMouseUp	N/A	Runs a routine when the user releases the right mouse button while the pointer is on the object
PageNo*	1	Holds the page number where object exists
Parent	N/A	An object reference that points to the parent form
Paste()*	N/A	Pastes contents of Clipboard
Release()	N/A	Removes the object definition from memory
ScrollBar	2-Auto	Determines if and type of scrollbars
SetFocus()	N/A	Gives focus to the object
ShowDeleted	.F.	Holds the value to authorize display of the object's delete box column
ShowHeading	.T.	Authorizes display of field name headings at the top of each column in the object
ShowRecNo	.T.	Holds the value for showing the record number column in the object
StatusMessage	""	A message displayed on the status bar
TabStop	.T.	Decides if the object can receive focus by pressing **Tab** or **Shift+Tab**
Text	BROWSE	The text string for the object displayed on the caption bar
Toggle	.T.	Authorizes the user to switch between display modes
Top	0	Holds the position of the top border
Undo()*	N/A	Activates the Windows undo function
Visible	.T.	Lets the object be visible or hidden
When	.T.	Specifies a condition that must be true before the user can give focus to the object
Width	12.00	Holds the width

* Items that have changed or are new to Visual dBASE.

THE CHECKBOX CLASS

Objects created from the Class CheckBox can be used to display a CheckBox in a form. It can be used as a graphical tool for representing or displaying the status of a logical state (.t. or .f.) from a field or memory variable.

The CheckBox object that lets a user graphically toggle between true (.T.) and false (.F.) using a small checkbox that places an **x** for .t., blank for false.

Objects created from a CheckBox Class must be contained in a form.

CheckBox example

The example creates a form containing a CheckBox object for the **Customer** table.

```
LOCAL xForm
xForm = NEW BrowseForm()
xForm.OPEN()
CLASS BrowseForm OF FORM
  this.width = 44
  this.view = "CUSTOMER.DBF"
  DEFINE CHECKBOX cBox1 OF this PROPERTY;
       top 2, left 4, width 14, text "Credit OK", DataLink
"Credit"
ENDCLASS
```

Figure A1–3 shows the form and a CheckBox object from the preceding code.

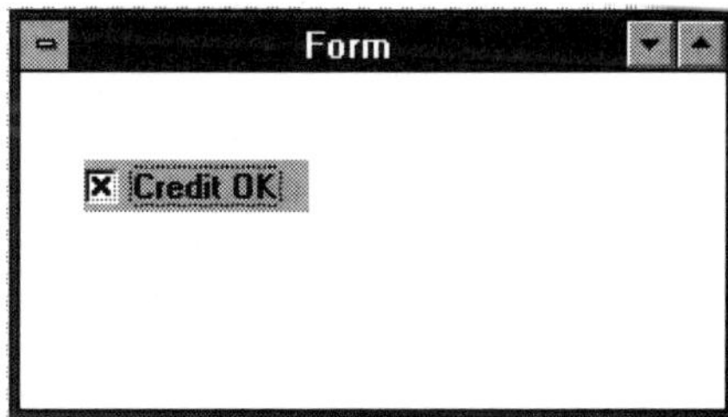

Figure A1–3. Using a CheckBox Class.

The properties and methods of a CheckBox Class

Table A1–3 shows all of the properties, their default values, and a short description.

Table A1–3. The CheckBox Class.

Property/Method	Default	Description
Before	N/A	Names the CheckBox object that precedes the tabbing order of the parent form
ClassName	CHECKBOX	Identifies the CheckBox object's class
ColorNormal*	BTNTEXT/BTNFACE	Holds the color of the object
DataLink	""	Holds the name of the link field to the object
Enabled	.T.	Can the CheckBox be selected?
FontBold	.F.	Will characters in the CheckBox prompt be displayed in bold type?
FontItalic	.F.	Will the characters be displayed in italic type?
FontName	MS Sans Serif	The name of the font to apply to displayed characters
FontSize	8.00	The size of the font in points
FontStrikeOut	.F.	Will the characters be displayed in strikeout type?
FontUnderline	.F.	Will the characters be displayed in underlined type?
Group	.F.	Starts an object group in the parent form
Height	2.00	Holds the height
HelpFile	""	Holds the name of the Windows Help file (.HLP) that contains context-sensitive Help topics
HelpID	""	Holds the context string or context number of a Help topic in a Windows Help file (.HLP)
HWND	N/A	Holds the CheckBox handle
ID	-1	The numeric value of the CheckBox
Left	0	The position of the left border
MarkCustom()*	N/A	
MousePointer	0	Holds the mouse pointer type when the pointer is over the CheckBox
Move()	N/A	Lets the CheckBox be moved or sized

Table A1–3. The CheckBox Class.

Property/Method	Default	Description
Name	CHECKBOX1	Holds the CheckBox name
OldStyle	.F.	Will the CheckBox be displayed in the default Windows style or in Borland style?
OnChange	N/A	Runs a program when the user changes values
OnGotFocus	N/A	Runs a program when the CheckBox receives focus
OnHelp	N/A	Runs a routine when the user presses F1
OnLeftDblClk	N/A	Runs a program when the user double-clicks the CheckBox
OnLeftMouseDown	N/A	Runs a routine when the user clicks the CheckBox with the left mouse button
OnLeftMouseUp	N/A	Runs a routine when the user releases the left mouse button while over the CheckBox
OnLostFocus	N/A	Runs a program when focus is removed
OnMiddleDblClk	N/A	Runs a program when the user double-clicks the CheckBox with the middle mouse button
OnMiddleMouseDown	N/A	Runs a program when the user clicks the CheckBox with the middle mouse button
OnMiddleMouseUp	N/A	Runs a program when the user releases the middle mouse button while the pointer is on the CheckBox
OnMouseMove	N/A	Runs a program when the user moves the mouse pointer over the CheckBox
OnOpen	N/A	Runs a program when the parent form is opened
OnRightDblClk	N/A	Runs a program when the user double-clicks the CheckBox with the right mouse button
OnRightMouseDown	N/A	Runs a program when the user clicks the CheckBox with the right mouse button
OnRightMouseUp	N/A	Runs a routine when the user releases the right mouse button while the pointer is on the CheckBox

Table A1–3. The CheckBox Class.

Property/Method	**Default**	**Description**
PageNo*	1	The page number object resides on
Parent	N/A	The object reference that points to the parent form
Release()	N/A	Removes the CheckBox definition from memory
SetFocus()	N/A	Gives focus to the CheckBox
StatusMessage	""	Holds a message to display on the status bar while the CheckBox has focus
SpeedTip*	""	Holds text for one-second delay bubble Help
TabStop	.T.	Holds the value to determine if the user can go to the CheckBox by pressing **Tab** or **Shift-Tab**
Text	CheckBox	Holds the text for the CheckBox
Top	0	Holds the position of the top border
Value	N/A	Holds the value in the CheckBox
Visible	.T.	Is the CheckBox visible or hidden?
When	N/A	Specifies a condition that must evaluate to true before the user can give focus to the CheckBox
Width	11.62	Holds the width

* Items that have changed or are new to Visual dBASE.

THE COMBOBOX CLASS

Objects created from the Class ComboBox can be used to display a selection of values in a list. The user can select from the list by entering characters in a Text box or by selecting the value directly from the list.

It is a graphical tool for displaying multiple items to be used to select one item. Objects created from a ComboBox Class must be contained in a form.

ComboBox Example

The example creates a form containing two ComboBox objects for the **Customer** table.

```
LOCAL xForm
xForm = NEW BrowseForm()
xForm.OPEN()
CLASS BrowseForm OF FORM
  this.width = 44
  this.view = "CUSTOMER.DBF"
  DEFINE COMBOBOX cBox1 OF this PROPERTY ;
       Top 2, Left 2, Width 12, Height 6, Style 1, ;
       DataSource "FIELD State_PROV"
  DEFINE COMBOBOX cBox2 of this PROPERTY ;
       Top 2, Left 18, Width 20, Height 8, DataSource "FILE
*.WFM"
ENDCLASS
```

Figure A1–4 shows the form and the two ComboBoxes from the preceding code.

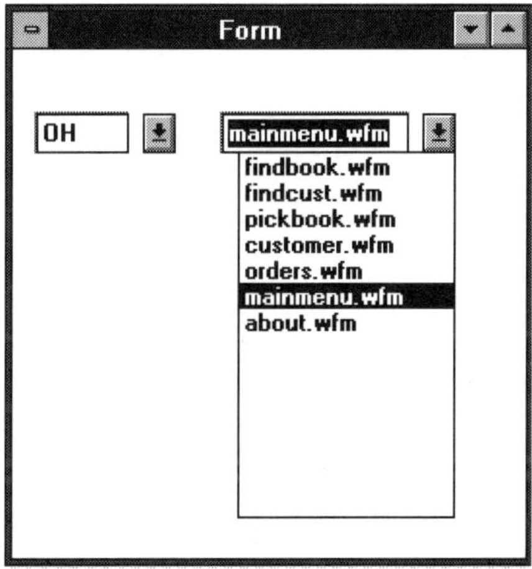

Figure A1–4. Using a ComboBox Class.

The properties and methods of a ComboBox Class

Table A1–4 shows all of the properties, their default values, and a short description.

Table A1–4. The ComboBox Class.

Property/Method	Default	Description
Before	N/A	Which object precedes the ComboBox in the tabbing order of the parent form?
ClassName	COMBOBOX	Identifies the ComboBox class
ColorNormal*	WindowText/Window	Specifies the color of the ComboBox
Copy()*	N/A	Copies contents of field to clipboard
Cut()*	N/A	Removes contents of field and puts in clipboard
DataLink	""	The field name linked to the ComboBox
DataSource	""	The display data source for the ComboBox
DropDownHeight*	6	Specifies the height for the drop-down box
Enabled	.T.	Can the ComboBox be selected?
FontBold	.F.	Can the characters be displayed in bold type?
FontItalic	.F.	Can the characters be displayed in italic type?
FontName	MS Sans Serif	The name of the font to displayed characters
FontSize	8.00	The size of the font in points
FontStrikeOut	.F.	Will the characters be displayed in strikeout type?
FontUnderline	.F.	Will the characters be displayed in underlined type?
Height	8.33	Holds the height
HelpFile	""	The name of the Windows Help file (.HLP) that contains context-sensitive Help topics
HelpID	""	The name of the context string or context number of a Help topic in a Windows Help file (.HLP)
HWND	N/A	The ComboBox handle
ID	-1	Holds the ComboBox numeric value
Keyboard()*	N/A	Lets you keyboard items to the object
Left	0	Holds the position of the left border
MarkCustom()*	N/A	

Table A1–4. The ComboBox Class.

Property/Method	Default	Description
MousePointer	0	The type of mouse pointer when it is over the ComboBox
Move()	N/A	Used to move or size the ComboBox
Name	COMBOBOX1	The name of the ComboBox
OnChange	N/A	Runs a program when the user moves from one prompt to another
OnGotFocus	N/A	Runs a program when the ComboBox receives focus
OnHelp	N/A	Runs a program when the user presses F1
OnLeftDblClk	N/A	Runs a program when the user double-clicks the ComboBox
OnLeftMouseDown	N/A	Runs a program when the user clicks the ComboBox with the left mouse button
OnLeftMouseUp	N/A	Runs a program when the user releases the left mouse button while the pointer is over the ComboBox
OnLostFocus	N/A	Runs a program when focus is removed
OnMiddleDblClk	N/A	Runs a program when the user double-clicks the ComboBox with the middle mouse button
OnMiddleMouseDown	N/A	Runs a program when the user clicks the ComboBox with the middle mouse button
OnMiddleMouseUp	N/A	Runs a program when the user releases the middle mouse button while on the ComboBox
OnMouseMove	N/A	Runs a program when the user moves the mouse in the ComboBox
OnOpen	N/A	Runs a program when the parent form is opened
OnRightDblClk	N/A	Runs a program when the user double-clicks the ComboBox with the right mouse button
OnRightMouseDown	N/A	Runs a program when the user clicks the ComboBox with the right mouse button

Table A1–4. The ComboBox Class.

Property/Method	Default	Description
OnRightMouseUp	N/A	Runs a program when the user releases the right mouse button while on the ComboBox
PageNo*	1	The page number for the object
Parent	N/A	The object reference that points to the parent form
Paste()*	n/a	Pastes contents from clipboard
Release()	N/A	Removes the ComboBox definition from memory
SetFocus()	N/A	Gives focus to the ComboBox
Sorted	.F.	Will the prompts be listed in sorted order?
StatusMessage	""	The message to display on the status bar
Style	0 (Simple)	Will the user use the text box, the drop-down list, or both?
TabStop	.T.	Will the object get focus by pressing **Tab** or **Shift+Tab**?
Top	0	The position of the top border
Undo()*	N/A	Undoes last change to field
Value	""	The value in the ComboBox
Visible	.T.	Will the ComboBox be visible or hidden?
When	N/A	Specifies a condition that must evaluate to true before the user can give the ComboBox focus
Width	12.50	The width

*Items that have changed or are new to Visual dBASE.

THE DDELINK CLASS

Objects created from the Class DDELink can be used to initiate and control a DDE link between dBASE and a Windows server application, allowing dBASE to send instructions and data-exchange requests to the server.

Objects created from a DDELink Class do not have to be contained in a form.

DDELink example

The example creates a DDELink object with the NEW operator. It attempts to initiate a server session with Quattro Pro for Windows with the Initiate method. Then it uses the Peek method to extract a value from the element HospCosts:C4 to a dBASE memory variable and Poke to place a new value in cell HospCosts:C5 of the QPW spreadsheet.

```
LOCAL xLinkObj
xLinkObj = NEW DDELINK()
IF xLinkObj.Initiate("QPW","Irwin.WB1")
  ? "I am connected to QPW OK"
ELSE
  ? "The connection to Quattro Pro for Windows failed"
ENDIF
mVal1=xLinkObj.Peek("HospCosts:C4")
? mVal1
xLinkObj.Poke("HospCosts:C5","198")
mVal2=xLinkObj.Peek("HospCosts:C5")
? mVal2
xLinkObj.Release()
```

The properties and methods of a DDELink Class

Table A1–5 shows all of the properties, their default values, and a short description.

Table A1–5. The DDELink Class.

Property/Method	Default	Description
Advise()	N/A	Asks the Server to notify the Client when an item in the Server document changes
ClassName	DDELINK	Identifies the DDELink object class
Execute()	N/A	Works with the Server to send instructions in its own language
Initiate()	N/A	Starts communication with a DDE Server application
OnNewValue	N/A	Runs a program when an item in the Server application changes
Peek()	N/A	Gets a data item stored in the Server document
Poke()	N/A	Puts a data item into the Server document
Reconnect()	N/A	Reactivates a DDELink that was terminated with Terminate()
Release()	N/A	Removes the DDELink object definition from memory
Server	N/A	Holds the name of the Server you specify with the Initiate() method
Terminate()	N/A	Terminates the DDELink with the Server application
Timeout	10.00	Waits for the specified amount of time for a transaction before returning an error
Topic	""	Holds the name of the topic you specified with the Initiate() method
Unadvise()	N/A	Asks the Server to stop telling the DDELink object when an item in the Server document changes

THE DDETOPIC CLASS

Objects created from the Class DDETopic can be used to receive requests from a DDE Client. This Class is used as the Server and determines what action will be taken by dBASE for Windows.

Objects created from a DDETopic Class do not have to be contained in a form.

DDETopic example

The example creates a DDE server to be used by Quattro Pro.

```
*** DDETopic.Prg
*
SET PROC TO DDETopic.PRG
********************
******   Part A   ******
********************
*  Following is the Initialization code for Server
*          It assigns a name to the _app.DDEServiceName
*          property and a function name to the OnInitiate
property
*
*      DDEServiceName is property that holds DDE session name
*      OnInitiate event property will run the function specified
*          when the Client attempts to initiate a DDELink
*
_app.DDEServiceName = "VdBServer"
_app.OnInitiate = StartHandler
*
*  End of Intialization code
*
********************
******   Part B   ******
********************
*   The following function will be started when the Client
*   initiates a DDE Link with this session of dBASE (VdBServer)
*
*   The parameter TopicName is passed to the StartHandler
function
*    by the Client program—NOT dBASE
*
FUNCTION StartHandler (TopicName)
  *       Create a custom DDETopic object
  xDDESrv1 = NEW SpdShtDDETopic(TopicName)
  ? "Server is ACTIVE"
  ? "The Topic is ", xDDESrv1.Topic
RETURN xDDESrv1
********************
******   Part C   ******
********************
*
CLASS SpdShtDDETopic(cTopic) OF DDETopic(cTopic)
  *
  *   code goes here for the new topic server and its
  *   functions. Depending on the type of actions the
  *   Client will be doing you will have to specify code
  *   for the OnPeek, OnPoke, OnExecute methods of
  *   the new object instantiated from this CLASS
  *
ENDCLASS
```

The properties and methods of a DDETopic Class

Table A1–6 shows all of the properties, their default values, and a short description.

Table A1–6. The DDETopic Class.

Property/Method	Default	Description
ClassName	DDETOPIC	Identifies the DDETopic object class
Notify()	N/A	Tells a Client application (or all if more than one) that a dBASE item was changed
OnAdvise	N/A	Runs a program when an external application creates a hot link
OnExecute	N/A	Runs a program when the Client application sends a command to dBASE
OnPeek	N/A	Runs a program when the Client requests information (values) from dBASE
OnPoke	N/A	Runs a program when the Client inserts a new value into a dBASE item
OnUnadvise	N/A	Runs a program when a Client removes a hot link from a particular item
Release()	N/A	Removes the DDETopic object definition from memory
Topic	N/A	The DDETopic object's topic

The Editor Class

Objects created from the Class Editor can be used to view and edit Text or Memo fields. It is the tool of choice for editing Memo fields in a window of a form. If you attempt to edit a Memo field in Visual dBASE, the editor will activate its own window inside dBASE (MDI = .t.). This can be a problem if you are working with forms that have MDI = .f. The user will not be able to view/edit his or her forms without switching (activating) the dBASE window. Objects created from an Editor Class must be contained in a form.

Editor example

The example creates two Editor objects. One for a memo field (that can be modified) and one for the program file itself (read-only). The difference is setting one property. It is using a table named **Customer**.

```
LOCAL f
f = NEW EditorForm()
f.Open()
CLASS EditorForm OF FORM
   this.View = "Customer.DBF"
   this.Text = "Editor Object example"
   this.Top = 1
   this.Left = 4
   this.Width = 65
   this.Height = 18
   DEFINE EDITOR MyEd1 OF this   PROPERTY;
        Top  11, Left  2, Width  42, Height  5, Wrap .T., ;
         DataLink "CUSTOMER->NOTES"
   DEFINE EDITOR MyEd2 OF this PROPERTY ;
        Modify .F., Wrap .T., Top 2, Left 2, Width 60, Height 7,
;
        DataLink "FILE TSTEDITR.PRG"
   DEFINE PUSHBUTTON Exit OF this PROPERTY ;
        Top 15, Left 50, Width 12, height 2, Text "Exit", ;
        OnClick {;Form.Close()}
   DEFINE TEXT MyTxt1 OF this PROPERTY ;
        Top 9.5, Left 3, Width 36, Height 1.2, FontSize 12, ;
        Text "A Memo field (editable)"
   DEFINE TEXT MyTxt2 OF this  PROPERTY;
        Top 0.1, Left 2, Width 58, Height 1.2, FontSize 12, ;
        Text "*** The Program File (View ONLY!) ***"
ENDCLASS
```

Figure A1–5 shows the form and the Editor objects from the preceding code.

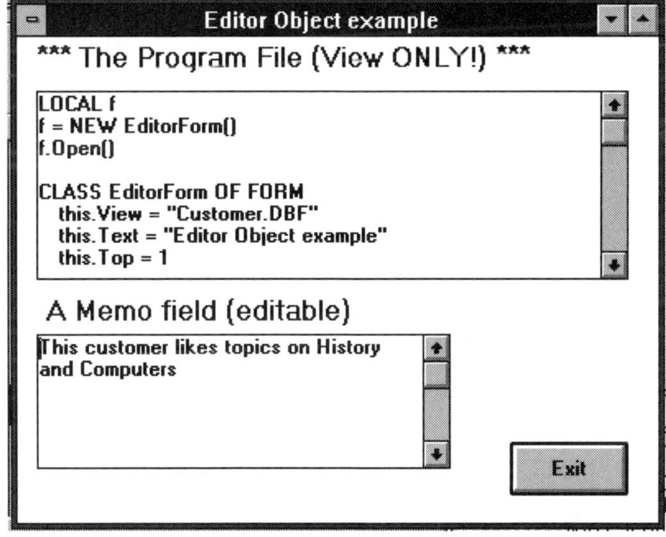

Figure A1–5. Using an Editor Class.

The properties and methods of an Editor Class

Table A1–7 shows all of the properties, their default values, and a short description.

Table A1–7. The Editor Class.

Property/Method	**Default**	**Description**
Before	N/A	Holds the name of which object the Editor object will precede in the tabbing order of the parent form
Border*	.T.	If a border is displayed or not
ClassName	EDITOR	Identifies the Editor object class
ColorNormal	N/W*	Holds the color value of the Editor object when it does not have focus
Copy()*	N/A	Copies the highlighted item to Clipboard
CUATab*	.T.	Determines how the **Enter** key/**Tab** key work
Cut()*	N/A	Removes the highlighted item to Clipboard
DataLink	""	The name of a Memo field, text file, or character field that is linked to the Editor object
Enabled	.T.	Can the Editor object be selected?
FontBold	.F.	Can characters be displayed in bold type?
FontItalic	.F.	Can characters be displayed in italic type?
FontName	MS Sans Serif	Which font is used for the characters in the display?
FontSize	8.00	What is the size of the font in point size?
FontStrikeOut	.F.	Are the characters displayed in strikeout type?
FontUnderline	.F.	Are the characters displayed in underlined type?
Height	10.00	The height
HelpFile	""	The name of the Windows Help file (.HLP) that contains context-sensitive Help topics
HelpID	""	The context string or context number of a Help topic in a Windows Help file (.HLP)
HWND	N/A	The Editor object handle
ID	-1	The Editor object with a numeric value

Table A1–7. The Editor Class.

Property/Method	Default	Description
Keyboard()*	N/A	Places keys into the object
Left	0	The position of the left border
LineNo*	1	Moves to the line number specified
MarkCustom()*	N/A	
Modify	.T.	Can the user change data in the Editor object?
MousePointer	0	Which mouse pointer type when in the Editor object?
Move()	N/A	Moves or sizes the Editor object
Name	EDITOR1	The name of the Editor object
OnChange	N/A	Runs a program when the user changes text in the Editor object
OnGotFocus	N/A	Runs a program when the Editor object receives focus
OnHelp	N/A	Runs a program when the user presses F1
OnLeftDblClk	N/A	Runs a program when the user double-clicks on the Editor object
OnLeftMouseDown	N/A	Runs a program when the user clicks on the Editor object with the left mouse button
OnLeftMouseUp	N/A	Runs a program when the user releases the left mouse button while in the Editor object
OnLostFocus	N/A	Runs a routine when focus is removed
OnMiddleDblClk	N/A	Runs a program when the user double-clicks on the Editor object with the middle mouse button
OnMiddleMouseDown	N/A	Runs a program when the user clicks on the Editor object with the middle mouse button
OnMiddleMouseUp	N/A	Runs a program when the user releases the middle mouse button while in the Editor object
OnMouseMove	N/A	Runs a program when the user moves the mouse in the Editor object
OnOpen	N/A	Runs a program when the parent form is opened

Table A1–7. The Editor Class.

Property/Method	Default	Description
OnRightDblClk	N/A	Runs a program when the user double-clicks on the Editor object with the right mouse button
OnRightMouseDown	N/A	Runs a program when the user clicks on the Editor object with the right mouse button
OnRightMouseUp	N/A	Runs a program when the user releases the right mouse button while in the Editor object
PageNo*	1	Holds the page number for the object
Parent	N/A	The object reference that points to the parent form
Paste()*	N/A	Pastes the Clipboard contents to object
Release()	N/A	Removes the Editor object definition from memory
Scrollbar	1 (On)	Will the Editor object have a scroll bar?
SetFocus()	N/A	Gives focus to the Editor object
StatusMessage	""	The message to display on the status bar when the Editor object receives focus
TabStop	.T.	Can the user go to the Editor object by pressing **Tab** or **Shift+Tab**?
Top	0	The position of the top border
Undo()*	N/A	Change last action taken against object
Valid	N/A	The condition that must evaluate true (.T.) before the user can remove focus from the Editor object
Value	""	The contents of the Editor object
Visible	.T.	Can the Editor object be visible?
When	N/A	The condition that must evaluate true before the user can give focus to the Editor object
Width	13.00	The width
Wrap	.T.	Can the Editor object wrap input text automatically?

*Items that have changed or are new to Visual dBASE.

THE ENTRYFIELD CLASS

Objects created from the Class EntryField can be used to input display and modify information that is stored in a table field or simply in the object itself. It is similar to the @ . . . GET command combined with a memory variable that the information is placed in. However, the similarity ends there. The entryfield is an object that can be updated, linked to a field, or stand alone (like a memory variable).

Objects created from an EntryField Class must be contained in a form.

EntryField example

The example creates two entryfields that are not attached to a table field and two that are. It will use a table named **Customer**.

```
LOCAL f
f = NEW EntrFldForm()
f.Open()
CLASS EntrFldForm OF FORM
   this.View = "Customer.DBF"
   this.Text = "EntryField Object example"
   this.Top = 1
   this.Left = 4
   this.Width = 65
   this.Height = 18
   DEFINE PUSHBUTTON Exit OF this PROPERTY ;
       Top 15, Left 50, Width 12, height 2, Text "Exit", ;
       OnClick {;Form.Close()}
   DEFINE ENTRYFIELD MyEntFld1 OF this   PROPERTY;
       Top  4, Left  5, Width  42, ColorNormal "W+/N", ;
       DataLink "CUSTOMER->Cust_Name"
   DEFINE ENTRYFIELD MyEntFld2 OF this   PROPERTY;
       Top  6, Left  5, Width  42, ColorHighlight "GR+/R",;
       DataLink "CUSTOMER->Address1"
   DEFINE ENTRYFIELD MyEntFld3 OF this   PROPERTY;
       Top  12, Left  5, Width  42,  Value "Type in anything
here"
   DEFINE ENTRYFIELD MyEntFld4 OF this   PROPERTY;
       Top  14, Left  5, Width  42, Value "Fill in the blank ...
"
   DEFINE TEXT MyTxt1 OF this PROPERTY ;
       Top 1, Left 2, Width 56, Height 1.2, FontSize 12, ;
       Text "An EntryField attached to a field"
   DEFINE TEXT MyTxt2 OF this  PROPERTY;
       Top 10, Left 2, Width 58, Height 1.2, FontSize 12, ;
       Text "*** Two EntryFields non-attached! ***"
ENDCLASS
```

Figure A1–6 shows the form and some EntryField objects from the preceding code.

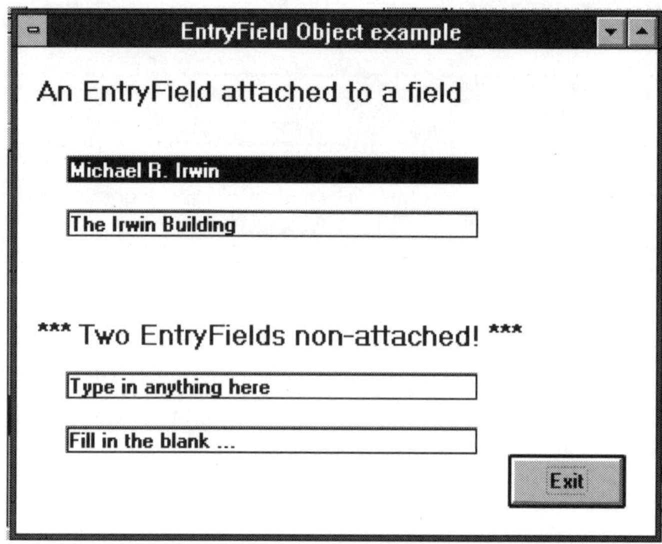

Figure A1–6. Using an EntryField Class.

The properties and methods of an EntryField Class

Table A1–8 shows all of the properties, their default values, and a short description.

Table A1–8. The EntryField Class.

Property/Method	Default	Description
Before	N/A	Holds the name of which object the entryfield precedes in the tabbing order of the parent form
Border	.T.	Will the entryfield be surrounded with a border?
ClassName	ENTRYFIELD	Identifies the EntryField class
ColorHighlight*	WindowText/dWindow	Holds the color of the entryfield when it is highlighted
ColorNormal*	WindowText/Window	Holds the color of the entryfield when it is not highlighted
Copy()*	N/A	Copies contents of object to Clipboard
Cut()*	N/A	Removes the contents of object to Clipboard
DataLink	“”	Holds the field name that is linked to the object
Enabled	.T.	Can the entryfield be selected?

Table A1–8. The EntryField Class.

Property/Method	Default	Description
FontBold	.F.	Can the entryfield display bold type?
FontItalic	.F.	Can the characters be displayed in italic type?
FontName	MS Sans Serif	Name of the font used to displayed characters
FontSize	8.00	The size of the font in points
FontStrikeOut	.F.	Will the characters be displayed in strikeout type?
FontUnderline	.F.	Will the characters be displayed in underlined type?
Function	""	Holds the format for the text based on the overall object
Height	1.33	The height
HelpFile	""	The name of the Windows Help file (.HLP) that contains context-sensitive Help topics
HelpID	""	The context string or context number of a Help topic in a Windows Help file (.HLP)
HWND	N/A	The entryfield handle
ID	-1	The entryfield numeric value
Key	N/A	Runs a program when the user presses a key
Keyboard()*	N/A	Copies keystrokes to the object
Left	0	The position of the left border
MarkCustom()*	N/A	
MaxLength	12	The scrolling width for the entryfield
MousePointer	0	The type of mouse pointer when it is over the entryfield
Move()	N/A	Moves or sizes the entryfield
Name	ENTRYFIELD1	The name of the entryfield
OldStyle	N/A	Will the entryfield be displayed in the default Windows style or in Borland style?
OnChange	N/A	Runs a program when the user changes a value
OnGotFocus	N/A	Runs a program when the entryfield receives focus

Table A1–8. The EntryField Class.

Property/Method	Default	Description
OnHelp	N/A	Runs a program when the user presses F1
OnLeftDblClk	N/A	Runs a program when the user double-clicks the entryfield
OnLeftMouseDown	N/A	Runs a program when the user clicks the entryfield with the left mouse button
OnLeftMouseUp	N/A	Runs a program when the user releases the left mouse button while over the entryfield
OnLostFocus	N/A	Runs a program when focus is removed
OnMiddleDblClk	N/A	Runs a program when the user double-clicks the entryfield with the middle mouse button
OnMiddleMouseDown	N/A	Runs a program when the user clicks the entryfield with the middle mouse button
OnMiddleMouseUp	N/A	Runs a program when the user releases the middle mouse button while on the listbox
OnMouseMove	N/A	Runs a program when the user moves the mouse over the entryfield
OnOpen	N/A	Runs a program when the parent form is opened
OnRightDblClk	N/A	Runs a program when the user double-clicks the entryfield with the right mouse button
OnRightMouseDown	N/A	Runs a program when the user clicks the entryfield with the right mouse button
OnRightMouseUp	N/A	Runs a program when the user releases the right mouse button while on the entryfield
PageNo*	1	The page where the object is located
Parent	N/A	The object reference that points to the parent form
Paste()*	N/A	Pastes contents of Clipboard to object
Picture	""	Holds the format for the text one character at a time
Release()	N/A	Removes the entryfield definition from memory

Table A1–8. The EntryField Class.

Property/Method	**Default**	**Description**
SelectAll	.F.	Is the initial value in the entryfield to appear completely selected (highlighted)?
SetFocus()	N/A	Gives focus to the entryfield
StatusMessage	""	The message displayed on the status bar while the entryfield has focus
TabStop	.T.	Can the user give focus to the entryfield by pressing **Tab** or **Shift+Tab**?
Top	0	The position of the top border
Undo()*	N/A	Undoes last action against object
Valid	N/A	Holds the condition that must evaluate to true before it can remove focus from the entryfield
ValidErrorMsg	""	Holds the message displayed on the status bar when the Valid property returns false (N/A)
ValidRequired	.F.	When true (.t.) will force the Valid property to apply any time the object is left
Value	""	The value in the entryfield (if blank or unlinked)
Visible	.T.	Is the entryfield to be visible
When	N/A	Holds the condition that must evaluate to true before the user can give focus to the entryfield
Width	11.5	The width

*Items that have changed or are new to Visual dBASE.

THE FORM CLASS

Objects created from the Class Form are the window. The window is more than a window. It can be used to contain other objects. Once it contains additional objects, it can be used to input and display information. The form can be more than just an entry/view screen. It can be a dialog box, a message box, even a completely integrated application.

Objects created from the Form Class are the actual containers that will be used to hold other objects.

Form example

The example creates three different forms using the DEFINE FORM command, the NEW METHOD command, and defining a new Class from the Form Class. The last form will have a pushbutton in it that will close all three forms. It also makes that last opened form Modal—it must be closed before moving to another one.

```
LOCAL MyFormCls
DEFINE FORM MyDefForm PROPERTY ;
   Text "Created with DEFINE", Top 1, left 2, Height 10, MDI  .f.
OPEN FORM MyDefForm
MyNewForm = NEW Form()
MyNewForm.Text = "Created with NEW command"
MyNewForm.Top = 4
MyNewForm.Left = 5
MyNewForm.Height = 12
MyNewForm.MDI = .f.
MyNewForm.Open()
fFrClsForm = NEW MyFormCls()
fFrClsForm.ReadModal()
CLASS MyFormCls OF Form()
    this.text = "The Form Example from a NEW Class"
    this.top = 8
    this.left = 12
    this.Height = 5
    this.MDI = .f.
    *
    DEFINE PushButton MyClosButn OF this  PROPERTY;
         Top 2.5, Left 50, Height 1.2, Text "E&xit", ;
         OnClick CLASS::CLOSForms

    PROCEDURE CLOSForms
       CLOSE FORM MyDefForm, MyNewForm
       CLOSE FORM
       RELEASE MyDefForm, MyNewForm, fFrClsForm
    RETURN
ENDCLASS
```

Figure A1–7 shows the form from the preceding code.

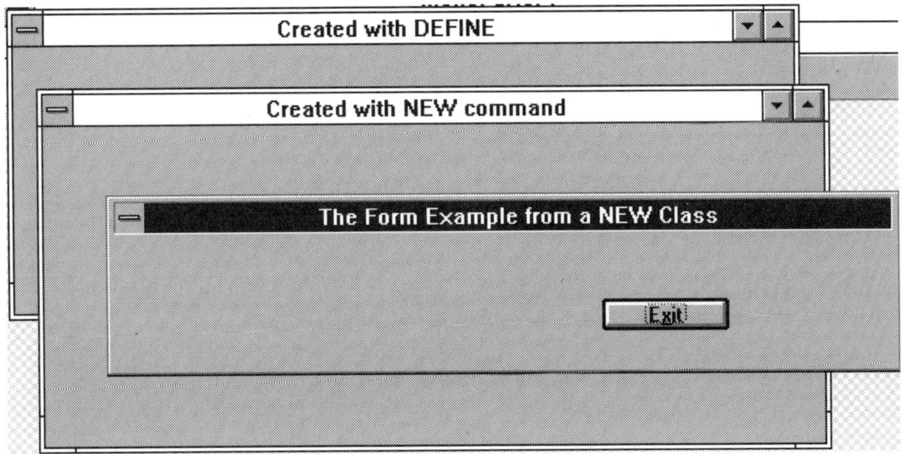

Figure A1–7. Using a Form Class.

The properties and methods of a Form Class

Table A1–9 shows all of the properties, their default values, and a short description. Those with an asterisk are new or changed in Visual dBASE (from dBASE for Windows version 5.0).

Table A1–9. The Form Class.

Property/Method	Default	Description
AbandonRecord()*	N/A	Abandons append to phantom record
ActiveControl	.f.	Holds the name of the object that has focus when the form is opened or gains focus
AutoSize	.T.	Will the form adjust itself automatically to contain its objects when the form is opened?
BeginAppend()*	N/A	Starts process to append to phantom record
CanClose*	N/A	Runs a program when user tries to close the form
CanNavigate*	N/A	Runs a program when user tries to navigate records
ClassName	FORM	Identifies the Form object class
Close()	N/A	Closes the form
ColorNormal*	BtnFace	The color of the form

Table A1–9. The Form Class.

Property/Method	Default	Description
DesignView*	""	Holds the name of a table/query to be used only for creating the form; it is temporary
Enabled	.T.	Can the form receive focus?
EscExit	.T.	Can the user close the form by pressing the **Esc** key?
First	N/A	The name of the object that will first be pointed to in the form
Height	15.00	The height
HelpFile	""	The name of the Windows Help file (.HLP) that contains context-sensitive Help topics
HelpID	""	The name of the context string or context number of a Help topic in a Windows Help file (.HLP)
HWND	N/A	The object handle of the form
Icon*	""	Name of icon to use when minimized
IsRecordChanged()*	N/A	Determines if record has changed
Left	2.00	The position of the left border
Maximize	.F.	Can the form be maximized?
MDI	.T.	Does the form conform to the Windows Multiple Document Interface (MDI) standards—forms will be contained inside the dBASE frame?
MenuFile	""	The name of the attached menu system for the form
Minimize	.F.	Can the form be minimized?
MousePointer	0	The mouse pointer type when it is in the form
Move()*	N/A	Move the form
Moveable	.T.	Can the form be moved with the mouse?
NextCol()	N/A	The next highest column position
NextObj	N/A	The name of the next object in the form
NextRow()	N/A	The next highest row position

Table A1–9. The Form Class.

Property/Method	Default	Description
OnAppend*	N/A	Runs a program when the user appends a record
OnChange	N/A	Runs a program when the user changes a value
OnClose	N/A	Runs a program when the form is closed
OnGotFocus	N/A	Runs a program when the form receives focus
OnHelp	N/A	Runs a program when the user presses F1
OnLeftDblClk	N/A	Runs a program when the user double-clicks the form
OnLeftMouseDown	N/A	Runs a program when the user clicks the form with the left mouse button
OnLeftMouseUp	N/A	Runs a program when the user releases the left mouse button while in the form
OnLostFocus	N/A	Runs a program when focus is removed
OnMiddleDblClk	N/A	Runs a program when the user double-clicks the form with the middle mouse button
OnMiddleMouseDown	N/A	Runs a program when the user clicks the form with the middle mouse button
OnMiddleMouseUp	N/A	Runs a program when the user releases the middle mouse button while in the form
OnMouseMove	N/A	Runs a program when the user moves the mouse in the form
OnMove	N/A	Runs a program after the user moves the form
OnNavigate	N/A	Runs a program when the user moves to a different record
OnOpen	N/A	Runs a program when the form is opened
OnRightDblClk	N/A	Runs a program when the user double-clicks the form with the right mouse button
OnRightMouseDown	N/A	Runs a program when the user clicks the form with the right mouse button
OnRightMouseUp	N/A	Runs a program when the user releases the right mouse button while in the form

Table A1–9. The Form Class.

Property/Method	Default	Description
OnSelection	N/A	Runs a program when the form data entry is completed, moving to the next record (submitted)
OnSize	N/A	Runs a program after the user resizes the form
Open()	N/A	Opens the form as a modeless window
PageCount()*	N/A	Returns the number of pages in form
PageNo*	1	The page number currently on in form
PopupMenu*	.f.	Holds pointer to popup menu if associated
Print()	N/A	Prints the form and the objects it contains
ReadModal()	N/A	Opens the form as a modal window (only when mdi = .f.)
Refresh()*	N/A	Forces a form to refresh
RefreshAlways*	.t.	Will force refresh automatically
Release()	N/A	Removes the form definition from memory
SaveRecord()*	N/A	Saves the record added to phantom record
ScaleFontName	MS Sans Serif	The name of the font the form is based on
ScaleFontSize	8.00	The size of the font in the coordinate plane of the form
Scrollbar	0 (Off)	The type of scroll bar the form will have
SetFocus()	N/A	Gives focus to the form
Sizeable	.F.	Can the user resize the form?
ShowSpeedTip*	.t.	Activates speed tips if present
StatusMessage	“”	Holds the message to display on the status bar while the form has focus
SysMenu	.F.	Can the form have a Control menu (System Menu)?
Text	Form	The text to be display in the caption bar
Top	0	The position of the top border
TopMost*	.F.	Determines if display on top of other forms
View	“”	The name of the query or table which the form uses

Table A1–9. The Form Class.

Property/Method	Default	Description
Visible	.T.	Will the form be visible?
Width	40.00	The width
WindowState	0 (Normal)	The state of the form—minimized, maximized, or normal

*Items that have changed or are new to Visual dBASE.

THE IMAGE CLASS

Objects created from the Class Image can be used to display bitmap images—.BMP and .PCX files. In addition to the .BMP and .PCX files, an Image object can hold bitmap images from a field or a Windows resource file.

Objects created from an Image Class must be contained in a form.

Image example

The example creates two Image objects. One of the images will be from an external file named **TREEMTN.PCX**. The other image will come from a Borland Windows resource #21.

```
LOCAL fImageForm
fImageForm = NEW ImageForm()
fImageForm.Open()
CLASS ImageForm OF FORM
   this.Text = "Image examples"
   this.Width =         38
   this.Top =          1
   this.Left =         25
   this.Height =         12
   DEFINE TEXT MyTxt1 OF this PROPERTY;
         Top 1, Left 3.5, Height 1.2, Width 25, FontSize 10, ;
         Text "External .PCX file"
   DEFINE IMAGE MyImage1 OF this PROPERTY;
         Top 2, left 4, Height 6, Width 32.5, ;
         DataSource "FILENAME TREEMTN.PCX"
   DEFINE TEXT MyTxt2 OF this PROPERTY;
         Top 10, Left 3, Height 1.2, Width 20.5, FontSize 10,;
         Text "From a Resource"
   DEFINE IMAGE MyImage2 OF this PROPERTY;
         Top 9, Left 26, Height 2.5, Width 9,;
```

```
        DataSource "RESOURCE #21"
ENDCLASS
```

Figure A1–8 shows the form with two Image objects from the preceding code.

Figure A1–8. Using an Image Class.

The properties and methods of an Image Class

Table A1–10 shows all of the properties, their default values, and a short description.

Table A1–10. The Image Class.

Property/Method	Default	Description
Alignment	0 (Top Left)	The positioning type for the graphic image in the Image object
Before	N/A	Holds the name of which object the entryfield precedes in the tabbing order of the parent form
ClassName	IMAGE	Identifies the Image object class
DataSource	""	The name of the file, DLL resource, or binary field that is the graphic image
Height	5.00	The height
HWND	N/A	The Image object handle
ID	-1	The numeric value of the Image object
Left	0	The position of the left border

Table A1–10. The Image Class.

Property/Method	Default	Description
MarkCustom()*	N/A	
MousePointer	0	The mouse pointer's type when it is in the Image object.
Move()	N/A	Moves or sizes the Image object
Name	IMAGE1	The name of the Image object
OnLeftDblClk	N/A	Runs a program when the user double-clicks the Image object
OnLeftMouseDown	N/A	Runs a program when the user clicks the Image object with the left mouse button
OnLeftMouseUp	N/A	Runs a program when the user releases the left mouse button while on the Image object
OnMiddleDblClk	N/A	Runs a program when the user double-clicks the Image object with the middle mouse button
OnMiddleMouseDown	N/A	Runs a program when the user clicks the Image object with the middle mouse button
OnMiddleMouseUp	N/A	Runs a program when the user releases the middle mouse button while on the Image object
OnMouseMove	N/A	Runs a program when the user moves the mouse in the Image object
OnOpen	N/A	Runs a program when the parent form is opened
OnRightDblClk	N/A	Runs a program when the user double-clicks the Image object with the right mouse button
OnRightMouseDown	N/A	Runs a program when the user clicks the Image object with the right mouse button
OnRightMouseUp	N/A	Runs a program when the user releases the right mouse button while on the Image object
PageNo*	1	Specifies the page containing the object
Parent	N/A	The object reference that points to the parent form
Release()	N/A	Removes the Image object definition from memory

Table A1–10. The Image Class.

Property/Method	Default	Description
Top	0	The position of the top border
Visible	.T.	Will the Image object be visible?
Width	8.00	The width

*Items that have changed or are new to Visual dBASE.

THE LINE CLASS

Objects created from the Class Line can be used to display a type of line on a form. Objects created from a Line Class must be contained in a form.

Line example

The example creates five Line objects in a form. They go horizontal, diagonal, and vertical. They are thin and thick; they are solid, dotted, dashed, and combined.

NOTE: If you want to have a line that is dotted or dashed it must have a Width of 1.

```
LOCAL fLineForm
fLineForm = NEW LineForm()
fLineForm.Open()
CLASS LineForm OF FORM
   this.Text = "Demonstration of Line Objects"
   this.Width =        50
   this.Top =         1
   this.Left =         4
   this.Height =        11
   DEFINE LINE MyLine1 OF this  PROPERTY;
         Top 1, Left 48, Right 4, Bottom 1, Width 1, Pen  3
   DEFINE LINE MyLine2 OF this  PROPERTY;
         Top 2, Left 26, Right 4, Bottom 8, Width 1, Pen  4
   DEFINE LINE MyLine3 OF this  PROPERTY;
         Top 2, Left 48, Right 48, Bottom 8, Width 6
   DEFINE LINE MyLine4 OF this  PROPERTY;
         Top 9.5, Left 4.5, Right 44.5, Bottom 9.5, Width 2
   DEFINE LINE MyLine5 OF this  PROPERTY;
         Top 2, Left 28, Right 46, Bottom 8, Width 1, Pen
2
```

```
ENDCLASS
```

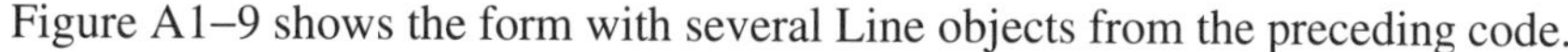

Figure A1–9 shows the form with several Line objects from the preceding code.

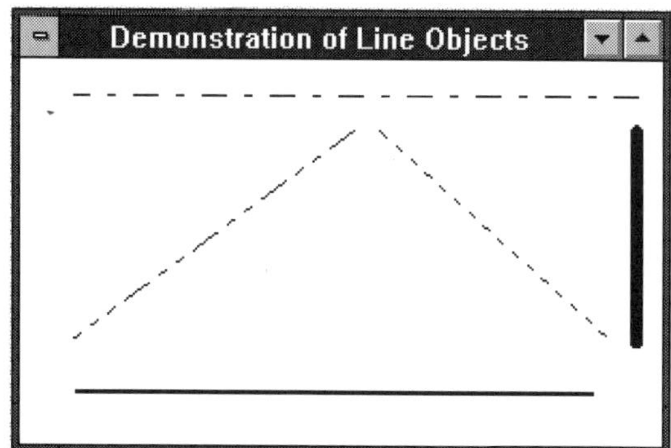

Figure A1–9. Using a Line Class.

The properties and methods of a Line Class

Table A1–11 shows all of the properties, their default values, and a short description.

Table A1–11. The Line Class.

Property/Method	Default	Description
Beforc*	N/A	Holds the name of which object the entryfield precedes in the tabbing order of the parent form
Bottom	10	The row position of the bottom (lower) end of the Line object
ClassName	LINE	Identifies the Line object class
ColorNormal	N	The color of the Line object
Left	0	The horizontal position of the left end of the Line object
MarkCustom()*	N/A	
Name	LINE1	The name of the Line object
OnOpen	.F.	Runs a program when the parent form is opened
PageNo*	1	Which page is object on?
Parent	N/A	The object reference that points to the parent form

Table A1–11. The Line Class.

Property/Method	Default	Description
Pen	0 (Solid)	The Line object's style (dotted, dashed, solid). If the width is greater than 1, it will always display solid.
Release()	N/A	Removes the Line object definition from memory
Right	10	The column position right end of the Line object
Top	0	The row position of the higher end of the Line object
Visible	.T.	Will the Line object be visible?
Width	1	The thickness of the Line object

* Items that have changed or are new to Visual dBASE.

THE LISTBOX CLASS

Objects created from the Class ListBox can be used to display a selection of values in a list. The user can select one or more items in a listbox. Objects created from a ListBox Class must be contained in a form.

ListBox example

The example creates two listboxes. The first one uses the Animals.dbf found in the samples subdirectory of Visual dBASE. As the user clicks in the listbox, the record pointer will automatically move to that record. This means that the Image object in the form will automatically update itself based on the BINARY field named **BMP** from the table **Animals.dbf**.

The second listbox uses the FILE option to use all files in the skeleton *.prg to be displayed in the listbox. This listbox uses its OnSelChange event property to run a program that will run the program ShowMsg. ShowMsg changes the text for two seconds and then the message returns the text to the original.

```
LOCAL ShowPics
ShowPics=NEW PickForm()
ShowPics.OPEN()
CLASS PickForm OF FORM
  this.Top=2
  this.Left=2
  this.Width=60
  this.Height=15
```

```
  this.Text= "a Listbox example"
  this.View="Animals.DBF"
  DEFINE TEXT MyTxt1 OF this PROPERTY;
    Top 1, Left 1, Height 1.2, Width 40, FontSize 12.00,;
    Text "Pick the Animal to see"
  DEFINE TEXT MyTxt2 OF this PROPERTY;
    Top 10, Left 25, Height 1.2, Width 40, FontSize 12.00,;
    Text "<<=== Select a file"
  DEFINE IMAGE MyImage1 OF this  PROPERTY;
    Top 2.5, Left 35, Width 20, Height 5, DataSource "BINARY BMP"
  DEFINE LISTBOX MyListBox1 OF this PROPERTY;
    Top 2.5, Left 6, Width 20, Height 4, DataSource "FIELD Name"
  DEFINE LISTBOX MyListBox2 OF this PROPERTY;
    Top 9, Left 6, Width 18, Height 4, DataSource "FILE *.prg" ,
;
       OnSelChange CLASS::ShowMsg

   PROCEDURE ShowMsg
       form.MyTxt2.Text = "I could run "+form.MyListBox2.Value
       sleep 2
       form.MyTxt2.Text = "<<=== Select a file "
   Return
ENDCLASS
```

Figure A1–10 shows the form with ListBox objects from the preceding code.

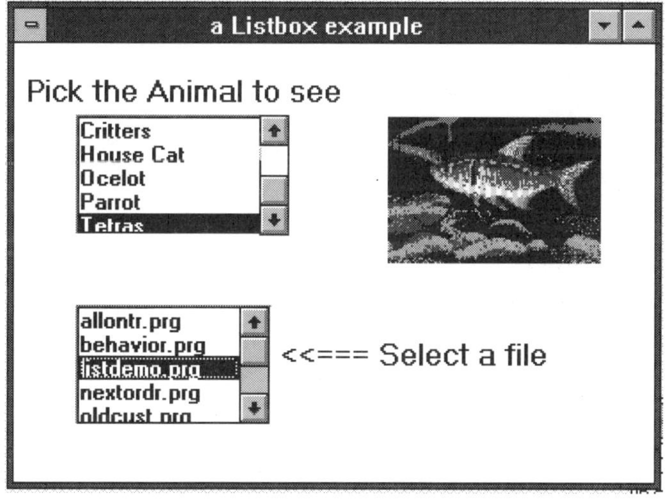

Figure A1–10. Using a ListBox Class.

The properties and methods of a ListBox Class

Table A1–12 shows all of the properties, their default values, and a short description.

Table A1–12. The ListBox Class.

Property/Method	Default	Description
Before	N/A	Names that the listbox object precedes in the tabbing order of the parent form
ClassName	LISTBOX	Identifies the listbox object's class
ColorHighlight*	HighLightText/HighLight	Holds the color of the object when it is highlighted
ColorNormal*	WindowText/Window	Holds the color of the object
Count()	N/A	Holds the number of prompts in listbox object
CurSel	0	Holds the currently selected prompt
DataSource	""	The source of data displayed in the listbox
Enabled	.T.	Can the listbox be selected?
FontBold	.F.	Will characters in the listbox be displayed in bold type?
FontItalic	.F.	Will the characters be displayed in italic type?
FontName	MS Sans Serif	The name of the font to apply to displayed characters
FontSize	8.00	The size of the font in points
FontStrikeOut	.F.	Will the characters be displayed in strikeout type?
FontUnderline	.F.	Will the characters be displayed in underlined type?
Height	2.00	Holds the height
HelpFile	""	Holds the name of the Windows Help file (.HLP) that contains context-sensitive Help topics
HelpID	""	Holds the context string or context number of a Help topic in a Windows Help file (.HLP)
HWND	N/A	Holds the listbox handle
ID	-1	The numeric value of the listbox
Left	0	The position of the left border
MarkCustom()*	N/A	
MousePointer	0	Holds the mouse pointer type when the pointer is over the listbox

Table A1–12. The ListBox Class.

Property/Method	Default	Description
Move()	N/A	Lets the CheckBox be moved or sized
Multiple	.F.	Can more than one item be selected in the listbox?
Name	LISTBOX1	Holds the listbox name
OldStyle	.F.	Will the CheckBox be displayed in the default Windows style or in Borland style?
OnGotFocus	N/A	Runs a program when the listbox receives focus
OnHelp	N/A	Runs a routine when the user presses F1
OnLeftDblClk	N/A	Runs a program when the user double-clicks the listbox
OnLeftMouseDown	N/A	Runs a routine when the user clicks the listbox with the left mouse button
OnLeftMouseUp	N/A	Runs a routine when the user releases the left mouse button while over the listbox
OnLostFocus	N/A	Runs a program when focus is removed
OnMiddleDblClk	N/A	Runs a program when the user double-clicks the listbox with the middle mouse button
OnMiddleMouseDown	N/A	Runs a program when the user clicks the listbox with the middle mouse button
OnMiddleMouseUp	N/A	Runs a program when the user releases the middle mouse button while on the listbox
OnMouseMove	N/A	Runs a program when the user moves the mouse pointer over the listbox
OnOpen	N/A	Runs a program when the parent form is opened
OnRightDblClk	N/A	Runs a program when the user double-clicks the listbox with the right mouse button
OnRightMouseDown	N/A	Runs a program when the user clicks the listbox with the right mouse button
OnRightMouseUp	N/A	Runs a routine when the user releases the right

Table A1–12. The ListBox Class.

Property/Method	Default	Description
		mouse button while on the listbox
OnSelChange	N/A	Runs a program when the highlighted section is moved from one prompt to another
PageNo*	1	What page is the object on?
Parent	N/A	The object reference that points to the parent form
Release()	N/A	Removes the listbox definition from memory
Selected()	N/A	Holds the currently selected prompt
SetFocus()	N/A	Gives focus to the listbox
Sorted	.F.	Should the listbox prompts be sorted before they are displayed?
StatusMessage	""	Holds a message to display on the status bar while the listbox has focus
TabStop	.T.	Holds the value to determine if the user can go to the listbox by pressing **Tab** or **Shift+Tab**
Top	0	Holds the position of the top border
Value	N/A	Holds the value in the listbox
Visible	.T.	Is the listbox visible or hidden?
When	N/A	Specifies a condition that must evaluate to true before the user can give focus to the listbox
Width	11.62	Holds the width

* Items that have changed or are new to Visual dBASE.

THE MENU CLASS

Objects created from the Class Menu are Windows style menus. Once created, they can be attached to a dBASE form.

Objects created from a Menu Class must be contained in a form to be used. They are specified in the form through a form property MenuFile.

Unlike DOS, each prompt of a menu is its own menu object. So a menu comprises a series of menu objects.

Menu example

The example creates a form and attaches the menu named **MenuDemo**.

```
LOCAL fMenuDemo
fMenuDemo = NEW MenuForm()
fMenuDemo.Open()
CLASS MenuForm OF FORM
   this.MenuFile = "CLSMENU.MNU"
   this.Text = "Menu Demo of Form"
   this.View = "Customer"
   this.Width = 63
   this.Top =  1
   this.Left =  1
   this.Height = 6

   DEFINE ENTRYFIELD MyEntrFld1 OF this PROPERTY;
         Top 2, Left 2, Height 1.5, Width 55, FontSize 14,
;
         DataLink "CUSTOMER->CUST_NAME"
ENDCLASS
```

The actual menu code that is used to create MENUDEMO.mnu is the following:

```
Parameter FormObj
NEW CLSMENU(FormObj,"Root")
CLASS CLSMENU(FormObj,Name) OF MENU(FormObj,Name)
   this.Text = ""
   DEFINE MENU File OF this PROPERTY;
      Text "&File"
      DEFINE MENU Open OF this.FILE PROPERTY;
         Text "&Open"
         DEFINE MENU Programs OF this.File.Open PROPERTY;
            Text "&Programs ..."
         DEFINE MENU Forms OF this.File.Open PROPERTY;
            Text "&Forms ...."
         DEFINE MENU Reports OF this.File.Open  PROPERTY;
            Text "&Reports ..."
      DEFINE MENU Exit OF this.File PROPERTY;
         Text "E&xit", Shortcut "Esc", OnClick {;form.close()}
   DEFINE MENU Records OF this  PROPERTY;
      Text "&Records"
         DEFINE MENU Next OF this.Records PROPERTY;
            Text "&Next", Shortcut "PgDn", OnClick {;skip}
         DEFINE MENU Prev OF this.Records PROPERTY;
            Text "&Prev", Shortcut "PgUp", OnClick {;skip -1}
         DEFINE MENU Top OF this.Records  PROPERTY;
```

```
            Text "&Top", Shortcut "Ctrl+PgUp", OnClick {; go top}
        DEFINE MENU Bottom OF this.Records PROPERTY;
            Text "&Bottom", Shortcut "Ctrl+PgDn", OnClick {;go
⇒           bottom}
ENDCLASS
```

Figure A1–11 shows the form with Menu objects from the preceding code.

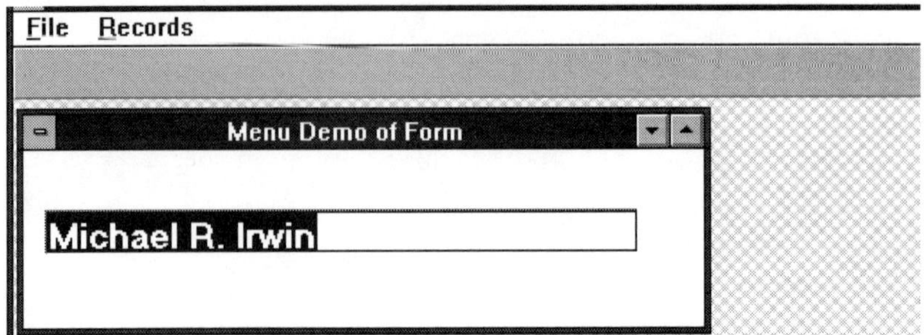

Figure A1–11. Using a Menu Class.

The properties and methods of a Menu Class

Table A1–13 shows all of the properties, their default values, and a short description.

Table A1–13. The Menu Class.

Property/Method	Default	Description
Before	N/A	Holds the name of another Menu object the Menu object precedes
Checked	.F.	Can a checkmark appear beside a menu prompt?
ClassName	MENU	Identifies the Menu object class
Enabled	.T.	Can the menu be selected?
HelpFile*	""	Holds the name of the Windows Help file (.HLP) that contains context-sensitive Help topics
HelpID*	""	Holds the context string or context number of a Help topic in a Windows Help file (.HLP)
ID	-1	The numeric value for the menu
Name	MENU1	The name of the menu item

Table A1–13. The Menu Class.

Property/Method	Default	Description
OnClick	.F.	Runs a program when the user chooses the menu
OnHelp*	N/A	Runs a routine when the user presses F1
Parent	""	The object reference that points to the parent form
Release()	N/A	Removes the menu object definition from memory
Separator	.F.	Is the prompt a menu item that the user cannot select (like a line separator)?
ShortCut	""	The key combination that will automatically execute the OnClick subroutine
StatusMessage	""	The message to display on the status bar
Text	""	The text to display in the menu prompt

* Items that have changed or are new to Visual dBASE.

The MenuBar Class

The MenuBar Class is new to Visual dBASE. It is similar to the Menu Class. Objects created from a MenuBar Class must be contained in a form to be used. They are specified in the form through the same form property, MenuFile, as the menu object.

The MenuBar Class lets you create a top level menu for a form. A top level menu does not contain any prompts or menu items. It is simply a container for child menu prompts and menu items. The child Menu object contains the form's actual menu items. These items are derived from the child class menu.

The advantage to using the MenuBar Class is the added ability to add standard Windows edit actions (Cut, Copy, Paste, Undo) and pull-down Windows to your forms.

MenuBar example

The code that drives a MenuBar is exactly the same as a Menu Class object.

The primary difference is the ability to specify edit actions against specific prompts of the menu. It has several new properties and methods that allow you to attach Windows edit actions to the menu items.

To examine an example of the code, view the Customer.mnu created in Chapter 15.

The properties and methods of a MenuBar Class

Table A1–14 shows all of the properties, their default values, and a short description.

Table A1–14. The MenuBar Class.

Property/Method	Default	Description
ClassName*	MENUBAR	Object instantiated from this class
EditCopyMenu*	.f.	Holds reference to the menu item object that will perform Windows copy actions
EditCutMenu*	.f.	Holds reference to the menu item object that will perform Windows cut actions
EditPasteMenu*	.f.	Holds reference to the menu item object that will perform Windows paste actions
EditUndoMenu*	.f.	Holds reference to the menu item object that will perform Windows undo actions
HelpFile*	""	Holds the name of the Windows Help file (.HLP) that contains context-sensitive Help topics
ID*	-1	The numeric value for the menu
Name*	MENUBar1	The name of the menu item
OnInitMenu*	""	Runs a program when the menu first initiates
Parent*	""	The object reference that points to the parent form
Release()*	N/A	Removes the menu object definition from memory
WindowsMenu*	.f.	Holds reference to the menu item object that will perform Windows window actions

* Items that have changed or are new to Visual dBASE.

THE OBJECT CLASS

Objects created from the Class Object can be used to design your own objects from scratch. It is simply an empty container with no built-in properties or methods. You can use the Object Class to create your own properties and methods.

This is a way you can create your own user-defined objects. Objects created from an Object Class do not have to be contained in a form.

Object example

The example creates a user-defined object that holds the name and address of a person.

```
MyPerson = NEW OBJECT()
MyPerson.LastName = "Irwin"
MyPerson.FirstName = "Michael"
MyPerson.Address1 = "The Irwin Building"
MyPerson.Address2 = "1234 Main Street"
MyPerson.City = "Washington"
MyPerson.St_Prov = "DC"
MyPerson.Country = "USA"
```

The properties and methods of an Object Class

There are no default methods or properties associated with the Object Class.

THE OLE CLASS

Objects created from the Class OLE can be used to display any OLE document that is stored in an OLE field. It will let the user start (initiate) an action in the Server application that originally created the OLE document by double-clicking on the OLE object in the form.

Objects created from an OLE Class must be contained in a form.

OLE example

The example creates an OLE object in a form. It uses the table named **PICTURES.DBF** that is in the Examples subdirectory under Visual dBASE. The OLE object is linked to the field named **BitMapOLE**.

If the user double-clicks on the picture object (OLE), paintbrush will automatically be launched.

```
LOCAL fOleForm
fOleForm = NEW OleForm()
fOleForm.Open()
CLASS OleForm OF FORM
   this.Text = "OLE object example"
   this.View = "pictures.dbf"
   this.Width =         68
   this.Top =          1
   this.Left =         25
```

```
   this.Height =          15
   DEFINE OLE MyOle1 OF this PROPERTY;
      Top 3, Left 33, Height 9, Width 29, ;
      DataLink "PICTURES->BITMAPOLE"
   DEFINE LISTBOX MyListBox1 OF this PROPERTY;
      Top         5, Left 4, Height 4, Width 16, ;
      DataSource "FIELD PICTURES->NAME"
   DEFINE TEXT MyTxt1 OF this PROPERTY;
      Top .5, Left 32, Height 1.8, Width 29, FontSize 16,;
      Text "The OLE Picture"
   DEFINE TEXT MyTxt2 OF this PROPERTY;
      Top 6, Left 24, Height 1.8, Width 6, FontSize 22, Text ">>"
   DEFINE TEXT MyTxt3 OF this PROPERTY;
      Top 2.5, Left 4, Height 1.8, Width 18, FontSize 16,;
       FontUnderline .T., Text "Pick A Pic"
   DEFINE TEXT MyTxt4 OF this PROPERTY;
      Top 12, Left 34, Height 1, Width 32, FontSize 7,;
      Text "*** Double Click to RUN PBrush"
ENDCLASS
```

Figure A1–12 shows the form with an OLE object from the preceding code.

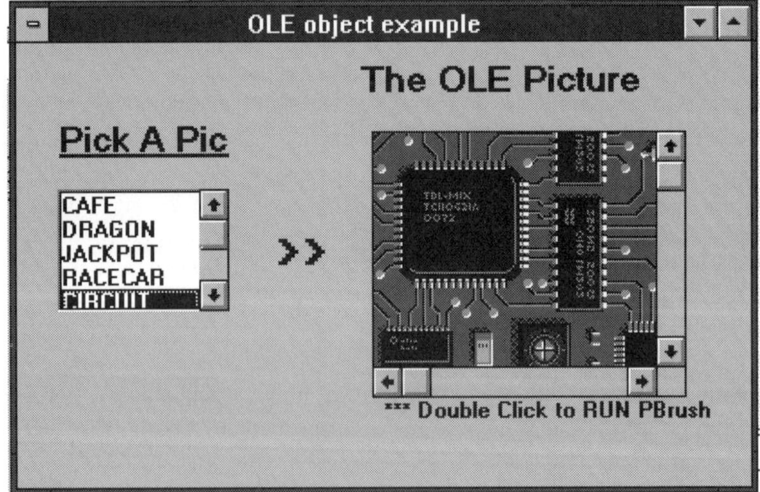

Figure A1–12. Using an OLE Class.

The properties and methods of an OLE Class

Table A1–15 shows all of the properties, their default values, and a short description.

Table A1–15. The OLE Class.

Property/Method	Default	Description
Before	N/A	The name of the object the OLE object precedes in the tabbing order of the parent form
Border	.T.	Can the OLE have a border?
ClassName	OLEITEM	Identifies the OLE object class
DataLink	""	The name of the field the OLE object is linked to
DoVerb()	0	Starts the OLE Server session and determines what type of Server session it is
Enabled	.T.	Can the OLE object be selected?
Height	8.00	The height
HWND	N/A	The OLE object handle
ID	-1	The OLE object's numeric value
Left	0	The position of the left border
LinkFileName	""	The name of the OLE document file (if any) that is linked with the current OLE field
MarkCustom()*	N/A	
MousePointer	0	The type of mouse pointer when the pointer is over the OLE object
Name	OLE1	The name of the OLE object
OleType	0	Returns a number that tells if an OLE field is empty, contains an embedded document, or contains a link to a document file
OnChange	N/A	Runs a program when the user changes a value
OnClose	N/A	Runs a program when the OLE Server session is ended
OnGotFocus	N/A	Runs a program when the OLE object receives focus
OnLostFocus	N/A	Runs a program when focus is removed
OnOpen	N/A	Runs a program when the parent form is opened
PageNo*	1	The page that holds the object
Parent	N/A	The object reference that points to the parent form

Table A1–15. The OLE Class.

Property/Method	Default	Description
Release()	N/A	Removes the OLE object definition from memory
ServerName	""	The Server application that is run when the user double-clicks on an OLE viewer object
SetFocus()	N/A	Gives focus to the OLE object
StatusMessage	""	The message to display on the status bar
TabStop	.T.	Can the user give the object focus to the OLE object by pressing **Tab** or **Shift+Tab**?
Top	0	The position of the top border
Visible	.T.	Can the OLE object be visible?
Width	12.00	The width

* Items that have changed or are new to Visual dBASE.

THE OLEAUTOCLIENT CLASS

Objects created from the Class OLEAutoClient can be used as a complement to OLE field support. Using Visual dBASE, you can control dynamically OLE 2 applications that provide server automation range requests to the server.

Objects created from an OLEAutoClient Class do not have to be contained in a form.

OLEAutoClient example

The following examples let you activate several OLEAutoClients. Once connected, you can view their properties and methods using the Inspect() function. These properties and methods can be set directly via Visual dBASE through the object model of Visual dBASE.

```
WinWordBasic = NEW OLEAutoClient("Word.Basic")
ExcelApp = NEW OLEAutoClient("Excel.Application.5")
MSGraph5 = NEW OLEAutoClient("MSGraph.Chart.5")
Oracle5Ses = NEW OLEAutoClient("OracleInProcServerr.
⇒xOraSession.1")
```

If you specify an identifier name, like "Word.Basic" or "MSGraph.Chart.5" that has not been registered as the identifier, you will not be able to create an autoclient link. To see the names of all programs identified by Windows in the Registry, you can run the program REGEDIT.EXE of Windows. Although it will not tell you if an application is OLE2 compliant, it will show you all of the programs that are registered and their specifics. The name that you supply to the OLEAutoClient Class must be a *valid* **identifier** name that is registered in REGEDIT.EXE.

The properties and methods of an OLEAutoClient Class

The OLEAutoClient has no built-in properties. Once you create an autolink to an OLE2 compliant application, the available properties and method of that application are available.

THE PAINTBOX CLASS

The PaintBox Class is new to Visual dBASE. It is simply a generic control that is displayed in a rectangular space that can be placed anywhere on a form. Objects created from a PaintBox Class must be contained in a form to be used.

The PaintBox Class lets you place a generic control in your form that can be used to create a wide variety of objects. It is strictly designed to allow advanced developers to create their own custom controls using the Windows API. It is simply a rectangular container that can be used to contain any type of object.

PaintBox example

The following code uses Windows function found in the USER.EXE and GDI.EXE programs. It will place the PaintBox control in the middle of the form. Then it will place a triangle in the middle of the PaintBox control. Finally, the user can click anywhere in the form and the program will move the PaintBox and its contents.

```
fBox =  NEW PBoxForm()
fBox.Open()
*
CLASS PBoxForm OF Form
  this.Width = 68
  this.Height = 12
  this.OnLeftMouseUp = CLASS::Form_OnLeftUp

  DEFINE TEXT Title OF this PROPERTY;
    Top 0.5, Left 2, Width 25, Height 1.8, Text"Click and Move
⇒   ",;
    FontSize 16, FontUnderline .T.
```

```
DEFINE TEXT Instruct1 OF this PROPERTY;
  Top 11, Left 22, Width 45, Text "- Click any where on form -"

DEFINE PaintBox PBox OF this PROPERTY;
  Top 2.5, Left 22, Width 22, Height 7, ;
  OnOpen CLASS::PBox_OnOpen, OnPaint CLASS::Pbox_OnPaint, ;
  OnLeftMouseDown CLASS::Pbox_OnLeftDown, ;
  OnLeftMouseUp CLASS:: pBox_OnLeftUp

Procedure PBox_OnPaint
 hFact = (256/43)
 vFact = (256/15.5)
 lWidth = Form.pBox.Width * hFact
 lHeight = form.pBox.Height * vFact
 form.pointarray = makepoint(lWidth/2,0)
 form.pointarray = form.pointarray + MakePoint(0,lHeight)
 form.pointarray = form.pointarray + makePoint(lWidth, lHeight)
 Local hDC
 hDC = GetDC(this.hWnd)
 hBrush = CreateSolidBrush(hDC, RGB(255,0,0))
 SelectObject(hDC, hBrush)
 SetTextColor(hDC, RGB(0,0,255))
 SetPolyFillMode(hDC, 2)
 Polygon(hDC, Form.Pointarray, 3)
 ReleaseDC(this.hWnd, hDC)
Procedure PBox_OnOpen
 Set Proc to Program(1) ADDITIVE
 EXTERN CHANDLE  GetDC(Chandle) USER.EXE
 EXTERN CINT     ReleaseDc(Chandle, Chandle) USER.EXE
 EXTERN CLOGICAL Polygon(Chandle, Cptr, Cint) GDI.EXE
 EXTERN CINT     SetTextColor(Chandle, Clong) GDI.EXE
 EXTERN CLOGICAL Ellipse(Chandle, Cint, Cint, Cint, Cint)
⇒ GDI.EXE
 EXTERN CLOGICAL FloodFill(Chandle, Cint, Cint, Clong) GDI.EXE
 EXTERN CINT     SetPolyFillMode(Chandle, Cint) GDI.EXE
 EXTERN CHANDLE  CreateSolidBrush(Chandle, Clong) GDI.EXE
 EXTERN CHANDLE  SelectObject(Chandle, Chandle) GDI.EXE
 this.Moving = .F.
Procedure Pbox_OnLeftDown(flags, col, row)
 this.Moving = .t.

Procedure Pbox_OnLeftUp(flags, col, row)
 this.Moving = .f.

Procedure Form_OnLeftUp(flags, col, row)
 if Form.Pbox.Moving = .f.
   Form.Pbox.Move(col, row, form.pbox.width, form.pbox.height)
   this.Moving = .f.
 endif
```

```
ENDCLASS
Function RGB(r, g, b)
  return b*65536+g*256+r

Function MakeRect(l, t, w, h)
  Return MakeInt(l)+MakeInt(t)+MakeInt(w+l)+MakeInt(t+h)

Function MakePoint(x, y)
  Return (MakeInt(x) + MakeInt(y))

Function MakeInt(int)
  return Chr(BitAnd(Int,255))+Chr(BitR(Int,8))
```

Changing the values for the RGB() calls in the pBox_OnPaint procedure will give you different colors for the triangle. Want to change the triangle to another shape, change the last value passed (number of lines) in the Polygon function in the pBox_OnPaint procedure? Try 6 and 9 instead of 3.

Figure A1–13 shows the PaintBox object in a form.

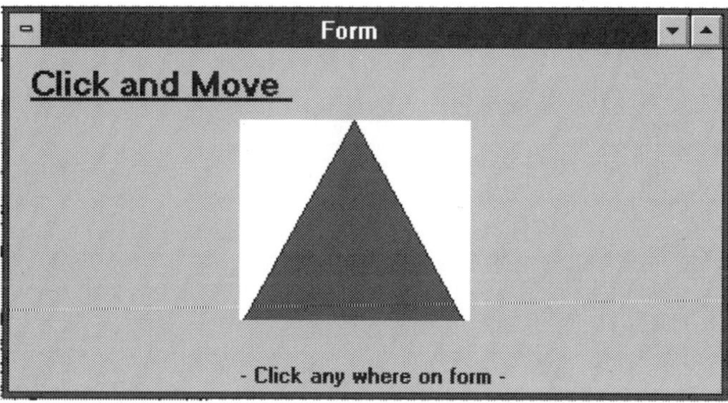

Figure A1–13. Running a form with a PaintBox object.

The properties and methods of a PaintBox Class

Table A1–16 shows all of the properties, their default values, and a short description.

Table A1–16. The PaintBox Class.

Property/Method	Default	Description
Before*	N/A	Points to the object this object precedes
ClassName*	PAINTBOX	Object instantiated from this class
ColorNormal*	WindowText/Window	Sets the color of the PaintBox object
Enabled*	.T.	Lets the PaintBox object be selected
Height*	5.00	Holds the height
HWND*	N/A	Holds the PaintBox handle
ID*	-1	The numeric value of the PaintBox
Left*	0	The position of the left border
MousePointer*	0	Holds the mouse pointer type when the pointer is over the PaintBox
Move()*	N/A	Lets the PaintBox be moved or sized
Name*	PAINTBOX	Holds the PaintBox name
OnChar*	N/A	Runs a program when a "printable" key is pressed
OnClose*	N/A	Runs a program when the object closes
OnDesignOpen	N/A	Runs a program when the form is opened in the design surface
OnFormSize*	N/A	Runs a program when the form is resized
OnGotFocus*	N/A	Runs a program when the object gets focus
OnKeyDown*	N/A	Runs a program when the user presses a key
OnKeyUp*	N/A	Runs a program when the user releases a key
OnLeftDblClk*	N/A	Runs a program when the user double-clicks the object
OnLeftMouseDown*	N/A	Runs a routine when the user clicks the object with the left mouse button
OnLeftMouseUp*	N/A	Runs a routine when the user releases the left mouse button while over the object
OnLostFocus*	N/A	Runs a program when focus is removed

Table A1–16. The PaintBox Class.

Property/Method	Default	Description
OnMiddleDblClk*	N/A	Runs a program when the user double-clicks the object with the middle mouse button
OnMiddleMouseDown *	N/A	Runs a program when the user clicks the object with the middle mouse button
OnMiddleMouseUp*	N/A	Runs a program when the user releases the middle mouse button while on the object
OnMouseMove*	N/A	Runs a program when the user moves the mouse pointer over the object
OnOpen*	N/A	Runs a program when the parent form is opened
OnPaint*	N/A	Runs a program when the object needs to redraw
OnRightDblClk*	N/A	Runs a program when the user double-clicks the object with the right mouse button
OnRightMouseDown*	N/A	Runs a program when the user clicks the object with the right mouse button
OnRightMouseUp*	N/A	Runs a routine when the user releases the right mouse button while on the object
PageNo*	1	Specifies the page of the form it exists on
Parent*	""	The object reference that points to the parent form
Release()*	N/A	Removes the menu object definition from memory
SetFocus()*	N/A	Gives focus to the object
StatusMessage*	""	Holds a message to display on the status bar while the object has focus
TabStop*	.T.	Holds the value to determine if the user can go to the object by pressing **Tab** or **Shift+Tab**
Transparent	.F	Holds the value to determine if PaintBox is transparent
Visible*	.T.	Is the object visible or hidden?
Width*	9	Holds the width

* Items that have changed or are new to Visual dBASE.

THE POPUP CLASS

Visual dBASE has added this new class. Objects created from the Class Popup are Windows-style popups. Once created, they can be attached to a dBASE form.

Objects created from a Popup Class must be contained in a form to be used. They are specified in the form through a form property MenuFile.

Popup example

The example creates a form and attaches the menu named **PopUpDemo**.

```
LOCAL fPopDemo
fPopDemo = NEW PopForm()
fPopDemo.Open()
CLASS PopForm OF FORM
    this.Text = "Menu Demo of Form"
   this.View = "Customer"
   this.Width = 63
   this.Top =  1
   this.Left =  1
   this.Height = 6
   this.OnOpen CLASS::Form_OnOpen

   DEFINE ENTRYFIELD MyEntrFld1 OF this PROPERTY;
         Top 2, Left 2, Height 1.5, Width 55, FontSize 14,
;
         DataLink "CUSTOMER->CUST_NAME"
   Procedure Form_OnOpen
     DO PopDemo.POP with this, "MyPopUp"
     form.PopupMenu = form.MyPopUp
ENDCLASS
```

Notice that the Popup program, POPDEMO.POP, was run, placing it in memory. Then the PopupMenu property of the form was set to the value of the Popup menu passed to the POPDEMO.POP program when it was run (MyPopUp). This program was run when the OnOpen event property of the form was triggered.

The actual Popup code that is used to create POPDEMO.pop is the following:

```
Parameter FormObj,PopupName
NEW MyPOPUP(FormObj,PopupName)
CLASS MyPOPUP(FormObj,PopupName) OF ;
                           POPUP(FormObj,PopupName)
   this.Top = 0
   this.TrackRight = .T.
   this.Left = 0
   DEFINE MENU xx1 OF THIS  PROPERTY Text "Choice 1  "
   DEFINE MENU xx2 OF THIS PROPERTY Text "Choice 2"
```

```
    DEFINE MENU xQuit OF THIS  PROPERTY;
          Text "&Close Form", OnClick {;form.Close()}
ENDCLASS
```

Figure A1–14 shows the Popup object called from a form.

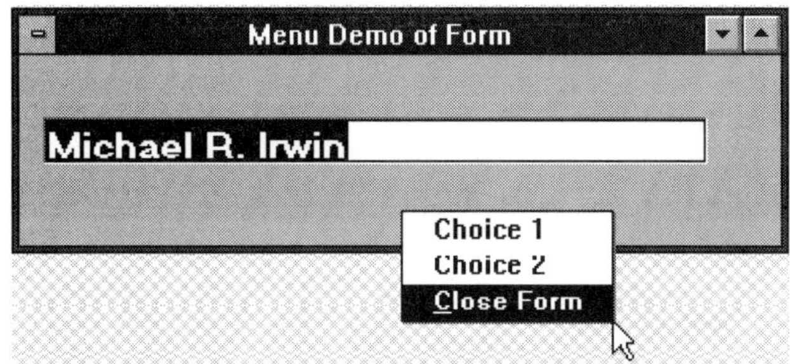

Figure A1–14. Running a form with a Popup object.

The properties and methods of a Popup Class

Table A1–17 shows all of the properties, their default values, and a short description.

Table A1–17. The Popup Class.

Property/Method	Default	Description
Alignment*	1 -Center	Specifies how to identify the text in popup
ClassName*	POPUP	Identifies the Popup object class
ID*	-1	The numeric value for the menu
Left*	0	Sets left-most position
Name*	POPUP1	The name of the menu item
OnInitMenu*	""	Runs code when the popup is opened
Open()*	N/A	Opens the popup
Parent*	""	The object reference that points to the parent form
Release()*	N/A	Removes the menu object definition from memory
Top*	0	The top, left corner position
TrackRight	.T.	Right mouse click for selection of menu item

* Items that have changed or are new to Visual dBASE.

THE PUSHBUTTON CLASS

Objects created from the Class PushButton can be used to launch some action. The action can be a method, a codeblock, even an external procedure or function.

Objects created from a PushButton Class must be contained in a form.

PushButton example

The example creates two PushButtons, one will close the form, the other will change its own text. The one that closes the form will display a bitmap picture of a red **x**.

```
LOCAL fPushBtn
fPushBtn = NEW PushBtnForm()
fPushBtn.Open()
CLASS PushBtnForm OF FORM
    this.Top = 2
    this.Left = 2
    this.Width = 50
    this.Height = 5
    this.Text = "Push Button example form"
    DEFINE PUSHBUTTON MyButn1 OF this PROPERTY ;
         Top 2, Left 4, Height 2, Width 20, Text "Click ME!", ;
         OnClick {;form.MyButn1.text =  ;
            IIF(form.MyButn1.text ="Click ME!", "Thank U", "Click
⇒            ME!")}
    DEFINE PUSHBUTTON MyButn2 OF this PROPERTY ;
         Top 2, Left 28, Height 2, Width 20, Text "Close Form", ;
         UpBitMap "RESOURCE #28", OnClick {;form.Close()}
ENDCLASS
```

Figure A1–15 shows the form with two PushButton objects from the preceding code.

Figure A1–15. Using a PushButton Class.

The properties and methods of a PushButton Class

Table A1–18 shows all of the properties, their default values, and a short description.

Table A1–18. The PushButton Class.

Property/Method	Default	Description
Before	N/A	Names which object the PushButton object precedes in the tabbing order of the parent form
ClassName	PUSHBUTTON	Identifies the PushButton object's class
ColorNormal*	BtnText/BtnFace	Holds the color of the object
Default	.F.	Is the pushbutton the default pushbutton?
DisabledBitmap	""	The graphic image to display when the button is disabled
DownBitMap	""	The graphic image to display when the button is pushed down by the user.
Enabled	.T.	Can the pushbutton be selected?
FocusBitMap	""	The graphic image to display when the button has focus.
FontBold	.F.	Will characters in the pushbutton be displayed in bold type?
FontItalic	.F.	Will the characters be displayed in italic type?
FontName	MS Sans Serif	The name of the font to apply to displayed characters
FontSize	8.00	The size of the font in points
FontStrikeOut	.F.	Will the characters be displayed in strikeout type?
FontUnderline	.F.	Will the characters be displayed in underlined type?
Group	.F.	Starts an object group in the parent form
Height	2.00	Holds the height
HelpFile	""	Holds the name of the Windows Help file (.HLP) that contains context-sensitive Help topics
HelpID	""	Holds the context string or context number of a Help topic in a Windows Help file (.HLP)
HWND	N/A	Holds the pushbutton handle

Table A1–18. The PushButton Class.

Property/Method	Default	Description
ID	-1	The numeric value of the pushbutton
Left	0	The position of the left border
MarkCustom()*	N/A	
MousePointer	0	Holds the mouse pointer type when the pointer is over the pushbutton
Move()	N/A	Lets the pushbutton be moved or sized
Name	PUSHBUTTON1	Holds the pushbutton name
OnClick	N/A	Runs a program when the pushbutton is clicked
OnGotFocus	N/A	Runs a program when the pushbutton receives focus
OnHelp	N/A	Runs a routine when the user presses F1
OnLeftDblClk	N/A	Runs a program when the user double-clicks the object
OnLeftMouseDown	N/A	Runs a routine when the user clicks the object with the left mouse button
OnLeftMouseUp	N/A	Runs a routine when the user releases the left mouse button while over the object
OnLostFocus	N/A	Runs a program when focus is removed
OnMiddleDblClk	N/A	Runs a program when the user double-clicks the object with the middle mouse button
OnMiddleMouseDown	N/A	Runs a program when the user clicks the object with the middle mouse button
OnMiddleMouseUp	N/A	Runs a program when the user releases the middle mouse button while on the object
OnMouseMove	N/A	Runs a program when the user moves the mouse pointer over the object
OnOpen	N/A	Runs a program when the parent form is opened
OnRightDblClk	N/A	Runs a program when the user double-clicks the object with the right mouse button
OnRightMouseDown	N/A	Runs a program when the user clicks the object with the

Table A1–18. The PushButton Class.

Property/Method	Default	Description
		right mouse button
OnRightMouseUp	N/A	Runs a routine when the user releases the right mouse button while on the object
PageNo*	1	Holds the number of the page control is on
Parent	N/A	The object reference that points to the parent form
Release()	N/A	Removes the pushbutton definition from memory
SetFocus()	N/A	Gives focus to the object
SpeedBar	.F.	Should the button be part of a speedbar (does NOT work in version 5.0)?
SpeedTip*	""	Holds a short message to display in a bubble when the user sits over 1 second on control
StatusMessage	""	Holds a message to display on the status bar while the object has focus
TabStop	.T.	Holds the value to determine if the user can go to the object by pressing **Tab** or **Shift+Tab**
Text	BUTTON1	The text on the button
Top	0	Holds the position of the top border
UpBitMap	""	The graphic image to display when the button is not selected (in the up position)
Visible	.T.	Is the object visible or hidden?
When	N/A	Specifies a condition that must evaluate to true before the user can give focus to the object
Width	9	Holds the width

* Items that have changed or are new to Visual dBASE.

THE RADIOBUTTON CLASS

Objects created from the Class RadioButton can be used to represent a single choice in a set of mutually exclusive choices. The first radiobutton needs its Group property set to **.T.**, and the others in the group are set to .F. Only one Value property can be set to .t. in the group. So whichever one you want to be the default value should be set to .t. and the remaining radiobuttons should be set to .f.

Objects created from a RadioButton Class must be contained in a form.

RadioButton example

The example creates a series of RadioButtons that are in a single group. They are used to trigger a calculation program for converting from U.S. measurements to metric. The value is entered in an entryfield object and then the calculation is performed by a method of the form object.

```
LOCAL fRadButn
fRadButn = NEW RadioBtnForm()
fRadButn.Open()
CLASS RadioBtnForm OF FORM
   this.Text = "Radio Button Example"
   this.Width = 64
   this.Top =  1
   this.Left =  5
   this.Height = 12
   DEFINE RECTANGLE MyRect11 OF this PROPERTY;
         Top 3.5, Left 25.3, Height 4.5 , Width 36.5, BorderStyle
⇒         2, Text ""
   DEFINE TEXT MyTxt1 OF this PROPERTY;
         Top 4, Left 26.5, Height 1, Width 10, Text "Solution :"
   DEFINE TEXT MyTxt2 OF this PROPERTY;
         Top 5, Left 30, Height 1, Width 30.5, Text ""
   DEFINE TEXT MyTxt3 OF this PROPERTY;
         Top 6.5, Left 30, Height 1.2, Width 30, Text "",
FontSize
⇒        12, ;
          FontUnderline .T.
   DEFINE TEXT MyTxt4 OF this PROPERTY;
         Top 1.5, Left 45, Height 1, Width 12.5, Text "<<===
⇒         Value"
   DEFINE PUSHBUTTON MyButn1 OF this PROPERTY;
         Top 9, Left 41, Height 2, Width 20, Text "Calculate", ;
         OnClick CLASS::PUSHBUTTON1_ONCLICK
   DEFINE RADIOBUTTON MyRadioBtn1 OF this PROPERTY;
         Top 1.4, Left 1.2, Height 1.1, Width 23.5, Group .T.,
⇒         Value .T.,;
         Text "US Gallons 2 Liters"
```

```
   DEFINE RADIOBUTTON MyRadioBtn2 OF this PROPERTY;
         Top 2.8, Left 1.2, Height 1.1, Width 23.5, ;
         Text "Inches 2 Centimeters"
   DEFINE RADIOBUTTON MyRadioBtn3 OF this PROPERTY;
         Top 4.2 , Left 1.2, Height 1.1, Width 23.5,;
         Text "Feet 2 Meters"
  DEFINE RADIOBUTTON MyRadioBtn4 OF this  PROPERTY;
         Top 5.6, Left 1.2, Height 1.1, Width 23.5, ;
         Text "Miles 2 Kilometers"
   DEFINE RADIOBUTTON MyRadioBtn5 OF this  PROPERTY;
         Top 7, Left 1.2, Height 1.1, Width 23.5,;
         Text "Pounds 2 Kilograms"
   DEFINE RADIOBUTTON MyRadioBtn6 OF this  PROPERTY;
         Top 8.4, Left 1.2, Height 1.1, Width 23.5, ;
         Text "Fahrenheit 2 Celsius"
   DEFINE ENTRYFIELD MyEntFld1 OF this  PROPERTY;
        Top 1, Left 28, Height 2, Width 16.5, FontSize 18, Value
⇒        "0"

   Procedure PUSHBUTTON1_OnClick
     DO CASE
        CASE form.MyRadioBtn1.Value
           form.MyTxt2.text = TRIM(form.MyEntFld1.value);
                              + " US gallons = "
           form.MyTxt3.text = LTRIM(STR(val(form.MyEntFld1.value)
⇒          * ;
                              3.79,4,2))+" Liters"
        CASE form.MyRadioBtn2.Value
           form.MyTxt2.text = TRIM(form.MyEntFld1.value) + "
⇒          inches = "
           form.MyTxt3.text = LTRIM(STR(val(form.MyEntFld1.value)
⇒          * ;
                              2.54,6,2))+" Centimeters"
        CASE form.MyRadioBtn3.Value
           form.MyTxt2.text = TRIM(form.MyEntFld1.value) + " feet
⇒           = "
           form.MyTxt3.text = LTRIM(STR(val(form.MyEntFld1.value)
⇒           * ;
                              0.3048,6,2))+" Meters"
        CASE form.MyRadioBtn4.Value
           form.MyTxt2.text = TRIM(form.MyEntFld1.value) + "
miles
⇒           = "
           form.MyTxt3.text = LTRIM(STR(val(form.MyEntFld1.value)
⇒          * ;
                              1.6093,6,2))+" Kilometers"
        CASE form.MyRadioBtn5.Value
           form.MyTxt2.text = TRIM(form.MyEntFLd1.value) + "
⇒          pounds = "
           form.MyTxt3.text = LTRIM(STR(val(form.MyEntFld1.value)
⇒          * ;
```

```
                                0.4536,6,2))+" Kilograms"
        CASE form.MyRadioBtn6.Value
           form.MyTxt2.text = TRIM(form.MyEntFld1.value) + ;
                                " Fahrenheit = "
           form.MyTxt3.text =
LTRIM(STR((val(form.MyEntFld1.value)
⇒             - ;
                                32) *0.5555556 ,6,2))+" Celsius"
     ENDCASE
ENDCLASS
```

Figure A1–16 shows the form with several RadioButton objects from the preceding code.

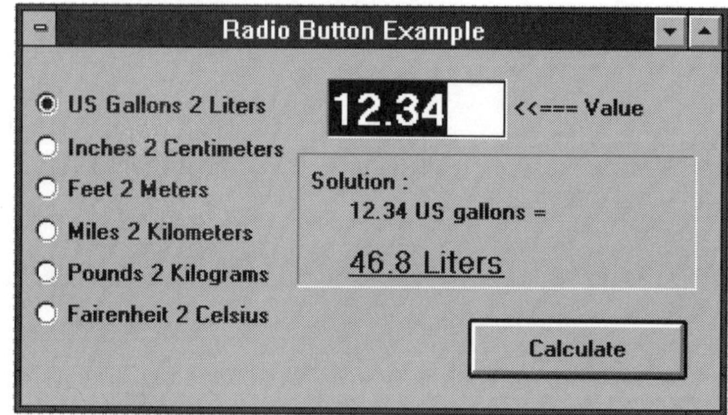

Figure A1–16. Using a RadioButton Class.

The properties and methods of a RadioButton Class

Table A1–19 shows all of the properties, their default values, and a short description.

Table A1–19. The RadioButton Class.

Property/Method	Default	Description
Before	N/A	Names which object the RadioButton object precedes in the tabbing order of the parent form
ClassName	RADIOBUTTON	Identifies the RadioButton object's class
ColorNormal*	BtnText/BtnFace	Holds the color of the object
DataLink	""	Links radiobutton to a field

Table A1–19. The RadioButton Class.

Property/Method	Default	Description
Enabled	.T.	Can the radiobutton be selected?
FontBold	.F.	Will characters in the radiobutton be displayed in bold type?
FontItalic	.F.	Will the characters be displayed in italic type/
FontName	MS Sans Serif	The name of the font to apply to displayed characters
FontSize	8.00	The size of the font in points
FontStrikeOut	.F.	Will the characters be displayed in strikeout type?
FontUnderline	.F.	Will the characters be displayed in underlined type?
Group	.F.	Starts an object group in the parent form
Height	2.00	Holds the height
HelpFile	""	Holds the name of the Windows Help file (.HLP) that contains context-sensitive Help topics
HelpID	""	Holds the context string or context number of a Help topic in a Windows Help file (.HLP)
HWND	N/A	Holds the radiobutton handle
ID	-1	The numeric value of the radiobutton
Left	0	The position of the left border
MarkCustom()*	N/A	
MousePointer	0	Holds the mouse pointer type when the pointer is over the radiobutton
Move()	N/A	Lets the radiobutton be moved or sized
Name	RADIOBUTTON1	Holds the radiobutton name
OldStyle	.F.	Should the radiobutton be displayed in the default Windows style or Borland style?
OnChange	N/A	Runs a program when the radiobutton is changed (user selects a different radiobutton)
OnGotFocus	N/A	Runs a program when the radiobutton receives focus

Table A1–19. The RadioButton Class.

Property/Method	Default	Description
OnHelp	N/A	Runs a routine when the user presses F1
OnLeftDblClk	N/A	Runs a program when the user double-clicks the object
OnLeftMouseDown	N/A	Runs a routine when the user clicks the object with the left mouse button
OnLeftMouseUp	N/A	Runs a routine when the user releases the left mouse button while over the object
OnLostFocus	N/A	Runs a program when focus is removed
OnMiddleDblClk	N/A	Runs a program when the user double-clicks the object with the middle mouse button
OnMiddleMouseDown	N/A	Runs a program when the user clicks the object with the middle mouse button
OnMiddleMouseUp	N/A	Runs a program when the user releases the middle mouse button while on the object
OnMouseMove	N/A	Runs a program when the user moves the mouse pointer over the object
OnOpen	N/A	Runs a program when the parent form is opened
OnRightDblClk	N/A	Runs a program when the user double-clicks the object with the right mouse button
OnRightMouseDown	N/A	Runs a program when the user clicks the object with the right mouse button
OnRightMouseUp	N/A	Runs a routine when the user releases the right mouse button while on the object
PageNo*	1	The page where the control is located
Parent	N/A	The object reference that points to the parent form
Release()	N/A	Removes the radiobutton definition from memory
SetFocus()	N/A	Gives focus to the object
SpeedTip*	“”	Holds message to display in bubble
StatusMessage	“”	Holds a message to display on the status bar while the

Table A1–19. The RadioButton Class.

Property/Method	Default	Description
		object has focus
TabStop	.T.	Holds the value to determine if the user can go to the object by pressing **Tab** or **Shift+Tab**
Text	RADIOBUTTON1	The text on the button
Top	0	Holds the position of the top border
Value	""	The value in the radiobutton
Visible	.T.	Is the object visible or hidden?
When	N/A	Specifies a condition that must evaluate to true before the user can give focus to the object
Width	14	Holds the width

* Items that have changed or are new to Visual dBASE.

THE RECTANGLE CLASS

Objects created from the Class Rectangle can be used to display a rectangle at a specific location in the form. It can appear to be sunken or raised or on the surface and have text associated with the box.

Objects created from a Rectangle Class must be contained in a form.

Rectangle example

The example creates three different Rectangle objects in a form with text inside the border.

```
LOCAL fRectangle
fRectangle = NEW RectangleForm()
fRectangle.Open()
CLASS RectangleForm OF FORM
   this.Text = "Rectangles in Form Example"
   this.Width = 64
   this.Top =  1
   this.Left =  5
   this.Height = 14
   DEFINE RECTANGLE MyRectl1 OF this PROPERTY;
```

```
      Top 1, Left 1, Height 9 , Width 25, BorderStyle 0, ;
      Text "I am Text for the Box"
   DEFINE RECTANGLE MyRectl2 OF this PROPERTY;
      Top 1, Left 27, Height 4 , Width 35, BorderStyle 1, Text
""
   DEFINE RECTANGLE MyRectl3 OF this PROPERTY;
      Top 6, Left 27, Height 4 , Width 35, BorderStyle 2, Text
""
   DEFINE TEXT MyTxt1 OF this PROPERTY ;
      Top 4, Left 3, Width 20, Text "These are in a"
   DEFINE TEXT MyTxt2 OF this PROPERTY ;
      Top 6.5, Left 3, Width 20, Text "normal Rectangle"
   DEFINE TEXT MyTxt3 OF this PROPERTY ;
      Top 2.5, Left 29, Width 30, Text "This is in a sunken
⇒     Rectangle"
   DEFINE TEXT MyTxt4 OF this PROPERTY ;
      Top 7.5, Left 29, Width 30, Text "This is in a raised
⇒     Rectangle"
   DEFINE PUSHBUTTON MyButn1 OF this PROPERTY ;
     Top 11, Left 45, Height 2, Width 15, Text "E&xit", ;
     OnClick {;form.Close()}
ENDCLASS
```

Figure A1–17 shows the form with several Rectangle objects from the preceding code.

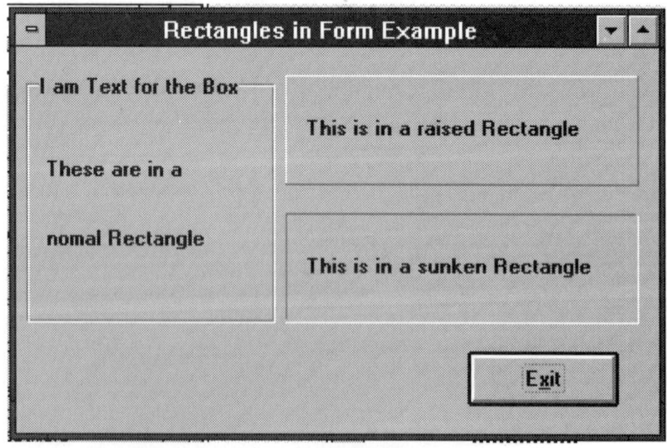

Figure A1–17. Using a Rectangle Class.

The properties and methods of a Rectangle Class

Table A1–20 shows all of the properties, their default values, and a short description.

Table A1–20. The Rectangle Class.

Property/Method	Default	Description
Border	.T.	Can the rectangle have a border?
BorderStyle	0 - Normal	What style of border—normal, raised, or sunken?
ClassName	RECTANGLE	Identifies the Rectangle object's class
ColorNormal*	BtnText/BtnFace	Holds the color of the object
FontBold	.F.	Will characters in the rectangle be displayed in bold type?
FontItalic	.F.	Will the characters be displayed in italic type?
FontName	MS Sans Serif	The name of the font to apply to displayed characters
FontSize	8.00	The size of the font in points
FontStrikeOut	.F.	Will the characters be displayed in strikeout type?
FontUnderline	.F.	Will the characters be displayed in underlined type?
Height	9.00	Holds the height
HWND	N/A	Holds the rectangle handle
Left	0	The position of the left border
MousePointer	0	Holds the mouse pointer type when the pointer is over the rectangle
MarkCustom()*	N/A	
Move()	N/A	Lets the rectangle be moved or sized
Name	RECTANGLE1	Holds the rectangle name
OldStyle	.F.	Should the radiobutton be displayed in the default Windows style or Borland style?
OnLeftDblClk	N/A	Runs a program when the user double-clicks the object
OnLeftMouseDown	N/A	Runs a routine when the user clicks the object with the left mouse button
OnLeftMouseUp	N/A	Runs a routine when the user releases the left mouse button while over the object
OnMiddleDblClk	N/A	Runs a program when the user double-clicks the object with the middle mouse button

Table A1–20. The Rectangle Class.

Property/Method	Default	Description
OnMiddleMouseDown	N/A	Runs a program when the user clicks the object with the middle mouse button
OnMiddleMouseUp	N/A	Runs a program when the user releases the middle mouse button while on the object
OnMouseMove	N/A	Runs a program when the user moves the mouse pointer over the object
OnOpen	N/A	Runs a program when the parent form is opened
OnRightDblClk	N/A	Runs a program when the user double-clicks the object with the right mouse button
OnRightMouseDown	N/A	Runs a program when the user clicks the object with the right mouse button
OnRightMouseUp	N/A	Runs a routine when the user releases the right mouse button while on the object
PageNo*	1	The page where the object is located
Parent	N/A	The object reference that points to the parent form
PatternStyle	0—solid	The Windows background hatching style
Release()	N/A	Removes the rectangle definition from memory
Text	RECTANGLE1	The text on the button
Top	0	Holds the position of the top border
Visible	.T.	Is the object visible or hidden?
Width	14	Holds the width

* Items that have changed or are new to Visual dBASE.

THE SCROLLBAR CLASS

Objects created from the Class ScrollBar can be used to increase or decrease a value. It can only be linked to numeric and date fields.

Objects created from a ScrollBar Class must be contained in a form.

ScrollBar example

The example creates two ScrollBar objects.

```
LOCAL fScrollBar
fScrollBar = NEW ScrollBarForm()
fScrollBar.Open()
CLASS ScrollBarForm OF FORM
   this.Text = "ScrollBars in Form Example"
   this.Width = 64
   this.Top =  1
   this.Left =  5
   this.Height = 14
   DEFINE SCROLLBAR MyScrlBar1 OF this PROPERTY;
         Top 2, Left 11, Height 10 , Width 3, ;
         RangeMin 100, RangeMax 1000
   DEFINE SCROLLBAR MyScrlBar2 OF this PROPERTY;
         Top 2, Left 35, Height 1.2 , Width 25, Vertical .F., ;
         RangeMin 1, RangeMax 10
   DEFINE TEXT MyTxt1 OF this PROPERTY;
        Top 3, Left 15, Text "- 10"
   DEFINE TEXT MyTxt2 OF this PROPERTY;
        Top 10.5, Left 15, Text "- 01"
   DEFINE TEXT MyTxt3 OF this PROPERTY;
        Top 3.2, Left 38, Text "01"
   DEFINE TEXT MyTxt4 OF this PROPERTY;
        Top 3.2, Left 55, Text "10"
ENDCLASS
```

Figure A1–18 shows the form with two ScrollBar objects from the preceding code.

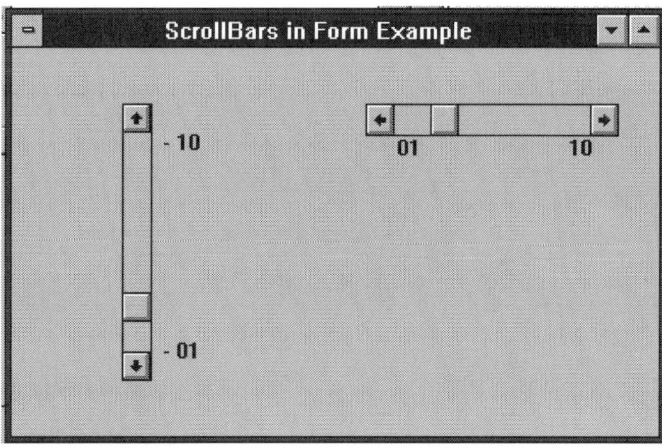

Figure A1–18. Using a ScrollBar Class.

The properties and methods of a ScrollBar Class

Table A1–21 shows all of the properties, their default values, and a short description.

Table A1–21. The Scrollbar Class.

Property/Method	Default	Description
Before	N/A	The object the scrollbar precedes in the tabbing order of the parent form
ClassName	SCROLLBAR	Identifies the ScrollBar object's class
ColorNormal*	SCROLLBAR	Holds the color of the object
DataLink	""	The name of the link field for the scrollbar
Enabled	.T.	Can the scrollbar be selected?
Height	8.00	The height
HelpFile	""	Holds the name of the Windows Help file (.HLP) that contains context-sensitive Help topics
HelpID	""	Holds the context string or context number of a Help topic in a Windows Help file (.HLP)
HWND	N/A	Holds the scrollbar handle
ID	-1	The numeric value for the scrollbar
Left	0	The position of the left border
MarkCustom()*	N/A	
MousePointer	0	Holds the mouse pointer type when the pointer is over the scrollbar
Move()	N/A	Lets the scrollbar be moved or sized
Name	SCROLLBAR1	Holds the scrollbar name
OnChange	N/A	Runs a program when the user moves the slider button on the scrollbar
OnGotFocus	N/A	Runs a program when the scrollbar receives focus
OnHelp	N/A	Runs a program when the user presses F1
OnLeftDblClk	N/A	Runs a program when the user double-clicks the object

Table A1–21. The Scrollbar Class.

Property/Method	Default	Description
OnLeftMouseDown	N/A	Runs a routine when the user clicks the object with the left mouse button
OnLeftMouseUp	N/A	Runs a routine when the user releases the left mouse button while over the object
OnLostFocus	N/A	Runs a program when the scrollbar's focus is removed
OnMiddleDblClk	N/A	Runs a program when the user double-clicks the object with the middle mouse button
OnMiddleMouseDown	N/A	Runs a program when the user clicks the object with the middle mouse button
OnMiddleMouseUp	N/A	Runs a program when the user releases the middle mouse button while on the object
OnMouseMove	N/A	Runs a program when the user moves the mouse pointer over the object
OnOpen	N/A	Runs a program when the parent form is opened
OnRightDblClk	N/A	Runs a program when the user double-clicks the object with the right mouse button
OnRightMouseDown	N/A	Runs a program when the user clicks the object with the right mouse button
OnRightMouseUp	N/A	Runs a routine when the user releases the right mouse button while on the object
PageNo*	1	Which page will hold the control?
Parent	N/A	The object reference that points to the parent form
RangeMax	100.00	The upper limit for the value linked to the scrollbar
RangeMin	1.00	The lower limit for the value linked to the scrollbar
Release()	N/A	Removes the scrollbar definition from memory
SetFocus()	N/A	Gives focus to the scrollbar
StatusMessage	""	The message to display on the status bar
TabStop	.T.	Can the user give focus to the scrollbar by pressing the

Table A1–21. The Scrollbar Class.

Property/Method	Default	Description
		Tab or **Shift+Tab** key?
Top	0	Holds the position of the top border
Value	1	Holds the value of the scrollbar
Vertical	.T.	Display vertical or horizontal
Visible	.T.	Is the object visible or hidden?
When	N/A	The condition that must be true before the user can give focus to the scrollbar
Width	2.00	Holds the width

* Items that have changed or are new to Visual dBASE.

The Shape Class

Objects created from the Class Shape place a region of color within a form. You can create circles, rectangles, and squares. This is a new class added to Visual dBASE.

Objects created from a Shape Class must be contained in a form.

Shape example

The following code will create a form and place three shapes inside it—a square, a circle, and a rounded-edge rectangle.

```
fShp = NEW Shapeform()
fShp.Open()
CLASS ShapeForm OF FORM
   this.Text = "Form"
   this.Width = 50
   this.Height = 16
   DEFINE SHAPE Square OF THIS PROPERTY;
       Top 0.5,Left 2, Width 20, Height 6,;
       ShapeStyle 5, ColorNormal "/W*"
   DEFINE SHAPE Circle OF THIS PROPERTY;
       Top 0.5, Left 25, Width 20, Height 6,;
       ColorNormal "/n"
   DEFINE SHAPE RndRectangle OF THIS PROPERTY;
       Top 8, Left 6.5, Width 36, Height 6,;
       ShapeStyle 0, ColorNormal "/R*"
ENDCLASS
```

Figure A1–19 shows the form with two Shape objects from the preceding code.

The properties and methods of a Shape Class

Table A1–22 shows all of the properties, their default values, and a short description.

Table A1–22. The Shape Class.

Property/Method	Default	Description
Before*	N/A	The object the shape precedes in the tabbing order of the parent form
ClassName*	SHAPE	Identifies the Shape object's class
ColorNormal*	WindowText/Window	Holds the color of the object
Height*	5.00	The height
Left*	0	The position of the left border
MarkCustom()*	N/A	
Move()*	N/A	Lets the shape be moved or sized
Name*	SHAPE1	Holds the shape name
OnOpen	N/A	Runs a program when the parent form is opened
PageNo*	1	Which page will hold the control?
Parent*	N/A	The object reference that points to the parent form
PenStyle*	0 Solid	The style used for the line
PenWidth*	1.00	The width of the pen for drawing the line
Release()*	N/A	Removes the shape definition from memory
ShapeStyle*	3—Circle	The type of shape to display
Top*	0	Holds the position of the top border
Visible*	.T.	Is the object visible or hidden?
Width	10.00	Holds the width

Items that have changed or are new to Visual dBASE.

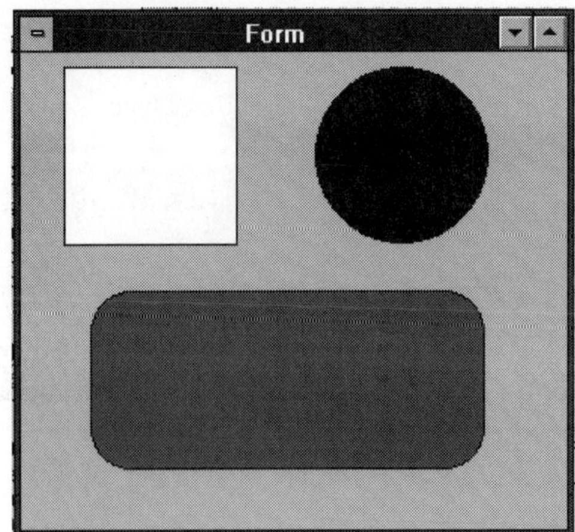

Figure A1–19. Using a Shape Class.

THE SPINBOX CLASS

Objects created from the Class SpinBox can be used to click a value up or down using a graphical tool or enter the value in a box.

Objects created from a SpinBox Class must be contained in a form.

SpinBox example

The example creates a SpinBox with a range of 1 to 10, and a decrement/increase value of 1, starting at 5.

```
LOCAL fSpinBox
fSpinBox = NEW SpinBoxForm()
fSpinBox.Open()
CLASS SpinBoxForm OF FORM
   this.Text = "SpinBox in Form Example"
   this.Width = 64
   this.Top =  1
   this.Left =  5
   this.Height = 6
   DEFINE SPINBOX MySpinBox1 OF this PROPERTY;
         Top 2, Left 11, Height 1.5 , Width 10, Step 1, Value 5
,;
         RangeMin 1, RangeMax 10, RangeRequired .T.
   DEFINE TEXT MyTxt1 OF this PROPERTY;
         Top 2, Left 22, Width 35, Text "Enter a number (1 to
10)"
```

```
ENDCLASS
```

Figure A1–20 shows the form with a SpinBox object from the preceding code.

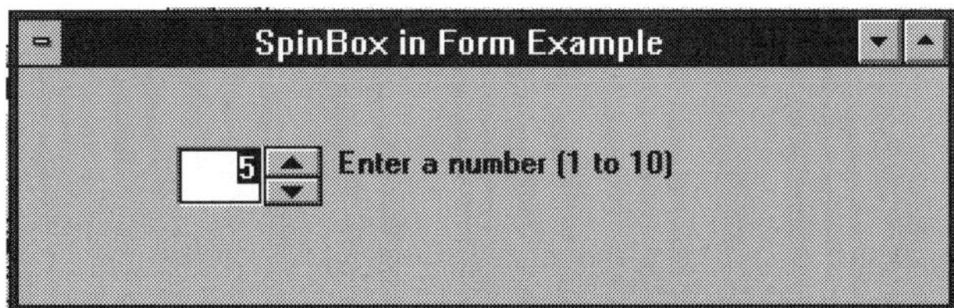

Figure A1–20. Using a SpinBox Class.

The properties and methods of a SpinBox Class

Table A1–23 shows all of the properties, their default values, and a short description.

Table A1–23. The SpinBox Class.

Property/Method	Default	Description
Before	N/A	Names which object the SpinBox object precedes in the tabbing order of the parent form
Border	.T.	Can the spinbox have a border?
ClassName	SPINBOX	Identifies the SpinBox object's class
ColorHighlight*	WindowText/ Window	Holds the color of the object when highlighted
ColorNormal*	WindowText/ Window	Holds the color of the object
Copy()*	N/A	Copies the contents of object to Clipboard
Cut()*	N/A	Cuts the contents of object to Clipboard
DataLink	""	The name of the field linked to the spinbox
Enabled	.T.	Can the spinbox be selected?
FontBold	.F.	Will characters in the spinbox be displayed in bold type?
FontItalic	.F.	Will the characters be displayed in italic type?

Table A1–23. The SpinBox Class.

Property/Method	Default	Description
FontName	MS Sans Serif	The name of the font to apply to displayed characters
FontSize	8.00	The size of the font in points
FontStrikeOut	.F.	Will the characters be displayed in strikeout type?
FontUnderline	.F.	Will the characters be displayed in underlined type?
Function	""	The format for the spinbox
Height	2.00	Holds the height
HelpFile	""	Holds the name of the Windows Help file (.HLP) that contains context-sensitive Help topics
HelpID	""	Holds the context string or context number of a Help topic in a Windows Help file (.HLP)
HWND	N/A	Holds the spinbox handle
ID	-1	The numeric value of the spinbox
Keyboard()*	N/A	Pass keystrokes to object
Left	0	The position of the left border
MarkCustom()*	N/A	
MousePointer	0	Holds the mouse pointer type when the pointer is over the spinbox
Move()	N/A	Lets the spinbox be moved or sized
Name	SPINBOX1	Holds the spinbox name
OldStyle	.F.	Should the radiobutton be displayed in the default Windows style or Borland style?
OnChange	N/A	Runs a program when the spinbox is changed (user selects a different spinbox)
OnGotFocus	N/A	Runs a program when the spinbox receives focus
OnHelp	N/A	Runs a routine when the user presses F1
OnLeftDblClk	N/A	Runs a program when the user double-clicks the object
OnLeftMouseDown	N/A	Runs a routine when the user clicks the object with the

Table A1–23. The SpinBox Class.

Property/Method	Default	Description
		left mouse button
OnLeftMouseUp	N/A	Runs a routine when the user releases the left mouse button while over the object
OnLostFocus	N/A	Runs a program when focus is removed
OnMiddleDblClk	N/A	Runs a program when the user double-clicks the object with the middle mouse button
OnMiddleMouseDown	N/A	Runs a program when the user clicks the object with the middle mouse button
OnMiddleMouseUp	N/A	Runs a program when the user releases the middle mouse button while on the object
OnMouseMove	N/A	Runs a program when the user moves the mouse pointer over the object
OnOpen	N/A	Runs a program when the parent form is opened
OnRightDblClk	N/A	Runs a program when the user double-clicks the object with the right mouse button
OnRightMouseDown	N/A	Runs a program when the user clicks the object with the right mouse button
OnRightMouseUp	N/A	Runs a routine when the user releases the right mouse button while on the object
PageNo*	1	The page that the control is on
Parent	N/A	The object reference that points to the parent form
Paste()*	N/A	Pastes the contents of the Clipboard to control
Picture	""	The format text for each character of spinbox
RangeMax	100.00	The upper limit for the value linked to the object
RangeMin	1.00	The lower limit for the value linked to the object
RangeRequired	.F.	Does the range specified with Max/Min apply to all data or just new data?
Release()	N/A	Removes the spinbox definition from memory

Table A1–23. The SpinBox Class.

Property/Method	**Default**	**Description**
SelectAll	.F.	Can the initial value be highlighted (selected)?
SetFocus()	N/A	Gives focus to the object
SpinOnly	.F.	Can the editing in box be performed or not?
StatusMessage	""	Holds a message to display on the status bar while the object has focus
Step	1	How much should be added to or subtracted from the value when pressing the buttons?
TabStop	.T.	Holds the value to determine if the user can go to the object by pressing **Tab** or **Shift+Tab**
Top	0	Holds the position of the top border
Undo()*	N/A	Performs a Windows undo on the last action
Valid	N/A	The condition that must evaluate to true before the user can leave the spinbox
ValidErrorMsg	""	The message to display on the status bar when the Valid property returns .F.
ValidRequired	.F.	Is the Valid property always enforced or just when the value changes?
Value	""	The value in the radiobutton
Visible	.T.	Is the object visible or hidden?
When	N/A	Specifies a condition that must evaluate to true before the user can give focus to the object
Width	14	Holds the width

* Items that have changed or are new to Visual dBASE.

THE TABBOX CLASS

Visual dBASE has added a new **Tab**-based control that can be used to move from page to page in your forms. Objects created from the TabBox Class must be contained in a form.

TabBox example

The example creates a TabBox object and places it on the form.

```
LOCAL fTab
fTab = NEW TabForm()
fTab.Open()
CLASS TabForm OF Form
   this.pageno = 1
   this.Width = 45
   this.Height = 10

    DEFINE TEXT Title1 of this PROPERTY FontSize 16, ;
       PageNo 1, Top 3, Left 3, Width 35, Height 1.8, ;
       Text "This is page 1"
    DEFINE TEXT Title2 of this PROPERTY FontSize 16, ;
       PageNo 2, Top 3, Left 3, Width 35, Height 1.8, ;
       Text "2 is the Page"
    DEFINE TEXT Title3 of this PROPERTY FontSize 16, ;
       PageNo 3, Top 3, Left 3, Width 35, Height 1.8, ;
       Text "The last page"
    DEFINE TABBOX MyTab of this PROPERTY ;
        DataSource 'ARRAY {"One","Two","Three"}',;
        OnSelChange {;form.pageno=this.cursel}
ENDCLASS
```

Figure A1–21 shows the form with a SpinBox object from the preceding code.

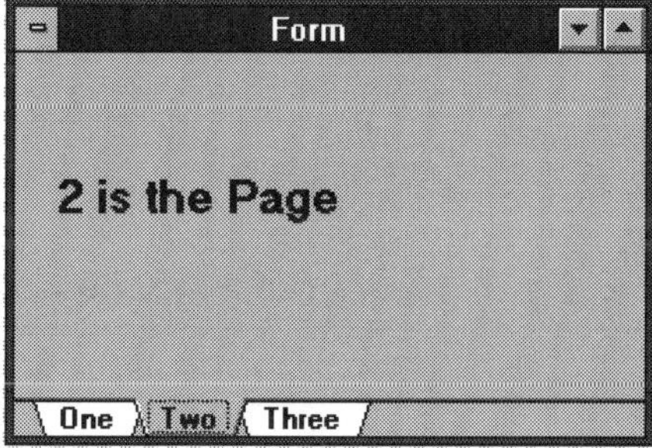

Figure A1–21. Using a TabBox Class.

The properties and methods of a TabBox Class

Table A1–24 shows all of the properties, their default values, and a short description.

Table A1–24. The TabBox Class.

Property/Method	Default	Description
Anchor*	1	Determines the position of the tabbox
Before*	N/A	Names that the TabBox object precedes in the tabbing order of the parent form
ClassName*	TABBOX	Identifies the TabBox object's class
ColorHighlight*	""	Holds the color of the object when highlighted
ColorNormal*	BtnText/BtnFace	Holds the color of the object
CurSel*	1	The currently selected tab
DataSource*	""	The prompts that are on the tabs
Enabled*	.T.	Can the tabbox be selected?
FontBold*	.F.	Will characters in the tabbox be displayed in bold type?
FontItalic*	.F.	Will the characters be displayed in italic type?
FontName*	MS Sans Serif	The name of the font to apply to displayed characters
FontSize*	8.00	The size of the font in points
FontStrikeOut*	.F.	Will the characters be displayed in strikeout type?
FontUnderline*	.F.	Will the characters be displayed in underlined type?
Height	2.00	Holds the height
HelpFile*	""	Holds the name of the Windows Help file (.HLP) that contains context-sensitive Help topics
HelpID*	""	Holds the context string or context number of a Help topic in a Windows Help file (.HLP)
HWND*	N/A	Holds the tabbox handle
ID*	-1	The numeric value of the tabbox
Left*	0	The position of the left border
MarkCustom()*	N/A	
MousePointer*	0	Holds the mouse pointer type when the pointer is over the tabbox
Move()*	N/A	Lets the tabbox be moved or sized

Table A1–24. The TabBox Class.

Property/Method	Default	Description
Name*	TABBOX1	Holds the tabbox name
OnGotFocus*	N/A	Runs a program when the tabbox receives focus
OnHelp*	N/A	Runs a routine when the user presses F1
OnLeftDblClk*	N/A	Runs a program when the user double-clicks the object
OnLeftMouseDown*	N/A	Runs a routine when the user clicks the object with the left mouse button
OnLeftMouseUp*	N/A	Runs a routine when the user releases the left mouse button while over the object
OnLostFocus*	N/A	Runs a program when focus is removed
OnMiddleDblClk*	N/A	Runs a program when the user double-clicks the object with the middle mouse button
OnMiddleMouseDown *	N/A	Runs a program when the user clicks the object with the middle mouse button
OnMiddleMouseUp*	N/A	Runs a program when the user releases the middle mouse button while on the object
OnMouseMove*	N/A	Runs a program when the user moves the mouse pointer over the object
OnOpen*	N/A	Runs a program when the parent form is opened
OnRightDblClk*	N/A	Runs a program when the user double-clicks the object with the right mouse button
OnRightMouseDown*	N/A	Runs a program when the user clicks the object with the right mouse button
OnRightMouseUp*	N/A	Runs a routine when the user releases the right mouse button while on the object
OnSelChange*	N/A	Runs a program when a new tab is selected
PageNo*	0	The page that the control is on default is 0, when 0 object displays on all pages
Parent*	N/A	The object reference that points to the parent form

Table A1–24. The TabBox Class.

Property/Method	Default	Description
Release()*	N/A	Removes the tabbox definition from memory
SetFocus()*	N/A	Gives focus to the object
StatusMessage*	""	Holds a message to display on the status bar while the object has focus
Top*	0	Holds the position of the top border
Visible*	.T.	Is the object visible or hidden?
When*	N/A	Specifies a condition that must evaluate to true before the user can give focus to the object
Width*	10	Holds the width

* Items that have changed or are new to Visual dBASE.

THE TEXT CLASS

Objects created from the Class Text can be used to display a string of text. This is similar to the @ SAY . . . command of DOS. Of course this is an object and works like an object.

Objects created from a Text Class must be contained in a form.

Text example

The example creates a Text object and places it on the form.

```
LOCAL fText
fText = NEW TextForm()
fText.Open()
CLASS TextForm OF FORM
   this.Text = "Text in Form Example"
   this.Width = 64
   this.Top =  1
   this.Left =  5
   this.Height = 6
   DEFINE TEXT MyTxt1 OF this PROPERTY;
         Top 2, Left 2, Width 35, Text "Enter a number (1 to 10)"
   DEFINE TEXT MyTxt2 OF this PROPERTY;
         Top 4, Left 2, Width 35, Text "This is a Text object"
```

```
ENDCLASS
```

Figure A1–22 shows the form with a Text objects from the preceding code.

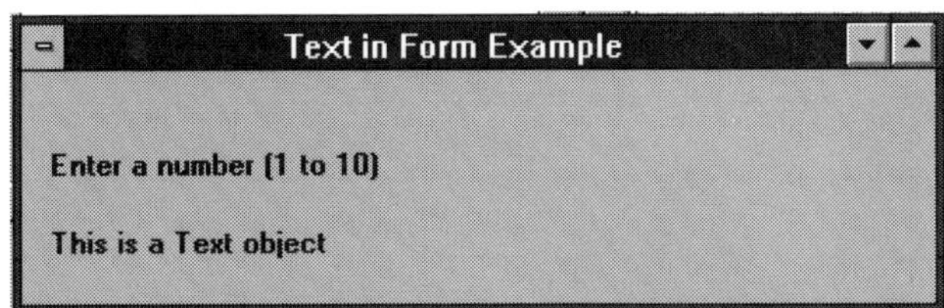

Figure A1–22. Using a Text Class.

The properties and methods of a Text Class

Table A1–25 shows all of the properties, their default values, and a short description.

Table A1–25. The Text Class.

Property/Method	Default	Description
Alignment	0 Top Left	The Text object position
Before	N/A	Holds the name of which object the Text field precedes in the tabbing order of the parent form
Border	.F.	Will the Text field be surrounded with a border?
ClassName	TEXT	Identifies the Text class
ColorNormal*	BtnText/BtnFace	Holds the color of the text when it is not highlighted
FontBold	.F.	Can the text display bold type?
FontItalic	.F.	Can the characters be displayed in italic type?
FontName	MS Sans Serif	Name of the font used to displayed characters
FontSize	8.00	The size of the font in points
FontStrikeOut	.F.	Will the characters be displayed in strikeout type?
FontUnderline	.F.	Will the characters be displayed in underlined type?
Function	""	Holds the format for the text based on the overall object
GetTextExtent()	N/A	The length of the Text object based on comparing its font to the font of the form

Table A1–25. The Text Class.

Property/Method	Default	Description
Height	1.33	The height
HWND	N/A	The text handle
ID	-1	The text numeric value
Left	0	The position of the left border
MarkCustom()*	N/A	
MousePointer	0	The type of mouse pointer when it is over the text
Move()	N/A	Moves or sizes the text
Name	TEXT1	The name of the text
OldStyle	N/A	Will the text be displayed in the default Windows style or in Borland style?
OnLeftDblClk	N/A	Runs a program when the user double-clicks the text
OnLeftMouseDown	N/A	Runs a program when the user clicks the text with the left mouse button
OnLeftMouseUp	N/A	Runs a program when the user releases the left mouse button while over the text
OnMiddleDblClk*	N/A	Runs a program when the user double-clicks the object with the middle mouse button
OnMiddleMouseDown *	N/A	Runs a program when the user clicks the object with the middle mouse button
OnMiddleMouseUp*	N/A	Runs a program when the user releases the middle mouse button while on the object
OnMouseMove	N/A	Runs a program when the user moves the mouse over the text
OnOpen	N/A	Runs a program when the parent form is opened
OnRightDblClk	N/A	Runs a program when the user double-clicks the text with the right mouse button
OnRightMouseDown	N/A	Runs a program when the user clicks the text with the right mouse button

Table A1–25. The Text Class.

Property/Method	Default	Description
OnRightMouseUp	N/A	Runs a program when the user releases the right mouse button while on the text
PageNo*	1	Page that the control is placed on
Parent	N/A	The object reference that points to the parent form
Picture	“”	Holds the format for the text one character at a time
Release()	N/A	Removes the text definition from memory
Text	TEXT1	The text displayed in the text object
Top	0	The position of the top border
Visible	.T.	Is the text to be visible?
Width	9	The width

* Items that have changed or are new to Visual dBASE.

THE TIMER CLASS

This Class is an undocumented Class that can be used to create timer events. It was also in dBASE for Windows 5.0. Using this Class, you can create a timer that will do something based on a specified time lapse.

Objects created from a Timer Class do not have to be contained in a form.

Timer example

The example creates a Timer object and uses it to update a text field with the time displayed in it. When using the Timer Class you can only create a Timer object using the NEW operator. DEFINE TIMER command will result in an error.

```
Local fTimer
fTimer = NEW TimeForm()
fTimer.Open()
CLASS TimeForm OF Form
   this.width = 45
   this.height = 10
   this.OnClose = {;xtimer.Enabled = .f.; form.Release()}
   DEFINE TEXT TimeTitle OF this PROPERTY ;
```

```
        FontSize 16, Top 0.2, Left 5, Width 42, Height 1.8,;
        Text "Time is:"

    xTimer = NEW Timer()
        xTimer.Interval = 5
        xTimer.Enabled = .t.
        xTimer.OnTimer = {;fTimer.TimeTitle.text="Time is:
⇒       "+time()}

ENDCLASS
```

Figure A1–23 shows the form with a Timer object active from the preceding code.

Figure A1–23. Using a Timer Class.

The Timer Class is an undocumented class that has very powerful potential. However, you must always remember to dis-enable it when it is not in use. It can also be released from memory using the RELEASE OBJECT or RELEASE command.

The properties and methods of a Timer Class

Table A1–26 shows all of the properties, their default values, and a short description.

Table A1–26. The Timer Class.

Property/Method	Default	Description
ClassName	TEXT	Identifies the Timer class
Enabled	.f.	Activates the timer
Interval	10	Specifies the seconds interval for the timer
OnTimer	“”	Runs a program based on the timer event

Appendix: Part Two

THE VISUAL dBASE FILE EXTENSIONS

The following is a complete listing of all the different file types, their extension, and purpose that are supported by Visual dBASE. The table is in alphabetical order based on the file extensions that are supported in Visual dBASE.

General rules

Note the following general rules about file extensions used by Visual dBASE:

The standard extension for dBASE tables is .DBF. This file extension is not required. For instance a .CAT (catalog) file is actually a dBASE table. It can be used just like any dBASE database that ends in .DBF. When naming tables, there are certain file extensions that cannot be used.

The table extension cannot end in an **X** or **T**. These extensions are reserved for producing Index and Memo files. If you create a table named MIKEDATA.HIJ, dBASE will create a Memo file named MIKEDATA.HIT and an Index file named MIKEDATA.HIX.

You should not use the letter **O** as the last character of the file extension if the file can be compiled. For instance, you can compile any text file that contains dBASE programming code. If you create a program named DOIT.bad, it can be compiled and run.

```
*** DOIT.bad
*
USE CUSTOMER
list
RETURN
```

With the code created, it can be compiled using the COMPILE or DO command specifying the extension. Once compiled you can run the code by typing in either command:

```
DO DOIT.BAO
DO DOIT.BAD
```

The extensions

The following table describes all of the file extensions and the type of files that they are.

Table A2–1. The Visual dBASE files.

Extension	Description
.BAK	Program (.PRG) or procedure backup file in dBASE for Windows only
.BAT	DOS batch file
.BFM	Binary form file for VBX controls
.BMP	A Windows bitmap file
.CAT	A dBASE catalog file
.CC	A dBASE custom control file
.CO	The compiled custom control file
.COM	A DOS command file
.COV	A dBASE coverage file
.CRR	Crystal Reports registration file
.CVT	dBASE table with change detection field
.DB	A Paradox table file
.DBF	A dBASE table file
.DBK	A dBASE table backup file
.DBT	A dBASE memo file
.DLL	A Windows Dynamic-Link Library file
.EXE	An Executable program file
.FMO	A compiled format file (.FMT)
.FMT	A dBASE III/IV format file
.FNF	Expression Builder database file
.FR3	The old III plus report form file (.FRM)
.FRG	dBASE IV generated report form file (from .FRM)

Table A2–1. The Visual dBASE files.

Extension	Description
.FRM	dBASE III plus report form file
.FRO	Compiled report form (.FRG) file
.GRP	A Windows group file
.H	A program Header file (# INCLUDE)
.HDX	A Help keyword index file
.HLP	A Windows format Help file
.ICO	A Windows icon file
.INI	A Windows initialization file
.LB3	Renamed old dBASE III label form
.LBG	A dBASE label form
.LBL	dBASE III Plus label form file
.LBO	A compiled label form file
.MB	A paradox blob/memo field
.MBK	Multiple index backup file
.MDX	A dBASE multi-index file
.MEM	A dBASE memory file
.MNO	A compiled menu (.MNU) file
.MNU	A dBASE menu file
.NDX	A single dBASE index file
.PCX	A PC Paintbrush format bit image file
.PIF	A Windows program information file for DOS apps
.PRF	Print form file
.PRG	dBASE source code program file
PRK	Program backup file in Visual dBASE only
.PRO	A compiled program (.PRG) file
.PRT	A printer output file

Table A2–1. The Visual dBASE files.

Extension	Description
.PX	A Paradox primary key file
.QBE	A dBASE query file
.QBO	A compiled query (.QBE) file
.QRY	A dBASE III plus query/filter file
.RPC	A Crystal Reports cross-tab report file
.RPL	A Crystal Reports for dBASE label file
.RPT	A Crystal Reports for dBASE report file
.SCN	An image of the results pane saved to a file
.TBK	A dBASE table memo backup file
.TXT	A text file
.UPD	A QBE update query file
.VAL	A Paradox validity check file
.VBX	A Visual Basic Custom control file
.VUE	dBASE III plus/IV query/ view file
.WAV	A Windows sound file
.WB1	A Quattro Pro for Windows notebook file
.WFK	A dBASE form (.WFM) backup file
.WFM	A dBASE form file
.WFO	A compiled form (.WFM) file
.WIN	A dBASE window save file
.WK1	A Lotus 1-2-3 version 2 file
.XGn	A secondary multifield index for Paradox tables
.Xnn	A secondary single-field index for Paradox tables
.YGn	A secondary multifield index for Paradox tables
.Ynn	A secondary single-field index for Paradox tables

Appendix: Part Three

NEW AND ENHANCED COMMANDS OF VISUAL DBASE

The following is a listing of all of the new and enhanced commands for Visual dBASE. This list does not include all of the property and event names of objects. To see them, refer to Appendix One.

Command or Function	New or Enhanced	Description/Purpose of Command or Function
{v1; v2, ..}*	N	Used for building arrays directly— MyArray = {1, 2, 3}
@ . . . say . . . get	E	HELPID <id> option added
abandon()	N	Abandon a transaction process
acopy()	N	Used to copy an array (one- or two-dimensional) to another array
activate menu	E	Retraced option added
activate screen	E	Save option added
adel()	N	Used to delete an element, row, or column from an array
adir()	N	Stores directory information in an array
aelement()	N	Returns the number of the specific element within a one- or two-dimensional array
afields()	N	Stores the field information from a table structure in an array
afill()	N	Stores a user-specified value into an array
agrow()	N	Adds elements to array
ains()	N	Inserts a value of .t. or .f. into an array

Command or Function	New or Enhanced	Description/Purpose of Command or Function
alen()	N	Returns the number of elements, rows, or columns in an array
ansi()	N	Returns the ANSI value corresponding to an OEM (DOS code page)
append	E	No wait option added
append automem	N	Adds new record stored in automem
append from	E	dBASE II, RPD, FW2, SYLK, DIF, and WKS types dropped Position option added, dBASE and PARADOX types added
aresize()	N	Increases or decreases the size of an existing array
ascan()	N	Searches an array for an expression, returning the first element that contains the value
asort()	N	Sorts the elements of an array, one- or two-dimensional
asubscript()	N	Returns the row or column number of a specified element in an array
begintrans(a,b)	N	To begin a transaction process
bitand()	N	Performs an AND comparison of the bits in two specific expressions
bitor()	N	Performs an OR comparison between two bits of different, specific expressions
bitRshift()	N	Returns the number generated by right-shifting the bits in a specific expression
bitset()	N	Indicates whether a bit in a specific expression is set to 1 (.t.) or 0 (.f.)
bitshift()	N	Returns the number generated by left-shifting the bits in a specific expression
bitxor()	N	Performs an exclusive OR (XOR) comparison between two bits

Command or Function	New or Enhanced	Description/Purpose of Command or Function
bookmark()	N	Returns an internal bookmark, similar to a recno(), for the current record
browse	E	<browse name> option added FOR and WHILE options added COLOR option added KEY [WITHIN] option added NORMAL, NOTOGGLE, NOWAIT options added TITLE option added ONGOTOFOCUS, ONLOSTFOCUS, and ONCLOSED options added
build[+]	E	Links code and builds EXE
cd	N	Changes the DOS directory
charset()	N	Returns the name of the character set that is current or being used by a table
chooseprinter()	N	Lets you activate a Printer dialog box that can be used to choose printers and options
class . . . endclass	N	Declares a class object and creates new properties, methods, and values
clear automem	N	Initializes a set of memory variables containing the same name as the fields of the current record being pointed to. Sets all value empty
clear program	N	Clears all compiled programs from memory that aren't currently being executed or opened with SET Proc/Library/Format
close	E	Database option added
close forms	N	Clears forms from memory
close printer	N	Closes the current printer
commit()	N	Ends a transaction and writes to the open files any changes made

Command or Function	New or Enhanced	Description/Purpose of Command or Function
compile	E	Compiles source code (AUTO, LOG)
copy binary	N	Copies the contents of a specified binary field to a file
copy table	N	Copies a specific table and associated files (.dbf, .mdx, .dbt)
create form	N	Opens the Form Designer to create a new (or modify existing) .WFM file
create menu	N	Opens the Menu Designer to create a new (or modify existing) .MNU file
create session	N	Creates a new work session
database()	N	Returns the name of the current database (SQL type or local)
dberror()	N	Returns the number of the last IDAPI error
dbmessage()	N	Returns the message of the last IDAPI error
define	N	Creates an object from a Class
define bar	E	SKIP [FOR <cond>] added
define color	N	Creates and names a user-created color
define pad	E	SKIP [FOR <cond>] added
define popup	E	PROMPT ARRAY and COLOR options added
delete table	N	Deletes a specific table and associated files (.dbf, .dbt, .mdx)
diskspace	E	<drive nNum> added
display coverage	N	Displays the contents of a coverage file (COV) and the percentage checked
display files	E	ON <drive> option added
dos	N	Displays the DOS prompt allowing execution of DOS commands
edit	E	<edit name> and <bookmar> option added FOR and WHILE added, COLOR added,

Command or Function	New or Enhanced	Description/Purpose of Command or Function
		KEY [WITHIN] added, COLUMNAR, NORMAL, NOTOGGLE, and NOWAIT options added TITLE option added ONGOTOFOCUS, ONLOSTFOCUS, and ONCLOSED options added
export	E	WB1 and dBASE options added DBASEII, RPD, FW2, FW3, PFS, WKS, and WK1 options removed
extern	N	Declares a prototype for non-dBASE functions (external) to be used by dBASE
faccessdate()*	N	Win 95 file access date
fcreatedate()*	N	Win 95 file create date
fcreatetime()*	N	Win 95 file create time
fdecimal()	N	Returns the number of decimal places in a specific field
flength()	N	Returns the length of the field specified
flush	N	Writes data buffers to disk and releases unallocated memory
fnamemax()*	N	Win 95 file name length—12 (8.3) for no file names; 255 for long filenames
for . . . next	N	Runs the statements in-between the For and Next the number of times specified
fshortname()*	N	Win 95 display short filename
funique()	N	Creates a unique filename
generate	N	Adds random records to a table
getcolor()	N	Activates a Color dialog box that lets you define a custom color or select a color
getdirectory()	N	Displays a Directory dialog box that lets you select a directory
getexpr()	N	Activates a Create/Edit an Expression dialog box and

Command or Function	New or Enhanced	Description/Purpose of Command or Function
		lets you create an expression
getfile()	N	Activates a File dialog box that lets you select a filename
getfont()	N	Activates a Font dialog box that lets you select a font filename
go/goto	E	<bookmark> option added
htoi()	N	Returns the decimal number equivalent of a specific hexadecimal number
id()	E	Returns name of user on network
IF	E	ELSEIF option added
import	E	WB1 option added dBASE II, RPD, FW2, FW3, PFS, WKS and WK1 options removed
index	E	Primary key added for Paradox tables
insert automem	N	Inserts record from automem
inspect()	N	Activates the Property Inspector dialog box to work with an object interactively
isalpha()	N	Returns a true (.t.) if the specific expression is alphabetic characters, (.f.) if false
istable()	N	Tests if a table exists in an SQL database
itoh()	N	Returns the hexadecimal equivalent of a specific decimal number
ldriver()	N	Returns the name of the language driver the current table is using
left()	E	No longer limited to 254 characters
len()	E	Null characters are counted
lennum()*	N	Returns length of specific number
listcount()	N	Returns the number of prompts in a listbox

Command or Function	New or Enhanced	Description/Purpose of Command or Function
listselected()	N	Returns the prompt of the listbox or combobox item selected by the user
load dll	N	Places a DLL file's pointers in memory; initiates it
local	N	Declares a variable as local
lock()	E	<book mark> option added
logout*	N	Log out of protected tables
md/mkdir	N	Creates a new DOS directory
mdown()	N	Determines if the mouse button is down, returns true (.t.) if it is, false (.f.) if not
modify form	N	Lets you modify an existing .WFM file
nextkey()	N	Returns the decimal value of a key or key combination held in the KEYBOARD buffer
oem()	N	Returns a character string that is the OEM (code page) value of the ANSI character expression
on neterror()	N	Executes a specified program when a network error occurs
on selection form	N	Runs a routine or codeblock when the user submits a form
open database+	N	Starts a connection to an SQL database. Has New AUTOEXTERN ability
open form	N	Opens a form and its contained objects
play sound	N	Plays a .WAV file
program()	N	Returns the name of the running program or UDF.
proper()	N	Converts a character string to proper case—michael r. irwin becomes Michael R. Irwin
protect*	N	Builds protection for dBASE tables
putfile()	N	Activates a File dialog box to save a file
readmodal()	N	Opens a form as a modal window

Command or Function	New or Enhanced	Description/Purpose of Command or Function
redefine	N	Modifies settings made with a Define without destroying the existing object
relation()	N	Returns the key expression defined with the SET RELATION command
release automem	N	Clears all automem variables from memory
release dll	N	Deactivates DLL files
release object	N	Removes an object definition from memory
rename	N	Used to rename an existing file
rename table	N	Changes the name of the table and associated files (.dbf, .dbt, .mdx)
replace automem	N	Returns values from memory variables back into the fields
replace binary	N	Adds or replaces the contents of a binary field
replace ole	N	Inserts an OLE document into an OLE field
replicate()	E	No longer limited to 254 characters
resource()	N	Returns a Windows string resource found in a DLL file
restore image+	N	Displays an image file
return	E	TO READ option added
rlock()	E	<bookmark> option added
save screen	E	TO FILE option added
seconds()	N	Returns the number of seconds that have elapsed since midnight (00:00:00)
SET (“proc”,2)	E	Procedure has a second option to specify the work area to look into
set color to+	E	Can use Windows screen element color strings
set coverage	N	Turns coverage on or off
set database	N	Sets the current database as the focus for table names
set dbtype	N	Sets the default local database type to dBASE or

Command or Function	New or Enhanced	Description/Purpose of Command or Function
		Paradox for file usage
set display	E	<MONO | COLOR | MONO43> no longer supported
set encryption*	N	Visual dBASE protection of dBASE tables
set error	N	Specifies one character expression to precede error messages and another character expression to follow them
set help to	N	Places the name of the .HLP file
set key to	E	LOW, HIGH, EXCLUDE options added
set ldconvert*	N	Language drivers versus Char/Memo fields
set message	E	AT option removed
set pcol	N	Sets the printer column position
set procedure	E	ADDITIVE keyword added to place more than one procedure file in memory
set prow	N	Sets the printer row position
set topic	N	Sets the top to display in the Help window when the Help command is issued (F1)
set wp to	N	Specifies which editor to use for viewing text memo fields
shell()	N	Removes or restores interactive dBASE environment when a form is open
show menu	N	Displays, not enables, a defined dBASE IV bar menu
show object	N	Displays an object without enabling it
sleep	N	Pauses a specific number of seconds
sqlerror()	N	Returns the error number from the SQL database
sqlexec()	N	Executes an SQL statement to the current database (SQL)
sqlmessage()	N	Returns the message from the SQL database
static	N	Declares a variable static
store automem	N	Stores the contents of the current record to memory

Command or Function	New or Enhanced	Description/Purpose of Command or Function
		variables of the same name
store memo	N	Stores the text of a memo field to an array-type memory variable
target()	N	Returns the name of the table linked to the current work area
type	E	MORE option added
updated()	N	Indicates whether you changed the contents of any @ . . . GET variable in the command window
user()*	N	Specifies name of user when security is on
validdrive()	N	Determines if a specific drive can be read (or exists)

* New to Visual dBASE.

+ In both dBASE for Windows and Visual dBASE (improved in Visual dBASE).

Appendix: Part Four

VISUAL dBASE AND WINDOWS 95

Visual dBASE is Windows 95 aware. This means that it can run the same executables in both Win 3.1 and Windows 95. It also means that Visual dBASE is able to support the long filenames and Universal Naming Conventions of Windows 95, as well as support the new UI style differences. Finally, it integrates well into the Windows 95 Explorer.

Most-recently-used (MRU) files list

Because of long filenames in Windows 95, long entries may exist in the MRU. The MRU is the list of files that appears appended to the end of the File menu. Visual dBASE will support the maximum length and add three dots in the middle of the name when it is too long (just like Windows 95).

Titlebar text

Visual dBASE will detect that it is running in Windows 95 and automatically display the text in the title bar following Windows 95 convention. The filename will be shown first, followed by a dash, and then the name of the dBASE component.

Navigator support for Windows 95

The Navigator has been modified to support long filenames when working in Windows 95.

Again, if filenames are too long to fit the user-specified spacing, it will be truncated. However, the three dots will be appended to the end of the truncated name.

Two new DBASEWIN.INI options are added under the [Navigator] section to add control for how files will be displayed.

```
ShowFileExtensions =
ShowBackUpFiles =
```

In Windows 95, backup files begin with the words BACKUP OF. If ShowBackUpFiles is set to 1, then they will be displayed.

Universal Naming Convention (UNC)

UNC allows network server names to be used in place of DOS drive letters in file pathnames. Visual dBASE supports this ability.

UNC is also used to identify network printers (avoiding the need to redirect output to a local printer). Visual dBASE supports the UNC for network printers that are configured using the *Users* Win.INI file.

Language improvements

Visual dBASE has added several new commands to work in Windows 95.

```
ADIREXT()
FACCESSDATE()
FCREATEDATE()
FCREATETIME()
FNAMEMAX()
FSHORTNAME()
```

ADIREXT()

This is the same as the ADIR() function. However, it will show additional columns in the array for new values in Windows 95—the alias filename, file create date/time, and file last access date.

FAccessDate()

This command reports the last file access date.

FCreateDate()

This command reports the file creation date.

FCreateTime()

This command reports the file creation time.

FNameMax()

This function is used to determine if a specific disk volume supports long filenames. The function returns a 255 for Windows 95 and a 12 (8.3) for Windows 3.1x. It supports one option for the drive—FNameMax ("D:\").

FShortName()

This function returns the alias name (short name) of Windows 95 filenames. If programs running in Windows 95 are not Windows 95 aware, they use the alias name instead of a long filename. This function lets you determine the alias name.

Appendix: Part Five

Visual dBASE and Security

Visual dBASE offers security against dBASE tables based on the dBASE/DOS security methodology. It fully supports the DOS security system for backward compatibility.

The new security commands only work against .DBFs. Paradox tables and SQL tables have their own security already built in, relying on the database engine for security.

The new commands and functions are:

```
PROTECT
SET ENCRYPTION
LOGOUT
ACCESS()
USER()
```

These are the same commands that exist in previous DOS versions of dBASE.

PROTECT

This command will activate a dialog box that is used by the Administrator to set up groups, uses, and privilege levels for individual DBFs.

Unlike dBASE DOS Protect, Visual dBASE security does not make a copy of the table being worked with. Rather, it makes the changes directly to the current table. In dBASE DOS, PROTECT created a CRP file. This file had to be manually copied using the DOS COPY command to the DBF, overwriting the nonprotected table. Visual dBASE does not create a CRP file; rather, it directly encrypts the existing table.

MODIFY STRUCTURE and COPY STRUCTURE extended commands

Once a table is encrypted, the MODIFY STRUCTURE command will not work against it. If you need to work with a different structure, you will need to copy the fields to a new table with encryption turned off.

SET ENCRYPTION ON/OFF

The command is used to enable security against the COPY, JOIN, and TOTAL commands. It works at session level so you can have one session with encryption on, another with it off. When off, you can copy encrypted data (as long as you have access rights to the table) to a nonencrypted file.

LOGOUT

This command will log the user out, closing all files in the session and activate a dialog box requesting a new group and user name. It only works when security is enabled via the Protect.

Access() and User() functions

The Access() function returns the access level of the current user. The User() function returns the name of the user.

Index

LICENSE AGREEMENT AND LIMITED WARRANTY

READ THE FOLLOWING TERMS AND CONDITIONS CAREFULLY BEFORE OPENING THIS DISK PACKAGE. THIS LEGAL DOCUMENT IS AN AGREEMENT BETWEEN YOU AND PRENTICE-HALL, INC. (THE ÒCOMPANYÓ). BY OPENING THIS SEALED DISK PACKAGE, YOU ARE AGREEING TO BE BOUND BY THESE TERMS AND CONDITIONS. IF YOU DO NOT AGREE WITH THESE TERMS AND CONDITIONS, DO NOT OPEN THE DISK PACKAGE. PROMPTLY RETURN THE UNOPENED DISK PACKAGE AND ALL ACCOMPANYING ITEMS TO THE PLACE YOU OBTAINED THEM FOR A FULL REFUND OF ANY SUMS YOU HAVE PAID.

1. **GRANT OF LICENSE:** In consideration of your payment of the license fee, which is part of the price you paid for this product, and your agreement to abide by the terms and conditions of this Agreement, the Company grants to you a nonexclusive right to use and display the copy of the enclosed software program (hereinafter the ÒSOFTWAREÓ) on a single computer (i.e., with a single CPU) at a single location so long as you comply with the terms of this Agreement. The Company reserves all rights not expressly granted to you under this Agreement.

2. **OWNERSHIP OF SOFTWARE:** You own only the magnetic or physical media (the enclosed disks) on which the SOFTWARE is recorded or fixed, but the Company retains all the rights, title, and ownership to the SOFTWARE recorded on the original disk copy(ies) and all subsequent copies of the SOFTWARE, regardless of the form or media on which the original or other copies may exist. This license is not a sale of the original SOFTWARE or any copy to you.

3. **COPY RESTRICTIONS:** This SOFTWARE and the accompanying printed materials and user manual (the ÒDocumentationÓ) are the subject of copyright. You may not copy the Documentation or the SOFTWARE, except that you may make a single copy of the SOFTWARE for backup or archival purposes only. You may be held legally responsible for any copying or copyright infringement which is caused or encouraged by your failure to abide by the terms of this restriction.

4. **USE RESTRICTIONS:** You may not network the SOFTWARE or otherwise use it on more than one computer or computer terminal at the same time. You may physically transfer the SOFTWARE from one computer to another provided that the SOFTWARE is used on only one computer at a time. You may not distribute copies of the SOFTWARE or Documentation to others. You may not reverse engineer, disassemble, decompile, modify, adapt, translate, or create derivative works based on the SOFTWARE or the Documentation without the prior written consent of the Company.

5. **TRANSFER RESTRICTIONS:** The enclosed SOFTWARE is licensed only to you and may not be transferred to any one else without the prior written consent of the Company. Any unauthorized transfer of the SOFTWARE shall result in the immediate termination of this Agreement.

6. **TERMINATION:** This license is effective until terminated. This license will terminate automatically without notice from the Company and become null and void if you fail to comply with any provisions or limitations of this license. Upon termination, you shall destroy the Documentation and all copies of the SOFTWARE. All provisions of this Agreement as to warranties, limitation of liability, remedies or damages, and our ownership rights shall survive termination.

7. **MISCELLANEOUS:** This Agreement shall be construed in accordance with the laws of the United States of America and the State of New York and shall benefit the Company, its affiliates, and assignees.

8. **LIMITED WARRANTY AND DISCLAIMER OF WARRANTY:** The Company warrants that the SOFTWARE, when properly used in accordance with the Documentation, will operate in substantial conformity with the description of the SOFTWARE set forth in the Documentation. The Company does not warrant that the SOFTWARE will meet your requirements or that the operation of the SOFTWARE will be uninterrupted or error-free. The Company warrants that the media on which the SOFTWARE is delivered shall be free from defects in materials and workmanship under normal use for a period of thirty (30) days from the date of your purchase. Your only remedy and the Company's only obligation under these limited warranties is, at the Company's option, return of the warranted item for a refund of any amounts paid by you or replacement of the item. Any replacement of SOFTWARE or media under the warranties shall not extend the original warranty period. The limited warranty set forth above shall not apply to any SOFTWARE which the Company determines in good faith has been subject to misuse, neglect, improper installation, repair, alteration, or damage by you. EXCEPT FOR THE EXPRESSED WARRANTIES SET FORTH ABOVE, THE COMPANY DISCLAIMS ALL WARRANTIES, EXPRESS OR IMPLIED, INCLUDING WITHOUT LIMITATION, THE IMPLIED WARRANTIES OF MERCHANTABILITY AND FITNESS FOR A PARTICULAR PURPOSE. EXCEPT FOR THE EXPRESS WARRANTY SET FORTH ABOVE, THE COMPANY DOES NOT WARRANT, GUARANTEE, OR MAKE ANY REPRESENTATION REGARDING THE USE OR THE RESULTS OF THE USE OF THE SOFTWARE IN TERMS OF ITS CORRECTNESS, ACCURACY, RELIABILITY, CURRENTNESS, OR OTHERWISE.

IN NO EVENT, SHALL THE COMPANY OR ITS EMPLOYEES, AGENTS, SUPPLIERS, OR CONTRACTORS BE LIABLE FOR ANY INCIDENTAL, INDIRECT, SPECIAL, OR CONSEQUENTIAL DAMAGES ARISING OUT OF OR IN CONNECTION WITH THE LICENSE GRANTED UNDER THIS AGREEMENT, OR FOR LOSS OF USE, LOSS OF DATA, LOSS OF INCOME OR PROFIT, OR OTHER LOSSES, SUSTAINED AS A RESULT OF INJURY TO ANY PERSON, OR LOSS OF OR DAMAGE TO PROPERTY, OR CLAIMS OF THIRD PARTIES, EVEN IF THE COMPANY OR AN AUTHORIZED REPRESENTATIVE OF THE COMPANY HAS BEEN ADVISED OF THE POSSIBILITY OF SUCH DAMAGES. IN NO EVENT SHALL LIABILITY OF THE COMPANY FOR DAMAGES WITH RESPECT TO THE SOFTWARE EXCEED THE AMOUNTS ACTUALLY PAID BY YOU, IF ANY, FOR THE SOFTWARE.

SOME JURISDICTIONS DO NOT ALLOW THE LIMITATION OF IMPLIED WARRANTIES OR LIABILITY FOR INCIDENTAL, INDIRECT, SPECIAL, OR CONSEQUENTIAL DAMAGES, SO THE ABOVE LIMITATIONS MAY NOT ALWAYS APPLY. THE WARRANTIES IN THIS AGREEMENT GIVE YOU SPECIFIC LEGAL RIGHTS AND YOU MAY ALSO HAVE OTHER RIGHTS WHICH VARY IN ACCORDANCE WITH LOCAL LAW.

ACKNOWLEDGMENT

YOU ACKNOWLEDGE THAT YOU HAVE READ THIS AGREEMENT, UNDERSTAND IT, AND AGREE TO BE BOUND BY ITS TERMS AND CONDITIONS. YOU ALSO AGREE THAT THIS AGREEMENT IS THE COMPLETE AND EXCLUSIVE STATEMENT OF THE AGREEMENT BETWEEN YOU AND THE COMPANY AND SUPERSEDES ALL PROPOSALS OR PRIOR AGREEMENTS, ORAL, OR WRITTEN, AND ANY OTHER COMMUNICATIONS BETWEEN YOU AND THE COMPANY OR ANY REPRESENTATIVE OF THE COMPANY RELATING TO THE SUBJECT MATTER OF THIS AGREEMENT.

Should you have any questions concerning this Agreement or if you wish to contact the Company for any reason, please contact in writing at the address below.

Robin Short
Prentice Hall PTR
One Lake Street
Upper Saddle River, New Jersey 07458